MW00528815

THE UNDYING STARS

The Undying Stars

*the truth that unites the world's ancient wisdom,
and the conspiracy to keep it from you*

David Warner Mathisen

Published by Beowulf Books, Paso Robles, California

Mathisen, David Warner.
The Undying Stars / David Warner Mathisen. – 1st ed.
Includes index.

1. Mythology. 2. Civilization, Ancient. 3. Spirituality

ISBN   978-0-9960590-1-5

Note of caution to literalist readers: This text examines evidence and arrives at conclusions which may be extremely damaging to the
foundations of literalist belief. Some literalist readers may not wish to know this information, preferring to believe in a literalist
paradigm in which they have a significant personal and psychic investment, rather than examine evidence which might undermine
that paradigm. Some readers, however, may decide that if the arguments and analyses presented herein are in error, then they can be
safely ignored; but if they are correct, then it is preferable to know the truth than to build one's life upon a lie. Those taking this view
can safely read on.

Dedicated to my Family

and to all my friends who left this life too soon

Johnny, Tommy, and Bill

and to all my family who have also gone before

may we all meet again together in the Akhemu one day . . .

and

to Santos Bonacci,

Flavio Barbiero,

the Rev. Robert Taylor,

Alvin Boyd Kuhn,

and

Gerald Massey,

and to those ancient Sages who preserved the ancient wisdom,

and all those who since then have sought after it,

as well as all those who have endeavored to teach it in truth.

CONTENTS

PREFACE

Sing, O ye heavens . . .
                Isaiah 44:23.

"Ancient wisdom, unlike the modern, included a knowledge of trance-conditions."
                Gerald Massey,
                Man in search of his soul during fifty thousand years
                and how he found it![1]

The myth is the only true narrative of the reality of human experience. It is the only ultimately true history ever written. It is a picture and a portrayal of the only veridical history ever lived. [. . .]

With transcendent genius the Sages formulated the systems of myths, allegories, fables, parables, numerological structures and astronomical pictographs such as the zodiac and the planispheres or uranographs to supplement the central ceremonial drama.   The whole structure was, however, fabricated with such esoteric subtlety that, the keys once lost, the system has defied the best of medieval and modern acumen to recapture its cryptic import.
                Alvin Boyd Kuhn
                Who is this King of Glory?[2]

This book explores a subject whose vast outline many have labored to share with the world before. It does not pretend to be the first or the last word on this subject, but seeing that the number of voices teaching lies (some doing so knowingly, others unwittingly and in sincerity because they themselves have been deceived) are so many and so clamorous, it seeks to add its own voice to those trying to share the truth, knowing that in so important a struggle no contribution, however small, is unwelcome.

In its examination of some of the connections between modern quantum physics, the holographic model of the universe of modern theoretical physicists such as David Bohm, and evidence that the ancient authors and artists – going back at least as far as Stonehenge – were describing the same phenomenon, perhaps it offers some new perspectives that will prove valuable in shedding light on the truth about our ancient forebears and the nature of the universe they seem to have understood so many millennia before the modern physicists.

In its examination of the evidence surrounding the violent suppression of the ancient wisdom by actors on the stage of Rome during the first three centuries AD, and the evidence that the "shamanic, holographic" model was abundantly represented in "the west"(certainly in ancient Egypt and in the *mysteria* found throughout the Mediterranean

i

and the Levant), and in its application of the historic details of that catastrophe as sketched out by Flavio Barbiero to the broader issue of the loss of the ancient wisdom, it also may be breaking some new ground towards discovering the thieves who "stole the gold from the temple" and replaced the deep truths with lies.

This subject is hardly one of merely academic or even esoteric interest – the evidence suggests that those who perpetrated that conspiracy in the days of the Roman Empire remain in control of the levers of power in "the west" today, and that in the intervening centuries they have devoted themselves to erecting a spiritual tyranny to deliberately enslave millions under their control, and at the same time to violently stamping out the ancient shamanic-holographic wisdom everywhere else.

In fact, many of those who are most familiar with ancient scriptures in the west today, specifically those found in the Old and New Testaments of the Bible, have been accustomed to study them only through a literalist lens. This is true not only of "fundamentalist" or other forms of strict literalistm, but also of those who may reject many strictly literal passages within those scriptures, while still believing that the Scriptures teach the existence of and demand belief in a historical figure named Jesus, his twelve disciples, their literal adventures in a region between Galilee and a terrestrial Jerusalem, themselves descendants of twelve literal tribes of Israel (specifically from the two which did not get "lost"), who also had literal adventures in the same geographic region centuries before, and who were descended from twelve literal sons of Jacob-Israel, who was a literal son of Isaac, the literal son of the historical figure named Abraham.

For the purposes of the discussions in this book, all those teachings which assert that these scriptures are primarily intended to be understood as describing literal historical figures are grouped under the term "literalist," while recognizing that there still exists a wide range within literalism regarding hermeneutics and doctrine. Those who would assert that the twelve tribes of Israel were no more (and no less) intended to be taken strictly literally than Heracles was in Greece or Coyote in North America, and that the same is true of the stories in the New Testament, are generally considered to have left the fold of orthodoxy.

For those who begin this book while still locating themselves somewhere within the literalist camp, I can only offer the perspective that I have been there myself, and the hope that they approach the evidence presented herein with the attitude that they would rather know the truth than accept the assertions of other (interested) parties that the literalist interpretation is the only way to believe that these scriptures are, in fact, True.

On the contrary, it may be that it is by understanding them esoterically, that is to say gnostically, shamanically, or even (if you will) holographically, that they are seen to be True, and that an honest reading of them will show that they were never intended to be understood literally or their truth to be limited to a literal, historical "truth."

It is a fact that for centuries they were not allowed to even be translated into the languages of the common people, so that the clergy could be the only ones to consult them in detail. The penalty for translating and publishing them was death, a penalty which was meted out to William Tyndale (1484 – 1536), among others who dared to oppose this oppressive, tyrannical, and unnatural measure. It should at least be considered that at least one very important reason for keeping these scriptures from widespread circulation and examination was the fear that their undeniably esoteric nature would be noticed, for the stories of the twelve tribes of Israel, or the adventures of Samson, or the cycle of the Christ and his twelve disciples, or even the graphic symbols of the book of the Apocalypse (the Revelation of John) all plainly correspond to the book of the sky: the motions of the sun, moon, and visible planets against the backdrop of the infinite heavens and their constellations – in particular the twelve figures of the zodiac.

In this, they take their place among all the other ancient esoteric sacred traditions of the world, from ancient Egypt to ancient Greece, to ancient China and all the other manifestations of the collective heritage of our planet. And in fact, as this book will argue, they teach the same thing. It is only due to a conspiracy which sought to steal this knowledge from the human race, and restrict it to a tiny few, while destroying every vestige of it everywhere else, that so many now accept the fiction foisted upon the world by the literalist believers in the historical Jesus and the historic twelve tribes, which severed one branch of faith from the rest of humanity, and set it against all the others. Its descendants and converts are still at it today.

Gerald Massey wrote in *The Natural Genesis* (1883) that the misunderstanding of typology (by which he meant the literalist misunderstanding) has led to a "most terrible tyranny in the mental domain," an apt metaphor.[3] For the conflict under investigation in this book is a war between those who would enslave others through their control of the high ground in "the mental domain" and those who believe that this high ground should be open to all who seek it. To give lies to the seeker when you possess the truth is abhorrent.

The treasure of mankind's ancient wisdom is the birthright of all men and women who earnestly seek to know the truth. What follows is offered in service to that truth.

PART I:

The Ancient System

1
The ancient treasure

Our forefathers in the most remote ages have handed down to their posterity a tradition, in the form of a myth, that these bodies are gods, and that the divine encloses the whole of nature. [. . .] one must regard this as an inspired utterance, and reflect that, while probably each art and each science has often been developed as far as possible and has again perished, these opinions, with others, have been preserved until the present like relics of the ancient treasure.

Aristotle, *Metaphysics*.[4]

In *Hamlet's Mill*, published in 1969, Professors Giorgio de Santillana and Hertha von Dechend examine a system of celestial metaphor in the world's mythology, a system so ancient that they write in the introduction (quoting an earlier 1959 essay by Santillana) that "The dust of centuries had settled upon the remains of this great world-wide archaic construction when the Greeks came upon the scene."[5]

Their text makes this great archaic world-wide construction more accessible, but they do not always spell out all the conclusions, or even all the stepping stones to their conclusions, often leaving the reader to make the final connections for himself or herself. This text will endeavor to spell it out all the way, with pictures when that might be helpful, and to examine the truly stunning ramifications of the structure that lies underneath "the dust of centuries."

The distinguishing feature of the ancient myths, as Santillana and Dechend demonstrate, is a constant dramatizing of the great procession of stars and other heavenly bodies, wheeling over our heads in majestic grandeur day after day, night after night. As we will see in abundant examples (and many more could be offered than those we will examine), this feature also characterizes the stories found in the Old and New Testaments.

This fact has been kept from nearly all those who approach the Bible for (at least) the past seventeen hundred years. While we can (and will) speculate as to the possible reasons for this secrecy, its unfortunate consequence has been that those who have through analysis discovered the undeniable connections to the heavenly motions in the ancient scriptures (Biblical or otherwise) have been at something of a loss to explain what these connections could actually mean.

This has had the additional unfortunate consequence of leading some to conclude that these pervasive celestial connections are simply remnants of a primitive groping to explain the awesome wonders of the physical world by mystified people living at the dawn of civilization. This conclusion, as this book hopes to demonstrate, could not be further from the truth. In fact, it appears that the framers of that "great world-wide archaic construction" may have known more about quantum physics, the holographic universe, man's place in the cosmos, and the practical and spiritual consequences of this knowledge, than anything we have been able to discover about them today. It is we, at this end of civilization, who appear to be groping in the dark, and not they.

An example from Greek myth, offered in *Hamlet's Mill*, may serve to illustrate the type of connection that can be found in these stories, before proceeding to a couple important examples from the Bible (one from the Old Testament, and one from the New).

In Chapter 11 of *Hamlet's Mill*, de Santillana and von Dechend point to a perceptive ancient writer who explained this very thesis almost two thousand years ago:

> Lucian of Samosata, that most delightful writer of antiquity, the inventor of modern "science fiction," who knew how to be light and ironic on serious subjects without frivolity, and was fully aware of the "ancient treasure," remarked once that the ludicrous story of Hephaistos the Lame surprising his wife Aphrodite in bed with Mars, and pinning down the couple with a net to exhibit their shame to the other gods, was not an idle fancy, but must have referred to a conjunction of Mars and Venus, and it is fair to add, a conjunction in the Pleiades.
>
> This little comedy may serve to show the design, which turns out to be constant: the constellations were seen as the setting, or the dominating influences, or even only the garments at the appointed time by the Powers in various disguises on their way through their heavenly adventures.[6]

This revelation turns out to be a major key to the entire "archaic construction," (or, as Aristotle referred to it, the "ancient treasure"). Most of us are taught by representatives of conventional academia that the planets were named after the gods of the ancients, but Lucian (and the entire thesis of *Hamlet's Mill*) argues that the gods were in fact named after the planets – and that the myths were made to allegorize or "mythologize" actual planetary events.

Here, Lucian is arguing that the well-known story of the liaison of the illicit lovers Ares and Aphrodite (which is recounted in the Odyssey by a bard during Odysseus' visit to Phaeacia) was not "an idle fancy" but rather an account describing a conjunction of two planets in our sky, Mars and Venus, in the "net" of the Pleiades.

In the above image from NASA, the planets Mars and Venus are seen on either side of the Pleiades. At times the three can be even closer together.

In the version of the myth found in the Odyssey, Ares (the god of war) and Aphrodite (the goddess of love, who is married to the smith Hephaestus) are first spied making love in the mansion of Hephaestus by the all-seeing eye of the Sun-god, Helios. Alerted to his wife's infidelity, Hephaestus in grim anger forges a gossamer-thin web of chains, so fine that they can hardly be seen even by another god. He drapes these over his bed, fixing them to the firm posts and to the rafter in the center of the ceiling, and then announces that he must take a business trip to visit some of his worshipers in a far-off country on earth.

No sooner has he departed than Ares strides in, grasps Aphrodite by the hand, and leads her off to bed, where after a night of lovemaking they eventually fall asleep. The cunning chains then descend on them, and the Sun-god, who has been keeping watch for Hephaestus, sees the two and notifies the angry husband. Hephaestus comes limping in and begins to roar with anger and sorrow, summoning all the immortals, who gather around and begin to laugh at the helpless couple, pinned down by the net in their bed of love (Hermes laughs that he would gladly trade places with Ares, even under chains with all the gods and goddesses gazing on, just to lie in Aphrodite's arms).[7]

Now that we have been alerted to them by the ancient satirist Lucian and by the authors of *Hamlet's Mill*, the celestial elements of the story could not be more clear. Note the important role played by the sun, twice mentioned as the one who spies Venus and Mars as they are lingering together. Note that Venus (along with Mercury) make their orbits within the orbit of the earth – closer to the sun than our own orbit – so that in order to see either Mercury or Venus one must be looking generally towards the sun. That's why Mercury and Venus are either seen near a sunrise or a sunset, and not long before or after the rising or the setting sun (Venus for this reason alternates between being the Morning Star and the Evening Star). Venus will never be seen racing across the middle of the sky – if we were to spot Venus high in the sky at midnight, when we are on the side of the earth facing away from the sun, it would mean that Venus had somehow broken free of her usual orbit and was now located farther from the sun than our earth!

Thus, to have a conjunction with Venus near the Pleiades, the Pleiades themselves must be located near the horizon at either sunrise or sunset, which they are during the time of year that the earth is turning towards Taurus and the Pleiades just before the sun pops up over the eastern horizon (in this age, during the month of June), or when the earth is turning towards Taurus just after the sun drops below the western horizon at sunset. From the context of the bard's song in the Odyssey, we can see that he is clearly talking about a sunrise, when the sun surprises the two lovers Ares and Aphrodite in the net of the Pleiades as he rises in the east.

Because all the planets generally cross the sky along the same arc that we see the sun travel (known as the ecliptic), they periodically come into "conjunction" with one another. Mars and Venus both pass by one another during a conjunction of Mars and Venus – which the ancients chose to memorialize as a sexual liaison. There are other myths which describe Jupiter pursuing Venus with amorous intent, as well as Venus seducing Mercury: all of these myths tend to confirm the theory proposed by Lucian of Samosata so long ago (he lived during the second century AD, roughly between AD 125 and AD 185).

But this incisive observation by Lucian is not limited to the story of Ares and Aphrodite pinned down in the net of the Pleiades, nor even to the other planetary conjunctions immortalized in myths: the assertion made in this book is that *all* sacred scripture, all ancient myth, deals with the stars of the vault of heaven, and the mighty objects in our solar system which pass between an observer on earth and that starry vault: namely, the sun, the moon, and the planets (particularly Saturn, Jupiter, Mars, Venus, and Mercury).

Metaphors of the starry heavens are not *all* that these sacred traditions are – they are considerably more, full of wondrous insight and depiction of the human condition, the deepest questions of ethics and morality, life and death – but they are certainly not *less*. Nevertheless, there have been and continue to be those who would strip them of this metaphorical nature, and try to reduce them to literal history, and in doing so impoverish – yes, impoverish – these sacred treasures of the human race.

For the above assertion applies not only to the tales of Zeus and Hermes and Aphrodite (which describe the motions of the planets Jupiter, Mercury, and Venus), but equally to the scriptures of the Old and New Testaments and to nearly all the other myths of the world's sacred traditions, which likewise describe the motions of the mighty vault of heaven, divided as it is into twelve sections conveniently demarcated by twelve groupings of stars (the twelve constellations of the zodiac, a constellation being a cluster or "tribe" of stars), and the intermediating objects through which we relate to the vast, silent, unchanging, unending universe: Saturn, Jupiter, Mars, Venus, Mercury, the moon, and the sun.

Now, it is important to clarify at the outset that the thesis just now stated is only the tip of the iceberg. For to declare that the sacred traditions of the human race – the collective body of beliefs which we call "religion" – describe celestial motions from start to finish is not intended to diminish them in any way, nor even to suggest that they are not "true." Far from it. Indeed, to say that the group of scriptures which we call the Bible are not literal history, but that they are celestial metaphors having to do with the vault of heaven, is not to say that they are not true. In fact, it is only in this sense that they *are* true – they are decidedly not "true" if stripped of their celestial content and shoehorned into an artificial and constrained literalism.

We will examine numerous examples from both the Old and New Testament to show that the exact same pattern demonstrated above for the liaison of Ares and Aphrodite takes place throughout the Bible – enough to prove the point several times over (and many more could be discussed). The first two are two that are discussed in *Hamlet's Mill*, and they are both very compelling. We will discuss one from the Old Testament and one from the New, beginning with the story of Samson in the Old Testament book of Judges.

In their seminal 1969 study *Hamlet's Mill* Giorgio de Santillana and Hertha von Dechend declare: "The story of Samson stands out in the Bible as a grand tissue of absurdities."[8]

They then proceed to demonstrate that, in common with so many other sacred scriptures and oral traditions from around the globe, the origin for many of the strange objects and incidents appearing in the story of Samson is to be found in the celestial realm – the realm of the stars and the planets.

The authors begin by examining Samson's weapon of choice for slaying Philistines in Judges 15: the well-known "jawbone of an ass" ("Sunday school pupils must long have been puzzled about his weapon for killing Philistines," they write). De Santillana and von Dechend demonstrate that a jawbone-shaped weapon shows up in other sacred traditions around the world, from the weapon known as Vajra of Indra in the Vedas (which is not depicted as shaped like a jaw, but which was made from the bones of a horse-headed giant, and hence may be related to the "jawbone of an ass," just as a horse is related to an ass), to the boomerang-shaped weapon of Marduk in the Babylonian creation epic, to the legends of the Central American natives who spoke of their hurricane-god Hunrakan using the jawbone of a tapir as a weapon, and even to the Maori of New Zealand, who relate that the hero Maui killed the Sunbird using a jawbone as a weapon as well – this time the jawbone of Muri Ranga Whenua, "his own respected grandmother."[9]

Why all the traditions around the world of a powerful god or hero using a jawbone as a weapon? The authors explain that it is because the Hyades are positioned directly above the constellation Orion, Orion being the constellation with the most bright stars in the entire sky, a figure who appears in sacred tradition the world over as a mighty god or hero.

If you go out into the night sky on a clear evening when Orion is up (he disappears for a 70-day period each year, when the earth is on the side of the sun opposite to the stars of Orion, when Orion is in the sky only during the day and hence invisible, mainly during the summer months in modern times), you can see exactly where all these legends come from. The stars of Orion and the jawbone-shaped Hyades are shown in the illustration below (the Hyades are the V-shaped group directly under the word "Taurus"):

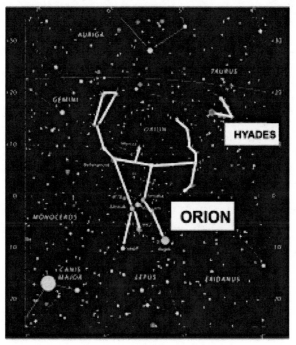

You can trace your own jawline and see that a jawbone (mandible) when detached from the skull makes a "V" shape, and that the Hyades *is* in fact very reminiscent of a jawbone. De Santillana and von Dechend explain that the Babylonians referred to the Hyades, which are located in the constellation Taurus the Bull (see illustration above) as "the jawbone of the Bull."[10]

Here is the passage from Judges 15 in which Samson uses the jawbone of an ass to slay the Philistines, beginning in verse 15:

> [15]And he found a new jawbone of an ass, and put forth his hand, and took it, and slew a thousand men therewith.
> [16]And Samson said, with the jawbone of an ass, heaps upon heaps, with the jaw of an ass have I slain a thousand men.
> [17]And it came to pass, when he had made an end of speaking, that he cast away the jawbone out of his hand, and called that place Ramathlehi.
> [18]And he was sore athirst, and called on the LORD, and said, Thou has given this great deliverance into the hand of thy servant: and now shall I die for thirst, and fall into the hand of the uncircumcised?
> [19]But God clave an hollow place that was in the jaw, and there came water thereout; and when he had drunk, his spirit came again, and he revived: wherefore he called the name thereof Enhakkore, which is in Lehi unto this day.
> [20]And he judged Israel in the days of the Philistines twenty years.

This passage is certainly difficult to understand when taking a literal approach. What is the meaning of the "hollow place that was in the jaw" providing water for Samson's thirst? The authors of *Hamlet's Mill* provide an explanation: because the jawbone represents the Hyades, and the Hyades were a harbinger of rain (known to poets as "the rainy Hyades").[11] Their very name contains the linguistic root for water, *hyd-*, reflecting this ancient knowledge, for their constellation Taurus anciently ruled the spring time of plowing and planting in the "April showers" that bring the later May flowers (and eventually the crops that would be harvested in the fall).

This single detail of the jawbone being associated with the Hyades is enough all by itself to cast serious doubt upon the assertion that we are to interpret every word of the scriptures of the Old and New Testaments in a literal fashion. It is quite evident that this jawbone, as de Santillana and von Dechend tell us, "is in heaven", and that the story of Samson thus represents some sort of celestial or astronomical knowledge, and does not represent a literal account of an earthly man who "judged Israel in the days of the Philistines" as an historical figure and who wielded an earthly jawbone as a weapon.

Note that Samson "put forth his hand" to take the jawbone before slaying his "heaps upon heaps" – and then look at the figure of Orion, who is raising his right hand to brandish a weapon (usually interpreted as a club) but who is "putting forth" his right hand towards the Hyades, reaching out towards them as if about to seize them for the gory task of slaying his thousand with the unlikely weapon.

This explanation – that the story of Samson slaying with the jawbone is meant to teach us about events taking place in the sky – certainly seems to be worthy of consideration as an alternative to the assertion that we are to imagine that Samson actually killed one man after another using the jawbone of an animal, slashing each with this unlikely weapon until he had killed . . . a thousand.

This single celestial detail – that Orion is reaching out his arm towards the jawbone-shaped Hyades – is enough to indicate that the entire doctrine of literal interpretation of the scriptures of the Old and New Testament (and many other sacred scriptures and traditions, as de Santillana and von Dechend demonstrate) is on shaky ground. However, if one single piece of evidence pointing to the celestial nature of the Samson account is not enough for some, it is possible to find many others.

For instance, in the Samson account, two chapters before the slaying of the thousand with the jawbone of an ass, Samson is shown slaying a young lion with his bare hands, and later discovering a swarm of bees inhabiting the carcass of the lion he had slain.

If we allow the possibility that the account of Samson (like the Greek myths and those of other ancients) preserves a record of celestial truths rather than literal human events, then the episode in which Samson slays a young lion which roared in meeting him in the vineyards of Timnath (Judges 14:5-6) becomes a significant clue. De Santillana and von Dechend assert in passing that this slaying of the lion by Samson is one of "his feats as a young Herakles, tearing a lion apart."[12]

Let's think about that for a bit and tease out some of the connections. Both Samson and Herakles (or Hercules) are preternaturally strong and willful, and both slay a lion with their bare hands (the Nemean lion, in the case of Herakles, whom the hero must slay without a weapon since no weapon can pierce its supernatural hide). In the passage in Judges, the Scripture is careful to point out that in the encounter with the lion, Samson "rent him [the lion] as he would have rent a kid, and *he had* nothing in his hand" (Judges 14:6).

The lion, of course, is a famous denizen of the night sky as well, in the form of the beautiful constellation of Leo the Lion, a member of the zodiac. There are twelve zodiac constellations, and there were twelve labors of Hercules, indicating that the myth of Hercules might have something to do with the passage of a strong and willful celestial power through each of the twelve stations of the zodiac, one of which is the Lion. Other zodiac constellations which appear to support this interpretation include Taurus the Bull (one of the twelve labors involves the Minoan or Cretan Bull) and the constellation of Hydra, which is located very close to Cancer the Crab.

In any case, the parallels between Samson's slaying of a lion barehanded and the same act by Herakles or Hercules is potentially significant, especially if the two heroes embody aspects of one or more celestial powers. While the authors of *Hamlet's Mill* spend some time pointing out connections between the character of Samson and the characteristics associated with the planets Mars and Saturn, it is also quite likely that the character of Samson – who encounters a lion, a beehive, the jawbone in Taurus, and ultimately a woman who binds him and brings him down to bondage in the land of the Philistines, where he meets his ultimate demise – represents the sun itself in its annual cycle, which climbs up through the summer months and exults in its strength in the season of Leo the Lion, but which descends towards the winter as it passes through the constellation of Virgo the Virgin, and ultimately towards a sort of death and resurrection at the winter solstice each year.

7

Note that in the Samson story, Samson is going "down towards Timnath" where he talked with a beautiful woman who pleased him well. Then he returned and came across the lion again (now a "carcase") and found a swarm of bees and honey in the lion.

The zodiac constellation "below" Leo as he is rising in the east is Virgo (remember, this was a "young lion" in the Samson story, which would probably indicate a rising Leo, especially as the woman Samson visited was "down" from the lion, as Virgo is when Leo is rising). The zodiac constellation above Leo as he is rising in the east is Cancer, a constellation of very faint stars but which does have right in the middle of it a "small hazy spot just visible without glasses under the best conditions" according to H.A. Rey in his wonderful guide to the night sky, *The Stars: A New Way to See Them*.[13] This cluster of many faint stars is known as *the Beehive*.

The celestial details in the short account of Samson meeting a lion on his way *down* to see a beautiful woman, and meeting a swarm of bees on his way back *up* from meeting her, are quite remarkable.

The passage of Samson *down* to a woman of Timnath through an encounter with a lion (the correct direction to Virgo – down – from Leo) and then upon his return to the lion to an encounter with a beehive is strong evidence that the Samson story in the book of Judges is meant to embody celestial knowledge, rather than a literal account of an individual person who judged Israel for twenty years.

Those who believe that the primary understanding of the Bible should be through a literal interpretation of the events as they are written have something of a problem when faced with what appears to be very strong evidence that the Samson story is not primarily literal but is instead metaphorical and related to the stars of the brightest constellation in the sky and the zodiac constellations nearby (Cancer, Leo and Virgo all follow closely behind – east of – Orion in the sky, and the Hyades are in Taurus, immediately above – north of – Orion).

They have a few options if they wish to continue to believe that the rest of the Bible should be interpreted literally. They can, of course, simply deny the very strong evidence and stubbornly continue to believe that the "grand tissue of absurdities" in the story still depicts literal events: that Samson literally slew one thousand men with the jawbone of an ass, that he slew a young lion with his bare hands and later found a beehive in its carcass, that he tied three hundred foxes together by their tails (after catching them himself) and "put a firebrand in the midst between two tails" (certainly a painstaking endeavor that would have taken perhaps more than a single night of work) before setting them loose in the fields of the Philistines, burning those fields and the nearby olive groves and vineyards as well. Or, they can admit that the Samson story is indeed primarily metaphorical for celestial events, and somehow explain this away as an anomaly and continue to maintain (through whatever path of argument) that the rest of the scriptures of the Old and New Testament are still to be interpreted literally.

However, far from an isolated example, the story of Samson turns out to be representative of the entire rest of the Bible (and the sacred scriptures and traditions of virtually every other culture on earth, as *Hamlet's Mill* makes clear). The entire assembly of events in the scriptures of both the Old and New Testaments can be very satisfactorily interpreted as a series of metaphors for celestial realities involving the sun, moon, and stars.

To visit another example (also discussed in *Hamlet's Mill*), this time from the New Testament, we can turn to the book of Revelation, in the first eleven verses of the ninth chapter, where we read:

> 1And the fifth angel sounded, and I saw a star fall from heaven unto the earth: and to him was given the key of the bottomless pit.
> 2And he opened the bottomless pit; and there arose a smoke out of the pit, as the smoke of a great furnace; and the sun and the air were darkened by reason of the smoke of the pit.
> 3And there came out of the smoke locusts upon the earth: and unto them was given power, as the scorpions of the earth have power.
> 4And it was commanded them that they should not hurt the grass of the earth, neither any green thing, neither any tree; but only those men which have not the seal of God in their foreheads.
> 5And to them it was given that they should not kill them, but that they should be tormented five months: and their torment was as the torment of a scorpion, when he striketh a man.
> 6And in those days shall men seek death, and shall not find it; and shall desire to die, and death shall flee from them.
> 7And the shapes of the locusts were like unto horses prepared unto battle; and on their heads were as it were crowns like gold, and their faces were as the faces of men.
> 8And they had hair as the hair of women, and their teeth were as the teeth of lions.
> 9And they had breastplates, as it were breastplates of iron; and the sound of their wings was as the sound of chariots of many horses running to battle.
> 10And they had tails like unto scorpions, and there were stings in their tails: and their power was to hurt men five months.
> 11And they had a king over them, which is the angel of the bottomless pit, whose name in the Hebrew tongue is Abaddon, but in the Greek tongue hath his name Apollyon.

Those who have interpreted this chapter literally have often taken it as a vision of a future apocalyptic war, with some modern commentators seeing the "locusts" that came out of the smoke as modern-day helicopters, which the revelator's vision interpreted as giant flying insects with great power.

However, as with the Samson account, a familiarity with some of the most prominent constellations of the zodiac leads to an entirely different possibility. Below is a diagram showing the Milky Way, which arcs like a great white hoop across the entire sky, and which is in fact the "thickness" of our galaxy viewed edge-on from our location on a planet inside that galaxy (and closer to the edge of it than the center of it). This is the view of the southern side of that beautiful starry arch, the point where it intersects the southern horizon, as it is rising up from the eastern horizon (for viewers in the northern hemisphere):

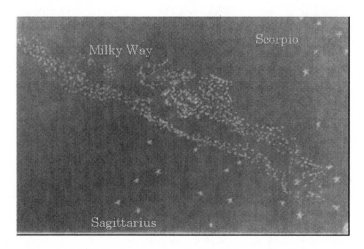

In the above diagram, Sagittarius is to the left of the Milky Way, and Scorpio to the right, with the tail or stinger of the Scorpion wrapping all the way around and into the base of the Milky Way.

These constellations quite closely match up with the description in Revelation 9, as pointed out by the German philologist Professor Franz Boll (1867 - 1924).[14] First, the smoke which arose out of the bottomless pit, "as the smoke of a great furnace," is clearly the Milky Way, rising up out of the southern horizon like a shining haze or a towering column of smoke.

Then, we are told that "there came out of the smoke locusts upon the earth: and unto them was given power, as the scorpions of the earth have power." The constellation of Sagittarius is generally depicted as a centaur carrying a bow (and pointing it in the direction of Scorpio). However, Sagittarius is also often described in modern times as a "teapot," which it does resemble with its brightest stars. When looking at the teapot of Sagittarius in the night sky, you will immediately perceive that these brightest stars of Sagittarius could also be envisioned as a large grasshopper (or locust), with its head facing left and its hind legs sticking up in a narrow triangle (below is a diagram of the "teapot"):

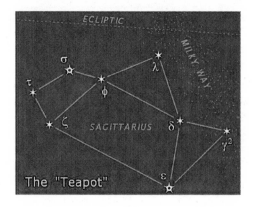

In this image, the teapot is seen with its handle on the left and its spout on the right, but it can also be a grasshopper or locust, with its head to the left and its angular hind legs rising up to make two triangles – and the effect is even more insect-like when viewing the actual constellation in person.

However, just so that we are sure we do not misinterpret the constellation we are dealing with, the passage goes on to tell us that these locusts are really like centaurs as well. In verse seven we read: "And the shapes of the locusts were like unto horses prepared unto battle; and on their heads were as it were crowns like gold, and their faces were as the faces of men."

So, the locusts are like horses with men's faces – a reference to centaurs, which Sagittarius traditionally represents – and they have "crowns like gold." Significantly, just to the right of Sagittarius is a faint arc of stars known as the Southern Crown (or *Corona Australis*), a fact that confirms the identification of these locust-centaurs with the constellation Sagittarius next to the rising smoke of the Milky Way.

Below is a diagram of Sagittarius, using the outlines proposed by H. A. Rey. The u-shaped arrangement of the stars of the Southern Crown *Corona Australis* are highlighted as well, forming an arc just to the left of the letter "A" in the words "Corona Australis," and you can easily see how close they are to the actual zodiac constellation of Sagittarius:

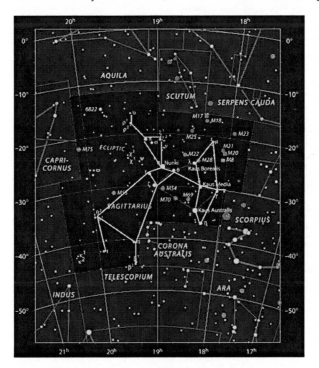

Sagittarius and Scorpio flank the rising smoke of the Milky Way in this part of the sky, and both are well-represented in the passage from Revelation 9. We have already seen that the locusts in verse three are described as having been "given power, as the scorpions of the earth have power," thus referring to each of the zodiac constellations that stand beside the smoke rising from the bottomless pit.

Later, in verse ten of the same chapter in Revelation, the constellation of the Scorpion is referenced again, when we are told of these terrifying locust-centaurs: "And they had tails like unto scorpions, and there were stings in their tails: and their power was to hurt men five months." You can easily see from the image above how close the stingered tail of the Scorpion comes to Sagittarius.

As with the Samson story, the Biblical account of the presence of locust-centaurs at the mouth of the smoking entrance to the bottomless pit finds parallels in sacred traditions all around the world. In *Hamlet's Mill*, de Santillana and von Dechend note that the shining path of the Milky Way is believed to be the road that souls travel in between incarnations in many cultures, including those of the Americas (North, South, and Central America) and Polynesia, and that there are many traditions in which the souls of the dead are received by a scorpion-goddess before they embark along that path.[15]

In ancient Egypt, this was the scorpion-goddess Selket, who can be seen protecting the burial shrine of Tutankhamun which held his three nested sarcophagi and the mummy itself (see below – she wears a golden scorpion on top of her head):

According to *Hamlet's Mill*, other scorpion-goddesses who meet the souls of the dead as they leave this world to cross the shining path of the Milky Way are Ishara of the ancient

Hurrians and the "Old Goddess with the scorpion's tail" of the Maya, who is depicted in the Maya Codex Tro-Cortesianus.[16] De Santillana and von Dechend also tell us that "In the Gilgamesh Epic Scorpion men watch the way to the other world; Virgil (*Aeneid* 6.286) makes it centaurs."[17]

The above should make it clear that, while some may persist in interpreting Revelation 9 as a literal prophecy of horrible creatures afflicting the earth at some future date, plenty of evidence exists to argue that Revelation 9 encodes details of the celestial motion of the important zodiac constellations stationed at the southern end of the glorious Milky Way in the sky. This conclusion, coupled with the evidence that Samson deals with a very similar subject, and the evidence that this very same subject was encoded using very similar metaphors around the world, has profound ramifications.

First, because this celestial connection (and its widespread resonance with similar sacred traditions from around the globe) is hardly common knowledge, we must ask ourselves how and why this way of interpreting the stories of the Old and New Testaments has been kept secret. In fact, as we will see, the examples from Judges and Revelation just discussed are by no means anomalies in the Holy Bible – they are some of the most accessible examples of a phenomenon that takes place from start to finish in every single book in a very similar manner.

Second, we must ask ourselves what it could possibly mean: why would the sacred scriptures and traditions of so many cultures take such an unexpected form?

The short answer to those two questions, which the rest of the book will attempt to support with evidence and analysis, is of immediate importance to our current situation in the moment of history in which we are living. The sacred scriptures and traditions of the world – including the Bible as well as many texts that were not included in the canon of the Bible and were vigorously suppressed – point the way to consciousness. They have been and continue to be deliberately twisted and obscured because malevolent forces have from time immemorial actively warred against consciousness, seeking to keep men and women imprisoned and unaware and in fact to prey upon them.

In other words, the teachings of mankind's most ancient traditions serve as guideposts to consciousness, and thus constitute key terrain in the war between consciousness and the enemies of consciousness, a war which continues to this day and in fact appears to have lately escalated in intensity and which may be reaching a climax.

2

What is the esoteric?

> The evidence is mountainous in bulk that pagan eyes pierced through the phenomena of nature to the truth of higher levels. Pagan spiritual discernment was all the keener for its close beholding of the natural world. The assumption that in his primitive infantilism the pagan stopped at nature, while the Christian went on to God, is rank heresy. It is defied by all the fact of antiquity. Rebuttal of this gratuitous depreciation of past civilization is firmly based upon the most exalted wisdom. The authors of these high revelations knew the realm of sublime truth that lay beyond nature, and they also knew the mighty fact that nature was the outer visible analogue of this other world of truth. Then as now, esoteric genius grasped the distinction between outer and inner, but ancient sapiency recognized better than modern the essential kinship of the two.
>
> Alvin Boyd Kuhn, *Who is this King of Glory?*[18]

Why might the most sacred texts and traditions of cultures around the world take such care to encode and pass on to future generations stories describing the motions of the sun, moon and stars?

The answer is that this knowledge relates to a task that is vital to every soul here in this plane of existence, namely the attainment of consciousness.

John Anthony West, author of the masterful 1976 publication *Serpent in the Sky: the High Wisdom of Ancient Egypt*, explained this concept very succinctly in an interview with Henrik Palmgren of *Red Ice Radio* which aired in 2008:

> And the doctrines are all basically the same – I mean they take it as a premise, as a given, that we human beings are not accidental glitches in an accidental universe, but that rather we have a specific role to play, which is the acquisition of a level of consciousness that we are not born with, but that we have the *potential* to reach, and this is what in Egypt is called the "Doctrine of Immortality" and what in other civilizations is called Samadhi or Nirvana or whatever – I mean, different names for it – but basically it's the same doctrine: that we're here for a reason, and that if we don't pursue that path, then we do so at our peril.[19]

Later in the interview, he points to Darwinism as a doctrine that leads to the opposite of this ancient belief, in that it teaches that there is not real purpose to human existence, and can thus lead to a pursuit of materialism and a neglect of the true goal of human existence, the acquisition of consciousness.

The scriptures of the Old and New Testaments teach the same doctrine which John Anthony West asserts was the goal of all the other ancient doctrines – that we are here for "the acquisition of a level of consciousness that we are not born with," but as the previous examples from the story of Samson and the account of Revelation 9, that purpose has been obscured, suppressed, and largely forgotten.

How does the motion of the sun, moon and stars relate to the attainment of consciousness? Why would a collection of scriptures such as the Bible, which purports to deal with profound matters of the soul, life, death, and behavior in this world, turn out to do so through metaphors relating to the motions of the heavens?

The answer is multifaceted and profound. One extremely compelling explanation has been expounded at length by Alvin Boyd Kuhn (1880-1963), most comprehensively in his 600-page tome *Lost Light: An Interpretation of Ancient Scriptures*, first published in 1940. His thesis is that all the ancient scriptures teach the descent of each individual's everlasting soul from the immaterial realm of spirit into the material realm of gross matter, in order to experience the things that can only be felt in the world of the physical and in order to learn lessons that can only be learned through such experience (as painful as such experience can often be), and then to re-ascend into the realm of spirit again, to return as often as is necessary for its own spiritual evolution.

Because the soul upon its descent to the world of matter largely forgot its true condition and its true spiritual origin, typified by being given a drink of strong liquor to make it forget, or a drink from the river Lethe which is the river of forgetfulness, the scriptures were imparted to mankind in order to help the soul to remember the truth. It did this through a series of metaphors which could transcend the dulled senses of the mind that was imprisoned in gross matter and which therefore had a harder time accepting those truths which transcend the physical realm of the five senses, and the most powerful metaphor the ancients used according to Kuhn was the constant descent of the heavenly bodies of the sun, moon, visible planets, and majestic constellations, endlessly plunging from the high spiritual realm of air and fire into the gross physical tomb of muddy earth and water, only to appear again on the opposite horizon and soar once more into the celestial realm.

In a chapter entitled "Loosing the Seven Seals," Kuhn explains:

> [. . .] the series of myths deals not with a wide variety of spiritual or cosmical situations, but only with the same one situation in endless repetition! There is but one story to religion and its Bibles, only one basic event from which spring all the motivations of loyalty and morality that stir the human heart. The myth-makers had but one narrative to relate, one fundamental mystery of life to dilate upon. All phases of spiritual life arise out of the elements of the one cosmic and racial situation in which the human group is involved; and all scriptural allegory has reference to this basic datum, and meaning only in relation to it. The myths are all designed to keep mankind apprised of this central predicament. It is the key to the Bible. And it is the loss of this key situation that has caused the Book to be sealed against the age-long assaults of our curious prying and delving. The restoration of this key to our hands will be seen at once to open the doors to a vision of clear meaning, where now stalks dark incomprehensibility. Cosmology has been almost wholly discarded from religion since Milton's day, yet a cosmical situation provides the ground for all adequate interpretation of Bible representation. *The one central theme is the incarnation.*[20]

In a follow-on text entitled *Who is this King of Glory?* which was published in 1944, Kuhn explains the aptness of the motions of the heavenly spheres in typifying the successive cycles of incarnation in matter followed by release and new incarnation:

The divinity in man being a portion of the ineffable glory of the sun, and necessarily therefore typified by it the great scenic portrayal was built upon the solar allegory, and the successive phases of man's divinization were enacted around the solar year in accordance with the significance of the orb's monthly and seasonal positions. Ancient religion was for this reason called solar religion or "sun-worship." Temples were built to the sun and hymns to the sun written to extol its splendor as typical of man's inner splendor. [. . .] a drama that was based on and interwoven with the most obvious of all natural phenomena – the rise and setting of the sun in the daily round and the larger counterpart of the same routine in the seasonal cycle. These two daily and annual operations, the alternate victory and defeat of the sun, typify of course the very gist of the whole human drama, the soul's descent into "death" in mortal body and its recurrent resurrection therefrom. This is the core of the central theme in all religious scripture.[21]

Alvin Boyd Kuhn's explanations plumb great depths and undoubtedly shed tremendous light on the true meaning of the ancient sacred myths of all cultures, and this book will refer to his work throughout the exploration of the subject as we continue. However, with the earth having now made some seventy additional turns around the sun since his explications were published, some additional developments have come to light which add even more layers to the deep meanings that he uncovered.

One of these developments has been the invention of lasers (beginning in 1960), which have the ability to create extremely concentrated beams of phased light, a development which makes possible (among many other applications) the creation of holograms, which cannot be created using typical light sources in which light disperses too much to allow the capture of the kind of detail necessary for a hologram. The creation of holograms and the subsequent discovery of some of their fascinating properties (beginning with the creation of the first practical holograms in 1962) led some insightful theoretical physicists to propose a model for our physical universe which opens valuable new vistas upon the ancients' consistent use of celestial metaphors to convey truths about human existence.

If the ancient scriptures, including the Old and New Testaments, teach truths about our innermost spirit using the incessant motions of the wheeling heavens, then it can be said that they are putting forth the assertion that the individual is somehow intimately related to the bigger drama above, and conversely that the motions of the outer world (even the motion of objects as far away as the planets Jupiter and Saturn) have some bearing upon the individual. In fact, as we will see, it can be said that these ancient astronomically-focused scriptures teach that the attainment of consciousness involves the apparently illogical realization that the soul in the body is a microcosm, a reflection or an embodiment of the universe that we see around us – that we contain in our microcosm of the individual self the entire macrocosm of the earth on which we live, and the wider cosmos we see above us in the sky, containing the sun by day and the infinite stars by night.

The well-known Hermetic dictum conveying this teaching declares, "As above, so below" (this dictum is found, for example, in the Hermetic text known as *The Emerald Tablet*, thought to have been written between AD 500 and AD 799 but containing concepts which are almost certainly many hundreds of years older). This identification of microcosm and macrocosm is not merely metaphorical – it is not just that we *reflect* "here below" what we see "there above," but that we actually *contain* it, we *are* it. By focusing at length and in great depth upon the motions of the great cyclical forces of nature, in our bodies, in the world around us, but most especially upon the largest stage of all, the infinite stage of the heavens, the ancients were finding and expounding truths that relate to the most internal and intimate aspects of who we are, aspects of our innermost spiritual being.

Interestingly enough, the principle that teaches that the smallest component part contains and reflects the larger whole of the universe is a crucial aspect of some of the most modern models which have been proposed by theoretical physicists to try to incorporate the almost-unbelievable aspects of quantum physics that began to come to light in the early twentieth century. One of these models is the "holographic" model, which has been put forward by physicists such as David Bohm and Karl Pribram.

As Michael Talbot explains at length in his *Holographic Universe* (1991), a hologram is very different from a conventional photograph or even digital photograph, in that a conventional or digital photograph is composed of many tiny components all colored or shaded differently to make up a picture, but a hologram is composed of many tiny components *which each embody the entire hologram* within themselves.[22]

This concept sheds a whole new light on the teaching of "As above, so below." It suggests that each of us actually contain in microcosm the entire macrocosm – that there is a unity which is difficult to comprehend logically, but which is nonetheless vitally important to understand, so important that the sacred texts of ancient cultures around the globe were centered on it.

It is to convey just such expansive concepts – concepts so transcendent that they are difficult or impossible for our logical and literal "left brain" intellect to grasp – that the technique of esotericism is so necessary. Esotericism can be broadly defined as the use of symbols or metaphorical pictures to convey truths of a spiritual nature, or truths about concepts that can defy the ability to convey them through any other method.

The truth that the mind-boggling variety of individuals on earth at this moment, and all those individuals who have lived on this earth in the past, each in some way embody the infinite wholeness of the entire universe is one such truth. *The Emerald Tablet*, the same Hermetic text which declares "as above, so below" also declares "all things have been and have come forth from One."[23] Such a concept is so contrary to the type of information that the "intellect" is designed to deal with that its first response is to simply ignore it, or tune it out, or scoff. It is abstract – it cannot be grasped by the aspects of our intellect designed to deal with the concrete world of the five senses – but it can be "concretized" in symbol or metaphor, which can then act as a kind of "Trojan Horse" to sneak the abstract truth in to the understanding.

In a book-length examination of the nature and use of esotericism, written in 1947 and first published in 1960, entitled *Esoterism & Symbol*, twentieth century alchemist, Hermeticist and philosopher R. A. Schwaller de Lubicz (1887-1961) made a distinction between what he labeled as "the intellect" or "cerebral intelligence" and what he called "intelligence of the heart" – and argued that that which is esoteric speaks to "intelligence of the heart."

He wrote: "Cerebral intelligence depends upon the senses, the recording of observed facts, and the comparison of ideas. No element of cerebral intelligence is abstract, and every qualitiative or abstract idea results from the comparison of concrete elements."[24]

Schwaller argued that the language of symbol – esoteric symbol – is designed to bypass the cerebral intelligence and convey powerful truths about the nature of consciousness and existence which the intellect cannot perceive. To do this, these symbols had to appeal to something else, which Schwaller de Lubicz called "the intuitive," "the innate," and "the intelligence-of-the-heart."[25]

To appeal to this intelligence-of-the-heart, the ancient Egyptian sages used symbol, including mythology, parable, play on words, artistic imagery, architecture, proportion, and number. All of these profound symbols could bypass the intellect and speak straight to the intuitive intelligence-of-the-heart, guiding the way to "illumination" or "consciousness" or "ex-stasis" (that which is outside of the material *stasis* of time and space, from which our word *ecstasy* is derived, which denotes the attainment of a state beyond the physical and beyond the intellect that deals with the material world perceived in terms of the five physical senses) – all terms found in the writings of Schwaller de Lubicz. He called this science of symbol "the Symbolique."[26]

These symbols or analogues or triggers for intuitive understanding of the cosmic truth that transcends the material will thus – of necessity – seem irrational or mysterious when considered by the intellect. This fact accounts for the conventional understanding of the word "esoteric" as describing "hidden truths" or teachings which deliberately intend to obfuscate, confuse, or conceal. However, Schwaller de Lubicz argues that this understanding of the concept of "esoteric" is a mistake. In fact, the esoteric is designed to *reveal*, not to conceal! It is only because it does so in terms that bypass the intellect and speak directly to the intelligence-of-the-heart that the esoteric appears to conceal.

As he writes in *Esoterism & Symbol*:

> Esoterism has no common measure with deliberate concealment of the truth, that is, with secrecy in the conventional sense of the term. [. . .] Esoterism can be neither written nor spoken, and hence it cannot be betrayed.[27]

Later in the same text he says:

> Esoterism is not a particular meaning hidden in a text, but a state of fusion between the vital state of the reader and the vital state of the author: this in the sense of a spiritual, spatial, synthetic vision which disappears at precisely the moment thought becomes concrete.

> Thus esoteric teaching is strictly *evocation*, and can be nothing other than that. Initiation does not reside in any text whatsoever, but in the cultivation of intelligence-of-the-heart. Then there is no longer anything occult or secret, because the intention of the enlightened, the prophets, and the "messengers from above" is never to conceal – quite the contrary.[28]

Schwaller teaches us that the consciousness of unity cannot be grasped by the intellect, because the intellect primarily divides and distinguishes, which is a function of breaking into pieces. The intellect can also assimilate, but once again this is a function of putting many pieces together to form a whole, as in a digital image or a conventional photograph. He writes that "The fundamental character of cerebral intelligence is that it is born of duality."[29] We might say that it is very good at seeing the world in terms of "either-or," but has a very difficult time with "both-and" (such as a man or woman being simultaneously a totally unique individual and at the same time reflecting and embodying the entire cosmos, the embodiment of which seems to defy individuation and swallow up everything into the vast "Oneness" of the universe).

Because of this problem, consciousness of unity (which is a form of ecstasy – a state beyond reason, in which the bonds of individuality and the body blur or are actually breached) must be conveyed through symbol, which does not speak to intellect. Because it does not speak to intellect, such symbol is often perceived as being deliberately obscure – of deliberately trying to hide the truth. However, Schwaller says, this appearance of deliberately obscuring is not the true case at all. Instead, the purpose of the esoteric is to convey what cannot be conveyed otherwise – it is not intended to hide the truth, but to illuminate it.

For Schwaller de Lubicz, one of the ancient symbols of the dividing mind, is the symbol of the serpent. The action of dividing, of choosing, of distinguishing, or of demanding "either-or" is the force which causes the motion of anything out of the condition of Unity or cosmic "One-ness" and into multiplicity. It is an event or a change which Schwaller called "The Primordial Scission."

In his indispensible 1979 explanation of and elaboration upon the work of Schwaller de Lubicz (which at that time had yet to be translated into English in any publication), entitled *Serpent in the Sky: the High Wisdom of Ancient Egypt*, John Anthony West explains:

> One, the Absolute or unity, created multiplicity out of itself. One became Two.
>
> This Schwaller de Lubicz calls the 'Primordial Scission' (Division, Separation). It is forever unfathomable and incomprehensible to human faculties (although language allows us to express what we cannot comprehend).[29]

To convey the concept of this Scission, the ancient Egyptians used the symbol of the serpent -- particularly the Egyptian cobra (which appears on the pharaoh's diadem as the *uraeus*, or rearing cobra). In his *Sacred Science: the King of Pharaonic Theocracy*, published in 1961, Schwaller de Lubicz writes:

> The uraeus is the *Naja* of Egypt, the dreaded though peaceful and timorous cobra, dangerous for its spit and deadly for its bite, but only if it believes itself attacked. The snake is the symbol of duality: It separates the right and left sides of the brain.[30]

We can immediately see that the serpent perfectly symbolizes "scission" or division. By its very body shape and means of locomotion it is constantly dividing into two whatever it passes through. Further, the rearing cobra which the Egyptians chose as their particular symbol for division, discernment, and discrimination is an even more precise and perfect choice. The cobra when rearing is in the very act of discriminating and discerning, of choosing between binaries: to strike or not to strike, threat or non-threat. When and if it does strike, this action is yet another perfect manifestation of discriminating or selecting. Thus the choice of the erect cobra to represent the discriminating aspect of intellect illustrates the genius of the ancients, genius which Schwaller de Lubicz and John Anthony West discover in countless other aspects of their art and architecture, proportion and number.

It also represents the exact same sort of symbolizing which Alvin Boyd Kuhn argued was at the heart of the method of properly understanding the ancient sacred myths of the world, and which literalistic approaches would always miss completely.

Mr. West elaborates still further on the concept which Schwaller de Lubicz mentions at the end of the passage quoted above, in which he notes that the brain itself -- seat of the intellect -- is divided by a serpentine line when viewed from above, into a left hemisphere and a right hemisphere (the familiar "left brain" and "right brain").[31]

Tutankhamun's diadem, which was found on the head of the mummy of the king (an excellent image of which can be seen on the website of the Dallas Museum of Art -- the image allows zooming in for detail in high resolution), shows that the Egyptians saw the Scission as somehow connected to the division of the brain. One possible explanation for this symbolism might be the assertion that with this art, the ancients were asserting that the Scission goes so far as to divide the individual even within himself or against himself (or herself), so to speak.

However, there is another possibility, and one which will become more clear as we continue deeper into this book, and that is a possibility that is suggested by modern quantum physics.

Quantum physics is a concept of which most people are at least dimly aware, but one which not everyone would be perfectly comfortable if called upon to explain. The basic outline of quantum theory is not particularly complicated. It should be something most people could at least describe at a basic level. It is probably safe to say, however, that more people could explain the basic principles which cause an internal combustion engine to operate than could explain the basic principles of quantum theory, even though the operation of an internal combustion engine is rather complicated compared to the basic outline of quantum theory, and even though many people who use internal combustion engines have never actually taken one apart themselves. However, because quantum theory cannot be discussed without running up against another one of those mysteries which defy by their very nature the discerning, dividing, "either-or" expertise of the cerebral intelligence. It is easier to "tune it out" or to ignore it. Quantum physics makes assertions which simply "do not make sense" to the intellect.

Quantum physics was necessitated by the mystifying results, demonstrated over and over again and now widely accepted, of experiments showing that tiny subatomic particles can actually exist in a state of "superposition," in which they exhibit traits which can be described as being in *two completely different places at the same time*, or being in two completely different states (a particle or a wave) at the same time. This is the aspect of quantum physics that makes our everyday, five-sense-processing cerebral intelligences revolt.

Even more astonishing, the experiments conclusively demonstrate that it is observation which brings these particles out of the state of superposition and causes them to manifest as either a wave or a particle, or to manifest in one location or another after being effectively *both*. It is the arrival of consciousness that brings them out of the "both-and" of pure potentiality and into the "either-or" of materiality.

In their outstanding book *Quantum Enigma: Physics Encounters Consciousness*, Professors Bruce Rosenblum and Fred Kuttner of the University of California at Santa Cruz provide what they call a "rough summary" of quantum theory:

> Quantum theory tells that the observation of an object can instantaneously influence the behavior of another greatly distant object – even if no physical force connects the two. These are the influences Einstein rejected as "spooky actions," but they have now been demonstrated to exist. Quantum theory also tells us that an object can be in two places at the same time. Its existence at the particular place where it happens to be found becomes an actuality only upon its observation. Quantum theory thus denies the existence of a physically real world independent of its observation.[32]

One of the foundational experiments of quantum physics is the "double slit experiment," in which a beam of single atoms or a beam of single subatomic particles is sent towards a partition containing two slits, through which they will pass and create a pattern on a screen beyond. The astonishing results of the experiment demonstrated that some portion of each of the quanta in the beam will somehow come through both slits and interfere with one another (the way a wave does), even when sent only one at a time towards the slits. The particle demonstrates the potential to be in two places at once. However, if the observer of the experiment only opens one slit, then the beam will act as if it is composed only of particles. The beam appears to have the potential to be *either* a wave or a particle, and to somehow change into one state or another depending on the actions of the observer!

In other words, it travels in the state of a wave if the observer decides to open two slits, and in the state of a particle if the observer decides to open only one slit. Did it know beforehand how many slits would be open when it arrived at the partition? Did the decision to open either one slit or two slits somehow "reach back into the past" and cause the stream to travel as either a particle or a wave? The experiment's results are not really that difficult to *describe*, but they are certainly difficult to believe!

Even more astonishing, the experiment could be rearranged to send a single particle into one of two boxes (a "box-pair"), where it would be trapped. The results of this version of the experiment show that the particle somehow exists in "superposition" in which it is simultaneously in both of the box-pairs, until again a consciousness interacts with it. If the observer of the experiment looks in one of the boxes, or opens one or the other to allow the particle (if inside) to escape, then the particle will be found to be in one box only. If the box first opened (or peeked into) does not contain a particle, then the particle will be found to be in the other box. But, amazingly enough, if *both* boxes are opened simultaneously, then the particle will escape in such a way that it creates an interference pattern, indicating that some of the particle was somehow in each box!

Here again the physicists performing the experiments run head-on into the perplexing question which Professors Rosenblum and Kuttner have termed the "quantum enigma." How did the particle "know" what the observer would choose to do? It is as if the decision to open only one box (or look into only one box) somehow caused the particle to manifest in one box or the other – and no evidence of it (or part of it) ever having been in the other box will be found. But, if the observer chooses to open both boxes at once, it will be as if the particle was always somehow "spread" across both of the boxes, even *before* the observer decided to open both the boxes! The decision seems to have created not just the result that happened *after* the decision, but also the history *leading up to* the decision.

These results completely defy "logical" explanation, which is why quantum physics has completely turned classical Newtonian physics on its ear, and why many physicists strenuously opposed it when experiments first began to point to the existence of such bizarre behavior by atomic and subatomic particles. Albert Einstein famously described the behavior of these particles as "spooky."

Rosenblum and Kuttner describe the quantum enigma that these experimental results raise:

> Did your free choice determine the external physical situation? Or did the external physical situation predetermine your choice? Either way, it doesn't make sense. It's the unresolved quantum enigma.
>
> [. . .] This mystery connecting consciousness with the physical world displays physics' encounter with consciousness.
>
> To a certain extent at least, our present actions obviously determine the future. But obviously, our *present* actions cannot determine the *past*. The past is the "unchangeable truth of history." Or is it?

Finding an atom in a single box means the whole atom came to that box on a particular *single* path after its earlier encounter with the semi-transparent mirror. Choosing an interference experiment would establish a *different* history: that aspects of the atom came on two paths to both boxes after its earlier encounter with the semi-transparent mirror.

The creation of past history is even more counterintuitive than the creation of a present situation. Nevertheless, that's what the box-pairs experiment, or any version of the two-slit experiment, implies. Quantum theory has *any* observation creating its relevant history.[33]

Here we find an example of a truth which we simply cannot logically grasp – and yet it is true. If our universe really is composed of such "super-logical" building blocks, then it only makes sense that esotericism was selected by the ancients to convey the truth of the universe. Esotericism supercedes logic – it teaches truths that cannot be grasped by logic alone, truths which *defy* logic.

To return to the symbolism of the Scission described by Schwaller, which he argued was evoked by the Egyptians using the esoteric symbolism of the serpent whose body twists its way along the dividing line of the human brain: if quantum theory says that the state of pure potentiality is ruptured by the intrusion of human consciousness – that it is the arrival of consciousness which brings particles out of their superpositional state of potential into the manifestational state of being one thing or another – then the symbolism employed by the Egyptians could not possibly be more appropriate! The Scission in esoteric terms is the rupturing of the state of superposition. It is the bringing of the particle out of the state of "both-and" and into the state of "either-or." The state of "either-or" is a division. Since quantum physics has demonstrated that it is consciousness which causes the particle to leave the state of superposition and manifest as either a wave or a particle (or as being in one box or the other), the serpent symbols on the human head are most apt.

It is the human mind which causes "the Scission" – it is human consciousness which brings the physical universe (in a very real way) into manifest discrete existence, out of the state of pure potentiality or "superposition."

We saw that the Egyptians (according to the arguments of Schwaller de Lubicz) used the serpent as a symbol of dividing, discerning, and deciding (just as a cobra rearing up discerns and decides between "strike" or "not strike"), and that they placed this cobra right at the seat of the intellect, with its body often depicted as a wave-form going right down the dividing line between the brain hemispheres. Some readers at this point will reject the possibility that the ancient Egyptians could have been symbolizing a "quantum universe," but we will see more and more evidence as we proceed throughout the investigation which will suggest that the ancients were possessed of an understanding of the nature of the cosmos that was sufficiently sophisticated as to allow that possibility and even to make it very likely.

For the present, suffice it to say that the abundance of ancient sacred texts whose stories are all based upon astronomical metaphors may all be demonstrating an assertion about the cyclical incarnation of the fiery spirit in the world of matter (as Alvin Boyd Kuhn so convincingly demonstrates in his extensive analyses), but that may not be all that they demonstrate: they may also demonstrate an awareness of the enigmatic connection between human consciousness and the material realm of physics, the realm that stretches out to the planets, stars, and galaxies. The infinite heavens are the obsession of modern physicists no less than they were the obsession for the authors of the ancient sacred scriptures. Quantum physics suggests an intimate connection between the human consciousness and the "stuff" of which planets, stars, and galaxies are made: so did the ancient scriptures.

Below is an image looking down upon the top of the head of the mummy of Tutankhamun, showing the king's embroidered skull-cap and the twin uraeus-serpents, raised to strike or not-strike, their undulating bodies framing the line between the two hemispheres of the brain, the seat of consciousness. It is a fitting example of all that esotericism can convey through the use of symbol, as a means to impart a truth that can be explained in paragraphs full of words, but which remains beyond the grasp of the cerebral intelligence no matter how many words are used.

Esotericism is not, then, a tool for hiding the truth: it is a tool for conveying the truth, when the truth is so enormous that it cannot fit into the "either-or," when it is "super-logical" to the point that the left brain cannot assimilate it without help.

Thus, those who try to reduce the esoteric scriptures to a false literalism are doing mankind a double disservice. First, they are declaring to be literal texts which demonstrably *were not intended* to be understood literally. We were never intended to believe that there was an historical figure named Samson who killed a thousand men with the jawbone of an ass.

Second, by collapsing these scriptures into false literalist history, those who urge this interpretation are short-circuiting the esoteric truths that these ancient sacred teachings were intended to convey. Obviously, when that happens, the "quantum" aspect that they embody cannot be conveyed, and they cannot teach the full picture. They thus are forced, when turned into a literalistic caricature, to teach an overly-simplistic view of the cosmos, and of mankind's place within it.

We will examine further the question of who would want to rob these ancient scriptures of their esoteric message to humanity, and when and how that robbery took place. First, however, we will explore more evidence that the scriptures of the Bible are of a piece with all the other ancient sacred traditions of mankind in their astronomical and esoteric nature.

3

The system of celestial metaphor

Millions of intelligent persons today have looked upon sun and moon throughout the whole of their lives and have never yet discerned in their movements and phases an iota of the astonishing spiritual drama which the two heavenly bodies enact each month, a drama disclosed to our own astonished comprehension only by the books of ancient Egypt. Hundreds of celebrities in the field of Egyptology have mulled over the same material and have not yet lifted as much as a corner of the veil of Isis. Primitive simplicity could not have concocted what the age-long study of an intelligent world could not fathom. Not aboriginal naïveté, but exalted spiritual and intellectual acumen, formulated the myths. Reflection of the realities of a higher world in the phenomena of a lower world could not be detected when only the one world, the lower, was known. You can not see that nature reflects spiritual truth unless you know the form of spiritual truth.

> Alvin Boyd Kuhn,
> *Lost Light: an Interpretation of*
> *Ancient Scripture.*[34]

In the passage above, Alvin Boyd Kuhn marvels at the unknown tutors who bequeathed to mankind a system of soaring spiritual grandeur, conveyed through a profound system of mythological drama, personifying what the ancients called "the Phaenomena" – the motions of the circling heavens, their complex cycles, and against this infinite backdrop the action of the primary heavenly bodies of sun, moon, and visible planets. He marvels that this body of myth could point to such sublime spiritual truth, and makes the insightful observation that the spiritual truth must have been first understood by the ancient authors of this system, before they could convey it through the esoteric symbols of the system itself.

This system is the inheritance of all of mankind – an inheritance that has, as we will see, been stolen away, hidden, and suppressed by those who sought to keep it for themselves. And yet, even today, as Alvin Boyd Kuhn says, for those who carefully examine the sacred traditions and scriptures of the world (including those of the Old and New Testaments) nothing is needed "but a mind free from bias to discern the unity, amounting virtually to identity, underlying all the old systems, which expressed so clearly the characteristic features of what appeared to have been a universal primal world religion, with the solar myth as its corner-stone."[35]

In order to understand this "unity underlying all the old systems," which Kuhn believes had "the solar myth as its corner-stone," some discussion of the solar cycle in its motions through the solstices and equinoxes each year, as well as through the backdrop of stars that inhabit the zodiac band, will be necessary. While what follows contains a bit of technical explanation, its application to the metaphors in the Bible will make that worthwhile. These details are the very key to the "ancient treasure" which was given to mankind in the myths of the world, and which Kuhn described as "a meaning deep as life itself, which they [the myths] were from the first designed to embody."[36]

We have seen evidence in previous chapters, following the analysis of Giorgio de Santillana and Hertha von Dechend in their 1969 text *Hamlet's Mill*, of the detailed celestial metaphors in familiar Biblical passages, including Samson from the Old Testament and Revelation chapter 9 from the New. However, there were even more thorough examinations of the "astro-theological" metaphors in the Old and New Testament scriptures written over a hundred years before *Hamlet's Mill* was published, by Robert Taylor of England (1784 – 1844), in two collections of his lectures entitled *The Devil's Pulpit, or Astro-Theological Sermons*, and *Astronomico-Theological Lectures*, both published posthumously in 1857. There have been others who have pointed out the same things, some of them predating Taylor by centuries, but for sheer comprehensive explication of the celestial metaphors in the Bible, the Reverend Taylor (who was imprisoned for his efforts) is hard to beat.

The diagrams below will be helpful references for the metaphors that Taylor uncovers in the scriptures of the Old and New Testaments, and in fact they are the key to a system of celestial metaphor which unites the metaphorical stories of the Bible with the parallel metaphorical mythologies of the rest of the world, from ancient Greece to the islands of the Pacific. The first diagram shown is very similar to the illustration Taylor provides at the beginning of his book *The Devil's Pulpit*, and to which he frequently refers back throughout his text, calling it "the cut at the beginning of the book." It depicts a typical "double hemisphere" map of the earth, such as were common in previous centuries, which shows on it the path of the sun throughout the year – the ecliptic path – as a graceful, serpentine arc tracing out a "sine wave" line above and below the line of earth's equator:

This particular map is the work of Peter Goos, from the year 1666. It is interesting to note that the continent of Antarctica was unknown to this mapmaker, and California is depicted as a long narrow island off the west coast of North America, itself unfinished to the north and west, as is Australia and New Zealand on the other side of the Pacific.

It is also interesting to note in passing the two largest birds depicted above each hemisphere, an eagle above the western and a swan above the eastern, depicted with wings outstretched and flying generally towards one another. This imagery has a celestial counterpart in the constellations Aquila and Cygnus in the night sky, who fly generally towards one another in the band of the Milky Way. Both constellations depict the two majestic birds with their wings outstretched and feet trailing behind, just as the birds in Peter Goos map above are drawn.

The sinusoidal path of the ecliptic throughout the year is the product of the earth's axial tilt (also known as its "obliquity"). Because the earth moves around the sun with a constant tilt to its poles (by a little over 23.4 degrees from its plane of orbit), the angle that the sun will trace through the sky as the earth rotates each day will be influenced by this tilt. This tilt causes the sun's path to be above the celestial equator during its daily journey for one entire one half of the year, and to cross below and afterwards be below the celestial equator during its daily journey during the other half of the year.

The celestial equator is that imaginary circle in the sky which is located ninety degrees of arc down from the north celestial pole, or ninety degrees of arc up from the south celestial pole. It can also be described as the imaginary circle created by projecting the earth's own equator up into the heavens. Thus, the sun's path being above this celestial projection of the earth's equator for one half of the year is shown in the "sine wave" arc of the sun's path which is drawn across the two hemispheres, and which crosses above and below the earth's equator in the diagram, spending half its time above and half below.

Although the arc is depicted as reaching its maximum northern point as it crosses Central America, and its maximum southern point in the ocean between Madagascar and Australia, this is only a convention: the sun's path reaches its maximum northern point at a time of year, not a specific point in Central America. Because a two-dimensional map on parchment cannot depict a spherical earth turning on its axis as it hurtles around the sun, with the sun's most direct rays falling further to the north as that hurtling earth approaches the June solstice, and then falling further to the south as it approaches the December solstice, the mapmakers have created a convention to symbolize in 2-D space the reality that happens in the 3-D. What the diagram is trying to convey is the fact that the sun's path reaches a maximum northern and a maximum southern point on our globe once each year, as it progresses around the sun with its axis tilted in relation to the plane of its orbit.

When the north pole is most directly oriented towards the sun (which happens at one moment during the entire year – the June solstice), the track of the sun will cut furthest north across the northern hemisphere. It will then be midsummer for those in the northern hemisphere, and midwinter for those in the southern. Conversely, when the south pole is most directly oriented towards the sun (which happens at one moment during the entire year – the December solstice), the track of the sun will cut furthest south. At that moment, the north pole will be oriented most directly away from the sun, and it will be midwinter in the northern hemisphere and midsummer in the southern. This concept is what the sinuous track of the ecliptic on the above double-hemisphere earth map is depicting. It is very common to see this "sine wave" on old double-hemisphere maps.

The important concept, and one very necessary for deciphering the metaphors in the Bible and other ancient scriptures and traditions, is the idea that the sun is "climbing" towards the midsummer point for half the year, after which it begins a "descent" towards midwinter (these concepts are usually expressed in reference to the northern hemisphere). For those in the northern hemisphere, this climb begins after midwinter on the December solstice, but until the March equinox (the spring equinox for the northern hemisphere) the days are still shorter than the nights.

After that, the climb continues with longer days than nights. There is a slight difference between the precise day of equality and the actual equinox moment, and this is due to the fact that the sun is a disc and not a tiny point, and to the fact that the atmosphere bends the rays of the sun as it rises and sets, just as a light will bend when it passes through a layer of water. However, at the midsummer point (June equinox is midsummer for the northern hemisphere), the sun and the ecliptic path begins to proceed towards the south again, "descending" towards midwinter. From midsummer until midwinter, the sun is on the descending path. From fall solstice until spring solstice, the days are shorter than the nights (although for the second half of the "shorter days" period the sun is actually "climbing" again).

Thus, we can envision the year as cut in half two ways. One way is "climbing" versus "descending," with climbing taking place from midwinter (lowest point on the sine wave on the map above) to midsummer (highest point on the sine wave). The other way to divide it is from "shorter days" to "longer days," with days that are shorter beginning when the ecliptic crosses the equator on the way down, and days that are longer beginning when the ecliptic crosses the equator on the way back up (again, the exact day of "Equalday/night" – as explained by Professor Gordon Freeman, author of *Hidden Stonehenge* – is slightly different than the moment the earth passes through its equinox point in either direction, due to the size of the sun's disk and the bend in light created by the thickness of the atmosphere at dawn and dusk).[37]

In some double-hemisphere maps, the curve of the "sine wave" ecliptic is marked with symbols indicating the signs of the zodiac, because as the earth goes around the sun and earth's tilt causes the ecliptic to move north and then south, the backdrop of stars changes as earth moves around its orbit. To envision this, we can think of earth orbiting the sun inside a large dining room or other room in a house: the stars on the walls that are visible will change as the earth makes its circular route inside the room. When the earth gets to the point of winter solstice, people on earth will be looking out at a different wall at midnight than the wall they will see on the other side of their circuit, when the earth is at the point of summer solstice.

The stars seen on "the wall" just before the earth's rotation brings the sun into view will be different as the earth makes its rounds each year, and these stars (the ones on the horizon ahead of the rising sun just before the earth's turning brings the sun into view) are the ones that indicate which "sign" the earth is passing through each month. The action of precession causes this to change (explained in detail in my previous book), but setting that discussion aside for the time being, the sign that occupied this point above the eastern horizon on the morning of March equinox (in a previous precessional age) was the zodiac constellation of Aries, and the sign that occupied that point above the eastern horizon on the morning of the fall equinox (in the same previous age) was Libra. With this in mind, consider the second important diagram, below:

Here, instead of a sinuous wave, the sun's path throughout the year is depicted in a circle, and the signs of the zodiac (the constellations through which the ecliptic passes) are marked along its edge. However, even though the sine wave has now been joined into a circle, the same concepts we just discussed still apply. The sun still "climbs" from the lowest point (at the bottom of the circle, marked by the sign of Capricorn, just to the left of the kneeling archer of Sagittarius in the above diagram) until it reaches its highest point of the year (near the top of the circle, marked by the sign of Cancer, which in the old diagram above looks more like a lobster than a crab). Note that these signs, in reference to the previous diagram of the double hemisphere, help us to understand why the line twenty-three and a half degrees north of the equator is called the "Tropic of Cancer" (it is the northernmost point reached by the sun's path each year), and why the line an equal number of degrees south of the equator is called the "Tropic of Capricorn." So, we see that the circle can also be divided into halves in which the sun is climbing for one half and descending for the other.

Alternately, the year can also be divided into a period of "longer days" and another period of "longer nights." This is depicted in the zodiac wheel below, in which the line dividing the year goes between the two equinoxes, rather than the two solstices. On the sun's upward journey (as it moves through the year in a clockwise manner in the diagram), the longer days commence as we cross the line to the left side of the circle, in the sign of Aries (March equinox, or spring equinox for the northern hemisphere). On the other side of the circle, we pass into the period of longer nights after crossing the equinox again, this time the September equinox, or fall / autumn equinox for the northern hemisphere. That takes place in the sign of Libra (the balances or scales).

The above discussion depicts the "Age of Aries," so named because the March or spring equinox took place in the constellation of Aries the Ram, and the March or spring equinox opened the sacred year in ancient cultures (note that both Passover and Easter are keyed to the spring equinox, and other ancient cultures had similar traditions). Since the Age of Aries, precession has shifted the actual constellations that occupy the position above the rising sun on the spring equinox ("delaying" the zodiac constellations, such that Pisces was there instead, a period known as the Age of Pisces, which itself is now drawing to a close, to be replaced by the long-anticipated Age of Aquarius).

However, it is important to understand that the convention shown above is still used among many astrologers, as if we were still in the Age of Aries, and this is because the traits that make one "an Aries" do not actually come from the far away stars but rather from the angles of the sun's rays impacting the earth at the time of year when the earth is passing through the March equinox, and the traits that make one "a Cancer" do not come from the far away stars of that constellation either, but from the angle of the sun's rays impacting the earth as they do in the time of year when the earth is passing through the June solstice.

In other words, the characteristics of the time of the earthly year and the angle of the light from the sun as it reaches the earth is determined by the earth's location on its orbit in relation to the sun. As earth passes winter solstice, for example, the angle of the sun's rays will be the same as they were as the earth passed winter solstice thousands of years earlier, even though the background constellations will have shifted due to precession. Therefore, the science of angles worked out by the ancients, encoded in scriptures using the signs from the Age of Aries, will still apply today even though the background stars have shifted into the Age of Pisces.

This concept is clearly explained by Thomas H. Burgoyne in his 1900 text *The Light of Egypt, or The Science of the Soul and the Stars, volume 2*, on pages 7 through 9. There, he writes:

> The shining Zodiac, with its myriad constellations and its perfect galaxy of starry systems, derives its subtle influence, as impressed astrologically upon the human constitution, from the solar center of our solar system, NOT FROM THE STARS which occupy the twelve mansions of space. *Aries*, the fiery, and *Pisces*, the watery, *are always there*, and instead of its being an argument against astrology, it is one of its grandest truths that, in all ages and in all times, Aries, the first sign of the Zodiac has been found *ever the same*, equally as well as Pisces the last. [. . .] [I]t is the angle at which we, THE INHABITANTS, receive this Sun's light that makes all the difference [. . .].[38]

In other words, the constellations of the zodiac are markers for the angle of between the earth and the sun, and more precisely for the angle created by the tilt of earth's axis which, as we circle the sun, causes the ecliptic plane to move up and down across the celestial equator throughout the year, causing the sun to rise further and further north during one half of the year, and then further and further south during the other half, and to follow an arcing path through the sky that is higher and higher through one half of the year, and then lower and lower through the other half. The angle of the sun's rays will be much more direct when the sun's arcing path is at its highest (on the summer solstice), and much more oblique when the sun's arcing path is at its lowest (on the winter solstice).

These angles give the different parts of the year their different character, and that character does not change when the constellation-markers "behind the sun" rotate due to precession. Thus the portion of the year governed by the *sign* of Aries does not change when the *constellation* of Aries is no longer behind the rising of the sun during that portion of the year: we can still refer to it using all the characteristics that the ancients attributed to the sign of Aries. It is *the sun* which moving through the signs that the ancient scriptures and tales are commemorating, not so much the signs themselves.

We have already seen that Alvin Boyd Kuhn argued that the whole system of myth used these esoteric stories to remind us of the truth that all men and all women in this world are spirits who have chosen to come down from the fiery realm of spirit and to incarnate in the material world of gross matter, taking on a body made up of water and earth, which they will one day leave behind again to ascend into the spiritual realm from whence they came. He argues that the motion of the sun, in its daily ascending and descending, as well as the motions of all the other heavenly bodies, formed the basis of the system designed to convey this esoteric truth. We will explore this interpretation of Alvin Boyd Kuhn, as well as the many other profound ramifications of this ancient system, in subsequent chapters.

This understanding of the sun's "climbing" and "descending" throughout the year, and its passing through the twelve signs of the zodiac as it goes through its "climbing half" and "descending half" (and its "longer-day" half and "shorter-day" half) proves to be a cornerstone for interpreting all the metaphors of the ancient sacred traditions, from Greek and Roman mythology, to the stories of the Old Testament, the stories of the New Testament, and the sacred traditions of many other cultures as well.

That half of the year when the Sun is on his upward path, climbing towards the summer solstice, is represented in the Old Testament as the Promised Land, a hill whose summit is the Heavenly City of Jerusalem, while that half of the year in which the Sun arcs downward to the winter solstice is the land of Egypt, the house of bondage. More broadly, the upper half of the year represents Heaven, and the lower half of the year represents Hell. In the Homeric accounts of the Trojan War, the upper half of the year represents the Achaeans or Danaans (the Greeks), while the lower half represents Ilium and the Trojans. In ancient Egypt, the upper half of the year was Upper Egypt, and the lower half represented Lower Egypt. This same pattern will be repeated over and over, in many different guises, throughout the sacred traditions the world over, but once we know the pattern, it will become more and more familiar and more and more recognizable.

A dramatic example of the way this system works should suffice to convince even the most skeptical reader that the ancient myths primarily allegorize these heavenly cycles, while at the same time proving quite convincingly the assertion that the stories of the Old and New Testaments follow the same pattern that is found among the "pagan" myths.

As we have seen in the forgoing discussion, the arc of the sun's daily path through the sky is located *above* the celestial equator during the summer half of the year: those months which stretch between the spring equinox at the beginning, to the summer solstice which is the "summit" of the year, and then down to the fall equinox, where the sun's ecliptic path crosses the celestial (and earthly) equator and the "lower half" of the year commences.

The ancient myths of many cultures choose to describe a sacrifice at the important crossing points where the sun's path crosses from being above the equator (in the "Promised Land" side of the year) to being below it (going down to the "house of bondage," or to Sheol). In the ancient Greek myth-cycle surrounding the story of the Trojan War, there is a powerful scene in which a sacrifice is demanding at just such a "crossing."

In the myths describing the descent of the Greeks to fight on the plains of Troy, and their eventual triumph and return, there is plenty of violence and bloodshed, and even evidence of human sacrifice, such as the sacrifice of Iphigenia daughter of Agamemnon and Clytemnestra, in order to enable the Argive fleet to reach Ilium. In this complex and important episode, some ancient traditions have it that Iphigenia was actually killed in the sacrifice, but in many other ancient portrayals of the sacrifice of Iphigenia, a stag is substituted for the maiden at the last moment. This dramatic sacrifice legend takes place at the crossing *down* to Troy, at the port of Aulis.

If the theory being proposed is correct, and the legendary Trojan War is actually a celestial allegory, then the "crossing" and the sacrifice of Iphigenia probably represents one of the two crossings that take place during the year, one at each equinox: one at the fall equinox when the sun crosses down into the land of winter and death, and another at the spring equinox when the sun triumphantly crosses back upwards into the land of summer and renewed life. If we can find clear parallels between the story of the sacrifice of Iphigenia which correspond to the stars near one of these two crossings, it would both illustrate the system that has just been described, and go a long way towards confirming that it is actually the system underlying the ancient sacred traditions of the world.

The sacrifice of Iphigenia (not directly mentioned in Homer but certainly a part of many of the ancient accounts of the Trojan War) takes place at a significant crossing, and one that is in a *downward* direction. It takes place at the point where the Argives plan to sail from their lands to the lands of the Trojans – in other words, at the crossing between the upper (Greek) half of the year and the lower (Trojan) half of the year. This corresponds to the September equinox, and as we can see in the zodiac wheel diagrams in this chapter, it is precisely at the September equinox that we find the sign of the Virgin, the sign which rules the period leading up to the crossing of the sun from being above the equator to being below it (the sign of Libra follows immediately after the September equinox).

Clearly, the constellation Virgo the Virgin is quite appropriate for Iphigenia, and also for the goddess Artemis / Diana, a virgin goddess and the one most commonly associated with the sacrifice of Iphigenia (in some accounts, Iphigenia must be sacrificed to Artemis to appease the goddess, after the Achaean warriors offend her in some way – the ancient accounts vary).

Since Iphigenia in most ancient accounts was saved from death by the substitution of a stag, we should suspect that perhaps there is a constellation near Virgo which gave rise to this tradition – a constellation which resembles a stag. But is there?

Directly below (from the perspective of northern-hemisphere observers) the constellation of Virgo the Virgin is the more southerly constellation of Centaurus, the Centaur. He is a large and fairly bright constellation, containing the very bright star Alpha Centauri. While he very much does resemble a centaur, a quick glance at the stars of this constellation confirms the fact that, in addition to resembling a centaur, the stars of Centaurus can also be seen as a deer with a wide rack of majestic antlers (see the image below).

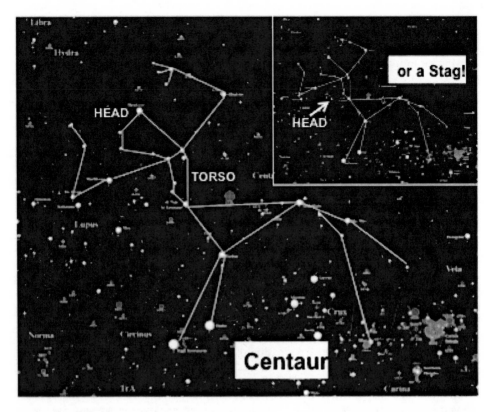

In the image, lines between the stars are depicted as suggested by H.A. Rey in his book, *The Stars: A new way to see them* (originally published in 1952). The centaur as drawn has a rather large head, and a small narrow human torso above the horse-like body. At the juncture between head and torso, two outstretched arms already resemble a deer's wide antlers. If the "cross-bar" that forms the top of the "head" area is removed, then we see that the centaur is instantly transformed into a mighty stag. The narrow torso of the original centaur becomes the deer's head, the arms become the outer sweep of the antlers, and the former "head" area of the centaur becomes two inner prongs on this rack.

That the maiden Iphigenia is saved from sacrifice at the hands of her parents by the appearance at the last moment of a substitutionary stag, and that the sacrifice takes place at a downward crossing, corresponding to the September equinox and the sun's downward crossing, and finally that the sign of the Virgin corresponds in the zodiac wheel to the downward crossing and that she has a stag-constellation beneath her feet, are all powerful confirming evidence that this celestial system underlies the myth. There are simply too many clear correspondences to attribute them all to coincidence.

I strongly suspect that this similarity of the constellation below the Virgin to a stag is also responsible for the story of Artemis and Actaeon (the unfortunate hunter who was transformed by Artemis into a stag and hunted down by his own pack of dogs). Also, the above interpretation of the Danaans and Trojans as inhabiting the upper and lower halves of the circle of the year is also echoed in the body (we will see that the metaphors in the scriptures that became the Bible also frequently have both a celestial and a human-body interpretation). Note that the "wide plains of Ilium" in the human body correspond to the wide-spreading bones of the pelvis, the largest and highest of which are designated the *ilium* in the human body.

Any reader familiar with the Old Testament has by this point no doubt noticed a strong correspondence between the story of Iphigenia, who was to be sacrificed by her parents but was saved by the substitution of a stag, and the story of Isaac the beloved son of Abraham, who was to be sacrificed by his father but was saved at the last possible moment by the substitution of a ram. In the Isaac story, however, the details are slightly different: Abraham and Isaac must trudge *up* to the top of Mount Moriah to reach the appointed place of sacrifice. This suggests that the sacrifice story, in this case, refers to an upward crossing, rather than a downward crossing as it does with Iphigenia.

The sun's upward crossing of the equator takes place each year at the spring equinox (the March equinox, in the northern hemisphere). Referring again to the zodiac wheel, we can see that the sign of Pisces immediately precedes the spring equinox, and that when the sun bursts across the line in the upward direction, he emerges into the sign of Aries – the Ram. Here again we have dramatic confirmation that the stories depict celestial allegories, and that the sacrifice corresponds to the equinoctial crossing (and was not intended to be understood as a literal or historical event).

These twin stories should dispel any doubt that the system described in this chapter is at work in both cases – and that the esoteric stories preserved in the Bible are close kin to those of ancient Greece, and in fact to those of the rest of the world's sacred traditions as well. The diagram below shows the parallels and places the two stories on their appropriate points on the zodiac wheel described previously:

Part I

The following two chapters will examine evidence of this pattern in numerous other stories from the Bible, first from the Old Testament and then from the New, before embarking on a discussion of the profound significance of these allegories, and the indication that the ancients who bequeathed them to mankind were possessed of a high wisdom far beyond anything suspected by the defenders of conventional history.

4
The Old Testament in the stars

And the *wilderness* literally is, and never was, and never meant any other, than that wild and confused jumble of stars, of which you can make neither head nor tail, till you have learned to *convoke*, or call them together, and group them into their respective constellations.

And then you will understand that *Benui Yesreile*, or *Children of Israel*, literally, really, and from the first use of that term in the ancient Phœnician language meant the Stars of Heaven; *Yesreile* being the Phœnician name of the planet Saturn, of whom all the celestial bodies within the range of his immense orbit are the children.

And among these children of Israel, the Lord, or the Lord God of Israel, is the leading constellation, or that which brings them up out of the land of Egypt, out of the house of bondage – that is, not out of any real land of Egypt, or house of bondage, but from below the horizon.

Robert Taylor,
Astronomico-Theological Lectures.[39]

As we embark upon an overview of some of the most important astronomical metaphors in the scriptures of the Old Testament, it may be helpful to present a brief outline of the principles which underlie the system, some of which we have already discussed in previous chapters, along with some very brief comments on the meaning of this esoteric structure, which will be explored in greater depth in subsequent chapters.

First, we have already touched upon the compelling thesis of Alvin Boyd Kuhn, argued at considerable length and with considerable supporting evidence by that author in his 600-page *Lost Light* and 460-page *Who is this King of Glory*, that the esoteric meaning conveyed in the stories of the endlessly ascending and descending stars (and sun, moon, and visible planets) is the incarnation of individual men and women, who like the stars (and sun, moon, and visible planets) descend from the empyrean of spirit (the realm of air and fire) into the material world, taking on bodies made of clay (earth and water).

It was Kuhn's assertion that the system found in the Old and New Testaments reflected directly the system found in ancient Egypt, and indeed came directly from Egypt (we will explore the evidence supporting this assertion, and its importance to the history of the deliberate suppression of the esoteric interpretation of the scriptures, in later chapters). Very briefly, Kuhn finds evidence in the Egyptian Book of the Dead and other sources that the Egyptians saw in the apparent motion of the heavenly bodies a perfect metaphor for the plunge of the human spirit into incarnation.

Taking for an example just the sun itself, when the sun plunged beneath the horizon, it became the sun in the realm of the dead, passing from the western horizon of sunset through the dark chambers of the underworld towards the eastern horizon. In this dark underworld, the sun was personified as Osiris, the mummified god – the sun entombed in the earth. Upon reaching the eastern horizon, however, the sun would then burst forth back into the airy realms free of the earth, and would be personified as Horus, the son of Osiris. In some of his manifestations, Horus was known as Horus-of-the-two-horizons: he was the sun god soaring into the sky, between the eastern horizon of his rising and the western horizon of his setting. Because in this phase he was free of the bonds of earth, he was often personified as a falcon, or a god with a falcon's head.[40]

The important thing to understand about Kuhn's thesis is that he believes that the realm symbolized by the soaring Horus-sun in the heavens represented the spirit-realm where the human souls come from and return to, but that the realm beneath the western horizon – the realm of earth and mire, ruled over by the mummiform Osiris-sun – represented this material world, in which those spirits are incarnated in these bodies we wear during our sojourn through this underworld. In other words, all the versions of the Osirian lower-realm (which is called in various versions of the myth-system "the house of bondage," or in the Book of the Dead "Amenta," or in the Hebrew scriptures "Sheol," or in the New Testament "hell") are nothing more than the expression of this very life which we are living right now. It is esoterically described that way because, in contrast to the realm of spirit from which we descend and to which we return, this material realm is lower, heavier, darker; in short, it is to the spiritual realm as the underworld (where the sun travels from nightfall to sunrise) is to the heavens (where the sun soars free again after bursting out from the eastern horizon at daybreak).

These two contrasting realms are depicted in the myth-systems (whether of ancient Egypt or Greece or the two halves of the Bible) as the lower realm and the upper realm, and the stories which take place in the upper realm are understood to describe the motions of the deathless stars and planets, and not the historical adventures of people here on earth. As we will see in the examination of the system as it manifests in the Hebrew Old Testament, the tribes of the Israelites are the starry bands of the zodiac constellations, who in their endless cycles plunge downward and then below the horizon (into the "land of Egypt") only to later rise again to ascend up that "holy hill" towards the upper houses of the year (on our zodiac wheel shown previously), and ultimately towards that shining city on the highest hill, Jerusalem (which is a heavenly city).

In the quotation that begins this chapter, we see the Reverend Robert Taylor (who will be one of our most important guides through the astronomical figures of the Old and New Testaments) asserting that the very name Israel is directly connected to the Phœnician name for the planet Saturn, and that the "Children of Israel" are the stars of heaven who were figured to be the children of that farthest-ranging of the visible planets.

This assertion is most significant for the system we have been laying out in these introductory paragraphs to this chapter's examination of the Old Testament, because Osiris himself has clear Saturnian characteristics, as Giorgio de Santillana and Hertha von Dechend demonstrate conclusively in *Hamlet's Mill*. Like Saturn, Osiris was once the ruler of a "Golden Age," but he "retires" to sleep in an underwater or underworld cave, promising to one day return (we will examine the world-wide Saturn myth in greater detail at a later point). In fact, the Egyptian name for the personified constellation Orion (closely associated by the Egyptians with Osiris) was *Sa* or *Sahu*, which may well be related to the Latin or Roman name of *Saturn*. We will see clear indications of Saturnian elements in the Old Testament as we proceed.

Finally, in sketching the outline of the system as seen in the scriptures of both the Old and New Testaments, we will see that the metaphors often have allegorical connections to both the "macrocosm" of the starry heavens and the "microcosm" of the human body. This aspect of the Bible and other ancient sacred tradition is very important, as it reinforces the assertions made by Alvin Boyd Kuhn that the scriptures remind us of our descent from and ultimate return to the world of spirit (returning many times – during each incarnation our body being a very important tool for learning the lessons we could not learn in our disincarnated, spirit-state). However, as we will see in the discussions of the implications of our examination of the stories of the Old and New Testament, this simultaneous "heavenly" and "bodily" allegorization may indicate that, in addition to what the esoteric scriptures teach us about our human condition during successive incarnations, they also teach us profound truths about the nature of our universe – truths which were not guessed-at by "moderns" until after the advent of quantum physics, and the "holographic universe" proposals that followed.

In an important passage in *Hamlet's Mill*, Giorgio de Santillana and Hertha von Dechend explain:

> The real actors on the stage of the universe are very few, if their adventures are many. The most "ancient treasure" – in Aristotle's word – that was left to us by our predecessors of the High and Far-Off Times was the idea that the gods are really stars, and that there are no others. The forces reside in the starry heavens, and all the stories, characters and adventures narrated by mythology concentrate on the active powers among the stars, who are the planets.[41]

The point being made by these authors is that there are actually very few actors on the celestial stage – in fact, there are really only seven – but that among these seven, they take on just about all the varied roles found in all the various myths. Many times, they play several different roles within a single culture's mythology. For example, *Hamlet's Mill* presents evidence to argue that Prometheus, Hephaestus, Phaethon, and Kronos are all among the many manifestations of the planet Saturn.

The final sentence declares that the planets are the "active powers among the stars" – the stars form a fixed backdrop, like the sets on a stage, through which the active powers move and create their drama. Once the overall pattern is understood, the observer of a drama based on this celestial design will begin to recognize the familiar planets and constellations, whether the story is from the ancient Vedas, the Norse Eddas, the traditions of the Pacific islanders in Hawaii or Aotearoa (New Zealand), or even the tales of ancient Japan.

As the metaphor employed by de Santillana and von Dechend suggests, the situation is directly analogous to the actors on the stage (or in the movies) who take on different roles and who can for a while be difficult to recognize. Then, in a flash of recognition, the viewer realizes the actor is a familiar one he or she has seen in many other different productions, a realization that often brings about a sense of resolution and satisfaction, especially if the viewer was trying to remember where he or she had seen that actor before.

This experience is no doubt familiar to everyone in the modern world – for instance, the actor Geoffrey Rush looks and speaks and dresses entirely differently in the movie *The King's Speech* (where he plays a speech therapist) than he does in the *Pirates of the Caribbean* movies (where he plays a pirate). In the same film (*King's Speech*), actor Timothy Spall (playing Winston Churchill) looks and speaks very differently than he does in the movie *A Series of Unfortunate Events* (playing Mr. Poe). Just as de Santillana and von Dechend declare, the "actors" on the stage of any given era or generation are fairly few, and they show up in different costumes and disguises and speaking with different accents in widely different productions. It was the same in the days of Shakespearean acting, and no doubt in the amphitheaters of ancient Greece and Rome.

In the same way, the "active powers" in the heavens – the sun, the moon, and the visible planets Mercury, Venus, Mars, Jupiter and Saturn – don different attire and speak different languages in the mythology of ancient Egypt, or in the Norse myths, or in the legends and traditions of the tribes and civilizations of North and South America, but like the actors who appear in different movies, they are the same planets and once we are familiar with the pattern, we will begin to recognize the actors even if they are wearing different costumes and makeup when appearing in a story from a different part of the globe.

As we have seen in our examination of the Biblical personages and events thus far, the constellations of the zodiac often play leading roles as the hero or heroine of the story, and do not leave the acting to the sun, moon and planets alone. We have already seen that the constellation Virgo may have been mythologized as both Iphigenia and the virgin goddess Artemis (Diana) in Greek myth, and we will see Virgo take on many other extremely important roles as we continue. This pattern will hold true in the Old Testament as well, with the players taking on different costumes and different names, while still recognizable to those familiar with the celestial key. In a passage in *The Devil's Pulpit*, Robert Taylor says that the Old and New Testaments are "so essentially interwoven" that they are "like different translations of the same original."[42]

Following the pattern we have already observed in our analysis of the sacrifice of Iphigenia (when the Greeks were going *down* to Troy), and which we observed to have mythologized characters taken from the constellations around Virgo, who presides over the region of the zodiac where the sun is crossing the equator on the way *down* to the lower winter half of the year, we can suspect that the Genesis story of *the Fall* might take place among the same constellations, for it is at that point in the zodiac wheel that we see the sun falling from the realms of air and fire and plunging below the horizon of the equator, into the realm of death and Hades.

Robert Taylor confirms this suspicion with his compelling explanation of celestial origin of each of the actors in the account of the Fall, in a lecture entitled "The Fall of Man" in his *Astronomico-Theological Lectures*. In that lecture, he argues that Eve is none other than the constellation Virgo. Her husband, Adam, is played by the nearby constellation of Boötes the Herdsman, a prominent figure in the night sky, marked by the brilliant red-orange star Arcturus (note that linguistic scholars assert that the root of name "Adam" means "red," and that other words containing the three consonants "*adm*" also relate to red in Hebrew and other Semitic languages).

Sure enough, there is a serpent below the constellation Virgo – the constellation Hydra, the longest constellation in the entire sky. Corvus the Crow and Crater the Cup, each constellations we will also encounter in conjunction with Virgo in the context of the New Testament, are perched on the back of the constellation of the Hydra-serpent.

The image below shows the sinuous line of the Hydra, with Corvus and Crater on its back, writhing through the sky ahead of the constellation Virgo, who is seen reclining on her back above Corvus and Crater, and Boötes who can barely be seen in the upper left of the chart:

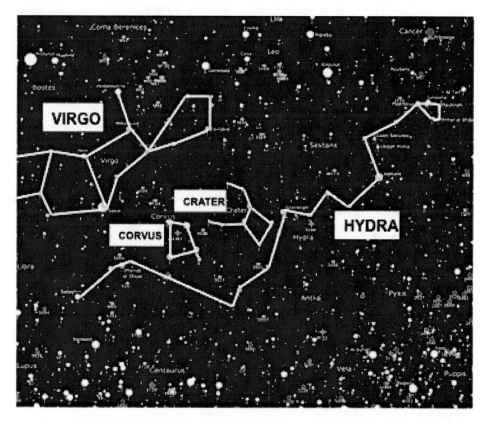

Because the rotation of the earth causes the stars to move across the sky from the east to the west, the stars in the above chart will move through the night towards the right-hand side of the image as we are looking at it above. Thus, the serpent of the Hydra will lead the woman towards the western horizon, and she in turn will be ahead of Boötes in this progression: he is further east than Virgo, who is further east than Hydra, and thus in the march towards the western horizon the procession will be led by the serpent, then the woman, then the man.

With these facts in mind, Robert Taylor shows that the events of the Genesis story of the Fall are a perfect fit for the celestial drama. Note that the events of the episode of the Fall take place in "a garden eastward in Eden" (Genesis 2:8) where God "put the man whom he had formed" (Genesis 2:8), a point which Robert Taylor argues is given to us to understand that the story deals with the motion from east to west of the constellations described above.[43]

> And there, in the garden of God, looking eastward among those flowers of the sky, which adorn the beautiful bosom of the night, will be seen depicted in the groups of Stars, the whole drama of Paradise.

> The constellation, or group of Stars, represented as falling within the imaginary outline of a Serpent rising in the east, and followed by the woman, whom he may therefore, in the most literal sense, be said to seduce, *seducere*, to lead on, as the woman with extended hand, holding a branch of fruit in her hand, is said to seduce, or lead on her husband, the celestial herdsman, Boötes: till, at the moment when the Virgin and the Herdsman, having run after the Devil through the whole garden, are seen to set on the western horizon, which is literally the fall of man; and at the moment of their setting on the western side, the constellation Perseus, the cherubim with the flaming sword, will be seen to rise on the opposite side (the east of the garden of Eden), and so to drive them out, with his flaming sword, which turned every way to keep the way of the tree of life.[44]

The celestial drama described can perhaps best be seen during the early spring months in our modern era, around the middle of April. At that time, Virgo begins rising in the east during the hours after sunset and begins to traverse the sky through the hours of the night, followed by Boötes. The entire journey takes almost twelve hours from one horizon to the other, at the latitude of the Great Pyramid (it takes less time the further north).

We can point out one other striking detail which adds tremendous weight to the parallels already noted, and that is the fact that the constellation Virgo has her arm stretched outwards from her body, a very distinctive feature of the constellation which we will see woven into other allegorizations which center on the stars of the Virgin. Looking at the diagram above, one can observe her outstretched arm, which is indicated by the bright star Vindemiatrix, which is labeled. Virgo's outstretched arm is envisioned between the star labeled Minelauva (*delta Virginis*) and Vindemiatrix (designated *epsilon Virginis*, even though it is the third-brightest star in the constellation). The name Vindemiatrix actually means "grape-gatherer" in Latin, which is appropriate because Virgo seems to be reaching out to pluck some *fruit*. Is it a coincidence that the Genesis story tells us that it was the woman who took the fruit from the tree, and who also gave it to her husband?

Taylor also points out another striking parallel between the constellations and the Genesis account, which is the fact that the constellation of Perseus with his raised sword rises in the east at about the same time that Virgo and Boötes are sinking below the edge of the western horizon.[45] This corresponds precisely to the events described in Genesis 3 verses 23 and 24, in which God drives out Adam from the garden of Eden (*translation*: the constellation connoting Adam is driven out of the sky), and we are specifically told in verse 23 that Adam is sent forth "to till the ground from whence he was taken" (*translation*: the constellation arose from the earth when it broke above the eastern horizon, and now it has descended again to "till the earth" as it goes down in the west). In verse 24, we are told that God placed "at the east of the garden of Eden Cherubims and a flaming sword which turned every way, to keep the way of the tree of life" (*translation*: the flaming angel is the constellation Perseus, who rises in the east of "Eden" [the heavens] as the constellations Adam and Eve are cast out of the heavens to sink below the western horizon).

To this day, an observer who knows what to look for during the right time of the year can watch the constellations of Virgo and Boötes cross the sky and sink down below the western horizon just as Perseus is rising up in the east. To see that take place in the early hours of the morning, it is best to wait until late April or even the month of May, when it will happen in the hours before dawn (a few minutes earlier each night).

Just as we saw with the story of Samson, and the story of the sacrifice of Isaac, the celestial correspondences are striking, and it would be difficult to argue that they are coincidental. If only one episode in the Bible matched up so closely, then it could perhaps be argued that the correspondences could be coincidental, but with so many other stories displaying the same level of celestial connection, the pattern becomes exceedingly difficult to dismiss.

Very briefly expounding on the celestial metaphor as regards to the story of Adam and Eve, we see that the promised curse – that on the day they ate of the fruit they would surely *die* – did in fact take place: the stars die in that they fall below the horizon (the Egyptians referred to those stars which are so close to the celestial north pole that they never go below the horizon as *the undying stars* or *the imperishable stars*). But, as Alvin Boyd Kuhn is at pains to demonstrate again and again throughout his books – and in particular throughout *Lost Light* – in the metaphor, *dying* meant incarnating in this world, the world of matter, the world of flesh, the world of death and the realm of the dead. The metaphorical sense of all the underworlds, journeys through the night realms, and hells of the ancient myths is *this very world we inhabit*.[45]

Thus the story of the Fall is the story of each of our souls' descent from the realm of spirit, the realm of Paradise, into our current incarnational state. For the spirit, it is a kind of death – entombed in the body of matter, dazed and confused by the strong drink of forgetfulness as to its true home – but it is only metaphorically a "death," for it is only a temporary state, from which the spirit will again rise at the end of the journey through this underworld.

In Genesis 3, we see that the man cast out of the garden is bound "to till the ground from whence he was taken." Certainly, the plunge of the stars – and esoterically the plunge of the soul into this incarnation – can be described as a plunge into *the earth* (Adam, after all, was given a body fashioned of clay or wet earth). However, as we will see, the celestial metaphors also describe the celestial actors as plunging beneath *the sea*, or the waters below, when they descend from the realm of the two higher elements (air and fire) into the incarnational world of the two lower elements (earth and water). The celestial allegory particularly describes as "the sea" the lower half of the year, when the sun's daytime ecliptic has crossed below the celestial equator, which occurs at the September equinoctial crossing-*down* and continues through the winter solstice at the bottom of the zodiac wheel, all the way until the March equinoctial crossing-*up*.

The authors of *Hamlet's Mill* explain the system as follows:

First, what was the "earth"? In the most general sense, the "earth" was the ideal plane laid through the ecliptic. The "dry earth," in a more specific sense, was the ideal plane going through the celestial equator. The equator thus divided two halves of the zodiac which ran on the ecliptic, 23 ½° inclined to the equator, one half being "dry land" (the northern band of the zodiac, reaching from the vernal to the autumnal equinox), the other representing the "waters below" the equinoctial plane (the southern arc of the zodiac, reaching from the autumnal equinox, via the winter solstice, to the vernal equinox).[46]

Later, they elaborate further on this definition.

Those four points [speaking of the two equinoxes and two solstices] together made up the four pillars, or corners, of what was called the "quadrangular earth."

This is an essential feature that needs more attention. We have said above that "earth," in the most general sense, meant the ideal plane laid through the ecliptic; meanwhile we are prepared to improve the definition: "earth" is the ideal plane going through the four points of the year, the equinoxes and the two solstices. Since the four constellations rising heliacally at the two equinoxes and the two solstices determine and define an "earth," it is termed quadrangular (and by no means "believed" to be quadrangular by "primitive" Chinese, and so on). And since constellations rule the four corners of the quadrangular earth only temporarily, such an "earth" can rightly be said to perish, and a new earth to rise from the waters, with four new constellations rising at the four points of the year. Virgil says: "*Iam redit et Virgo . . .*" (already the Virgin is returning). (It is important to remember the vernal equinox as the fiducial point; it is from this fact that a new earth is termed to rise from the waters. In reality, only the new vernal equinoctial constellation climbs from the sea onto the dry land above the equator – the inverse happens diametrically opposite. A constellation that ceases to mark the autumnal equinox, gliding below the equator, is drowned.) This "formula" will make it easier to understand the myth of Deucalion, in which the devastating waves of the flood were ordered back by Triton's blowing the conch: the conch had been invented by Aigokeros, i.e., Capricornus, who ruled the winter solstice in the world-age when Aries "carried" the sun.[47]

For readers unfamiliar with the precession of the equinoxes, to which de Santillana and von Dechend are referring in the above passages when they describe the "changing of the guard" of the four zodiac constellations who rule the four corners of the "earth" (in other words, who rule the four points of March equinox, June solstice, September equinox, and December solstice), it is thoroughly explained in both the *Mathisen Corollary* book and blog, and in many other books and resources. The important points in the above discussion for the next examination of Old Testament metaphor are those points which refer to the waters, and specifically to the Flood. Reference is made to the Greek legend of Deucalion, who survived the flood sent by an angry Zeus by building an ark-like chest in which he and his wife rode out the deluge in safety.

As the authors of *Hamlet's Mill* argue in the above passages, the lower half of our zodiac wheel was allegorized as the sea (in addition to being allegorized as Hell, Sheol, Hades,

Amenta in the ancient Egyptian system, and many other "lower realms"). Of the zodiac signs which occupy the lower part of the wheel, we find numerous animals (including one that is half-man, that being the centaur-figure of Sagittarius) and we find one man: Aquarius. Appropriately enough, the figure of Aquarius is pouring out twin streams of water, and in doing so starting a deluge in the celestial realms.

It is this zodiac sign, Aquarius the Water-Bearer, which Robert Taylor associates with the Old Testament figure of Noah. Taylor argues that Aquarius is the sign which begins to lead the zodiac band upwards, following the sign of Capricorn who rules over the lowest part of the year – which in the system described by de Santillana and von Dechend above is allegorized as the lowest depths of the waters.[48] We see that the Greek myths also seem to hint that these lowest zodiac signs are associated with the flood-story, for as the passage from *Hamlet's Mill* cited above points out, Deucalion heard Triton blowing the conch-horn to order the flood-waters to retreat, and Triton must in this case figure the sign of Capricorn. So Capricorn announces the receding of the waters of the Flood (being the sign at the very bottom of the wheel), and Aquarius – who stands for Deucalion and for Noah – presides over their retreat, being the sign that begins to lead the zodiac band back upwards out of the waters.

Interestingly enough, the ancient Latin author Gaius Julius Hyginus (c. 64 BC – AD 17), in Part II of his *Astronomica*, has this to say of the constellation Aquarius:

> Many have said he is Ganymede, whom Jupiter is said to have made cupbearer of the gods, snatching him up from his parents because of his beauty. So he is shown as if pouring water from an urn.

> Hegesianax, however, says he is Deucalion, because during his reign such quantities of water poured from the sky that the great Flood resulted.

> Eubulus, again, points out that he is Cecrops, commemorating the antiquity of the race, and showing that men used water in the sacrifice of the gods before wine was given to them, and that Cecrops ruled before wine was discovered.[49]

Here we see another example of the principle that a constellation or other celestial power can play many different roles in many different myths. The constellation Aquarius no doubt plays all three of the roles mentioned by Hyginus, as well as many others. The fact that Hyginus cites a now-unknown author named Hegesianax, who says that Aquarius is Deucalion, is significant confirmation of our analysis above, and would suggest that Noah is Aquarius as well.

The passage from Hyginus is also significant in revealing another ancient tradition, cited in the third myth that Hyginus suggests for Aquarius – that of a ruler who came from a time when "men used water in the sacrifice of the gods before wine was given to them," the ruler Cecrops who "ruled before wine was discovered."

Importantly, Biblical tradition has it that Noah was the first to make wine: he is specifically described as doing so only *after* the Flood, and it is the first time in the Bible that wine or the making of wine is mentioned (the immediate consequence, as one might expect for someone who has just made wine for the first time in human history, is that

Noah passes out drunk and naked in his tent). In Genesis 9:20-21, we read "And Noah began *to be* an husbandman, and he planted a vineyard: and he drank of the wine, and was drunken; and he was uncovered within his tent." The fact that we have evidence from ancient Latin authors of a pagan tradition associating Aquarius with both Deucalion who rode out a flood in an ark and with Cecrops a ruler who ruled before wine was discovered is important confirmation of the identity of these ancient myths with Aquarius and of the identity of Noah with Aquarius. The reader might also note that the tradition associating a transition from water to wine associated with Aquarius will be important to remember when we get to the New Testament.

Both Noah and Deucalion ride out their respective Floods in a box-shaped vessel. De Santillana and von Dechend present compelling evidence to associate cube-shaped objects with the Flood, and with Saturn – Saturn is closely associated with the Flood as well, because Saturn is universally depicted as presiding over a lost Golden Age, as we will see shortly, a Golden Age that was ended by the Flood.[50] However, while this connection is no doubt important, and explains the box-shape of both Noah and Deucalion's arks, there is also a rather "boxy"-looking ship constellation not far from Aquarius in the heavens, and one that is undoubtedly associated with the legend of Noah and of Deucalion.

The ship Argo Navis is a very southern constellation, and thus one which sits well below the celestial equator (which *Hamlet's Mill* has already informed us was often depicted by ancient astrologers as the line in the sky below which constellations were said to be "watery" or submerged in the celestial "sea"). In fact, it contains the very significant star Canopus, a very bright but very southern star, the star which the ancient myths portrayed as being the great weight which rested at the very bottom of the celestial "waters below." In describing the system of the "dry" and "wet" halves of the celestial sphere, de Santillana and von Dechend have this to say of Canopus:

> At the "top," in the center high above the "dry" plane of the equator, was the Pole star. At the opposite top, or rather in the depth of the waters below, unobserved from our latitudes, was the southern pole, thought to be Canopus, by far the brightest star of these regions, more remarkable than the Southern Cross.[51]

The reason we can be quite certain that this ship is the ark of both Noah and Deucalion is the fact that this celestial ship is accompanied by a dove. Plutarch (c. AD 45 – c. AD 120) informs us in *De Sollertia Animalium* ("On the intelligence of animals"), found in his *Moralia*, that Deucalion used a dove to ascertain whether the waters had receded enough for the birds to find land, just as Noah does with a dove in the Genesis account. In the section numbered 13 in that essay by Plutarch, which is numbered 968 in the modern reference system for the entire *Moralia*, paragraph F (or 968f), Plutarch writes:

> Now the story-books tell us that when Deucalion released a dove from the ark, as long as she returned, it was a certain sign that the storm was still raging; but as soon as she flew away, it was a harbinger of fair weather.[52]

While many authors have seen this passage as evidence that Plutarch must have had contact with the Old Testament and imported that detail from Noah's flood experience, there is no reason to believe that it was not an original feature of the Deucalion myth, for the simple reason that the constellation of Columba the Dove is located right beside the constellation of Argo Navis the heavenly ship.

Columba is often described as a "modern constellation," since it was not included in the forty-eight constellations discussed by Ptolemy in his *Almagest*. But, while Ptolemy may not have mentioned the Dove, that does not necessarily mean that Columba was not an ancient constellation. Clement of Alexandria (AD 150 – AD 215), an early Christian author, in a passage in *Paedogogus*, most of which is devoted to rather severe admonishments regarding the adornment of the body, says that finger-rings are allowable (but not ear-rings or nose-rings!) due to the need for signet seals (but not for ornamentation), and says that we should "let our seals be either a dove, or a fish, or a ship scudding before the wind, which Polycrates used, or a ship's anchor, which Seleucus got engraved as a device."[53]

It has been argued that here Clement is evincing ancient awareness of the constellation of the Dove, since all of the "seals" he suggests are clear constellations: the Fish of Pisces or of Piscis Austrinus, the Ship of Argo Navis, and the Dove of Columba, although the anchor is not a commonly-recognized constellation today. It is possible that the anchor represents the constellation Crux (the Southern Cross), which the Maori people of New Zealand do refer to as the Anchor. However, since Clement does not specifically and explicitly say that he is referring to constellations as the acceptable source for signet-ring seals, we cannot say with certainty that this passage from the *Paedogogus* indicates an ancient convention of seeing the stars of Columba as a Dove. It is notable, however, that Clement mentions the dove and the ship in close proximity in this passage.

Long before Clement, however, the Greek myth of Jason and the Argonauts associated a dove with the ship *Argo*. It was a dove who assisted the Argonauts in safely negotiating the Symplegades, or the Clashing Rocks: the Argonauts were instructed to release a dove and if it made it through the dangerous passage, then they too would be safe. The dove made it through in time, although the rocks snapping together clipped its tail feathers. Then, the *Argo* went through, and just like the dove the ship made it through safely, although the Clashing Rocks came together and crushed its aft-most stern-ornament. Thereupon, the rocks sprang open and remained open, creating a new passageway or a new channel: the authors of *Hamlet's Mill* explain that the creation of such a new gateway is emblematic in the celestial allegory of having a new sign at the March equinox, because the equinox crossing is (metaphorically) like the sun passing through a narrow gate. The action of precession periodically opens a new "crossing point" at the equinoxes roughly every 2,160 years. Because the Argonauts were in search of the golden fleece of a ram, it is likely that the transition to the Age of Aries was meant by their mythological journey.

The fact that Columba the Dove is located right next to the *stern* of the celestial ship is strong indication that the myth of the Argo and the Symplegades mythologizes these constellations. The fact that so many ships of ancient sacred tradition – that of Jason and his Argonauts, that of Deucalion in the Flood, and that of Noah – all involve stories which contain a helpful dove indicates that the constellation was known long before Clement of Alexandria, and long before Ptolemy.

The presence of a dove constellation next to a ship constellation, and the use of a dove in legend in conjunction with the memorable ship-myths of the Argonauts and the

Symplegades, Deucalion and the Flood, and Noah and the Flood, strongly suggest that all these are "of a piece" with one another: they are the same "actors" (in this case, the constellations Argo Navis and Columba, as well as Aquarius in the case of Noah and Deucalion) appearing in different "plays" on different "stages" in world culture.

Note that this identification of Noah and his Ark with stars in the sky does not of necessity mean that there never was a world-wide flood: it is quite possible that the ancients – who possessed the level of sophisticated knowledge that we will later see evidence that the unknown civilization which bequeathed all these myths to the people around the globe clearly possessed – knew that the earth had once been violently flooded by water, as the geology of this planet and the evidence elsewhere in our solar system strongly suggest. However, that discussion is not entirely germane to the question of whether or not the story of Noah as it is presented in the Old Testament is historical and literal, or if it in fact is celestial and esoteric, as the evidence strongly suggests that it is.

Alvin Boyd Kuhn expounds at some length upon the esoteric significance of the Ark and the Flood in *Lost Light*, where he devotes the entire seventeenth chapter to the subject. There, he suggests that the story "exemplifies the eternal alternation of spirit and matter, soul and flesh, discarnate and incarnate existence in the universe of life."[54] Expounding further, he explains:

> When we transfer the reference from external symbol to subjective reality, the myth is seen to be a somewhat fanciful but lucid pictorialization of the reciprocal relation of the two bodies of man's constitution, physical and spiritual, as well as a formula for the routine of evolutionary growth. In life the material body is the ark in which the soul is carried over the sea of sense and realism; in the heavenly state the ark is the spiritual body that enwombs the seeds of physical creation. From the moment of first entry into incarnation the soul is borne across the waters of earthly existence, from west gate of life to east gate through the dark underworld, in the ark of the physical body. But when the six water signs of the zodiac have been traversed, and the soul comes to the point of emergence from the sea, it then embarks anew on the ark of Ra on the eastern marge and is borne up the ascent of heaven to the Paradise about the Pole, to join the company of the gods and the stars (souls) that never set (incarnate). The ark below matches and reflects the structure of the ark above, but in inverted form. The tabernacle was to be fashioned after the pattern of things in the mount. And the lower and the higher tabernacles were to enwomb each other in turn.[55]

As Robert Taylor asserts in his *Astronomico-Theological Lectures*: "We treat the Scriptures with respect and reverence, – when with the clue thus put into our hands, we endeavor to wind the maze of their occult significancy." The clue that enables us to wind or trace our way through the maze in search of their hidden ("occult") meaning, according to Taylor, is the understanding that "all the events [. . .] are emblematical pictures of the phænomena of the universe."[56]

One of the most significant personalities of the Old Testament is the character of Abram / Abraham. His genealogy is recorded in Genesis 11, where we learn that he is the son of Terah, son of Nahor, son of Serug, son of Reu, son of Peleg, son of Eber, son of Salah, son of Arphaxad, son of Shem, son of Noah.

Immediately after the recitation of his genealogy, we are told that the LORD directs Abram to leave his country, Ur of the Chaldees, "unto a land that I will shew thee: And I will make of thee a great nation" (Genesis 12:1-2). This is the first of the promises to Abram that he will be the father of many children – so many, in fact, that they will be beyond numbering: as numerous as the stars of the sky. His name *Abram*, in fact, means "Father" or as Robert Taylor argues, "Father of Elevation."[57] When his name is later changed to *Abraham* (Genesis 17:5), the addition signifies amplification or exaltation – "Father of a Great Multitude" or "Father of Many Nations," we are told in the text.

Robert Taylor presents extensive evidence for understanding Abraham to represent the heavenly body Saturn, the highest (farthest away) of the visible planets, with the longest orbit: truly the "Father of Elevation."[58] There is some evidence that ancient authors described the religion of the Jews as connected to Saturn-worship, with passages in Eusebius (quoting Philo of Byblos and other ancient sources less well-established) declaring that the ancient Phoenician name for Kronos was "El" or "Elus," and the Roman historian Tacitus asserting in his *Histories* that the Jews worshipped Saturn.[59] Saturn in the Greek myths was Kronos, the father of the Olympian gods, and the father of Zeus by his consort Rhea, so this "father" characteristic of Abraham may indeed be one clue of his Saturnian identification. Taylor points out that Vesta was both the wife of Saturn but also his sister – a characteristic that Sarah the wife and sister of Abraham shares as well.[60]

The child-devouring deity Kronos was in some ways identified with devouring Time (which eventually "devours" all its children, meaning we ourselves when we leave the timeless realm of spirit and enter this material realm of Kronos), and even today we sometimes refer to the personification of Time as "Father Time," just as Abraham is often styled "Father Abraham." De Santillana and von Dechend devote extensive analysis in *Hamlet's Mill* to the mythological characteristics of Saturn across many cultures, and to the assertion that "Saturn gives the measures" (because he is the planet with the longest orbit, taking thirty years to orbit the sun) associates him with Time, which measures out our lives and all the periods within our lives.[61] All measures of distance are also measures of time (as we can see by the measures of distance upon our rotating globe, in which a "minute" is both a measurement of time and a measurement of distance through which our earth turns in that amount of time, and as we can see from Einstein's argument that time and space are two aspects of the same thing), and so we can understand why the one who gives the measures of time was also the one who gives the measures of distance and every other form of measurement. Many cultures call the deity associated with the planet Saturn the "Lord of Measures" (de Santillana and von Dechend point to ancient Sumer, ancient Mesopotamia, ancient Egypt, and ancient China as examples).[62]

Taylor points out that there are many intriguing passages in the Bible which seem to link Abraham to the concept of time and the measuring out of time.[63] Among these are "Before Abraham was, I AM," a New Testament passage given as the words of Jesus (John 8:58), which Taylor interprets as a declaration that he existed before time ("before Abraham, that is Kronos, that is to say *Time* even existed, I AM").[64] Also, "Your father Abraham rejoiced to see my day – he saw it and was glad" (John 8:56). Here again we see Abraham referred to as one who is watching over Time, measuring out the days, waiting for the beginning of a New Age: the Age of Pisces the Fish (Jesus), replacing the Age of Aries the Ram (Moses).

Taylor offers further evidence linking Abraham and the complex character of Saturn. As already noted, Genesis tells us that Abraham is the son of Terah. Kronos / Saturn, of course, is the son of Uranus (Ouranos) and Gaia, and the Latin form of the word *Gaia* was *Terra*, a goddess who was the Roman version of the Greek Gaia and whose name of course gives us words such as "terrestrial," "terrarium," and "territory." It is singularly notable that both Abraham and Saturn were described as being the son of Terah or Terra.[65]

Several ancient writers indicate that there were clear traditions of Saturn sacrificing his own son, just as Abraham is commanded to do upon Mount Moriah. Ancient historians including Eusebius, Plutarch, and Diodorus Siculus all explain that Saturn sacrificed his favorite son. Ancient Greek and Roman historians also explain that surrounding peoples, especially the Phoenicians, practiced child sacrifice to their Saturn deity (sometimes called Cronus, sometimes El). Taylor cites the sacrifice of the son motif present in the mythology surrounding Saturn as another piece of evidence linking Abraham to Saturn.[66]

Perhaps the most obvious evidence linking Abraham to Saturn involves the Saturnian traditions and strictures followed by the "children of Abraham." Most distinctive among these, of course, is the honoring of a Sabbath-day, which was (and still is) observed on the seventh day of the week, Saturday.[67] This day was Saturn's Day in many ancient cultures of the Mediterranean.

Additionally, and remarkably, the practice of circumcision Taylor believes was associated with the planet Saturn. He believes that the rings of Saturn, which are not visible to the naked eye and were not even seen as rings by Galileo when he constructed his first telescope, may have given rise to the ancient myths that depict Kronos / Saturn committing suicide by self-emasculation (castration), or in other versions meeting his death by being castrated. Taylor believes this is a reference to the "starry ring which appears cut off from that planet."[68] In recognition of this circle that is "cut off" from Saturn, Taylor says that the worshippers of Saturn "have never ceased to inflict on their own persons a cruel commemorative exhibition of the fabulous suicide of Saturn" – that is, the commemorative marking of the male genitals through circumcision.[69]

Note that circumcision is not mentioned in Genesis until Abraham. The practice is specifically associated with Abraham. God commands it of Abraham when he changes his name from Abram to Abraham (Genesis 17:11-14). It is even possible – in fact, it is likely – that the circular yarmulke worn on the head by male children of Abraham is a mark of respect for Saturn the ringed planet, especially since the traditional color for this headgear is the color black, one of the colors associated with the planet Saturn (the other is the color yellow).

Modern scholars might scoff at the idea that the ancients could have been aware of the rings of the planet Saturn. The rings are not visible with the naked eye. They are not even visible through binoculars. Even Galileo with his first telescope in 1610 could make out that there was something blurry around the planet Saturn, but his telescope did not have enough resolution to enable him to identify that blur as the Saturnian rings. That identification would have to wait another forty-five years, when Christiaan Huygens would describe the rings as a disc around the planet Saturn, in the year 1655. If astronomers equipped with telescopes (albeit early telescopes) could not even identify the rings, how is it possible that the ancients could have known of them?

And yet there seems to be evidence that knowledge of the rings of Saturn was known anciently, and that this knowledge was passed down in myth and sacred tradition through the ages. The circumcision and castration traditions associated with Saturn / Abraham are one body of evidence, but before we accept that as evidence we should look to see if there are other mentions of rings around Saturn from other sources.

In fact, there are. One of the clearest traditions comes from the islands of Aotearoa (New Zealand), where the Maori legends describe Saturn as a beautiful but wayward woman, who wears a circlet around her head.

In *The Astronomical Knowledge of the Maori, Genuine and Empirical*, written by Elsdon Best (1856 – 1931) and published in Wellington, NZ in 1922, there is preserved a host of accounts from the Maori themselves of their star-lore and planet-lore.

Although Mr. Best indulges in some unfortunate condescending and paternalistic sentiments (such as his reference to "uncultured races" and "puerile superstitions"), the book itself contains a wonderful treasury of Maori astronomical lore, including Maori names for many of the stars and planets, as well as discussions of celestial navigation.[70]

Among the many fascinating revelations contained in the book is the fact that the Maori name for the sun, found in many of the *hakas* which are reproduced in the book, is *Ra*.[71]

Another amazing discussion concerns the celestial body known to the Maori as Parearau. Mr. Best explains that this name was given to an important bright planet, either Jupiter or Saturn, said to be the leader or "puller" of the Milky Way, and described as having a ring![72]

Mr. Best explains:

> Parearau, say the Tuhoe people, is a *wahine tiweka* (wayward female), hence she is often termed Hine-i-tiweka. One version makes her the wife of Kopu (Venus), who said to her, "Remain here until daylight; we will then depart." But Parearau heeded not the word of her husband, and set forth in the evening. When midnight arrived she was clinging to another cheek, hence she was named Hine-i-tiweka. Parearau is often spoken of as a companion of Kopu. Of the origin of this name one says, "Her band quite surrounds her, hence she is called Parearau" – which looks as if our Maori friends can see either the rings of Saturn or the bands of Jupiter with the naked eye.[73]

This planetary knowledge is certainly remarkable, in that even with a telescope, Galileo could not perceive that Saturn has a ring or rings!

Of this amazing perception, Mr. Best writes that it "looks as if our Maori friends can see either the rings of Saturn or the bands of Jupiter with the naked eye." Back in 1922, when he wrote his book, Mr. Best could not know that astronomers would later determine that Jupiter has rings as well, and so he speculated that if Parearau represented Jupiter, then the "ring" must refer to the bands of clouds across the face of that planet (which are also not visible to the naked eye, or even to the eye aided by binoculars). While the bands of

Jupiter can be seen with a telescope, only the most powerful modern earth-bound telescopes can detect the rings of Jupiter, which were not discovered until unmanned spacecraft passed by the planet in the 1970s.

Another quotation from the Maori about Parearau found in the discussion in Mr. Best's book is cited: "That green-eyed star is Parearau; that is the reason why she wears her circlet."[74] It certainly seems to have been part of Maori lore that Parearau wears a ring!

Could the Maori really see the rings of Saturn or the bands or rings of Jupiter with the naked eye? Or, did they have some other way of knowing that Saturn or Jupiter are ringed planets?

Robert Taylor cites evidence from ancient historians indicating that the ancients were possessed of more advanced technology than modern historians are willing to give them credit for. He points out that the Odyssey of Homer appears to describe the Phaecaians as possessing a technology that enabled them to navigate through the fog, through the night, and outside of the sight of the coastline, and notes that Homer describes it as resembling an "arrow."[75] In the same pages, Taylor testifies to his belief that the ancients also had telescopes, in some cases built into the solid rock at their observatories.

The planet Saturn has a complex relationship as a sort of adversary to the sun. De Santillana and von Dechend show throughout *Hamlet's Mill* that Saturn-figures are often portrayed in myth as the Sun that has been deposed, the king who has been cast-down from ruling over a lost Golden Age.[76] The same legends often depict him as being banished to a murky and watery place, such as the cave of Ogygia in Greek legend. There, the Saturn-figure is often depicted as sleeping in an enchanted sleep, some day to reawaken and return, bringing back with him the Golden Age that has been lost. The fate of King Arthur, taken down into a watery cave by the Lady of the Lake, there to sleep until some future time, is a medieval version of this theme.[77]

Saturn figures in world legend include Osiris in ancient Egypt, who was deposed by his brother Set and entombed in a coffin that was floated out to sea. They include the figures of Kukulkan / Viracocha / Quetzlcoatl in Central and South America, who ruled over a Golden Age and then departed over the sea with a promise to one day return. Saturn figures also include Yama of the Vedas, and Yu the Great of ancient China, who "once upon a time [. . .] had plumbed out the utmost depth of the sea."[78] He is also Yima Xsaeta or ancient Persia (note the linguistic connection of the second part of his name to the Latin name *Saturn*), Jamshyd of later Persia, and Sigu of the Guyanas in South America, and also Ptah of the ancient Egyptians in addition to Osiris.[79] Saturn figures are civilizers, who teach mankind the arts of agriculture and the times and seasons of planting and reaping. Prometheus, who was imprisoned upon a rock for the crime of giving mankind the gift of fire, is also a Saturn figure, according to de Santillana and von Dechend.[80]

From earlier discussions, we know that Alvin Boyd Kuhn argued that Osiris was the sun in the underworld, during the portion of its daily journey when it traversed the caverns beneath the earth's surface after dropping below the western horizon on its way back to the east (there is abundant evidence that the Egyptians knew the earth was a sphere, by the way, and did not literally believe that the sun went into an underground portion of a flat earth – this is a metaphor like the rest of the myths). Thus, Osiris – who was a

Saturnian figure, sleeping in a cave in the underworld – is the Lord of the Underworld of incarnation: that is, the lord of those incarnate beings who are traversing this material world. This connection to Osiris helps explain the Saturnian aspects we are discovering in the Old Testament, and the reason that the Old Testament seems to reverence Saturn as the lord of this world.

The complex role of Saturn as the opposite of the sun, the one who has fallen or been thrown down, the one who sleeps in a watery cave or at the bottom of the sea (or, in the case of King Arthur, the Lake), and the one who is bound to a rock in the case of Prometheus can all be understood by studying the astrological associations of the seven celestial wanderers with the familiar zodiac chart we have used up to this point. Note that this chart, which comes from the text *Opus Medico-Chemicum* by Johann Daniel Mylius (c. 1583 – 1642), published in 1618, has as its centerpiece the emblem of the sun surrounded by a six-pointed star containing the symbols of the other six "visible planets" in our sky: the moon (a crescent symbol), and working clockwise from the symbol of the moon the symbols for Venus, Jupiter, Saturn, Mars, and Mercury (see below):

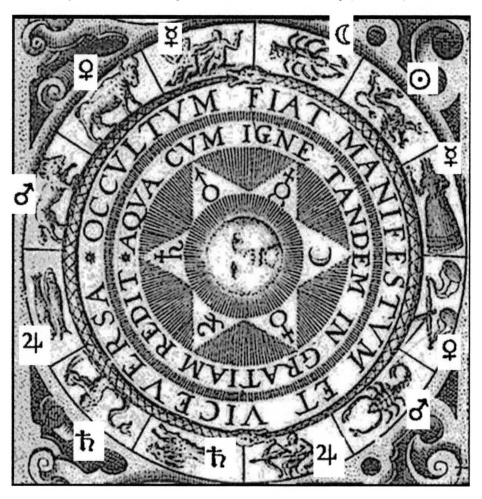

In the above diagram, the signs of the sun, moon, and planets have been placed on the zodiac wheel in accordance with the traditional system. Their respective locations on the wheel will help explain the Saturnian characteristics and mythologies described above.

The symbol of the sun, a circle with a dot in the center (the great eye of Horus or the great eye of Ra in Egyptian mythology), has been placed in the house of Leo the Lion, the sign that rules over the hottest part of the year, July-August.

Just before the sun, the symbol for the moon is placed in the sign of Cancer the Crab, a water sign. From the sun and the moon, who are central to the system, the rest of the five visible planets are placed on either side of this pair, starting with Mercury (the planet closest to the Sun) and moving outwards all the way to Saturn (the farthest).

Thus, on either side of the sun and moon, we first encounter the symbol of Mercury, in the signs of Gemini and Virgo. Next comes the symbol of the planet Venus, on either side of the two signs containing Mercury: Taurus and Libra. Next comes Mars, the Red Planet, whose symbol has been placed in the houses of Aries and Scorpio. Next is the sign of Jupiter (Jove), in the houses of Pisces and Sagittarius. Finally, in the signs furthest from the sun in Leo and the moon in Cancer, we find the symbol for the planet Saturn, in Capricorn and Aquarius.

In astrological terms, the sign on the opposite side of the wheel from another is known as its "adversary," as Taylor explains in *Astronomico-Theological Lectures*, "a diameter drawn from any one of these signs of the Zodiac, would pass into its adversary; and any two persons, standing opposite to each other, are adversarii, in relation to their respective positions."[81]

With this understanding, and the diagram above, we can now understand how the Saturn figures in mythologies around the world all play the role of a sort of "dark sun," or adversary to the sun, because the position of Saturn on the wheel is opposite to that of the sun (Saturn in Capricorn is the "adversary" to the sun in Leo). We can also see why Saturn in myth is often depicted as being "thrown down" (as, for example, Hephaestos and Phaethon), for Saturn's location is in the very depths of the zodiac wheel, far below the Sun in the summer months.

We can also understand why Saturn sleeps in an underground or underwater cave (or, in the case of Prometheus, is chained to a rock), because his sign is located in the Pit or the Abyss of the zodiac wheel. His portion of the wheel is literally under the earth (or under the ocean) when Leo is transiting across the meridian or highest north-south line of the celestial globe.

And yet, he is depicted in myth as the "first Sun" or the "first Father," the one who ruled over a previous Golden Age, and was cast down by his own kin, betrayed. As de Santillana and von Dechend explain, Saturn was the only god who was ever depicted as coming and dwelling among mankind, during that lost Golden Age.[82] They write:

> No one but Saturn dwelt among men. Says an Orphic fragment: "Orpheus reminds us that Saturn dwelt openly on earth and among men." Dionysius of

Halicarnassus (1.36.1) writes: "Thus before the reign of Zeus, Kronos ruled on this very earth" to which Maximilian Mayer crisply annotates: "We find no mention anywhere of such an earthly sojourn on the part of Zeus." In a similar way, Sandman Holmberg states with respect to Ptah, the Egyptian Saturn: "The idea of Ptah as an earthly king returns again and again in Egyptian texts," and also points to "the remarkable fact that Ptah is the only one of the Egyptian gods who is represented with a straight royal beard, instead of with a bent beard."[83]

The reason that Saturn is the one god who is depicted as dwelling with us is clear if we accept Kuhn's argument, that the myths of the world type our incarnational state as an imprisonment in matter in the "underworld" realm into which the celestial bodies plunge when they meet the western horizon. Osiris and Saturn are the ones most associated with this incarnational underworld – they are the aspects of the sun in its dark, underworld aspect, rather than in its Horian, soaring, fiery aspect. The myths teach this esoteric meaning by explaining that Saturn was the god who dwelt among men, who taught them to plant grains and get their "daily bread."

From his position on the "inverted" side of the zodiac, ruling over the opposite world, comes the Saturn tradition of inverted relationships (such as during the Saturnalia). De Santillana and von Dechend write, in a continuation of the passage above:

> The Saturnalia, from Rome to Mexico, commemorated just this aspect of Saturn's rule, with their general amnesties, masters serving slaves, etc., even if Saturn was not always directly mentioned. When this festival was due in China, so to speak "sub delta Geminorum" – more correctly, delta and the Gemini stars 61 and 56 of Flamsteed – "there was a banquet in which all hierarchic distinctions were set aside . . . The Sovereign invited his subjects through the 'Song of Stags.'"[84]

Taylor argues that the use of the term "the Father" found throughout the scriptures of the Old and New Testaments refers to Father Abraham or Father Saturn, and points out several aspects of the New Testament prayer we know as the Lord's Prayer which have Saturnian imagery. The prayer is addressed, of course, to the "Father in heaven." Its first request is "Thy kingdom come" – expressing a desire for the return of that millennial Golden Age that is associated in all ancient mythologies from Egypt to the Maya with the millennial reign of Saturn.[85]

The next request, "Give us this day our daily bread," Taylor argues, is also Saturnian. The reference to *daily* bread acknowledges Saturn's role as the "Lord of Measures" (measures of time preeminent among them). And, as already mentioned, Saturn was the one who taught man to plant seed and to farm, and his implement was the scythe or the sickle used to harvest grain (which forms the basis for his astrological symbol in the diagram above). Taylor writes:

> And they further prayed to Saturn, 'Give us this day our daily bread.' Because the very name of *Saturn* was derived from the word *Satu*, to sow, as corn is sown in the earth, and Sator, the sower: and Saturn it was, who was believed in that happy *golden age*, to have taught mankind the art of agriculture, and to raise their bread out of the earth; agreeably to which conceit, they represented him with his sickle or scythe in his hand, wherewith to cut down the corn, and piously

pledged themselves to desire from him no more than that vegetable diet, that simple bread, with which the happy denizens of the golden age had been entirely content. And it was to be in a particular sense *quotidian,* or *daily* bread as being the especial gift of Saturn, the 7th of the planets, the 7th of the days of the week, and the genius or demon of TIME.[86]

The foregoing discussion of the Saturnian aspects of Abraham, which clearly show that Saturn plays a central role in the Old Testament and one that continues to weave through the New Testament as well, does not mean that the term "the Father" always refers to Abraham, or that the Old Testament is entirely devoted to Saturn – far from it. In fact, the sun and the twelve houses of the zodiac play as central a role in the Old Testament as in the New, as Taylor demonstrates in his discussion of the twelve tribes of Israel.

The starry heavens themselves, which the Greek myths associate with the father-god Ouranos, who is the father of all living through mother Earth or Gaia, is in a very real sense the father or "pattern" (a word related to the term "father" or *pater*) of all that is below, as we will see. Saturn, as the planet closest to the heavenly sphere – the closest to that silent starry host, which turns on and on in placid, unchanging, unending *unmoved moving,* takes on some of the aspects of *that* Uranian father, but only in a derivative sense (as Saturn / Kronos in the myths usurps the place of Ouranos his own father, only to be cast down in his turn by Jove / Zeus – his son).

The vast expanse of the stars beyond the planets, then, may be more correctly identified with "the Father" than Saturn, for they are infinite, unchanging, unhurried, and they seem to more accurately reflect the nature of the unmoved mover of all.

Nevertheless, as the farthest of the visible planets, Saturn acts in a sense as a sort of mediator between earth-bound mortals and the unending heavens. However, in another sense, as Taylor explains, it is the sun who acts as the mediator between those heavens (the father, Ouranos) and mankind, for it is the sun which interposes itself between us and the zodiac constellations and through which (or through *whom*) we know them. In *The Devil's Pulpit,* speaking of the role of Christ as the mediator, Taylor says:

> Christ, that is, the SUN, is most literally the Mediator, or go-between, between Gad and man, because the fixed stars which compose or make up the tribe of Gad, and all the other tribes of the celestial Israel, are suns to the systems of their own: and our earth's annual motion round the sun throws the sun, or makes him seem to go, between us and those measurelessly remote fixed stars.
>
> As, only walk round the table with your eyes steadily directed to any fixed object on the table, you will see that object, with relation to the distant parts of the room, exactly opposite them, changing its point of opposition as you change your situation. And thus, while you alone are moving, the object on which your eye is fixed will seem to be moving; and thus, will be a mediator, or intercessor, at all times between you and the more distant fixed objects, by which alone you can measure the change which is going on, not in their positions, but yours.[87]

With this passage, the esoteric system which teachers such as Robert Taylor and Alvin Boyd Kuhn are expounding begins to come into view: it is the same system in the Old

Testament as in the New, but using different figures. In the Old Testament, the Saturnian Abraham is a central figure, and a mediator between earth-bound (incarnated) man and the starry heavens. He plays a role very similar to the incarnated Jesus in the New Testament – he proceeds into the material realm, to make children as numerous as the stars in heaven. That is to say: he connects us, in our incarnational state, with our heavenly, spiritual origin. Both the Old Testament and the New Testament (and all the other myths of the world) had this role, in Alvin Boyd Kuhn's opinion. They were sacred texts to remind us of our true nature, which in our dizzying plunge into incarnation we have forgotten, because we are stupefied with the wine of forgetfulness on our way from the celestial world into this one.

Expounding on this interpretation of the Abraham mythos, Alvin Boyd Kuhn writes:

> The angels in *Revelation* pour out the contents of their censers over the earth, granting a nucleus of solar "fire" to each mortal to divinize him. As the *Timaeus* of Plato reports, the deity was to furnish the collective seed of what was to be immortal in humanity.
>
> In *Old Testament* allegorism the doctrine is found most unexpectedly to be the core of meaning in the Abraham story. Like the Prodigal Son of the *New Testament* he was sent out from his home, country and kinsfolk (in the heavenly Eden) to go to a strange land (incidentally to the West, where was the Tuat, or gate of entry to the earth!). There his seed was to multiply until it filled the earth with his children, the heirs of supernal grace.[88]

Although Alvin Boyd Kuhn does not directly discuss the identification of Abraham with Saturn (his analysis is not as directly "astronomico-theological" as that of Robert Taylor, for instance), his next assertion about Abraham provides quite powerful confirmation of the connections we have been making between Abraham and Saturn. Recalling that Saturn – as the farthest of the visible planets – is the closest to the unchanging fixed-stars of the heavens, and thus was depicted by the Greeks and Romans as the son of Ouranos, we see a direct parallel in this argument from Alvin Boyd Kuhn:

> But the hidden sense of the name Abraham or Abram has escaped notice, and it is of great moment, as are all Bible names. Scholars may protest, but it seems obvious that the word is simply A-Brahm, (Hindu), meaning "not-Brahm." Abraham, the Patriarch or oldest of the aeons or emanations, was not Brahm, the Absolute, but the first emanation from Brahm. He was the first manifestation of the Not-Self of Brahm; the first ray, the first God, perhaps equivalent to the Ishwara of the Hindus. He was the first life that was not Absolute, yet from the Absolute. He was to go forth into the realms of matter, divide and multiply, and fill the world with his fragmented units. To return to Abraham's bosom would be just to complete the cycle of outgoing and return, to rest in the bosom of the highest divinity close to the Absolute.[89]

No less important in the Old Testament than the character of Abraham is the character of Moses. In his sermons and lectures, Robert Taylor also demonstrated that the Trinitarian Godhead of Father, Son and Holy Ghost in the New Testament have esoteric connection to Fire, Water, and Air as well as to Fire, Water, and Anointing Oil, and that these elements are personified in the Old Testament as well as the New.[90] He devotes several lectures to demonstrating that the character of Moses is related to water and salvation by water, while Aaron the brother of Moses is related to sacred oil and salvation by oil (a point he makes most explicitly on page 374 of his *Lectures*, based upon a carefully constructed chain of analysis). He also shows that Moses, who turns out to be a very complex and important figure and one to whom we will return later to find even more layers of meaning, is also related to the sign of Aries the Ram, just as Aaron is to Taurus the Bull, and their sister Miriam to Virgo the Virgin (just as her New Testament counterpart Mary is connected to Virgo, Miriam and Mary being essentially the same name linguistically).

We are told in Exodus 2:10 that Pharaoh's daughter called Moses by his name specifically because she drew him out of the water, where we read "And she called his name Moses: and she said, Because I drew him out of the water."

This name is clearly appropriate for a personification of Aries, the constellation that leads the zodiac band out of the lower part of the year, the portion of the circle which was often encoded in myth as "the sea" or "the ocean" or "the waters." It is also appropriate for one who will lead his people out of Egypt, for the lower half of the circle was also associated in the allegorical stories of the Old Testament with the land of Egypt.

Taylor also argues that the name Moses is related to the Greek goddesses known as the Muses, who were nine in number.[91] The Nile flooded for three months out of the year, and the other nine were the months of the year that were figuratively speaking "drawn out of the water."

In *Astronomico-Theological Lectures*, he explains:

> It was in Egypt especially that the nine Muses – that is, as these divinities were formerly called the nine *Moses*, received divine honors: their name being exactly the same as Moses, and of the same signification, and for the same reason, signifying *drawn out of the waters*, and even out of the very same waters: those of the Nile, out of which Moses is said to have been drawn, the real exposition of the fable being, that the worship of these deities grew upon the respect shown to the nine emblematical figures which were exhibited among the Egyptians, to denote the nine months of the year, during which the country was free from the inundation of their great river. Hence these Moses were said to be *drawn out*, or *saved from the waters*, and were represented each as holding some instrument or symbol, as a pair of compasses, a flute, a mask, a trumpet, &c., expressive of the one or the other months of the year, over which they severally presided. And the whole group were represented as dancing round the Sun, who, personified as the god Bacchus, was always represented as attended by the Muses, and presiding in the midst of them: and, by the metonymy of language, which always gives a common name to things which have an essential relation to each other, Bacchus himself acquired the name, precisely the same name, MOSES, and was worshiped and adored under that name.[92]

The evidence in the scriptures of the Old Testament to support this interpretation is plentiful. Moses is associated in many instances with waters – the waters of the Nile, out of which he was drawn, the waters of the Red Sea across which he led his people, the water gushing from the rock.

Taylor also cites as evidence 1 Corinthians 10:1-2 which declares, "Moreover, brethren, I would not that ye were ignorant, how that all our fathers were under the cloud, and all passed through the sea; And were all baptized unto Moses in the cloud and in the sea." This New Testament passage, associating baptism with Moses, is quite significant. Further, as Taylor says, it clearly supports the association of Moses with "salvation by water," in that "Moses in the cloud, and Moses in the sea, are none other than a hieroglyphical way of meaning the waters in the cloud, and the waters in the sea, – the sea and the clouds being the great primary reservoirs of all the waters."[93]

Further supporting Taylor's analysis of the character of Moses, and his connection with the Egyptian personification of nine months of the year free of the inundation of the Nile, we note that the historical books of the Old Testament, which are Genesis, Exodus, Leviticus, Numbers, Joshua, Judges, Ruth, Samuel and Kings are nine in number – exactly as Herodotus divides the portions of his *Histories* detailing the histories of Egypt into nine chapters.[94]

Taylor is referring to Book 2 of the *Histories*, chapters 2 through 11, which concern Egypt and the Egyptians. While some readers will note that the Old Testament as we have it today usually contains two books called Chronicles after Kings, in older times the books today known as First and Second Chronicles were known as Third and Fourth Kings; thus, if all the books known as "Kings" (which were once called 1, 2, 3, and 4 Kings but today are called 1 and 2 Kings and 1 and 2 Chronicles) are counted together, the historical books of the Old Testament are nine in number. The nine chapters of Herodotus which deal with Egypt have subdivisions also, just as the book of Kings has, so this observation of Taylor retains its validity.

Taylor also notes that Moses was often depicted as having horns – both because the Nile River with its delta was referred to as being crowned with horns, and because he is a personification of Aries the Ram.[95] See for example the famous statute of Moses by Michelangelo. Taylor explains:

> And Moses' horns are accounted for, in common with those of Bacchus, by the demonstrated fact that they are both of them personifications of the river Nile; the Nile always being represented and emblemized as wearing horns, and as identified with Bacchus, with Dionysius, with the Ocean (which was believed to flow from it), and with the Sun, from which it was believed to flow, is addressed in those solemn invocations of the Orphic Hymns [. . .].[96]

At the end of the passage above, Robert Taylor quotes lines from the Orphic Hymns. The first line is from Hymn 44, *To Dionysius Bassareus Triennialis*, which in the 1792 translation of Thomas Taylor is rendered, "Come, blessed Dionysius, various nam'd, / Bull-fac'd, begot from Thunder, Bacchus fam'd."[97] In that same hymn, Dionysius / Bacchus is called "Furious inspirer, bearer of the rod," which is certainly consistent with Robert Taylor's assertion that Moses is a Dionysus / Bacchus figure (Moses carries a rod which features prominently in various miraculous signs, including turning into a snake and giving the Israelites victory in battle). Elsewhere in the Orphic Hymns, Bacchus is specifically addressed as "Two-horn'd" (in Hymn 29, *To Bacchus*).[98]

Taylor spends some time treating the incident of the golden calf, which he sees as an allegory depicting the precessional shift from the Age of Taurus to the Age of Aries. Due to the inexorable action of precession, the constellation Aries took over the heliacal rising position on the spring equinox that had previously been held by Taurus (just as Taurus, 2,160 years earlier, had usurped the spring equinox heliacal rise position held by Gemini and nearby Orion, giving rise to the mythology of Set – associated with Taurus – usurping the throne of Osiris – associated with Orion – as explained in greater detail in my previous book).[99]

Aaron, associated with Taurus according to Taylor's analysis, takes the opportunity afforded by the absence of Moses upon Mount Sinai to prepare a golden calf, and to declare to the children of Israel that, "These be thy gods, O Israel, which brought thee up out of the land of Egypt" (Exodus 32:4). The fact that he calls a single calf idol by the plural word "gods" indicates that he is referring to a constellation, made up of stars, according to Taylor.[100]

He is basically saying to the tribes of Israel (who themselves represent the zodiac constellations): "These are the stars of Taurus, the spring equinox constellation that led you (you, the rest of the zodiac) up out of the portion of the wheel that is below the equinox line (the portion of the wheel that we call *Egypt*, as well as the Pit, the Abyss, the watery deep, etc.)." In other words, during the Age of Taurus, when Taurus occupied the house of the rising sun on the day of the spring equinox, and thus could be said to be the sign that led the procession across the line out of the "lower" half of the year and into the upper, Taurus could have been rightly said to be the group of stars which leads the twelve tribes "up out of the land of Egypt." Moses, who represents Aries, is incensed at this declaration – Taurus is no longer entitled to be the leader of the zodiac wheel, having been replaced by Aries.

From this concept, we can understand that the entire account of the Exodus out of Egypt, and the crossing of the Red Sea, has an astrological and celestial message: it represents the annual crossing of the lower part of the year, and in particular the five winter months presided over by Scorpio, Sagittarius, Capricorn, Aquarius, and Pisces. These are the months allegorically identified as "Egypt" in the Old Testament, the house of bondage. Moses leads his people out, because he is identified with Aries the Ram, the sign which begins with the spring equinox, when the sun finally emerges from the period of the year in which night is longer than day.

As Taylor explains in his *Astronomico-Theological Lectures*, the character of Miriam is very revealing evidence in support of this argument as well. In the book of Exodus, after crossing the Red Sea, Miriam rejoices and the scriptures record the song of Miriam: "Sing ye to the LORD, for he hath triumphed gloriously; the horse and his rider hath he thrown into the sea" (Exodus 15:21). A review of the zodiac wheel will immediately reveal that when the rising sun has reached the sign of Aries, and is thus leading the children of Israel (the twelve houses of the zodiac, as we will soon see) out of the Red Sea, the sign of Sagittarius – "the horse and his rider" – is near the lowest portion of the wheel.

Days Longer than Nights

Nights Longer than Days

Taylor asks:

> And who is this 'horse and his rider' whom this Lady Mary is so pleased to have 'thrown into the sea?' See ye not *there*, in the Sagittarius of November, that very 'horse and his rider,' who must necessarily sink into the sea, when the Lord triumphs gloriously – that is, when the Sun shines brightly; and in bringing up the children of Israel into the regions of long days and summer months, throws 'the horse and his rider' (the gloomy genius of November) below the horizon?[101]

Continuing this argument (with a flash of his occasionally cutting wit), Taylor points out:

> Nor, if there had been any intended historical congruity in its being an Egyptian army, could there have been any horse at all thrown into the sea; for sure we shouldn't forget our lesson so fast, as not to remember that all the horses in Egypt had just before died of the murrain. And it must have been rather hard to kill 'em first and drown 'em afterwards.[102]

In other words, the text can never have been meant to have been interpreted literally, although that is generally the only way they have been "allowed" to have been interpreted and taught to the public for nearly seventeen centuries. Taylor points out that all the Egyptian horses were previously declared to have been killed in the ten plagues that struck Egypt and which finally caused Pharaoh to relent and allow the Hebrews to depart. If that fact is taken literally, then what horses were the Egyptians riding in pursuit of the Israelites, and what beasts were pulling the Egyptian chariots which were drowned when the Red Sea closed back in over their heads? And yet Exodus 14:9 specifically states that "the Egyptians pursued after them, all the horses *and* chariots of Pharaoh, and his horsemen, and his army," as if it is very important that we note the presence of horses and horsemen. This makes no sense if it is a literal history, but it makes perfect sense if the story refers to the zodiac wheel, and the horses and horsemen refer to the sign of Sagittarius, "thrown down" to the bottom of "the sea" at the point in time that the sign of Aries leads the "Israelite band" through the very significant *crossing* of the March equinox.

Here as so many other places in the Old and New Testaments, we find that – as Taylor eloquently puts it – "When we look into the derivative or first sense of all the terms, and phrases, and periphrases, by which divine revelation is spoken of, we find that first sense is absolutely an astronomical one, and we are obliged to strain and transpose, and do no small violence to the first principles of language to make them bear any other than an astronomical one."[103]

As we have been implying in some of the explanation thus far, the allegorical, metaphorical and celestial nature of the character of Moses holds true as well for the twelve tribes of Israel, or the children of Israel, who form such a central part of the allegorical stories of the Old Testament scriptures.

In one of his *Astronomico-Theological Lectures* entitled "The Twelve Patriarchs," Taylor points to a verse in Acts chapter 7 in which the word "patriarchs" is used to denote the children of Jacob / Israel: "And the patriarchs, moved with envy, sold Joseph into Egypt: but God was with him" (Acts 7:9).[104] We know from Genesis that it was Joseph's brothers who sold him into Egypt, and therefore if the author of Acts is speaking accurately, this indicates that the term "patriarchs" was at least sometimes anciently used to refer to those twelve tribes of Israel.

Being now acutely aware that the number twelve in sacred tradition almost always points us to the twelve signs of the zodiac, we should immediately investigate evidence that might confirm the suspicion that the twelve tribes of Israel also encode the zodiac signs. Before running through the characteristics of the twelve children of Israel, which correspond quite closely with the zodiac signs, Taylor prepares his listeners by giving some sweeping explication of the entire system of encoding the celestial phenomena in the symbolic (or "hieroglyphical") language of the scriptures:

> And as the stars, in this hieroglyphical language, are so evidently meant – and all that is meant – by our *Fathers or Patres*, we have the clue in our hands to lead us to the discovery, as to who were the Patriarkai or pre-eminent and great arch-fathers, or patriarchs in the system, in the never-to-be-forgotten essentiality of the system, that they were exactly twelve of them, nor more nor fewer, answering exactly to the number of the twelve signs of the Zodiac – that is, those twelve groups of stars which lie in the course which the sun appears to pass through in the heavens in that annual revolution which constitutes the twelve months of the year.

[. . .]

An imaginary character and imaginary history were referred to these groups, analogous to the character and history of nature pending that portion of the year, during which the Sun appears to be in that part of the heavens, over which the Stars that make up that group spread themselves.

And the sun itself, by the ordinary metonymy of language, took the name and character, and was the imagined genius of each of these groups of stars, pending the period of time that he appeared to be passing through it. And as the Sun was always the Supreme God, so each of these signs of the Zodiac were all of them Gods in their turns: so spoken of, so adored and worshiped, and so one or other adopted by different nations, as the Great Father or Patriarch, from which they imagined themselves to be descended.[105]

The zodiacal characteristics of the twelve tribes of Israel are most clearly seen in the final blessing of Jacob / Israel, who gathers his sons to him in Genesis 49, before he dies. There is a similar passage in Deuteronomy 33, before the death of Moses, in which Moses "blessed the children of Israel before his death" (Deuteronomy 33:1), using many of the same images and symbols as those found in the blessing of Jacob, with some notable differences.

As Taylor interprets these passages in *Astronomico-Theological Lectures*, the twelve sons of Jacob / Israel correspond to the following zodiac signs:

- Reuben – Aquarius ("unstable as water," Genesis 49:4).
- Simeon and Levi together – Pisces ("instruments of cruelty are in their habitations," Genesis 49:5, referring to the fish hooks, spears, nets, and harpoons of the fishermen, according to Taylor).[106]
- Judah – Leo ("Judah is a lion's whelp: from the prey, my son, thou are gone up: he stooped down, he couched as a lion, and as an old lion; who shall rouse him up?" Genesis 49:9).
- Ephraim – Taurus (not discussed in Genesis 49, but found in Deuteronomy 33:17, where we read "His glory is like the firstling of the bullock, and his horns are like the horns of the unicorn: with them, he shall push the people together to the ends of the earth: and they are the tens of thousands of Ephraim, and they are the thousands of Manasseh").
- Dan – Scorpio ("Dan shall be a serpent by the way, an adder in the path, that biteth the horse heels, so that his rider shall fall backward," Genesis 49:17, describing the Scorpion as a serpent, biting the heels of Sagittarius "the horse and his rider," and the falling backwards image corresponds quite well to the stars of Sagittarius, shown below using the outline proposed by H.A. Rey).

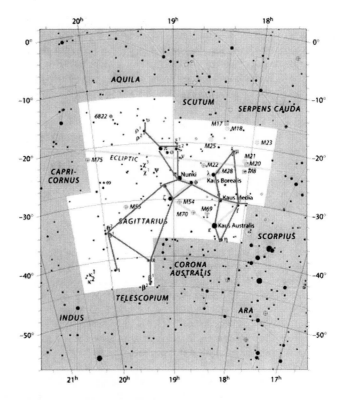

The backwards-leaning angle of the archer of Sagittarius is clearly evident in this outline, although H.A. Rey does not envision a horse in his system of outlining the constellation. Note the tail of Scorpio (labeled "Scorpius" in this diagram) is evident at lower right. If we imagine a horse underneath the rider above, and if the tail of Scorpio is stinging its heels, then the rider is leaning backwards towards the rear of the horse as Scorpio stings the heels of its rear legs. The rider is aiming his bow backwards as he rides: the details in the Biblical text precisely match the details in the constellations themselves.

- Zebulun or Zebulon – Capricorn ("shall dwell at the haven of the sea," the Goat of Capricorn being depicted as terminating with a fish's tail in the same way that a mermaid's lower body is a fish's tail, and the sign of Capricorn dwelling at the lowest part of the lower half of the zodiac wheel, the half that represents the deep).

- Issachar – Cancer ("a strong ass couching down between two burdens," Genesis 49:14). This reference may seem obscure for the constellation of Cancer the Crab, but in fact the two faint center stars of this faintest of zodiac constellations have been known from antiquity as Asellus Borealis and Asellus Australis – the Northern Ass (actually colt or foal of an ass) and the Southern Ass. Between them is the Beehive star cluster (known today as Messier object 44 or M44), also known as Praesepe "the Manger." Below is a diagram of the stars of the constellation Cancer the Crab, showing the stars labeled with their Greek letters under the Bayer designation system (after Johann Bayer, 1572-1625, who created this naming system in 1603), in which the stars of constellations are given a Greek letter, usually starting with the brightest star of the constellation as alpha although not always, coupled with the Latin name of that constellation in the genitive (or possessive) form – thus the star *alpha Centauri* means "the Centaur's alpha." The diagram below shows the stars of Cancer, with the outline suggested by H.A. Rey. The star *gamma Cancri* (Cancer's gamma) is marked with the lower-case Greek letter *gamma* (ϒ), which is the star Asellus Borealis (the northern). The star *delta Cancri* is below it, marked with the lower-case letter *delta* (δ) and corresponds to the star Asellus Australis (the southern). Close between them you can see M44, the Beehive or the Manger.

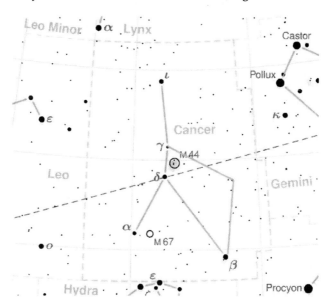

- Gad – Aries ("a troop shall overcome him, but he shall overcome at last," Genesis 49:19, an apt description for the constellation that had been the last of the zodiac troop when Taurus ruled the March equinox in a previous age, but which had ascended to the first position – the head of the troop, so to speak – in the Age of Aries).
- Asher – Gemini ("blessed with children" in Deuteronomy 33:24).
- Naphtali – Virgo and Libra ("a hind let loose: he giveth goodly words," Genesis 49:21. Even Taylor admits this is "a deeply couched enigma."[107] He notes that "goodly words" are associated with the god Mercury / Hermes / Thoth, and that the sign of Virgo is associated with Mercury, as can be seen in the zodiac diagram with planetary signs introduced earlier during the discussion of Saturn. He also argues from Deuteronomy 33:23 where in the blessing of Moses Naphtali is called "satisfied with favour, and full with the blessing of the LORD," which should correspond to the autumn months dominated by Virgo and Libra, when the wheat is brought in. Virgo is not only depicted as holding a sheaf of wheat, but also is often depicted as holding the scales of Libra, from whence we have our image of Justice personified as a woman holding the scales. However, Robert Taylor does not appear to have been aware of the most important clue of

all: the fact that the constellation Centaurus which is below Virgo strongly resembles a stag and that there is clear evidence from Greek mythology to support this connection, as we have already seen from our examination of the myth of Iphigenia and the myth of Artemis and Actaeon. This fact strongly confirms Robert Taylor's suspicion that Naphtali, associated in the Genesis text with a stag, corresponds to Virgo.

- Joseph and Benjamin – Sagittarius (we are told of Joseph that "his bow abode in strength" in Genesis 49:24, the bow being a singular symbol of the sign of Sagittarius, and of Benjamin that he "shall ravin as a wolf: in the morning he shall devour the prey, and at night he shall divide the spoil" (Genesis 49:27). The constellation Lupus the Wolf being located south of and between Scorpio and Libra, Taylor argues that "The constellation Sagittarius in the Zodiac, immediately precedes the celestial Wolf, which hardly falls within the Zodiac. But the character of ravening as a Wolf, indicates the hungry and black character of the deep winter, and the devouring the prey in the morning, and dividing the spoil at night, the extreme shortness of the days at that season of the year").[108]

There is certainly some room to argue with a few of these identifications, although many of them are very clearly indicative of their corresponding zodiac signs. I would tend to break Libra out from Virgo and assign that zodiac station to Benjamin, because the constellation of Lupus the Wolf is actually one of the "decans" of Libra, under the system discussed later in which three nearby constellations were anciently associated with each of the twelve zodiac constellations, giving rise to the forty-eight classical constellations (four times twelve, counting each zodiac constellation itself plus three decans along with it for a total of four). Naphtali would then be connected only with Virgo, and not with Virgo and Libra as argued by Robert Taylor.

While the references to a stag and to a wolf, constellations not actually part of the zodiac twelve, may be obscure and may seem to argue against the assertion that the twelve children of Israel are in fact associated with the twelve constellations of the zodiac band, we find that they are perhaps some of the strongest pieces of evidence *in support* of such an assertion. The fact that there is in fact a constellation Lupus the Wolf right next to Libra (and associated with it as one of the decans of that sign, in astrological tradition), and a constellation Centaurus which looks like a stag (or "a hind let loose") right underneath Hydra and Virgo, are both powerful celestial connections to the descriptions of Naphtali and Benjamin in the blessing of Jacob/Israel in the Genesis account. This connection makes the argument for a celestial rather than a literal interpretation of the tribes of Israel even more difficult to deny.

The fact that the "tribes" of Israel are actually groupings ("tribes") of stars along the zodiac band is, of course, profoundly significant. Spiritually, it is a powerful picture to convey the esoteric meaning that Alvin Boyd Kuhn argues to be the purpose of all ancient sacred myth: the lesson that we on earth are all "descendants" of the stars, for the sinking of the stars into the western horizon as the earth revolves through each night is a powerful image of our own spiritual condition as souls who have come down from the pure realm of spirit to be imprisoned for a time in a body of flesh, to wander for a generation in the material "desert."

Kuhn explains: "Many passages from the Old Testament books refer to the Israelites as captives, outcasts, expatriates and exiles, matching Greek, Egyptian and Gnostic terminology, and alluding of course to the expulsion of the angelic hosts from a celestial Paradise to a bleak earthly exile."[109] Like all the other myth-systems of the world's people, these stories were intended to teach us powerful truths about the human condition and the nature of our universe, and were not intended to be taken as literal histories.

There are many other amazing and beautiful celestial connections latticed throughout the entire structure of the Old Testament, far too many to treat in this chapter. The main purpose here has been to strive to introduce this vitally important concept, and to provide enough evidence to clearly demonstrate the system, one which has been deliberately hidden throughout the centuries and which continues to be deliberately kept hidden to this day. As we explore the implications of this celestial system, and the reasons why certain parties have through the ages desired to obscure it, we will have occasion to visit some of the other important Old Testament themes in order to better examine some of the esoteric teachings that these can illustrate.

5

The New Testament in the stars

> It is the purpose of the present volume to set forth to the modern mind the extent of the wreckage which splendid ancient wisdom suffered at the hands of later incompetence. [. . .] It involves the reversal of that mental process which in the days of early Christianity operated to change myth and allegory in the first instance over to factual history. As third century ignorance converted mythical typology to objective history, the task is now to convert alleged objective history back to mythology, and then to interpret it as enlightened theology. The almost insuperable difficulty of the project will consist in demonstrating to an uncomprehending world, mistaught for centuries and now fixed in weird forms of fantastic belief, that the sacred scriptures of the world are *a thousand times more precious as myths than as alleged history.*

Alvin Boyd Kuhn, *Lost Light*.[110]

In the New Testament letter of Paul to the Corinthians known as 1 Corinthians, a juxtaposition of the roles of Adam in the Old Testament and Christ in the New can be found in the following verse, from the fifteenth chapter and beginning at verse 45: "And so it is written, The first man Adam was made a living soul; the last Adam was made a quickening spirit." The first Adam obviously is the Adam of Genesis and the Fall, and "the last Adam" is generally understood to refer to Christ. So there is a pairing here, of Adam and Christ, one being a sort of "negative Adam" and the other a "positive" or "quickening" ("life-giving") Adam. There is also some interesting language about the first (falling) Adam being "made a living soul" and the second (or "last") Adam being described as a "spirit."

The verse makes reference to both Genesis 2 (particularly verse 7) and Romans 5 (beginning in verse 12). In Romans 5:14, the same assertion about a first and a last Adam is less explicitly put forth, where we read: "Nevertheless death reigned from Adam to Moses, even over them that had not sinned after the similitude of Adam's transgression, who is the figure of him that was to come." Like the passage from 1 Corinthians, this verse implies that the Adam "that was to come" (generally understood to mean Christ) is a "second Adam" who fixes the transgression of the first.

In *The Devil's Pulpit*, Robert Taylor (who at one time must have believed the "orthodox" or literalist teaching about these verses, because he went through the effort of being ordained a minister in England, until he was separated because of his teaching, which he continued afterwards and which ultimately landed him in prison two times, for a total of three years behind bars) explains that the "first Adam" refers to the "falling Sun" – the sun during the half of the year between summer solstice and winter solstice, when the days are progressively shortening and the sun's rising point on the eastern horizon is further south each day (for observers in the northern hemisphere).[111] Let's refer again to one of the diagrams shown previously:

According to Robert Taylor, the first Adam corresponds to the part of the year seen on the right half of the above diagram, in which the days are growing shorter, and the sun's rising point is moving to the south. This portion of the year commences after the June solstice for the northern hemisphere, when the north pole and the northern hemisphere reach the moment in which they point most directly towards the sun in the earth's annual trek.

After reaching that most northerly point (at the June solstice), the sun begins to "fall" towards the south (because earth is progressing around its orbit, on its way towards the moment in which the north pole and the northern hemisphere are pointed most directly away from the sun). While it is still the "same Sun," the sun in this portion of the year is metaphorically "Adam" – it is falling, it has "transgressed" (literally meaning it has "crossed over") – it is playing a "different role" in the heavenly drama.

After the winter solstice (the December solstice), however, the sun crosses over its point of most southerly rising and setting, and begins to move back towards the north, and the days begin to lengthen again. The sun now takes on a different role. It is now the "Second Adam" – it is the rising, life-giving sun – it is no longer the falling, dying, declining sun. This idea that the same sun can take on different "roles" in the heavenly drama is a very important concept for the unlocking of the esoteric sense of the stories of the Old and New Testaments, and in the rest of the world's mythologies. Here, the sun is taking on the role of Adam (the transgressing, "south-ing" or "falling" Sun) during one entire half of the year, and it is taking on the role of the "second Adam" or "Christ" during the other half of the year (the rising, "north-ing" half of the year). But the sun will also take on the identity of the twelve smaller subdivisions of the year as well, passing through each house of the zodiac band (which is divided into twelve signs) and taking on the role of each or the characteristics of each.

Another way of stating the same concept would be to say that the authors of the ancient allegories, using the phenomena of the infinite universe stretched out above our heads as material to convey their profound spiritual teachings, would often use the same heavenly object to convey different messages, and in doing so would personify that same object as different or distinct characters in their scriptures or legends.

Thus the sun in its declining half of the year is a perfect manifestation in the physical world of the spiritual process by which our souls descend from the heights of the spiritual realm to incarnate in a body, becoming "a living soul," while the sun in its ascending half of the year perfectly allegorizes the process of the spirit's awakening to its original nature, surmounting the animal nature of its material bonds, and ascending towards the spiritual life that is its true inheritance, becoming a "quickening spirit." There is strong evidence that the author of 1 Corinthians understood these two Adams in a primarily esoteric sense, not in a literalistic sense, as we will see in Part III of this book.

So, we can see that in some sense the mirrored actions of the first Adam and the second Adam act to "bridge" the Old and New Testaments. A second concept which acts to bridge them is the concept of the *covenant*, which Robert Taylor points out means quite literally a "coming together" (from the Latin word *venere*, which gives us the Spanish word *venir* and which is found in other English words such as "convene," "convention," "intervene," and "reconvene," among others).[112] Robert Taylor provides evidence for the assertion that these "covenants" refer to the "coming together" of the plane of the ecliptic (the sun's path) and the celestial equator, which happens two times each year (halfway between the extremes reached at the solstices), at each of the two equinoxes.

At the spring equinox, the sun's path crosses the celestial equator such that the ecliptic is above the celestial equator during the day, and below it during the night (the zodiac constellations are below the celestial equator at night during the period stretching from spring to autumnal equinox). This portion of the year is the "upper half" of the year in our familiar zodiac wheel, when the days are longer than the nights.

At the autumnal equinox, however, another "convention" or "covenant-point" is reached, when the ecliptic again crosses the celestial equator. After this point, the Sun enters the lower half of the above diagram, in which days are shorter than nights and the rising and setting points are on the southern half of their annual swing between their solstice boundaries.

If we run an "animation" of the motion of the ecliptic in our minds, then, we might imagine ourselves standing at a northern hemisphere latitude – perhaps at the latitude of the Giza pyramids – and facing towards the south. Across the sky, rising up from the eastern horizon like a great arc and crossing the sky exactly ninety degrees down from the north celestial pole (indicated by the star Polaris, behind our heads as we face south) would be the celestial equator, glowing in the night sky like a great luminescent line drawn along the inside of a huge glass globe (for purposes of this "animation"). All through the year, the great glass globe would turn through the night, night after night, bringing up various constellations in the east which progress across the sky to sink back into the west, but the line of the celestial equator would never move: it would remain fixed, exactly ninety degrees down from the north celestial pole (which is that point around which the entire heavens would seem to revolve).

However, if our animation could create a second glowing luminescent line to represent the ecliptic path, this too would create a great arc across the southern part of the sky as we stood on the plateau of Giza. This line would be very much like the fixed arc of the celestial equator, and it would stretch from the eastern horizon and arc across the southern part of the sky to sink down into the western horizon. This line would be that line that the sun travels during the day, and that the visible planets follow as well (the planets being only visible at night, or at the periods of dusk and dawn and sometimes for a very brief time even after the sun has come up or before it has fully gone down).

As we have already seen, this line moves "up and down" quite a bit throughout the year, yawning well above the celestial equator (during the day) from spring equinox through the summer (when it reaches its maximum elevation above the celestial equator on the summer solstice) and on to fall equinox, as the arc of the sun's path moves higher and higher through the heavens in the summer months. Then the yawning gap between ecliptic and equator closes down like the closing jaws of a great fish as summer draws towards autumn, until it actually crosses the celestial equator at the September solstice and then begins to open the gap in the opposite direction, getting wider and wider below the celestial equator during the winter months.

Thus, the two equinoxes are the two "coming-together" points for these mighty celestial "hoops." They are meeting-places, and they are *covenants*. There is an old convention within orthodox Christianity which refers to the Old Testament and the New Testament as the Old Covenant and the New Covenant.

Robert Taylor argues that the "upper half" of the year, when the sun is "above" the celestial equator each day (during the day), corresponds to the "Covenant of Works," during which half of the year all the work is done to plant the crops, sustain the crops, and ultimately harvest the crops.[113] During the "lower half" of the year, when the Sun is "below" the celestial equator each day, from the Autumn equinox until the Spring equinox, the earth is in the "Covenant of Grace," in which the work is over and the inhabitants of the earth can enjoy the bread and wine that are the products of the working months, which will sustain them through the winter until the ecliptic again meets the celestial equator and ushers in the spring and the beginning of the planting cycle once again.

These two examples bridge the Old and New Testaments. The first involves one way of dividing the year in half: from solstice to solstice, into a "falling sun" and a "climbing sun," in which the Old Testament figure of Adam corresponds to the falling Sun and the New Testament figure of Christ represents the "second Adam" who reverses the course of the first.

The second involves another way of dividing the year in half: from equinox to equinox. The equinoxes divide the year in to two "covenants," with the "Covenant of Works" in this case being the "upper half" or "sunny half" of the year (in which agricultural work is done), and the "Covenant of Grace" being the "lower half" or "wintery half" of the year (in which the fruits of the work must sustain mankind while he rests from his labors). We have already seen that the upper half and lower half of the year, when divided by the equinoxes, are represented by many other important metaphors, among them the metaphor of the "house of bondage (Egypt)" which represents the lower half of the same equinoctial division and which is counterpoised by the upper half that is allegorized as Paradise, Eden, the Promised Land, and the Kingdom of Heaven. This allegorical system, which we have already explored in some detail, has some aspects which will be critical to any effort to unlock the New Testament metaphors, and so a brief review and elaboration upon the system will be helpful here.

Another common metaphorical theme used to describe this upper half and lower half of the annual cycle consists of the imagery of a mountain, up which the sun climbs during the year, reaching the summit at the summer solstice. At the other side of the cycle, the sun descends into a deep abyss, a pit, reaching the bottom at the winter solstice. Note that when someone talks about *the* Abyss or *the* Pit, it is understood that they are speaking of Hell, and this is an important connection, because the lower half of the year – and particularly the section of the year denominated by the five signs stretching from Scorpio to Pisces (Scorpio, Sagittarius, Capricorn, Aquarius, and Pisces) – actually represents Hell, and every myth or legend which discusses Hell should be carefully examined for indications of clues indicating that the legend is actually referring to the wintery section of the year, clues which careful analysis will almost invariably find.

We have already seen that another trope that winds through ancient celestial metaphors across cultures is the association of the lower half of the great annual wheel with the sea or the ocean. Again, we see evidence of this connection in the word "abyss," which is not only used to describe a deep chasm or pit on the earth's surface, as well as "Hell below," but which is also associated with the watery deep, the vast depths beneath the surface of the ocean.

Hamlet's Mill contains an entire chapter entitled "The Depths of the Sea" which explores this theme, noting for instance the significant fact that Saturn or Kronos is hurled down to Tartaros (Hell) by Jupiter / Zeus, and that the same Saturn / Kronos who has been hurled down to Hell is also often depicted in ancient myth as sleeping in the depths of the sea, or dwelling in a cave beneath the sea, or in the mysterious island of Ogygia.[114] Its authors also give extensive evidence throughout their work that Saturn / Kronos parallels the Babylonian deity Ea, "whose 'town' is Eridu/Canopus, the very depth of the sea."[115]

Elsewhere in the same chapter, de Santillana and von Dechend discuss the fact that the Saturn figure in the world's myths was the lord of time, the "giver of measures," and that many legends and sacred traditions around the world depict the "giving of the measures" in conjunction with the feat of diving to the "navel of the deep" or "plumbing out the utmost depth of the sea."[116] At the end of this discussion of Saturnian "diving," de Santillana and von Dechend explain:

> In any case, whether the description is sublime or charmingly nonsensical, it is literally the "fundamental" task of the Ruler to "dive" to the topos where times begin and end, to get hold of a new "first day."[117]

They don't explicitly tell the reader why this is so, but the probable explanation involves the beginning of the year near the winter solstice, which is located on the very lowest point in the cycle of the great zodiac wheel, and the association of the lower regions of that wheel with the depths of the sea.

Finally, the reader is reminded that one other important metaphor for the lower half of the wheel is the subterranean realm, a deep cave in the earth, or even a tomb (all of which were presided over by Osiris in the Egyptian mythology). In particular, the period when the sun reaches its lowest point (for the northern hemisphere) at winter solstice – its lowest arc across the sky, and its most southerly rising point on the eastern horizon – which falls on or around December 21 each year and where the sun remains for about three days before turning back towards the north, becomes the time when the sun in the allegorical legends was depicted as being shut up within a cave, or entombed in a rock.

Note that at midnight on any given night of the year, one can think of the sun as being entombed directly beneath the earth below one's feet, because at that particular moment (midnight) the turning of earth brings the entire bulk of the planet between the observer on the surface of the earth and the sun, which is shining on the exact other side of the world (where it is high noon).

Keeping this in mind, and then adding the metaphor of the deep pit or abyss we have been discussing with regard to the lower half of the year (and especially the lowest point of the year), one can immediately grasp the reason that the legendary birth of Mithras (*Sol Invictus*, or the Unconquered Sun) was held to take place exactly at midnight on the end of the 24th of December and the beginning of the 25th of December, out of a rock or a cave. That is the point in time that the sun is metaphorically bound deep within the heart of the earth, and the point in the year when the sun is about to begin its annual turn back towards the north and towards longer and longer days, ascending the heavenly mountain to the summit at the opposite solstice (the reason the "birth" takes place at midnight on the third day after the traditional December 21 date of solstice is that the sun's rising point on the eastern horizon appears to "stand still" at solstice for three days before turning back towards the north and rising further and further north along the eastern horizon again as the days lengthen).

And now we can transition to an examination of the stories of the New Testament and their celestial allegory, for there is a clear parallel to the birth of Jesus, traditionally celebrated on the 25th of December as well, and often at midnight on Christmas Eve (the 24th), at the very beginning of December the 25th, for the reasons just discussed.

The most detailed account of the Nativity scene is found in Luke's gospel, and in three lectures on "The Star of Bethlehem (Part I, Part II, and Part III)," found in *The Devil's Pulpit*, Robert Taylor expounds the astronomical allegory of the details found in those scriptures. His overarching argument throughout is that the stories of Jesus and the twelve disciples correspond to the motions of the sun and the twelve signs of the zodiac. If this argument is correct, then the "birth of the sun" at the winter solstice (also allegorized by the birth of Mithras out of a rock or a cave at the same point of the annual cycle) makes perfect sense in light of the diagrams presented earlier in this chapter.

The zodiac wheel helps us grasp the reason that the gospel accounts chose to have the Nativity of Jesus take place in a "manger" rather than in a rock or a cave like Mithras. At the bottom of the zodiac wheel, the winter solstice takes place at the juncture between the signs of Sagittarius and Capricorn, signs representing a centaur (half-man and half-horse) and a goat (Capricorn is actually depicted most often as half-goat and half-fish: a goat with a fishlike tail instead of rear legs, like a mermaid but instead a "mer-goat"). Horses and goats are "barnyard animals," and so the allegories chose to describe the birth of the sun at the winter solstice as taking place in a stable.

Later on, in the same series of lectures on "The Star of Bethlehem," Taylor unpacks the other allegorical details of the Nativity scene, particularly the identity of the Virgin Mary. It is quite clear that if we are to look for a zodiac sign that would correspond to the Virgin Mary in the gospels, the most obvious candidate would be the sign and constellation of Virgo, the Virgin, a sign of great importance in ancient sacred tradition.

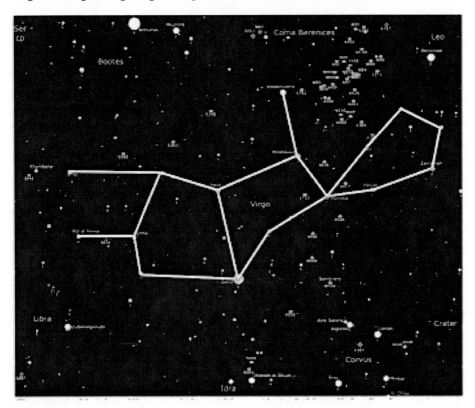

During the time of year that the sun is rising in the house of the sign of Sagittarius, the sky at midnight is very different from the sky at sunrise. During this time of year at midnight, Virgo is rising up in the east, following Leo who is striding up the arch of the eastern half of the sky towards the zenith point. Leo follows the constellation Cancer the Crab, a very faint constellation but one which contains the beautiful and distinctive nebula known as the Beehive (which we encountered in the first discussion of Samson's celestial metaphors, and which must have been known to the ancients because the Samson legend has Samson encountering a swarm of bees in conjunction with the lion he slays on the way *down* to see a beautiful Philistine maiden, i.e. a Philistine virgin, or the constellation Virgo).

In addition to being known as the Beehive, this shimmering nebula had another name by which it was known to the ancients: *Praesepe*, a name by which it is still sometimes referred today. This Latin word means "manger." The cluster probably received that name because it is located between the two stars known as the two donkeys, as we have already seen (Asellus Borealis and Asellus Australis, the northern and southern colts of an ass or donkey). The Beehive or Manger reaches its highest point in the heavens right at midnight during the same time of the year that the sun rises in the house of Sagittarius / Capricorn (which used to occur at winter solstice during the Age of Aries, but which has now been delayed to later in the year due to the action of precession).

We can now understand why the gospel of Luke tells us that Jesus was born in a manger. Just as the legend of Mithras tells us that he is born at *midnight* on the juncture between the 24th and the 25th of December, and in a rock or cave (because the sun is then trapped in the depths of the earth, directly below our feet as we pass through the point of midnight in earth's daily rotation), even so the Sun is being born at midnight in a manger in the gospel account, when Praesepe passes overhead at midnight in the starry sky on the juncture between December 24th and December 25th (in the Age of Aries). One version of the legend (that of Mithras) describes the birth in terms of the great "rock" that the sun is beneath at the moment it is "born" to begin its ascent from the year's nadir to the year's summit, while the other version of the legend (that of Jesus) describes the birth in terms of the contents of the sky at the moment the sun is being "born" to begin the same ascent. Because the Beehive cluster, Praesepe the Manger, stood at the highest point in the sky at that moment of midnight, the heavenly birth of the sun was described as taking place in a manger (between two stars known as the donkeys).

Robert Taylor explains the entire cast of the scene in the *Devil's Pulpit*:

> [. . .] if you rectify your celestial globe to the moment of twelve o'clock midnight, between the 24th and 25th of December, you will find the constellation of the stable of Bethlehem, in which Christ is said to be born, the moment he achieves his first degree of ascension, at the lower meridian, while you shall see the constellation of the Virgin, who is said to bring him forth (in no disparagement to her eternal virginity) at that moment, come to the line of the horizon; and thus said to preside over his nativity.

> [. . .] he tumbles down into the stable, the nadir, or lower meridian, the precise astronomical position of the Sun at that moment.

> Now, sirs, at that moment, to the accuracy of the setting of a watch, what is the state of the visible heavens, in the construction of the planisphere? Why, it is this: at the lower meridian you have the stable of Bethlehem, in which Christ is born; on the eastern point of the horizon you have the sign of the Virgin, with the great star *Vindemiatrix*, in her elbow, just peering above the horizon, of which Star the magi, or wise men, express themselves – "*We have seen his star in the east.*" At the upper meridian, you have the constellation *Cancer, the Crab*, which includes the cradle of Jupiter, literally the Io-Sepe – that is, the manger of Jao, from which mistaken words, have been formed the name of the imaginary husband of the Virgin, *Joseph*. While on the western horizon, you have the Lamb of God, that taketh away the sins of the world; immediately above which, you will see the Epiphany, or "manifestation of Christ to the Gentiles," which is none other than the beautiful constellation, *Orion*, which you may see this very evening; those three bright Stars, which constitute his belt, being the three

Magian kings, who, looking directly across the horizon, see his Star in the east, and are come to worship him, which they do by presenting gold, frankincense, and myrrh, the emblematical oblations in all ages, consecrated to the honor of the Sun.[118]

This very scene as Taylor describes it can now be observed in the night sky during the months from February to April (although the Beehive only transits the meridian or line through the highest point in the sky on one particular night, the scene itself can be observed in its general details during the course of several weeks). Virgo is rising, with her outstretched arm coming up first (a fact which may, Taylor asserts, account for her description in the gospels as the *hand*-maid of the Lord, which he discusses in his lecture entitled "Virgo Paritura," which contains a complete examination of the evidence supporting the identification of Mary with the constellation and sign of Virgo).[119] Cancer, ahead of Leo, with its Beehive or Manger, is near zenith. Orion, which had dominated the central panels of the southern night sky during the winter months, is now retreating in the west, and his distinctive belt-stars are sinking down to the horizon. There, they take on the role of the *Three Kings* or *Three Magi* who saw the star in the east announcing the divine birth – for they truly look to the east from their position near the horizon in the west.

The visit of the magi is described in the gospel of Matthew, where they do indeed say, "Where is he that is born King of the Jews? for we have seen his star in the east, and are come to worship him" (Matthew 2:2). Why does Taylor assert that Vindemiatrix is the star they are calling "his star" in this verse? Perhaps it is because, in addition to being seen as the upraised hand of the constellation Virgo, this star could also be seen as the head of a child being held in the lap or at the breast of the Virgin (refer again to the chart above showing the stars of Virgo, and you can envision this interpretation for yourself). Below is a statue from ancient Egypt showing the goddess Isis nursing the infant sun-god Horus at her breast, while seated in the same posture that the stars of the constellation Virgo depict. This Egyptian scene is clearly almost identical to later depictions of the Madonna with Christ-child from Christian iconography, because in both cases the iconography is probably originally inspired by the positions of the stars in the zodiac constellation:

The fact that the celestial Manger in Cancer the Crab was also the birthplace of Zeus or Jupiter, as Taylor mentioned in the passage cited, is supported by the legend telling us that Zeus was nursed or suckled by a miraculous goat, Amaltheia. If the divine child was born at the end of Sagittarius and the start of Capricorn, then it only makes sense that its nursing was done by a goat: Capricorn.[120]

In the second chapter of Luke's gospel, we find the prophecy of Simeon, who had been waiting in Jerusalem to see the Lord's Christ (Luke 2:25-26). His words to Mary become more clear when we understand the celestial foundation of the scriptures: "And Simeon blessed them, and said unto Mary his mother, Behold, this *child* is set for the fall and rising again of many in Israel; and for a sign which shall be spoken against" (Luke 2:34). This makes perfect sense if we understand that *Israel* refers to the starry host, and especially to the zodiac band. Esoterically, it teaches that we "fall" into incarnation, but are destined to "rise again" out of the material and into the spiritual, by the recovery or remembering of the "Christ within" toward which the scriptures of the world were designed to point us.

Whenever the New Testament speaks of "signs," such as in this verse, it is a good practice to investigate the possibility that the text is referring to a specific sign of the zodiac, or (more precisely) *the sun occupying* a specific sign of the zodiac. To which of the signs of the zodiac could Simeon be referring in the above prophecy?

It is important to clarify that Jesus does not correspond to a single "sign" of the zodiac – he corresponds to the sun moving through all twelve of the zodiac signs (his twelve companions, the twelve disciples). Throughout the gospel accounts, the episodes involving the character of Jesus (the sun) are seen to reflect the attributes of whatever sign he is passing through during the annual cycle. This concept may seem a little strange at first, but Robert Taylor provides some explanation throughout his sermons. One way to understand it, he says in the *Devil's Pulpit*, is to consider the fact that the sun passing through each zodiac sign is a "mediator" to those of us on earth, which can be understood using the analogy of a dining room table. As the earth goes around the sun, the sun will always be between the observer on the earth and the stars the observer looks toward just prior to sunrise on any given morning. Thus, the sun is the "mediator" of the constellation in which the sun rises on any given morning. Robert Taylor explains:

> [. . .] our earth's annual motion round the sun throws the sun, or makes him seem to go, between us and those measurelessly remote fixed stars.
>
> As, only walk round the table with your eyes steadily directed to any fixed object on the table, you will see that object, with relation to the distant parts of the room, exactly opposite them, changing its point of opposition as you change your situation. And thus, while you alone are moving, the object on which your eye is fixed will seem to be moving; and thus, will be a mediator, or intercessor, at all times between you and the more distant fixed objects, by which alone you can measure the change which is going on, not in their positions, but yours.[121]

When the sun "enters" each sign, it becomes identified with that sign, and the portion of the year associated with that stage on the earth's annual circuit can be metaphorically depicted using the imagery associated with that sign. Thus, as we have already seen, the sun arriving at the juncture between Sagittarius and Capricorn, at the lowest point of the entire year, is allegorized as the Christ-child being born in a stable.

By far the most common sign with which Jesus identifies himself during the gospel narratives is the "sign of the Son of Man," and it is with this sign that I believe the prophecy of Simeon has to do. What is this "sign of the Son of Man," and why was it such an important sign in the zodiac – a sign that was "set for the fall and rising again of many in Israel"?

It will become abundantly clear from the many discourses of Jesus given in the New Testament gospels that the sign of the Son of Man is the constellation Aquarius, depicted in the star chart below:

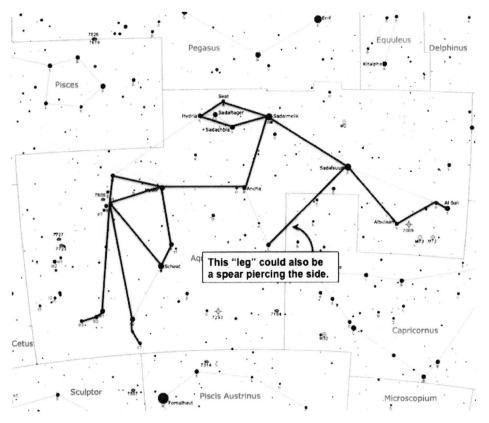

This "leg" could also be a spear piercing the side.

Note that Aquarius depicts a man pouring out water from a vessel, and who appears to be running as he leans forward or falls forward, with one "leg" stretched well out in front of him. That "leg," however, could also be interpreted as a sword or a spear, pointing directly into his side. This possibility, of course, later features prominently in the account of the crucifixion, but it is also clearly present in the blessing of Simeon given in Luke chapter 2, for in the verse following the one previously quoted, Simeon tells Mary "(Yea, a sword shall pierce through thy own soul also,) that the thoughts of many hearts may be revealed" (Luke 2:35). Note that the arm of Virgo could also be seen as a piercing sword!

But why is the sign of the Son of Man so important? Because it marks the end of a precessional "Age," which is metaphorically described as the "end of the world." We previously saw evidence that the confrontation between Moses and Aaron over the golden calf in the Old Testament esoterically encoded the transition from the Age of Taurus to the Age of Aries, when the sign of Aries took over the point of March equinox from the sign of Taurus which had ruled there previously, and could thus be seen as the zodiac group which "leads the children of Israel up out of the land of Egypt." It so happens that the gospels as we know them today were formulated near the dawn of a new precessional age, when Pisces was taking over from Aries. The sign that would thus be seen at the end of that precessional age would be the sign of Aquarius, and its arrival would mark another "end of the world" – that is, the end of the Age of Pisces and the dawning of the Age of Aquarius. We are only just now reaching that point in the precessional cycle, each precessional age lasting approximately 2,160 years.

This analysis thus reveals that the formulators of the ancient system used multiple levels of natural and celestial phenomena in the system of allegory they devised to preserve their precious spiritual teachings. We are all familiar at some level with the daily motion of the sun, moon, and stars, rising in the east and setting in the west. We are also familiar with the monthly cycles of the moon, and with the annual cycle of the seasons. But there is another cycle that is far longer than all of these – the great precessional cycle of 25,920 years (discussed at length in *The Mathisen Corollary* and in many other books which deal with the ancient myths and monuments left to us from the dawn of human civilization).[122] This precessional cycle is clearly the foundation for many ancient myths and legends, from the usurpation of the throne of Osiris by his brother Set in ancient Egypt, to the nostalgia over the lost "Golden Age" of Saturn found in numerous cultures around the world, to the quest for the Golden Fleece by Jason and the Argonauts, to the confrontation between Moses and Aaron at the scene of the golden calf, and to the sermons attributed to the character of Jesus in the gospels, describing an "end of the world" which accompanies the arrival of the "sign of the Son of Man."

In the New Testament book of Matthew, in the twenty-fourth chapter, we find a version of the words attributed to Jesus known as the "Olivet discourse," because it was delivered on the Mount of Olives. It begins by telling us:

> [1]And Jesus went out, and departed from the temple: and his disciples came to him for to shew him the buildings of the temple.
> [2]And Jesus said unto them, See ye not all these things? Verily I say unto you, There shall not be left here one stone upon another, that shall not be thrown down.

The Matthew passage then says, "And as he sat upon the mount of Olives, the disciples came unto him privately, saying, Tell us, when shall these things be? and what shall be the sign of thy coming, and of the end of the world?" (Matthew 24:3).

This verse lets us know that the discourse which took place upon the Mount of Olives (which, according to the esoteric interpretation, would be a celestial location rather than an earthly location, and one that probably refers to the high point of the zodiac wheel), deals with the end of the world, the time when the current "structure" of the heavens would be torn down and replaced by another.

Because of this subject matter, the Olivet discourse has also been termed the "little Apocalypse," a word which is Greek for "unveiling," as in the unveiling of things that are hidden or things that are yet to come. As such, the Greek-derived word *apocalypse* is identical to the Latin-derived word *revelation*, which also means "unveiling" (revelation meaning "to reveal" or to lift the veil which previously hid something). In fact, the last book of the canonical New Testament, the Revelation of John, was in previous centuries also commonly referred to as the Apocalypse of John.

We have already seen in our examination of just one chapter of the Revelation of John that the imagery contained therein strongly suggests that it deals with celestial events having to do with the constellations of the zodiac (in the case of Revelation 9, with the zodiac constellations of Scorpio and Sagittarius and their positions flanking the beautiful arc of the Milky Way galaxy, where it rises up like smoke from a constellation known as Ara the Altar).

Can we find a similar celestial symbology in the Olivet discourse, which treats a similar theme to the Revelation of John?

Indeed, we find startling celestial symbology. The most important of these concerns the identity of "the Son of man." In Matthew 24, verses 28 through 30, we read the following:

> 28For as the lightning cometh out of the east, and shineth even unto the west; so shall also the coming of the Son of man be.
> 29Immediately after the tribulation of those days shall the sun be darkened, and the moon shall not give her light, and the stars shall fall from heaven, and the powers of the heavens shall be shaken:
> 30And then shall appear the sign of the Son of man in heaven: and then shall all the tribes of the earth mourn, and they shall see the Son of man coming in the clouds of heaven with power and great glory.

If we are attuned to the possibility that the authors of these ancient scriptures were encoding important celestial symbols in their writing, then a phrase which tells us "and then shall appear the sign . . . in heaven" will immediately ring an alarm bell indicating the possibility that the sign in heaven being described may have a celestial correspondence, possibly to a zodiac constellation or other important constellation in the heavens. Notice that *the scripture text itself* tells us that the sign which shall appear will be a sign in heaven; the fact that the scriptures themselves tell us plainly that they are dealing with celestial symbology no doubt explains the fact that the literalist church sought to keep the scriptures out of the hands of the populace for over a thousand years, and punished those who translated them out of the ancient languages and into the "vulgar" language of the people with grisly public execution and the desecration of their corpse afterwards.

Which heavenly sign could be signified by the "sign of the Son of man" described in Matthew chapter 24? The answer has already been given. As other writers have pointed out, there is only one zodiac sign which represents a man, and that is Aquarius.

When the New Testament came into being, the inexorable march of the precession of the equinoxes was bringing the turning of ages from the Age of Aries into the Age of Pisces. In terms of celestial mechanics, the motion of precession was causing the dawn of the March equinox sun to rise in the house of the sign of Pisces, rather than the sign of Aries.

Pisces *precedes* Aries in the zodiac's normal east-to-west motion of nightly rotation. This is why the ages-long motion that brings the sunrise on any specific day of the year (such as the day of the March equinox) into the *preceding* sign is called "precession."

The sign which precedes Pisces is Aquarius.

Thus, if the Olivet discourse is set at the beginning of one precessional age (the Age of Pisces, the Fish), and if it is talking about the "end times" as in the *end of a precessional age,* then the end of that age would very certainly be that time when the sign of Aquarius appears in place of Pisces over the March equinox sunrise.

For confirmation that this identification of the sign in question as Aquarius is in fact correct, we can find a verse later in the same Olivet discourse, from chapter 25. There, in verses 31 through 33, we find the following description (still talking about the events of the "end times"):

> ³¹When the Son of man shall come in his glory, and all the holy angels with him, then shall he sit upon the throne of his glory:
> ³²And before him shall be gathered all nations: and he shall separate them one from another, as a shepherd divideth his sheep from the goats:
> ³³And he shall set the sheep on his right hand, but the goats on the left.

These verses provide stunning confirmation that the passage is indeed talking about the zodiac sign of Aquarius, for Aquarius indeed "divideth his sheep from the goats." The constellation Aquarius, which is the only fully-human zodiac sign besides Virgo and Gemini, and the only one of the zodiac signs that would be described as a "Son of man" (Virgo being a woman, and Gemini being two youths and thus not a singular "son"), follows immediately after the constellation Capricorn, the Goat. It precedes Pisces the Fish, but not far beyond them is the constellation of Aries the Ram. Thus, Aquarius stands between the Goat and the Ram, and the Ram of course represents a male sheep; Aquarius thus separates the "sheep" from the "goats." Clearly, this passage from the Olivet discourse supports the interpretation of the "sign of the Son of man" as representing the zodiac sign of Aquarius.

Notable also is the verse found at the beginning of the first Matthew 24 passage quoted above. That verse, Matthew 24:28, reads: "For as the lightning cometh out of the east, and shineth even unto the west; so shall also the coming of the Son of man be."

This passage is very interesting, but it does not seem to make much sense if interpreted literally. What does it mean that "lightning cometh out of the east, and shineth even unto the west"? As discussed earlier, the constellations of the night sky, like the sun itself, rise in the east and move towards the west, due to the direction of the rotation of the earth. This unusual mention of "lightning" which comes from the east and then moves to the west, which immediately precedes a verse talking about a zodiac sign – the sign of the Son of man – raises the possibility that the passage is discussing heavenly bodies, which move from the east to the west.

Giorgio de Santillana and Hertha von Dechend spend some time in *Hamlet's Mill* demonstrating that myths involving the word "fire" often refer to the "equinoctial colure" – the pathway traced out by the sun as the earth rotates towards the east.[123] In light of that, it is very likely that Matthew 24:28's "lightning" also refers to the sun. If we test out that hypothesis by substituting the word "sun" for lightning in the passage, and the sign of Aquarius for "Son of man" based on our discussion above, then Matthew 28 would read something like this:

> For as the *sun* cometh out of the east, and shineth even unto the west; so shall also the coming of the *sign of Aquarius* be [at the end of the Age of Pisces].

The passage alerts us to the fact that we are talking about heavenly phenomena, and the apparent reference to the sun's rising (flashing in the east and shining towards the west) also alerts us to the fact that we are probably talking about a heliacal rising. When the Age of Pisces draws to a close, the rising of the sun in the east on the March equinox will be in the constellation of Aquarius instead of Pisces.

However, it would be a mistake to conclude from the foregoing that Jesus in the gospels is associated with one sign, Aquarius, only – even though he does often refer to himself in the third person as "the son of Man" throughout. Instead, the textual evidence suggests that it would be more accurate to identify him with the sun itself, moving through each of the zodiac signs. These twelve signs of the zodiac correspond to the twelve disciples or twelve apostles, in the same manner that they correspond to the twelve tribes of Israel in the Old Testament.

Robert Taylor finds confirmation of this interpretation in the fact that each of the twelve disciples "has a house of his own, while the Savior has not where to lay his head – the constellations retaining their fixed relative positions, while the Sun, in seeming to pass through them, wanders from house to house."[124] In this quotation, Taylor is citing the words of Jesus from Matthew 8:20 and also Luke 9:58, in which Jesus said, "The foxes have holes, and the birds of the air *have* nests; but the Son of man hath not where to lay *his* head."

Taylor presents compelling arguments throughout his sermons to conclude for example that Peter corresponds to the "head-strong" sign of Aries, while Philip – whose name means "lover of horses" – corresponds to Sagittarius, and Thomas to Cancer the Crab, the sign which occupies the position just after the summer solstice at the very top of the zodiac wheel. Taylor argues that the name *Thomas* is actually linguistically very close to that of the Sumerian god *Tammuz*, who was a vegetation god and ruled over productive summer months of the year.[125] There was an ancient festival of mourning for Tammuz every year at the summer solstice, when the women would weep for Tammuz (because the sun would begin declining towards the Pit after the passing of the summer solstice).

In the gospels, Jesus is similarly glorified at the "summit" of the year, prior to undergoing his own descent and agony, in the story of the Transfiguration, which is recorded in the three canonical synodic gospels (Matthew, Mark, and Luke). In those accounts of the Transfiguration, each begins by telling us that Jesus took Peter, James and John and led them "up into an high mountain" (Matthew 17:1, Mark 9:2, Luke 9:28 – the account in Luke only calls it "a mountain," rather than a "high mountain"). Is it significant that the text in each says "into" a mountain, rather than "upon" a mountain? Perhaps: if the text indeed refers to the sun's progress through the houses of the zodiac, going "into" the houses at the top of the wheel is metaphorically like going "into" a high mountain, and the preposition "into" would be more appropriate than the preposition "upon."

In either case, we see that the sun approaches the summit of the year as it passes through the sign of Gemini – the Twins – at the end of which we find the summer solstice (on or around June 21 each year, at the end of the sign of Gemini and the beginning of the sign of Cancer). In light of this fact, Robert Taylor finds it significant that Jesus brings along on this trip the brothers James and John, who are often mentioned almost as if they were one person (i.e., as if they were twins – and in fact they are both the sons of Zebedee, given the nickname "Boanerges" or "sons of thunder").[126]

In the account of the Transfiguration, Jesus is literally "metamorphosed" in front of the astonished disciples, turned into a being who shines so brightly that he and his raiment are "glistering" (Luke 9:29). In a sermon entitled "On the Transfiguration of Jesus" published in Robert Carlile's periodical, *The Lion*, in December of 1829, Taylor argues that this transformation is meant to reveal the fact that Jesus is meant to actually personify the Sun itself, just as the twelve disciples represent the twelve signs of the zodiac, and just as the angels represent the starry host (and the archangels, or "ruling angels," the first magnitude stars among that heavenly army).[127]

In that sermon on "The Transfiguration," Taylor asserts: "You see the language actually labours to exclude any other sense than that of the visible sun as the meaning of the words *Christ* and the *Son of Man*."[128] For supporting evidence, he points to (among other examples) the declaration by Christ before Pilate that "my kingdom is not of this world" (John 18:36), to which Taylor replies, "Assuredly not; it was the kingdom of heaven, the visible starry heavens"[129] Elsewhere in the sermon, Taylor points to the declaration by Christ that "In my Father's house are many mansions" (John 14:2) as additional evidence of the same concept (in this case, referring to the twelve houses or signs of the zodiac).[130]

As the sun continues from the highest part of its annual journey, it begins to decline again towards the next equinox, approaching the months of autumn. This progression brings it into the sign of Virgo, stretching from late August to late September, and the sign of Libra, and the autumnal equinox which takes place at the end of Virgo and beginning of Libra, on or around September 22 each year.

At this point, the ecliptic path of the sun, which has been above the celestial equator since the spring equinox, will cross the celestial equator again. The path of the sun, which has been north of the celestial equator each day for observers in the northern hemisphere, will intersect the celestial equator again, and then as earth continues around its orbit, the ecliptic will be below the celestial equator, days will be shorter than nights, and the path of the sun through the sky will be lower and lower – closer and closer to the southern horizon – on the way to the winter solstice again.

We have already seen from our examination of the Greek myth of Iphigenia (replaced by a substitutionary stag) and in the Old Testament story of the sacrifice of Isaac (replaced by a substitutionary ram) that death and sacrifice are associated with the equinoctial crossing, whether the crossing takes place on the way down (as in the case of Iphigenia) or on the way back up (as in the case of Isaac). According to the argument of Robert Taylor, the *crossing* of the ecliptic and the celestial equator is represented in the gospel allegories as a crucifixion, and the metaphor is an apt one for the motion of the ecliptic line crossing over the celestial equator. In the image below, we see again the traditional "double hemisphere" world map, with the sinuous path of the ecliptic traced over it between the two lines of the tropics: it crosses the equator twice, marked in this instance by a black arrow and two white arrows (the two white arrows are actually pointing to the same place on the globe and on the equator):

In the diagram, the ecliptic crosses <u>below</u> the equator at the black arrow (corresponding to autumnal equinox) and then crosses back <u>above</u> the equator at the white arrow (corresponding to the spring equinox). As we will see, there are actually *two crucifixions* in the scriptures of the New Testament, with imagery corresponding to each of these two crossings of the equator by the sun!

Note that this parallels the earlier discussion of two *covenants* – the covenant is a "coming together" (which happens at the equinoxes) – and the same bi-annual event can also be described as two *crucifixions*.

The crucifixion that takes place as the sun passes through autumnal equinox is marked by imagery of bread and wine, because the fall season is the time of harvest for both wheat and grape. The sign of Virgo, which immediately precedes the autumn equinox, is associated with the harvest of wheat, and Virgo has since ancient times been depicted as holding a sheaf of wheat in one hand (corresponding to her brightest star, Spica). The image below, from the early 1800s, shows a traditional depiction of Virgo with a sheaf of wheat:

The arrow points to the location of the star Spica, and the artist's depiction of the constellation shows a sheaf of wheat in the Virgin's hand corresponding to the location of Spica.

Very close to Virgo is the constellation of Corvus the Crow (the entire constellation is visible in the first star chart of Virgo presented in the previous chapter). Corvus is a bright group of stars, arranged such that the bird seems to be gazing intently at the star Spica – as H. A. Rey puts it in his delightful book on the constellations, "The Crow's bill is pointed toward the Virgin's jewel, Spica, as though he were waiting for a chance to grab it."[131]

Immediately on the other side of the Crow from Spica (behind the head of the bird, if you will) is the constellation of Crater, the Cup. It is perched on the back of the serpent-constellation Hydra. All three of these constellations – the Virgin, the Cup, and the Crow – will play a role in the crucifixion stories found in the gospels.

The image below shows the stars of Crater, a somewhat faint constellation, in relation to Corvus. Some of the stars of the constellations Virgo and Leo are visible near the upper edges of the chart as well:

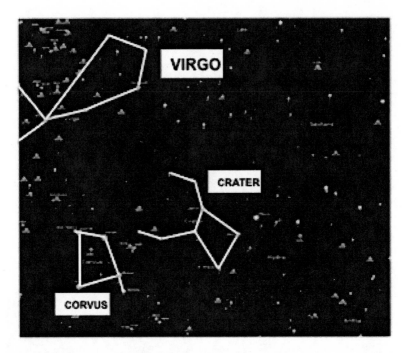

The location of Crater the Cup near Virgo (the sign associated with the period of time leading right up to the September equinox), is extremely significant, according to Robert Taylor, for the autumnal equinox metaphorically represents the "crucifixion" of the sun: one of the two points in the annual cycle where the ecliptic path crosses the celestial equator. Moreover, the autumnal equinox is the "crossing" at which the sun is descending towards the Pit (the winter months), and thus is the more dolorous of the two crossings (on the spring equinox, the crossing is triumphant, as the sun is ascending out of the winter months on its way to the "high mountain" again).

As the sun crosses the equator, it leaves the sign of Virgo and enters the sign of Libra, the Scales – a symbol of justice, as well as of equality and balance (the days and nights reaching equilibrium at the equinox). This autumn crossing at the end of the sign of Virgo, Taylor demonstrates, furnishes the imagery which shows up in the New Testament depictions of the crucifixion.[132]

First, of course, there is the Last Supper, with the bread and the wine, symbolizing the harvest season of autumn when the wheat is cut down and ground into bread, and the grapes are brought in and trampled into wine. Not only do the Last Supper and some of the imagery of the crucifixion in the New Testament accounts embody these terrestrial symbols from the agricultural year, but they also reflect the fact that the sign of the Virgin carries a sheaf of wheat, and that just beyond her in the night sky we find the celestial goblet of Crater the Cup. This celestial imagery becomes the bread and the cup described in the Last Supper.

Next, of course, is the fact that Mary the mother of Jesus (whom we have already seen to be associated with the constellation of Virgo) is specifically described as standing near the cross at the crucifixion. The gospel according to John tells us in its account of the crucifixion that three Mary's stood by the cross: "Now there stood by the cross of Jesus his mother, and his mother's sister, Mary the wife of Cleophas, and Mary Magdalene" (John 19:25). We will return to the importance of the name Mary itself later, but the close proximity of Mary to the cross is seen by Taylor as evidence of the fact that the crucifixion here corresponds to the autumnal equinox, located at the end of the sign of Virgo.

Taylor elaborates on the identification of Mary and Virgo:

> Who, then, is that heavenly maid, that hand-maid of the Lord, that Judith so remarkable for her arms, that warms the true David; *but* that constellation of Virgo, that city of refuge, as the ultimate end for which the whole year exists, and which the sun enters in the warm month of August, so expressly and literally defined in the New Testament, as "a virgin in the sixth month," when "he crowneth the year with his goodness. And the valleys also stand so thick with corn, that they do laugh and sing."

> Hence, this virgin of the Zodiac, without any contradiction, without any absurdity, was worshipped by the ancient Tsabaists, under the characteristic epithet of Virgo Paritura – that is, *the virgin that shall bring forth*; because it is really and physically the month of August, which brings forth the fruits of the earth: and for the fruitfulness of which, expectation waits through all the circling year.

> Hence, though a pure virgin – that is, most literally, a *fire* virgin – that is, a virgin whose form is made up of those bright fires, which stud the starry bosom of the night – she is yet the tender mother of all animal life, who provides the food on which we are to be sustained throughout the year – that "openeth her hand and filleth all things living with plenteousness." Thus, all is beautiful, all is magnificent, grand, harmonious, and intelligible; elegant as art, and convincing as science, when interpreted by the true key of astronomical allegory.

> Where stands the virgin mother, in the gospel, but near the cross of Christ?

> Where stands the virgin mother in the Zodiac? but just as near the cross which the sun makes over the equinoctial line, in September, when, after having expended his last fervors in ripening the corn, he passes into his church of Laodicea – that is, literally, the just people – that is, the group of stars which form the scales of justice, in which it is neither hot, nor cold, but lukewarm: but where the solar heat every day diminishing, he begins to descend with sorrow to the grave.[133]

This passage displays some of Robert Taylor's deep knowledge of both language and literature, and deserves a little "unpacking" or explication. He makes numerous Biblical references without telling his listeners or readers where they come from – evidence of both the depth of his familiarity with the Bible, and the Biblical literacy of his audience in the early nineteenth century, which could be generally taken for granted then but can no longer today.

In the first paragraph of the above-quoted passage, Taylor quotes the 65th Psalm (actually, a Psalter version of the 65th Psalm, rather than that found in the version known commonly as the "King James Version"). The relevant passages of that Psalm to which he makes reference are found in verses 11 through 13, where we read:

> 11 Thou crownest the year with thy goodness; and thy paths drop fatness.
> 12 They drop upon the pastures of the wilderness: and the little hills rejoice on every side.
> 13 The pastures are clothed with flocks; the valleys also are covered over with corn; they shout for joy, they also sing.

Taylor argues that these verses describe the harvest-time, the period in which the year is "crowned with goodness," and the valleys ("pastures," in the King James translation) are so thick with corn (which is to say, *wheat*, the crop associated with Virgo, rather than the maize of the New World which is known as "corn" in American English) that they sing and shout for joy.

The reference to the "virgin of the sixth month" is a reference to the annunciation, when the angel Gabriel visited Mary, in the sixth month of her cousin Elizabeth's pregnancy with John the Baptist. Note that Virgo presides over the sixth sign from Aries, Aries being the leader of the zodiac parade and the sign of the spring equinox. The fact that the months were once counted from Aries is still evident in our calendar today, for our month of *Sept*ember is the *seventh* from Aries (not from January), and our month of *Octo*ber is the *eighth* from Aries (it is the tenth from January), as Taylor explains in *Devil's Pulpit* (obviously, *Nov*ember and *Dec*ember continue the pattern).[134]

When he says that Virgo is a "pure virgin – that is, most literally, a *fire* virgin," Taylor is referencing the fact that the word "pure" has its origins in the Greek word *pyros*, which means fire or having to do with fire (as in "pyrotechnics," "pyromaniac" or "funeral pyre"). From this remark, he goes on to extol the importance of the time of harvest, through which the virgin of Virgo literally becomes the mother of all living, that harvest upon which all life depends, furnishing the plant food which sustains all the plant-eating animals, and therefore indirectly all the meat-eating animals as well. In this poetic passage, we catch a glimpse of the basis for the reverence of the ancients who worshipped the Great Goddess, whether under the name of Rhea, Cybele, Ishtar, Ashtoreth, Ceres, or Demeter.

In the final paragraph of the cited passage, Taylor describes the motion of the personified sun passing from the house of Virgo the Virgin into the house of Libra the Scales, the sign of judgment, and the beginning of the waning of the year, when days once again become shorter than nights after the earth reaches the autumnal equinox and proceeds on its orbit towards the months of winter and the "grave" of winter solstice.

Here Taylor makes another literary reference that will be familiar to the very Biblically literate but which might be unfamiliar to those who have spent less time in the New Testament, and that is his reference to the Revelation (or Apocalypse) of John, when he identifies the sign of Libra with the church of Laodicea referenced in Revelation chapter 3, where we read in verses 14 through 16:

¹⁴And unto the angel of the church of the Laodiceans write; These things saith the Amen, the faithful and true witness, the beginning of the creation of God;

¹⁵I know thy works, that thou art neither cold nor hot: I would thou wert cold or hot.

¹⁶So then because thou art lukewarm, and neither cold nor hot, I will spue thee out of my mouth.

Just as Libra is the seventh sign after Aries, so also is Laodicea the seventh in the Revelation listing of the seven churches of Asia, which Taylor elsewhere explains are the seven summer signs beginning in Aries.[135] As Asia was the "land of fire," the seven churches are the fiery summer months (although Laodicea is only "lukewarm," as it is the sign that follows the autumn equinox and ends the seven warm months, setting the stage for the five painful months or signs beginning with Scorpio and proceeding to Pisces).

The churches described in Revelation chapters 2 and 3 – which correspond to the seven "warm" signs of the year – correspond to the following zodiac signs, according to Taylor's explication:

- Ephesus, mentioned first (Revelation 2:1-6), corresponds to Aries, the first of the zodiac and the sign of spring equinox (in March). It has "left its first love" and is told to "remember therefore from whence thou art fallen," and it is threatened with having its candlestick removed: all metaphors for the fact that precession took away the equinox from the sign of Aries when the end of the Age of Aries ushered in the Age of Pisces.[136]
- Thyatira Taylor identifies with the sign of Taurus the Bull, which is described as being characterized by "patience," "service," and "works" (Revelation 2:19) all aspects of the patiently plowing bull of early spring.[137]
- Philadelphia (Revelation 3:7-13), the city whose name means "brotherly love," is clearly Gemini the Twins.[138] It is told that "him that overcometh will I make a pillar in the temple of my God" (verse 12), and Taylor elsewhere explains that the "solstitial colure," that great circle which runs between the summer solstice (which comes at the end of the sign of Gemini), the north celestial pole, and the winter solstice (found at the end of Sagittarius) is depicted as a pillar in ancient myth and oral tradition (we will later see that this same pillar is the Djed-column of ancient Egypt). Gemini is bounded by a pillar, that is to say that it ends on a solstice. For clear supporting evidence of this analogy, Taylor shows us that Philip – whose name means "lover of the horse" and who personifies Sagittarius – was traditionally held to have been executed by being "hanged against a pillar."[139] In his case, it was the pillar with its base in the winter solstice, which ends Sagittarius, whereas here in Revelation the pillar for those of Philadelphia who persevere to the end refers to the top of the same pillar, which runs all the way up to the summer solstice, which comes at the end of Gemini.
- Pergamos (Revelation 2:12-17), whose name also has the root of *pyros* or "fire" and means literally "height of fire" in Taylor's opinion, stands for Cancer, the sign of the height of summer, commencing after the summer solstice.[140]
- Sardis (Revelation 3:1-5) is told more than once to "be watchful," and Taylor believes that Sardis corresponds to the zodiac sign of Leo the Lion, often depicted as a watchful guardian. Gateways and doorways are often adorned with statues of lions as guardians against thieves or evil spirits, and Sardis is

warned to be on the watch for the one who "will come on thee as a thief" (Revelation 3:3).[141]

- Smyrna (Revelation 2:8-11) represents Virgo according to Taylor's reading. The city's name means "bundle of myrrh" according to Taylor, which was one of the gifts brought to the rising constellation of the Virgin by the Three Magi (three stars of Orion's belt, setting in the west and looking to the east) as we saw earlier in the discussion of the celestial origins of the Nativity scene.[142]

- Finally, Laodicea (Revelation 3:14-22) represents Libra and the "lukewarm" part of the year over which it presides. Note that the passage describing Laodicea and quoted earlier is full of references which can be construed as connecting to the Scales as a symbol of justice. There is the word "witness" in verse 14, and a reference to Laodicea as being "blind" in verse 17 (an attribute of the personified goddess of Justice, the holder of the Scales).[143]

To return to the imagery of the autumnal equinox which Taylor was discussing in the quoted passage, not only do the Biblical accounts contain references to the bread of Virgo (made by the wheat gathered at harvest) but even more so do they contain references to the wine that is made when the grapes are gathered at the same time of year, and which are trampled out in that great winepress that is associated with the Day of Judgment in the Old Testament imagery of the book of Isaiah (particularly in Isaiah 63:3) and also quite tellingly in Lamentations 1:15, in which we read that "the Lord hath trodden the virgin, the daughter of Judah, as in a winepress" (the virgin here must be Virgo, and her identification as the "daughter of Judah" is appropriate for the sign that follows Leo, the Lion – the animal with which Judah is associated).

In his lecture entitled "The Cup of Salvation" in *The Devil's Pulpit*, Taylor elaborates on the winepress imagery in the crucifixion narratives that correspond to the sun's crossing of the equinox in autumn. He explains that the crucifixion takes place "outside the gate" of Jerusalem (that heavenly city) because Jerusalem represents the warm months or signs of March through September, the "city on a hill" when the sun is traversing the upper part of the zodiac wheel (which we earlier said was often encoded in myth and story as a mountain or hill), and at the equinox the sun passes "through the gate" and leaves that city on the hill.[144]

With these sorts of arguments, Taylor advances his case that the crucifixion imagery primarily relates to the autumnal equinox, and the depth and volume of the connections certainly makes this a strong thesis. The fact that so many other aspects of the Old and New Testaments appear to have very clear celestial connections to the houses of the zodiac and the passage of the sun each year through the great wheel makes the interpretation of the crucifixion in these terms almost certainly the correct interpretation.

Turning now to the other day of the year when the ecliptic crosses the celestial equator again, this time on the way back "up" out of the months of winter, is there evidence that this equinox is also commemorated in the Bible with celestial imagery? In fact there is. Taylor argues that the spring equinox takes place in the sign of Aries the Ram, and the gospels contain plenty of references to the "crucifixion of the Lamb."

In spite of all the detail-rich imagery explained above connecting the crucifixion to autumn, the harvest of wheat and the pressing of the vintage, we know from established tradition that the crucifixion is annually celebrated in the spring, alongside the celebration of the Passover, at a date which is tied to the spring equinox (the details of the calculation are complicated, and importantly they also involve the moon, but beyond that these details need not concern us here: the fact that the calculation is directly connected to the solar phenomenon of the spring equinox is the pertinent fact for demonstrating that the crucifixion involves imagery from both the points at which the ecliptic *crosses* the equator).

In *The Devil's Pulpit*, Robert Taylor explains these "two crucifixions" in the annual cycle:

> That it is the Vernal Crucifixion, or crossing of the Equator by the Sun, when he enters the sign of *Aries*, the Ram, as he does on the 21st of March, and crucifixion of any man, nor any even that happened upon earth, that was the subject of the Fast of Good Friday, and the Feast of Easter, that follows; is demonstrated in the historical fact, that this Fast and Feast have been religiously observed in the Spring of the year in every country of the world, and in every era of time, of which a record of any sort has descended to our own; and observed, too, with the very same ceremonies, to the very same significancy, and even with the very same words. And the Christ of the Spring Crucifixion is celebrated; because, after the Passover, he ascends into Heaven, and we look forward to the joyful Summer. But the Christ of the Autumnal Passover descends into Hell; and we must prepare for the gloomy Winter.[145]

That descent into hell after the autumnal equinox, of course, refers to the descent into the bottom of the metaphorical wheel of the year, and it is referenced both in the Apostles' Creed ("was crucified, dead, and buried; he descended into hell") as well as in the epistles, where in 1 Peter 4:6 a controversial passage declares "For this cause was the gospel preached also to them that are dead, that they might be judged according to men in the flesh, but live according to God in the spirit."

Notice also that there are two passages in Acts chapter 2, in the sermon of Peter on the day of Pentecost, in which Peter cites language from Psalm 16 declaring that "thou wilt not leave my soul in hell, neither wilt thou suffer thine Holy One to see corruption" (Acts 2:27) and tying this explicitly to the resurrection of Christ in verse 31, by saying "He [David, the Psalmist] seeing this before spake of the resurrection of Christ, that his soul was not left in hell, neither his flesh did see corruption" (Acts 2:31). These passages imply that Christ after the resurrection did go down to hell, as the Apostle's Creed proclaims, but that "he was not left in hell" – a passage which makes complete sense if the astronomical interpretation is applied.

With his descriptive and evocative language, Taylor explains this same concept in *The Devil's Pulpit*: "by means of death – that is, being crucified, and ducking under the Equator, he might redeem and fetch up the stars which were in a state of transgression, by being under the line of the first Covenant."[146] The downward motion of the sun after the autumnal equinox, then, is responsible for these Biblical teachings. The upward motion of the sun after the spring equinox translates into the Easter imagery of the resurrection and the celebration of new life.

Those who have a hard time accepting that the crucifixion imagery in the Bible comes from two different parts of the year should consider the point that Taylor makes in his sermons, which is that the canon of the New Testament contains a reference to Christ being crucified in Egypt, in addition to the more well-known crucifixion at Golgotha in Jerusalem. As Taylor points out, Revelation 11 verse 8 tells us, "And their dead bodies shall lie in the street of the great city, which spiritually is called Sodom and Egypt, where also our Lord was crucified."[147]

It could of course be argued that this passage in Revelation is referring again to Jerusalem, and saying that Jerusalem is "spiritually" called Sodom and Egypt, although the text only says "the great city," not Jerusalem explicitly. Furthermore, the use of the word "also" in this verse, as in "Egypt, where *also* our Lord was crucified," seems to imply that the text is referring to a location *in addition to* the Golgotha crucifixion.

The conundrum is solved with the astrological interpretation, since there are in fact two crucifixions in the annual cycle, where the sun is "crucified" between the crossing of the ecliptic line and the line of the celestial equator. Furthermore, one of them is at the gateway to the lower half of the year: Egypt, just as the Revelation passage tells us.

If the lower half of the year is metaphorically the land of Egypt, then the sun's escape from this land as it crosses the equinox once again in the spring is a passing-over of that period, and indeed we find that both the Passover and Easter are to this day celebrated in conjunction with the spring equinox.

The crucifixion of the spring equinox is the crucifixion of the Lamb, because it is in the sign of Aries. Remembering the discussion in the previous chapter that the "four corners of the world" were in the ancient celestial myth-system the four signs at the spring equinox, summer solstice, fall equinox and winter solstice, and adding to that knowledge the understanding that the spring equinox was chosen by many ancient cultures as the start of the year (and hence the beginning of "the world"), we can perceive an astronomical interpretation of the phrase "the Lamb slain from the foundation of the world" found in Revelation 13:8.[148] If the world's foundation each year is in Aries, at spring equinox, then this mysterious phrase has a hidden meaning that makes perfect sense when the celestial interpretation is applied.

Elsewhere in Revelation, Christ declares that he is *the Alpha and the Omega*, the first and the last (Revelation 1:11). If we choose a point on the zodiac circle to be the beginning, it stands to reason that this same point will also be the end of the circle – it will be the first and the last.

The zodiac code even explains the tradition of fasting during Lent, the season of forty days leading up to the resurrection. Taylor points out the zodiac connection:

> [. . .] this lamb-eating [of Easter meals], always follows after the long fast of Lent, during which, it was always the most damnable sin, that a man could commit, to eat anything but fish, as here you see the constellation of the Lamb comes immediately after that of the Fishes.[149]

Another lamb reference which Taylor points out is the reinstatement or restoration of Peter, in which the risen Christ says to Peter three times, "Feed my sheep," or "feed my lambs." Elsewhere, Taylor goes into the fascinating interpretation of the various twelve apostles, through whose houses the sun traverses during the year, and examines evidence supporting the identification of Peter with Aries the Ram (leading as he does the others, and also being marked by something of a headstrong disposition).

One of the most important aspects of Peter which indicate the association with Aries is the declaration that Peter shall have the keys to the kingdom of heaven.[150] Taylor points out that the two crossing points of the equinoxes are like doorways or gateways, and the kingdom of heaven would be the arch of the zodiac wheel that stretches above the two equinox crossings (from Aries through to Virgo).[151]

If the restoration of Peter after his denial of Christ is significant for its Aries imagery, the denial itself should also strike a chord with readers who are becoming familiar with the methodology of the celestial code, involving as it does "a maid" who sees Peter on the night before the crucifixion (a "maid" is a virgin – so we might immediately suspect she represents Virgo again), and a cock which crows after the second or the third denial.

The cock that is near Virgo is none other than the constellation of Corvus the Crow, but described as a cock. This association is supported by the Greek myths, in which the crow is said to watch over the pregnant princess who is to give birth to Asclepius, an important god-man. The expectant mother in that Greek myth, of course, is Virgo once again, and the crow is Corvus. We know from other sources that Asclepius was associated with the cock or the sacrifice or offering of a cock, and from that fact we have evidence that the ancients sometimes saw the constellation of Corvus as a rooster rather than a crow. Plato records the last words of Socrates to have been, "Crito, we ought to offer a cock to Asclepius. See to it, and don't forget."[152]

So, the evidence appears fairly clear that the episode of Peter's denial of Christ and the subsequent restoration of Peter mirror the motion of the sun through the two equinoxes as well. In Peter's denial, there are indicators meant to suggest the constellations of the autumnal equinox – when the sun is sinking down towards the grave (the virgin by the fire, the cock that crows three times). In his restoration, there are multiple references to lambs and sheep – indicators of the constellation at the spring equinox.

The constellations of Virgo and Corvus are referenced by the maid who is described as being *by the fire* and who declares that Peter was with Jesus, which he denies (Luke 22:56-57, as also Mark 14:66-69 and Matthew 26:69-75). That the equinoxes were depicted with fire imagery is quite clear from the tauroctony scenes of the ancient temples of Mithras, where two youths in Phrygian caps and their legs crossed (whose names are Cautes and Cautophanes) hold torches to represent the ecliptic crossing the celestial equator, the torch of one of them pointing down (autumnal equinox) and the torch of the other pointing upwards (spring equinox), discussed in my previous book and based upon observations made by David Ulansey in *Origins of the Mithraic Mysteries*.[153] Hertha von Dechend and Giorgio de Santillana also spend some time in *Hamlet's Mill* demonstrating that the "equinoctial colure" was metaphorically depicted as a ring of fire, or other sorts of fire imagery, in mythologies from the Greek to the Norse to the tribes of North America.[154]

After the denial by the fire when confronted by the maid, Peter denies one more time, and the scripture tells us that "immediately, while he yet spake, the cock crew" (Luke 22:60).

In the reinstatement of Peter, found in John 21 verses 15 through 18, the risen Christ demands of Peter three times that he declare his love, and commands Peter three times, "Feed my lambs," "Feed my sheep," and again, "Feed my sheep." This restoration of Peter, significantly enough, also takes place by a fire, for John tells us in verse 9 of the same chapter that the disciples had been out fishing through the night, and as they came to shore they were hailed by Jesus, and as they landed "they saw a fire of coals there, and fish laid thereon, and bread." Of course, the zodiac sign that precedes the spring equinox and the advent of the sign of Aries the Ram (or Lamb) is none other than Pisces, the Fishes. The spring equinox is the rising equinox, when the sun is triumphantly crossing above the celestial equator again after passing through the dreary signs of winter. It is appropriate, then, that this encounter between Christ and Peter contains imagery of sheep and lambs, indicating the sign of Aries, as well as a fire and fish, since the equinoctial line (the fire) runs between Pisces and Aries.

These are just some of the abundant clues Taylor analyzes, found throughout the scriptures of the New Testament, which indicate that the content is almost entirely celestial in its references. Interested readers will find Taylor's explication of the others full of even more connections at which to marvel, and his analysis very difficult to contest. However, those offered so far should be sufficient to prove the point.

As with our examination of the Old Testament, these revelations proving that the entirety of the New Testament stories rest upon an esoteric foundation have profound ramifications. Certainly, the revelation that the references to "hell" and "hellfire" describe the lower half of the zodiac circle will be a relief to the hundreds of millions living today who have been mentally terrorized by the threat of literal hellfire for themselves or their deceased family members and loved ones. But the implications go far deeper than that. We will spend the remainder of the book examining the profound implications of this ancient esoteric system, as well as the ages-long conspiracy to keep the knowledge of this truth from the people of earth, for reasons that appear to be nefarious.

Part II:

What Does It Mean?

6

The holographic universe

Does consciousness collapse wavefunctions?   That question, raised at the beginning of quantum theory, cannot be answered.   It can't even be well posed. Consciousness itself is a mystery.

Bruce Rosenblum and Fred Kuttner,
Quantum Enigma:
Physics Encounters Consciousness.[155]

The foregoing chapters have presented evidence to establish that the scriptures collected as the Old and New Testaments were never intended to be interpreted literally but rather metaphorically and esoterically.   If the number of examples and the explanation of the metaphors was insufficient to establish that beyond reasonable doubt, the interested reader can find hundreds more examples in the books of Robert Taylor, as well as those who have come after him in the more than 150 years since his astronomico-theological analyses were first published.

The reader may be forgiven, however, for a sense of quizzical bewilderment at this point – an urge to exclaim, "But what does it all mean?"   Why would the ancients go to so much trouble to preserve as divine revelation a collection of astronomical allegories?   Why would they do so not only in the stories of the Old Testament and then again in the New Testament, but also in culture after culture around the world, from Sumer to Babylon to Egypt to Greece to India, China, Australia, and the islands of the Pacific?

The stock answer of many of the adherents of that secular orthodoxy which has come to dominate western academia over the past century might be to smugly conclude that all religious thought is nothing more than a relic of mankind's "primitive" past, the product of that dim period in which men and women tried to make sense of the powerful forces of nature which so dominated their world that they made into gods all the actors of the world they saw around them – the sun, the moon, the stars, the rivers, the woods, the mountains, the seas, and in some cases the animals.

If the Bible stories reflect a reverence for the motions of the sun, moon, planets and zodiac, it is because they are an outgrowth of that ancient primitive impulse, according to this interpretation.   They may be more sophisticated and poetical, and they may be adorned with truly sublime moral teaching in some cases, but they are really just an ornate outgrowth of an erroneous starting-point (the erroneous attribution of mystical powers to natural objects that in the end are really nothing more than balls of gas or rocky objects, whirling through the indifferent and uncaring void of space).   In this naturalistic view, a prayer offered to an imaginary deity derived from a primitive awe for the sun or the moon is nothing more than a waste of breath, a futile plea to a figment of the imagination.

Robert Taylor himself appears to voice such a view at times, while asserting at other points in his lectures that he does hold the scriptures in high esteem and that he believes the skeptic (meaning the atheist) to be as mistaken as the literalist. At one point in his *Astronomico-Theological Lectures*, he offers this possible hypothesis for the origin of "these astronomical illustrations," saying:

> As no account has been kept, nor could have been kept of the millions of the races of squeeling savages, ourangoutangs and wild men of the woods, who were the ancestors of the human race, these astronomical illustrations supplied the place of history: each individual was believed to have a particular star or group of stars, that had presided over his nativity, and that would continue over him a guardian protection through all his life, and receive him into his own bright sphere of happiness and glory after death. [. . .]

> A feeling of relationship, and a sentiment of gratitude and piety, grew on the pleasing fiction, and it became duty and virtue not to suffer themselves to be disabused of the impressions the fiction had made upon them.

> [. . .]

> Thus were the stars their fathers; and thus were the phænomena which the priests described in relation to the stars supposed to be the real history of what had occurred to those from whom they believed themselves to have descended.[156]

It is interesting to note that these lectures were only published in 1857, a couple years after Darwin published his *On the Origin of Species*, and even more interesting to note that the lectures themselves were given in the 1820s (Taylor having been arrested for heresy and standing trial in October of 1827, and after being convicted serving a total of three years behind bars). This would make his assertion that mankind was descended from "ourangoutangs and wild men of the woods" seem somewhat to anticipate the later publication of Darwin's controversial theories.

However, older usage of the word "ourangoutang" meant "wild man of the woods" and not necessarily an actual ape, so Taylor is not necessarily here advancing a theory that modern man literally descended from the animal we today call the orangutan, or even from apes in general, but the tenor of his comments makes clear that he is here advocating the theory that mankind began in a primitive state, as "squeeling savages," and slowly advanced into a more and more sophisticated state.

This view of generally linear upward progress from "squeeling savage" to scientific and sophisticated modern has, in the intervening centuries (almost two centuries now since Taylor lectured in the 1820s), become the dominant and accepted paradigm through which most of us have been taught to view the history of the human race. So much has this paradigm prevailed, in fact, that we tend to forget that for many cultures around the world – and certainly for most of the ancients – an entirely different view held sway.

Most of the ancient histories (whether from Hesiod or Herodotus in ancient Greece, or from even more ancient cultures including Egypt, Sumer and Babylon), and most of the sacred teachings of the world (from the Vedas of ancient India to what we know of the remnants of the teachings of the Maya and the Inca of Central and South America) taught that mankind had successively degenerated through a series of ages, beginning with a lost golden age, which gave way to a silver age, and so forth, each less enlightened and more degenerate than the one before (if not in these exact terms, in some variation on this theme).

If we set aside the condescending assumption that we must of necessity know more about the human condition and the universe we inhabit than did the "primitives" or "early humans" whose superstitious anthropomorphisms supposedly became the seeds which grew into the celestial allegories we have just examined at some length, we may find that this different perspective opens a new window on the teachings in the ancient writings.

In fact, I believe that the esoteric texts we have already examined at some length, coupled with some of the implications of quantum physics, and some of the conclusions that physicists and scientists have in recent decades drawn from the new models of the world that have been developed in light of quantum discoveries, suggest that the ancients who preserved these celestial allegories in the scriptures of the Old and New Testaments – and in other sacred traditions found around the world – were far from the "squeeling savages" and "ourangoutangs and wild men of the woods" that Taylor describes.

Far from being mere "pleasing fictions," these allegories may teach profound truths which reveal that our ancient ancestors were in possession of an extremely sophisticated cosmology and an understanding of the reality of the universe and mankind's place in it which far outpaced anything possessed by modern civilization. We have already seen numerous examples of the incisive analysis of Alvin Boyd Kuhn, which he backs with piles of evidence drawn from his voluminous knowledge of the Bible and Greek and Egyptian myth, arguing that the ancient scriptures together expound a system of describing the invisible spiritual truths regarding the incarnation of human souls in human bodies, as the most important process in their spiritual evolution, and that they teach these spiritual truths by using physical examples from the physical universe around us – most especially the motions of the heavenly phenomena, which together comprise the most perfect material for spiritual metaphor imaginable.

Kuhn makes the argument, previously cited at the beginning of chapter 3, that such sophisticated spiritual allegorization in and of itself belies the hypothesis that these myths originated in an era of primitive "early humans" who simply personified nature around them with deific powers, creating the forerunners of the myths which later evolved into more sophisticated moral and spiritual allegories. He declares:

> Primitive simplicity could not have concocted what the age-long study of an intelligent world could not fathom. Not aboriginal naïveté, but exalted spiritual and intellectual acumen, formulated the myths. Reflection of the realities of a higher world in the phenomena of a lower world could not be detected when only the one world, the lower, was known. You can not see that nature reflects spiritual truth unless you know the form of spiritual truth.[157]

Indeed, our understanding of these ancient myths appears to have gone from more sophisticated and esoteric to more primitive and literal over the millennia, rather than the other way around!

Another important aspect of these ancient scriptures, and one of which Alvin Boyd Kuhn was keenly aware, is the fact that even as they contain an undeniable celestial interpretation (often incorporating details of the celestial mechanisms into the story in ways both delightful and ingenious), they also incorporate metaphors which can be interpreted in terms of the human body and human form – often at the same time! In other words, the virtuosity of the ancient revelation is such that a story can reflect a heavenly pattern and a "human body" pattern simultaneously – an incredible accomplishment, and yet one that the scriptures demonstrate effortlessly, over and over again.

For instance, we have already seen that the "crossing of the Red Sea" has a clear celestial interpretation. On the zodiac wheel, it refers to the "bringing up" of the starry band from the land of Egypt, which served as the designated "land of bondage" in the Old Testament version of the metaphor, but which represented a heavenly reality: the lower half of the year when the sun's arc across the sky is below the celestial equator, and the days are shorter than the nights, and the world is plunged in winter and hardship. Specifically, the myth as told in the story of the Exodus has Moses (who is an Aries-figure, often depicted with horns in older iconography) leading the crossing, with the crossing itself representing the March equinox, when the sun crosses *up* out of the lower half of the year, just as the Israelites crossed *up* out of Egypt.

And yet, as clear as these zodiacal parallels are within the story, Alvin Boyd Kuhn and other authors amply demonstrate that the crossing of the Red Sea also can be simultaneously interpreted as referring to this human body in which we make our "crossing" through this world of materiality, through this incarnation. In *Lost Light*, Alvin Boyd Kuhn explains:

> "Egypt" is just this earth, or the state or locale of bodily life on it. It even at times connotes the physical body itself, as in "the flesh pots of Egypt." Hence the descent of Abraham, and later of the twelve sons of Jacob, into "Egypt" are again the fable of the soul's adventure here.[158]

In a later and much shorter book, entitled *The Esoteric Structure of the Alphabet*, Alvin Boyd Kuhn elaborates even further:

> The Bibles of antiquity have but one theme: the *incarnation*. The vast body of ancient Scripture discoursed on but one subject, – the descent of souls, units of deific Mind, sons of God, into fleshly bodies developed by natural evolution on planets such as ours, therein to undergo an experience by which their continued growth through the ranges and planes of expanding consciousness might be carried forward to ever higher grades of divine being. These tomes of "Holy Writ" therefore embodied their main message in the imagery of *units of fiery spiritual nature plunging down into water*, the descending souls being described as sparks of a divine cosmic *fire*, and the bodies they were to ensoul being constituted almost wholly of water. (The human body is seven-eighths water!)
>
> It can indeed be said that the one sure and inerrant key to the Bibles is the simple concept of fire plunging into water, the fire being spiritual mind-power and water being the constituent element of physical bodies, – as well as the symbol of matter. Soul (spirit) as fire, plunged down into body, as water, and therein had

its *baptism*. Hence soul's incarnation on earth was endlessly depicted and dramatized as its crossing a body of water, a Jordan River, Styx River, Red Sea, Reed Sea. Since the water element of human bodies is the "sea" which the soul of fire has to cross in its successive incarnations, and it is red in color, the "Red Sea" of ancient Scriptures is just the human body blood. [159]

Thus, the "crossing of the Red Sea" is simultaneously celestial, pointing to the zodiac stars shining from the infinite depths of space and yet individual, referring to the human experience of every single person, at the level of intimacy of the blood flowing through his veins. In this sense, the scriptures are simultaneously depicting the macrocosm of the entire universe, and the microcosm of the individual incarnated soul, and tying them together. The smallest component unit – the individual person – contains and reflects the infinite whole.

The scriptures do this simultaneous macrocosm-microcosm allegorization so regularly and so unmistakably that the message cannot be shrugged aside. In the Old Testament, for instance, in the story of Jacob's Ladder (Genesis 28), esoteric interpreters have suggested that the "stone" on which Jacob rests his head represents the hard, flat fused bones of the human sacrum, and that the "ladder" stretching up to heaven upon which angels ascend and descend is the spinal column itself. This would mean that "heaven" is not only the vaulted dome of the celestial sky, but also the vaulted dome of our skull, in which we each carry around a universe every bit as infinite as the one we see when we gaze out into the vastness of the night sky.

This interpretation of Jacob's Ladder is bolstered by the fact that the New Testament gospels clearly have celestial foundations, but at the same time they appear to incorporate the same "Jacob's Ladder" metaphor. Jesus himself is crucified at a place called "the Skull" (*Calvary* in the Latin-derived translation, *Golgotha* in the Aramaic, but both mean the same thing). He traditionally lived for thirty-three years: the human spinal column contains a total of thirty-three vertebrae.

In light of this evidence, it is by no means too farfetched to suggest that the sacred traditions containing metaphors of both the celestial heavens and the human body were intended to convey the esoteric message that the universe is holographic: that it is contained in the human body – that in fact it is made manifest *only through* the human consciousness!

Modern physics experiments (such as those which gave rise to the category now termed "quantum physics") suggest that in a very real sense, sub-atomic particles do not actually manifest without the presence of consciousness. Taken in their entirety, could we not interpret the simultaneous celestial and human body/brain metaphors of the scriptures as teaching the same thing? Everything we see manifested around us, all the way out to the infinite reaches of space, however remote they may seem, is in some way so connected to our internal perception and consciousness that there is actually no division. "As above, so below," declares the famous Hermetic formula mentioned previously.

We are units of that grand expansive, infinite cosmos – embodied in flesh, to be sure, but in a very true and real sense still part of that infinite origin, and containing in our selves all that is also out there.

This concept would later find an analogue in the hologram – an invention not even possible until lasers could be produced, in the twentieth century. As we have already seen, and as the thinkers who pioneered the concept of the holographic universe discovered, every subdivision of the hologram contains the entire three-dimensional image within itself. This message, or something very much like it, may well be what the ancient scriptures were trying to convey.

The very insistence with which the scriptures and traditions of the world demand that we pay attention to the stories of the sun, moon and stars indicates that they are trying to "bridge the gap" between the macrocosm and the microcosm. By insisting that the motions of the heavens have implications for men and women on this earth, they argue a connection or an identity between them.

By turning the sun, moon and stars into characters who resemble men and women, they make this identity still more explicit. Is it not possible that by this endless analogizing of the celestial actors into figures in a human drama, they are saying that the distance we perceive between ourselves and the endless universe is an illusion?

Note that quantum physics has demonstrated that atoms and particles and even larger compositions of atoms become "entangled" such that they can influence one another instantaneously, even over great distances. The atom described earlier which exists in "superposition" in two boxes simultaneously demonstrates this principle: when an observer looks into one box, for instance, and sees (or does not see) an atom there, then the other box will instantaneously *not have* the atom (or have it, if it was not seen in the first box), no matter how far apart the boxes are located. The overwhelming message of the ancient scriptures, which demonstrate not just that the heavens above have an influence upon the individual, but that in some sense the individual and the heavens interpenetrate and embody one another, can almost be described as a doctrine of *entanglement*!

The evidence for such a message becomes even stronger when we encounter the evidence that these esoteric stories, while built upon a foundation of heavenly bodies, contain a distinct and undeniable analogue to our earthly bodies as well. It is well established that the ancients assigned the signs of the zodiac to the sections of the body, beginning at the top of the head with Aries and moving all the way down to the feet with Pisces. This convention makes explicit the connection between macrocosm and microcosm that we have been arguing that the Bible and all the other sacred scriptures are trying to teach to us.

And yet is such knowledge simply too much to attribute to the ancient authors of the world's esoteric scriptures? Could they possibly have had an inkling of concepts that modern quantum physicists have only begun to discover in the past hundred years – concepts so rarified that Albert Einstein even had difficulty accepting them?

As it turns out, there is more than enough evidence both within ancient tradition and in the architecture and art that they left behind to support the assertion that the ancients somehow possessed a depth of knowledge that we have not even begun to fathom.

For starters, it is plainly evident that the authors of the most ancient writings, including the scriptures of the Old Testament, understood the precession of the equinoxes (we saw evidence, for instance, that the incident of the golden calf in the book of Exodus has a precessional meaning). As I have detailed in my previous book, and as other authors have pointed out, precession is a very subtle phenomenon, and one that is not easy to detect.[160] The action of precession "delays" the heavens by only a tiny amount from one year to the next – so tiny, in fact, that after seventy-two years of observation of an individual star or group of stars, that star or constellation will be delayed by only one degree.

Additionally, this one degree of delay can only be measured for a star at exactly the same position in earth's orbit from one year to the next – for example, the location of the star Spica at exactly midnight on the summer solstice. If the exact location of Spica at midnight on the summer solstice can be recorded for upwards of seventy years, then after seventy-two years, the location of Spica will be found to be a mere one degree behind where it was measured on the exact same night at the exact same time and from the exact same observer's location seventy-two years previously.

Such a calculation, clearly, requires a fairly high degree of sophistication. It requires the ability to know when the earth has returned to exactly the same point on its annual orbit around the sun. Note that conventional calendar dates do not give the degree of precision required for such a measurement, because our calendar "slips" a bit each year, due to the fact that the time that it takes earth to get to the exact same point in its orbit each year does not match up with an even number of days (rotations of the earth around its axis).

Because of this mismatch, we use the convention of "leap years" to keep the calendar from slipping too far in either direction from telling us the general point that our planet has reached on its annual track, but simply measuring the location of Spica at midnight on June 21 each year will not be precise enough to determine that precession delays the heavens by one degree in seventy-two years. It might be enough to determine that precession is taking place (after enough years of careful observation), but it would not be enough to determine that the rate of precession, also known as the "constant of precession," is 72 (actually, it is 71.6). There is ample evidence that the ancients knew this constant of precession *before the Great Pyramid was designed and constructed!*[161]

Additionally, there is evidence that the Great Pyramid was built with a sophisticated understanding of the size of the spherical earth, and that its proportions relate to the proportions of our globe by a ratio which incorporates the constant of precession. And this fact is by no means an anomaly among ancient architecture and ancient myth – again and again we are confronted with evidence suggesting that the most ancient ones were the most advanced, and that successive ages brought a degradation in understanding.

In fact, researchers such as Graham Hancock, Carl P. Munck, and Joseph P. Farrell have found evidence that the Great Pyramid was the base node in a *global, self-referential* "grid" of megalithic architecture and coded structures located on carefully selected sites in both the Old and New World. One aspect of this "self-referential" system which Graham Hancock has demonstrated in books such as *Heaven's Mirror*, is the fact that important and well-known sacred sites can be found precisely seventy-two degrees of longitude *east* of the Giza pyramids in Egypt (Angkor Wat in Cambodia), as well as seventy-two additional degrees of longitude east of that (Kiribati in the South Pacific, an island chain containing stone structures of unknown origin, as well as mysterious stone paved pathways leading into the ocean).[162]

Hancock also shows that well-known sacred sites lie one hundred eight degrees *west* of Giza (Paracas, on the west coast of South America); 108 is a very significant precessional number equal to the precessional constant of 72 times 1.5 (or, stated differently, 72 plus its own half of 36), and it appears constantly in ancient sacred traditions around the world, as well as in ancient monuments.[163] Giorgio de Santillana and Hertha von Dechend in *Hamlet's Mill* point out that the ritual of the Agnicayana, which continues to this day in some parts of India and has been described as the world's oldest surviving ritual, involves the building of a brick altar using 10,800 bricks, a number which incorporates the precessional number 108 (there are literally hundreds of other examples of the use of 108 in the sacred traditions of the world).[164] This fact evinces of a level of advanced geodetic knowledge during periods of history and among farflung cultures that far surpasses what conventional historians commonly teach. Certainly the ability to accurately measure longitude, and to precisely measure the rate of precession, were not present among the early modern European states until well after the dawn of the sixteenth century.

Joseph P. Farrell has defined this grid in his *Grid of the Gods: the Aftermath of the Cosmic War and the Physics of the Pyramid Peoples* as follows: "Ancient sites, temples, and structures are laid out upon a grid whose significance is determined by their placement at mathematically significant places upon the surface of the Earth, or in correspondence with celestial, astronomical alignments, or both, and often incorporate these and other mathematical analogues in the structures themselves."[165] In that book as well as in others, Drs. Farrell and de Hart argue that this grid may provide evidence of an ancient cosmic war, and that this war might explain the continuity of the hidden and esoteric "ancient wisdom" that is the subject of this book, and the possibility is certainly intriguing.

Such advanced achievement at such an ancient epoch casts doubt upon the conventionally accepted narrative of linear progression from primitive to modern. A right understanding of what the Bible and other ancient sacred literatures are trying to tell us with their constant reference to the "personages" of the celestial realm (sun, moon, planets, and stars) provides additional confirmation of an ancient wisdom that was higher than we would expect under the conventional historical paradigm – higher, perhaps, than anything we have produced since.

Readers who are perhaps willing to accept that the ancients may have somehow been able to know to an astonishing degree of accuracy the size and shape of our globe, even before the building of the Great Pyramid, may yet balk at the idea that they could somehow have had knowledge of sophisticated concepts related to physics including the properties of particles and waves, let alone that they may have had a grasp of quantum physics. But here again there is substantial tangible evidence from ancient history which suggests that in fact they may have understood far more than conventional history has been willing to grant. They may, in fact, have understood what is today called "the holographic universe theory."

In his ground-breaking publication *The Holographic Universe*, Michael Talbot explains in the first chapter that one of the origins of the holographic theory was the inability of conventional materialist models to explain certain results of brain and memory experiments beginning in the 1940s. Mr. Talbot explains that one of the pioneers of the holographic theory, Karl Pribram, became very excited when he learned about holograms while reading an article published in *Scientific American* in the 1960s, realizing that the concept of the hologram might provide a solution to the puzzling findings that he and other scientists had encountered in their study of the brain.

Mr. Talbot explains that understanding the reason Pribram became so excited requires understanding of the methodology behind producing holograms, which involve the interference patterns created by any waveform phenomena, including waves on the surface of a body of water as well as light waves, sound waves, and radio waves. He explains that to create a hologram, however, an extremely concentrated form of light is required to create the interference patterns: normal light is too diffuse.[166]

Mr. Talbot explains that in order to create a hologram, a laser is split, with one half of the laser's light illuminating the object to be recorded and then continuing towards the two-dimensional medium (the film), while the other half of the laser's beam is allowed to interfere with the first half as it reaches the film, producing an interference pattern which is recorded on the two-dimensional film and which enables the evocation of the three-dimensional hologram later on. Thus, it is the interference pattern itself which enables the storage of three-dimensional information in two dimensions.

Mr. Talbot's book explores the possibility, discussed in the previous chapter and supported by experimental evidence from many different areas of science, that the three-dimensional universe which our brains encounter can be understood to be an evocation of the interference pattern created by waves of energy.[167]

Mr. Talbot then goes on to explain the aspect of holograms that caused scientist Karl Pribram to make the amazing connection between the mysterious experimental results he had been studying and the concept of the hologram. Pribram had been involved in experiments with a scientist who had been trying to remove portions of rats' brains to cause them to lose specific memories, such as the memory of how to navigate a specific maze which they had previously learned. The experiments found that the memories appeared to remain intact even when just about every part of the brain had been removed. They removed different parts of the brain in different rats, until all parts had been tried without "success" – that is, without eradicating the memory of how to navigate the maze. It should go without saying that such experiments are worse than cruel – they are abhorrently inhumane and monstrous.

When Dr. Pribram read in the *Scientific American* that each subordinate part of a hologram-generating interference pattern contains the information to create the entire hologram, he realized that this fact might help to shed light on the mysterious results in this and other brain and memory experiments that he and other scientists had encountered.

Mr. Talbot explains:

> Three-dimensionality is not the only remarkable aspect of holograms. If a piece of holographic film containing the image of an apple is cut in half and then illuminated by a laser, each half will still be found to contain the entire image of

the apple! Even if the halves are divided again and then again, an entire apple can still be reconstructed from each small portion of the film (although the images will get hazier as the portions get smaller). Unlike normal photographs, every small fragment of a piece of holographic film contains all the information recorded in the whole.[168]

This aspect of holographic reproduction sparked a revelation in Dr. Pribram's awareness, leading him to consider the possibility that the brain may encode memory in much the same way.

Even more astonishing, however, is the idea that the ancients may have had a similar understanding of the nature of reality – may, in fact, have had that understanding as far back into the dawn of human history as it is currently possible for us to probe through archaeology!

Stonehenge in England is one of the most well-known – and most ancient – megalithic sites in the world. While some more recent discoveries are pushing back the most-ancient timeline of human history available to archaeologists, Stonehenge remains a monument of extreme antiquity. Current consensus among conventional historians maintains a date of perhaps 3000 BC for the earliest development of the Stonehenge site: over 5,000 years ago.

Stonehenge has been studied from all kinds of different angles and different fields of science, and new and innovative approaches continue to yield new and important findings. Read the following passage by scientist Steven J. Waller, in light of the above discussion of holograms:

> Two sound sources, such as bagpipes playing the same tone, can produce an interference pattern. Zones of silence radiating outward occur where sound waves from one source cancel out the sound waves from the other source; zones of loudness occur where sound waves add together to reinforce each other. People unaware of the wave nature of sound would intuitively expect two pipes to sound louder than one pipe. The complex interference effect of alternative zones of silence and loudness must have seemed quite mysterious, since normally when noise occurs, quiet can only be experienced when the sound is blocked by large dense objects casting acoustic shadows on the listener.
>
> The first study presented below demonstrates that passing through zones of silence of a dual source sound wave interference pattern can be misinterpreted as passing through acoustic shadows from a ring of massive invisible objects that closely match the structure of Stonehenge. The second study shows that the actual acoustic shadows cast by the megaliths of Stonehenge form a sound pattern that closely recreates a dual source sound wave interference pattern. Thus sound wave interference patterns and Stonehenge each give an auditory illusion resembling the other to such a remarkable degree that it suggests a possible relationship between the two.[169]

Below is an image from Dr. Waller's article, which is entitled "Stonehenge-like Auditory Illusion Evoked by Interference Pattern," presented November 01, 2011 to the 162nd Acoustical Society of America meeting in San Diego, California.

Dr. Waller's remarkable work at archaeological sites around the world – many of them in North America – suggests that these sites may well have incorporated sophisticated acoustic features which played some sort of a role in shamanic ceremonies or other rituals held at those monuments.

Dr. Waller begins the Stonehenge paper cited above with the remarkable observation that, "The results of two experiments with sound show there may be some truth to the old British legend that the stones came into being when two magical pipers enticed maidens to dance in a circle."[170]

In other words, in addition to all the other amazing features of the Stonehenge monument, it also appears to be a sort of manifestation in physical stone of a pattern created by invisible interference patterns of sound waves!

It is also interesting to note that one of Dr. Waller's experiments involved blindfolded participants who were led about in an open meadow, in the center of which Dr. Waller had set up a device with two pipes, each playing its own constant tone, creating an interference pattern in the field. The blindfolded participants were led about the field and then asked to draw what they thought had caused the varying levels of sound that they had experienced while blindfolded. Those participants were not told of any connection between this experiment and theories about Stonehenge in any way.

What is remarkable to note is the fact that the participants drew diagrams that envisioned large rectangular objects arranged in a circle, even though there were no such objects at all (the patterns of sound that they heard having been entirely the product of interference). In other words, they had created *in their minds* a sort of "virtual Stonehenge," which they had imagined to be the cause of the patterns that they heard.

Dr. Waller's experiment, and the companion experiment which shows that Stonehenge itself is laid out in such a way that its stones create patterns of shadows nearly identical to an interference pattern produced by two sound sources near its central point, indicates that the designers of this amazing ancient monument have accomplished an incredible feat: they have captured in stone something that normally only exists as invisible waves of energy! Or, to say it in a slightly different way, they have memorialized in the physical medium something which *exists in the mind* of a listener experiencing an interference pattern of sound waves.

If Dr. Waller is correct, this information adds to an already-lengthy list of aspects of ancient monuments such as Stonehenge which are extremely difficult to explain according to conventional historical theories.

Although modern "history channel"-type films and documentaries about Stonehenge persist in dressing up re-enactors in animal furs, long scraggly beards, and dirty faces, the very feat of bringing the huge stones to their current location implies a level of advancement far greater than a "hunter-gatherer" society would be expected to possess. This statement should not be misconstrued as implying that the author believes hunter-gatherers to be unsophisticated or unintelligent, but the point is that hunting and gathering is a precarious way to eke out an existence, and does not afford the kind of time for the development of unrelated skills such as the quarrying of enormous stones (over twenty-four feet above the ground) and the organization of large numbers of people to move them, to say nothing of the invention of devices for their transport. More than the time limitation is the food limitation – hunting and gathering requires lots of area for roaming and frequent traveling to new areas. It is not conducive to the erecting of labor-intensive stone structures, let alone the development of the specialized skills that would be necessary to plan and then create very complex megalithic monuments such as Stonehenge.

The remains of the monument of Stonehenge attest to an astonishing range of sophisticated skills. The unique mortise-and-tenon architecture that held the mighty lintel stones upon the upright pillar stones speaks to a level of mastery in the construction of huge stone structures that is difficult to explain among people living the kind of rude hand-to-mouth existence implied in the "*National Geographic*-style" re-enactments.

It is thought that the stones that make up this enormous monument came from quarries twenty-five miles away, which makes the transport of these megaliths difficult to explain, but that is just the beginning of the mysteries surrounding Stonehenge. Many people are now aware that Stonehenge contains precise astronomical alignments. The alignments at Stonehenge reach a level of sophistication far beyond that usually discussed in superficial discussions of the site.

Those who spend much time studying Stonehenge hear a lot about solstice alignments built into the ancient megalithic structure (particularly summer solstice alignments), but very little about equinoctial alignments. In his amazing work *Hidden Stonehenge*, Professor Gordon R. Freeman explains that there are in fact subtle equinoctial alignments built into Stonehenge, in addition to subtle lunar alignments and the beautiful (and more widely-recognized) solstice alignments.

More precisely, Professor Freeman found that Stonehenge contains alignments to the rising and setting of the sun on "Equalday/night" (as previously mentioned, a day slightly different from the equinox). Professor Freeman discovered the distinction by careful observation of the Sun Temple Ring *Ómahkiyáahkóhtóohp* in modern Alberta, Canada (located, interestingly enough, at a latitude very close to that of Stonehenge: 50.585 north latitude for *Ómahkiyáahkóhtóohp* and 51.178 north latitude for Stonehenge).[171] His observations found that the sacred circle site there contains clear alignments for days near the days we call the equinoxes, but slightly before that date in March and slightly after it in September.

In his book, Professor Freeman explains:

> [. . .] the time of an *Equinox* is selected "theoretically" as the time when the centre of the Sun is directly above the Equator, and the "theoretical" Sun rise is when the *centre* of the Sun is *physically* horizontal from the observer. "Theory" treats the Sun as if it were a tiny dot, instead of its actual broad disk. The radius of the Sun is one-quarter of a degree, and the near-horizontal light of the first flash from the Sun's tip is bent downward more than one-half of a degree as it penetrates the Earth's atmosphere, so the first flash of sunlight appears when the centre of the Sun is more than three-quarters of a degree below the horizon. So the observed rise time is a few minutes before the "theoretical" sun rise.
>
> Similarly, the last flash occurs a few minutes after the "theoretical" Sun set. At the latitude of *Ómahkiyáahkóhtóohp*, five minutes are added to each end of the day and taken from each end of the night. The so-called Equinox days are 12.2 hours long and the nights are 11.8 hours. So the 12.0-hour-day/12.0-hour-night, or the Equalday/night, occurs two to three days, an average of 2.8 days, before the Equinox as the days lengthen in March, and two to three days after the Equinox as the days shorten in September.[172]

Professor Freeman goes into a great deal more detail about this important concept in his book, which is an absolutely essential reference and full of gorgeous photography and clear and detailed explanation.

Regarding the alignments at Stonehenge which encode Equalday/night, Professor Freeman deserves credit for being the first in modern history to rediscover these. He notes, "Strange as it may seem, during a century of speculation about a possible calendar in Stonehenge, nothing was published about an attempt to observe an Equinox Sun rise or set there."[173]

Professor Freeman explains that the observation lines for the winter solstice sunset and the summer solstice sunrise were well known, and aligned to some of the most massive stonework in the complex, but that the summer solstice sunset and the winter solstice sunrise both used a subtle alignment through the notches carved in Sarsen 58 of the "West Trilithon" (the trilithon composed of Sarsen 58 and Sarsen 57, and topped by the mighty lintel stone 158). This trilithon can be seen in the image at top, on the right-hand side of the picture -- the notches in Sarsen 58 are clearly visible and form little "windows" with the edge of Sarsen 57 in the photo.

Below is a photograph showing Sarsen 58 and some of the other nearby stones, with their numbers indicated for ease of reference.

Amazingly, Professor Freeman found that the dramatic "windows" on Sarsen 58 also figured in the alignments for the Equalday/night sunrise and sunset, which makes the design and construction of this ancient site all the more mind-boggling in its sophistication.

A sample chapter from his book which is available online explains the Equalday/night sunrise and sunset alignments in detail, with beautiful photographs showing the "sight windows" created by the ancient builders to frame the sunrise and sunset on these important days (the resolution of the online version is not great, but the photographs in the book itself are wonderful and well worth the price of the book all by themselves).

The discussion of Stonehenge's Equalday/night alignment begins on page 116 in that online chapter (same pagination as the book itself). The photograph marked "Figure 4-45" on page 126 of that file (and the actual book) is perhaps the most dramatic, clearly showing the window formed by the lower notch on Sarsen 58 framing the setting sun of Equalday/night (taken on September 24, 2002). That photograph shows that Sarsen 3 (on the other side of the circle from the image above) forms the left edge that creates the window with the notches in Sarsen 58.

The photograph above is looking towards 58 from almost due west of the center of Stonehenge, with a view towards the northeast, and so the beam of light from the setting sun can be imagined coming in from the left side of the above picture and piercing through the notch in Sarsen 58 on its way towards an observer on the other side of the stones, on the other side of the circle.

In order to visualize this phenomenon more clearly, the numbered diagram below is provided. It is from *Wikimedia commons* here, and originally came from a 2008 book by Anthony Johnson called *Solving Stonehenge*, which Professor Freeman praises highly and regarding which he at one point declares, "I just want everyone to know that Johnson's work is more important than even he imagined."[174]

Professor Freeman explains that the sight-line for the Equalday/night sunrise ran along the northern edge of Sarsen 20 (no longer present), which was on the circle just below Sarsen 21 (still standing and visible in the left side of both the photograph above and in the map diagram) and just to the east and a bit north of the fallen lintel stone marked 120 on the map above (you can see 120 lying embedded in the earth in the photos). From the north edge of 20, the Equalday/night sight-line ran across the circle to the southern edge of a Sarsen on the far side of the circle, Sarsen 2 (still standing and holding up a lintel designated 102, which is also supported by circle Sarsen 1).

The Equalday/night sun*set* line ran in the opposite direction (of course), and an observer on the eastern side of the Sarsen circle looking west would use the northern edge of Sarsen 3 as the "near sight" and the notched southern edge of Sarsen 58 as the "far sight" to frame the setting sun. The image on page 126, referenced earlier, shows this important sunset taking place between the edges of Sarsens 3 and 58.

Even after so many thousands of years, the precision of these alignments is breathtaking. The fact that they are executed using such enormous stones makes the achievement even more so, and the fact that these same stones incorporate solstice and Equalday/night alignments, as well as the more complex lunar rise and set patterns, is almost incomprehensible.

But that's by no means all. Professor Freeman also discovered that Stonehenge, like *Ómahkiyáahkóhtóohp* in Canada, incorporates mechanisms to track a four-year "leap year" pattern (created by the fact that the earth itself does not turn an equal number of times during its circuit from one March or September Equalday/night to the next March or September Equalday/night each year). Because the earth turns an additional one-quarter of a rotation (almost) during its annual circuit each year, this has the effect of "adding a day" every four years.

Professor Freeman found that the very precise window created by Sarsen 58 frames the setting sun crossing from left to right (heading from the south to the north, as one looks to the west) during March (a few days after the spring equinox) and frames the setting sun crossing again from right to left (heading from the north back towards the south on its way to the December solstice) in September. The alignments are constructed such that the sun *rises* can be seen looking east through Sarsens 2 and 3 (as described above) against even further mounds on the horizon which indicate the *first* two years of this four-year cycle, and such that sun *sets* are seen in the Sarsen 58 window during the *last* two years of this four-year cycle![175]

This kind of precision beggars belief. Even more intriguing is the fact that Professor Freeman was alert to such a mechanism at Stonehenge because he had already found a similar "four-year" or "leap-year" mechanism encoded in the alignments at the sacred circle in Canada!

As he explains in his book, Equalday/night varies greatly by latitude on the globe. *Ómahkiyáahkóhtóohp* in Canada is very close to 51° north latitude, as is Stonehenge all the way across the width of the North American continent plus the width of the Atlantic Ocean, over in England!

One final observation is in order, and it is an insightful one which only Professor Freeman could make (because he is the first in modern history to discover these Equalday/night alignments at Stonehenge). He points out that the designers of these incredible sites had to have their alignments already planned out before they began to place stones on the ground.[176] That means that the widths of the stones at Stonehenge (such as Sarsen 58 and Sarsens 2 and 3 and 20 discussed above), as well as the widths of the trilithons and all the other stones were dictated by these very precise alignments that the architects wanted to establish!

In other words, the builders of Stonehenge didn't just haul up a bunch of huge stones to the site and see what kinds of alignments they could make with them -- it is not in any way a haphazard arrangement. They knew what they were doing before they did it, which means they knew what sized stones they would need before they obtained and transported them. The sophistication of this site, executed in such a ponderous medium, speaks to the genius of the ancients.

Added to all of the above, the fact that Stonehenge also appears to be a very precise physical manifestation of a dual-source wave interference pattern should be absolutely astounding! This means that the designers of this site were able to create a monument which would simultaneously contain incredibly precise alignments demonstrating their knowledge of the most subtle cycles of the interaction between the earth, sun, and moon, and their knowledge of standing wave interference patterns, and then execute that monument using enormous stones transported from miles away – all of it with such skill that the site continues to perform its function and mutely proclaim its vital message more than five thousand years later!

What message does the site proclaim? If it indeed manifests in stone a standing wave pattern, then I would suggest that Stonehenge is telling us something very crucial about who we are and what kind of a cosmos we inhabit. It is telling us that, like the mighty circle of stones, we and everything around us are also manifestations of interference patterns of energy! And, by virtue of its precise alignments keyed to the rising and setting of the sun, moon, and possibly other celestial bodies including stars and constellations, Stonehenge is also telling us in a different format the same message proclaimed by the ancient scriptures: that we are souls who have descended from the immaterial realm into the material realm and taken on physical form, but who will re-ascend like the celestial objects whose rising it commemorates. This would be in line with the interpretation Alvin Boyd Kuhn has argued in his books and essays.

Further, we have seen that the ancients appeared to have demonstrated awareness that it is consciousness that makes the difference between the realm of potential (the realm of "superposition") and the realm of manifested materiality.

This message is very much the same as the message modern-day physicists have drawn from the results of their experiments, including the foundational experiment of the quantum age, the double-slit experiment. In the double-slit experiment, we learn that everything we see around us is in some mysterious way the manifestation of a "wave" of possibilities into temporary physical form. In the holographic universe theory, we learn the same thing. Now it appears, from the work of Dr. Steven Waller, that Stonehenge is telling us the very same thing!

Did the ancients really have such knowledge? The massive physical fact of Stonehenge is very hard to deny.

There are other clues from the ancient world which appear to corroborate the conclusion that the ancients were somehow telling us that physical matter is a kind of "petrification" of wave energy. If Stonehenge is a kind of "turning to stone" of the interference pattern of wave energy, then we might suspect that the most famous mythological being associated with turning things to stone – the gorgon Medusa – might also contain some clues that can help us in our investigation. Close examination of the evidence left to us by the ancients regarding Medusa and her sisters reveals that this suspicion is well-founded.

The story of Medusa is a famous ancient myth, depicted in ancient Mediterranean art from Greece, Rome, and the Etruscans (among others). In Ovid's version of the story, told in *Metamorphoses* IV, he tells us that Medusa was once a stunningly beautiful maiden, fought over by numerous suitors, with dazzlingly beautiful hair, but that she was transformed into a monster by Athena. Her most notable feature as a human became her signature physical feature as a monster, a head of fearsome serpents.[177] From then on, Medusa had the horrible ability to turn anyone who looked on her into stone, and the lonely island where she and her horrible sisters lived was scattered with the petrified remains of unfortunate men and beasts who had glimpsed the petrifying monsters.

The most ancient images of Medusa and the Gorgons share a typical stylized set of features: staring, bulging eyes, grinning mouth with tongue protruding downward and sometimes two tusks curving upward from the corners, round face with flattish nose, and ringed with short and fat worm-like snakes. Below are a few examples from ancient art, all of them from around 600 BC or from the sixth century BC (which stretches from 600 BC to 501 BC):

The above bas-relief is from the Temple of Artemis on the island of Corfu, sixth century BC. Note the protruding tongue and the serpents entwined for a belt. This is a typical posture for an ancient Gorgon – legs in the peculiar "lunge" position shown, arms bent at the elbows with the rear forearm pointing downward and the lead forearm pointing upward, almost like a human swastika or spinning disk (a symbol which we will see appears to have been associated in some way with the Gorgons, and which may have anciently be interpreted as having to do with transformation or incarnational cycles).

Above we see a vase from Etruria from the sixth century BC, depicting two Gorgons chasing Perseus after he slays Medusa (her headless body, not visible in the above image, is shown immediately behind the two Gorgons who chase Perseus). Again, the staring eyes and long protruding tongue are clearly visible. Note the "serpent" hair looks almost like a lion's mane – the serpents are quite short and fat in the above image.

Above is another Gorgon or Medusa image, this time on pottery found on the island of Rhodes and also from around 600 BC. Here, the strange round face with staring eyes is quite evident, as is a small downward-protruding tongue and upward-curving tusks. Also noteworthy are the numerous swastika-like or spiraling designs, one of which is on the calf of her outthrust leg, as well as the cross-symbols.

Some modern observers have noted that the strange features of these ancient Gorgons and Medusas resemble patterns created in the science of cymatics, the study of wave forms created in a physical medium (that sounds familiar!). In *Serpent in the Sky*, John Anthony West explains:

> Cymatics, the study of wave forms, illustrates dramatically the relationship between frequency and form. Specific materials subjected to specific vibrations assume specific forms. A given form can only be summoned forth at its corresponding frequency; form is a *response* to frequency. Form is what we call 'reality' but that reality is obviously conditional – for it is the structure of our organs of perception that is responsible for the ultimate picture.[178]

One of the first modern explorers of this fascinating subject was German physicist and musician Ernst Florens Friedrich Chladni (1756 - 1827), who demonstrated the principle by causing thin metal plates to vibrate (such as by drawing the bow of a violin across their edge), causing a thin layer of sand or other fine particles on the surface of the plate to create beautiful geometric shapes and patterns on the surface of the plate in response to the vibration. Below is a diagram from a book published in the 1800s and illustrating the technique, with a violin bow (note that the alteration of the frequency by the pressing down of the fingers of the hand alters the pattern evoked from the particles):

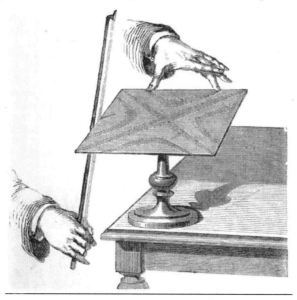

Below is a diagram of a modern Chladni plate with a coating of sand, creating a more complex pattern in response to the vibrations it receives:

Interestingly enough, the vibrations sometimes cause wiggling worm-like formations to ring a central circular image, and some observers argue that these cymatic designs are reminiscent both of the staring faces of ancient Gorgons and the faces of "Green Men" who adorn the interior masonry of many medieval cathedrals and chapels and which have many features in common with the ancient Gorgons (staring eyes, wavy hair – in their case foliage and not snakes, and gaping mouths which often sprout vines from the corners in similar fashion to the tusks found in some Gorgon mouths).

Below is a drawing based on a diagram from a book entitled *Ley Lines and Earth Energies* by David Cowan:

In the caption, the author explains:

> When isochronous (simultaneous) progressive waves meet each other from opposing directions, turbulent vortices are produced which will exhibit, when driven to chaotic states, remarkable geometrical patterns. When plane waves of the same frequency, amplitude and wavelength and speed meet at one point in space when they are traveling in opposite directions, a standing wave, with nodes and anti-nodes, will form.[179]

Cowan says, "Thus the gods always presented angry faces," and then he notes the similarity of the above images to both the faces of ancient Medusas and Gorgons, and to those of the medieval Green Man.[180]

Below are a few examples of the Green Man (all from centuries before the birth of Chladni) – note the similarities between the features of the Green Man and the classical Gorgons:

The above image, taken by Simon Garbutt and posted to Wikimedia commons, depicts a Green Man atop a column in a church in Oakham Church in England, from the 14th century AD. Note the upward-curving branches and foliage emerging from the corners of the mouth, just like the tusks on a Medusa or Gorgon. The eyes and splayed nose are also reminiscent of the Gorgons.

The above image is a Green Man from Castle Campbell in Scotland. Like the Medusa and Gorgon images, it almost resembles a lion. The staring eyes are in evidence, just as in ancient Gorgon depictions. We can tell this face is a Green Man because its jaw is decorated with an oak-leaf, just below the protruding tongue – remarkably similar to the protruding tongues of the Gorgons.

Above is one more Green Man carving, this time from a monastery in Sweden, the Gudham Monastery. Again, we see foliage emerging from the mouth, and staring eyes.

It is also worth noting another important connection, to art predating even the Greek and Etruscan depictions of the Gorgons, and that is the connection to the ancient Egyptian deity named Bes, a short, squat, lion-headed god who was a protector deity, particularly of women and children. Ancient Egyptian depictions of Bes frequently show him with the same wide, staring eyes that we have noted in the above images from later cultures, and with a grinning mouth and protruding tongue. The fact that the faces of the Medusas, Gorgons, and Green Man figures often resemble the face of a lion is significant in this context. Below is an image of a statue of Bes from the Egyptian temple at Dendera, in which the staring eyes and protruding tongue are clearly visible:

Note the very serpentine aspect of the beard that fringes the round face in the above statue. Also note that Bes appears to have a leonine face or symbol on his chest.

The connection to ancient Egypt is important, in that it suggests that the knowledge behind the images of Medusa and the Gorgons goes back much further than the ancient Greeks. There is other evidence that the Egyptians – at least at some point in their remote past – possessed a sophisticated understanding of the connection between wave-energy and matter, or were in close contact with someone who did.

If the ancient Gorgons and Medusa images depict some aspect of cymatics – in which normally-invisible waves of energy take on visible, physical form – then they must fall into the same category that Dr. Waller believes Stonehenge falls into: the ancient depiction of the "petrification" of wave energy, an acknowledgement that all that is physical is actually a form of wave energy made "static." How appropriate that the dreadful power of Medusa and the Gorgons was to *turn to stone* all who gazed upon them!

Perhaps the hidden message of that myth is that we are all in some way victims of Medusa in our journey through this world – we are all spirit energy, imprisoned temporarily in static form. Here we return to the usefulness of the modern "holographic universe theory" -- just as a hologram is an evocation of three-dimensional form from the interference patterns, so perhaps are we and everything else we encounter in the "physical" universe around us.

Noting the recurrence of cross-iconography in the ancient depictions of the Gorgons, this discussion of the meaning of the cross from Alvin Boyd Kuhn is most appropriate to the line of investigation we are following:

> This most ancient, perhaps, of all religious symbols (by no means an exclusive instrument of Christian typology) was the most simple and natural ideograph that could be devised to stand as an index of the main basic datum of human life – the fact that in man the two opposite poles of spirit and matter had crossed in union. The cross is but the badge of our incarnation, the axial crossing of soul and body, consciousness and substance, in one organic unity. An animal nature that walked horizontally to the earth, and a divine nature that walked upright crossed their lines of force and consciousness in the same organism. The implications of this situation are all that the great symbol ever connoted.[181]

It is worth examining more closely the belt of intertwined serpents worn about the waist of some of these ancient Medusa figures, very suggestive of the intertwined strands of DNA (many have noted the similarity of the serpents on the caduceus to the double-helix of DNA, but the connection to Medusa and DNA may be equally significant). It is through the action of DNA that *information* is turned into *matter* – the coded information in the twisted strands telling the proteins to make the parts of the body that will become an elephant, a palm tree, or a man or woman. Thus DNA is very closely related to the mythological function of the Gorgons – it takes "potential" and "freezes it," just as the electrons in the famous double-slit experiment leave the realm of "pure potential" and "choose" a form, becoming a particle, and thus becoming a *particular* thing.

The clear connections between the depictions of Medusa and the action of DNA, and between the depictions of Medusa and the wave-interference patterns which make possible the creation of holograms (but only after the invention of lasers), are simply astounding.

While many moderns might at first scoff at the suggestion presented in earlier chapters (and explored in greater detail in subsequent chapters) that the celestial imagery of ancient sacred tradition might in fact reveal the possession of a sophisticated understanding of the "holographic" nature of the *apparently* static cosmos by the most ancient civilizations, and that their thorough understanding of this holographic universe extended to the deliberate practice of the techniques of *ecstasy* (the act of transcending the static), the evidence from Stonehenge and from the Gorgons appears to support the assertion. The Gorgons and Stonehenge depict the *petrification* of wave energy – perhaps a metaphor for the imprisonment of the spirit in the physical. The techniques of ecstasy and the knowledge depicted in the celestial sacred scriptures and traditions of the world pertain to the opposite end of this process – the release of the spirit from the illusory bounds of the apparently static, of the physical, of the holographic.

From this survey of ancient art and monument, it appears quite likely that the same deep knowledge encoded in the ancient scriptures is behind the physical art and monuments which we can still see and touch to this day. The evidence of sophisticated understanding of concepts displayed in the Gorgon iconography and in the masterpiece of Stonehenge bolsters the argument that the ancient scriptures could also manifest the same sophisticated understanding.

From the ancient scriptures' ubiquity of "astronomico-theological" themes, we can also deduce another important ramification of the astronomico-theological dissection of the Old and New Testament, which is the assertion that the ancient wisdom of the human race was, at one time, in a state of agreement, even in a state of harmony, with no division between "pagan" myth and the myth-system found in the Biblical scriptures. The ancient sacred traditions of the planet, which in some parts of the world have survived down to the nineteenth and even the twentieth centuries, were *all* built upon a foundation of celestial mechanics – and those ancient sacred traditions include, quite emphatically, the scriptures that found their way into the canon of the Old and New Testaments. Somewhere along the line, the keepers of the Old and New Testaments advanced the paradigm that their sacred texts were markedly different from those of the "pagans," in that their scriptures were based on historical verities, while the rest of the world followed "cunningly devised fables," but the evidence we have examined argues the opposite. In reality, there is an astonishing unity running through all the ancient sacred writings and teachings – a unity that has been deliberately denied and obscured for some reason.

7

Consciousness unbound

> But the essential schema is always to be seen, even after the numerous influences to which it has been subjected; there are three great cosmic regions, which can be successively traversed because they are linked together by a central axis. This axis, of course, passes through an "opening," a "hole"; it is through this hole that the gods descend to earth and the dead to the subterranean regions; it is through the same hole that the soul of the shaman in ecstasy can fly up or down in the course of his celestial or infernal journeys.
>
> Mircea Eliade, *Shamanism:*
> *Archaic Techniques of Ecstasy.*[182]

In preceding chapters, we examined extensive evidence that the Bible is not to be taken literally, even though for seventeen long centuries that is the only way people have generally been allowed to take it – sometimes upon pain of death.

When various critics in more recent centuries have challenged the literal interpretation, it has generally been to mock and ridicule the scriptures as a collection of contradictory fables, or else to see them as a collection of fables and parables for the general improvement of morality and behavior.

But these interpretations may well be as wide of the mark as a literal interpretation. Instead, it was proposed in the preceding chapters that the actual texts which were later designated as the canonical scriptures of the Bible, along with other ancient scriptures and traditions found in ancient cultures around the world (and in cultures in more isolated regions who survived into the modern era outside the reach of those who were violently stamping out all opposition to acceptance of the Bible as literally true), actually contain a set of very layered metaphors which point to both the macrocosm and the microcosm at the same time, and were intended to convey profound truths, including the assertion that, "In a very real sense, the entire universe is in an intimate intertwined relationship with our interior microcosm." This fact is what the sacred scriptures (including the Bible) teach.

If so, then the ancient sacred traditions of mankind appear to be proclaiming, in their own set of metaphors, the very conclusions which quantum physicists have been reaching in recent decades, almost against their will.

In a lecture entitled *The World as Hologram* (delivered on June 28, 2011), Professor Leonard Susskind of the Stanford Institute for Theoretical Physics explains that the idea that the entire universe resembles more than anything else a hologram is a conclusion which physicists have been forced to settle on after eliminating every other possibility.[183] Quoting "a famous intellectual by the name of Sherlock Holmes," Professor Susskind says: "When you have eliminated all that is impossible, whatever remains must be the truth, however improbable."[184] He then goes on to say:

The thing that I am going to tell you tonight is one of those things – it seems nutty, it seems wildly improbable, but it wasn't just something that some of us – I wasn't alone in saying this – that some of us just said, "Oh!" – one day – "Oh! You know, maybe the world is a hologram!" That's *not* the way it happened. The way it happened was *exactly* this way: when you eliminate everything that's impossible, whatever is left over must be the truth.[185]

What is this wildly-improbable truth that Professor Susskind says was the last possibility standing after eliminating every other possible theory as invalid? He explains: "The answer is, that in a certain sense, in a certain peculiar sense, the world is a hologram."[186]

It turns out that the direction of physics throughout the twentieth century and into the twenty-first century have led some physicists (apparently, unless they are all lying) to conclude that the world we experience may at some level be constructed by consciousness.

The evidence on which these physicists have constructed this remarkable theory has most recently and most dramatically come from black holes, as Professor Susskind explains in the lecture quoted above, but prior to the more recent evidence from black holes, evidence from the experiments which launched the field of "quantum physics" (including the "double-slit" experiments and other related experiments which we have already discussed), whose results pointed to the conclusion that particles can inhabit a realm of infinite possibility until observed by a conscious soul, or a measuring device or observing device that will report the particle's behavior to a conscious soul, at which time the subatomic quanta will "pop into" a single possibility out of the realm of infinite possibility.

This conclusion has staggering implications. The conclusion that physicists drew from the double-slit experiments declared that the very "building blocks of matter" remain in a state of absolute possibility – infinite potential – and do not actually take on a concrete material nature until they interact with consciousness. In other words, the material world is at some very real level *the product of consciousness*, and not the other way around.

(*Materialism*, of course, argues that consciousness is the product of the material world – specifically, that our consciousness is generated by the brain through chemical and electrical processes, and that once that brain dies or is destroyed, the consciousness it was generating disappears forever).

The evidence for a holographic universe which comes from theoretical examinations of black holes begun in the early 1970s, beginning with the work of Professor Jacob Bekenstein, then a student, who started investigating models for understanding the amount of information that could be added to black holes. His work ultimately led to the conclusion that information held by black holes can be thought of as being encoded on a two-dimensional boundary surface (as a function of area), rather than in three-dimensional volume as one might initially expect.[187]

Based upon this work, and the related work of other physicists including Stephen Hawking, Gerard t'Hooft, Charles Thorn, and Raphael Bousso, Professor Susskind and others realized that three-dimensional information stored in two dimensions defines a hologram. Taken far enough, their work leads to the conclusion that the information of less massive things than black holes is also proportional to surface area and not to volume, leading to the further conclusion that volume could in some sense actually be illusory! In other words, like a hologram, the information in the universe is actually stored in two dimensions, which beings such as ourselves, focusing our consciousness using the tools we have at hand, construct into a three-dimensional "reality" which is actually an illusion (or, perhaps it might be better to say, more like what we would call "an illusion" than we are accustomed to think it).

To put it more precisely, Leonard Susskind in the talk cited above explains this concept this way:

> Can it be that somehow our world, or at least the surface of a black hole, can be described both in three-dimensional terms and two-dimensional terms? It seems impossible, on the face of it. Three-dimensions and two-dimensions just seem very different. Can you take three-dimensional information and re-express it: voxels instead of pixels? Well, the answer is "yes," but there's always a big cost. And the big cost is, when you take the three-dimensional data and try to lay it out in two dimensions, the result is always to scramble it horribly. It's always going to be incredibly mixed up. An example is a hologram. A hologram is a piece of film. When I say the word *hologram*, I don't mean the image: I mean the piece of film that the hologram is stored on. This is about what a piece of holographic film would look like: incredibly scrambled, lots of scratchy little things. If you looked at it through a microscope, you would see no pattern and you would not be able to tell in a million years what this thing was a hologram of. It's incredibly scrambled, and it's two-dimensional. But if you know the rule – and in this case, the rule is an experimental rule – you shine light on the hologram, and an image forms. A full, three-dimensional image: you can find out whether this clown has hair on the back of his head. How do you do it? You go around to the back of the hologram and you take a look. Three-dimensional information. Of course it doesn't contain the three-dimensional information of what's *inside* the clown's head, but if you made the hologram from an MRI scan, you could actually code the full three-dimensionality, including the brain and everything else, on the holographic surface here. So a hologram is a very good example. Let's call it compressing data down to a two-dimensional surface, but in the process scrambling it beyond recognition – unless you know the detailed code.[188]

Is it possible that our three-dimensional universe is the three-dimensional projection, but that there is a "film" somewhere that contains all the information in another form, a compressed form, a data form, a form which is "scrambled horribly" but which relates intimately and directly to the "projection" we see around us, for those who "know the rule," so to speak? We have already seen, from our study of the iconography of the Gorgons, that their most-dreaded power involves the power of "turning into physicality," and that they are often depicted with serpent "belts" as well as serpent hair – belts which resemble the caduceus-symbol of intertwined serpents, or the double-helix strand of DNA: that molecule whose stored data is turned into three-dimensionality by the action of proteins and all the other little "factories" of the body. Could it be that the ancients knew that there was a sort of "film"-world which was not the same as this three-dimensional world which we all inhabit, which somehow contained the data for this world in *compressed* form, or "seed-form," a world of pure potentiality, and that this was the world of the gods? The gods, who are normally invisible to human eyes, but who sometimes would manifest in this world, like the wave-forms which are normally invisible to our human eyes, but which manifest in the Chladni-forms for us to see, with their staring eyes and tusked grins? Is it possible that the ancients not only knew of this "holographic film realm," but knew how to visit it?

This idea that there might be such a realm may not be as far-fetched as it seems at first. First of all, Leonard Susskind has already explained that physicists have now arrived at a model for describing the data they have been discovering for the past hundred years which views the universe as akin to a hologram: data stored in compressed form and projected using a mathematical rule (he explains that, unlike the hologram which is used for an analogy, the data is not projected by simply "shining a light" on the holographic film). He says, "What I'm going to tell you next is, that it's not just black holes which are holograms: but in a certain sense the entire universe can be represented as a hologram, or any finite region of the universe, any big chunk of the universe, can be represented as a hologram."[189]

Perhaps it is human consciousness which in some way enables us to "construct" or "project" the material world out of the data stored in the "holographic medium," during our incarnation in this realm. Again, as we have seen from the results of the foundational experiments of quantum physics, such an assertion is not as far-fetched as it may seem. Further, as many of the authors who discuss this concept explain, we now know that the brain itself sits inside the sealed chamber of the skull, where nerves bring it electronic impulses that it then interprets, constructing the world out of those signals.

No light actually reaches the brain directly, at any time: light enters the eyes and goes as far as the back of the eyeball, and after that the impressions that the light makes upon the specialized structures of the retina (the cones and rods) are converted into electronic signals which travel down the optic nerves to the brain.

Similarly, the brain itself never reaches out to feel the texture of anything in the world around it. Instead, various forms of pressure upon the skin are transformed into electronic signals, which the nerves conduct to the brain, which then interprets them into the model of the three-dimensional world which it has been constructing out of all these signals since birth.

Proprioception, the sense of where we are in space and what direction we are facing and how much distance there is to anything that we see or hear, is also a construct of the brain, which decodes the vast numbers of signals that it is constantly receiving from sensors all over the body, and from sensors inside the inner ear and other specialized structures, to create a sense of its position in three-dimensional space. The same can be said for all the other inputs which the brain receives and translates into "a world."

We can conduct a thought-experiment in which we imagine removing a brain from its normal space within a sealed skull and placing it in a different container, such as a glass jar full of solution that will bathe it and keep it alive, and connecting all the nerves that normally bring it electronic information – the optic nerve, the aural nerve, the nerves running to the cochlea and inner ear, the nerves which gather together and conduct the signals from the nerves coming in from all over the body – to a powerful supercomputer that is capable of generating identical impulses to those nerves (impulses which the eyes, ears, and all the other sensors normally generate).

With such a computer, one could conceivably make the brain believe it is in its regular body, walking through a beautiful alpine meadow, looking at a majestic backdrop of mountains, listening to birds and a bubbling brook, smelling the mountain air and the wildflowers, and feeling a slight breeze against the forearms and face. With such a computer, one could conceivably allow the brain to believe it is in a body that is capable of flying, or in a body of a person of the opposite sex (or any number of the other transformations that take place in Ovid's *Metamorphoses*), or in a body that can breathe under water – all while it is safely motionless inside that same glass jar full of saline solution and connected to the supercomputer.

Once we have conducted such a thought-experiment, we can then understand why author and speaker David Icke refers to the body as "the body-computer."[190] Like the supercomputer in the thought experiment, our bodies contain the sensors which change data into electrical impulses sent to the brain, thus feeding our brain all the electronic signals which it then interprets as the three-dimensional world, with the brain constructing that world based on the impulses it receives from the body (just as it would construct a world from impulses received from a computer).

This concept parallels the famous thesis of the 1999 movie, *The Matrix*. In that film, of course, people are kept in appalling conditions, stationary inside liquid-filled shell-like pods, connected into a computer via numerous rubbery cables that pierce the body and skull at various points, and are fed electronic impulses from an enormous computer network so that they believe they are experiencing life in a three-dimensional world, when in fact they are stationary inside a vast hive.

In that movie, perceiving the true situation seems to be almost impossible: the simulation is so real to the brains that have been fed artificial computer signals from birth that they cannot even know that they are in a prison. While that ground-breaking film explored numerous other important themes, it also provides a perfect illustration of the conceptual possibility that the brain is very much dependent upon the signals that come to it through electronic impulses, and that it really *constructs* its own reality based upon those signals, regardless of whether they are coming from a computer or from an eyeball.

Of course, just because the brain *could* conceivably be tricked by a supercomputer into constructing an artificial world does not mean that this situation is actually the case. However, there are numerous bits of evidence from a variety of different fields of human endeavor, some of them quite well documented, which could be interpreted as arguing for a view of reality that is in some ways reminiscent of *The Matrix*.

One category of evidence involves the accounts of near-death experiences which have been reported by many individuals who experienced severe physical trauma or extreme forms of surgery, in which their point of perception seemed to leave their body, often hovering above their body, and during which they heard and saw conversations and activities which they were later able to report accurately to witnesses at the scene. In an extremely thorough examination of the subject entitled *Science and the Near-Death Experience: How Consciousness Survives Death*, Chris Carter examines accounts of near-death experiences (or NDEs) from around the world and from various centuries, and their implication for questions of consciousness and the brain.

In one of the most-famous NDEs of all time, an amazing 1991 surgical operation known as a "standstill operation," a young woman named Pam Reynolds had suffered a major aneurysm on the wall of the basilar artery on the base of her brain and needed to undergo a harrowing procedure in order to allow doctors to reach that artery. This risky operation is discussed in detail in Chris Carter's book, as well as in a book by cardiologist Dr. Michael Sabom entitled *Light and Death*. During the operation, in order to relieve the life-threatening pressure on the aneurysm and then enable them to operate, the surgeons had to reduce Pam's body temperature to sixty degrees Fahrenheit, stop both her heart and her breathing, ensure that all electrical activity in her brain had stopped, and then drain all the blood from her head.[191]

According to the description by Dr. Sabom, Pam was given general anesthesia at 7:15 am, her skull was cut open by a bone saw at 8:40 am, her blood was re-routed to a cardiopulminary bypass machine through her femoral artery and vein at 10:50 am in order to cool her core temperature, her heart was arrested at 11:05 am with injections of potassium chloride, her body temperature was measured at "a tomblike 60 degrees Fahrenheit" at 11:20 am in the words of Dr. Sabom, and then at 11:25 am -- as described by Dr. Sabom -- "the head of the operating table was tilted up, the cardiopulminary bypass machine was turned off, and the blood was drained from Pam's body like oil from a car."[192]

The operation itself is unbelievable -- the fact that Pam recounted a detailed NDE after the successful surgery and her subsequent revival is even more astonishing. The fact that she was able to accurately describe the appearance of the bone saw (her eyes were taped shut and she had been unconscious for over an hour before that instrument was even uncovered on its table) and the conversation during the search for her femoral artery and vein (which did not take place until 10:50 am, and which would not be expected to be heard since she had form-fitting earplugs in each ear producing rapid high-decibel clicking so that the surgeons could monitor her EEG to see if her brain was processing sound signals at all) makes her particular NDE account even more stunning.[193]

If anyone deserved to be described as "mostly dead," it was the patient in that particular operation.

While there are skeptics who have tried to question the implications of the Pam Reynolds operation, the fact is that her particular near-death experience – as astonishing as it is – counts as only one of literally thousands of such accounts.

Accounts like these have tremendous implications for our understanding of human consciousness and the question of whether consciousness is in fact dependent upon the physical mechanism of the brain, as Chris Carter discusses in his book.

The descriptions of the state of Pam Reynolds' brain during her NDE, and the accurate descriptions she was able to provide from a consciousness that appears to have continued during some portion of the time that her brain was being drained of blood and measured as having no responsive activity, suggest that consciousness may not be dependent upon the brain in the way that most hard-core materialists continue to insist must be so.

The reason this information is pertinent to the preceding discussion about brains in jars of saline solution, or in *The Matrix*, is that NDE accounts like the one above indicate that whatever is "driving" our "body-computer" (the consciousness receiving all of the electrical impulses which allow the brain to construct its "reality") may not actually reside in the brain! In fact, the experience of Pam Reynolds indicates that the temporary incapacitation of the entire body-computer (to include the brain) switches off the electrical inputs coming from the body, but that some aspect of individual consciousness can then move to a completely different way of receiving signals. In other words, the ability to turn the signals we receive into the universe we experience may reside or derive from some place *other than* the physical material of the brain or body.

This information, of course, carries all kinds of ramifications for a variety of subjects, but one of them is the idea that "we" are not necessarily "located" inside the mechanism that is receiving the electrical impulses.

If you could imagine flying a remote-controlled aircraft, equipped with high-definition video cameras that instantly transmitted everything the aircraft saw to a big high-definition screen in front of your control panel, and equipped with sensitive audio sensors that instantly transmitted everything that they picked up to high-quality headphones on your head, you might be able to imagine that after hours and hours of flying this remote craft and seeing what it sees and hearing what it hears, you might begin to feel not just as if you were *flying* the craft, nor even that you were actually *in* the craft (even though you might be miles away), but that *you* were actually becoming the craft itself – that the line between it and you was growing very faint.

If someone were to say to you, "Where are you now?" you might answer "Oh, I'm flying over a forest!" even though you yourself were not actually anywhere near the vehicle you were piloting from a distance. Because you were receiving so much visual and audible information from the remote aircraft, you would start to feel as though you were there.

The point of this discussion is to ask the question: If our bodies are actually providing an interface to a "consciousness" that is not necessarily physically tied to the body itself, then where does that consciousness need to be? In other words, if NDEs show that the "operator" of our body can (at least temporarily, and in extreme situations) continue to operate even when the body is lowered into a state that we would describe as "mostly dead," then where is that operator? Not in the brain, evidently! Like the pilot of the remote aircraft, it seems logical to conclude that the "consciousness" that is receiving the impulses from the "computer-body" could in fact be very far away, perhaps even in another dimension, although it could still very much "feel" like it is "right there" inside the body that is sending it signals.

All this to say that the idea that the world may resemble *The Matrix* in many important ways might not be as far-fetched as it appears at first blush. In fact, in addition to the evidence from theoretical physicists examining black holes and electrons passing through double-slit experiments, there appears to be an extensive array of additional scientific evidence which has been viewed by scientists as providing additional support "hologram" model of the universe. The interested reader is encouraged to go check it out in the many fascinating books, videos of lectures, and scientific papers on the subject.

This discussion should help throw more light on the critical concept of "ecstasy" – the quality of being *ex stasis*, or passing beyond the confines of the "static" physical world we perceive with our physical senses. Someone experiencing an NDE, it would seem, could be described as moving (temporarily, at least) ex stasis: the consciousness of that individual is not tied to the physical condition of the body and brain, and is operating in direct contradiction to what we would expect from an examination of the physical conditions (for instance, if we were to examine the body and brain of Pam Reynolds during her famous surgery, we would say there was no way she could be maintaining consciousness at all, let alone gathering visual and audible sensations from the operation taking place around her inert body).

But if consciousness is separate from the body, like the operator of the remote-controlled aircraft just described, it is certainly conceivable that consciousness can at times leave the body-vehicle, and travel beyond the body and its impressive array of signal-gathering sensors. The substantial documented evidence of NDE ex stasis activity supports this possibility. There are also traditions, stretching back into antiquity but continuing even to the present day, of shamanic *ex stasis* activity – in which the shaman leaves the world of the static or physical, and travels temporarily to an unknown realm, much like the patient who undergoes a near-death experience.

Significantly, descriptions of shamanic travel often feature the movement of the consciousness of the shaman through a "hole" or a "tunnel" – closely corresponding to the descriptions used time and again by those who have returned from near-death experiences to tell about what they perceived during their out-of-body travel. For instance, in the quotation at the beginning of this chapter, Mircea Eliade – who compiled an exhaustive description of shamanic practice from around the world, often citing first-hand participants, and published them in 1951 (decades before the first popular descriptions of NDEs by medical practitioners and patients) – describes the common feature of a "hole" or "opening" through which "the soul of the shaman in ecstasy can fly up or down in the course of his celestial or infernal journeys."[194]

Elsewhere, he cites the fact that the traditional costume of the Yakut or Sakha shamans of the Lake Baikal region south of Siberia features a symbol of the "Hole of the Spirits" by which shamans could travel to the other realm.[195]

Eliade provides a first-hand account of a prophet of the Ghost-Dance Religion, an ecstatic movement among North American Indians which sprang up after its founder had a trance-vision in 1890 during which he was instructed to resist the incursions of the white men into the ancestral lands of the Lakota. The prophet describes his personal experience, in words which have tremendous resonance with the descriptions of those who have had NDEs and who presumably never read anything about this account from the Ghost-Dance movement:

> All at once I saw a shining light – a great light – . . . I looked and saw my body had no soul – looked at my own body – it was dead . . . My soul left body and

went up to judgment place of God . . . I have seen a great light in my soul from that good land . . . [196]

The fact that the accounts of shamans accord very closely with the accounts of those who went through near-death experiences is very significant. It suggests that perhaps the participants are going to "the same place" when their consciousness separates from their body and moves into the other realm.

Michael Sabom collected numerous descriptions of NDE survivors who describe floating above their body, looking down upon it and seeing it appear "dead," and then going through "tunnels," "holes," or "shafts" and emerging into a place of great light. Here is one of them – the account, in fact, of Pam Reynolds herself:

> The feeling was like going up in an elevator real fast. And there was a sensation, but it wasn't a bodily, physical sensation. It was like a tunnel but it wasn't a tunnel.
>
> At some point very early in the tunnel vortex I became aware of my grandmother calling me. But I didn't hear her call me with my ears. . . . It was clearer hearing than with my ears. I trust that sense more than I trust my own ears. The feeling was that she wanted me to come to her, so I continued with no fear down the shaft. It's a dark shaft that I went through, and at the very end there was this very little tiny pinpoint of light that kept getting bigger and bigger and bigger.
>
> The light was incredibly bright, like sitting in the middle of a lightbulb. It was so bright that I put my hands in front of my face fully expecting to see them and I could not. But I knew they were there. Not from a sense of touch. Again, it's terribly hard to explain, but I knew they were there. . . .[197]

As we will see, the holographic model of the universe harmonizes very well with the evidence of such ex stasis travel. In the holographic model, there is a projection (the universe we see around us, which appears solid and three-dimensional, although it may not be as solid and static as it we perceive it to be), and there is the holographic medium, where the data of the hologram is stored in a sort of "seed form." Is it possible that those who undergo near-death experiences, or shamans who deliberately travel to the "other realm," are somehow switching their perception from the holographic projection to the holographic medium (the film)?

Given the undeniable celestial content of sacred scriptures such as the Bible, and the possibility that their celestial metaphors are describing the "holographic model" of the universe, and given the evidence that shamanic ecstatic travel has been going on for a very long time (all the way back, at least, to the early dynasties of ancient Egypt), it is very possible that the holographic model of the universe may be more accurate than any model developed so far – and it is very possible that the ancients understood this model far better than we do today.

8
The serpent on the pole

Uraeus, the name, evidently derives from *Ur*, the original creative fire, and *aei*, meaning in Greek "ever, always." They were the "eternal fires" that forged the various creations. They create life below the level of mind, but must be lifted up to be changed into spiritual intelligences. They begin around the feet of the gods and goddesses, and end up on their foreheads. In man physiologically they are brought up from the base of the spine and crown the human development by opening up the latent faculties of divine intelligence locked up in the pineal gland and pituitary body in the head. A line from the *Ritual* dispels all doubt as to their higher or lower rating and nature. It reads: "The seven Uraeus divinities are my body." They are the fiery formative energies of matter, not of mind. They are the energy in the atom, seven blind forces, which, however, draw the chariot of creation and must therefore be directed by intelligence.

Alvin Boyd Kuhn, *The Lost Light:*
An Interpretation of Ancient Scriptures.[198]

In a previous chapter, we encountered the assertion of esotericist Alvin Boyd Kuhn from a text entitled *The Esoteric Structure of the Alphabet* and published in 1900, that "The Bibles of antiquity have but one theme: the *incarnation.*"[199]

"The vast body of ancient Scripture," he writes – implying not only the scriptures of the Old and New Testament but including by the sweeping phrase "vast body of ancient Scripture" all the ancient writings and traditions from Egypt to Greece to India and so on around the globe – "discoursed on but one subject, the descent of souls [. . .] into fleshly bodies [. . .]"[200]

In that short treatise, Kuhn gives examples of the esoteric use of *symbol* to convey this message and its implications for our sojourn in this body. In this case, the symbols he examines as bearers or transmitters of esoteric content are the very letters themselves, the Hebrew, Greek, and Latin letters, the latter most familiar to the western reader of today, as they are still in use, having been imposed upon much of the world by the power of Rome through the centuries.

In other words, not only are the scriptures that we have been examining (in this case, the scriptures of the Old and New Testaments) bearers of esoteric wisdom through their allegorical portrayal of the macrocosm and microcosm, but also the very letters of which they are composed and through which they were transmitted (first the Hebrew and the Greek letters, and later the Latin letters into which they were translated) were in and of themselves similar pictures conveying the same esoteric truths! If this revelation is not a most powerful embodiment of the holographic principle of the macro contained in the micro, what could possibly embody the idea better?

It is as if the letters themselves stand in relationship to the whole of the scriptures as the individual man or woman stands in relationship to the macrocosmic universe. They embody in themselves the story of the incarnation and ascension, just as the words and verse and chapters and books formed out of them tell the story of the incarnation and ascension. In the same way, the individual man or woman is a microcosm, containing within himself or herself the same truths that are reflected on a much larger scale in the vast reaches of space.

Alvin Boyd Kuhn's treatise deserves to be read in its entirety, but a few of the examples he gives to support his primary assertion are repeated here. Introducing his thesis that the very shapes of the letters are esoteric symbols which convey spiritual truths, he says of their forms:

> They are true ideograms. The capital letter A, for instance, is obviously the cardinal letter I, the symbol of primordial unity (since it is also the number 1), split apart from the top into the creative duality of spirit and matter, the cross-bar indicating the interrelation which dynamically subsists between them. The U (V) symbolizes, exactly as it is drawn, the descent of spirit into matter and its return above.[201]

Later on, at the very summit of his argument, he provides even more amazing evidence:

> It is now to be announced that the great meaning-structure discovered in the alphabet outlines this descent of soul-fire into water and its return to its native empyrean. If one arranges the letters in a circular arc downward from A to the last letter of the first half of the alphabet, and then begins the upward return with the first letter of the second half and completes the arc to the final letter, describing the *lower* half of a circle, one will have blueprinted the organic structure here revealed. On the thesis just presented, one would challenge the claim of such a structure to demonstrate that the first letter or letters were somehow charactered as *fire,* and the two middle letters at the bottom or turning-point of the semi-circle were charactered as *water.* We are proclaiming that the structure meets that challenge and therefore proves itself as true and correct. The result is that, along with every other symbolic device of ancient meaning-form, even the alphabet embodied the central structure of all ancient literature, – the incarnation, the baptism of fire-soul in and under body-water. If this is to be confirmed, we must find *fire* at the top or beginning of the descending arc, and *water* at the bottom or turning-point. It must now be shown that the conditions our thesis requires to prove itself are precisely met in the alphabet. The discovery was made and certified when it was perceived that *the alphabet did fulfill these precise conditions.* The top or beginning letters are A and B, and should, the A alone or combined with B, represent *fire*; the middle letters coming at the base of the arc are M and N, and *mirabile dictu,* they represent *water!* From A to M, then, the descending arc traces the downward or involutionary plunge of fire into water, reaching its lowest depth with M; from N back to the final letter, whatever it be in different languages, the upward return arc represents the arising out of water and the return through evolution of the heavenly fire to its true home, completing the cycle.[202]

Using Biblical examples, the author points to the "solar fire" of AB linked to "the Egyptian RA, the radiant solar diety," in the name of the patriarch Abram.[203] He writes, "The

Hebrew word for *father* being *ab*, *Ab-ra-m* is 'Father Ra,' as clearly as Hebrew can say it. *Ram* would be this creative fire immersed in water, matter."[204]

The addition of the letter M to the word "Ra," in other words, adds the concept of the descent into matter, for the letter M, by its very shape resembling waves upon the ocean, represents water. If the prefix or phonic "AB" signifies "father" (note that the New Testament has Christ tell the disciples to call upon the Father by saying, "Abba, Father"), the prefix or phonic "AM" signifies "mother," as Alvin Boyd Kuhn explains.[205] From this analysis, it is hardly surprising that the Virgin mother in New Testament scripture is named Mary, a word which clearly contains within it the word for the watery sea or ocean as well (*mare*, from which we get *mariner, maritime, marine,* and many others).

What does all this have to do with the incessant allegorizing of celestial events in the scriptures of the ancients (including the scriptures of the Old and New Testaments)? The celestial metaphors in the scriptures do not just refer to the cosmos above – they refer simultaneously to the microcosm in each man and woman. In each one of us, the fire of the stars has descended into a watery incarnation (in a body that is seven-eighths water, and which depends for its survival on the ceaseless tides of its own internal "Red Sea," the blood pumping through the veins and arteries and each tiny capillary). Each of us, in other words, is an Abram, and a Mary.

The ancients quite clearly and explicitly taught a connection between the zodiac wheel that encircles the earth and the microcosm of the human body. Each of the signs of the zodiac was connected with a part of the body, beginning with Aries at the top of the head and continuing all the way around the zodiac to Pisces at the feet (proceeding in the direction that the signs pass through the rising-point of the sun throughout the year, Aries-Taurus-Gemini-Cancer and so on).

This convention was well established by the time of the Hellenistic astrologers. Vettius Valens of Antioch (AD 120 – c. 175), a contemporary of Ptolemy and of Marcus Aurelius, who has been described as "the single most important surviving source for the study of the Hellenistic tradition of astrology due to the fact that he was a practicing astrologer," describes the signs' associations with the body as follows:[206]

- Aries – "Aries is indicative of the head in general, the sensory faculties, and the eyesight."
- Taurus – "Taurus is indicative of the neck, face, gullet, eyebrows, and nose."
- Gemini – "Gemini is indicative of shoulders, arms, hands, fingers, joints, sinews, strength, courage, change, the birth of women, speech, mouth, blood vessels, the voice."
- Cancer – "Cancer is indicative of the chest, stomach, breasts, spleen, mouth, the hidden parts, the dimming of vision and blindness because of the nebula."
- Leo – "Leo is indicative of the flanks, the loin, the heart, courage, vision, sinews."
- Virgo – "Virgo is indicative of the belly, the internal organs, and the internal reproductive organs."
- Libra – "Libra is indicative of the hips, buttocks, the colon, the genitals, the hind parts."
- Scorpio – "Scorpio is indicative of the genitals and the rump."
- Sagittarius – "Sagittarius is indicative of the thighs and the groin."

- Capricorn – "Capricorn is indicative of the knees, the sinews, and internal and external sprains because of its mysterious character."
- Aquarius – "Aquarius is indicative of the legs, calves, sinews, and joints."
- Pisces – "Pisces is indicative of the feet, the sinews, and the toes."

Thus, not only does this system tell us that each sign rules a part of the body, which in and of itself implies a powerful connection between the macrocosmic and the microcosmic, but it also means that we can envision the great band of the zodiac itself as a grand expansive human form, encircling the heavens, with the top of the head beginning at Aries and continuing all the way around until the feet are reached at Pisces. Again, this understanding reveals an ancient understanding of the holographic principle that the smallest element of the whole contains and reflects the entirety.

Further, while the more-accessible writings of the Hellenistic astrologers provide the clearest evidence of the antiquity of this system, there is reason to believe that these astrologers were transmitting truths that came from Egypt and which thus may have been much older than the Hellenistic period. Indeed, many of the writings of the Hellenistic period are quite explicit in their acknowledgement of the original Egyptian source of their knowledge, as are some of the earlier philosophers including Plato and the traditions surrounding many of the pre-Socratics including Pythagoras.

The zodiac signs, as we have already seen, are those constellations which are stretched along the ecliptic plane. Due to the angle of the earth's tilt in regard to the ecliptic plane (this tilt is also known as the "obliquity of the ecliptic"), the ecliptic path crosses above and then below the celestial equator throughout the year, tracing a graceful sine wave as it does so, above and below the equator (we have already seen this on the older double-hemisphere maps). This sinuous path of the ecliptic resembles a serpent as it travels above and then below the equator.

If the zodiac signs that stretch along the ecliptic can be seen as a human form (beginning at Aries at the top of the head and continuing to Pisces at the feet), then we can by analogy understand the idea that we ourselves contain an internal equator, and a serpentine energy line tracing sine waves back and forth across that equator. The symbol of the caduceus, the staff with two serpents twisting gracefully around it, surmounted by two wings, can be seen as representative of the human body (which we see from its adoption as the symbol of medicine) as well as of the motions of the heavens.

In parts of the world which were insulated for centuries from the deliberate destruction of the ancient wisdom that took place in "the west," places such as India, Tibet, and China, the tradition that the body contains a series of energy nodes or *chakras* along the spinal column to the top of the head, as well as two intertwining energy lines which trace a caduceus-like double-helix along this central path, crossing at each of the chakras, provides further evidence that the ancient wisdom taught such a concept.

Interestingly enough, the Americas represent another part of the globe that was isolated (by virtue of the oceans) from the deliberate destruction of the ancient wisdom (a destruction we will examine in greater detail in later chapters). There is strong evidence that the peoples of the Americas also understood the system of chakras or energy nodes. In the *Book of the Hopi*, Frank Waters published the ancient traditions related to him and

Oswald White Bear Fredericks over the course of three years during tape recorded sessions with a group of twenty-seven Hopi elders during the 1950s. From the recordings, Mr. Waters and Mr. Fredericks created a manuscript, which the elders reviewed and approved (an important point which counters the allegations some have made that Mr. Waters changed what he heard into what he wanted it to be).

In the manuscript, the Hopi elders relate:

> The living body of man and the living body of the earth were constructed in the same way. Through each ran an axis, man's axis being the backbone, the vertebral column, which controlled the equilibrium of his movements and his functions. Along this axis were several vibratory centers which echoed the primordial sound of life throughout the universe or sounded a warning if anything went wrong.

> The first of these in man lay at the top of the head. Here, when he was born, was the soft spot, *kópavi*, the "open door" through which he received his life and communicated with his Creator. For with every breath the soft spot moved up and down with a gentle vibration that was communicated to the Creator.[207]

Other vibratory centers described include those at the brain, the throat, the heart, and the navel. While slightly different than the chakra system of India and the east (there are five in the Hopi system as described, but seven in the eastern tradition), there is clearly a strong correspondence between these concepts, separated as they are in space by the entire half-circumference of the globe.

Note the strong parallels the elders draw between the microcosm (the body of man) and the macrocosm (in this case, the "body" of our planet earth). It is also notable that the chakra system used in India and other nearby cultures assigns a correspondence between each of the seven chakras of the human body and the seven major visible solar system objects (sun, moon, Mercury, Venus, Mars, Jupiter, and Saturn). Here again there is a clear microcosm/macrocosm message.

Similarly, the system of Chinese medicine ascribes planetary influences to each of the major organs of the human body, which seems to reflect the same theme.

The connections between microcosm and macrocosm at this point go deeper still. In a previous chapter, we examined the argument of Robert Taylor in his *Astronomico-Theological Lectures* that Moses of the scriptures is related to the waters of the Nile, and that the traditions of depicting him as having horns relate to the "horned" nature of the Nile, with its delta spreading out like rays emanating from its head.

Below is an image of the deity Okeanos (Oceanus) from classical antiquity, who was depicted by both the Greeks and the Romans as having horns very similar to those found in depictions of Moses.

Mosaic of Okeanos. 2nd Century AD, Spain.

image: Wikimedia commons

In *Hamlet's Mill*, Giorgio de Santillana and Hertha von Dechend explain that Okeanos is a very important figure in ancient myth, and they cite Professor R. B. Onians' work *Origins of European Thought*, in which he advances the argument that Okeanos is an aspect of Achelous, the primal river "conceived as a serpent with human head and horns."[208]

They quote an extensive passage from Professor Onians, who argues that: "Okeanos was, as may now be seen, the primeval psyche and this would be conceived as a serpent in relation to procreative liquid" and who made the important connection from there to "the procreative fluid with which the psyche was identified, the spinal fluid believed to take serpent form." De Santillana and von Dechend remark that this idea is undoubtedly related to "the 'kundalini' of Indian Yoga."[209]

They also argue that Okeanos does not refer only to the earthly ocean which surrounds all continents, but to the celestial ocean. Citing a 1904 text by German mythologist E. H. Berger, they note that:

> The attributes of Okeanos in the literature are "deep-flowing," "flowing-back-on-itself," "untiring," "placidly flowing," "without billows." These images, remarks Berger, suggest silence, regularity, depth, stillness, rotation – what belongs really to the starry heaven. Later the name was transferred to another more

earthbound concept: the actual sea which was supposed to surround the land on all sides. But the explicit distinction, often repeated, from the "main" shows that this was never the original idea. If Okeanos is a "silver-swirling" river with many branches which obviously never were on sea or land, then the main is not the sea either, *pontos* or *thalassa*, it has to be the Waters Above. The Okeanos of myth preserves these imposing characters of remoteness and silence. He was the one who could remain by himself when Zeus commanded attendance in Olympus by all the gods. It was he who sent his daughters to lament over the chained outcast Prometheus, and offered his powerful mediation on his behalf. He is the Father of Rivers; he dimly appears in tradition, indeed, as the original god of heaven in the past. He stands in an Orphic hymn as "beloved end of the earth, ruler of the pole," and in that famous ancient lexicon, the *Etymologicum magnum*, his name is seen to derive from "heaven."[210]

This is compelling evidence indeed to support the assertion that Okeanos personifies the deep ocean of space (an ocean that is "without billows"), and not originally the ocean of the earth. If so, then this is another important ancient indicator of the connection between microcosm and macrocosm. Okeanos is simultaneously the untiring circle of the heavens, and the "psyche" inside every one of us, "the spinal fluid believed to take serpent form."

This connection reinforces the thesis that the ancients understood (or had in the distant past received) the "holographic universe" theory. The quantum physicists tell us that particles in superposition do not actually manifest until they are observed by a consciousness. The ancient personage of Okeanos, who personifies simultaneously both the infinite depths of the universe and the watery cerebro-spinal fluid of the human body (or the kundalini fluid), implies a connection between our consciousness and the universe, between our chakras and the celestial bodies.

The Orphic Hymn to which the above *Hamlet's Mill* passage makes reference is number 82, addressed to Okeanos. Here is the 1792 translation by Thomas Taylor of that 82nd Hymn:

> OCEAN I call, whose nature ever flows,
> From whom at first both Gods and men arose;
> Sire incorruptible, whose waves surround,
> And earth's concluding mighty circle bound:
> Hence every river, hence the spreading sea,
> And earth's pure bubbling fountains spring from thee:
> Hear, mighty fire, for boundless bliss is thine,
> Whose waters purify the pow'rs divine:
> Earth's friendly limit, fountain of the pole,
> Whose waves wide spreading and circumfluent roll.
> Approach benevolent, with placid mind,
> And be for ever to thy mystics kind.[211]

De Santillana and von Dechend note that the ninth line, which Taylor has here translated "Earth's friendly limit, fountain of the pole" is yet another indication that Okeanos refers to the starry heavens. The actual Greek here reads *terma philo gaies, arche polou* – "beloved end of the earth, ruler of the pole" as de Santillana and von Dechend put it.[212] Okeanos is addressed as the ruler (*arche*) of the pole, that point in the sky around which the entire heavens appear to turn (the point in the heavens above the earthly pole).

The final line of the Orphic Hymn to Okeanos refers to mystics, which also suggests the macrocosm-microcosm theme. The mystics of Okeanos ("thy mystics") would be those who are able to achieve a mystic union or identification or merging with Okeanos, "whose nature ever flows." They are those who perceive the connection, who transcend the static. The prayer to Okeanos, then, suggests that he has mystics, and that in fact the one who offers this prayer is including himself (in the grammatical third person) among those to whom he hopes Okeanos will be forever kind.

The fact that Robert Taylor provides conclusive evidence to indicate that Moses of the Hebrew scriptures personified the River Nile provides some interesting insights when juxtaposed with the above discussion on Okeanos. Many modern analysts who depart from the conventional historical framework put forth in academia, such as Graham Hancock and Robert Bauval, have argued convincingly that the ancient Egyptians consciously constructed monuments along the Nile to mirror heaven.

They find extensive evidence, in the layout of the monuments that remain, as well as in the ancient Egyptian texts, that the physical Nile itself was seen as a reflection of or earthly counterpart to a "celestial Nile." For instance, in their 1996 text *Keeper of Genesis: A Quest for the Hidden Legacy of Mankind*, Graham Hancock and Robert Bauval write:

> One of the most salient features of the *Duat*, as it is described in the ancient Egyptian texts, is its relationship to a great cosmic 'river' called the 'Winding Waterway.' Several studies have confirmed beyond any serious doubt that the 'Winding Waterway' was the magical band of light meandering across the sky that we know as the 'Milky Way.' It is also evident that the ancient priest-astronomers who compiled the Pyramid Texts identified the terrestrial counterpart of this 'Winding Waterway' in the sky as the River Nile and its yearly flood, the 'Great Inundation,' which also happened to coincide with the summer solstice.
>
>> The Winding Waterway is flooded, the Fields of Rushes are filled with water, and I am ferried over thereon to yonder eastern side of the Sky, the place where the gods fashioned me . . . [Orion's] sister is Sothis [Sirius] . . .
>> I have come to my waterways which are in the bank of the Flood of the Great Inundation, to the place of contentment . . . which is in the Horizon . . .
>> May you lift me and raise me to the Winding Waterway, may you set me among the gods, the Imperishable stars . . .
>
> As Sir E. A. Wallis Budge rightly observed: 'the Egyptians . . . from the earliest times . . . depicted to themselves a material heaven [the *Duat*] . . . on the banks of a Heavenly Nile, whereon they built cities.' And similarly the philologist Raymond Faulkner, who translated the Pyramid Texts and much of the other religious literature of ancient Egypt into English, could not avoid making the obvious correlations between the 'celestial river,' the 'Winding Waterway' and the Milky Way.

The stars of Orion and Sirius are located on the right bank of the Milky Way, which – at the summer solstice in the Pyramid Age – would have appeared as a vertical 'cosmic river' in the pre-dawn in the east.

To the ancient Egyptians, therefore, the *Duat* could not possibly have been seen merely as some vague, blank, rose-tinted region somewhere over the eastern horizon. On the contrary, it clearly had an extremely specific address in the sky – the 'Dwelling Place' of 'Orion and Sirius' on the banks of the 'celestial Nile':

> Be firm O Osiris-King [Orion] on the underside of the sky with the Beautiful Star [Sirius] upon the bend of the Winding Waterway . . .
> Betake yourself to the Waterway . . . May a stairway to the *Duat* be set for you to the place where Orion is . . .
> O King, you are this Great Star, the companion of Orion, who traverses the sky with Orion, who navigates [in] the *Duat* with Osiris . . . 213

Based on their identification of the Nile with the Milky Way, then, Robert Bauval and Graham Hancock advanced the now-famous thesis that the three pyramids of Giza correspond to the belt-stars of the constellation Orion. The important point for our discussion of Okeanos and Moses, however, is the fact that the River Nile was seen as a reflection of the celestial river, and therefore we can take the observation of Robert Taylor that Moses personified the Nile and connect it with the observation of de Santillana and von Dechend (based on the work of E. H. Berger and R. B. Onians) that Okeanos personified the celestial waters as well.

In other words, we see a very clear kinship between Okeanos and Moses. Both personify the heavens or the Waters Above. And yet, as Professor Onians and the authors of *Hamlet's Mill* argue, there is evidence to support the conclusion that Okeanos (and hence Moses) also personify "the procreative fluid with which the psyche was identified, the spinal fluid believed to take serpent form" and therefore "the 'kundalini' of Indian Yoga."

This is a powerful example of "as above, so below." The Waters Above and the Waters Below are connected – and the Waters Below refer not only to the earthly oceans and the earthly Nile, but even more so to the waters within the human body – in this case, the spinal fluid.

The reference to the concept of the *kundalini* by de Santillana and von Dechend is also significant. The kundalini is usually depicted as a serpent, rising up the spinal cord along the line of the chakras, just as the two serpents entwine the staff in the symbol of the caduceus. The practice of lifelong disciplines, such as yoga, could impart to the practitioner the ability to raise the kundalini-serpent from the base chakra to the crown chakra.

Note that Moses in Genesis is described as having a staff that had the very interesting ability of turning into a serpent! This fact reinforces the identification of Moses with Okeanos and with the kundalini serpent energy within the human being.

In addition, those familiar with the scriptures of the Old Testament will know that Moses, in a very significant act which is referenced by Christ in the gospels of the New

Testament, *raised* upon a pole an image of a brazen serpent in the wilderness to save his people from a plague of vipers, in an act that Christ specifically compared to the raising up upon the cross of his own body to save his people.

In Numbers 21:8-9, we read:

> 8And the LORD said unto Moses, Make thee a fiery serpent, and set it upon a pole: and it shall come to pass, that everyone that is bitten, when he looketh upon it, shall live.
> 9And Moses made a serpent of brass, and put it upon a pole, and it came to pass, that if a serpent had bitten any man, when he beheld the serpent of brass, he lived.

In John 3:14-15, we find this incident referenced, when Christ says:

> 14And as Moses lifted up the serpent in the wilderness, even so must the Son of man be lifted up:
> 15That whosoever believeth in him should not perish, but have eternal life.

It is very interesting that the depiction of this serpent raised upon the pole by Moses is often drawn with the same sinuous curve that artists invariably impart to the image of Christ upon the cross.

Take for example, the illustration below of the scene from Numbers 21, from the Foster Bible Pictures of 1899:

http://commons.wikimedia.org/wiki/File:Foster_Bible_Pictures_0079-1_Moses_Pointing_to_a_Great_Snake.jpg

In the illustration, the serpent's pole is almost crucifix in form, and the most distinct curve of the serpent's body (in the middle of the serpent) goes to the left as we look at the image and then back to the right. Notice that in this image, Moses is drawn with horns, but they are very subtle and drawn in such a way as to look almost like curls of his hair upon his forehead. The curls, however, are in the correct position where the horns are traditionally found (the same location, for example, as in the statue of Moses by Michelangelo). Okeanos was depicted with the same horns, as we have seen in the Roman mosaic shown earlier in this chapter.

Here is another illustration of the same scene from Numbers, this time by Gustave Doré from 1866:

http://upload.wikimedia.org/wikipedia/commons/6/6f/042.The_Bronze_Serpent.jpg

Here, the cruciform shape of the "pole" on which the serpent is raised is much more obvious. The "horns" on Moses are also much more distinctive, although Doré has imagined them as rays of light. Nevertheless, they are clearly reminiscent of the horns shown on the image of Okeanos from the 2nd century AD. Again, we see that the serpent's main coil goes to the left of the pole as we look at the image.

Remembering that the kundalini-serpent rises through the spinal region, we now look at an image of the crucifixion of Christ, done by El Greco in 1566 but generally reflecting artistic conventions that are centuries old:

http://upload.wikimedia.org/wikipedia/commons/1/10/El_Greco_%28Domenikos_Theotokopoulos%2C_called%29_-_Christ_on_the_Cross_-_Google_Art_Project.jpg

Significantly, the curve of the body is very similar to that depicted in the renditions of the brazen serpent. The body curves to the left and then back to the right. The sinuous shape is very reminiscent of the serpent, and of the "sine-wave" form that the ecliptic takes as it crosses back and forth over the celestial equator – the very celestial motion which Robert Taylor believes forms the basis for the crucifixions in the scriptures.

Very notably, this sinuous curve has a clear analogue in the celestial realm, in the serpentine shape of the important constellation Scorpio. Below is a star map showing the shape of the constellation:

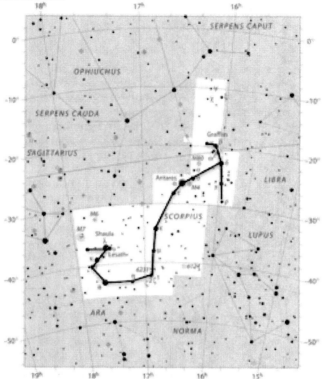

The outline of the constellation clearly comes down from the "outstretched arms" and then curves gracefully to the left of the centerline before arcing back to the right towards the bottom. It then curves hard to the left again to finish in the "stinger" area (a curve which can be seen in the dip or saddle in the hills to the left of the base of the cross as we look at it in the painting by El Greco – note that in his painting there is a little "stinger" at the very end of this curve, disguised as the trunk of a tree).

It is difficult to dispute the assertion that the artistic renditions of Christ on the cross – and the depictions of the brazen serpent of Moses – reflect this heavenly "serpent," Scorpio. When we note that Robert Taylor believes that the crucifixion of the fall equinox takes place just before the sign of Scorpio (at the end of the sign of Virgo the Virgin and the beginning of the sign of Libra the Scales, which immediately precede Scorpio), this connection becomes even more justifiable.

The connection, then, runs from the crucifixion of Christ, back to the figure of Moses, who is associated with the figure of Okeanos, whom R. B. Onians associates with Achelous, the primal river depicted as a serpent with a horned head of a man, as well as with the spinal fluid, which is connected to the kundalini-serpent and the raising of consciousness through the raising of the kundalini through the chakras.

145

This connection suggests that the "raising of the brazen serpent" and indeed the raising of the man on the cross have an analogue not only in the heavens (which they certainly do) but also in the human body. The raising of the brazen serpent by Moses was not a literal serpent being raised to save, but a symbol akin to the raising of the kundalini to activate the crown chakra and in doing so to *overcome* in a spiritual sense, rather than in the literal sense described in the incident in Numbers 21, an incident which is an allegory and not historical.

This extended example should serve as evidence supporting a number of the assertions made at the end of the previous chapter. First, it is evidence that the ancient wisdom embedded in the scriptures is "of a piece" with the ancient wisdom embodied in the traditions of other ancient cultures. The connections between Moses and Okeanos – and indeed with the "celestial Nile" discussed in the passages from the Egyptian texts cited by Graham Hancock and Robert Bauval – demonstrate a profound connection between these ancient sacred traditions, suggesting a unity of the ancient wisdom. The examples given also support the assertion that the stories encode not only the motions of the heavens but also teachings about our human condition in the body, about the descent of the spirit into matter and about the re-ascent through practices such as the "raising of the serpent" by disciplines such as yoga.

Before leaving the subject of Moses and Okeanos and the raising of the kundalini serpent, it is also important to recall the evidence presented by Bauval and Hancock in the quoted passage above which indicates that the ancient Egyptians located the Duat along the banks of the "heavenly Nile." As we will see later, the Duat is an extremely important concept in the holographic-shamanic theory. The fact that it can be clearly connected to the "raising of the serpent" is significant and bears noting now for further examination subsequently.

There are many other examples which could be offered of symbols which also have a dual reference to the celestial realm and the human body, found throughout the ancient texts which were included in the Old and New Testaments. Let us examine in slightly greater depth some which have already been mentioned, Jacob's Ladder and the crossing of the Red Sea (both of which are clearly connected to the spine and to Moses, and hence to the Nile, to Okeanos, and to the Duat).

Many esoteric authors in the Hermetic tradition have explained that the dome of the skull which arches over the brain (the seat of our consciousness) and the dome of the heavens which arch over us in the sky, are microcsomic and macrocosmic reflections of one another. Based on this, they have explained that the story of Jacob's Ladder, found in Genesis 28, refers to the spinal column in the human body.

In that account, Jacob arrives a certain place on his journey from Beersheba to Haran, and because the sun had set he prepares to spend the night there. We are told that he "took the stones of that place, and put them for his pillows, and lay down in that place to sleep. And he dreamed, and behold a ladder set up on the earth, and the top of it reached to heaven: and behold the angels of God ascending and descending on it" (Genesis 28:11-12). The ladder is the spine, reaching all the way to heaven – the skull – and the stones which Jacob used for his pillows are the fused bones at the very base of the spine, which form one large flat bone in the coccyx, but which is made up of several bones fused together.

Manly P. Hall outlines this interpretation in his *Occult Anatomy of Man*, saying:

> The spinal column is Jacob's ladder connecting heaven and earth, while its thirty-three segments are the degrees of Masonry and the number of years of the life of Christ. Up these segments the candidate ascends in consciousness to reach the temple of initiation located on the top of the mountain.[214]

Another metaphor with both heavenly and human-body interpretations is the Red Sea. Under the celestial allegory, we have seen that "crossing the Red Sea" refers to the sun's passage through the lower half of the zodiac circle, through the signs of darkness and winter, between the September equinox in which the sun is crucified and the March equinox in which he bursts forth to "rise again" into the season of longer days between Aries and Virgo.

However, the Red Sea also allegorizes the blood flowing through our veins. This is the Red Sea through which the fiery soul, which descends from the ether, must traverse during its incarnation in the physical world of matter, in which it inhabits a body. Alvin Boyd Kuhn writes of this Red Sea connection in several beautiful passages in his *Esoteric Structure of the Alphabet*. In a passage that continues from one cited earlier, he writes:

> It can indeed be said that the one sure and inerrant key to the Bibles is the simple concept of fire plunging into water, the fire being spiritual mind-power and water being the constituent element of physical bodies, – as well as the symbol of matter. Soul (spirit) as fire, plunged down into body, as water, and therein had its *baptism*. Hence soul's incarnation on earth was endlessly depicted and dramatized as its crossing a body of water, a Jordan River, Styx River, Red Sea, Reed Sea. Since the water element of human bodies is the "sea" which the soul has to cross in its successive incarnations, and it is red in color, the "Red Sea" of ancient Scriptures is just the human body blood. When the red fire of spirit-soul was gradually introduced into and permeated the original sea-water which was the bodily essence of earliest living creatures on earth, it changed colorless salt water into its own color, red. The "Red Sea" never could have meant anything other than the human blood. The Scriptures reiterate that "fire descended from heaven and turned the sea into blood." This transformation of course took place in man's body, not in the world oceans. This is a clarification that alone can reillumine old Scriptures with a flashing new and enlightening orientation of meaning. Egypt said that souls came down to "kindle a fire in the sea," to "create a burning within the sea," verily to set the ocean on fire. This has actually been done, but in man's veins and in his passions, not in the seven seas.[215]

Personally, I disagree with the assertion that "The 'Red Sea' never could have meant anything other than the human blood" – as we have seen in the previous examination of the wheel of the zodiac as a key to the depictions in scripture (both the Biblical scripture and the other "Bibles" to which Kuhn above refers), symbols such as the "Red Sea" can refer simultaneously to a celestial and to a bodily interpretation. Indeed, this duality is vital to perceiving the esoteric meaning that the scriptures want their readers to perceive through their endless procession of such symbology. That esoteric meaning, I believe, involves the "holographic" concept that the microcosmic unit (the individual man or woman) contains the macrocosmic whole. It is the Hermetic teaching of "as above, so below."

Elsewhere in the same treatise, Alvin Boyd Kuhn shows how the "microcosmic" units of the scriptures – the very letters of Hebrew, Greek, or Latin – tell forth the same esoteric meaning in their own shape and structure:

> Every letter of the Hebrew alphabet, beside carrying a number value, also has attached to it a symbolic monograph: B is *beth* and means *house*; G is *gimel* and means *camel*; D is *daleth* and means *door*; H is *he* and means *window*, etc. When we come to M, we find it is named *mem* and means – *water*! N is called *nun* and means that which is the animal life in water, – *fish*! Its character letter is simply a short line indented to indicate *seven waves*, as our English script *m* is a succession of three waves. M therefore in the Hebrew, and in English as well, marks the nadir of soul's descent into water, and N, at the same level and therefore also signifying water (or as *fish* the organic life in water), marks the turning-point for return, the Mount Sinai of evolution. Its reference is undoubtedly to this earth, which true symbolic insight discovers is itself – and not any hill on its surface – the "mount" or "hill of the Lord," on which God meets man in a cloud of fire, and on which all sermons are preached by his inner deity to man, and all temptations, crucifixions, spiritual initiations and final transfigurations take place.
>
> From A, the point of emanation of the spiritual fire, the creative stream of living energy, the river of vivification, as the Greeks called it, proceeded and swept downward until at M it had immersed its fiery potencies in the water of the human body, therein to begin to do its evolutionary work of kindling its own bright flame of spiritual consciousness in the red sea of the human blood. And now it is known that this red blood was originally sea water. As fire causes water to evaporate, the ancient allegorism represented the divine fire as drying up the water of the bodily sea, permitting souls to pass over the watery terrain dryshod. Variant symbolism had the Christ nature walking on the water without sinking into its depths. Egyptian figurism had the fire causing the water to boil, with the soul subjected to the danger of being scalded thereby.
>
> So the graph of the soul's descent and return swings down from the fire-height of AB to MN and there turns back upward to end in the final letter.[216]

Intriguingly, in light of the foregoing discussion of Moses, Okeanos, Achelous, and the kundalini, the same author's later discussion of the letter S points back to the same theme of fiery spirit incorporated into watery matter:

> It may be asked, why, since the tenth letter YOD represents the flame of the divine creative fire, and indeed gives its name to *God*, the *shin* (S or SH) has come in for so much of the divine fire symbolism. Our answer can not be categorical or dogmatic. It can be speculated that as the YOD represented the flame in its primal oneness, the *shin* represented it when it had differentiated into the triplicity, for it contains three YODS. It does not seem a wild assumption to think also that the letter chosen to carry the hissing sound of S and SH should

depict the threefold divine fire, for the fire became triple only when it entered the watery composition of the body, and the S and SH sound is precisely that produced by fire plunging into water! [. . .]

It has often been said that the S (SH) sound is derived from the *hiss* of the serpent. This tradition seems more likely to come from the ancient symbolism of fire plunging into water (symbol of soul descending into body) than from the inaudible "hiss" of the snake. For, again coincidental as it may seem, the creative fire was by the ancients called the "serpent fire," expressly by the Egyptians the great *uraeus* snake, "a serpent of fire."[217]

Note that in the Numbers 21 incident, it is expressly *fiery* serpents which bite the people: "And the LORD sent fiery serpents among the people, and they bit the people; and much people of Israel died" (Numbers 21:6). This may have a celestial counterpart in addition to the spiritual meaning which Alvin Boyd Kuhn outlines above, for the ecliptic path (along which the sun traces out its journey across the heavens) was depicted in ancient symbol as a fiery band, for obvious reasons.

The equinoctial figures in the Mithraic temples, for example, each hold a torch – one pointing upwards and one pointing downwards, to indicate the crossing of the ecliptic as it ascends above the celestial equator, or descends below it each year.[218] As we have already seen, Robert Taylor provides extensive evidence to support the interpretation of the crucifixions as connected to these crossings of ecliptic and equator, and as we have seen, the raising of the serpent has been portrayed in art as a sort of crucifix, and indeed the words of John 3:14 expressly point to this interpretation.

Thus, the serpent of heaven is both a fiery one and a watery one. We have seen that Achelous / Okeanos / Moses is associated with the horned Nile and also with the "celestial river" – the Milky Way. The Milky Way itself is sometimes depicted as a serpent, especially as a great serpent in a ring, with its own tail in its mouth – the *ouroboros*. The galaxy indeed resembles a great serpent in a ring, and it can be seen to grasp its own tail in its mouth right at the widening point (the Galactic Center) which is located just above the point where it rises between Scorpio and Sagittarius.

Below is an image of the entire Milky Way, which cannot be seen all on one night (this image stitches many photographs together to depict the entire ring of the Milky Way as a single band). Instead, the "ring" of the Milky Way appears to rotate slowly around the earth throughout the year, as we travel in our annual orbit, like a great hoop flipping slowly over and over the sky. What we are really looking at is the great, largely flat body of our galaxy, which is like a great pancake with a bulge in the center, or a fried egg. When we look out into space in the direction of the "pancake," we see a brighter band (we are inside the pancake itself). When we look in other directions, the heavens are much darker and the stars much more spread-out. Thus, the flat pancake of the galaxy appears to us, from earth, as a ring in the sky, or a river, or a great serpent. The central bulge of the galaxy appears to be the widest part of the river or hoop or serpent. The galactic bulge can be envisioned as the head of the serpent-river, biting its own tail.

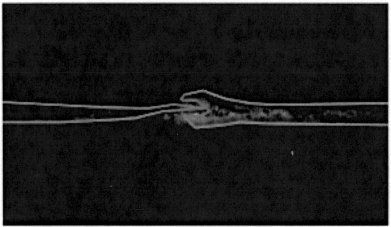

image: http://upload.wikimedia.org/wikipedia/commons/6/60/ESO_-_Milky_Way.jpg

Clearly, the serpent motif is of tremendous importance to the discussion. It finds a heavenly pattern in both the Milky Way, and in the sinuous form of the constellation Scorpio (which may well be the heavenly pattern for the sinuous depiction of the Christ upon the cross). Note also that the shape of the stars of Scorpio appear to be the model not only for the depictions of the crucifixion, but also of the Latin letter "S." Its curves are arranged in the same pattern as the stars of Scorpio. All of this discussion appears to support the assertions of Alvin Boyd Kuhn, that the great motif of the fiery soul being incarnated in the watery matter of flesh is conveyed in these stories and symbols.

Even more amazing, a point which has been noted by many other observers, is the remarkable correspondence between the serpents on the caduceus and the double-helix structure of DNA, the gene-bearing material that encodes the material form of our incarnation. The depictions of the energy channels that wrap around the central rod of the spine in the eastern religions (called the Ida and the Pingala) form the same double-helix spiral.

This similarity is remarkable, for although it could be argued that the motion of the path of the sun and the planets back-and-forth across the celestial equator traces out such a path, and that therefore the ancients only copied this and did not in any way know about the structure of DNA, it is still astonishing to learn that the motions of the celestial bodies and the structure of the DNA molecules that tell our bodies what shape they will take fit together in perfect harmony. This fact provides still further confirmation of the holographic / Hermetic truth that we embody in our individual microcosm the infinite macrocosm.

In addition, I believe there is ample evidence that the ancients somehow understood this double-serpent structure of DNA, and its importance in dictating the form we take in this incarnation. We are generally blinded to this possibility by the assumptions of the historical paradigm that is drummed into us from our earliest schooling through to the university and even post-graduate levels, but as we will see later, there is evidence that this insistently-repeated paradigm is false – deliberately false, in fact.

Evidence of an awareness of the role of DNA can be found in the ancient myths. The poetry of Ovid, especially his influential *Metamorphoses*, is full of the assertion that our material forms are more fluid than we think – that the boundaries between man and animal, or between male and female, or between earthly and celestial, are all subject to constant change. Although Ovid wrote his epic in the 1st century AD, the subject matter which he bent to his masterful verse is far older, stretching back to the ancient Greeks and (as *Hamlet's Mill* demonstrates) much further into the past before the Greeks as well.

The episode from Greek mythology which perhaps most clearly reveals the awareness of the role of DNA is the tale of the blind seer Tiresias of Thebes, and his transformation for a time into a woman. Ovid tells us in Book III of the *Metamorphoses* that Tiresias was once called upon to settle a dispute between Jove and Juno (Zeus and Hera to the Greeks) over Jove's theory: "Women get far more pleasure out of sex than men do" (verse 412).[219]

Juno denied this assertion, and so they called upon the sage Tiresias, who was at that time not yet blind. Ovid explains that the reason Tiresias could weigh in on this matter was the fact that he had spent seven years as a woman. Once, while walking through a leafy forest, Ovid says, he had come across "the coupling of two enormous serpents," and interrupted their mating with a blow from his walking stick (III.416-418).[220]

Upon doing so, Tiresias found himself immediately transformed into a woman as an unexplained consequence for striking them, and he remained a woman for seven years. At the beginning of the eighth year, however, Tiresias came upon the same two serpents again, and reasoned that since striking them had previously caused him to switch into the opposite sex, striking them again might cause another such transformation – and having done so he found himself transformed again into "the image of his former self" (III.419-426).[221]

When, however, Tiresias alleged that Jove was correct in his assertion that the woman receives far more pleasure than the man, Juno punished him with "eternal blindness" (III.433).[222] Since Jove could not undo the act of Juno, he compensated Tiresias with the gift of preternatural foresight to replace his lost vision.

The mechanism given for the transformation from man into woman, and later back again, is worth careful consideration. It was the disturbance of the coupling of two serpents which caused Tiresias to cross over from man to woman, and then back again after seven years' time. Is it not noteworthy that the "coupling serpents" evoke the double-helix of the DNA strand? These "coupling serpents" dictate everything about our material form: the color of our eyes, the shape of our limbs, the appearance of our face . . . literally everything. Metaphorically speaking, it was the disruption of the DNA's coupled serpentine strand that allowed the physical identity of Tiresias to become fluid, so fluid in fact that he *became* a woman, capable of judging which sex has the most pleasure from carnal intercourse.

While the inclusion of two coupling serpents in this tale does not *conclusively* prove that the ancient source of these myths understood the power of DNA, the possibility is certainly intriguing. The shape of the caduceus staff, symbol of Hermes (Mercury) and its similarity to the structure of DNA is another tantalizing hint of such a possibility as well.

The transformations of Tiresias are surrounded by myriad other transformations from ancient myth, most of them rendered by Ovid in far more graphic detail than is devoted to the episode of Tiresias. Collectively, they powerfully convey the mutability of all things in this universe – the message that all solidity is illusory, and of the fundamental liquidity of the material world.

This doctrine accords perfectly with the models of our universe being proposed by theoretical physicists in the age of quantum physics. If the experiments prove that the "binariness" of a subatomic particle is actually illusory – that individual electrons fired at a double-slit seem to go through *both* slits until a consciousness is watching them, at which time they amazingly seem to manifest as a particle that chooses one of the two slits – then it seems that the view of the universe offered by Ovid and his ancient predecessors stretching back into the mists of time is astonishingly accurate. The episode known as the "Judgment of Tiresias" illustrates an overcoming of "binariness" that is extremely suggestive of the fundamental principles of quantum physics.

If a subatomic particle (or even an atom or a molecule) can switch back and forth between a wave and a particle, or being located in one box or two, based (as far as we can tell) *entirely upon the presence of human consciousness,* then why cannot the matter that is composed of these particles, atoms, and molecules likewise pass effortlessly between man and woman, animal, mineral and vegetable, during successive incarnations of human consciousness, or even somehow through the encounter with human consciousness in one incarnation? As Bernard Knox says in his introduction to Charles Martin's translation, in the world described by Ovid's *Metamorphoses,* "People are changed into animals, birds, fish, insects, flowers, plants, trees, rivers, fountains, rocks, mountains, islands, and stones; stones are turned into people, as are ants; men are changed into women and vice versa; and, in one famous case, a statue is changed into a woman."[223]

In a line that is part of a larger passage we shall examine at length later, Ovid himself reveals something of the message that his poem should convey. He "frames" his own work with discussion at the end, using the voice of various other speakers. For example, speaking words he attributes to Pythagoras, in Book XV he says that everything changes constantly, moving fluidly back and forth between the boundaries of human and animal, but that the spirit "is always the same" even as it takes on successive new incarnations (XV. 209-217).[224]

The startling truth revealed by the teachings of the ancients, then, is that the material world is mutable, and that our spirit is eternal and "always the same."

It is a truth that the mysteries of modern quantum physics seems to verify – the world around us is mutable, and the force that can change it is actually human consciousness. In other words, one powerful conclusion of the grand teaching of the ancients is that *consciousness can change the world.* This assertion is not meant in some vague, dreamy way: it is an assertion that we each can, in some way, bring about in the physical universe ideas which originate inside our minds. Art is one example of this principle: a concept in the imagination becomes physical form. Many other forms of human creativity and innovation manifest the same principle, whether designing a building or a semiconductor, or creating an idea that captures the imagination of many other people and leads to profound changes on other levels.

Further, it is not just an assertion that *consciousness can change the world* in a spiritual or intangible way: quantum physics and the sacred scriptures of the ancients teach that *consciousness can change the physical world* – physically change it. The results of the double-slit experiment confirm the truth of "mind over matter" in a way that appears to be undeniable.

As we let the ramifications of that ancient teaching sink in, the reasons that some malevolent force might have wanted to suppress this knowledge and keep it from the mass of humanity begin to become more apparent. If the universe is in some sense "a hologram," as described by Leonard Susskind and other theoretical physicists, then it is possible that those who know the real teachings of the ancient scriptures but who wish to keep these teachings from others are keeping those teachings to themselves in order to control mankind.

If, as we saw previously, the brain could be suspended in a jar of saline solution and *fed* signals from a supercomputer, and relying on those signals the consciousness connected to that brain could experience the illusion of reality even while suspended in a jar of fluid, then this knowledge – and the knowledge of the techniques of manipulating the inputs that the brain receives – could be very powerful. It could be described as a form of *mind control* – as a means of altering the "reality" of those at the receiving end of those signals. Further, if (as we saw) the universe itself is like a hologram, which is "constructed" in some way by the consciousness that interacts with it, then those who know how to manipulate that process can impact not only those who are receiving signals from the universe, but can actually impact the universe itself, and this knowledge is very powerful indeed. We can begin to see why evil actors on the world stage might want that ancient knowledge surpressed, why they might want to keep it all to themselves.

In an interview recorded for *Red Ice Radio* in July of 2009, researcher Sofia Smallstorm – the creator of a documentary film entitled *9-11 Mysteries* (2006) – made the following comments, which resonate strongly with the subject matter examined in this chapter:

> Well, again I am no expert – no expert at all. But I'll tell you this: everything in the world is a collection of frequency – everything. Solids, things that aren't solid, our thoughts, our feelings. And *we* are participants and observers in the activity of those frequencies. The people who *control* us (you could say) know all about that, and that's why they can control us as well as they can. Because you see, we don't know about that. So we are at the receiving end of – very sophisticated . . . I would call it even metaphysics. It's a combination of science, and physics, and metaphysics. And we can't even see our way out of the maze, because we don't know that we're in one.[225]

There are other clear implications of these ancient teachings which are potentially world-changing as well.

9

The shamanic

"Shaman" is a Tungusian word. Shamanism has its epicenter in Ural-Altaic Asia, but it is a very complex phenomenon of culture which can be explained neither by psychologists nor by sociologists, but only by way of historical ethnology. To put it in a few words, a shaman is elected by spirits, meaning that he cannot choose his profession. Epileptics and mentally unhinged persons are obvious privileged candidates. Once elected, the future shaman goes to "school." Older shamans teach him his trade, and only after the concluding ceremony of his education is he accepted. This is, so to speak, the visible part of his education. The real shamanistic initiation of his soul happens in the world of spirits – while his body lies unconscious in his tent for days – who dismember the candidate in the most thorough and drastic manner and sew him together afterwards with iron wire, or reforge him, so that he becomes a new being capable of feats which go beyond the human. The duties of the shaman are to heal diseases which are caused by hostile spirits which have entered the body of the patient, or which occur because the soul has left the body and cannot find the way back. Often the shaman is responsible for guiding the souls of the deceased to the abode of the dead, as he also escorts the souls of sacrificed animals to the sky. His help is needed, too, when the hunting season is bad; he must find out where the game is. In order to find out all the things which he is expected to know, the shaman has to ascend to the highest sky to get the information from his god – or go into the underworld. [. . .] The shaman's soul ascends to the sky when he is in a state of ecstasy; in order to get into this state, he needs his drum which serves him as a "horse," the drumstick as a "whip."

Giorgio de Santillana and
Hertha von Dechend, *Hamlet's Mill*.[226]

We have now examined substantial evidence suggesting that the celestial and human body metaphors in the ancient scriptures, and the visible and even physical metaphors in ancient art, iconography, and monumental architecture all point to a sophisticated understanding of the holographic nature of the universe. We will now turn to examine the evidence which suggests that the ancients possessed an advanced understanding not just of the holographic model (which was not even dreamed about by "modern science" until the advent of quantum physics, in the twentieth century), but also of the "technologies" which human beings can use to travel back and forth between the different "planes" of existence that are implied by the holographic model.

In other words, they possessed "techniques of ecstasy," techniques of deliberately traveling beyond *stasis*, beyond the apparently static plane in which we normally operate and into a very different realm, and then returning, possibly with new levels of understanding that could be useful in this plane, and possibly after effecting changes in the other world that would impact the manifestations of matter and energy in this one.

The term "techniques of ecstasy" comes from the landmark study of shamanism published in 1951 by Mircia Eliade and entitled, *Shamanism: Archaic Techniques of Ecstasy* (originally published in French, with the title *Le Chaminisme et les techniques archaïques de l'extase*, translated into English in 1964). Thus, by extension, we can say that the sacred traditions around the world including the scriptures known today as the Old and New Testament, with their obsessive allegorizing of things celestial and their identification of them with our human condition, and even with our human form, which contains and reflects the cosmos, have something to do with shamanism on a very profound level, and that shamanism likewise has to do with the concept of the holographic universe which we have seen the scriptures to contain.

Later on, we will explore the subject of how this holographic-shamanic understanding was truncated in one specific region of the world, how a counterfeit understanding was substituted in its place, and how the representatives of that new "non-shamanic" understanding then proceeded to aggressively stamp out the shamanic wherever and whenever they could do so – a process which (the evidence strongly suggests) continues to this very day.

To further establish the connection between shamanic ecstasy, the holographic universe theory, and the scriptural "As above, so below" imagery we have been examining, let us continue to examine the subject of near-death experiences (NDEs) and other "modern" manifestations of the out-of-body experience (OBE).

Does the "holographic" model of the universe have a logical connection to such a subject?

Michael Talbot, building upon the analysis of evidence of the near-death experience and out-of-body experience offered by numerous previous researchers, argues that it does. He writes that Dr. Kenneth Ring, a University of Connecticut professor of psychology who has closely studied the NDE phenomenon argues that NDEs represent a shift in consciousness away from (in Talbot's words) "the ordinary world of appearances and into a more holographic reality of pure frequency."[227]

Nineteen years after Michael Talbot published his *Holographic Universe*, Chris Carter published an in-depth and exacting examination of the Near-Death Experience phenomena. In his *Science and the Near-Death Experience: How Consciousness Survives Death*, Chris Carter provides exhaustive and well-documented evidence for the reality of NDEs. He also analyzes explanations from those who do not believe that human consciousness can actually survive the death of the body, and who therefore attempt to propose models by which the NDE can be explained as hallucination, fantasy, wishful thinking, imaginative reconstruction, semiconscious perception, and a host of other explanations which avoid the possibility that consciousness can exist independently of a functioning body and brain, and he argues persuasively and with supporting evidence that these explanations do not stand up to scrutiny

One of the most compelling NDE examples described in Chris Carter's book, but absent from Michael Talbot's examination, is the "standstill operation" on Pam Reynolds that took place in August of 1991 (which explains why it did not make it into Michael Talbot's book, which was published in April of 1991). We have already examined the remarkable similarities between the accounts Pam Reynolds gave of her out-of-body travel during that operation and the out-of-body account given by a Ghost-Dance practitioner from the 1890s.

If Pam were merely hallucinating or dreaming in some semi-conscious state, the EEG would have registered that brain activity. The fact that the EEG was flat, despite the high-decibel clicking in each ear, and despite the fact that she reported observing the bone saw and listening to the conversations of the surgeons, indicates that Pam's consciousness was making these observations *absent of the brain*, absent of the body!

Michael Talbot mentions this aspect of NDEs in his book, because there had been other instances in which people returned from a situation in which their EEG had been flat and yet reported out-of-body experiences during that period of time. He says:

> Under normal circumstances whenever a person talks, thinks, imagines, dreams, or does just about anything else, their EEG registers an enormous amount of activity. Even hallucinations measure on the EEG. But there are many cases in which people with flat EEGs have had NDEs. Had their NDEs been simple hallucinations, they would have registered on their EEGs.[228]

While there are skeptics who have tried to question the implications of the Pam Reynolds operation, the fact that her particular near-death experience – as astonishing as it is – is only one of literally thousands of such accounts, and the many similar details which NDE experiences share across cultures, across individuals, and across decades, argues that they are a valid source of evidence about the nature of our consciousness and our universe. Just because they are a source of evidence which severely undermines the dominant conventional view of our consciousness and our universe does not mean they should be marginalized, ridiculed, attacked or ignored.

Accounts like these have tremendous implications for our understanding of human consciousness and the question of whether consciousness is in fact dependent upon the physical mechanism of the brain, as Chris Carter discusses in his book.

The descriptions of the state of Pam Reynolds' brain during her NDE, and the accurate descriptions she was able to provide from a consciousness that appears to have continued during some portion of the time that her brain was being drained of blood and measured as having no responsive activity, suggest that consciousness may not be dependent upon the brain in the way that most hard-core materialists continue to insist must be so.

A very common feature among the accounts of those who have experienced this phenomenon of leaving the body during a near-death experience, not surprisingly, is a loss of the normal fear of death coupled with a greatly increased level of belief in an afterlife. Chris Carter discusses this aspect of NDEs, saying:

> Most of the individuals who have had an NDE feel that it has been the single most significant event of their lives. The nature of the NDE may be controversial, but there is little disagreement that the experience usually has profound, life-changing aftereffects. These typically include: a thirst for knowledge; increased compassion and tolerance for others; reduced competitiveness; reduced interest in material possessions; an increased interest in spirituality, coupled with a decreased interest in sectarian religion; a greater

appreciation for life, coupled with a greatly reduced fear of death; and most strikingly, a greatly increased belief in an afterlife.[229]

He provides quotations from some representative individuals who have undergone an NDE, and hearing in their own words the changes they see in themselves is quite powerful. One woman wrote: "I now feel that every day is a new gift to me. Material things are not nearly as important as they used to be and I now look forward with peace and joy to the day of my death." Another said: "Certainly my life changed. I am less frightened of dying personally, and I do believe there is life after death. But it hasn't made me more 'religious'; what I do feel is that there are so many religions in the world, why should our God be the only one or indeed the correct one?"[230]

While NDEs, by definition, are generally precipitated by a traumatic event, Gary Talbot makes the important observation that, "One does not have to be in a life-threatening crisis to visit the afterlife dimension. There is evidence that the ND realm can also be reached during OBEs."[231] In other words, he is suggesting that the plane of existence which those experiencing a near-death experience visit may be the same as that described by those individuals who have out-of-body experiences (OBEs) which are triggered by something other than a brush with death.

Talbot points to various studies conducted by researchers into this phenomenon which appear to indicate that at least 1 in 10 people surveyed, and in some studies as many as 1 in 5 people surveyed, report having had some type of OBE – often occurring spontaneously and unexpectedly, but in some cases produced by the individuals "at will."[232] Talbot writes that reported OBEs appear to occur most often during instances of severe pain or illness, but also during meditation or even sleep, during which the experiencer perceives his or her point of consciousness suddenly separate from the body, often hovering above it and able to fly to other locations at will.[233]

Just as many aspects of NDEs appear to agree with a "holographic" paradigm of existence, the evidence we have from the research that has been done into the OBE phenomenon appears to support the holographic universe model as well. Talbot argues that just as an image stored in holographic film has no distinct location on that film (it is located throughout the film), in the holographic universe "everything is ultimately nonlocal, including consciousness."[234]

Talbot points out that when we dream, we usually appear to have a location for our consciousness as we move through whatever landscape or situation we inhabit in our dream, but in fact our consciousness inhabits and animates everything in the landscape or situation, including all the other people and objects we encounter, since we are creating the dream (or, as he puts it, since the dream itself "is unfolding out of the deeper and more fundamental reality of the dreamer").[235] The extensive evidence we have from the reports of NDEs and OBEs throughout the years appears to point to the conclusion that the universe itself may operate on much the same principle.

Note how well these discussions harmonize with the findings of quantum physics and the holographic universe models that quantum physics inspired. In quantum physics, particles (very small particles, it is true) can exist in "superposition" – a state of potentiality, a state of being in two different places or two different states at the same time. It is consciousness which in some way (not fully understood by physicists) summons the particles out of this superpositional state of potentiality and into "materiality." We have seen that the ancients dropped numerous hints of understanding such a view of the universe, such as in their depiction of the Gorgons and their connection to the Chladni patterns of wave-energy turned into visible physical form. If the universe is in fact in some sense holographic, summoned into materiality by the power of consciousness, then shamanic travel, as well as OBE and NDE travel, may represent the ability of human consciousness to transcend the holographic and in a sense "illusory" realm of materiality and reach towards the disincarnate realm – the realm of superposition, the realm of potentiality, the "spirit world."

The fact that some people even today are apparently able to detach the "viewpoint of their consciousness" from the mechanism of the body and traverse the boundary between the physical world and the world of potentiality has very ancient precedents, stretching all the way back – in the opinion of some analysts – to the very earliest original texts we have extant today: the Pyramid Texts of ancient Egypt.

In his remarkable and important book *Shamanic Wisdom in the Pyramid Texts: The Mystical Tradition of Ancient Egypt* (2005), Professor Jeremy Naydler argues that the events described in the Pyramid Texts describe deliberate shamanic out-of-body journeys undertaken by *living* pharaohs, and are not primarily the hopeful descriptions of the afterlife travels of the soul of deceased pharaohs as they are usually interpreted by conventional scholars.

Dr. Naydler provides evidence from careful textual analysis, as well as other supporting archaeological evidence, to bolster his thesis that the prevailing lens through which much of ancient Egyptian culture -- including the pyramids -- is currently viewed is incorrect. Instead of being primarily funerary, he believes the pyramids were constructed in order to conduct initiatory and mystical rites during which the participant (usually the pharaoh) deliberately underwent a death and rebirth experience that opened his consciousness to a world beyond ordinary material human experience -- as Dr. Naydler explains, "the king was brought to the threshold of death in order to travel into the spirit world."[236]

Dr. Naydler believes that this extraordinary experience most likely took place during the private portion of the very important Sed festival which was traditionally held during the thirtieth year of the reign of a pharaoh but which Dr. Naydler demonstrates could be held before that and could be held multiple times (it was not limited to once every thirty years). We note in passing the celestial significance of the thirty-year cycle, discussed extensively in *Hamlet's Mill*: the orbital period of the planet Saturn, the "giver of measures," is 29.8 years, a number which is rounded to 30 years for incorporation in ancient myth and ceremony.[237] The Sed festival consisted of very public ceremonies, including the "measuring" of Egypt by the king, who would conduct a symbolic run wearing symbolic garments (the "dedication of the field" ceremony, and one replete with celestial imagery), but after the public ceremonies came the secret and private ceremonies conducted by the priests alone with the king. Naydler argues that these were conducted inside the specially-built pyramids, and that the pinnacle of these rites was the initiation of a deliberate, death-like, shamanic out-of-body experience, which the pharaoh underwent on behalf of the entire kingdom.

We have already encountered the thesis of Alvin Boyd Kuhn, which argues that the discussions of the realm of the dead found in the Egyptian Book of the Dead (of which the Pyramid Texts are an early version, with numerous common sections and themes clearly recognizable) actually describe *this material life*, which is metaphorically taking place in an "underworld" compared to the spiritual realms of fire and immateriality in which the soul dwells before and after incarnations. We have seen compelling evidence to support Kuhn's thesis, including the metaphors found in Egyptian mythology, describing the sun and stars as plunging into the underworld as they encounter the western horizon, and journeying through the chambers of the dead until they reach the eastern horizon. We have seen that the different aspects of Osiris and Horus clearly correspond to such an interpretation, and further that the oft-repeated metaphoric content of the Old and New Testaments seem to support Alvin Boyd Kuhn's thesis as well (as do the mythologies and sacred traditions of other cultures).

However, just because we accept Alvin Boyd Kuhn's thesis does not mean we have to reject Jeremy Naydler's assertion that the Pyramid Texts also describe shamanic journeys which took place during this incarnational life. The two theories are not mutually exclusive. It is quite possible that the sacred texts of ancient cultures around the world both describe *our human condition* in our incarnated state within the holographic world (a world composed of waves-energy, perhaps superpositional energy, and somehow rendered into material form through the encounter with consciousness) and also describe *the techniques of transcending* that incarnated state, transcending the normal human condition that they describe so well. In that sense, Jeremy Naydler's work harmonizes with Alvin Boyd Kuhn's thesis quite well.

Archaeologically, one of the strongest arguments for Jeremy Naydler's thesis is the fact that many of the pyramid sites contain sarcophagi which, when found, contained no burial remains -- even if the site was undisturbed when found. In some cases, sarcophagi were found that were still sealed, and yet empty. They do, however, often contain extensive texts, architecture, and murals of images referring to the Sed festival. Dr. Naydler takes us through the pyramids one after another and demonstrates that they may or may not have had a funerary purpose, but they almost certainly had a Sed festival purpose.

He notes that even the "very first pyramid to have been built, if we accept the orthodox chronology," the pyramid of Third Dynasty King Zoser at Saqqara, appears to have been constructed with a Sed festival purpose in mind, and that although mummy remains were found in the central granite chamber beneath the pyramid, they have been determined to have come from several centuries after Zoser: there is no evidence at all that Zoser was ever buried in his pyramid, but clear evidence from the pyramid's art and hieroglyphs that he used it for the Sed festival.[238]

Naydler continues chronologically, discussing next the stepped pyramid of Sekhemkhet, which was excavated in the 1950s and appeared to have never been previously breached. The inner chamber was intact, and when the archaeologists entered it in the 1950s they found a sealed alabaster sarcophagus. When opened, it was completely empty.[239]

Naydler notes that this does not necessarily mean that the sarcophagus was never used. He discusses evidence that a sarcophagus may have played a role in the "secret rites" of the Sed festival, perhaps as part of a deliberate enactment of the king's death, during which he underwent his shamanic journey. He points to other evidence that Sekhemkhet's pyramid, "in the center of a complex designed on similar lines to Zoser's pyramid complex," was likely associated with the Sed festival as well.[240]

He then goes on through the later periods, each time noting evidence connecting the pyramid to the Sed festival, but also noting the absence of evidence that the king was actually buried there. After Sekhemkhet, he discusses the "seven provincial step pyramids" attributed to either Huni (the last king of the Third Dynasty) or Sneferu (the first king of the Fourth Dynasty), then the Bent Pyramid at Dahshur, the Red Pyramid of Sneferu, the Giza Pyramids (also containing empty sarcophagi), the large unfinished Fourth Dynasty pyramid at Zawiyet el-Aryan south of Giza (which also contained a sealed, empty sarcophagus), the pyramid complex of Userkaf (first king of the Fifth Dynasty) which also contained an empty sarcophagus and possible Sed festival imagery, and on through the Fifth Dynasty to the pyramid of the last king of the Fifth Dynasty, Unas.[241]

Although there is some evidence that at least some of the Fifth Dynasty pyramids may have been used as tombs (some contained canopic jars, for example, into which the organs of the mummy would be placed), Naydler points out that "evidence of their use in the funerary cult does not preclude the possibility of their prior use by the living king for the conducting of mystical rites. [. . .] For the king to be buried in the same place where he first underwent initiation would not be in the least contradictory."[242] However, the numerous pyramids which contain empty sarcophagi or no traces of funerary evidence whatsoever, but which do appear to have been connected to the Sed festival of the king, provides extremely strong evidence in support of Dr. Naydler's revolutionary thesis.

The most extensive evidence for his thesis, however, comes from the Pyramid Texts themselves. *Shamanic Wisdom in the Pyramid Texts* contains Dr. Naydler's extensive, section-by-section analysis of the texts from the Pyramid of Unas (who probably reigned in Egypt from around 2353 BC to 2323 BC, according to James P. Allen and Peter Der Manuelian in *Ancient Egyptian Pyramid Texts*, although other scholars put his reign slightly earlier, from 2375 BC to 2345 BC).[243]

The Pyramid Texts from the pyramid of Unas are not only the earliest such texts we have, but also the most complete. As Dr. Naydler explains, there are nine pyramids at Saqqara, but four are badly damaged and missing large sections of text, three more lack an inscribed antechamber and thus do not contain the full text as represented by those pyramids that have inscribed antechambers, and of the two remaining, only the pyramid of Unas has all of its original inscriptions undamaged (the other, that of Pepi II, is larger and actually contains far more utterances than any of the others, including that of Unas, but some of its walls are damaged and missing texts, and so it is impossible to view its corpus of texts in their entirety, the way we can for the Unas pyramid).[244]

Dr. Naydler's analysis of the inscriptions in the pyramid of Unas is extensive and detailed, and deserves to be read in its entirety. The interested reader is encouraged to read his argument in the original in *Shamanic Wisdom in the Pyramid Texts*. Reading it with a complete copy of the texts themselves would be even better. Fortunately for those of us born into an era of electronic access to a tremendous amount of information via the web (information that was more difficult to find in previous decades and centuries), the entire corpus of texts from the pyramid of Unas is available online at sites such as Vincent Brown's outstanding *Pyramid Texts Online* website.[245] Here, visitors can read the utterances of the pyramid of Unas as they were intended to be read -- as a sort of "three-dimensional book" in which the location of various utterances is extremely significant. As Dr. Naydler explains: "Unlike a modern printed book that can be more or less read anywhere on the planet, the Pyramid Texts are wedded both to the chambers and to the walls on which they are inscribed. A north-wall sarcophagus-chamber text could not be transposed to the east wall of the antechamber without losing a whole dimension of significance."[246]

Visitors can see a diagram of the layout of the chambers in the interior of the pyramid, and click on the different walls of the chambers to read the utterances that are found in each area. As one goes through the pyramid of Unas, the text of Dr. Naydler is an essential guide, and his book contains excellent 3-D representations of the chambers as well as diagrams of each wall showing the partitioning of various utterances and their locations on each wall. However, the *Pyramid Texts Online* site is also an essential supplement to Dr. Naydler's book, as it allows readers to peruse every single utterance in its entirety.

Further, the online tour of the pyramid of Unas contains viewable photographic plates of each inscribed surface of the interior chambers, allowing visitors to see the hieroglyphs themselves in full color -- Dr. Naydler describes the first view the visitor to the actual temple has of the texts themselves:

> At the end of the corridor, the first chamber of the pyramid to be entered is the antechamber. The antechamber is right at the center of the pyramid. The exact center of the pyramid is the center point of the antechamber ceiling. Here it is possible to stand up, and to have the experience of being encompassed on all sides by the blue-tinted hieroglyphs, which seem almost tangibly to emanate a magical power and to saturate the chamber with a mysterious potency.[247]

The *Pyramid Texts Online* site enables the viewer to see a glimpse of this magical blue color of these earliest extant human texts. The hieroglyphs themselves are beautiful – a writing system that is a masterpiece of design. As John Anthony West explains in *Serpent in the Sky*:

> The hieroglphyic system was complete at the time of the earliest dynasties of Egypt. It continued in use for sacred and religious texts throughout the millennia of Egyptian history, and even beyond: the last recorded discovered hieroglyphs come from the island of Philae, just below the first Nile cataract, and date from the fourth century AD.[248]

Describing hieroglyphs carved into wood from the tomb of Hesire, vizier to the Third Dynasty pharaoh Zoser at Seqqara, he says:

> The hieroglyphs are already complete, and later Egypt will never succeed in carving them with more power or purity. Still earlier hieroglyphs are no less complete, but in general less well executed. Nothing supports a postulated

'period of development.' But it is possible that guardians of the ancient tradition required a number of generations in which to bring artists and artisans up to this standard.[249]

The beauty of the hieroglyphs in the Pyramid Texts of Unas is undeniable, and some measure of this beauty can be appreciated through the color photographic plates of the online site. John Anthony West sees them as yet another piece of evidence that Egypt was somehow a repository or recipient of an extremely advanced base of knowledge. Like their level of skill demonstrated in so many other areas, he points out that their sophistication appears nearly full-blown in almost every case, demolishing the conventional view that their sciences somehow "evolved" over centuries of trial-and-error.

But to return to the argument of Dr. Naydler in his book, the texts in the Unas pyramid which have so regularly been interpreted as being funerary in nature can satisfactorily be interpreted as describing a dangerous ritual in which the king takes leave of his body, encounters certain beings in another plane of existence, and then must return safely to his still-living body at the end of the journey.

To support this interpretation, Dr. Naydler takes the reader through each of the utterances of the pyramid, beginning in the sarcophagus chamber and moving along the walls in a fashion that is generally west to east and south to north. The order in which the walls were intended to be read has been a subject of intense scholarly debate over the years, and Dr. Naydler takes the reader through the various arguments that have been offered.

His order of interpretation is depicted in the diagram below, and he explains his decision with reference to the symbolic import of the cardinal directions. As we have already seen from the analysis of Alvin Boyd Kuhn, the movement of the incarnated soul was seen as being a movement from west to east through the underworld: an analogue of the movement of the sun and stars from their point of "death" at the western horizon (where they leave the world of spirit and are "entombed" in the underworld of matter) back to their point of "rebirth" on the eastern horizon. Jeremy Naydler explains that the texts move from west to east in the Pyramid Texts as well, but that they also have a south-to-north movement which has its own profound significance:

> Utterance 219, at the east end of the south wall, actually spills over onto the east wall at its southern end and has to be continued in a northerly direction. The significance of the south-north axis is that the south is the direction of the southern constellations, which change through the cycles of the year, whereas north is the direction of the "imperishable" northern stars, apparently immune to time and change. The south is also a direction, like the west, particularly associated with the Dwat. Whereas in the east the king experiences solar rebirth, in the north he experiences stellar rebirth.[250]

The "imperishable" northern stars are those whose proximity to the north celestial pole keeps them from ever dipping below the horizon – earning them the name of the "undying stars" or the "imperishable stars." They thus represent the condition beyond the incarnational cycles. If Dr. Naydler is correct in his belief that the Pyramid Texts should be read both west-to-east and also south-to-north, then the profound implication is that they describe the movement from "death" in matter to new life in the spiritual realm (west to east) but also the movement from the cycle of incarnations to the blessed condition beyond that cycle, among the undying stars (south to north).

In the diagram below, capital letters indicate the various sections and rooms of the pyramid "substructure" (below the surface of the ground). The capital letters in the diagram run from A to F. Also in the diagram, the lower-case letters indicate the walls of the pyramid's chambers that contain texts. To avoid confusion between the two sets of letters, these lower-case letters run from lower-case "L" to lower-case "Z" (from l. to z.).

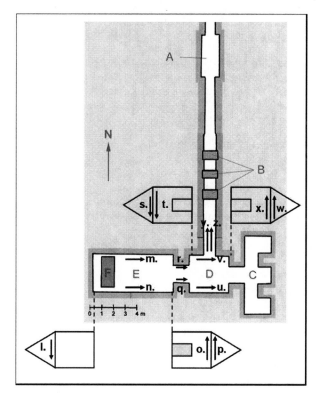

The substructure is accessed by a passage descending into the ground at the northern face of the pyramid itself (see diagram below showing the Unas pyramid complex, and showing the substructure in relation to the pyramid itself). At the base of the descending passage, one reaches the area marked "A" above, which is known as the "vestibule," which is level (its floor is level, not descending). Continuing south, a level passageway leads out of the vestibule at A and through three separate granite portcullises, marked "B," which sealed the chambers beyond through the millennia. Of the passageway beyond the portcullises, Dr. Naydler says that because hieroglyphs tell the reader (based on the direction that the symbolic images are facing) whether to read the lines from left to right or from right to left, and because the hieroglyphs in the passage all indicate that they should be read from "the inside of the pyramid out and not from the outside in," the reader is left with the clear impression that the long northern passageway is "an exit rather than an entrance."[251]

Beyond this, one reaches the room marked "D," which is known as the "antechamber." To the west of this, the room marked "E" is known as the "sarcophagus chamber," and in it was found the black granite sarcophagus nearly filling the west end of the chamber. The sarcophagus location is marked "F" on the diagram above. To the east of the antechamber is the area marked "C," which Dr. Naydler describes as "an undecorated and uninscribed triple chamber, or *serdah*, the purpose of which is not known for certain."[252] The sarcophagus chamber and the antechamber have high vaulted roofs, and the walls on the east and west side of these chambers thus have high gables, indicated by the triangular sections of the wall section projections in the diagram above (the dashed lines indicate their location in the chamber).

The inscriptions are indicated by lower-case letters on the diagram above, and the order in which Dr. Naydler argues they should be read is indicated by the letters, ascending from the lower-case letter "l" to the lower-case letter "z" in the diagram, along with arrows to indicate the direction of the hieroglyphs and the text. Dr. Naydler argues for this order:

l. sarcophagus chamber west gable, north to south (only the gable has hieroglyphs on this particular wall).
m. sarcophagus chamber north wall, west to east.
n. sarcophagus chamber south wall, west to east.
o. sarcophagus chamber east wall, south to north.
p. sarcophagus chamber east wall gable, south to north.
q. passage between sarcophagus chamber and antechamber, south wall, west to east.
r. passage between sarcophagus chamber and antechamber, north wall, west to east.
s. antechamber west wall gable, north to south.
t. antechamber west wall, north to south.
u. antechamber south wall, west to east.
v. antechamber north wall, west to east.
w. antechamber east wall gable, south to north.
x. antechamber east wall, south to north.
y. "entrance" passage west wall, south to north.
z. "entrance" passage east wall, south to north.

Below is a diagram showing all this substructure in relation to the pyramid and the rest of the Unas pyramid complex.

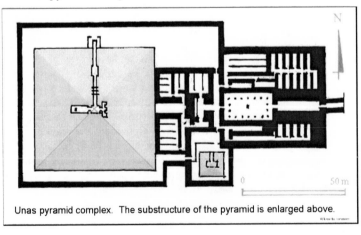

Unas pyramid complex. The substructure of the pyramid is enlarged above.

Dr. Naydler goes through each of the walls and discusses the texts on each wall, showing how they can be interpreted to support the theory that they refer primarily to a spiritual journey undertaken by the king *while alive*. The heavily-symbolic imagery of these texts leaves scholars plenty of room for argument as to what exactly they mean. It is clear that the texts can be interpreted as preparing Unas for a spiritual journey, and guiding him through that journey, but it is by no means certain that this journey must necessarily be one taken after death. One can see how the proponents of the funerary argument (which includes pretty much everyone prior to Dr. Naydler, other than Alvin Boyd Kuhn as we have seen) can interpret them as describing an after-death journey. However, there are a few places which seem to provide particularly strong arguments in favor of Dr. Naydler's theory of an out-of-body shamanic journey undertaken by a living pharaoh.

The texts on the sarcophagus chamber begin the journey, according to Dr. Naydler's ordering of the texts outlined above. Beginning on the wall marked "l." in the diagram, the gable area of the west wall of the sarcophagus chamber, we find eighteen texts which read from north to south and which Dr. Naydler describes as "mainly protective spells against snakes and relate to similar spells at the other end of the pyramid on the antechamber east wall."[253]

After that, the north wall of the sarcophagus chamber (the wall marked "m." in the diagram) contains 118 texts, which describe the following rites: rite of purification, rite of Opening of the Mouth, preliminary presentation of offerings, anointing with the seven holy oils, and an offering feast.[254] During the rite of purification, one of the acts is the censing rite, through which Dr. Naydler explains "the king became inwardly divinized. Thereby he could go forth with his ka, just as do the gods, with freedom to move in any direction he wanted."[255]

Of the famous Opening of the Mouth ceremony, Dr. Naydler argues that although it is usually described as primarily funerary in nature, conducted on the mummy of a dead person, the Opening of the Mouth rite should really be seen as representing the opening of "a channel between the spirit world and the physical world."[256] The texts describe the king being nourished by divine milk from the breast of a goddess (possibly Iat), and then participating in a feast that follows contains "adult" food offerings, "which the newborn king can now graduate to," in Dr. Naydler's analysis.[257] Following this come the offering of holy oils.

Dr. Naydler notes that in the Sed festival "secret rites" of Niuserre – the king who preceded Djedkare-Isesi (the penultimate king of the Fifth Dynasty), who preceded Unas (the last king of the Fifth Dynasty) – who left us very detailed images of his Sed festival, "the living king underwent an Osiris identification," in which "*sesefetch* oil (referred to in utt. 74) was used."[258] This fact is another important piece of evidence that the preparations being described in the sarcophagus chamber texts may refer to rites performed during the secret, private portion of the king's Sed festival, and not necessarily to funerary rites.

The assertion by Jeremy Naydler that the Opening of the Mouth ceremony may have been primarily for the living finds strong confirmation in the assertions of Alvin Boyd Kuhn, who believes that all the Book of the Dead texts (to include the Pyramid Texts) metaphorically or symbolically describe the journey of the incarnated soul in *this world*, which is the true underworld (and below which there is no other).[259] He argues that the act of Opening the Mouth symbolizes the awakening in the incarnate soul of the memory of its divine origin, after which the soul can speak words of truth to itself and to others (having begun to perceive the true nature of our human incarnate existence). Kuhn writes:

> One of the supreme features of Horus' mission was to open dumb mouths, or to give mouths to the dumb. This was to cause their lives to express the words of power and truth. *Isaiah* sings that "the dumb are to break forth into singing and the lame to leap for joy." Jesus was silent when accused. This is all to typify the infant god in the flesh, who has not yet learned to articulate the living reality of the spiritual truth. As the human infant is speechless for an initial period of some two years, so the god is silent in the expression of his divine nature for a corresponding period at the beginning of his incarnate sojourn.[260]

In this explication, we see the true potential for compatibility between the theory put forward by Alvin Boyd Kuhn in 1940, and that put forward by Jeremy Naydler in 2005. The theory of Kuhn argues that the texts metaphorically describe the situation of the divine soul, imprisoned in incarnation, and needing to remember its divine origin. The theory of Naydler argues that the shamanic ritual opened to the participant's understanding the fact that he or she is a being from another dimension, capable of traveling beyond this incarnate realm even during this life, and impressing this reality upon the participant by the fact that the participant experienced the ecstasy of departure from the body by the shamanically-activated consciousness.

The texts on the south wall of the sarcophagus chamber (marked "n.") continue onto the east wall (marked "o.") of the sarcophagus chamber (they wrap around the corner). Here, there is a sequence of twelve texts. Dr. Naydler explains that the series "begins with seven texts that describe a series of mystical experiences in which the spirit of 'Osiris Unas' travels to the southern stars, where he undergoes purification and rebirth. It is emphasized that Unas is 'not dead'."[261] A visit to the Pyramid Texts Online collection for the south wall of the sarcophagus chamber reveals the tremendous number of times the formula that *Unas lives*, that *Unas is not dead*, is repeated in these utterances. In utterance 213 we read:

> O Unas, you have not departed dead,
> you have departed alive
> to sit upon the throne of Osiris,
> your *'aba* scepter in your hand
> that you may give orders to the living,
> your lotus-bud scepter in your hand
> that you may give orders to those whose seats are hidden.[262]

Of these lines, Dr. Naydler writes that they again can be seen as strong evidence in support of his argument that this journey is being undertaken by a living king, for they describe the king as taking part in a coronation ceremony that enables him to give orders to both the living and "to those whose seats are hidden," that is to say, the dead – implying that the text describes the process whereby a living king (who can give orders to the living) opens a channel to the other world, so that he can also influence the hidden realm.[263]

Following these texts comes an important passage in which the king becomes a falcon, so that he can go up and be by the side of the god, and purify himself with the pure water of the stars. The transformation into a bird of prey for the journey to the heavens, as Dr. Naydler points out, is one of the most characteristic features of shamanic journeys (which are undertaken by a *living* shaman) around the world.[264]

A little later on the same wall, in Utterance 219, we find a formula repeated a total of twenty-four times declaring:

> He lives – this Unas lives!
> He is not dead – this Unas is not dead!
> He is not destroyed – this Unas is not destroyed!
> He has not been judged – this Unas has not been judged!
> He judges – this Unas judges![265]

Building on the analysis of W.R. Fix in *Star Maps* (1979), Dr. Naydler notes that:

> From a mystical or initiatory point of view, the text may be interpreted as stating that Unas, rather than coming before Osiris in his role of judge of the dead, escapes the fate of being judged altogether. In other words, it is just because his soul is not judged that he can be said still to be alive, with power over his own heart.[266]

With these and other texts, Dr. Naydler provides detailed analysis to support his argument that the Pyramid Texts should be interpreted as describing the shamanic journey of a living king.

One of the most powerful arguments in favor of this thesis comes from utterances 223 and 224, from the east wall of the sarcophagus chamber. Here, the king is urgently commanded to awaken, to turn himself about, to stand up, and to "put on" the body again.

Reading them in the *Pyramid Texts Online* site, the translations there contain bracketed attempts to explain these commands in terms of speculation that they may refer to some kind of "courtyard circular procession (?)," because the conventional approach that these texts address the spirit of the dead king makes them somewhat confusing to the traditional translator.[267]

However, under Naydler's theory, they make perfect sense: the king (still very much alive) has undergone a profound and dangerous mystical experience in which his consciousness has taken leave of the body and journeyed into astral realms beyond the boundaries of ordinary human experience. Now, the attendant priests are urgently requesting that he return, and again "clothe himself" with the body.

As Naydler writes in discussion of these utterances, they make much more sense if they are describing a living king who has been undergoing an out-of-body experience than if they are being addressed to a dead king whose body is now mummified. Instead, Dr. Naydler argues that at this point in the ritual, the king is being commanded to "return" to his body, so that the journey actually ends right where it began, just as the cycle of twelve utterances ending with the command to return appear to end right back where they began.[268]

Readers are encouraged to examine the full text of Dr. Naydler's work for his complete discussion of all the Pyramid Texts from the pyramid of Unas, and the complete explication of his important theory. However, the texts cited above should be more than sufficient to illustrate the argument. The larger question, of course, is *why* this ritual was undertaken. Once that overarching question is examined, it would also be important to know *how* the king was able to go through such an experience, if indeed his consciousness truly departed from his body and entered into another plane of awareness.

In her important 2010 book *Approaching Chaos: Can an Ancient Archetype Save 21st Century Civilization*, Lucy Wyatt offers some possible answers to those questions. Seeing the significance of Jeremy Naydler's thesis regarding the shamanic aspects of the secret rites of the Sed festival, she connects his observations to the possibility that shamanic journeys provide a window to knowledge that cannot be obtained any other way, and that the consultation of such knowledge actually formed the basis of ancient civilization – the very ancient advanced civilization that was lost, or deliberately destroyed. She makes this connection by examining what Jeremy Naydler argues was the purpose for the Sed festival secret rites, and then examining what some observers and participants believe may be taking place in some of the shamanic activities in the few remote locations on our planet where such rites and practices still survive today.[269]

Jeremy Naydler proposes that one of the primary reasons for the Sed festival in ancient Egypt was "to reach across to the more subtle spirit world that upholds and vitalizes the physical world, in order to ensure a beneficent connection with it and an unhampered flow of energies from it into the physical."[270] The king's activities during the Sed festival, then, were not primarily self-aggrandizing (as many conventional interpretations argue) but rather beneficent: the king undertook the rituals on behalf of the entire kingdom, to bring balance and positive energy for the benefit of the land and its people.

In describing these rites, and the possibility that other ancient cultures, such as the ancient Mesopotamians had a very similar rite in which the king renewed the world, Dr. Naydler writes: "certain passages in the Pyramid Texts [. .] indicate that through the king's transformation and rebirth, the land of Egypt was renewed, the grass was made green, and the fields became fertile."[271]

This was most true of the secret rites described above in the analysis of the Pyramid Texts themselves, in which the king crossed over to the "invisible world." Naydler writes, "The central rite of the Sed festival needs to be understood in this context of the king's harmonizing the relationship between the invisible and visible worlds for the benefit of the whole country. As we have already seen [. . .], the central rite involved the king crossing the threshold between worlds in order to stand in direct relationship to the normally hidden spiritual powers."[272]

We will examine this subject further presently, but Lucy Wyatt notes that shamanic out-of-body travels (which share numerous very clear metaphors with the language describing the king's mystical journey in the Pyramid Texts, as Dr. Naydler discusses at length, and as de Santillana and von Dechend also perceived and discussed decades earlier in *Hamlet's Mill*) are also undertaken on behalf of the people.[273] In surviving examples of shamanic practice, and in accounts from shamanic practice in previous centuries, the purpose for the shaman's mystical journey is very often for the healing of individual maladies, but also sometimes for other community needs.

In his landmark study of shamanism around the world, Mircea Eliade provides numerous examples of shamans from various traditions going into an altered state of consciousness in order to discern the cause of an illness or malady, and in order to learn the proper restorative action necessary to relieve the problem. For example, among the Paviotso of North America, he describes at length the process of shamanic healing, and the shaman's use of a trance state in order to consult with unseen powers regarding the diagnosis and treatment:

> After some time the shaman rises and walks around the fire in the center of the house. If there is a dancer, she follows him. He returns to his place, lights his pipe, draws a few puffs from it, then passes it to those present, who, at his invitation, smoke one or two puffs in turn. During all this time the songs continue. The next stage is determined by the nature of the illness. If the patient is unconscious, he is obviously suffering from "soul loss"; in this case the shaman must go into trance (*yaíka*) at once. If the illness is due to some other cause, the shaman may go into trance to establish the diagnosis or to discuss the proper treatment with his "powers." But this last type of diagnosis is used only if the shaman is powerful enough.[274]

But how does travel to the spiritual world, or the trance world, or the invisible world, really allow the shaman to receive actionable medical advice? If we knew this, then perhaps we could understand how such travel also benefited the people of Egypt through their king. Here is where Lucy Wyatt introduces an important connection. She points to the work of Jeremy Narby, published in his book *The Cosmic Serpent: DNA and the Origins of Knowledge* (1999). There, Dr. Narby described his experiences among the *Quirishari* of the Peruvian Amazon, during which he used the "trance-inducing substance" *ayahuasca* to gain "special insight into shamanism":

> The first point of interest is that, while in his hallucinating state, Narby encountered a pair of enormous snakes who were able to communicate with him [Narby, 1999, p7]. Although this odd experience unnerved him considerably, he decided to compare his experience with what he found in the literature on ancient myths and legends, and came to the realization that snakes and serpents have always been seen as the source of knowledge (not least in the Garden of Eden) – and may explain the connection between Egyptian gods, ntr, and the proto-Indo-European for snake, *netr.

> But what particularly struck Narby was the visual parallel between the image of entwined snakes, such as in the caduceus, and that of the double helix of DNA. Narby then came to the fascinating conclusion that the parallel was more than visual: it was actual. Shamans, he concluded, were communicating at the level of molecular biology, of DNA itself: 'DNA was at the origin of shamanic knowledge.' He was surprised to discover in the technical literature that the shape of the double helix of DNA is 'most often described as a ladder, or a spiral staircase,' which compares with the frequent references made worldwide to climbing a ladder during a shamanic trance [Narby, 1999, p108, p63].

[. . .]

Narby thus discovered how native people acquired their knowledge of medicinal plants. These plants were often highly toxic and required critical special preparation before use – otherwise these plants would kill you before you had chance to experiment with them and find out their healing properties. Even the ayahuasca had to be combined with another plant and boiled for hours before it was of use. The native people also knew precisely which plants to choose out of 80,0000 Amazonian plant species [Narby, 1999, p40, pp10-11]. The means by which they knew this non-empirical knowledge, he was told and he personally experienced, was through shamanism.[275]

From this connection, Lucy Wyatt draws the conclusion that, if entry into the unseen world could enable the inhabitants of the Amazonian rainforest to safely and effectively navigate through 80,000 different plant species (some of them deadly poison), then this technique may also explain the incredible civilizational achievements of the ancients who practiced the same out-of-body travels (through rites such as the Sed festival secret rites, for example).

In an essay published on the world wide web in 2010 and entitled "Megaliths, Shamanism, and the City-Builders – the hidden connections," she expands on this argument. She shows that many of the civilizational developments we take for granted could not have been achieved through trial-and-error, the way conventional historians argue that mankind advanced.[276]

The creation of domesticated grains, for example, would have taken many human generations of breeding before the use of grain was at all more convenient than hunter-gatherer existence – how many generations of hunter-gatherers would have continued the experiment (with no idea of the possibility of future success) long enough to make it finally come to fruition so that they could "settle down" from their hunter-gatherer lifestyle? Yet modern historical textbooks generally tell us casually that once upon a time, hunter-gatherers realized the benefits of farming and just "settled down" from the rigors of nomadic life.

Similarly the creation of domesticated animals from their wild predecessors would have taken many generations as well, and without knowing the end from the beginning it is difficult to imagine many generations of hunter-gatherers continuing with such a project.

Some modern analysts who have recognized the magnitude of these problems have posited that alien beings must have engineered the first domestic grains and the first domestic animals. While this is a possibility that should not be discounted, Lucy Wyatt has proposed a fascinating alternative explanation, via the mechanism of out-of-body travel. The resemblance of the DNA strands to intertwined serpents, and the fact that Jeremy Narby actually reports seeing such serpents during his *ayahuasca* sessions, also provides a fascinating alternative to those who argue that ancient mythologies describing alien beings from other planets must have been responsible for the mysteries of mankind's ancient past. It may be that the "serpent-beings" to which the ancients refer are not aliens from another planet, but the DNA strands of the plants and animals around them which they consulted, and within themselves! And it is certainly appropriate to recall that the ancient myth of Tiresias, who encountered two copulating snakes and was turned into a woman until he encountered them again, seems to support this interpretation.

As a side note to this fascinating story from antiquity, Mircea Eliade provides evidence from many cultures of a tradition wherein the shaman crosses over the boundaries of sex roles, often dressing as a member of the opposite sex at certain times and in certain circumstances, a piece of evidence which seems to have some resonance with the life of the seer Tiresias.[277] It is clear that the shaman is one who is capable of crossing over boundaries, including the most seemingly solid or seemingly impenetrable barriers, including the boundary between the material and the spiritual, but also the boundaries between human and animal, between living and dead, and between male and female.

But there is yet another crucial connection to be made, and it is suggested by Jeremy Naydler's outstanding explication of the meaning of the concept of the *Duat* or *Dwat*, that mysterious realm to which the pharaohs of Egypt were described as journeying in the inscriptions of the Pyramid Texts (and later dynastic texts as well). We have already seen from Lucy Wyatt's analysis of Jeremy Narby's work that the ancient kings may have in some way been traveling to a realm which involves seeing DNA, and even communicating with it somehow (stemming from Jeremy Narby's original and crucial observation that knowledge impossible to explain through the techniques known to followers of the "scientific method" may be explained by shamanic travel and communication with other entities, or with DNA itself). However, as Jeremy Naydler explains in *Shamanic Wisdom in the Pyramid Texts*, and as other scholars also interpret the ancient texts, the Duat (or Dwat) is associated with fairly specific *celestial* regions.[278] In other words, this analysis suggests yet another layer of connectivity between the microcosm (in this case, the microscopic microcosm, at the level of DNA) and the macrocosm (of the stars).

And there is more. Listen to Jeremy Naydler's description of the importance of the Duat, in a section entitled "The Living in Relation to the Dead." While conventional Egyptology asserts that the importance of the celestial region of the Duat lies in the belief of the ancient Egyptians that the Duat (or Dwat) region was the "realm of the dead," Dr. Naydler's analysis suggests something far deeper:

> Death was a realm – not a physical realm but a subtle realm that they referred to as the Dwat. Furthermore, the realm of the dead was for them an ever present factor of life, interpenetrating the world of the living. In the realm of the dead, invisible forces, powers, and energies – gods and demons as well as the spirits of the dead – are active, and their activity impinges directly on the world of the living. The Egyptians were intensely aware that the world they lived in was more than just the world perceptible to the senses. It included a vast and complex supersensible component as well.

> It would be a mistake, then, to regard the Dwat as simply the realm of the dead. It is the habitation of spirits, of beings that are capable of existing nonphysically. These include the essential spiritual energy of those beings and creatures that we see around us in the physical world. In the Dwat, everything is reduced to its spiritual kernel. Just as the forms of living plants, when they die, disappear from the visible world as they are received into the Dwat, so when the young plants unfold their forms again in the new year, they unfold them from out of the Dwat. This "hidden realm" (literally *amentet*, another term for the realm of the dead) is the originating source of all that comes into being in the visible world.[279]

Does anything in the above passage sound at all familiar? It is as if the ancient Egyptians understood and anticipated the holographic universe theory by well over four thousand years! Consider the last several sentences of the above quotation, and then compare them to Michael Talbot's discussion of David Bohm's concept of the "implicate order" (in a passage we have already examined before):

> One of Bohm's most startling assertions is that the tangible reality of our everyday lives is really a kind of illusion, like a holographic image. Underlying it is a deeper order of existence, a vast and more primary level of reality that gives birth to all the objects and appearances of our physical world in much the same way that a piece of holographic film gives birth to a hologram. Bohm calls this deeper level of reality the *implicate* (which means "enfolded") order, and he refers to our own level of existence as the *explicate*, or unfolded, order.
>
> He uses these terms because he sees the manifestation of all the forms in the universe as the result of countless enfoldings and unfoldings between these two orders.[280]

We could almost meld these two paragraphs into one and write:

> One of ancient Egypt's most startling assertions is that the physical world we see around us is really only a part of the whole, just as some physicists in the twentieth century would conclude. Underlying it is a deeper order of existence, a vast and more primary level of reality that gives birth to all the objects and appearances of our physical world in way that physicists over four millennia later would compare to holographic film giving birth to a hologram. The ancient Egyptians would call this deeper level of reality the *Duat*; some twentieth-century physicists would call it the *implicate order*. Both saw this unseen region, which underlies and interpenetrates the visible or physical universe, as the source of everything in the visible world, which exists in the other realm in "kernel" form (or, to use the more modern metaphor, in a form that is similar to holographic film, in which each portion of the film contains the "kernel" of the whole). In both views, everything we see in the visible world "unfolds" from the unseen world (the Duat, or the implicate order) and then enfolds back into it, endlessly.

The possibility that the Duat of ancient Egyptian understanding and the implicate order of the holographic universe theory are referring to the same concept has enormous implications.

For one, it implies that extremely ancient cultures possessed an extremely sophisticated understanding of the nature of reality – and an extremely accurate understanding of the nature of reality, if the models being proposed by modern physicists in response to the results of quantum experiments are in any way accurate. Note that the pyramid of Unas is the first ancient Egyptian pyramid with inscribed texts. We have some texts from before Unas, but none in any way as extensive as the Pyramid Texts. Unas reigned somewhere before 2300 BC, and by the time his pyramid was built and inscribed, we can assume the sophisticated understanding of the nature of consciousness and reality – the understanding of the Duat and the ability to undertake out-of-body travel to the Duat –

was already quite mature. It may have stretched many centuries into the past prior to the creation of the Unas pyramid. How did they come by their sophisticated understanding of the nature of the holographic universe, and of the means of traversing its modalities?

This sophisticated "holographic" understanding constitutes yet another piece of evidence in a huge pile of evidence pointing to the conclusion that the ancient history of mankind is far different than we have been led to believe. Indeed, the title of Jeremy Naydler's book, *Shamanic Wisdom in the Pyramid Texts,* indicates that the ancient Egyptian wisdom evidenced in the pyramid of Unas survives in the various shamanic traditions around the globe, found from Africa to Siberia to Mongolia to North, Central and South America to Australia to the islands of the Pacific (which, although they have significant differences, share many of the features found in the Pyramid Texts, as we shall see). While conventional timelines of human history might assert that shamanic types of mysticism came first and eventually "developed" or "evolved" into more elaborate types of ritual such as the Sed festival rites, there are reasons to believe that reality is the other way around – that the shamanic traditions surviving around the world into the nineteenth, twentieth, and in some remote locations even into the twenty-first centuries descended from the rites of the ancient Egyptians (and perhaps other advanced ancient civilizations, or from a single advanced lost civilization or culture whose influence was world-wide and whose legacy is shared by cultures spread across the globe).

Mircea Eliade, for example, cites numerous examples of traditions within shamanism of the "decadence" of current shamans in comparison to their remote ancestors in shamanism. There is so much evidence of this tradition given by shamans worldwide that Eliade's *Shamanism* contains an index entry for "decadence, of shamans" with sixteen different areas in the book that discuss this subject.[281]

Again, while the discussion of the Duat (or Dwat) from Jeremy Naydler's work is on its surface very different from the view of the Duat (or, as Kuhn calls it, the Tuat) found in the work of Alvin Boyd Kuhn, the discussions actually harmonize very well. Whereas Naydler refers to the Duat as the "realm of the dead [. . .] interpenetrating the world of the living," also called "'the hidden realm' (literally *amentet,* another term for the realm of the dead)," Alvin Boyd Kuhn believes that this hidden realm of *amentet* (or, as he refers to it, the realm of *Amenta*) is in fact the world of the incarnate living, the world into which our spirits descend upon incarnation, just like the stars of heaven which descend into the "hidden realm" when they reach the western horizon (the entrance to Amenta) and sink into the underworld.[282]

Note the root *Amen* ("hidden") in the word "Amenta" or "amentet." It is significant (and Alvin Boyd Kuhn discusses it at length) that this word is related to the name of the Egyptian god Amun or Amen (who, in some of his aspects, is "the hidden god") and in the Christian formula "amen" or "amen and amen" which is found throughout the gospel narratives.[283]

The implication is that the realm in which we dwell, the realm of incarnation, is only *apparently* material, only *apparently* solid, and only *apparently* separated from the realm of the unseen. The barriers over which we are conditioned to think we cannot cross, barriers that appear intractably "real," can in fact be crossed, through the techniques of *ex stasis* or the techniques of shamanism. The ancient Egyptians appear to have possessed detailed and sophisticated knowledge of those techniques, and to have practiced them and preserved them for thousands of years. The texts and monuments which they left behind, which we have been conditioned to believe had only to do with the world of the dead, had everything to do with the world of the living as well. The Egyptian Book of the Dead and the Pyramid Texts describe the interconnectedness and mutual interpenetration of the "seed world" of the implicate order and the "material world" that is its "unfolded" or "explicate" manifestation – its "holographic projection," in the language of the holographic universe theory.

Thus, it may be that to say that Alvin Boyd Kuhn interprets "Amenta" merely as "this underworld" of earthly material incarnate existence is too simplistic. He recognizes that this underworld is interpenetrated by the hidden realm – that we are material beings containing the *hidden* seed of the spiritual realm from whence we came and to which we will return (only, in many cases, to come back again). This hidden seed in each of us is the "hidden god," Amen (Amun).

Those who understand this mutual interpenetration of the implicate and explicate realms can, with the proper methodologies, cross over the boundaries which seem to separate the two, and can do so in order to gain knowledge or to effect changes which cannot otherwise be gained or effected by people who are conditioned to believe that the explicate realm is all that exists, and that no travel to the implicate realm can possibly be "real." Those who are able to cross over those boundaries are shamans.

We are seeing a developing case which suggests that all the ancient wisdom of the world was in a sense shamanic. The cultures which retain knowledge of the shamanic are now widely scattered, and in many of them there is a strong tradition which maintains that their shamanic knowledge and power is only a shadow of the shamanic knowledge and power of the shamans of old.

Part III:

How the Ancient Wisdom was Stolen from Humanity

10

Out of Egypt

The entire Christian Bible, creation legend, descent into and exodus from "Egypt," ark and flood allegory, Israelite "history," Hebrew prophecy and poetry, Gospels, Epistles, and Revelation imagery, all are now proven to have been transmission of ancient Egypt's scrolls and papyri into the hands of later generations which knew neither their true origin nor their fathomless meaning. Long after Egypt's voice, expressed through the inscribed hieroglyphics, was hushed in silence, the perpetuated relics of Hamitic wisdom, with their cryptic message utterly lost, were brought forth and presented to the world by parties of ignorant zealots as a new body of truth.

Alvin Boyd Kuhn,
Who is this King of Glory?[284]

At this point, we have seen enough evidence to conclude that the ancients possessed a deep and rich understanding of what modern physicists, building from the results of quantum experiments beginning in the twentieth century, have called the "holographic universe" theory. We have seen that their very thorough understanding of this paradigm certainly predated the construction of the most ancient extended texts we have found so far, the Pyramid Texts inscribed in the stone of the pyramid of Unas and his successors, dating back to 2345 BC – perhaps predating Unas by many centuries.

We have examined the possibility that some of the aspects of megalithic monuments including Stonehenge (believed to have been constructed even earlier than the pyramid of Unas) might also exhibit a sophisticated understanding of some aspects of the same "holographic" nature of reality, such as the idea that our material world is a manifestation of the interference patterns of energy waves, and that we are in some ways a form of "petrified" or incarnate energy, as is everything around us. We have seen that the myths of Medusa and the Gorgons might evidence the same understanding, and that the ancient depictions of Medusa and the Gorgons seem to express an awareness of the materialization of waves into physical form – of the "petrification" of energy into matter.

And we have seen extensive evidence to support a reading of the scriptures of the Old and New Testaments as teaching a holographic understanding of man and the cosmos as well. Rather than being intended as the record of literal events depicting the interaction of God and long-dead individuals, they endlessly incorporate celestial metaphors and simultaneous human-body metaphors, pointing to a unity or at least a harmony of macrocosm and microcosm. Indeed, this repeated metaphor can be said to be the allegorical depiction of the true, ongoing, and endless interaction of the divine and the human.

Finally, we have examined clear evidence that the ancients who possessed this profound knowledge also possessed the ability to act on it – to deliberately disconnect their consciousness from the material world of the seen and to enter into the world of the "implicate order" that underlies the hologram, the realm of the Duat that underlies and interpenetrates our visible world. Their understanding of this unseen world included the understanding that it was the source, the kernel, of all that "unfolds" in the visible material world. This understanding is very like to that proposed by modern physicist David Bohm, who sees the implicate order as the source and wellspring of all that unfolds into the explicit order. Again, the ancients appear to have had this knowledge at least as early as the time of Unas, and no doubt long before Unas as well.

We have also glimpsed numerous pieces of evidence suggesting that this knowledge lived on in various forms in certain parts of the world, sometimes for centuries – and in some places it may still exist. There is clear evidence to suggest that shamanism as it existed until very recently (and in some areas still exists) in parts of the world as widely separated as Siberia, Africa, the Americas, Australia, Central Asia, and far northern Europe, has clear connections to the rites of ancient Egypt and the ability to deliberately leave the physical and visible realm. There is plenty of other evidence that the ancient "holographic" worldview and its attendant knowledge and capabilities spanned the globe and that this ancient knowledge-set survived in some form in many places – everywhere, in fact, except those parts of the world which became what we still call "the west." Everywhere, that is, except those parts of the world that were conquered by the Roman Empire.

It is time to begin to address the question of how this knowledge was lost (or destroyed) in the areas where it was lost – that is, the west. If the scriptures that made their way into what is known as the Bible teach this knowledge, how has that interpretation been forgotten – or forbidden? Who might have had the motivation to effect such a suppression of this knowledge and its attendant "shamanic" practices, and what might those motivations have been (or continue to be)? We will explore some possibilities and the evidence that supports or refutes those various possibilities. While it may be that the body of evidence does not yet support any dogmatic conclusions, we can say with a fair amount of certainty that the possibilities that the evidence does support have the potential to completely alter our view of human history.

Perhaps the new perspectives that this examination opens up will suggest new and fruitful avenues of research, and perhaps further exploration down these paths will in the future lead us to even clearer views of what has taken place.

When it comes to definitive history of literal individuals and peoples, the further back we go into the misty past, the more difficult it usually becomes for researchers from the present to make definitive pronouncements regarding what took place and when – at least in terms of the question of what happened to suppress the "ancient wisdom" we are discussing here. We have already seen that there is good reason to believe that much of the description of the activities of the Israelites contained in the scriptures of the Old Testament may in fact be allegorical and indeed celestial. We have seen evidence which suggests that the Moses of the Bible does not refer to a specific historical individual, but rather a manifestation of Okeanos (who in turn represents both the earthly Nile and the heavenly Nile, as well as that mystical "river" which flows along the human spine and the line of the seven chakras), and that the "twelve tribes of Israel" refer to the twelve groupings of stars in the zodiac band (and who in turn are associated with twelve parts of the human body, beginning with Aries at the top of the head and progressing through to Pisces at the feet).

We have seen similar evidence that the Jesus of the Bible and his twelve disciples may in fact in many ways refer to the Sun and the twelve houses of the zodiac – as Robert Taylor says, the disciples are often depicted as having houses, but Jesus tells them that "the Son of Man has nowhere to lay his head," for he wanders through all of them in the course of the year.[285] Thus, it is dangerous to try to go back and make historical pronouncements based upon a literal or historical reading of texts that were primarily intended to convey allegorical and celestial events – although many histories do in fact try to do so. It is as dangerous as trying to begin an examination of the history of the Greeks based upon an historical and literal reading of the accounts of the Trojan War – which we have seen may well be primarily allegorical and celestial also.

It is, of course, quite possible and even likely that some of the figures who were worked into these allegories were once historical figures, and there is a thriving body of literature which attempts to work backwards from the scriptures to find their historical antecedents. There may well have been an historical Agamemnon, or an historical Abraham, and some aspects of their personalities, or at the very least some version of their historical names, might have been selected when composing the latest incarnation of the ancient story, in which the old roles are acted out by new actors in new costumes. However, the themes and plotlines remain allegorical in nature and celestial in content, and the existence of an historic Agamemnon or Abraham should not cause us to jump to the conclusion that we must then accept the actions attributed to those figures in the Iliad or the book of Genesis: those actions are primarily describing the motions of the heavens.

Because of this danger, the discussion which follows will deliberately be more limited in scope when it comes to deep forays into the distant past. What follows is not intended as a dogmatic assertion of one single theory of how the advanced "holographic universe" knowledge was suppressed, but rather as an exploration of some of the possibilities, with an effort to stay within what we might call "literal history" as much as possible, and to avoid accidentally making the mistake of confusing allegorical and celestial scriptures for literal and historical records.

To begin our examination, let's go back to an event that almost certainly did take place in literal, historical time: the Roman conquest of Judea, in the first century. It is quite clear that this event is central to our examination, as the Roman occupation of Judea clearly features prominently in the scriptures of the New Testament, and in the allegories of Jesus and his disciples. Somehow, this period of time is crucial for the introduction of the contents of the Hebrew scriptures into the Roman Empire, as well as the appearance in Greek of another set of celestial allegories found in an apparently new version of the old drama, this one set in the period of the Roman conquest (a few decades before the destruction of the Temple), and centered around the region of Galilee and Jerusalem.

We will, of course, have to look back into the centuries before that event as part of this investigation, but the further we go in that direction the more speculative in many cases our examination will necessarily become, for the mists of legend (or, more accurately, of allegory) become thicker and thicker from that point. This important fulcrum point of history can serve as a sort of undersea "base station" for our dives into the deep past, from which we can launch deeper expeditions into the murkier waters below but to which we will have to return periodically, as historical pronouncements concerning the fate of the "ancient wisdom" become more and more difficult to make the further down into the depths of time we go.

It is safe to say that the Romans did conquer Judea in the first century AD, and that they did destroy the Temple that was at the center of the religious life of the people who were conquered (the Jews). However, if those people whose Temple was destroyed and whose land was conquered were not descended from twelve *literal* sons of Israel, then from whom were they literally descended?

With this question we peer from our deep-sea "base station" into the murkier depths of history, where speculation is rife. However, the work of some alternative researchers suggests the radical conclusion that the Jews of Judea might well have been descendents of Egyptians, with a culture reflecting many aspects of that descent. Author Ralph Ellis has provided extensive and convincing arguments for this thesis, arguing that the account of the wandering shepherds fleeing from Egypt to Canaan depicted in Genesis and Exodus are actually thinly-disguised retellings of the line of Hyksos Shepherd-Kings of Lower Egypt who reigned from the 17th century BC to the 16th century BC until they were driven out by Ahmose I, the founder of the 18th dynasty of Egypt.

In a series of books beginning with *Jesus, Last of the Pharaohs*, Mr. Ellis presents a host of different lines of investigation which appear to support his startling thesis. Among the most amazing of these is his detailed examination of the genealogies in the Old Testament, wherein he finds clear parallels to the historical names of the kings of Egypt of Egypt, some of whom are listed by Manetho (and later by Josephus), and some of whom are also known to modern historians through other texts and archaeological evidence. In *Jesus, Last of the Pharaohs*, he presents this remarkable list:

Manetho	Bible	Egyptian history
Salatis	Sem	
Apachnat	Arphaxad	
[Cian]	Cainan	[Ciaan] Khyan
	Salah	
Bnon	Heber	[Eecbher] Yakubher
	Peleg	
	Ragau	[Raqu] (Aquenenre) Apepi
	Seruch	Apepi (Auserre)
Necho [per Josephus]	Nachor (Nahor)	Nehesy (Aaserre)
Assis	Thara (Terah, Azar)	(Aasahra) Nehesy [Aahssi]
	Abraham	Sheshi
	Isaac	Anather
	Jacob	[Jacoba] Jacobaam[286]

The bracketed names are those Ralph Ellis has altered based on his analysis of the hieroglyphs in the royal cartouches of those kings, as opposed to the traditional readings – his reasoning is discussed in detail in his writings. The names in parentheses on the list of known historical kings of Egypt indicate throne names of those kings.

This list alone provides a powerful argument in favor of the possibility that those people living in Canaan (the Promised Land: Biblical Israel and Judea) and venerating the scriptures containing characters bearing these names may have been Egyptians, either living as part of Egypt or as "renegade Egyptians" who had split off from the main kingdom and started their own independent project at a safe distance (perhaps because they had been driven out).

But Ralph Ellis provides additional supporting evidence throughout his books to support his radical proposal. Among these is an extended discussion of the events in Genesis 12, in which Abram and Sarai journeyed "toward the south [. . .] into Egypt to sojourn there; for the famine was grievous in the land" (Genesis 12:9-10). For one thing, Ellis points out, although Egypt is south of the Promised Land, it is really more west. He argues that Abram was the pharaoh Sheshi, whose throne name was Mayebra.[287] This name, when the syllables are reversed, is very close to "Abram" – Ayebra-M. If Abram were really a king of northern Egypt (Lower Egypt) at the time of the famine described in Genesis 12:9-10, then he would travel directly to the south to reach Upper Egypt and to encounter another pharaoh there, as described in the Genesis account. Ellis provides numerous other examples of pharaonic names which were often written and pronounced with their "component parts" reversed, such as Akhen-Aton (sometimes written Aton-Akhen) or Khaf-Ra (sometimes referred to as Ra-Khaf), providing precedent for his argument that Sheshi/Mayebra was Abram/Abraham.[288]

Ellis argues that the strange incident of Abram describing Sarai as his sister and not his wife in this chapter provides another clue that the Genesis and Exodus accounts describe pharaohs of northern Egypt. When Abram journeys to the south during the famine described in Genesis 12, he tells her to say she is his sister rather than his wife (verses 12 and 13 in that chapter). Ralph Ellis writes of this incident:

> The true explanation of this strange story is more likely to be that Sarah was not just beautiful, but that she also looked very similar to Abraham, for she was actually his full sister. If Abraham were the northern pharaoh, the Hyksos pharaoh, he would have married his sister according to pharaonic tradition. This likeness between Abraham and his sister-wife *would* have made the southern pharaoh angry: for marrying a sister was primarily a pharaonic tradition, so the royal status of Abraham would have been obvious.[289]

Elsewhere, Ellis provides many other arguments that support the idea that the stories of the Pentateuch at least involve Egyptians (or exiled Egyptian Hyksos). For instance, he points out the strange fact that the mighty pyramids of Egypt, the most massive buildings in the ancient world, seem to have escaped direct mention in the Biblical texts at all, in spite of all the times that "going down to Egypt" takes place. He then puts forth the theory that it is not really the case that the pyramids are not mentioned, but rather that they – like the true identity of Abraham and his descendents – are disguised in the Biblical texts. What, one might ask, could be the disguise for a pyramid? Ellis provides the startling answer: mountains! In particular, he argues that Mt. Sinai, upon which Moses meets with God and receives the Ten Commandments, was actually the Great Pyramid of Giza.

Ellis bases this assertion on the fact that the Biblical accounts describe the people of Israel all being arrayed at the bottom of the mount, but with the strict instruction not to touch the mount on pain of death. This would be rather hard to interpret if we were talking about a natural mountain out in the wilderness, whose boundaries and exact point of beginning are somewhat ambiguous, but the Exodus account found in chapter 19 is perfectly understandable if the mount which Moses ascends and descends is actually the Great Pyramid:

> [10]And the LORD said unto Moses, Go unto the people, and sanctify them to day and tomorrow, and let them wash their clothes,
> [11]And be ready against the third day: for the third day the LORD will come down in the sight of all the people upon mount Sinai.
> [12]And thou shalt set bounds unto the people round about, saying, Take heed to yourselves, that ye go not up into the mount, or touch the border of it: whosoever toucheth the mount shall be surely put to death:
> [13]There shall not an hand touch it, but he shall surely be stoned, or shot through; whether it be beast or man, it shall not live: when the trumpet soundeth long, they shall come up to the mount. Exodus 19:10-13.

The idea of setting bounds for the people, and warning them not to reach out so much as a hand to touch "the mount" suggests that we are talking not about a mountain in the wilderness but about a pyramid upon the plain of Giza, according to Ralph Ellis. He sets forth the details of this remarkable theory at length in his sequel to *Jesus, Last of the Pharaohs*, which is entitled *Tempest & Exodus*.[290]

Returning to his arguments based on the identification of Abraham as a pharaoh, Ellis points to an interesting assertion made by Josephus in his histories, in which Josephus writes that:

> Pharaoh Necho, King of Egypt at the time, descended on this land with an immense army and seized Sarah the Princess, mother of our nation. And what did our forefather Abraham do? Did he avenge the insult by force of arms? Yet he had three hundred eighteen [army] officers under him, with unlimited manpower at his disposal![291]

As Ralph Ellis points out, this passage seems to indicate that Abraham was something more than he is made out to be in the Biblical accounts. If Abraham had three hundred eighteen officers, and if each of them commanded only 30 other men then Abraham, as Ellis writes, "had a standing army over 11,000 strong."[292] Note that a unit of only 30 other men would be the size of a modern platoon, making these "officers" only junior lieutenants – in reality Josephus could be referring to officers of much higher status, perhaps in charge of ten times more than that number.

Ellis notes that Genesis interestingly refers to Abraham as having an identical number (ie, three hundred eighteen) of individuals available for help in matters requiring force of arms, but calls them "servants" and does not indicate that they are in charge of anyone underneath them. Genesis 14:14 reads: "And when Abram heard that his brother was taken captive, he armed [or "led forth"] his trained servants, born in his own house, three hundred and eighteen, and pursued them unto Dan." Comparing the Genesis text and the Josephus reference, Ralph Ellis writes, "it would appear that Josephus' version of the Old Testament holds the more reliable account."[293]

Perhaps it would be more accurate to have said, "it would appear that Josephus reveals here that he knows more than what the Old Testament account makes plain on its surface." Ellis has already observed that the Biblical accounts are notably vague about the names of any of the pharaohs – perhaps because the Hyksos kings were in bitter conflict with the kings of Upper Egypt, from whom they were divided, perhaps over a deep article of religious faith.[294] Josephus, however, mentions the name of "Pharaoh Necho," which again appears to indicate that Josephus knew more than the texts that make up the Pentateuch tell the reader.

As we will see, Josephus was proud of his status as a priest of the children of Israel, from a long and distinguished family line of priests of the children of Israel. In naming "Pharaoh Necho" as an adversary of Abram – when the Genesis texts do not – and in identifying Abram's three hundred eighteen armed "servants" as three hundred eighteen military officers, Josephus may be revealing the fact that as a learned priest of the Temple, he had been taught far more about his people's origins than was found in the texts themselves.

He is also revealing the possibility, as Ralph Ellis observes, that Abraham was in some sort of armed conflict with his grandfather (or possibly his own father), since Necho is obviously located on the list of Egyptian kings above, a pharaoh whom Ellis identifies as the Egyptian Nehesy (throne-name Aaserre).

Ellis believes that the reason for the conflict may have been over a fundamental matter of religious faith, and he finds support for this assertion in a passage of the Koran which indicates that Abraham rebuked his father over the worship of multiple deities. Ellis writes:

> Like the pharaoh Akhenaton, who will be discussed in detail later in the book, Abraham had renounced the plethora of Egyptian gods and worshipped the one, almighty god. Akhenaton would call this supreme deity Aton, a manifestation of Amen-Ra; while Abraham would have known this god as Adhon, and added an 'Amen' to the prayers in a strikingly similar fashion. The problem for Abraham was that his father did not share these beliefs:
>
> > Tell of Abraham, who said to Azar, his father: 'Will you worship idols as your gods? Surely you and all your people are in palpable error.'
>
> This is the reason for Abraham becoming the primary biblical patriarch, the father of a new religion and the 'Father of the Nation'. He made a significant break with tradition at this point, effectively starting a new dynasty, and it was a divergence that would prove to be fatally divisive; like Akhenaton's similar, but later, religious reforms, it would result in civil war.[295]

One other detail argued by Ralph Ellis is significant as support for the theory that the Old Testament texts and the people of Israel had an Egyptian origin, and that is the fact that Abraham is described by Josephus as being a learned astronomer.[296] Ellis argues that this fact also supports the Egyptian thesis, as the priests and kings of Egypt were clearly accomplished astronomers. In fact, Josephus goes further and argues that Abraham was *responsible* for bringing the celestial science into Egypt, and that "before Abraham came into Egypt, they were unacquainted with those parts of learning," referring to both arithmetic and astronomy.[297]

This assertion, while supporting a connection to Egypt as the origin of the Biblical texts (which we have already seen are richly astronomical in content), somewhat undermines Ellis' thesis that Abraham was actually a king in the sixteenth dynasty (if Josephus is correct), for the Egyptians obviously possessed a highly advanced mathematical and astronomical science long before the construction of the Giza pyramids or the Saqqara pyramids of Unas and his successors, all of which took place in much earlier dynasties. Josephus, of course, could be recounting what he had been taught as a descendent of Abraham.

We will see later that Josephus may be a very unreliable source for ancient history, with a king-sized agenda of his own to preserve. The very fact that he treats throughout his works people such as Abraham and Isaac as literal people, and the story of the sacrifice of Isaac as a literal event (going so far as to tell us that it took place when Isaac was about twenty-five years of age) shows that he either believed these events to have been literal, or (if he knew they were celestial allegories) had a reason to portray them as literal to the wider populace (the latter being much more likely than the former), either option showing that one who holds to the theories already outlined in this book cannot take the writings of Josephus at face value.[298]

However, the fact that Abraham and Isaac were (according to the theory proposed in this book and supported by overwhelming astronomical evidence) not literal persons does not destroy the insightful connections Ralph Ellis discovers which link the ancient inhabitants of Judea to the culture of Egypt. In fact, the celestial nature of Abraham and Isaac comports rather well with the theory, given the undeniably central role the Egyptians ascribed to the study of the motions of the heavens.

Expanding on the Egyptian focus on the stars, and Abraham's skill in the astronomical sciences, Ellis believes that the source of the religious dispute described above (between the Hyksos and the traditional priests of Egypt) may have been astronomical as well, and one centered on a disagreement regarding the shift of the zodiac constellation rising heliacally on the morning of the spring equinox from the sign of Taurus the Bull to Aries the Ram, a shift which took place at an epoch roughly equivalent to the Hyksos period in question.[299] He believes that Abraham and his followers recognized the shift, but that the change was too much for a conservative faction of priests and the people, who wanted to continue the worship of the bull. In fact, Ellis makes the fascinating connection that the Hyksos may have been called "Shepherd-Kings" precisely because they gave honor to Aries the Ram as the new leader of the zodiac, rather than to Taurus the Bull.[300]

Clearly, astronomical themes including the transition from the Age of Taurus to the Age of Aries occupy a central place in the Old Testament texts, but this fact does not mean that the events described – including those in the life of Abram / Abraham – are intended to represent literal characters.

Ellis reveals one of the problems with the literal interpretation when he tries to explain away the recurrence of the situation in which Abraham tells someone that Sarah is his sister. We have already seen one instance in which he does so, in the Genesis 12 account. Later in Genesis, Abraham is depicted as doing the same thing as he "journeyed [. . .] toward the south country" between Kadesh and Shur, in a place called Gerar, in Genesis chapter 20. Here, Abraham encounters Abimelech, king of Gerar, and tells him that Sarah his wife is his sister and not his wife, in exactly the same fashion as the Genesis 12 episode.

Abimelech is fooled, and is only saved from committing adultery with Sarah by a dramatic dream intervention in which God himself says to him, "Behold, thou art a but a dead man, for the woman which thou has taken; for she is a man's wife" (Genesis 20:3). The following verses tell us that Abimelech reasons with God, arguing that he had not come near her, and pleading for mercy upon his nation, since Abraham had told him directly that she was his sister, and she had confirmed it herself saying he was her brother. Then God said to him in the dream, "Yea, I know that thou didst this in the integrity of thy heart; for I also withheld thee from sinning against me: therefore suffered I thee not to touch her" (Genesis 20:6).

Later still, in Genesis 26, after the death of Abraham, we read that there is another famine in the land. True to form, Isaac goes down to Gerar and takes his wife, Rebekah. He tells the men of his country that Rebekah is his sister and not his wife. Apparently, Abimelech is again taken in by this ruse, in spite of the dramatic events just described from Genesis chapter 20 in which Abimelech had been personally visited by God and threatened with death, and had then pleaded with God and learned that he and his people would be spared, and that in fact God himself had preserved Abimelech from touching another man's wife. This gullibility on the part of Abimelech a second time is truly difficult to accept, if we have already read of the dream visit from Genesis 20! And yet in Genesis 26 we read that it was not until after Isaac and Rebekah had been there in Gerar a long time that Abimelech observed Isaac "sporting with Rebekah his wife" and realized the truth that she was his wife and not his sister (Genesis 26:8).

Ellis recognizes that these three repetitions of the exact same pattern are extremely hard to take literally. His explanation, however, is scarcely easier to accept, for he believes that the duplication of the episode is due to simple "scribal error." He argues that, "Of course, it is not possible that exactly the same event occurred three times; the scribes were simply being over-enthusiastic and wrote down everything they heard or read. [. . .] Quite clearly, this same peculiar event could not have happened three times – the separate traditions that evolved into the story known as 'Genesis' are simply confused about *when* it really happened."[301]

This explanation, while possible, is not very satisfactory if we are supposed to believe that the Old Testament records describe literal historical individuals. Of course there is the possibility of "scribal error," but the Hebrew scribes were actually extremely careful, with systems for cross-checking individual letters, letter by letter. An "error" of this magnitude would be nearly impossible to miss – and miss twice.

It is far more satisfactory, I believe, to consider the likelihood that these stories are metaphorical and astronomical in nature, and that they were not intended at all to be understood as describing literal flesh-and-blood individuals from history. The story of a prominent man and a prominent woman "going down" towards either Egypt or Gehar most likely refer to the constellation Boötes (the man) and Virgo (the woman – who is also a queen and always very beautiful) sinking downward into the lower parts of the sky.

Boötes and Virgo are positioned reasonably close to one another, and numerous celestial-metaphor stories describe their motion through the heavens according to Robert Taylor, including the story of Adam and Eve, Abraham and Sarah, Isaac and Rebekah, Jacob and Rachel, Joseph and Mary, and many others in the ancient sacred traditions of the world. Taylor expounds on this connection at length in *Astronomico-Theological Lectures*, and argues that this explanation satisfactorily provides the reason that Sarah never becomes old or undesirable (the literal-historical reading has some difficulty explaining that, just as it has trouble explaining away the three-fold repetition of the exact same story). He says:

> So it is the self-same 'Mother of us all,' in the Eve of Paradise, who is revived again, in the same conceit re-modelled, in *Sarah*, the Princess of Smiles, and mother of the miraculously born *Isaac*, whose very name is retained in the Astarte of the Zidonians, the *Sarah Apis*, or Serapis of Egypt, – and whose very attribute of that eternal laughter was sculpted in the exquisite Venus Urania, or heavenly Venus of Praxiteles, with the mouth a little open, and the lip so nicely turned, as if so archly smiling she would fain deny that she had smiled at all; and as if the very allegorical dialogue were going on while you gazed on her transcendent beauty, and she were retorting her pretty fib, 'I laughed not,' to her entranced admirer, who couldn't but say, 'Nay, but thou didst laugh!'

> For the scriptural allegory has called our observance to note that Sarah was very fair, and very young; and what is chiefly to be noted, none the less fair nor the less young when she was ninety years old.[302]

Taylor's explanation has no problem with the revival again of the same pattern for Isaac and Rebekah:

> The scriptural allegorist is so evidently pleased with this personified Universal Mother, who is the Cybele, or Mother of the Gods of the mythology, the Virgin Deipara, or God-bearer of the Zodiac, the Virgin Mary, or Christ-bearer of the gospel, and the Wonder, or Woman in Heaven of the Apocalypse, – that having allegorically buried her in the allegorical cave of Machpelah, he revives the self-same character again in the person of Rebekah, to be the wife of Isaac, with the self-same story of her being his sister, as well as his wife, and her being exceeding handsome, as Sarah had been, and Isaac selling her again to Abimelech, King of Gerah, just as Abraham had sold his Sarah to the same Abimelech, King of Gerah.

> And having done with her, in the character of Rebekah, the wife of Isaac – he actually brings her on the stage again, the third time in the character of Rachael, the wife of Jacob, who is the same goddess of beauty and of smiles, and makes precisely the same covenant with her maid Billah, which Sarah had made with her maid Hagar.[303]

That these events represent celestial allegories, which play themselves out in the heavens over and over just as they play themselves out in the scriptures and in other mythologies over and over, would seem to be a far more likely explanation than the idea that the scribes somehow mixed up an actual historical event, mixing up when during the life of Abraham and Sarah it happened, and with which southern king – and then mixing up whether it actually happened with Abraham and Sarah or with Isaac and Rebekah!

As Robert Taylor points out in a line of argument quoted earlier, the gospels provide a very clear key to understanding these stories. When Jesus is confronted by the Saducees in Matthew 22, he says to them in verses 31 and 32:

> [31]But as touching the resurrection of the dead, have ye not read that which was spoken unto you by God, saying,
> [32]I am the God of Abraham, and the God of Isaac, and the God of Jacob? God is not the God of the dead, but of the living.

The same teaching, with slight differences in content, is found again in Mark 12:27 and Luke 20:38. Robert Taylor's interpretation of this passage is that it teaches us that Abraham does not grow old and die, nor does Sarah grow old and unattractive, because these stories are concerning "heavenly things" – events which take place in the heavens above, and which can be seen every night in the stars, weather and time of year permitting.[304]

The fact these stories are most likely celestial metaphors does not, however, in any way invalidate the important work that Ralph Ellis has done in demonstrating the likelihood that the Old Testament may have strong connections to ancient Egypt, and perhaps to the Hyksos Shepherd-Kings.

We have already seen that the celestial metaphors have no problem putting on different costumes and being played-out by different actors, whether the stage is set to resemble a scene in ancient Egypt, ancient Greece, or the Old Testament times or New Testament times. They move equally smoothly over to the sacred traditions of the Maya, the Aztec, and the Polynesians of the broad Pacific. If the names selected for the characters who play out the celestial stories as they are found in the Old Testament can be shown to be the names of Egyptian kings, and if instead of setting the stories in Egypt proper the stories are placed in a thinly-veiled facsimile of Egypt (in which Mt. Sinai, for example, is substituted for Giza), then this information may indeed tell us that the people who carried the Old Testament stories into the lands we think of as Israel were indeed Egyptians – and perhaps descendents of a line of exiled Egyptian kings.

However, these connections do not mean that we need to make the leap of taking the stories themselves literally. Just because they use historical names does not make them history, any more than Shakespeare's plays are meant to be understood as history just because their author chose historical settings for his dramas, and gave real historical names to his characters (or *her* characters, if you subscribe to the theory, supported by some evidence, that Shakespeare's plays were actually written by someone other than an historical personage named "William Shakespeare," one version of which theory holds that the plays are the work of a woman).

In fact, the writings of Josephus, who (as we will see later) may well have known far more than his writings reveal at face value, but who was also capable of revealing more than he says, to those who can "read between the lines," may provide rather startling confirmation of some of the framework of Ralph Ellis' theory. Ellis asserts that the Hyksos left Egypt over a dispute involving the precessional change of ages, from the Age of Taurus the Bull to the Age of Aries the Ram. In the discussion of Abraham found in *Antiquities of the Jews*, Josephus has this to say about the patriarch:

Now Abram, having no son of his own, adopted Lot, his brother Haran's son, and his wife Sarai's brother; and he left the land of Chaldea when he was seventy-five years old, and at the command of God went into Canaan, and therein he dwelt himself, and left it to his posterity. He was a person of great sagacity, both for understanding all things and persuading his hearers, and not mistaken in his opinions; for which reason he began to have higher notions of virtue than others had, and he determined to renew and to change the opinion all men happened then to have concerning God; for he was the first that ventured to publish this notion, That there was but one God, the Creator of the universe; and that, as to other [gods], if they contributed any thing to the happiness of men, that each of them afforded it only according to his appointment, and not by their own power. This his opinion was derived from the irregular phenomena that were visible both at land and sea, as well as those that happen to the sun, and moon, and all the heavenly bodies, thus: -- "If [said he] these bodies had power of their own, they would certainly take care of their own regular motions; but since they do not preserve such regularity, they make it plain, that in so far as they co-operate to our advantage, they do it not of their own abilities, but as they are subservient to Him that commands them, to whom alone we ought justly to offer our honor and thanksgiving." For which doctrines, when the Chaldeans, and other people of Mesopotamia, raised a tumult against him, he thought fit to leave that country; and at the command and by the assistance of God, he came and lived in the land of Canaan.[305]

This description by Josephus hints at the very subject that Ellis believes may have been the root of the theological dispute that led to the migration of the "Shepherd" faction (the Aries faction) into Judea, and their break from the theological hierarchy maintained by the "Bull" faction in Egypt. It states that "Abram" (whom Josephus treats as an historical personage, whether or not Josephus actually knows better) perceived something very subtle in the motions of the stars, which led to his rejection of the doctrines of polytheism and a "new" notion – "That there was but one God."

What was it that caused Abram to reach this conclusion? According to Josephus, it was the discovery that the heavenly bodies could not "take care of their own regular motions," but somehow failed to preserve their regularity. We know that the stars actually do preserve a tremendous degree of regularity, rising year-in and year-out on their appointed day in the appointed time, but that there is a subtle "failure to preserve their regularity" which takes place so slowly and so gradually that it is barely possible for one man to perceive it: the motion of precession, which "delays" the heavens and the appointed rising of a star by only one degree in seventy-two years. This delay, or slippage of the heavenly gear, would after approximately 2,160 years cause the stars of Aries to replace the stars of Taurus in the house of the rising sun on the March equinox, just as Taurus had replaced Gemini before, and just as Pisces would later replace Aries, and just as Aquarius is now poised to replace Pisces. It seems quite likely that this failure to "take care of their own regular motions" is what Josephus is hinting at in the above passage, a failure that led to the declaration that the powers of the stars, whatever those might be, must be subservient to a higher power, the power of the one true God behind it all.

The fact that Josephus tells us that Abraham was seventy-five just before launching into this discussion of his perception of the stars' failure to take care of their regular motions is another possible clue that precession is the subject of the discussion, for the precessional rate is one degree every 71.6 years – very close to the seventy-five years that Josephus cites.

It may be that Josephus is being deliberately vague with Abram's age, in order to keep his hidden message hidden from the regular reader, while being close enough to alert the esoteric reader. It would have been something of a giveaway, for instance, if he had said that Abram "had left the land of Chaldea when he was 71.6 years of age," or even if he had said he had left at "seventy-two years of age." Or, it may be that Josephus was not aware of the precise precessional constant and used seventy-five instead of seventy-two The precessional constant of seventy-two *was* apparently known with that level of specificity by then, for when Plutarch (a contemporary of Josephus, Plutarch having been born around AD 46 and living until AD 120, and Josephus living from around AD 37 until AD 100) describes the Egyptian myth of Isis and Osiris and the murder of Osiris by Set, Plutarch gives Set seventy-two henchmen who help carry out the dastardly deed. Jane B. Sellers demonstrates quite convincingly that the murder of Osiris by Set allegorizes the end of the Age of Gemini and the advent of the Age of Taurus, and the use of the number seventy-two shows a very sophisiticated level of precision in determining the precessional constant no later than the time of Plutarch (and probably much earlier, since the legends of Osiris, Set, Horus and Isis are of tremendous antiquity, and clearly have precessional elements in their fundamental outline).[306]

Whether or not Josephus was aware of the precise constant of precession, or whether he used seventy-five as a close approximation (there is even the possibility that he was using a much older number than that known to Plutarch, and that the action of precession has been slowing down over the ages, just as the obliquity of the earth itself has declined over the ages), the passage quoted above makes it quite possible that he saw the foundation of monotheism to have been built upon the awareness of precession, and the realization that the stars could not be the ultimate arbiters of destiny in the universe, since they could not even take care of their own regular motions.

That Josephus assigns this realization to a literal and historical personage named Abram, who was seventy-five years of age when he left Chaldea over his discovery of the precessional motion, does not necessarily mean that the discovery happened that way, nor even that Josephus believed the literal details of the account he was publishing. It may be that Josephus was privy to the full knowledge of precession, but that he did not publish those details in his books. The important thing to take from this discussion is the strong possibility that Josephus is hinting at the discovery of precession, that he links this discovery to theological doctrines concerning the debate over "one God" versus "many gods," and his assertion that this theological argument over the implications of the irregularity of the heavenly phenomena became the foundational event of the faith of the "descendents of Abraham."

There are indeed other reasons to believe that the possessors of the Old Testament scriptures at the time of the Roman conquest may have been the direct descendents of Egyptians. For one thing, the worship of the sun played a very central role in the worship of ancient Egypt, and we have already seen that the scriptures from first to last concern the movements of the sun through the circle of the year. In fact, Ralph Ellis is clearly aware of many of the celestial aspects of Old Testament scripture, and devotes extended discussion and analysis to the solar and lunar roots of Old Testament worship in *Tempest & Exodus* and *Eden in Egypt*, which continue the arguments developed in *Jesus, Last of the Pharaohs*.

In many of his works, Alvin Boyd Kuhn discusses additional reasons to believe that the patterns of the Old and New Testament descend directly from the theologies of ancient Egypt. In addition to the evidence we have already seen which links the "horned" entity Moses with the horned Nile and the horned Okeanos, Kuhn points out the linguistic and symbolic resonance between other concepts of the Egyptian theology and the characters and stories of the Old and New Testaments.

For instance, in a remarkable passage in *Lost Light*, Kuhn explains that the ancient Egyptian religious center, known to the Greeks as Heliopolis but to the Egyptians as the city of On or A-NU, "where the death, burial, and resurrection of Osiris or Horus was re-enacted each year," had a name whose etymology was literally *not* – *nothing* (the prefix *a*- being a "privative" just as it is in English where words such as *a-theist* and *a-gnostic* signify one declaring "non-theism" or "non-knowledge/gnosis"). By extension, then, he argues that the word means "manifestation" or "matter" – the physical stuff into which pure or "virginal" spirit descends and from which it later re-ascends:

> A-NU would then mean "not-nothingness," or a world of concrete actuality, the world of physical substantial manifestation. Precisely such a world it is in which units of virginal consciousness go to their death and rise again. A-NU is then the physical body of man on earth. The soul descends out of the waters of the abyss of the NUN, or space in its undifferentiated unity, with is the sign and name of all things negative. The NUN is indeed our "none." Life in the completeness of its unity is negative. To become positively manifest it must differentiate itself into duality, establish positive-negative tension, and later split up into untold multiplicity. This brings out the significance of the Biblical word "multiply."[307]

Kuhn notes that the zodiac signs just prior to the two equinoxes (that is, Pisces just prior to the March equinox, and Virgo just prior to the September equinox) were seen and encoded in ancient scriptures as the two "mothers" of the first and second birth. The first birth, when the soul-consciousness descends into fleshly matter, is a sort of death, and it takes place just after the sign of Virgo. Remember that Virgo holds a sheaf of wheat (signified by the star Spica) and thus is associated with bread. The second birth, when the soul-consciousness rises in resurrection, is symbolized by the sun's crossing back into the heavens at the March equinox, after crossing through the sign of Pisces, the Fishes.

Thus we have loaves and fishes – symbology that is clearly of great importance in the New Testament! But Kuhn points out that the ancient Egyptian texts, such as the Book of the Dead, explicitly refer to ANU as "the place of multiplying bread."[308] One manifestation of this Egyptian pattern in the Old Testament is the man Joshua, who is a prototype of the Christ of the New Testament, and who is described as the son of Nun.[309] This epithet of Joshua, which is repeated no less than twenty-nine times in the Old Testament, hearken back to the Egyptian concept of ANU as that place where the death and resurrection of the gods is enacted. Even further, the Hebrew word NUN, as Alvin Boyd Kuhn reminds us, literally means "fish" – a piece of evidence which underscores the Old Testament connection to the resurrection symbology of Pisces at the gate of the March equinox, and which also suggests a connection between the Hebrew language and the esoteric symbology of ancient Egypt.

The fact that Joshua son of Nun and Jesus of the New Testament are symbolically related – even symbolically identical – can be seen from the fact, which Alvin Boyd Kuhn also explores, that the Bethany and Bethlehem of the New Testament provide linguistic evidence of the connection. The Hebrew word *beth* meaning "house" was attached to ANU to yield "Beth-ANU," or Bethany.[310] It was also attached to the Hebrew word for bread (*lechem* or *lekhem*) to yield "Beth-lechem" or Bethlehem.[311]

It was at Bethlehem (the House of Bread – corresponding to Virgo in the above symbology, where the soul-consciousness crosses the equator downwards) that the Christ came down into flesh (born, it need hardly be pointed out, of *a virgin*), and it was at Bethany (named for ANU, that place in Egypt where the resurrection of Osiris was annually re-enacted) that Jesus called Lazarus forth from the rock tomb. Alvin Boyd Kuhn points out that the linguistic derivation of Lazarus is tellingly close to Azar, or Osiris, and that Horus (the divine son) calls forth the mummified Osiris from a cave to restore him to life in the Egyptian theology, just as Jesus (the divine son) calls forth the mummified Azar or Lazarus from the cave-like tomb in the gospel accounts.[312]

These harmonies leave little doubt that the pattern of many of the most powerful stories in both the Old and New Testament came from Egypt.

If most of the Old Testament stories refer to celestial motion, then adapting these patterns from one geographical location to another would be fairly simple. Stories developed using "Upper Egypt" and "Lower Egypt" to represent the upper and lower halves of the annual cycle, for instance, could be rewritten replacing the "Promised Land" and "Egypt" for the upper and lower halves. As we will discuss in a later chapter, there is good reason to believe that Egyptians, living in the land we think of as the Promised Land, were taken captive by Babylon, and that it was during this captivity and subsequent return that the literal understanding of the books of the Pentateuch was substituted for the esoteric understanding that had prevailed until then. After that, these people (who had been Egyptians) began to think of themselves as the literal descendants of the esoteric and allegorical figures described in the books of Genesis through Joshua. It is also possible that at the end of the captivity in the east, the original Egyptian stories were re-cast in their present form, with Abraham coming out of "Chaldea" or "Ur of the Chaldees," and the original Egyptian characters transformed into their now-familiar roles as shepherds and nomads and (later) kings and warriors.

As we will see, perhaps the most startling confirmation of the suggestion that the people controlling Judea at the time of the Roman conquest were descendents of Egyptians – or of renegade Egyptians – will be the actions they take when they gained control of the Roman Empire which, as we will see, appears to be exactly what happened in the centuries following the destruction of the Temple at Jerusalem, as startling as that assertion may seem on the surface. One of the first things they did was to end any vestiges of the shamanic practices that had been carried on in Egypt for millennia, and to destroy the library at Alexandria, perhaps the greatest repository of ancient wisdom on the planet. They then began a systematic campaign of stamping out other vestiges of that ancient wisdom wherever in the world it tried to hide, a campaign which lasted for seventeen centuries and which may indeed still be ongoing.

11
Before the lights went out

The existence of similar or identical features in the cosmologies, myths, names, ceremonies, artefacts and even units of measure of such widely separated countries as China, Egypt, Britain and America implies that their cultures were derived from a common source, from some greater tradition of which they each preserved certain relics. [. . .] Ever and again, studies of ancient civilizatios trace them back from their declines to their high origins – beyond which the trail ends, with no trace of any previous period of cultural development. The great riddle in the quest for the origin of human culture is that civilizations appear suddenly, at their peak, as if ready-made. The version of history that constantly suggests itself is Plato's, given in his account of that long-vanished world which he called Atlantis.

John Michell, *New View Over Atlantis.*[313]

In this chapter, we will examine evidence which strongly suggests that techniques of altered consciousness – the ability to traverse the boundary between the "implicate order" and the "explicate order," to cross over into the Duat and return – were well known to an advanced ancient civilization which predated dynastic Egypt, that they continued to be known in "the west" through the long span of millennia encompassed by dynastic Egypt, and that they even continued to be known in some fashion in the west into the first two or three centuries AD. At some point after that, they went "underground" and were no longer widely known, accepted, or even acknowledged in the west.

By examining these three periods – the most ancient "pre-existing" period that predated Egypt, the period that encompassed dynastic Egypt and stretched into the end of "antiquity," and the period that came after and stretches to the present -- we can begin to build a case to explain "what happened." Using those three periods, we can see evidence to support the pattern (from oldest to present) of "had," "had," and then "did not have." This segmentation can help us identify where the break took place.

Note that during the final segment of time – the segment which stretches from the end of the fourth century AD to the present – the knowledge of the "holographic" model and the ability to deliberately traverse the boundary between the implicate and the explicate was lost in the west, but it can be demonstrated that it was not lost in the parts of the world which were not conquered by the Roman Empire. In fact, it can be demonstrated that this knowledge continued to the present at least among shamanic cultures, some of which survive to the present and many more of which survived in largely unaltered form up until the nineteenth and even twentieth centuries.

In the examination of the loss or extermination of the knowledge and techniques of consciousness, we can safely say based on the evidence examined so far that the ancients as far back as the time of Unas – in the oldest extant complete texts we have (disregarding short inscriptions) – possessed a sophisticated grasp of both the knowledge and the techniques. They could deliberately journey to the unseen realm of the Duat and return, and they perceived this journey as essential to the health, continuance, and preservation of their culture and civilization. This deliberate shamanic travel was not marginalized – it was central to the entire civilization of ancient Egypt.

Today, the idea of the shamanic journey has been completely eradicated from "western" civilization (we will examine this concept of "the west" at a later point). Where it was once central – undertaken during the rites associated with the great Sed Festival, by the king himself accompanied and enabled by his most knowledgeable priests – it became completely marginalized. It survived in regions where deliberate use of overwhelming force did not stamp it out, and if it survived in the west it was pursued by figures on the margins of society, never acknowledged or sanctioned or portrayed in a positive light.

Based on the thesis of Jeremy Narby, the travel to the unseen realm may enable "discussions" with DNA, and perhaps the attainment of information far beyond what we would believe possible with our "modern" methodology. In addition to their level of achievement in the realm of the spiritual or in the realm of "consciousness" (becoming an *akh*), which are difficult to document but of which we can catch glimpses from the still-mysterious texts they have left to us, the ancient Egyptians clearly possessed wondrous engineering ability, artistic ability, and medical knowledge.

And there is overwhelming evidence that the achievements of cultures such as ancient Egypt were the product of those who had inherited what are only the remnants of an even more ancient and awesome civilization. The most ancient cultures the world over appear to have used the largest and most massive megaliths in their construction, and their successors seem to have lost the ability to construct monuments using stones as massive as their predecessors. But the sophistication of the network of megaliths and alignments that they left behind goes far beyond the sheer size of their construction.

In *The View Over Atlantis* (1969) and *The New View Over Atlantis* (1983) John Michell lays out the evidence that the most ancient monuments from Stonehenge to Giza to the sacred *ceque* lines of South America and the *luhng mei* (dragon paths) of China mark a globe-encircling grid, displaying a precise awareness of the size and shape of the earth as well as of energy lines and nodes of which we remain largely ignorant, and an awareness of earth's relationship to the other visible planets and our moon and sun as well. In *Grid of the Gods* (1999), Joseph P. Farrell builds a case that the ancients who constructed this grid appear to have been aware of extremely sophisticated concepts of physics and the energy forces created by the torque of the spinning earth, as well as of the energy created by the interaction of the other major heavenly bodies in our solar system.

The evidence for the existence of an ancient civilization predating the Egyptians is overwhelming, and has been treated in detail by numerous authors. In *New View Over Atlantis*, John Michell explains:

> A great scientific instrument lies sprawled over the entire surface of the globe. At some period, thousands of years ago, almost every corner of the world was visited by people with a particular task to accomplish. With the help of some remarkable power, by which they could cut and raise enormous blocks of stone, these men created vast astronomical instruments, circles of erect pillars, pyramids, underground tunnels, cyclopean stone platforms, all linked together by a network of tracks and alignments, whose course from horizon to horizon was marked by stones, mounds and earthworks.[314]

After presenting overwhelming evidence to support the conclusion that the designers of this ancient world-wide network possessed a sophisticated understanding of the size and shape of our earth, as well as knowledge of earth energies which are not well understood even today, Michell delves into some of the possible reasons for the construction of this globe-spanning grid:

> There is evidence for the existence of a strong tradition of flight in the ancient world with or without the help of airships. [. . .] And the tradition is that the people of a previous age knew the secret of more subtle forces, now totally forgotten, by which solid vehicles, perhaps made of stone like the airship of Mog Ruith, could be transported through the air.

> The indications of a former knowledge of the art of levitating or lightening stone blocks are strong and numerous. No one can say how the monstrous stones, some 70 feet long, of the Baalbek platform in Syria were taken up from their quarry, and even today the problem of moving them would appear almost insoluble. It is also generally admitted that the task of raising from sea level the massive blocks found in the mountain-top cities of the Andes would be beyond the resources of modern technology. The degree of accuracy, comparable to that required of a jeweler, with which the stones of the Great Pyramid were cut and set could at no time within the historical era have been repeated, and all over the world the scale and precision of ancient stonework is of the same remarkable order. Everywhere the stories by which the local people explain the construction of megalithic monuments refer to some magic, often involving the use of sound, by which great stones could be induced to float in the air or to grow lighter and easier to handle as is the case when a stone is moved through water.[315]

In other words, John Michell is here exploring the possibility that the ancient designers, whoever they were, had access to a technology – apparently based upon the manipulation of sound waves and the inherent energies of our planet in conjunction with other solar system bodies – which enabled them to levitate stone, not only to build their massive megalithic structures, but to travel along the "ley lines" that stretch between the earth-energy centers in a gigantic world-encompassing grid.

> Stone levitated by sound could become a flying chariot, moving along the line of a certain magnetic intensity, whose course was marked out on the ground by alignments of stones and earthworks, linked by raised causeways and forest rides. With the earth's magnetic field regulated, and the streams that run through it diverted to conform to straight lines, the stone craft and its navigator could float from centre to centre, picking their way through a canal network of alternating currents and choosing the level of intensity to which their vibrations were attuned.[316]

If this theory is correct, Michell notes, it could explain why the ancients held the knowledge of the celestial motions of the sun, moon, and planets in such high regard, and why many of the most important megalithic sites that form the nodes of this worldwide network incorporate alignments that could enable their designers to predict solar and lunar eclipses with a high degree of accuracy. Because the electromagnetic energy of the sun, and the motions of the other major bodies in our solar system (including the moon), have such an impact on the natural earth energies which the ancients were using for their levitation and travel, the ability to predict their cycles and conjunctions would have been critical to anyone traveling through the air on such stone ships:

> There was one danger to which the aviator on magnetic currents would always be susceptible: that of a sudden and unexpected drop in the level of magnetic activity. Sunset or the moon sinking below the horizon would produce such an effect, but these events can easily be foreseen. Much more dangerous would be an eclipse. This could be why people of the ancient world had such fear of eclipses and attached such importance to their prediction. With the loss of the old power this importance waned together with the whole art of astronomy. The accuracy of the Chaldean astronomers' eclipse predictions was never regained until modern times, and even the memory of the former astronomical achievements became lost. The learned Chinese at the beginning of the Christian era acknowledged that the science of calculating eclipses had degenerated since the time 500 years earlier when it had been exact. An unpredicted eclipse has been the event most dreaded by the Chinese throughout history, and when it took place they shouted, beat gongs and let off fireworks to maintain the power of the dragon current.[317]

The network of ancient alignments noticed by Alfred Watkins in his native England in 1921 and analyzed in John Michell's books has since been clearly demonstrated to be world-encompassing. More recent analysts have perceived that ancient sites – apparently built centuries or even millennia apart and separated from one another by vast oceans and thousands of miles – are incontrovertibly located along lines and great circles which span the surface of our planet.

In articles published on-line, for instance, Jim Alison analyzes the locations of ancient sites around the world and concludes that great circles drawn across our globe link so many significant ancient sacred sites that there is no way to dismiss the occurrence as a coincidence. For any two points on our earth, a "great circle" can be traced which intersects those two sites and which has as its center the center of our planet. Such a great circle, for instance, could be drawn which contained on its perimeter the far-removed sites of the Great Pyramid and the island of Rapa Nui (Easter Island). Jim Alison demonstrates that the perimeter of that great circle also intersects Nazca, Ollantaytambo, Paratoari, and Tassili n'Ajjer – an astonishing revelation which goes a long way towards proving that such sites are either part of an ancient world-wide plan, or that their builders were responding to the grid of natural earth energies described above (or both). He further demonstrates that numerous additional sites are located within one tenth of one degree from the same great circle, including Petra, Persepolis, Khajuraho, Piyay, Sukothai, and Anatom Island.[318]

Mr. Alison presents these remarkable findings on his website in an illustrated article (thirteen web-pages in length) entitled *The Prehistoric Alignment of World Wonders: A New Look at an Old Design*.

Even more remarkable are the relationships that he demonstrates between many of these sites, such as his finding that Ollantaytambo (in Peru) is 108° along the great circle from Giza (in Egypt). As he points out, 108 is an extremely significant number, and the location of these historic sites 108° apart is unlikely to be a coincidence (the idea that the locations of all these sites along a great circle of the globe could be a coincidence is likewise extremely unlikely -- when we find that two of the sites are separated by 108° along a global great circle, the possibility of coincidence becomes even more remote).[319]

The number 108 is an important precessional number, as is the number 72, which Mr. Alison demonstrates to be operating between Giza and other sites. He notes in a different article on the same subject, this one published on Graham Hancock's website, that Giza and the site of Angkor Wat in Cambodia are very nearly 72° apart along the same great circle, and that Easter Island (Rapa Nui) is located at a point on the circle that is very nearly equal angles of arc to Angkor going in one direction and Giza going in the other. Mr. Hancock also discusses the significant separation angles of various sites around the globe (including Rapa Nui, Angkor, and Giza) in his book *Heaven's Mirror* (and movie of the same name).[320]

Also extremely significant is the fact that Easter Island / Rapa Nui is located directly across this great circle from the Indus Valley. This relationship (as well as the one discussed above for Angkor, Rapa Nui, and Giza) can be easily seen in the diagram of the great circle in Mr. Alison's essay. The mysterious (and as-yet undeciphered) writing systems of both of these sites (Rapa Nui and the Indus Valley) are almost certainly related. The undeciphered script of the Indus Valley is generally known as the "Indus Valley Script" and the undeciphered writing of the tablets found on Easter Island (preserved, in fact, by the people living there when the first European ships arrived) is known as "Rongo Rongo" (and the tablets known as "Rongo Rongo Tablets").[321] The similarities between these mysterious writing systems -- separated by half the globe along this great circle discovered by Mr. Alison, as well as by thousands of years of time -- can be clearly seen in an honest comparison of the many remarkably similar glyphs between the two writing systems.

The idea that these sites could be completely unrelated and just somehow happen to lie upon the same great circle of the globe -- at significant intervals on that circle, including angles of arc corresponding to clear precessional numbers – does not seem to be the most likely explanation for the evidence.

In an important book entitled *The Grid of the Gods: the Aftermath of the Cosmic War and the Physics of the Pyramid Peoples*, Joseph P. Farrell and his co-author Scott D. de Hart build upon the analysis of John Michell and conclude that the world-spanning grid of ancient sacred sites suggests that its designers understood the manipulation of the physical energy of the rotating earth and the other major heavenly bodies in our solar system, as well as the manipulation of human consciousness, all through the same earth-encompassing mechanism of carefully-selected sites containing precise celestial alignments.

Drs. Farrell and de Hart provide evidence which indicates that the anomalous yields from the early thermonuclear tests conducted by the US and the Soviet Union may have been produced by a property called *dynamic torsion* produced by the massive rotating bodies of our universe, including our own earth, sun, and the planets and other large bodies that accompany our earth in its travels through space around our sun. Building on the work of Russian astrophysicist Nikolai Kozyrev (1908 – 1983), Drs. Farrell and de Hart argue that the location of a thermonuclear test on our spinning planet – its latitude and longitude – was found to have a profound impact on the yield of the detonation, because the dynamic torsion imparted by massive spinning bodies opens a "gate" of torsion into the thermonuclear reaction.[322]

Based on this, they conclude that the earth along with the sun and other solar system bodies make up a vast "celestial machine." The motions of this machine impact space-time, producing dynamic torsion that is little understood today. However, it is possible – indeed likely – that the ancient predecessor civilization or civilizations (whoever they were) did understand this celestial machine, and that they built the world-spanning grid to tap into its power. Drs. Farrell and de Hart write: "the celestial machine with its component bodies functions in itself as a kind of a grid system, which is mirrored on the Earth by the placement of structures deliberately aligned with celestial markers. It is thus possible that thermonuclear testing, to some degree not fully understood, taps into the actual earth Grid system, as it in turn taps into the celestial one."[323]

Citing John Michell, they argue that the world-encompassing network of sites was not only designed to tap into physical energy, but also spiritual energy: that it manipulated not only "the physical medium" but also human consciousness itself. Drs. Farrell and de Hart write:

> *Bloody, and Human, Sacrifices* were also associated with *some* aspects and sites on the world Grid – one need only think of the blood and gore of the Meso-American sites – but not with all of them. As noted, Michell suspected that this was due to the concept that somehow such sacrifices were able to intensify the magical manipulation of whatever forces the ancients thought to be involved at the site. It was thus implied that the technology of such sites itself, which we have argued was for the ultimate purpose of the manipulation of the physical medium itself, may also have been involved in the manipulation of consciousness, and sacrifice was somehow a means to this end, though in ways we have yet to examine.[324]

This level of sophistication – to the point of designing a world-wide network which taps into the space-time impacts caused by our massive, rotating sun and the whirling planets of our solar system, in conjunction with our own rotating and orbiting planet – goes far beyond anything countenanced by conventional academia and currently-accepted historical timelines and models.

Both the work of John Michell and that of Drs. Farrell and de Hart suggest that the manipulation of this "earth and solar-system energy" and of human consciousness were somehow related. In *New View over Atlantis*, John Michell writes that: "The Druids in common with the shamans of Asia and North America are said to have accomplished magical flights, often from those very mounds and hilltops where the great heroes of mythology achieved their apotheosis. There may be something about such places which attracts those forces capable of modifying the normal influences of gravity, or which, alternatively, reacts upon an intensified field of human magnetism to produce circumstances conducive to levitation."[325]

It is reasonable to conclude that the extremely sophisticated knowledge of the predecessor civilization included both the manipulation of the physical world (possibly to the extent of being able to levitate massive stones and even travel along ley lines on ships powered by an energy field which we today do not understand) and the manipulation of aspects of human consciousness (almost certainly to the point of enabling out-of-body shamanic travel, perhaps for the purpose of conversing with one's own DNA as well as that of plants and other creatures, or with the *neters* that exist in the "implicate" medium that underlies the "holographic" or "explicate" universe which our consciousness normally inhabits).

The thesis of an advanced predecessor civilization (or civilizations) which possessed such knowledge may seem far-fetched to those who have grown accustomed to the timelines pushed on students in all levels of the conventional academic matrix, and supported by almost all the books written by conventional authors purporting to explore mankind's ancient past, but we have already seen abundant evidence which supports just such a thesis. Many aspects of ancient Egyptian civilization – a culture which has left us a treasure-trove of archaeological and textual evidence – appear to point to the same conclusion.

Interestingly enough, the cosmology that appears to be displayed in ancient Egyptian texts such as the Pyramid Texts points to their knowledge of the "holographic universe" concept as well. We will see that aspects of this very ancient knowledge – including the importance of initiatory or shamanic out-of-body travel (probably the product of the predecessor civilization) – appear to have survived all the way into the Roman period before being stamped out during the fourth century AD.

While certain aspects of ancient Egyptian civilization clearly indicate that some portion of the knowledge of this more ancient "predecessor" civilization survived in some form into dynastic Egypt, it is equally apparent that much of that predecessor civilization's knowledge did not survive. There are some indications of world travel or trade during dynastic Egypt – including alleged traces of tobacco and coca fiber among the mummy wrappings of individuals from dynastic times – but there is little evidence to suggest that the ancient Egyptians were piloting levitating stone vehicles across the oceans, for example. However, much of the evidence from ancient Egypt suggests that they were performing astonishing feats of engineering, possibly using technologies we cannot fully explain. And, as we have already seen, it is quite reasonable to conclude that the science of deliberate, out-of-body "shamanic" travel was well-understood far into the dynastic period, that historical kings guided by the priests undertook shamanic travel, and that this practice was somehow extremely central to the preservation of Egyptian civilization for millennia.

Ancient Egypt provides us with perhaps the greatest wealth of evidence in the form of monuments, art, and inscriptions to have survived the ravages of time of all the world's most ancient known civilizations. Many who have analyzed this evidence agree that it points to the existence of a predecessor civilization of even greater antiquity and possibly even greater sophistication.

In fact, as many observers including R.A. Schwaller de Lubicz and John Anthony West have observed, key elements of the civilization of ancient Egypt appear to spring almost fully-developed into existence with no clear forerunners, suggesting, as John Anthony West writes, that "Egypt did not 'develop' her civilisation, but inherited it."[326]

He continues, "The implications of this alternative are obvious. If the coherent, complete, and interrelated system of science, religion, art and philosophy of Egypt was not developed by the Egyptians but inherited (and perhaps reformulated and redesigned to suit their need), that system came from a prior civilization possessing a high order of knowledge."[327] It is clearly possible that this prior civilization possessed a higher order of knowledge, and that only some of their ancient knowledge was passed on to successor civilizations such as dynastic Egypt, but it is clear from some of the foregoing examples (such as their ability to undertake shamanic travel, their feats of advanced architectural engineering, their sophisticated medical knowledge, and their profound spiritual wisdom, which contains hints that they understood aspects of what we call "quantum physics" and that they would have found the "holographic universe" theory familiar as well) that Egypt at least inherited some understanding of the sophisticated cosmology we've been discussing, and some knowledge of the techniques of traversing between the visible and invisible realms for the enhancement of the kingdom and for the enlightenment of the individual traveler as well.

Closely tied to the concept of the Duat in ancient Egypt was the concept of the *Akhet*, another aspect of the unseen world, but one of spiritual illumination – the place where the human soul becomes an *akh* or shining spirit.[328] While it is difficult from the evidence we have at hand to know what may have become of the "prior civilization" that existed before dynastic Egypt, it is clear that they left their successor civilizations with techniques for achieving at least some level of illumination or enlightenment – of transforming into an *akh*. Some aspects of this knowledge appear to have survived into the end of the ancient period in the Hermetic tradition and in the Hellenistic mystery cults, and may still survive today in some form in regions of the world where it was not stamped out (the techniques of shamanism, for example, appear to have a direct connection to the rites that took place during the early Egyptian dynasties). The remnants of this knowledge, however, were very clearly stamped out in the regions of the world that became known as "the west." While the events that marked the departure of the "prior civilization" may have taken place so far back in time that little or no historical record from that transition survives, the stamping out of the technology that they passed on to Egypt can be dated more accurately, and they took place during centuries from which we do have sufficient knowledge to piece together what might have happened.

Based on the fact that the "shamanic" knowledge involving the ability to journey to the Duat and to transform the soul into an *akh* involved spiritual illumination or enlightenment or consciousness, we can broadly label the forces that oppose this knowledge and seek to suppress or actually eliminate it the enemies of illumination, enlightenment, or consciousness. These forces may have been in operation long before the time of the conquest of Jerusalem, and indeed they probably were, but we can begin to clearly see in the historical record a concerted effort to oppose, suppress, and eliminate this knowledge during the centuries following the conquest of Jerusalem.

If Ralph Ellis is correct, the Hyksos kings who left northern Egypt were characterized by a virulent opposition to the idea of multiple gods. In his shamanic out-of-body travel, according to Jeremy Naydler's theory, the living king entered the unseen realm where he encountered the gods – or *neters*, in the ancient Egyptian – as well as numerous other spirit beings. Basing his description on the Pyramid Texts themselves, Naydler writes:

> Inhabiting these inner worlds are a number of different spiritual beings. There are the dead, the royal ancestors in particular, who come to meet the king as he stands on the threshold of the spirit world (utt.306). There are also helping spirits, in the form of spirit wives who consort with the king (utt. 205), spirit mothers who suckle him (utts. 41-42, 211, 269, and 308) and spirit guides who guide him through the Otherworld regions (both Sothis and Wepwawet in utt. 302). Various gods observe the arrival of the king, welcome him, and may also assist him in his ascent to heaven by providing or holding a celestial ladder (utts. 271, 305, 306, and 269). There are also formidable opponents, whose wish seems only to obstruct the king [. . .].
>
> For the Egyptians, then, the spiritual dimension is full of beings. The breakthrough in plane is a breakthrough not into simplicity but into a complex and multifaceted world that presents many challenges to the human being who accomplishes it. The spirit world is a dangerous world that requires both knowledge and skill to negotiate, and not a little magic power. [. . .].[329]

A reading of Mircea Eliade's *Shamanism* will provide abundant confirmation of the fact that the shamanic view of the unseen world resembles very closely the view described above. Perhaps that is because this is the way a human consciousness understands the "implicate order" when it somehow reaches beyond the bounds of the "hologram." We have already seen that Lucy Wyatt has made the connection between the Sed-festival journey of the Egyptian king and the *ayahuasca*-impelled journey into another state of consciousness taken by Jeremy Narby, who reported an encounter with a pair of enormous snakes who were able to communicate with him.[330] Perhaps when we journey to the "implicate order" we are inclined to interpret the "wavelengths" we find there in terms of the types of beings and objects we encounter here in the "explicate order" of our more-familiar "physical" world – in other words, if we encounter a strand of DNA, perhaps we interpret it as "snakes that can talk."

Michael Talbot explores this possibility in his book on the holographic universe. He writes that Robert Monroe, a television executive who began experiencing OBEs in the 1950s and published two books about his travels, *Journeys Out of the Body* and *Far Journeys* believed that both we and the universe we inhabit is really a "vibrational pattern [comprised] of many interacting and resonating frequencies" which "our mind converts into various holographic forms."[331]

Talbot notes that while out-of-body travelers can frequently describe the remote locations they visit accurately, there are occasionally strange errors in their observations, such as seeing some object in the wrong color, and that this pattern of slight inconsistencies may support the holographic explanation, if it is caused by the fact that the out-of-body traveler is now perceiving with their consciousness and not their physical sense organs, and therefore may make slight errors because they have not yet mastered "the art of converting the frequency domain into a seemingly objective construct of reality."[332]

Thus, it is possible that the spiritual beings encountered in travels to the Duat are the way our minds interpret the energy fields we encounter there, often doing so in "terms" that come from our experience in this world. An out-of-body experience recorded later in Michael Talbot's book seems to support this conclusion. Describing an ayahuasca experience undergone by anthropologist Michael Harner in 1961, Talbot writes that Harner described encountering "dragonlike beings" which he later described as being reminiscent of DNA, although at the time (in 1961), "he knew nothing of DNA." Harner also recounts that when he recounted his experience and what the beings had told him to a Conibo shaman, the shaman replied "Oh, they're always saying that."[333]

This experience suggests that there is something objective that individuals are experiencing when they travel into the "implicate order" realm. It also provides a fascinating parallel to the "talking snakes" Narby encountered, which he also believes might have something to do with DNA, and supports the idea that journeys into the unseen realm might somehow involve "communication" with DNA, either one's own or the DNA of other organisms. This suggests that such travels could explain aspects of myth, such as the Egyptians view of the Duat realm as the realm inhabited by the ancestors (DNA, of course, comes from and embodies aspects of our ancestors) and as the realm of possibility, where things exist in their "kernel" form.

It is also possible, of course, that travelers to the unseen world are in fact encountering other consciousnesses, including the consciousnesses of individuals who are no longer living. The number of near-death experiences in which the subject encounters deceased persons known to them – and, in some cases, persons known to them whom they did not know at the time were deceased but whom they later learned had died not long before the NDE in question – seems to confirm this possibility.[334] And, it is also possible that travelers to the unseen realm encounter other conscious entities as well. None of these possibilities precludes the possibility that some of the "beings" they encounter there have something to do with DNA.

Finally, it is important to again point out that these discussions of shamanic travel and the holographic universe model do not contradict the important work of Alvin Boyd Kuhn in his interpretation of the ancient sacred scriptures, and his thesis that these scriptures consistently encode the esoteric message that our physical bodies each hide an immaterial spirit, which cannot be seen or felt but which is real nonetheless, which came down from an immaterial spirit realm in order to be encased in matter, and which will return one day (at our physical death) to the spirit world. This truth, Kuhn argues, is usually coded in language which calls our incarnation a "death," and our travels through this material realm the voyage through the "underworld," or the "realm of the dead," presided over by Osiris. This is because, for the immaterial spirit, the incarnation in this mortal coil, this body of clay, is a kind of a "death," and the end of the physical life is a kind of "re-birth" for the spirit.

However, as has been argued previously, Kuhn's thesis harmonizes quite well with the theory that these ancient texts also imply knowledge of the techniques of ecstasy and shamanic travel. Participation in such travel during our sojourn in this life would only serve to reinforce the truth that we come from another realm, a spiritual realm – the very message which Kuhn argues is the purpose of the scriptures and ancient sacred traditions (they were written to teach us the truth that we forget when we take the dizzying plunge from the worlds of air and fire into this world of water and earth, according to Kuhn's interpretation).[335]

That Kuhn is inclined to interpret many or all of the half-animal demons encountered in texts such as the Egyptian Book of the Dead as symbolic of the soul's prime danger in this incarnate life, the danger of becoming wedded too closely with the animal nature in which it is entombed (this body), and through entanglement with the lusts of the flesh fall into a near-animal condition instead of learning lessons needed for greater spiritual transformation, does not in any way invalidate the possibility that the spiritual realm itself is also peopled with other spiritual beings, some of which may be malevolent.[336] Kuhn himself seems to admit as much when he discusses the famous episode of Genesis 6, in which the "sons of God saw the daughters of men that they were fair: and they took them wives of all which they chose" (Genesis 6:2). Of this incident, Kuhn writes "This is not empty imagery. It has had historical actualization in a strange way."[337]

In any event, it is possible to speculate that acceptance of the "holographic universe" and travel to the unseen realm goes hand-in-hand with the acceptance of the existence of multiple *neters* and spiritual beings, and that conversely the rejection of the holographic model and the rejection of multiple gods go hand-in-hand.

Where this rejection of the holographic universe crept in to the cultures in possession of the scriptures that became the Old and New Testaments is difficult to say for certain. It is possible that the Egyptians who left Lower Egypt (northern Egypt) for the land that became Judea left over just such a rejection of the old gods, as Ralph Ellis maintains. It is possible that it had to do with the time of the captivity under Assyria and later under the Babylonians. It seems clear that the tension between the belief in multiple gods and the rejection of the belief in multiple gods runs through the Old Testament in particular.

It is also possible that the clue we have discussed above, from the works of Josephus, indicates that those who left Egypt were aware of the motion of precession, and held that its metaphysical or theological implications involved the rejection of the previous system of celestial allegory and its "gods and goddesses" enacting the message found in the stars. Those who left may have kept the stories and scriptures which had come from the old system, while rejecting the esoteric "as above, so below" system which held the original key to their meaning.

It also seems clear from the analysis already presented that the Old Testament contains clear evidence of an underlying knowledge of the "holographic universe." How literally was it interpreted during the centuries before the conquest of Jerusalem in AD 70? We cannot be sure. It is possible that an initiated elite understood the deeper "holographic" or even shamanic interpretation of the texts, while teaching a literal interpretation to the masses. It is also possible that different sects or schools held to different interpretations of the texts, and struggled with one another over them, and that a literal interpretation eventually won out. The struggles between the Saducees and the Pharisees described in the New Testament gospels may be indicators of exactly this type of interpretive struggle.

We have already seen that using the scriptures themselves as a source of historical evidence is problematic. We have also seen evidence that some of the authors of the New Testament scriptures appear to include hints that they knew that the Old Testament scriptures were not intended to be interpreted in a literal and historical fashion (for example, the quotation attributed to Jesus that "God is not the God of the dead, but of the living").

Leaving the question of "the break" for the present, it is quite clear that the shamanic-holographic world-view we have been proposing was well understood during dynastic Egypt. We have also seen that this world-view was probably understood at an even more sophisticated level by the "predecessor" civilization or civilizations which almost certainly predated Egypt and which bequeathed some of its advanced knowledge (perhaps in a diminished form or in an imperfectly-understood form) to the civilizations of ancient Egypt and the other ancient cultures of the earth.

The world-view we are describing is a world-view which understands the universe as "holographic" (to use our modern metaphor – ancient cultures of course used different means of describing it): holographic in that the individual "microcosm" reflects and embodies the entirety of the "macrocosm," and holographic in that the "unfolded" or "explicate" realm which we inhabit is seen as springing from the "folded" or "seedlike" or "implicate" realm (the realm that the Egyptians called the Duat). It was also a world-view which valued the techniques of crossing from the explicate into the implicate and saw such travel as beneficial to the consciousness and well-being of the traveler and his or her community.

Not only was this holographic world-view on display in Egypt, but there are reasons to suspect that it was fairly widespread in "the west" in late antiquity in cultures that were probably influenced by Egypt. We can see traces of the same aspects of this world-view among the secret, initiatory, participatory rituals and sacred traditions which the ancient Greeks and Romans called "the mysteries" (*mysteria*; they were also commonly referred to as *orgia* or "rites" and as *teletai* or "initiations," somewhat interchangeably) and which are today referred to in aggregate as "the mystery religions" or "the mystery cults."[338]

The content and meaning of the *mysteria* remains a disputed subject to this day, largely because those who participated in these rites (the initiated) were sworn to secrecy as to their content, under the threat of severe punishment and opprobrium.

Further, as Hugh Bowden has argued in his *Mystery Cults of the Ancient World* (2010), it is possible and even likely that many (or all) of the participants and even many (or all) of the officiants of the rites did not "understand" them in the sense that we might expect, because they were primarily "imagistic" as opposed to "doctrinal." These terms, Bowden explains, are recent categories proposed by anthropologists to contrast "two distinct ways in which experience and understanding of the divine is transmitted through religion."[339] He explains these two different "modes" as follows:

> The imagistic mode is characterized by very infrequent, but very dramatic, ritual events. [. . .] The imagistic mode of religion can be contrasted with the doctrinal mode, normally associated with larger, more hierarchical communities. Mainstream Christianity is typical of the doctrinal mode, involving regular rituals repeated week-by-week or day-by-day throughout the year. Christian services involve low levels of arousal when compared to the Baktaman initiations [which are offered as an example of the imagistic mode], but they also offer clear verbal explanations of what they are about, and through them worshippers acquire an authorized account of the nature of the divine and their relationship to it.

Infrequent intense events, once experienced, are never forgotten. The memory of this kind of event is called an episodic or 'flashbulb' memory. In contrast, doctrinal religion works with semantic memory, that is, the kind of memory that allows people to carry out activities like driving a car or riding a bicycle – one remembers how to do these things not because of a single moment of revelation but as a result of habituation through repeated actions.

It is characteristic also of imagistic religious experience that it is non-verbal – those who have gone through the ritual are able to reflect on what took place, but they are generally unable to communicate the experience to others.[340]

Bowden proposes that these "modes" defined by recent anthropology are helpful in the examination of the mysteries – suggesting that these ancient rites fit the description of the imagistic rather than the doctrinal.

The anthropologists who came up with these two "modes" as a tool for categorizing the "experience and understanding of the divine" follow the conventional framework of human history (which argues a fairly steady progression from "primitive" to "more advanced") and posit the "imagistic" as "the earliest form of religious experience" with "origins [that] are bound up with the earliest appearance of art in the cave paintings of the Upper Paleolithic period, around 30,000 years ago."[341] However, the segmentation proposed in this chapter – progressing from most ancient and most sophisticated, to the period of our earliest accepted history (dynastic Egypt and other extremely ancient civilizations up through late antiquity), to the period we are in today in which much of this knowledge was lost or deliberately stamped out – turns this conventional understanding on its head. Under this alternative paradigm, the *mysteria* of late antiquity were the last widespread *western* manifestation of an ancient – and extremely sophisticated – understanding of the holographic universe world-view, which was descended in some way from the "predecessor civilization" (or civilizations) that knew the size and shape of the earth, as well as the means of tapping into its earth energies and the energies of the other massive denizens of the solar system, for the purpose of manipulating the physical environment (to include, possibly, flight) and for the purpose of manipulating human consciousness.

There are several aspects of the ancient mysteries which support this theory. I believe that these aspects have remained un-remarked upon by most academic analysts of the ancient mysteries to date. The aspects of the ancient rites which suggest the continuation in some form of the world-view described above, possessing of a "holographic universe" cosmography and the ability to deliberately cross into the realm of the "implicate order," include:

- Clear macrocosm / microcosm symbology, in the incorporation of deities and actors who clearly embody elements of the celestial machinery in much the same way that the scriptures of the Old and New Testament have been shown to incorporate celestial machinery and portray them as characters and entities.
- Techniques of ecstasy, in the incorporation of orgies, rites and rituals through which the participants and/or the officiants would cross into the realm that the

Egyptians called the Duat, and experience a close encounter with the *neters* or gods.

- Shamanic themes, including the depiction of people with the heads of animals, a common feature of shamanic imagery and experience, and one which clearly relates to the themes explored by Ovid in his *Metamorphoses* that we have touched on previously, a work which can be seen as revealing a "holographic" world-view on many levels.

- In some cases, rites and rituals in which the boundaries between masculine and feminine are confused or inverted, and men take on the aspects of women or women take on the aspects of men, which is a theme that we have seen manifested in the *Metamorphoses* of Ovid as well, and which suggests the liquidity of the boundaries of the world which we take to be solid but which the holographic world-view suggests is something quite other than solid (and which is, as we have already noted, a sub-current in shamanic cultures which has been remarked upon by Mircea Eliade and other chroniclers of shamanic tradition).

- The transformation of the consciousness of the initiates or participants, to the point that they realized that this physical world is not the only world nor even the "most real" world, and that physical death is not the end of life: a revelation which has the power to transform the rest of their life after it is internalized.

Each of these points strongly suggests that the ancient *mysteria* (or *orgia* or *teletai*) were in some way connected to or descended from the rites of ancient Egypt which also evinced understanding of the holographic world-view. We will look at some evidence for each of the five points in turn (although not in great detail – much more could be said, but the scope here is simply to prove that the holographic world-view survived in the west in fairly widespread form all the way through the end of the third century AD and the beginning of the fourth, before it was eradicated or lost). However, in addition to all of the above five areas, we will also see that ancient art associated with the mysteries also incorporates very clear costume imagery reminiscent of the Sed festival rites of ancient Egypt – a very powerful clue that the *mysteria* should be understood as a continuation of the knowledge of ancient Egypt, or at least that they were closely related to and perhaps came from the same source at a much earlier time.

This new understanding of the mysteries should dispel the notion that they are a "more primitive" form of religious experience that was eventually displaced by the more modern "doctrinal" form. In fact, it may well be that the "modern" doctrinal-form religions are usurpers of a sacred tradition that was originally an imagistic *mysteria*-type tradition. In other words, it may be that the stories of the Old and New Testament were imagistic enactments in a system of cosmic understanding that we would today describe as "shamanic," but which were later hijacked and used as the foundation for a literal and dogmatic religious system. Nevertheless, the distinction between doctrinal and imagistic modes is valuable and can help us to understand how the mysteries differ from the form of religious experience that ultimately came to dominate "the west" and why their meaning remains in dispute to this day.

We will examine the mysteries and their importance to "the case of the suppression of shamanic holographic consciousness" more closely in the following chapter.

12
The mysteries

The whole intent of the drama and the Mystery ceremonials was to bring the force of the most impressive living realization home to the inner consciousness of the audience personnel, and to stamp in the most vivid manner upon the susceptibilities of the participants the deepest sense of the incarnational drama in which all mortals are adventuring.

Alvin Boyd Kuhn,
Who is this King of Glory?[342]

In his book *Ancient Mystery Cults* (1987), Walter Burkert argues that the ancient mysteries should not be called "religions," because that term conveys all kinds of implications which do not apply to the ancient *mysteria*. He writes:

In this book a decidedly pagan approach to the ancient mysteries is followed, which abandons the concept of mystery religions from the start. Initiation at Eleusis or worship of Isis or Mithras does not constitute adherence to a religion in the sense we are familiar with, being confronted with mutually exclusive religions such as Judaism, Christianity, and Islam. Whereas in these religious there has been much conscious emphasis on self-definition and on demarcating one religion as against the other, in the pre-Christian epoch the various forms of worship, including new and foreign gods in general and the institution of mysteries in particular, are never exclusive; they appear as varying forms, trends, or options within the one disparate yet continuous conglomerate of ancient religion.[343]

Evidence suggests that the mysteries were being practiced by the eighth century BC, and possibly much earlier. The earliest we have evidence of today come from ancient Greece, although there is evidence of mysteries in Anatolia that is nearly as old. There is evidence of Bronze Age occupation of the site of Eleusis, home of one of the most important ancient mystery cults, from a period prior to 1,200 BC, but whether or not the Mysteries of Eleusis were practiced at that time is not currently known from the evidence available.

While there were significant differences between the mysteries, stretching as they did across many centuries (at least from the eight century BC through the fourth century AD), and across many geographical regions and cultures, there are distinctive features which enable scholars to discuss them in the aggregate as well as individually. The mysteries usually involved ritual initiation, during which secret rites were performed which could not be revealed to non-initiates. In some of the cults, notably the Eleusinian Mysteries, these initiations only took place once a year (at a festival of eight days), while at others initiations could take place any time during the year.

During the initiations, initiates were ritually mocked, were immersed in darkness punctuated by light as well as loud music and other startling noises, and were subjected to frightening or startling experiences in a process which was described by various ancient participants as somehow terrifying. In the Eleusinian Mysteries at least, it seems that initiates were required to search for something in the dark, calling loudly, while officiants alternately revealed scenes or images using torches and bright bursts of light, and then the initiations culminated in the appearance of the goddesses Demeter and Persephone (or Kore, the Maiden – each of these goddesses were addressed by different names throughout the ancient world, and particularly in the various places in which they played a central role in mystery cult practices). Also at the culmination of the initiation, secret and sacred objects of veneration were revealed to the initiates, although what these were also remains a subject of debate.

The deities at the center of the mysteries varied, but the most well-known and widely followed appear to have been the mysteries involving Demeter and Persephone (or, in some cases, just one of these two figures), the mysteries involving Dionysus, those centered around the cult of Orpheus, and the mysteries involving the Great Mother (also known as the Mother of the Gods, or the Great Goddess, or the Queen of Heaven and sometimes by specific names including Cybele and Atargatis, with evidence that at least some of the ancients identified this Great Goddess with the Greek goddesses Rhea and Demeter, the Roman goddess Hera, the Babylonian Ishtar, the Sumerian Inanna, and the Egyptian Isis). There were also mysteries of possibly very ancient gods whose identity is still in question, and who may have been unknown even to the ancient participants in their *mysteria*. These unknown deities were sometimes called the Great Gods, the Nameless Gods, the Kabeiroi, and the Corybantes. Finally, elements of the *mysteria* appeared to take form later, in the Roman and Hellenistic periods, in the appearance of the mysteries of Isis, Serapis, and Mithras, as well as other less well-known deities.

While modern commentators have shed varying degrees of light on aspects of the mysteries, few if any have commented on the obviously celestial component of the mysteries – a component which may be one of the most important aspects for grasping the significance of these ancient rites.

For example, commentators spend a great deal of time trying to argue the various origins of the Great Goddess, discussing her probable emergence from the eastern portion of the Mediterranean at an early date, as well as describing her distinctive accompanying symbology (she is often depicted seated upon a throne, accompanied by a lion, or pulled in a chariot by lions, and holding a cymbal as well as in some cases a sheaf of wheat). The clear zodiacal aspects of this imagery, however, are almost never discussed.

An 1889 drawing of a 4th century BC relief of
the Mother of the Gods, seated on a throne with
a lion and a crescent arch.

In the circle of the zodiac, the constellation Virgo follows immediately behind Leo the Lion: Virgo, the constellation we have seen before being portrayed in myth and sacred scripture in various roles including Eve the mother of all mankind, Mary the Queen of Heaven who is present at the crucifixion, Iphigenia the daughter sacrificed at the crossing of the Argive ships (but saved at the last moment and replaced by a substitutionary stag, which is probably the Centaur constellation below Virgo which as we have already discussed looks very much like a stag), and Diana the virgin goddess who turns Actaeon into a stag.

The imagery of the Great Goddess clearly suggests Virgo. She is often depicted as seated on a throne, and the stars themselves can be seen to suggest a seated posture. In the star chart below, the constellation is shown recumbent, as it appears when crossing the sky and passing its zenith, but if rotated counter-clockwise (as it appears when rising in the east) then it clearly could be interpreted as representing a seated goddess.

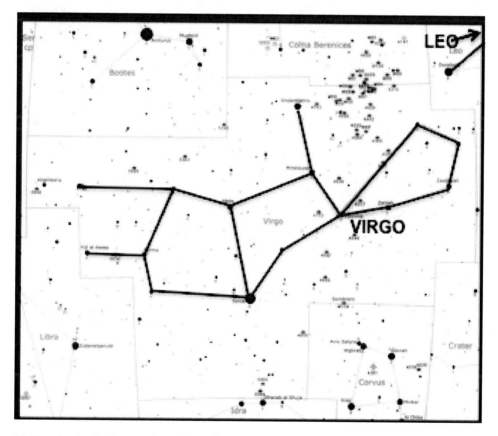

Notice also in the image above how closely Virgo follows Leo: the tail of the Lion (with the bright star Denebola) is visible in the corner of the chart above just to the right and up from the head of the Virgin.

The image below is from the Pergamon, from an altar built in the second century BC, and shows Rhea or Cybele, the Great Goddess, riding on a lion. Her posture is very similar to the constellation pictured above – slightly recumbent, with an arm extended, and a bend at the waist that very closely resembles the bend in the constellation of the Virgin.

Rhea / Cybele riding on a lion, Pergamon altar.
2ⁿᵈ century BC. Image: Wikimedia commons.

Scholars often write that Cybele the Great Mother originated in Anatolia or Phrygia, regions in modern-day Turkey. This area is not far from ancient Babylon and Sumer, where the great goddesses were Ishtar and Inanna, both of whom were associated with love and sexuality, and both of whom were associated with lions. The famous Ishtar Gate, of course, features lion imagery. Scholars of ancient mythology from this region associate Ishtar and Inanna, as well as the Ugaritic Ashtoreth or Asherah.

Thus, it is certainly possible that the Great Goddess imagery from Greece and Rome came from further to the east. However, it is also possible that all these regions are reflecting celestial imagery that was passed down from some predecessor civilization whose influence was felt both in ancient Mesopotamia but also in ancient Egypt. The Egyptian goddess Isis is depicted in the stele of Qadesh as riding on a lion (see the image below). She is also holding a sheaf of some plant (probably papyrus) in the hand which normally holds a sheaf of wheat in later depictions of the zodiac constellation of Virgo.

The Stele of Qadesh is a stele thought to have been erected by Seti I of Egypt, whose reign is thought to have been from 1290 BC until 1279 BC. It was found in modern-day Syria, and is thought to have commemorated an Egyptian military campaign by Seti, who was the son of Rameses I and the father of Rameses II.

The fact that the celestial imagery is being depicted in this way at this early date is significant, since many modern scholars try to argue that the zodiac imagery was a much later creation. Note that the image of the goddess above has a serpent in the hand that is not holding the sheaf. The sheaf corresponds to Virgo's upper hand, which is often depicted as holding a sheaf. Below the constellation of Virgo, however, is the constellation Hydra, a long and sinuous serpent of stars which has on its back both Crater the Cup and Corvus the Crow. Thus, the depiction of a serpent in the hand opposite the sheaf in the ancient Egyptian stele above is almost certainly related to the stars of the Virgin, and it shows that the zodiac symbology we have to this day was already well established by the reign of Seti I, in the thirteenth century BC.

Further east, the Hindu goddess Durga is also often described or depicted as riding a lion to slay her enemies. Below is a frieze from India which shows Durga on a lion. Note again the prominently extended arm (in this case holding what appears to be either a bow or a sword) which is consistent with the constellation Virgo, as well as the angle or bend of the hip which is likewise consistent with the heavenly Virgin.

The Hindu goddess Durga, riding on a lion.
image: Wikimedia Commons, http://en.wikipedia.org/wiki/File:Durga_Slays_Mahisasura.jpg

What is emerging is the picture of a very consistent ancient series of celestial goddesses, some of them found in very ancient cultures (those of India, Sumer, and Egypt are among the most ancient known to conventional historians), suggesting either ancient cross-contact among them, or else the possibility of an even more ancient predecessor culture which influenced all of them, and from which they may in some way be descended.

We can also see that the mystery cults of the ancient world, right up to the fourth century, appear to have been in some way carrying on a very ancient tradition that goes right back to the predecessor civilization.

Many other mysteries from all around the ancient world have similar celestial connections, and again most of these are similarly unremarked-upon by modern scholars. Despite overlooking the celestial imagery surrounding the Great Mother cults, Hugh Bowden in his *Mystery Cults of the Ancient World* does identify the possibility that the "Nameless Gods" or *Kabeiroi*, associated with the Mysteries of Samothrace, Lemnos, and Boetia, while associated by different ancient writers with numerous different gods and goddesses, were associated with the Dioscuri by at least some ancients.

First, he brings forth evidence that the Nameless Gods were not always identified by the name Kabeiroi. The Mysteries of Samothrace were celebrated for deities identified only as the Great Gods in any of the inscriptions found at the site itself so far.[344] However, Herodotus makes a reference to "the rites of the Kabeiroi which the Samothracians learned from the Pelasgians and now practice."[345] Other ancient writers also identify the unnamed gods of the Mysteries of Samothrace with the Kabeiroi and also with the Corybantes, although Bowden points out that Strabo (who lived from about 64 BC until AD 24) throws some doubt upon the accuracy of this identification.[346]

Bowden cites ancient evidence for identifying the Great Gods of the rites of Samothrace and the Kabeiroi of Lemnos and Boetia with some or all of the following: the Mother, Demeter (the Mother and Demeter were also conflated by some ancients), Persephone, Prometheus and his son Etnaeus, Hades, Hermes, Pan, Cadmus, and finally the Dioscuri, or Youths of Zeus: Castor and Polydeuces, or Castor and Pollux as they are called in Latin.[347]

Castor and Pollux, of course, are quite clearly identifiable as having a celestial counterpart, just as we have seen the Great Goddess to have a celestial counterpart in Virgo. Castor and Pollux form the important zodiac constellation Gemini the Twins, the starry heads of whom to this day bear the names Castor and Pollux.

Bowden notes this celestial connection during his discussion of two surviving ancient inscriptions which appear to at least suggest the identification of the Kabeiroi and the Twins. First he points to an inscription in an ancient sanctuary on the island of Delos which was known anciently as both the Kabeireion and the Samothrakeion. The inscription calls the priests of that place "priests of the Great Gods of Samothrace, the Dioscuri, the Kabeiroi," although Bowden argues that this may perhaps best be read as a noncommittal and somewhat questioning statement, meaning "Gods of this sanctuary, whether you be the Great Gods of Samothrace, or the Dioscuri, or the Kabeiroi."[348]

He then notes a coin which has survived into modern times, from the island of Syros in the Aegean Sea, bearing the image of two young men, each with a star on his head, and an inscription wrapping around the outer edge of the image which reads, "The Divine Kabeiroi of Syros."[349] Bowden writes, "This is the usual iconography for the Dioscuri, who are associated with the constellation of Gemini, with its two brightest stars, Castor and Pollux, represented as the heads of two brothers."[350]

Thus the clear celestial connections of the important mystery figure of the Great Goddess are not an anomaly – we see that at least some ancient sources identified other mysteries with celestial figures as well.

Let us examine the importance of the zodiac constellation of Gemini the Twins, associated with the mysteries of the Kabeiroi, more closely. In *Hamlet's Mill*, Giorgio de Santillana and Hertha von Dechend present extensive evidence for their thesis that virtually all of what we think of as "ancient religion" or belief descended from a coherent celestial model of enormous antiquity. According to their thesis, all of the central myths of the ancient mystery religions could be explained as referring to the great celestial machinery of the heavens.[351]

De Santillana and von Dechend demonstrate that the precessional mechanism which we have seen to be central to so many ancient myth systems underlies the ancient myth of Osiris, killed by his brother Set and his body thrown into the sea, to be avenged by Horus the son of Osiris – a pattern which surfaces over and over through history, for example in the story of Hamlet (whose father was killed by his brother, leaving Hamlet to play the role of Horus and avenge his murdered father).[352] Modern readers may notice that the pattern is quite clearly evident in the Disney movie, the *Lion King*.

Osiris is associated with Orion, and Set with Taurus the Bull and its red star Aldebaran (the color red was associated with Set by some ancient writers, including Plutarch). The diagrams below show how the delaying action of precession can be allegorized as Set "drowning" his brother Osiris and usurping his throne.

In the precessional age *prior* to the Age of Taurus, the sun rose in the constellation of Gemini on the morning of the March equinox (which is the spring equinox for the northern hemisphere). The situation is shown in the simplified drawing below. Note that the mighty constellation of Orion – the constellation containing the greatest ratio of bright stars per total stars out of any constellation – can be clearly seen coming up above the horizon along with the Twins when the sun makes its appearance on the equinox morning. The horizon is represented in this simplified diagram by the arc of the horizontal dark line.

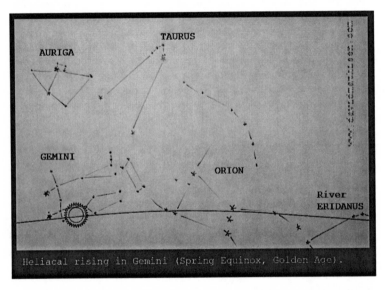

Heliacal rising in Gemini (Spring Equinox, Golden Age).

However, as the centuries roll by and the action of precession delays the sky by a tiny fraction of a degree each year, the background stars will be delayed on the morning of the spring equinox by a tiny amount. We can represent this in the diagram by depicting the morning sunrise and the line of the horizon as slowly creeping "upwards" in the diagram (because the turning of the background sky with its constellation is "delayed").

After an entire precessional age, the diagram would look like the second picture, shown below. Now the sky has been delayed to the point that the sunrise on the March equinox is in Taurus instead of Gemini -- a new age has dawned. Orion and Gemini are still below the horizon, but Taurus (as well as Auriga the Charioteer) can be clearly seen above the horizon before the sun pops up.

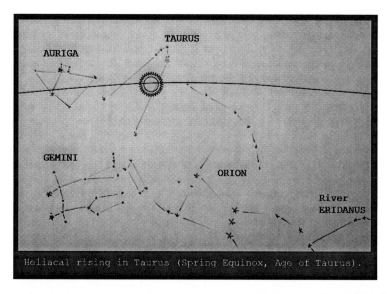

Heliacal rising in Taurus (Spring Equinox, Age of Taurus).

In mythological terms, we can describe this transition as Orion (or Osiris) being drowned or deposed or otherwise disposed-of, and the new usurping king Taurus (or Set, associated with the red star Aldebaran in Taurus) taking his place.

We know that the ancient Egyptians associated the bright star Sirius (the brightest star in the heavens, besides our sun) with the goddess Isis, consort of Osiris. Sirius is located below Orion in the images above, not visible below the lower border of the image. In the myths, Isis bewails the death of Osiris, and then goes on a world-wide search for his body.

This search for the "hidden god" or the murdered god is very significant: Robert Taylor remarks upon it at length in his *Astronomico-Theological Lectures*.[353] De Santillana and von Dechend discuss it in some detail as well, especially in light of ancient traditions and festivals surrounding the death of the god Pan and the wailing for him and search for him by his devotees.[354] And, in light of the centrality of a night-time search amidst disorienting and apparently terrifying conditions during the initiations of the Eleusinian Mysteries (one of if not the most important, most revered, and most widely-attended of all the ancient *mysteria*), this ancient pattern of the search for the missing god becomes significant to our analysis of the importance of the mysteries in general.

Note from the two charts above that the constellation of Auriga, located close to Taurus, figures prominently in the celestial cast of characters surrounding the deposition of Orion and Gemini at the start of the Age of Taurus and the end of the Golden Age of Gemini. We might expect the constellation Auriga to play an important role in ancient mythology connected to precessional motion, and in fact it does. In *Hamlet's Mill*, the authors demonstrate that Auriga, the Charioteer, is almost certainly connected to Phaethon, the youth who rashly asked to drive the Chariot of the Sun but could not control the celestial horses and who had to be cast down to earth and his own death.[355] They show that this important ancient myth has many precessional connections (for Auriga was a constellation whose rising along with Taurus on the March equinox heralded the end of the Golden Age of Gemini and Orion depicted in the diagrams above).[356]

In the constellation of Auriga the Charioteer is a bright star called Capella (also known by its modern designation following the system designed in the 1600s as *alpha Aurigae,* "Auriga's alpha"). By an insightful chain of reasoning and detective work, Giorgio de Santillana and Hertha von Dechend demonstrate the possibility that this star is connected to Rhea (who is associated with Cybele the Great Mother Goddess or the Mother of the Gods by many ancient authors, and who was in fact the mother of the Olympian gods) as well as to Demeter.[357] And Demeter, of course, with her search for her daughter Persephone, was at the center of the rites of the Eleusinian Mysteries.

In a chapter entitled "The Fall of Phaethon," the authors of *Hamlet's Mill* explain that "in the Golden Age, when the vernal equinox was in Gemini, the autumnal equinox in Sagittarius, the Milky Way had represented a visible equinoctial colure."[358] By this they mean that the band (or "colure," which means hoop) of the Milky Way actually ran through the constellations that marked the two solstices – Gemini and Sagittarius. We have already seen that the Milky Way rises between Scorpio and Sagittarius to cross the sky – it is very noticeable at that point. The author of Revelation encoded this connection between the Milky Way and Sagittarius (and Scorpio) in the imagery of chapter nine, as we have already seen.

Thus, de Santillana and von Dechend argue, the Age of Gemini was a sort of "Golden Age," when this important heavenly pathway of the Milky Way (which they also demonstrate was described as a pathway for souls in between incarnations) connected the important equinoctial constellations. When precession shifted it away, the Golden Age came to an end, because now Taurus and Scorpio occupied the equinoctial points and the Milky Way no longer acted as an "equinoctial colure."

The Age of Gemini was also a Golden Age in that it was the age of Orion, who while not a zodiac constellation was certainly a dominant figure rising out of the eastern horizon on the morning of the vernal (spring) equinox. Orion was associated with Osiris, the deposed king, a benevolent figure who walked among human beings and taught them agriculture and other civilizing skills. In this association, this lost age of a benevolent king has echoes around the world – in ancient Greece both Kronos and Prometheus have the same characteristics.[359]

Kronos would be called Saturn by the Latins, and this god and planet is associated with the color yellow (as well as with the color black), and this also helps us understand why the Age of Gemini (which we might also call the Age of Orion) was a "Golden Age." In China, legends speak of the Yellow Emperor, the benevolent Huang-ti, and von Dechend and de Santillana argue that he also shows Saturnian characteristics and presided over a lost Golden Age.[360]

With this in mind, we can now follow the argument of the authors of *Hamlet's Mill* in detailing the importance of Auriga and the connection to Rhea – and Demeter. In the Golden Age, they write,

> The three great axes were united, the galactic avenue embracing the "three worlds" of the gods, the living and the dead. [But, when precession shifted the ages from the Age of Gemini to the Age of Taurus, then] This "golden" situation was gone [. . .] There was no longer a visible continuous bond fettering together

immortals, living and dead: Kronos alone had lived among men in glorious peace.

And here there is a proposition to be made. In order to evaluate it, one has to consider the fact that alpha Aurigae is Capella, the Goat. This remarkable figure was the nurse of infant Zeus in the Dictaean Cave, and out of her skin Hephaistos was later to make the Aegis: Amaltheia. Capella-Amaltheia's Horn was the Horn of Plenty for the immortals, and the source of Nectar and Ambrosia. Mortals called it "second table," dessert so to speak. But there are two shreds of Orphic tradition which seem to be revealing, both handed down to us by Proclus. The first says that Demeter separated the food of the gods, splitting it up, as it were, into a liquid and a solid "part," that is, into Ambrosia and Nectar. The second declares that Rhea became Demeter after she had borne Zeus. And Eleusis, for us a mere "place name," was understood by the Greeks as "Advent" – the New Testament uses the word for the Advent of Christ. Demeter, formerly Rhea, wife of Kronos, when she "arrived," split up the two kinds of divine food having its source in alpha Aurigae. In other words, it is possible that these traditions about Demeter refer to the decisive shifting of the equinoctial colure to alpha Aurigae.[361]

This line of argument provides an incredibly important insight into the ancient mysteries, and indeed may be the decisive revelation that shows that they were indeed closely connected in their manner of allegorizing with the Isis and Osiris story and the most ancient sacred traditions of Egypt. What de Santillana and von Dechend are implying is that Demeter, the goddess at the center of the Eleusinian Mysteries, is Rhea, whom we have seen is also associated with Cybele the Great Goddess. Not only that, but they are showing that these mysteries are closely connected with the loss of the Golden Age (by the Capella connection), the very subject of the legends of Osiris and Set, the precessional event which initiated the mourning of Isis and her search for her slain husband.

This line of reasoning puts the mysteries squarely in the tradition of the most ancient religious traditions – traditions which may have been handed down to Egypt, Sumer and other ancient high civilizations by an incredibly advanced predecessor civilization. Note that the discovery of precession is no easy task, and its motions take place over literally thousands of years. How long before the legends of Osiris and Isis were written down the observation must have begun, and how long before the legends of Osiris and Isis were written down the understanding of this celestial machinery was arrived at, are impossible for us to say at this point in history. However, there are plenty of references to Osiris in the most ancient original texts in our possession (the Pyramid Texts), and so we know that this knowledge is extremely ancient – possibly thousands of years more ancient than the Pyramid Texts themselves.

From here we can see that the many other mysteries can be interpreted as fitting into this same tradition. We have already seen that the Dioscuri or the Twins may have been associated with at least some of the ancient mysteries. We have seen the names of Prometheus, and of Pan mentioned as well – both figures associated with the Golden Age and the loss of the Golden Age, as de Santillana and von Dechend explain at length.[362] And we have seen that Demeter and Rhea are every bit as connected with the end of the Golden Age as is Osiris the deposed king. Demeter's loss and her searching, then, is not only a mythological representation of the annual seasonal change from winter into spring (as it is usually interpreted by conventional scholars) but is also connected to the searching of Isis for her lost Osiris, a searching which is associated with the loss of the Golden Age, and with the inexorable grinding of the heavenly mill through the motion of precession.

And here we see that the mysteries concern the very same subject matter that our earlier analysis reveals the Old and New Testaments to treat as well: that is, they are intensely concerned with the motions of the celestial actors, and treat the heavenly machinery as having profound import for our understanding of our human condition in this body on this earth, and our condition after the death of that body. The fact that the mysteries incorporate the celestial characters so completely hints that they are also pointing to the macrocosm / microcosm connection. By participation in the mysteries, initiates somehow saw beyond their temporarily incarnated condition, and grasped the fact that they are eternal souls, sojourning in a physical body, destined to continue after the death of the body.

In fact, Alvin Boyd Kuhn, whose analysis is supported by so many of the points we are uncovering in this examination, believed that the entire concept of the "hidden god" or the "lost divinity" related to our condition in this incarnate life: we have fallen into a state of forgetfulness of our divine origin, and have lost our awareness of the "hidden god" inside each of us.[363] This mystery was encoded in numerous esoteric allegories throughout the ancient sacred texts. Kuhn writes:

> Deep inside the ark was the shrine for Deity; buried in the secret depths of every physical man is Amen-Ra, the hidden Lord.[364]

And again:

> The Prodigal Son remembered his forgotten Father's house on high. Away off in that "far country," the Vale of Lethe and Land of Oblivion, the exiled soul begins to recover from its amnesia, and the divine nostalgia sets in to lead it back home.
>
> [. . .]
>
> The figures of both Jesus and Jonah, fast asleep in the holds of their respective ships in the storm are variant types of this oblivion of the god in his mundane journey. In a similar episode in the career of Horus, "there was deep slumber within the ship."[365]

This slumbering, hidden divine principle inside each incarnate man and woman is the subject of all the scriptures, according to Kuhn. The purpose of these texts was to reawaken the sleeping one, to bring the one suffering from amnesia back to a true realization of who he or she was, to cause the prodigal son described in the parable found in Luke chapter 15 – eating among the brute swine – to come to his senses and remember the estate from which he has fallen.

We now see in a flash that this was no less the purpose of the ancient mysteries as well! Note well the metaphor cited by Alvin Boyd Kuhn at the end of the quoted passage above: the image of Jesus or Jonah, fast asleep in the holds of their respective ships in the storm at sea. This image of the sleeping god, in a narrow hold, below the surface of the sea, is a perfect parallel of the classic image of the Osiris-Saturn-Kronos figure! The Kronos archetype is always banished to the cave in the depths of the sea (the cave of Ogygia), there to slumber until the return of the Golden Age. King Arthur, banished to the enchanted sleep beneath the waters of the lake, is another manifestation of the identical pattern.[366]

We have seen that the mysteries are intimately concerned with this Saturnian figure, drowned by the motion of precession. Alvin Boyd Kuhn teaches us that the ancient system sought to use the motions of the heavenly bodies as metaphors for our human condition, that condition being the plight of the immortal soul trapped within a clay-form body, oblivious to its divine origin. The nightly procession of the stars figures this message, the daily descent of the sun into the western horizon (where it enters the underground kingdom of Osiris) figures this message, and most majestically of all perhaps the inexorable grind of the mighty gears of precession figure this message of the crushed king, the drowned king, the deposed god in all his cultural manifestations, whether Osiris, or Kronos, or Saturn, or Jamshyd, or Janbûshâd or Yima, or Yama, or the Great Pan, or Tammuz, or Jesus.[367]

Thus the mysteries, whether they were of the Queen of Heaven, of Rhea or Demeter or Ceres, of Kore or Persephone, of the Nameless Gods or Kabeiroi whom we have seen to have been identified with the Twins, or of Osiris or Isis - all of them appear to have been dramatizing this same truth, and performing the same function which the scriptures were designed to perform as well: the reawakening at the deepest level of the awareness of the soul to its true identity, the realization of our true human condition.

It is the awareness that came over the prodigal son in the parable, dining on husks among the pigs: our true condition is not one of mere physical animal, regardless of the many ways this message is drummed into us to this very day by those who wish to keep this knowledge from the people. The ancient mysteries conveyed this truth, profoundly and powerfully to all who chose to come and be initiated. But the mysteries have now been stamped out, deliberately and thoroughly. The ancient scriptures attest to it as well, but their message has been deliberately obscured.

Many ancient authors attest to the fact that participants in the mysteries emerged with a new perspective on their life, a perspective which included the loss of the fear that death formerly held for them.

In his *Greek Anthologies*, speaking of the mysteries of Eleusis, which is located in the Attic peninsula near Athens, Crinagoras (70 BC - AD 18) writes:

> Even if yours has always been a sedentary life, and you have never sailed the sea, nor walked the roads of the land, you should nevertheless go to Attica, so that you may witness those nights of the festival of great Demeter. For then your heart may be free of care while you live, and lighter when you go to the land of the dead.[368]

In a fragment from the play *Triptolemos*, the poet Sophocles (497 BC - 406 BC) writes of the mysteries of Eleusis:

> Thrice blessed are those mortals who have seen these rites and thus enter into Hades: for them alone there is life, for the others all is misery.[369]

But what could it be about these mysteries that could somehow remove the fear of death? Was it merely that initiates were now promised a better condition in the afterlife? Or is there something more to these assertions than that? Again, ancient texts on the subject are not overly plentiful, and scholars continue to debate their meaning today, but we have already seen a good explanation through careful examination of the content of the ancient mysteries in conjunction with the insights of Alvin Boyd Kuhn, and the later work of Giorgio de Santillana and Hertha von Dechend.

In addition, there are hints that the mysteries could somehow convey to their participants a vision akin to the crossing into the other realm.

In a famous passage from Plutarch, himself an initiate into the cult of Isis and possibly a priest of some status, we read his description of the soul at death, comparing it to the experience of an initiate in the mysteries:

> The soul suffers an experience similar to those who celebrate great initiations. . . Wandering astray in the beginning, tiresome walkings in circles, some frightening paths in darkness that lead nowhere; then immediately before the end all the terrible things, panic and shivering and sweat, and bewilderment. And then some wonderful light comes to meet you, pure regions and meadows are there to greet you, with sounds and dances and solemn, sacred words and holy views; and there the initiate, perfect by now, set free and loose from all bondage, walks about crowned with a wreath, celebrating the festival together with the other sacred and pure people, and he looks down on the uninitiated, unpurified crowd in this world in mud and fog beneath his feet.[370]

This description contains features that are remarkably reminiscent of the descriptions of near-death experience reported time after time by individuals who have perceived their point of consciousness leaving their body, traveling through some sort of "tunnel," and breaking out into a realm of intense light where they are met by "other sacred and pure people."

Plato in his famous dialogue *Phaedrus* also makes reference to the similarity between the mystery experience and the vision of the soul when it is not imprisoned in a body (the condition in the body Plato likens to being bound like an oyster within its shell):

> They could see beauty shining, when the divine chorus they beheld the blessed sight and vision – we following after Zeus and others after other gods – and we went through the initiations which it is right to call most blessed, which we celebrated in complete wholeness and without any touch of the ills which followed us in later time, seeing, as *mystai* and *epoptai*, entire and whole and calm and happy visions in pure light.[371]

The terms Plato uses (or rather, his character Socrates uses in the dialogue), *mystai* and *epoptai*, refer to participants in the *mysteria*, the first term for those undergoing the experience for the first time, and the second term for those who have been through them before. Thus Plato is implicitly asserting that the experience of the mysteries is intended to impel the participants into the realm beyond the physical realm, the realm in which their souls dwelt before they were imprisoned within the body like an oyster in a shell, the realm – if we may be so bold as to connect the experience with that undertaken by the pharaohs during the secret portion of the Sed festival rites – of the Duat, or the implicate order.

There has been much speculation as to how the mysteries enabled participants to cross over to that realm, but before discussing the possibilities, it is important to do so in the context of the thesis that such a realm may in fact exist – that the model of a universe with implicate and the explicate orders may be an accurate depiction of the cosmos that we inhabit. We have seen much evidence to suggest that this is the case, and that the ancient sacred traditions all taught it in some way (whether explicitly or implicitly), and even that an even more ancient predecessor civilization knew this fact thoroughly and knew the techniques for crossing between the explicate and the implicate with relative ease. However, for reasons we can explore in more detail in a later chapter, this vision of the true nature of the universe was brutally suppressed at a certain point in history, and even today it is unwelcome.

Modern scholars, largely supportive of a completely materialistic vision of the universe and in danger of various forms of censure if they stray too far from such a vision, are almost entirely silent about the voluminous evidence which points to the existence of a predecessor civilization. And when they take up the question of ecstatic experience, and the techniques with which cultures have brought about the condition of ecstasy, they often treat the subject as if these techniques were a trick with which to fool the consciousness into believing something that is not real, or with which to dull the consciousness so that it is susceptible to experience something that is not real, rather than techniques which just may *in fact* lead the participant into an actual realm which is connected to this one, but in much the same way that holographic film is connected to a projected hologram.

And yet, we have seen that even today, modern shamans in the Amazon have knowledge of remedies and tonics made from the dizzying array of plants, knowledge which can scarcely be explained by trial and error (Jeremy Narby's work being seminal in this regard, and in complete harmony with the earlier work of John Anthony West who shows the same thing about the medicinal knowledge of the ancient Egyptians in *Serpent in the Sky*). When asked how they acquired such knowledge, the shamans have simply stated, "The plants told us." If we were to expand on this statement, we might speculate that they mean, "The plants told us while we were in the realm of the implicate order, the realm the Egyptians called the Duat, where they said that beings exist in a kind of 'seed' form. Western participants in the *ayahuasca* ritual have reported experiences in which they feel they can actually 'talk' to DNA – and what is DNA if not a kind of 'seed' form of all life?"

In other words, there is abundant evidence that the Duat, or the implicate order, the place where shamans travel in their ecstasies, is a real place (or plane of existence), and any examination of the techniques used in the ancient mysteries to cause their participants to catch a glimpse of this plane should be undertaken with that possibility in mind.

The techniques of inducing ecstasy in the human consciousness are many and varied, and have been well documented elsewhere. In *Shamanism: Archaic Techniques of Ecstasy*, Mircea Eliade catalogues many of the rituals and practices used by shamans around the world to enter altered states of consciousness, including ecstatic dance, whirling, rhythmic drumming, chanting, songs, music involving various instruments and especially flutes, fasting, the use of entheogenic substances derived from plants, the use of difficult exercises or postures similar to or including Yoga, the undertaking of deliberate spirit quests, the use of constricted and enclosed spaces, the use of very crowded spaces, the imposition of long periods of solitude, rubbing the body with rock crystals, rubbing together two stones for days or weeks on end, elaborate initiatory processes involving experienced guides, and many others, as well as many variations and combinations of the techniques listed here.[372]

Sometimes, shamans obtain the ability to cross into the spirit world through an accident, such as being struck by lightning, bitten by a snake, or enduring a serious illness.[373] This feature in and of itself should cause us to consider the similarity to aspects of modern reported out-of-body experiences and near-death-experiences, which overwhelmingly involve extremely serious trauma, surgeries, or illnesses. If the theory being expounded in this chapter (and in this book) is correct, then this correspondence between circumstances of "accidental" shamanism and "accidental" near-death-experience or modern out-of-body experience should be expected, because in both cases the traveler is *visiting the same place*: the Duat, the implicate order, the realm of the dead, the other land.

This conclusion is reinforced by the similarity of some shamanic accounts to the descriptions given by near-death-experience accounts, particularly the appearance of a hole or a tunnel through which the consciousness floats, or flies, to journey to the other planes of experience or existence. We have already examined accounts which support this connection, and the thorough cataloging of shamanic trances and ecstatic journeys found in Eliade's pioneering work provide many more.

The point to be made is that the techniques of inducing ecstasy in the human consciousness are profuse and multifarious – suggesting that the human consciousness is perhaps *designed* to be naturally capable of achieving this state – and that therefore the techniques that were used by the mystery cults may have included almost any combination of those listed, as well as many others. From our distance in history, and with the ruthless and effective eradication to which these cults were subjected, as well as their own insistence on secrecy, it is nearly impossible to say with certainty what methods were employed by the mysteries in the west, but there are some clues.

Some have made well-reasoned arguments that hallucinatory plants or entheogenic mushrooms were the primary methodology of inducing the dissolution of the "explicate" world during the mysteries. There certainly seems to be room for accepting this possibility – particularly the descriptions of the initiations as terrifying, inducing sweats, and inducing tremendous dread: all feelings that would seem to be difficult to produce simply through the use of darkness, light, and music (although the skillful manipulation of those elements can certainly contribute to emotional response and no doubt played an important role in many of the rites).

Hugh Bowden downplays the hallucinogen theory in his discussion of the ancient mysteries in general and the Eleusinian Mysteries in particular, arguing that the ergot fungus which some have suggested as the hallucinogen can cause hallucinations but typically at doses which are always very painful and often fatal, and that regulating the dosage would have been extraordinarily difficult. Added to this he notes that ancient theater possessed a wide repertoire of special effects, and that "If we are to look for an external explanation for the power of the Eleusinian experience, the theatre seems a better place to look than the kitchen or brewery."[374]

However, he mentions but does not specifically refute the arguments for the use of mushrooms as a hallucinogen, which many authors beginning with Robert Graves and including John Allegro and Terence McKenna have suggested as the main hallucinogen in the ancient mysteries, advancing cogent arguments in support of this thesis.

In *Food of the Gods*, McKenna gives arguments for a hallucinogenic substance as the sacrament consumed in the Eleusinian Mysteries, as well as arguments against the ergotized wheat theory. He writes that "There is little doubt that Eleusis something was drunk by each initiate and each saw something during the initiation that was utterly unexpected, transformative, and capable of remaining with each participant as a powerful memory for the rest of their life," and then goes on to argue that the "something" was most likely either hallucinogenic mushrooms or a product of hallucinogenic mushrooms, citing for example the work of Robert Graves, who believed that ancient recipes for preparing the Eleusinian substance "contained ingredients whose first letters could be arranged to spell out the word 'mushroom' – the secret ingredient."[375]

McKenna adds a worthwhile exegesis of a version of the Greek myth of Glaukos as additional evidence that the ancient Minoans, later Cretans, and Greeks had knowledge of the use of entheogenic mushrooms, and that Glaukos in the myth represents a mushroom. Interestingly, the version cited involves the resurrection of Glaukos by an herb brought by a serpent to its mate, details that McKenna points out as significant and details which resonate with some of the observations we have already encountered regarding "communication with plants" and the possibility that shamanic cultures could communicate with DNA, perhaps seeing it in the form of two serpents.[376]

Once again, the thesis put forth by Terence McKenna – arguing that the consumption of hallucinogenic substances and especially mushrooms played a central role in the development of a peaceful and shamanic ancient human culture, which was later destroyed by an anti-shamanic and violent culture – appears to be largely complementary rather than antagonistic to the thesis being developed thus far in this book.

McKenna does not pursue the celestial aspect of ancient scriptures to any extent – at one point, for example, he argues that "The angel with flashing sword who guards the return to Eden seems an obvious symbol of the unforgiving harshness of the desert sun and the severe drought conditions which accompany it" (as supporting evidence for his argument that a Saharan Eden was destroyed by climatic change and drought, leading to the disruption of the peaceful Edenic shamanic culture), while we have already seen that Robert Taylor over a hundred years before had published a much more compelling argument showing that the angel with flashing sword almost certainly represents the constellation Perseus.[377]

I also remain unconvinced by McKenna's basic acceptance of a Darwinian evolutionary narrative, which basically asserts that advanced apes who discovered mushrooms were propelled into creating the worldwide civilization that built the megalithic monuments and the pyramids. Whle that is a theory that bears examination, we have already seen evidence that the ancient worldwide grid was constructed by a culture or civilization that may have been far more advanced than our own. Explaining this fact seems to cause some difficulty for the Darwinian narrative. Even more devastating, perhaps, is the fact that the Darwinian narrative has a difficult time accounting for the possibility of the evolution of a non-material soul, let alone a soul which reincarnates multiple times. If the ancient originators of the truths expounded in the mystery rites and the sacred texts were correct about their assertions, then the Darwinian thesis may be wrong. If they were wrong about their view of the spirit incarnated in each man or woman, then we have to say that their mushroom trips sent them on a tremendous wild goose chase.

However, even if there are some serious points of disagreement between the theory put forward in this book and the theory of Terence McKenna, his work has important insights which contribute to this theory. It is undeniable that the consumption of hallucinogenic plants plays a central role in the techniques of ecstasy of many shamanic cultures around the world, and that the evidence that ancient mystery cults used hallucinogenic plants to some extent is also compelling. While there are some differences between the arguments here and McKenna's work, both agree on the vital importance of the shamanic worldview and the recognition that this worldview has been suppressed to humanity's detriment.

Various authors have suggested that the ancient Egyptians had an understanding of electricity, producing various arguments including observations that the deep recesses of many of the pyramids and tombs lack signs of torch smoke or other deposits we would expect if candles or lanterns burning wicks had been used to light the way for workmen or artists or burial processions or other rites and rituals (other analysts have disputed this assertion, arguing that the carbon deposits found today could not all have been made by archaeologists in the modern period, and that there is evidence for hundreds of years of ancient torch use in some sites).

Some researchers, however, do believe that the ancients may have had some understanding of the manipulation of electricity. Lucy Wyatt, whose important work *Approaching Chaos* explores the implications of Jeremy Naydler's shamanic theory, points to the possibility that the Ark of the Covenant described in the Old Testament shows clear signs of carrying powerful electric charge (it had to be carried by wooden poles, and it knocked down or killed those who touched it).[378] She also points to the strong possibility that the Old Testament culture emerged from Egypt as further evidence for the possibility that the Egyptians possessed knowledge of electricity.[379]

Based on that possibility, Lucy Wyatt puts forth the extremely interesting possibility that the manipulation of electricity was involved in the secret portions of the Sed ritual in which the king undertook his journey to the Duat. She notes that the rites involved a tunic known as the *qeni* garment, or the "embrace of Osiris," which may have been designed to protect the heart of the king from stopping or from being disrupted by the electrical current, and she advances the theory that the famous "opening of the mouth" ritual was done to the king as he entered the trance in order to prevent him from swallowing his tongue![380]   Such an eventuality would be a clear possibility if the technique of inducing an OBE employed by the Egyptian priests and kings involved the use of powerful currents . She also points out that the kings often had special Sed festival beds made for them which were made of gold or overlaid with gold – an excellent conductor of electricity.[381]   Such beds have survived in some tombs, notably that of Tutankhamun.

Another possibility Lucy Wyatt explores is the possibility that gold itself can be an ecstasy-producing medium, particularly if it is somehow transformed into a powdery-white form. She points out that some archaeologists have discovered large amounts of mysterious white powder with strange properties in Egyptian tombs, and that hieroglyphic inscriptions in the Pyramid Texts and elsewhere speak of a special bread which "flies up" to the king during the feast that precedes the shamanic journey.[382]

The accounts recorded by Eliade, cited earlier, of shamanic traditions which accord importance to lightning, to shamans being struck by lightning, or being otherwise "chosen" or marked out by lightning, adds a curious possible support to the electrical-current theory of Lucy Wyatt.

Whether some of the mystery cults – many of which, especially during the Roman and Hellenistic periods were associated with Egypt or said to have come out of Egypt – had knowledge of some of the techniques guarded by the priests of Egypt down through the millennia is very difficult to say at this remove. It is as though a concerted effort has been made at a very early date to eradicate ancient accounts that could have shed more light on the ancient mysteries. Alvin Boyd Kuhn voices the opinion that "It is by no means an unwarranted assertion to him that the hostile attitude toward esotericism has been an item in the policy of a grand conspiracy, operative since the third century, to diminish the influence of the ancient teachings."[383] We will examine the evidence to support such a "not unwarranted assertion" in the following chapters.

Hugh Bowden offers convincing evidence that breathing techniques, loud rhythmic music, and the "charge" produced by a group of participants as they become more and more caught up in the pattern of the ritual can and do induce ecstatic experience even today, without the use of drugs or chemicals or any of the more exotic methods just discussed. He provides a very insightful in-depth examination of the ecstatic experience involved in the snake-handling sects of fundamentalist Christians in the United States in the twentieth century (and beyond to the present day).[384]

How the participants or their guides induced the journey to the ecstatic, however, is really secondary to the fact that the participants in the ancient mysteries really appear to have undergone a major change in perspective after their experience, which suggests that the initiations were (at least for many participants) capable of inducing an altered state of consciousness. Contact with the "other realm" – the realm of the Duat or the implicate order – seems to produce a major change in those who experience it. This fact is one of the most constant features of NDE reports, as Chris Carter demonstrates in his books *Science and the Near-Death Exeperience* and *Science and the Afterlife Experience*, and as Michael Talbot documents in *The Holographic Universe* in his chapters on NDE accounts.

In this light, Hugh Bowden's comments on the transformative power of the mystery rite experience are extremely revealing.   He explains that in the Odyssey, Menelaus learns that after death he will enjoy the Elysian fields, rather than the normal gloomy and miserable afterlife most mortals experience – and that the reason given is that he married Helen, which makes him a son-in-law of Zeus. This proximity to the gods is the transformative element. From this insight, Hugh Bowden concludes:

> The afterlife promised to initiates looks very similar to that of Menelaus, and the explanation for it is the same: like Menelaus, initiates have been in close contact with a god. But just as Menelaus did not marry Helen in order to reach the Elysian fields, so those who participated in mystery cults did not do so in order to have a better time after death.[385]

This extremely valuable insight suggests a connection with some of the assertions made so far in this book: that the "realm of the gods" is the realm of the "implicate order" (a modern name for the same concept), which is actually the realm that those who experience an NDE travel to and return from (often reporting that the experience profoundly changes their life and removes their fear of death). It is the realm to which shamans travel in their ecstatic flights. It is the realm to which the Egyptian kings traveled during their Sed festival secret rites – rites which that civilization saw as extremely beneficial, even crucial to their survival.

Travel to this realm, then, appears to have serious potential benefits, raising what we might term (although the word has been pressed into service to mean perhaps too many different things), "consciousness."

It appears increasingly clear that the mystery cults, which flourished in "the west" from at least 800 BC (possibly earlier) until the fourth century AD, were involved in the raising of consciousness, before they were eliminated.

We might add a few more pieces of evidence to support this thesis. One is the fact that artwork associated with *mysteria* sometimes depicts the participants as taking on the heads of animals. This can be seen in artwork from the region of Lycosura in southern Arcadia in Greece, in fragments which may be associated with the Mysteries of Demeter and a daughter named Despoina.[386] The travel into the other world in the form of a bird or animal is a common theme in shamanic tradition, and depiction of the shaman with an animal or bird's head is a common motif in shamanic imagery. The Olmec figurine below, for instance, shows a human with an eagle's head and other birdlike features, and is widely thought to represent a shaman transforming into an eagle or hawk (a common shamanic motif world-wide). The depiction in Egyptian art of gods, the denizens of the other realm, as having heads of animals is of course well-known and can be seen in countless examples of Egyptian art and statuary.

Another telling piece of evidence from ancient artwork depicting mystery rites are images of priests or priestesses officiating at the mysteries wearing a leopard-skin tunic or garment – an important symbol of the Egyptian priesthood. This fact suggests that the mysteries may indeed have had an Egyptian connection, or that they at least shared a common source with the rituals of ancient Egypt.

The god Dionysus was the center of widespread mystery rites, and he is often depicted in ancient Greek art as wearing a leopard-skin cape. His bacchants, the usually female participants in his *mysteria*, are sometimes depicted wearing leopard-skin capes as well, or sometimes holding a small leopard by the tail in one hand.

A bacchant wearing a leopard-skin cape can be clearly seen to the right of Dionysus on the beautiful cup painted by the "Kleophrades Painter" from the 5th century BC in Athens, in the Munich collection Antikensammlungen #8732.

Did such garments signify that the wearers, like the shaman of more recent centuries, could deliberately undertake journeys to the other world (the Duat, the implicate order)? Combined with the evidence from Professor Jeremy Naydler already discussed, which indicates that specific Egyptian rituals involved the deliberate travel to the other realm, this conclusion seems quite possible.

In sum, it seems that the practice of the "shamanic" is extremely ancient, and that it involves an understanding of the nature of the universe akin to the model which certain modern physicists have come to propose in light of the evidence which began to surface from their quantum experiments during the twentieth century. Not only did the ancient shamanic practitioners possess an intimate understanding of the "holographic" nature of the universe, and the ability to describe it quite precisely (using imagery not of holograms, as did some of the twentieth-century physicists, but of the Duat, the "seed" realm, the other world, the language of the mysteries), but they also demonstrate the ability to enter it deliberately, possibly through a variety of ecstatic technique.

The fact that the most ancient civilizations we know of possessed such knowledge raises numerous important questions which we must consider. Where did such sophisticated awareness come from? The evidence suggests that *all* ancient sacred tradition may have been, in some sense, shamanic and holographic in its teaching – including most of the scriptures we find collected in what we today call the Bible. This raises another question: where did such sophisticated awareness go? How was it eradicated among a large section of the earth – the section which today is often referred to as "the west" (that is to say, the part of the world that was at one time conquered by the Roman Empire, as well as the later colonies of Britain such as the US, Canada, Australia and New Zealand)?

For we can see from the discussion in this chapter that many aspects of modern shamanism, as it survived in those parts of the world not conquered by Rome, appear to stretch in an unbroken line all the way back to Egypt (and possibly beyond, depending on how we answer the first question regarding the original origins of such sophisticated knowledge and technique). This fact gives us a clue to the second question of what happened in the past to obscure this knowledge, a clue we will explore in subsequent chapters.

Another important question is whether this observation (that the shamanic is extremely ancient, that the shamanic is extremely sophisticated, and that most ancient civilizations give evidence of some level of shamanic knowledge in their sacred traditions) can help explain the origin of some or all of the advanced knowledge which they demonstrated. We have already touched on the fact, which some analysts have pointed out, that explaining the knowledge of medicinal applications for the teeming variety of plants found in the Amazon is difficult or nearly impossible using conventional explanations. Trial and error, the traditional fallback, is not satisfactory, particularly when it comes to the combinations of plants and plant derivatives, including the combination of derivatives which by themselves might be toxic but in combination are medicinal.

As we have seen, it is quite possible that the plants – or their DNA – do somehow "communicate" with individuals who are able to cross the threshold into the other realm (the realm of the implicate order). In other words, shamanic journeys to the "seed world" of the Duat may help us to understand the acquisition of knowledge which seems impossible to explain to those using the conventional paradigm (a paradigm rooted in the rejection of the shamanic for some reason, perhaps due to historical events which we will explore).

This explanation may be particularly helpful for historical problems (which conventional historians tend to gloss over or to ignore completely) such as the question of where mankind obtained domestic animals and domestic grains – questions which are "genetic" in nature (if the DNA of the Amazon flora can communicate with shamans, perhaps the DNA of the predecessors of todays domestic plants and animals communicated with shamanic travelers in the most distant past). We have already mentioned some of Lucy Wyatt's important arguments which make it difficult to accept the idea that ancient hunter-gatherers somehow determined that selective breeding could make some grains useful for cultivation and some wild animals useful for domestication – a process that would take generations of human lives. Could the shamanic explain this process more satisfactorily, as Lucy Wyatt suggests? If so, can it explain other ancient knowledge which is difficult to explain under conventional (non-shamanic) paradigms?

Finally, if in addition to what we might term "technological" advantages, the ability to cross over into the shamanic realms has beneficial consequences for what is broadly termed "consciousness," then why would anyone want to suppress the shamanic, or even stamp it out? The answer seems obvious – malevolent actors might seek to suppress the shamanic, and suppress human consciousness, in order to enslave, to control, to pacify, and to lord it over others. If consciousness is one of the highest aims of a human soul in its sojourn in this physical realm, then some might wish to thwart the attainment of it for their own selfish purposes, or out of malevolent intent towards those souls.

We will now turn to some of the traces in the historical record which might help us to understand how this astrologic/shamanic/holographic knowledge was violently suppressed in "the west" around the time of the cessation of the mystery religions.

13

Where did literalism come from?

It is a grave question whether the ecclesiastical system and movement known as Christianity has any right to its name. So far from being the cult that brought in a true Christ-worship for the first time in "heathen" darkness, it was indeed – after the third century – the one system that destroyed such a true worship. Ancient cults bent all effort upon the cultivation of the god within man. This is the nucleus of the only true Christianity.

Alvin Boyd Kuhn,
Who is this King of Glory?[387]

In the previous chapter, we examined evidence that the ancient mysteries incorporate clearly astronomical material, and in fact can even be said to be entirely founded upon metaphors that are celestial in nature, and which reveal a vision of human existence that parallels the cyclical motions of the heavens.

For instance, many of them were centered around some aspect or incarnation of the Great Goddess or Great Mother, whom we have seen can be associated with the zodiac constellation of Virgo, whose figure appears to be seated – like a queen upon a throne – and who follows Leo the Lion, just as the Great Goddess is often accompanied by one or more lions, or pulled in a chariot drawn by lions. Other mysteries involve the searching for a lost or hidden god or goddess, which we have seen can be connected to the celestial phenomenon of precession, which "delays" the motion of the heavens by a tiny amount each year, such that over great lengths of time constellations who once "ruled" important stations of the year (such as the March equinox) are replaced by new rulers. This motion of precession was also seen to bring about new "ages," and many myths around the world (as well as some of the imagery from the mysteries), concern the loss of an ancient "Golden Age," which may refer to the Age of Gemini, when Orion could be seen coming over the horizon in the predawn sky on the day of March equinox. In legend, the constellation Orion is associated with Osiris as well as Kronos, Saturn, Quetzlcoatl, King Arthur, the Yellow Emperor of ancient China, and other benevolent and civilizing rulers who eventually disappeared across the waves or under the waves, often with a promise of eventual return and restoration of the Golden Age.

We have argued that the identification of the celestial with the realm of the gods may have much deeper significance than merely representing the "primitive superstition." It may well indicate a sophisticated understanding of the macrocosm-microcosm view of mankind, the view that each individual embodies the entire cosmos, just as each tiny sub-section of the holographic medium embodies the data needed to project the entire hologram. It may indicate that the ancient sources of the world's sacred traditions understood this aspect of reality and preserved it in sacred scripture and legend. It may indicate, as Alvin Boyd Kuhn argues, their view that men and women are incarnate beings from a fiery realm of spirit, and that the hidden god reflects the truth we all carry around with us, a truth we forget upon our entry into this realm, and a truth to which we should reawaken through participation in the mysteries, or through the esoteric message of the texts. It may also indicate (along with other evidence) the ability to deliberately cross over into the other side of the hologram – to interact with the holographic medium or holographic "film" – to have a direct encounter with the realm of the "implicate order," or the Duat: the place of the gods.

We know that shamans use celestial imagery when they go to the place of the gods and spirits, and we have explored evidence that the participants in the ancient mysteries may also have experienced an encounter with the gods or with the other realm, and that this experience was understood to change their status in a profound way. Like Menelaus, who was promised a different and better afterlife not because of any good deeds in this life but simply because he had experienced close interaction with the gods, those who participated in the mysteries – like the shamans and the pharaohs who undertook deliberate journeys into the Duat or the spirit realm – and who experienced a direct encounter with the "other side" or "other realm" were profoundly changed by their experience, with evidence that it gave them an entirely new perspective on life and death.

We have examined extensive imagery running throughout the scriptures of the Old and New Testament which suggest that these sacred texts were founded upon the very same types of celestial metaphors as the other ancient sacred traditions, including those of ancient Egypt, ancient Greece, and the ancient mysteries. And yet the Biblical texts are decidedly *not* viewed in this manner by the vast majority of those who interact with them today, nor have they been viewed in such a manner by the vast majority of those who interacted with them over the past seventeen centuries. In fact, to suggest that the scriptures of the Bible are celestial in nature, and possibly shamanic, would have been viewed as damnable heresy for most of the past seventeen centuries – and would in fact still be viewed as dangerously heretical by many adherents of religions purportedly based on these scriptures right now in the present day.

What happened? How can we explain this set of circumstances?

In recent decades, there have been many alternative histories published which explore the tumultuous events during the early imperial era of the Roman period which led to the emergence of the Christian religion. Noteworthy among these are *The Jesus Mysteries* (1999) by Timothy Freke and Peter Gandy and *Caesar's Messiah* (2009) by Joseph Atwill. Although the explanation proposed in this book will ultimately be different than those proposed in those books, the work of Freke and Gandy, and the work of Joseph Atwill, both contain many important insights worth considering, many of which are likely accurate.

Freke and Gandy examine evidence suggesting that a version of the ancient mysteries, adapted for the land of Judaea and the Jewish people during the first century AD, attracted a wide variety of followers and initiates, but that this version was understood primarily esoterically by many of its earliest adherents (including the Christian gnostics). They posit, however, that after the fall of Jerusalem in AD 70, many adherents who did not understand the esoteric nature of these teachings, but who instead tended to have a more literal understanding, were scattered throughout the empire, giving birth to literalist churches which eventually suppressed and silenced everyone else.[388]

The "fall of Jerusalem" which they mention is an extremely important event in any examination of the birth of Christianity and the question of "what happened to the mysteries" and we will look at it in some detail in the chapters which follow. It refers to the campaigns undertaken by the Roman general Titus Flavius Vespasian (AD 9 – AD 79) who had been sent to Judea to deal with the violent rebellions that were taking place there, which he suppressed ruthlessly after several battles, exterminating many of the Jewish religious leaders and gutting the Jewish Temple and burning it.

Freke and Gandy offer several compelling lines of argument in support of their theory. First, they trace out the many parallels between the content of other ancient mystery cults (including the Mysteries of Eleusis, the Mysteries of Samothrace, and especially of Mysteries of Dionysus, or Osiris-Dionysus, or Bacchus) and the stories in the New Testament gospels. Parallels they identify include the central figure of a god-man, who is killed by his followers or his enemies (in fact, in some cases, crucified, as both Dionysus and Bacchus are in some traditions said to be), and the commemorative meal involving bread and/or wine (both agricultural products that are made from raw materials which must be "beaten" or "crushed" after the harvest in order to create the finished product).[389]

After noting these parallels, Freke and Gandy posit that the New Testament gospels represent the importation of a familiar ancient motif, fitted onto figures that would be more appropriate for those living in Judea at the time. They argue that whoever created these "Jewish Mysteries" did not simply import the Greek mysteries directly, without alteration. Instead, the creators of this "new mystery cult" selected the figure of the expected Messiah to play the role that Osiris played in Egypt and Dionysus or Bacchus played in Greece or Rome. The figure of the Messiah was a central figure in Judaism, but the inventors of the "Jewish Mysteries," in the view of Freke and Gandy, created a different version, one more like Osiris or Dionysus: a Messiah transformed into a suffering god-man.[390]

Freke and Gandy argue that this same sort of transformation took place when various mysteries arrived in Greece from other cultures (they argue, for instance, that Dionysus was a relatively minor god-figure, but that when the Pythagoreans wanted to import the Osirian Mysteries into Greece, they altered the original legends of Dionysus to parallel the life, death, and rebirth of Osiris).[391] They then argue that the same sort of transformation took place with the creation of "The Jesus Mysteries."

Freke and Gandy also offer compelling evidence to support their assertion that the original understanding of these mysteries was not literal, but esoteric. Much of this evidence comes from the texts discovered at Nag Hammadi, in Egypt near Alexandria, which have sometimes been called "the gnostic gospels."

Nag Hammadi is located near the dramatic bend in the Nile just north of Luxor, which in ancient Egypt was called Thebes, the mighty ancient capitol of Upper Egypt (southern Egypt, the "upstream" and thus "upper" portion of Egypt, since the Nile flows south-to-north). The map below shows the region and its terrain, along with a red arrow (lower arrow) indicating Nag Hammadi and a blue arrow (upper, longer arrow) indicating the Jabal al-Tarif, a massif with steep cliff-sides; at the base of the cliffs of this massif the jar containing the Nag Hammadi texts was buried.

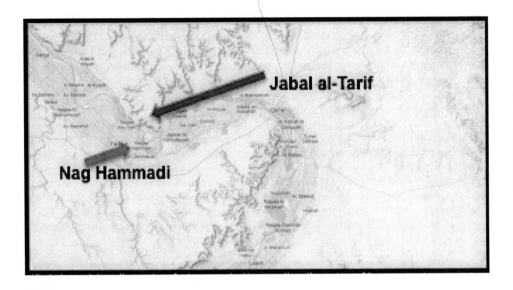

The texts are described by Marvin Meyer in his 2005 book *The Gnostic Discoveries: The Impact of the Nag Hammadi Library* as falling into five basic groups: a first group of gnostic texts characterized as "the Thomas texts," and including the Gospel of Thomas, the Book of Thomas, and a text called the Dialogue of the Savior whose style and content probably merits inclusion in this group; a second group of texts from what is known as "the Sethian school," reflecting the traditions and teachings of Seth, the son of Adam and Eve after the Cain and Abel catastrophe, who was held to be representative of an ideal human being; a third group categorized as Valentinian, after the second-century Alexandrian teacher Valentinus, a Christian gnostic, because they were either written by Valentinus himself or reflect his teachings; a fourth group containing Hermetic texts, of which there were three in the Nag Hammadi library, two of which had been previously known from other ancient sources, and a third new one which had never been seen by modern scholars, known as the Discourse on the Eighth and Ninth; and finally a fifth group which might be called the "other" category, consisting of gnostic texts which do not fit neatly into any of the previous categorizations.[392]

Such is the categorization suggested by Marvin Meyer and other scholars. Others may perhaps organize or categorize them differently. However they are categorized, their significance is profound on many levels and for many reasons. First, as Marvin Meyer explains elsewhere in the same book, "Prior to the discovery of the Nag Hammadi library, 'gnosticism' typically was considered to be an early and pernicious Christian heresy, and much of our knowledge of gnostic religion was gleaned from the writings of the Christian heresiologists, those authors who attempted to establish orthodoxy and expose heresy in the early church. [. . .] Since the discovery of the Nag Hammadi library and related texts, the study of gnostic religion and its impact upon ancient and modern religion has been fundamentally transformed."[393]

Second, the deliberate burial at the base of a cliff after sealing the texts into a jar suggests that those who valued these texts were hiding them from those who wanted to suppress or even destroy them, and this brings up the entire theme of the destruction of ancient

230

knowledge. Marvin Meyer provides evidence that these texts may have been buried upon the publication of the Festal Letter of Athanasius, Archbishop of Alexandria, in AD 367, also known as the 39th Festal Letter.[394] This letter lists the texts considered canonical and condemns as heretical those that are (in his words) "an invention of heretics."[395] It is arguably the first such letter whose list matches the twenty-seven New Testament texts considered canonical by the later church councils (notably Trent), and that matches the canon accepted by churches today.[396]

The existence of the Nag Hammadi texts attests to a thriving community following a completely different understanding of the scriptures from that which became the dominant "orthodoxy." The fact that the keepers of these texts carefully and deliberately sealed them in a large vessel and buried them under the loose scree at the base of the Jabal al-Tarif indicates that possession of these texts, which was once acceptable, had become a punishable offense – that the keepers of the doctrines that would harden into orthodoxy were consolidating their power and silencing other voices that could challenge their paradigm.

We will later examine in greater detail the chain of events set in motion by the fall of Jerusalem in AD 70 which led to the consolidation of the orthodoxy that would silence all opposing voices by the end of the fourth century and the reign of the emperor Theodosius. For now, however, let us return to the thesis of Timothy Freke and Peter Gandy, who propose that the teachings and texts which constituted a kind of mystery religion of Judea were originally understood by initiates in a metaphorical sense: expounding a view of human existence and the nature of the universe which its adherents believed to be true, without requiring that the contents of the texts themselves be understood literally.

This understanding of the significance of the Christ is characteristic of the ancient gnostics, who taught that there is a mystical or esoteric application of the events such as the crucifixion and the resurrection. For instance, Freke and Gandy explain:

> The Gnostic Illusionist view of the crucifixion was not meant to be taken as a historical account of events. It is a myth that encodes the perennial mystical teachings that a human being is made up of two parts: an earthly part which suffers and dies (the eidolon), and an eternal spiritual witness (the Daemon), which is untouched by suffering and experiences this world as a passing illusion.[397]

Similarly, the gnostics taught that the resurrection was not understood as either "a historical event that happened once only to someone else, nor a promise that corpses would rise from the dead after some future apocalypse. The gnostics understood the resurrection as a mystical experience that could happen to any one of us right here and now through the recognition of our true identity as the Daemon."[398]

They believe that these gnostic and esoteric interpretations were known to those who had been initiated into the higher levels of the mysteries (possibly signified by the baptism of the elements air and fire), but not to those who had only been through the first level (signified by the baptism of the element of water). Jesus is depicted as instituting these three levels of baptism in the gnostic Book of the Great Logos, the fragments of which survived ancient purges and were among those which helped shed light on the teachings of the gnostics even prior to the discovery of the Nag Hammadi library.[399]

Freke and Gandy cite numerous ancient sources which were known before the Nag Hammadi discovery, as well as numerous passages from various Nag Hammadi texts, to support this thesis. Supporting their argument with quotations from Origen as well as texts found in the Nag Hammadi library including the Gospel of Philip and the Acts of John, as well as the famous Pistis Sophia, and a discourse on the Mysteries of Dionysus by Proclus, they argue that there were progressive levels of greater and greater understanding in ancient mysteries, including the Christian mysteries. In both Christian and non-Christian mysteries, "The initations leading from one level to the next were symbolized by elemental baptisms":[400]

> Baptism by water symbolizes the transformation of the Hylic person, who identifies solely with the body, into a Psychic initiate, who identifies with the personality or psyche. Baptism by air symbolizes the transformation of the Psychic initiate into a Pneumatic initiate, who identifies with his Higher Self. Baptism by fire represents the final initiation, which reveals to Pneumatic initiates their true identity as the Universal Daemon, the Logos, the Christ within, the "Light Power" [. . .].[401]

Elaborating further, they argue that those who had experienced the first baptism had only been initiated into the "outer mysteries" and understood the story of Jesus on a literal level. Those who had experienced the second baptism understood the story allegorically, "encoding teachings about the spiritual path traveled by each initiate."[402] This understanding was given when the initiate was granted access to the secrets of the "inner mysteries." Finally, those who realized their own identity as the Christ "transcended the need for any teachings, including the Jesus story."[403]

Freke and Gandy then present evidence that Paul, who is traditionally viewed as "a bastion of orthodoxy and a crusader against the heretical Gnostics," may in fact have been a gnostic teacher.[404] They point out that "the great Gnostic sages of the early second century CE called Paul 'the Great Apostle' and honored him as the primary inspiration for Gnostic Christianity. Valentinus explains that Paul initiated the chosen few into the 'Deeper Mysteries' of Christianity, which revealed a sacred doctrine of God. These initates had included Valentinus' teacher Theudas, who had in turn initiated Valentinus himself."[405] Further, they note that many gnostic groups claimed to have been founded by Paul, that history demonstrates that gnostic groups calling themselves "Paulicians" were active until the tenth century AD in spite of the fact that the literalist church tried to stamp them out, that Paul was quoted in numerous clearly gnostic texts from antiquity, and that Paul's epistles were sent to cities which are known by scholars to have had active gnostic communities during the second century, communities led by the gnostic Marcion, who held Paul to have been the only actual apostle.[406]

As we will see later, there is strong evidence that Paul was a historical person, living prior to AD 70 and the fall of Jerusalem. While some of the letters attributed to him in the canonical New Testament (in particular the "pastoral letters" to Timothy and Titus) may have been written later by literalist authors and attributed to him, the earliest letters to the seven churches are probably genuinely Paul's. But Freke and Gandy point out: "It is a completely remarkable fact, however, that Paul says nothing at all about the historical Jesus! He is concerned only with the crucified and resurrected Christ, whose importance is entirely mystical."[407]

Further, they note that this understanding of Paul as a gnostic teacher makes sense of passages which pose serious difficulty for literal interpretors, such as a passage in Galatians 3 (verses 1-3) in which the author appears to chide the Galatians for having adopted a too-literal understanding of the resurrection. Freke and Gandy write:

> Paul criticizes the "Stupid Galatians," "before whose eyes Jesus Christ was openly displayed on the cross!" for looking to a "material" rather than "spiritual" understanding of salvation. Are we really to believe that this Christian community in Asia Minor had witnessed the crucifixion in Jerusalem and that Paul, who never claimed to have known Jesus, felt justified in calling such witnesses "stupid?" Paul's comment would make sense, however, if the Galatian Christians had rather witnessed a dramatic representation of Christ's passion [as initiates into other mysteries such as those at Eleusis, Freke and Gandy explain, might have experienced in a similar fashion]. It is this, Paul states, that will make them "perfect" – or to use the more accurate translation, "initiated"![408]

Citing more recent criticism of the canonical New Testament texts, Freke and Gandy argue that Paul's letters to the churches penned in the decades prior to the fall of Jerusalem are authentic, but should be understood in a gnostic paradigm. They argue that later, in the decades after the fall of Jerusalem, the gospels were written, including Mark, Matthew and Luke, and then John. These were penned to give geographical and historic trappings to what had originally been an esoteric mystery. Later still, the Acts of the Apostles was penned, to flesh out the stories of the various disciples / apostles. Finally, additional letters attributed to Paul and other apostles (such as Peter and John) were forged by literalists, primarily to attack gnosticism and those with an esoteric understanding – those who "confess not that Jesus Christ is come in the flesh" (a quotation found in 2 John 1:7, and there are similar passages in 1 John as well) – in the final decades of the second century and the first decades of the third.[409]

Freke and Gandy propose that after the fall of Jerusalem in AD 70 there was a scattering of the former inhabitants of the region far and wide, and many with only a literal understanding (who had undergone the first initiation, into the outer mysteries alone) carried on the faith but without the higher levels of understanding or initiation. This could explain the reason that texts providing literal details of the life of Jesus began to appear in the decades following AD 70.[410]

They also argue that literalism provided powerful incentives for those who wished to exert their power over others, and to silence those they deemed heretics. By claiming direct and unbroken succession of authority from literal apostles, the leaders of the new literalist faith could argue "that this invested their bishops with the authority of the original apostles."[411] This "fabricated lineage," Freke and Gandy argue, supplied "a powerful weapon in their battles with the Gnostics."[412]

This argument is compelling. We will see, however, that although it is heading in the right direction, it may not go far enough! Another author has supplied an even more compelling explanation for what may have happened during these decades, an explanation which does not refute the points made by Freke and Gandy just discussed, but in fact largely complements their research while going far beyond it in terms of historical detail and possible motive. It is an explanation backed by extensive evidence (much of it, perhaps, circumstantial, but taken together quite compelling nonetheless). We will also see that, about a hundred years before Freke and Gandy published their arguments, the self-taught English philosopher Gerald Massey (1828 – 1907) published numerous books elucidating the possibility that Paul was a gnostic, and that he provides some extremely important insights which bear directly on the shamanic-holographic thesis.

First, however, let us examine briefly in passing another important contribution to this topic, from Jospeh Atwill. In his book, *Caesar's Messiah*, Atwill examines the gospel accounts closely and compares them to the Judean campaigns of Flavius Vespasian and his son Titus, both of whom would later became emperor (first the father, then his son) after crushing the Jewish rebellions and ultimately sacking Jerusalem and the Temple. Atwill concludes that the gospels closely parallel the detailed descriptions of these Roman campaigns found in the well-known histories of the ancient Jewish author Josephus – a figure of great importance whom we will meet in greater detail momentarily.

Based on these parallels, Atwill concludes that the entire Christian religion was fabricated by the Romans to pacify the Jews, as a substitute to replace their long-expected violent Messiah (one who would overthrow the oppressors of the Jewish people and institute by divine might the Kingdom of God on earth) with a meek and gentle one, a Messiah who preached that his Kingdom was "not of this earth" and that his followers should not resort to violence but instead "turn the other cheek" and "render unto Caesar that which is Caesar's" and unto God that which is God's.[413] The selection of the campaigns of the conquering legions under Vespasian and Titus as the framework for these counterfeit Roman gospels, Atwill believes, was a kind of cruel and ironic Roman version of an inside joke.[414]

This theory is a very interesting development, and one which appears quite plausible. After all, the Jewish rebellions that Vespasian and Titus had been sent into Judea to crush were only the latest in a long century of violent uprisings led by those claiming to be the Messiah or those who were calling for uprising against the Romans as part of a preparation for the coming of this violent, Kingdom-establishing Messiah-figure. To replace this idea with a spiritual Messiah, who would preach peace and who would tell his followers to seek a spiritual rather than a temporal Kingdom appears to be a plausible goal for the Roman conquerors in dealing with a recalcitrant region filled with violent followers of a particularly virulent strain of religious faith.

Further, Atwill's discovery of astonishing parallels between the events described in the *Jewish Wars* penned by Josephus and the events of the New Testament gospels – events presented, moreover, in many cases in the *exact same order* in the canonical gospels and in the works of Josephus – bolsters his already-compelling thesis with significant textual evidence.

Among the events Joseph Atwill examines which may be seen as parallels between the events in the gospels (especially the synodic gospels of Mark, Matthew and Luke) are:

Josephus, *War of the Jews*	Event described in the gospels
Start of the campaign of Titus in Judea, described as sent by his father (Vespasian) tells his followers not to be afraid references Chorazin	Start of the ministry of Jesus described as sent by his Father tells his followers not to be afraid later also references Chorazin
Sea Battle at Gennesareth in which the rebels were caught like fish	Jesus at shore of Gennesareth calls his disciples and tells them they will be "fishers of men."
Battle at Gadara, capture of 2,200 rebels of the Sicarii, after being driven to the river and forced unwillingly to jump in	Confrontation with the demoniac driving out of legion of demons which are sent into swine, about 2,000 in number, which jump into the sea and drown
Judgment of two leaders of the rebellion, Simon and John, the taking of Simon to Rome, where he was bound and led in the triumphal parade of Titus and then killed, and the imprisonment of John	Judgment of Simon Peter and John at the conclusion of Jesus' ministry and the prediction that Simon would be bound and led and martyred, and that John would "remain."
A powerful leader of the rebels named Eleazar [Lazarus] is captured on the Mount of Olives, scourged and beaten, and threatened with crucifixion. He exhorts his followers to make peace with the Romans.	Parallels to the capture of Jesus at the Mount of Olives and his crucifixion. Atwill notes that the Eleazar in *War of the Jews* is also described as driving out demons.[415]

Further, Joseph Atwill analyzes an extended passage in *War of the Jews* concerning a certain mysterious root from a place called Baaras, which could dispel demons.[416] In conjunction with his analysis of the numerous passages about the messianic rebel leader Eleazar (who could dispel demons and who was captured at the Mount of Olives), Atwill concludes that these passages present a series of puzzle-pieces which, when fitted together, point to the conclusion that the Roman general Titus "plucked" Eleazar, and then created a new messianic substitute by "grafting" himself in as the Messiah in his place.

These puzzle pieces include the parallels between the description of the capture of Eleazar and the methods of safely plucking this demon-dispelling root, the fact that Titus orders Eleazar to be "pruned" and then returned to his followers after Eleazar has decided to sue for peace, and a passage in a different work by Josephus (*Life*, section 27) in which Josephus begs Titus to spare the lives of three captured rebels who are suffering on crosses at a place called Thecoa outside Jerusalem. After being taken down, two died despite the attentions of a physician, while the third survived. Noting that Josephus bar Matthias (the son of Matthias) is linguistically very similar to the "Joseph of Aramathea" who is described in the New Testament gospels as being the one who brings the body of the crucified Jesus down from the cross, Atwill argues that all these elements were woven together in the gospel accounts of the crucifixion outside Jerusalem, and that the Jesus presented there is a "pruned" or domesticated version of the messianic and rebellious Eleazar.[417] The fact that the events in the gospels mirror the events in the campaigns of Titus the son of Vespasian (both of whom became emperors and both of whom declared their own divinity) indicates in Atwill's analysis that the author of the gospels wanted to identify Titus as the new Messiah in place of the messianic rebellious leaders that the Romans were fighting to pacify and bring into submission.

But how can we reconcile these two different hypotheses, the gnostic / mysteries hypothesis presented by Freke and Gandy, and the Roman-conquest hypothesis proposed by Atwill? Were the doctrines which eventually became literally-interpreted Christianity originally gnostic teachings spread by Paul and others, which they intended to be understood esoterically by initiates of the inner mysteries, and which only later came to be twisted into histories? If so, how can Joseph Atwill's assertion that the gospels are parallels of the *Jewish Wars* by Josephus possibly be correct?

Moreover, how can we square the theories of both Freke and Gandy on the one hand, and Joseph Atwill on the other, with the thesis of this book – the thesis that all religions were originally presenting a complex series of celestial metaphors, intended to be understood esoterically? How could that possibly be the case, if (for example) Joseph Atwill is correct and the New Testament gospels are a mocking spoof of the conquest of Jerusalem and the rest of Judea by two Roman generals who later became emperors?

The solution lies in an incredible book, which in my opinion has not received enough attention from analysts of this crucial juncture in human history: *The Secret Society of Moses*, by Flavio Barbiero, originally written in Italian and published in an English translation by Steve Smith in 2010. It provides the key which can reconcile the insightful analysis of Freke and Gandy on the one hand, and of Joseph Atwill on the other. Moreover, while Barbiero's examination does not touch on the celestial theory presented in this book in any way, and in fact spends considerable time treating Moses and other figures of the Old Testament as literal figures, this in no way invalidates the celestial thesis and can be seen to harmonize with it quite well (as the following chapters will discuss).

In fact, the celestial and shamanic-holographic theory provides an important new perspective on the hypothesis of Flavio Barbiero – a hypothesis which I believe is almost certainly correct in almost all of its details, and a hypothesis which is of tremendous importance in understanding the history of the "western world," and one which (I believe) has ramifications far beyond even the astonishing ramifications that Flavio Barbiero himself discusses in his book.

14
The ransom of Josephus

But when Titus had composed the troubles in Judea, and conjectured that the lands which I had in Judea would bring me no profit, because a garrison to guard the country was afterward to pitch there, he gave me another country in the plain. And when he was going away to Rome, he made choice of me to sail along with him, and paid me great respect: and when we were come to Rome, I had great care taken of me by Vespasian; for he gave me an apartment in his own house, which he lived in before he came to the empire. He also honoured me with the privilege of a Roman citizen, and gave me an annual pension; and continued to respect me to the end of his life, without any abatement of his kindness to me [. . .]. I also received from Vespasian no small quantity of land, as a free gift in Judea; about which time I divorced my wife also, as not pleased with her behaviour [. . .]. However, the kindness of the emperor to me continued still the same; for when Vespasian was dead, Titus, who succeeded him in the government, kept up the same respect for me, which I had from his father; and when I had frequent accusations laid against me, he would not believe them. And Domitian, who succeeded, still augmented his respects to me; for he punished those Jews that were my accusers, and gave command that a servant of mine, who was an eunuch, and my accuser, should be punished. He also made that country I had in Judea, tax-free, which is a mark of the greatest honour to him who hath it; nay, Domitia, the wife of Cæsar, continued to do me kindnesses.

Josephus, *Life*.[418]

Joseph Atwill's analysis of the parallels between the events recorded by Josephus and the events described in the gospels of the New Testament is compelling, as is his thesis that the gospels represent a successful campaign to replace the messianic traditions inspiring violent rebellion in Judea with a version that would make the people more amenable to Roman occupation, but it runs into some difficulties in explaining some of the evidence. It is also difficult to reconcile with the theory of Timothy Freke and Peter Gandy, a theory which also has many compelling elements and which seems to explain other pieces of evidence and to mesh well with some of the "shamanic" and "holographic" themes we have been exploring.

I believe that these difficulties can be almost completely surmounted by incorporating the brilliant analysis of Flavio Barbiero published in 2010.

One of the difficulties for the theory of Joseph Atwill is the assertion that Christianity was almost exclusively the creation of the Flavians (with Josephus) after the violent pacification of Judea and the destruction of the Temple at Jerusalem. Joseph Atwill's books argue that the Romans (along with Josephus) created the entire fabric of the gospels based upon events that took place during the campaigns of AD 66 through AD 73, and Atwill finds parallels in the histories written by Josephus for the main events of the gospels, including the crucifixion.

There is a problem with this theory, however, in that at least some of the letters of Paul appear to have been written prior to AD 66, and to mention Christ and a crucifixion. Timothy Freke and Peter Gandy provide evidence, supported by some New Testament scholars, that some of Paul's letters were written as early as AD 50, while others (particularly the "pastoral" letters such as those addressed to Timothy and Titus) may have been much later forgeries not written by the same person at all. These early letters, Freke and Gandy point out, do not treat Christ as a historical figure – that would come later, during the period they believe the gospels were written, after AD 70.[419]

They present evidence to support the possibility that the author of those early Pauline letters such as Galatians and Colossians may have taught a gnostic understanding of a "dying and resurrecting godman."[420] Of course, if Joseph Atwill is correct, and the inspiration for the crucifixion came entirely from events that took place during the Roman pacification campaign, then these references from letters written a decade or more earlier would be quite prophetic. However, the two theories can be reconciled if we posit that the author or authors who later added historical details to what was once a more general and gnostic storyline borrowed from the events described by Josephus (or if the author was Josephus himself). This possibility fits quite well with the theory put forward by Flavio Barbiero.

Flavio Barbiero's theory is stunning in its scope and astonishing in its ability to explain a vast amount of historical evidence stretching across centuries, including historical evidence which is very difficult to explain otherwise. The heart of his theory – which again should be read in full in his own book in order to do true justice to the tremendous amount of evidence and detailed analysis which he presents – is the assertion that when the Roman general Vespasian and his son Titus put down the uprisings in Judea, a member of the Jewish priestly line surrendered to Vespasian and turned over the bulk of the treasures that had been accumulated under the system of Temple worship. This treasure was essential to Vespasian's ability to continue to pay his army and to install himself as emperor (Vespasian would be succeeded by his son Titus a few years later).

In return for the treasure whose funds enabled them to secure this greatest of prizes, Vespasian and Titus bestowed tremendous privilege on the priest who made it possible, and in addition spared many other members of the priestly lines who would otherwise have been killed by the Romans, but whose lives were saved at the specific request of the priest who had gone over to Vespasian and who had betrayed the location of the hidden treasures of the Temple. Flavio Barbiero demonstrates that those members of the priestly lines moved to Rome and set in motion a slow but steady campaign to gain control of the entire Roman empire, which they in fact accomplished – and that their success led to their descendents becoming the kings and queens and nobility of Europe for the next nineteen centuries, all the way up to the present day.

According to Flavio Barbiero's thesis, that priest who went over to Vespasian and who set in motion this grand design was none other than Josephus.

For his initial supporting evidence, he cites the works of Josephus himself, showing that Josephus begins his autobiography with the very clear statement that he is a member of the priestly class, which consisted of approximately twenty-four families, and that he in fact was a member of one of the most distinguished of these families, with an impeccable lineage. The significance of this fact – a fact which Josephus himself clearly held to be of the utmost significance – will become clear as the new approach offered by Flavio Barbiero unfolds.

Barbiero then demonstrates that the account given by Josephus of his surrender to Vespasian is highly suspect, and that it is almost certainly intended to mask the truth of the betrayal that actually took place. According to his own published history of the Jewish Wars, Josephus led the resistance against the Romans in the region of Galilee, where his forces were eventually surrounded inside the fortress of Jotapata by Titus Flavius Vespasian.

With defeat imminent, Josephus and the other high-ranking leaders hid in an underground cistern within the grounds of the fortress, and swore a suicide pact that they would kill themselves rather than allow themselves to be taken alive by the Romans. According to his own account, they decided to draw lots to determine the order that they would run one another through with their swords, with the plan being that the last two left alive would run one another through simultaneously.[421]

In his own account, Josephus drew the last position of the forty, and when he and only one other were left of the original group (having killed the rest), he suddenly realized that God had ordained that the Romans would be victorious, and decided that he could better serve God by living rather than by ending his life right there. In his account, Josephus says he gave himself up and asked to speak to the general himself, and when he was brought to Vespasian, Josephus told the general that he had received a prophecy from God that Vespasian was divinely ordained to become the emperor in Rome. According to the account of Josephus, it was this prophecy that caused Vespasian to gratefully spare his life, and that was the reason that Josephus was later adopted into the family of the emperor (Josephus became Josephus Flavius) and was even given a place to live in the Italian villa in which Vespasian himself had previously lived, once Vespasian had become emperor and built an even more palatial villa for himself.[422]

Flavio Barbiero points out that this treatment seems a little excessive if all Josephus did for Vespasian was relay a prophecy that Vespasian was destined to become emperor. He notes that there had been numerous such prophecies made about Vespasian already – the addition of one more would hardly warrant such lavish reward. Barbiero writes:

> Suetonius testifies that this prophecy made by Josephus was only the last in a series of similar predictions, which started on the day that Vespasian was born. Everybody knew of the existence of these prophecies – it was thus totally absurd to imagine that Vespasian covered a vanquished rebel with unprecedented favors simply because he had repeated an omen that was generally known. There must have been something else. The Roman general was under a terrible handicap in his race for the imperial purple robe: he was broke (it is Suetonius again who confirms this), but in order to become emperor, he needed ample financial means. Josephus provided them.[423]

Based on the evidence from other ancient writers, who attest to the fact that the prophecy delivered by Josephus was by no means the first time Vespasian had heard such a declaration, which scenario seems more plausible: that the Roman general saved an enemy leader who had just been fighting against him based on a supposed prophecy from the God worshiped by that enemy, or that the Roman general saved him because he promised immediate access to treasure now and to far greater treasure when they got to Jerusalem?

Flavio Barbiero cites passages from the works of Josephus himself indicating that, as the erstwhile governor of Galilee before the war began, Josephus had been able to gather a considerable amount of treasure, which he had set aside for the building of a wall for the city of Taricheae.[424] But the real treasure-store was the gold and silver of the Temple itself, which by clear and insightful analysis, Flavio Barbiero demonstrates to have been given over to Vespasian and Titus by Josephus to secure his release.

He points out the fact that the treasure of the Temple featured prominently in the triumph celebrated in Rome by Vespasian and Titus after their victory in Judea. This is testified to in the works of Josephus, who describes the triumph and states that among all the treasure on display in the procession, that treasure which had been taken from the Temple of Jerusalem stood out above the rest (in *War of the Jews* Book VII, Josephus explains that it was decided that Vespasian and Titus would share in a common triumphal procession, and the spoils of that triumph are described in some detail in Book VII part 5). Even more positive proof is the depiction on the Arch of Titus, which still stands today, of the spoils of the Temple being carried in the triumph.[425]

"There is no doubt, then, that Vespasian took possession of the treasure of the Temple," writes Flavio Barbiero, "but how and when did this happen? Reading of the circumstances in which the siege of Jerusalem and the final attack on the Temple took place, we should expect that when the Romans succeeded in capturing it, little remained of the original treasure: the Temple had been occupied for months by the Zealots, who had not hesitated to strip it completely."[426] The defenders were so adamant that nothing fall into the hands of the Romans that they burned the Temple itself when defeat became inevitable. They would not have let the most precious items of their faith, including the golden Menorah and the copy of the Law, fall into the hands of the enemy – and yet the writings of Josephus and the reliefs which can be seen to this day upon the Arch of Titus testify that these did fall into the hands of the Romans, intact.

Flavio Barbiero then points out that Josephus' description of how this could have happened is "somewhat confused and contradictory."[427] In his account of how it happened, Josephus states that a priest named Jesus and another priest named Phineas handed over the solid gold artifacts of the Temple, along with a great quantity of other precious goods and sacred objects used in worship, in exchange for their safe conduct. At the same time, other priests were summarily executed by Titus, according to Josephus' account, since Titus said that after the defenders had burned the Temple down themselves, the time for clemency to their priest-leaders had passed: "it was only right, therefore, for the priests to be exterminated together with their sanctuary," Titus told them.[428]

While this seems plausible on its face (after all, escaping execution and buying safe conduct from the Romans by paying them with treasure is believable – in fact, it is how Josephus himself escaped death according to Barbiero's theory), Barbiero demonstrates that there are several huge holes in this explanation:

There are some inaccuracies in this passage, and several details are omitted. First of all, the capture of the two priests takes place when the Temple had already been gutted by fire and what remained of it was in Roman hands. Consequently, it was impossible that, as Josephus tells us, the objects were lowered down by Jesus "from the top of the sanctuary wall." Further, it is unlikely that this happened before the fall of the Temple, because the walls were teeming with defenders who would never have allowed such an operation. Next, he presents the two priests as low-ranking figures, though they must have been at the top of the priestly organization in order to be the custodians of the Temple treasure. Last, he covers up the fact that the objects handed over had obviously been hidden in some secret hiding place. Phineas could not have had them with him at the time of his capture.[429]

These points become glaringly obvious once they are pointed out and once we consider them critically.

Further, as Flavio Barbiero demonstrates, the last of these points has some very powerful archaeological evidence to back it up – in one of the most famous archaeological discoveries of the twentieth century, the discovery of the Dead Sea Scrolls.

Barbiero presents evidence which describes a fascinating story, a story that would profoundly change the shape of history, with consequences that would echo down through the centuries to this very moment in time, a story of betrayal, cunning, buried treasure, and a long-lost treasure map – a map which resurfaced nearly two thousand years after the events surrounding the fall of the Temple. The story involves the mysterious Copper Scroll, discovered among the Dead Sea Scrolls in cave 3Q at Qumran, in 1952. It is called the Copper Scroll because, unlike the other Dead Sea Scrolls, it was actually engraved on the inside of three sheets of copper, joined together and rolled up like a scroll. Due to its age and condition, the scroll could no longer be unrolled, but it was taken to England and carefully cut into vertical strips, which were then cleaned and translated by a team of Qumranists, including the iconoclastic scholar John Marco Allegro, whose theory about the purpose of the Copper Scroll clashed with that of most of the other Qumranists.[430]

The Copper Scroll wastes no time with introductions or explanations, but gets right to business. Here is what it says (in a translation by J.T. Milik, which can be read online at the University of Memphis website; interpolations in that online version are shown here with brackets, as they appear in the translation itself):

1. At Horebbah which is in the Vale of Achor under the stairs which go eastwards forty cubits: a box [filled with] silver weighing in all seventeen talents.
2. In the tomb of . . . the third: 100 gold bars.
3. In the great cistern which is in the courtyard of the little colonnade, at its very bottom, closed with sediment towards the upper opening: nine hundred talents.
4. At the hill of Kohlit, containers, sandalwood and ephods [priestly garments]. The total of the offering and of the treasure: seven [talents?] and second tithe rendered unclean. At the exit of the canal on the northern side, six cubits towards the cavity of immersion.
5. In the hole of the waterproofed refuge, in going down towards the left, three cubits above the bottom: forty talents of silver.

6. In the cistern of the esplanade which is under the stairs: forty-two talents.
7. In the cave of the old Washer's House, on the third platform: sixty-five gold bars.
8. In the underground cavity which is in the courtyard of the House of Logs, where there is a cistern: vessels and silver, seventy talents.
9. In the cistern which is against the eastern gate, which is fifteen cubits away, there are vessels in it.
10. And in the canal which [ends] in it: ten talents.
11. In the cistern which is under the wall on the eastern side, at the sharp edge of the rock: six silver bars; its entrance is under the large paving-stone.
12. In the pond which is east of Kohlit, at a northern angle, dig four cubits: twenty-two talents.
13. In the courty[ard of] . . . in southerly direction [at] nine cubits: silver and gold vessels of offering, bowls, cups, tubes, libation vessels. In all, six hundred and nine.
14. In the other, easterly direction dig sixteen cubits: 40 tal. of silver.
15. In the underground cavity of the esplanade on its northern side: vessels of offering, garments. Its entrance is in the westerly direction.
16. In the tomb on the north-east of the esplanade three cubits under the trap [?]: 13 tal.
17. In the great cistern which is in the . . . , in the pillar on its northern side: 14 tal[ents].
18. In the canal which goes [towards . . .] when you enter for[ty-o]ne cubits: 55 tal. of silver.
19. Between the two tamarisk trees in the Vale of Akhon, in their midst dig three cubits. There there are two pots full of silver.
20. In the red underground cavity at the mouth of the 'Aslah: 200 tal. of silver.
21. In the eastern underground cavity at the north of Kohlit: 70 tal. of silver.
22. In the heap of stones in the valley of Sekhakha dig (. . .) cubits: 12 tal. of silver.
23. At the head of the water conduit . . . [at] Sekhakha, on the northern side under the large . . . dig [thr]ee cub[its]: 7 tal. of silver.[431]

The scroll continues with fully forty more descriptions of hiding places containing treasure, for sixty-three in all by the reckoning of József Tadeusz Milik (1922 – 2006), one of the first scholars to work with the Copper Scroll and to publish a translation (along with John Marco Allegro, with whom Milik disagreed on a number of important points).

Among the other treasures that are listed in the subsequent forty more locations added to the twenty-three shown above are tusks (perhaps of elephants), great lists of "talents" which sometimes specify whether they refer to silver or gold or both, and sometimes only specify the amount but not the metal in question, sometimes as many as 300 talents of gold (at the western side of a pond) and 900 talents of silver (at the western entrance of a tomb), as well as offering vessels and "devoted things."[432]

At the very end of the list there is one more item listed, perhaps more important than all the others. It states: "In the underground cavity which is in the smooth rock north of Kohlit whose opening is towards the north with tombs at its mouth there is a copy of this writing and its explanation and the measurements and the details of each item."[433] J. T. Milik numbered this "line 64."

The amount of treasure described is enormous. The amount is so vast that Milik insisted that these enormous amounts of treasure clearly indicated that the Copper Scroll was nothing but a work of fiction, perhaps the outline for some kind of story or tradition. As we will see, Milik, who was a Catholic priest, was part of an institution which may well have a strong motive for insisting that the treasure described in the Copper Scroll never existed. If such a vast treasure did indeed exist, and if Josephus was indeed able to deliver it in secret to Vespasian and Titus, then this fact would instantly explain the high regard with which Josephus was treated the rest of his life by the members of Vespasian's family, as well as the wealth, lands, and tax-free status which they bestowed upon Josephus.

Commenting upon that final, crucial line of the Copper Scroll, Flavio Barbiero concludes that the Copper Scroll found at Qumran, which survived to the present day, is thus only a backup copy of the original scroll, which must have been hidden at a cave or underground cavity at Kohlit among the tombs, as the Copper Scroll declares. Barbiero notes that whoever had been responsible for securing this treasure from the Roman invaders had laid their plans carefully, creating two copies of the treasure list, inscribing the list on the nonperishable substance of copper to guard against loss by fire or water, and hiding those two treasure scrolls carefully. He concludes that the entire plan must undoubtedly have been organized by the heads of the priestly family lines in charge of the Temple.[434]

Barbiero believes that Josephus, having been the first of the priests to surrender to the Romans (the Roman campaign having commenced in the region of Galilee, a point that Joseph Atwill argues as a support for his theory that the gospel accounts mirror the progress of Vespasian and Titus), bargained for his life by offering not only the treasure he had managed to accumulate as the priest in charge of the Galilee region *but also* access to the far larger treasure of the Temple itself, which had been carefully hidden in the secret places described in the two copies of the treasure-directory. One of those two copies, the Copper Scroll, remained undisturbed down through the centuries – until it was discovered by archaeologists in cave 3Q, where it would receive the designation "3Q15" by the modern Dead Sea Scroll scholars.

Josephus, according to this theory, led the Romans to the first scroll, the one that was hidden in a cave at Kohlit, near Jerusalem itself. He then helped the Romans to locate all the cryptically-described caves, chambers, cisterns, tamarisk trees, and ponds where the treasure was buried. Barbiero notes that Josephus came from the first of the priestly families (by his own admission and declaration at the beginning of his autobiography), that Josephus was obviously a trusted and respected member of the ruling class, having been made the governor of Galilee and the man in charge of the defense of that region (where the first blow from the invading Roman armies would fall), and that he had spent three years of his youth in the very deserts where the treasure was buried; based on all these facts, Barbiero says, it is not unreasonable to believe that Josephus knew about the strategy of hiding the treasure, knew where the instruction scrolls would be found, and would have had no problem locating all the secret points described in the Copper Scroll.[435]

This theory has much else to support it. It explains the otherwise inexplicable treatment afforded to Josephus, the first of the rebel commanders to surrender to Vespasian. In addition to later being given Vespasian's own former villa as his home, Josephus was also given "a robe and other objects of value" by Vespasian as gift immediately after the two came to an agreement.[436] Josephus was also given a maiden who was among the captives from the city of Caesarea (in Galilee) to be his wife, he was given the release of his brother and fifty friends in the region of Galilee, he was allowed to free friends and acquaintances that he recognized after the fall of the Temple totaling about 190 persons by Josephus' own account, he was able to have all these people (whom Barbiero believes were probably fellow members of the priestly class) restored to their original estates and conditions after the war, he was given the privilege of adoption into the family of the Flavians and took their name, and after Vespasian became the emperor, Josephus was given a lifetime annuity paid by the state treasury of the empire in addition to his substantial villa and additional lands and estates.[437]

The idea that such a jaw-dropping list of favors was given simply because a vanquished rebel commander emerged from his hiding-place in an underground cistern after the fall of Jotapata and told Vespasian that he had a divine message for him is quite simply unbelievable. The theory that during his private audience with the Roman general Josephus convinced him of his ability to deliver the hidden treasures of the Temple, on the other hand, explains this historical mystery quite well.

It also explains why nobody has ever been able to find any of the treasures in any of the locations described in the Copper Scroll in the decades since it was deciphered. For many – including J. M. Allegro, who wholeheartedly disagreed with his fellow-Qumranist J. T. Milik – spent considerable effort deciphering the terse descriptions of various treasure locations in 3Q15 and then searching for the ancient artifacts that would simultaneously prove that the scroll was what it appeared to be and constitute an archaeological find of incredible significance.

Finally, it explains why the Copper Scroll itself was left to slowly oxidize with the rust of nearly two millennia in a cave, a forgotten treasure map to a long-lost treasure, and a silent testimony to one of the greatest acts of betrayal and survival in human history. It was now useless as a guide to that long-stolen fortune.[438]

All of this analysis, and the story of that ancient betrayal of the hiding place of the treasure, after which it was seized by the Romans and used to vault a new imperial dynasty into power, is indeed fascinating, but the question remains, why would this event have world-changing consequences which continue to this day?

The answer to that question is this: the actions of Josephus vaulted a member of the *priestly class* into a position of tremendous wealth and influence within the Roman Empire, into a position from which he and the other members of that class (whose lives he had saved by his deal-making abilities) could exert their knowledge of the principles of human consciousness – and its suppression. They would create the religious hierarchy which would eventually make its mission the seizing of a treasure of far greater value – the ancient deep wisdom given to humankind, which the descendents of Josephus would take for their own and attempt to deny to everyone else.

15
The Mystery of Mithras

We may say, then, that the existence in Mithraic art of various symbols representing changing world ages and cycles of time offers strong support for our hypothesis that the Mithraic bull-slaying symbolizes Mithras's power to end one cosmic cycle and begin a new one, which he has by virtue of his control over the fundamental structures of the universe. [. . .]

We may now carry the argument one final step further by focusing on the word *invictus* (unconquered) in the title *Mithras sol invictus*. When Mithras is referred to as the *un*conquered sun, one naturally becomes curious as to whether or not there is also somewhere a *conquered* sun. And here, of course, Mithraic iconography gives us an absolutely explicit answer: all of those scenes depicting the sun god kneeling before Mithras or otherwise submitting to him make it abundantly clear that it is the sun itself who is actually the conquered sun. Mithras, therefore, becomes the *un*conquered sun by conquering the sun. He accomplices [*sic*] this deed, as we saw earlier, by means of the power represented by the symbol of the celestial pole which he holds in his hand in the "investment" scenes, a power which consists in his ability to shift the position of the celestial pole by moving the cosmic structure and which clearly makes him more powerful than the sun. And so we may say that Mithras is entitled to be called "sun" insofar as he has taken over the role of *kosmokrator* formerly exercised by the sun itself.

David Ulansey,
The Origins of the Mithraic Mysteries.[439]

The writings of Josephus testify that he was able to save hundreds of his friends, family, and acquaintances from death after the fall of Jerusalem to the Romans. Flavio Barbiero notes that among these there were certainly at least fifteen members of the priestly lineage of the Jews, whom Josephus lists in Book VI, chapter 2 of his *War of the Jews*.[440]

The priestly line, consisting of families descended from specific families of the priestly branch that returned to their homeland after the Babylonian captivity (events which Barbiero discusses in the earlier chapters of his book), had influenced tremendous power over the people for centuries leading up to the final destruction of the Temple in AD 70. Yet, as Flavio Barbiero points out, after the fall of the Temple, this ancient priestly line of families effectively disappears from history, never again to be mentioned in surviving texts – as if they wanted to hide their trail.[441]

From the testimony of Josephus, we know that a substantial number of those families were spared (most likely due, as we saw, to a secret deal that Josephus cut with Vespasian after the first major Roman victory in the Galilee region, a deal that promised the Temple treasure to the conquering general who would become the emperor). Josephus tells us that those families (undoubtedly very wealthy and influential families in the region of Jerusalem) even had their former wealth and possessions restored to them.

While history only provides us with information about the subsequent activities of Josephus, Flavio Barbiero reasons that the other members of the priestly class who had been spared would have sought to leave Judea for Rome. Staying in Judea, they would have been seen as traitors, but in a cosmopolitan city such as the capitol, they could start anew.[442]

From there, Barbiero reasons, they began to rebuild the Temple, which had been the basis of their power as well as the focus of their faith. However, there would be one major difference: this time, they would rebuild an *invisible* Temple, instead of a visible. It would be a spiritual Temple.[443]

If that idea sounds familiar, it is because the concept of the spiritual temple is very explicitly stated in the doctrines of Christianity, specifically discussed in New Testament verses such as 1 Corinthians 3:16-17, as well as 2 Corinthians 6:16 and also Ephesians 2:21. It is the astonishing thesis of Flavio Barbiero, backed up with extensive evidence presented in his book, that Josephus and the members of the priestly class used their knowledge and their experience to erect a spiritual Temple that would enable their descendants to take over the entire Roman Empire by the end of the fourth century, and then later, after they had discarded the empire that they no longer needed and which had become an obstacle, to secure themselves in positions of control over "Christendom" for the nearly seventeen centuries that have elapsed since their victory was complete.

To support this thesis, Barbiero cites a wide range of evidence. First, as we have already seen, are the voluminous writings of Josephus himself. Barbiero argues, with plenty of textual support some of which we have already examined, that one of the main purposes of Josephus' prolific literary efforts after he came to Rome was to cover up the terms of the deal he had cut with Vespasian – a deal by which Josephus had become a traitor to his people and by which he had delivered up to the Romans "the most precious things that existed for a Jew."[444]

Secondly, he examines three historic institutions which contain masses of evidence testifying to the deliberate construction of this "spiritual Temple" by the survivors of the priestly family in the Roman Empire (led, undoubtedly by Josephus himself). Those three institutions which testify to the success of Josephus and his associates are the institution of Mithraism, the institution of Masonry societies which have as a central focus the building of a spiritual Temple, and the institution of hierarchical Christianity under the bishops and priests – an institution which Flavio Barbiero believes was the public and popular version of the secret and esoteric Mithraic system, and which became the vehicle for open control once Christianity was strong enough and it was judged that the secret vehicle of Mithraism should be discontinued.

In addition to these two sources of evidence (the writings of Josephus and the three institutions just mentioned), he provides substantial additional evidence from world history, in particular the history of the Roman Catholic church and the European royalty and nobility during the Middle Ages, all of whom he argues were primarily led by descendants of those priestly families who had forged a new life for themselves and their lineages after the fall of the Temple in Jerusalem.

Barbiero's theory is that the vehicle established by the priestly family lines to gain control of the empire and ensure not only their survival but their lasting success was not, as some might have expected, the religion of Christianity but rather the secret society of Mithraism in conjunction with Christianity. Christianity would become Mithraism's public twin while the real plans and plots were discussed in the secrecy of the mithraea, until Christianity had consolidated enough political power to officially discard the Mithraic underground.[445] He then shows that Masonry very closely parallels the institution of Mithraism and is probably the surviving version of that institution (which could still be used in places or times in which open influence of the mechanisms of power by the church was impossible or impractical).[446]

Mithraism, whose astronomical and precessional symbology is discussed in some detail in a chapter in my previous book (building on the groundbreaking work of David Ulansey's *Origins of the Mithraic Mysteries*), was an ancient secret society restricted exclusively to men, with a hierarchical organization structure of seven levels, which met in underground "mithraea" (or above-ground buildings designed to resemble underground grottos) adorned with esoteric symbolism of very clear astronomical character.[447] Flavio Barbiero shows that the circumstantial evidence linking Mithraism to the Judaic priestly families who came to Rome with Vespasian and Titus is quite strong.

First, we know from history that Mithraism was very strong among the Roman army, and particularly among the Praetorian Guard, those troops dedicated to the protection of the imperial household and located in Rome itself. Barbiero argues that the infiltration of the Praetorian Guard probably began under the Flavians, who had seized control of the empire to found the first dynasty after the original Julians (Augustus, Tiberius, Caligula, Claudius and Nero, whose dynasty ended in AD 68 with the suicide of Nero, after which there was a struggle among possible successors, initiated by the prefect of the Praetorian Guard himself).

After the death of Nero in AD 68, Galba seized power with the support of Spanish legions, only to be assassinated by the Praetorian Guard and replaced by Otho in AD 69, who in turn was replaced by a general Galba had placed in charge of the legions in Germany, Vitellius, just a few months later. Only a couple of months later, Vitellius learned that the legions of Egypt and Judea had declared Vespasian emperor probably, as Flavio Barbiero explains, after Vespasian bribed the legions of Egypt with gold from obtained from Josephus.[448]

Although Jerusalem had not yet fallen, Vespasian had taken Josephus with him to Egypt (Josephus had been captured after the battle of Jotapata in AD 67), no doubt as a way of convincing the commanders there that he would soon have the funds to pay them off, and to keep the very precious asset (which Josephus had now become) under his control. Vitellius realized that the alliance of legions now in Vespasian's camp had effectively sealed his fate, and Vitellius made plans to surrender to Vespasian, who was marching against him and who took control of Rome in December of AD 69. He did not have the opportunity: the Praetorian Guard ordered Vitellius back to Rome, where he was murdered when Vespasian entered the capitol.

Josephus in the meantime had been sent back to Judea where he remained with Titus the son of Vespasian, who continued the campaign there through to the ultimate defeat of the Jewish insurrection and the destruction of the Temple in AD 70. When Titus returned victorious to Rome, Josephus was on board the same ship.[449]

Based on this tumultuous series of events, in which the Praetorian Guard played a leading role in deciding when an emperor would be deposed, it is unsurprising that Vespasian and his son would entrust their personal guard to freedmen from the conquest of Judea.

Flavio Barbiero argues that Vespasian and his successors decided to install those whose treasure had bought him the empire, and whose future success in Rome now depended upon Vespasian and his family, as the members and indeed leaders of the Praetorians. After all, Barbiero notes, these priestly families all "had glorious military traditions, starting from the Maccabees and ending with Josephus Flavius."[450]

While some readers might question the wisdom of such a move, Barbiero argues that it actually made more sense than leaving the Praetorian Guard in the command of fellow Romans, who after all had been instrumental in turning against Nero and supplanting the Julians: the Jewish freedmen whose lives they had spared had every reason to want their imperial protectors to remain in power, whereas a Praetorian Guard made up of Romans could easily turn against the new Flavian dynasty, especially if it were filled with descendents of any of the old Senatorial families, or others who might have connections to some rival who craved the throne for himself.[451]

The fact that Mithraism appears to have spread first among the Praetorian Guard thus becomes a key piece of circumstantial evidence which supports the theory that it represented a continuation (in disguise) of the esoteric religion that the priests of Judea had guarded for centuries prior to the Roman conquest.

Our own examination in this book so far, of the solar and astronomical symbology that completely saturates the Old Testament, provides powerful additional support for Barbiero's thesis. As discussed in my previous book, and as Professor David Ulansey has demonstrated in his book *Origins of the Mithraic Mysteries* (1989), the symbology and hierarchy of Mithraism is completely astronomical and solar and precessional – just as we have seen the symbology of the Old Testament to be.

Mithraism is also known as the cult of Sol Invictus (the "Unconquered Sun" or the "Unconquerable Sun"), one of the titles of Mithras (as Ulansey explains in some detail). This fact powerfully connects Mithraism to the pattern found in the Old and New Testaments, which we have examined in some depth. Further, many of the details that Ulansey examines in his 1989 text indicate that Mithraic iconology utilized symbols which were common to ancient Egypt. This fact appears to support the theory of Flavio Barbiero even more strongly, if the "out of Egypt" theory examined in earlier chapters is correct. If Mithraism was the vehicle used by Josephus and the relocated priestly families when they arrived in Rome, the fact that those priestly families were privy to the ancient system of esoteric celestial symbology which utilized the motion of the sun successively through the twelve houses of the zodiac each year, as well as the motion of precession which turned the backdrop of the "fixed" stars forward through the zodiac over the ages-long cycle of the Great Year, would explain the clear use of zodiac and precessional imagery found in every mithraeum. The fact that some of the iconography uses very distinctive Egyptian imagery would seem to suggest the possibility that the priestly class who had been in charge of Temple worship prior to the campaigns of the Romans which culminated in the Temple's destruction were well educated in the celestial system of ancient Egypt.

Perhaps the most striking example of this "Egyptian connection" in Mithraism are the friezes showing Mithras holding a joint of meat representative of "the bull's shoulder." Ulansey explains that, in addition to the "tauroctony" scene found in every mithraeum (a scene which shows Mithras slaying a bull while surrounded by zodiac animals: a clear precessional symbol which Ulansey interprets as indicating that Mithras was attributed with the power of turning the precessional ages and thus wielding even greater power than the power of the sun itself, which is "subject" to precession) friezes found in mithraea often show the sun-god Helios kneeling before Mithras.[452]

Ulansey writes:

> Mithraic iconography often portrays Mithras involved in various activites in conjunction with the sun god (Helios or Sol). Many of these scenes clearly represent Mithras as a power superior to Helios. For example, we find a number of monuments showing Helios kneeling before Mithras in a gesture of submission, the so-called investiture scenes (see Figure 7.9). In some of these "investiture" images, Mithras is shown holding in his hand something which looks like the shoulder or leg of an animal while Helios crouches in front of him (see Figure 7.10).[453]

Ulansey then notes that the shoulder of a bull was commonly used in ancient Egypt to represent the constellation of the Great Bear, Ursa Major, the constellation which contains the Big Dipper, and which turns about the north celestial pole. He cites the analysis of Roger Beck and R. L. Gordon concerning a portion of the ancient Greek text known today as the Paris Codex or Papyrus 574 of the Bibliotheque Nationale in Paris, thought to have been compiled in the early fourth century AD, a section found in lines 475 – 834 of that codex known as the "Mithras Liturgy."[454]

The connection of the contents of the "Mithras Liturgy" with Mithraism is disputed – some believe that it has nothing to do with Mithraism at all. However, Ulansey argues that because the text describes a god holding a bull's shoulder and because the iconography of mithraea sometimes show Mithras holding a bull's shoulder, the possibility that the Mithras Liturgy does indeed have some connection to Mithraism is strengthened.[455] In the Mithras Liturgy, the god Mithras is described as "holding in his right hand a golden shoulder of a young bull: this is the Bear which moves and turns heaven around, moving upward and downward in accordance with the hour."[456] Ulansey notes that Roger Beck in his analysis makes the direct connection that "in Egypt the Great Bear was known as the Bull's Shoulder."[457] This Egyptian identification can be easily corroborated by examining the Dendera Zodiac, in which the foreleg of a hoofed animal is clearly seen near the center of the circle of the sky, next to the female hippopotamus holding the pole.

Below is a sketch of an image showing Helios (identifiable by his radiant nimbus or halo around his head) kneeling before Mithras (in his distinctive Phrygian cap), who holds the Bull's Shoulder in one hand, and places his other hand atop the head of the kneeling Helios (this is the relief depicted in Figure 7.10 referenced in the block quotation from Ulansey above, CIMRM 1430 C5).

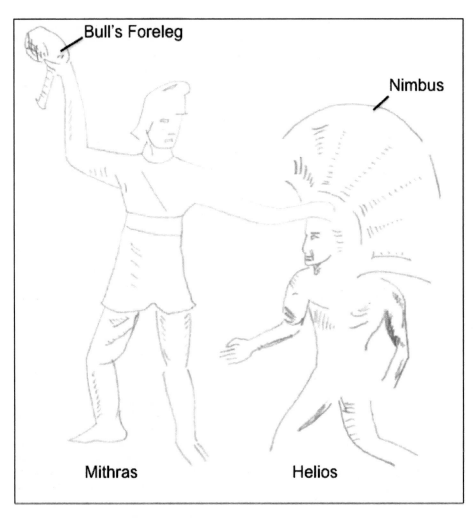

Bull's Foreleg

Nimbus

Mithras

Helios

In an essay entitled "Why the Shoulder?: A Study of the Placement of the Wound in the Mithraic Tauroctony," author Glenn Palmer notes that the Bull's Foreleg was placed in the sky after the defeat of Seth or Set by Horus, as a way of preventing Set from using it to murder anyone again. He notes that in the Papyrus Leiden I, thought to date to the time of Rameses II, the murder of Osiris by Set takes place when Set turns into a bull and tramples Osiris underfoot:

> A version of the murder of Osiris has Seth transformed into a bull when he commits the act. The Papyrus Leiden I states that Seth stomped Osiris to death with his bovine foreleg:
>
>> The stars of the northern sky are called "the never setting ones." They guard in the seven-star heavenly body the bull leg, the leg of Seth, with which he – as a bull – killed Osiris, and thereby prevent that a fight

arises again. Fatigue in the southern sky and fight in the northern sky endanger the course of the earth. A lamentation [or complaint] before Re can bring it [i.e., the course of the earth] to a stop. After the ritual against evil, both skies could move towards each other. The southern sky could pull the northern sky into its movement, so that it moves also towards the West, and both finally fall down. (*Pap. Leiden* I.348, Verso XI, 5ff. [Schott 1959:328])

Although the Foreleg has been imprisoned, it is still a threat and requires a retinue of keepers (Fig 17.4). The "never setting ones" in this passage are the sons of Horus, numbering four or seven depending on the source. They are considered guardians more in the sense of prison guards, rather than as maintainers of celestial function. The *Mithrasliturgie* employs these guardians as the seven Pole-Lords that turn the polar axis.

In order to prevent Seth from harming other gods, Horus, the son of Osiris, cut the Foreleg from Seth's shoulder:

And after he had cut out his foreleg he threw it into the sky. Spirits guard it there: the Great Bear of the northern sky. The great Hippopotomus goddess keeps hold of it, so that it can no longer sail in the midst of the gods. (*Pap. Leiden* I.348, Verso XI, 5ff. [Schott 1959:328])

The Hippopotomus goddess is an Egyptian constellation near the North Pole that represents a manifestation of Isis.[458]

The mythical events described in the Papyrus Leiden are clearly another esoteric version of precession, in which the constellation Taurus "tramples down" Orion and usurps the rule of the March equinox. The association of the motion of precession with the stars around the north celestial pole, as Ulansey explains, stems from the fact that the motion of precession causes the north celestial pole to move in a circle over the course of the entire cycle of the Great Year.[459] In this version of the precessional mythography, the Foreleg or Big Dipper is the "lever" by which the motion of precession is accomplished, and hence the Foreleg is a dangerous instrument (it brought about the demise of Osiris).

The important point to be made here is the fact that the iconography of Mithras has clear connections to ancient Egyptian iconography – to symbols which stretch to the time of Rameses II, in fact. Palmer notes in the same essay that:

There has been relatively little consideration of the effect of Egyptian belief on the development of Mithraic doctrine and iconography. Certainly late Egyptian belief was known to Mithraism. Statues of Isis have been found in association with Mithraic icons. Her consort Sarapis was often equated with Mithras, Jupiter, or Saturn/Kronos on Mithraic monuments. Some Mithraic statues also hold the Egyptian ankh. Priests of Isis are known to have belonged to the higher grades of Mithraic initiation.[460]

Palmer adds in a footnote that Roger Beck posits the possible transmission of Egyptian knowledge into Mithraism through a Roman astrologer named Tiberius Claudius

Balbillas (AD 3 – AD 79).[461] However, if the thesis of Flavio Barbiero is correct, then the explanation for the understanding of esoteric Egyptian symbology, to include the extremely precise symbol of the Bull's Foreleg, can be explained by the fact that according to his theory, Mithraism was almost entirely the creation of the priestly families who came to Rome with Josephus (note that to this day scholars are not aware of examples of Mithraic architecture or inscription prior to the first century AD). If those families were in possession of ancient Egyptian esoteric knowledge (because they and their Old Testament were descendents of Egyptians of Egyptian myth many centuries before), then this would explain the origins of the precise esoteric Egyptian symbology in the Mithraic iconography.

Flavio Barbiero explains that we can track the spread of Mithraism by dates on surviving dedicatory inscriptions at mithraea, many of which survive throughout the reaches of the former empire.

He points out that the very first extant written evidence referencing Mithraism "is a dedicatory inscription to Mithras left by a certain Titus Flavius Hyginus Ephebianus, almost certainly a freedman of the emperor whose name he assumed: Titus Flavius. He was likely a Jew who came to Rome after the destruction of Jerusalem, and it is more than likely that he was one of the priests of the circle of Josephus Flavius."[462] His name indicates that he was a freedman of emperor Titus, which Barbiero explains is good reason to believe that he came from Judea, where the campaigns of Vespasian and Titus had taken place. This inscription dates to the reign of the emperor Domitian, another son of Vespasian who succeeded his brother Titus in AD 81.

The second is "a statue dedicated to Mithras by a certain Alcimus," who was one of the two commanders of the emperor's personal guard under Trajan, successor to Domitian after the two-year reign of Nerva.[463] After this early dedication by a member of the Praetorian Guard, Flavio Barbiero explains, the cult of Mithras and the Praetorian Guard became closely intertwined, to the extent that the vicinity of their barracks now contains the heaviest concentration of mithraea in the capitol region.[464]

From there, the cult appears to have spread to the rest of the army, as well as into the bureaucracy of the empire, through the apparatus of the collection of various taxes, particularly at the customs-houses.[465] The next large concentration of mithraea after Rome is in Ostia, the port closest to the capitol, where a huge percentage of the imports bound for Rome would arrive.

At the same time that the cult of Sol Invictus was spreading throughout the empire, a certain form of Christianity was spreading right alongside it. Barbiero examines several pieces of evidence suggesting that, far from being rival religions as they are often portrayed, Christianity and Mithraism were actually two different aspects of the same plan to infiltrate and eventually control the Roman Empire.[466]

First, he points out the numerous parallels between Mithraism and Christianity, including the traditions that Mithras was born on December 25th out of a rock, or even out of a stable to a virgin (we have already discussed the celestial reasons why this would be the case), the fact that Mithras was venerated on the day of the sun each week (i.e., Sunday), the fact that he was depicted with a halo around his head, and that he celebrated a last supper with his followers before ascending to heaven where he would return in the last days.[467]

The locations of mithraea were often below Christian churches, including the most important and influential mithraeum of them all, which was located in a grotto on the Vatican hill in Rome, where Constantine would later construct the basilica of St. Peter.[468] In fact, the grotto under the basilica of St. Peter was still in use as a mithraeum for over sixty years after the basilica was built and put to use in the service of Christianity! He points out that it is unlikely that so many Christian churches would be built on top of mithraea that were still in use, and that followers of Mithras would permit the ongoing use of mithraea on the same real estate, if the two institutions were really rivals with one another.[469]

He notes that, while historians often generalize by saying that early Christian tradition often incorporated pagan traditions and practices and "Christianized" them, it is actually primarily the traditions of Mithraism that were incorporated. These include many aspects of the liturgy, the use of candles and incense and bells, many of the solar symbols, the veneration of certain days of the year corresponding to the annual solar cycle, the attire of the priests, and the office of the *pater patrum*, which became the office of the Pope.[470]

There are many other pieces of historical evidence, including the fact that when Mithraism was finally abolished in the fourth century, the entire senate which had been thoroughly populated by members of the cult of Sol Invictus suddenly "discovered" that they were actually Christian instead![471]

Perhaps one of the most important clues Barbiero offers in support of this thesis is the fact that wherever mithraea appeared during the spread of Mithraism throughout the empire (concentrated wherever legions were garrisoned), a Christian community sprang up at the same time.[472]

"Wherever Mithras arrived," writes Flavio Barbiero, "the Christians arrived too."[473] He notes that the archaeological remains of early Christian churches from the period are very often discovered right next to mithraea, or even built right above mithraea – including the ancient basilicas of St. Clement, St. Stephen Rotundus, St. Prisca, and others.[474]

The ultimate explanation for all of this evidence, according to Barbiero's theory, is that the cult of Sol Invictus Mithras was not really a cult at all – it was an exclusive secret society that functioned as the brain or nerve center of the expansion of control by the priestly family. Barbiero shows evidence that none could participate in the upper levels of the Mithraic order (above the third rank) unless he was a son of one of the priestly lines.[475] The secret and exclusive meetings of small groups in the confined, windowless mithraea set the policy that would be followed in the expansion and steady consolidation of power – using the public and inclusive religion that they controlled, Christianity, whose leaders after AD 70 were increasingly chosen from the priestly families exclusively as well.[476]

Flavio Barbiero concludes that the Mithras cult was the secret fraternal arm of the priestly family in the empire, and that it was in full control of the more public Christian cult, which was open to women and the pagan world. The center of this organization was located in Rome, where there was a mithraeum in the grotto of the Vatican, whose leader set the policy for the entire family organization, with power that was identical to the high priest under the Temple system back in Judea. With this strategy, Christianity could take the heat and bear the attacks from enemies and opponents, while those in charge of the Sol Invictus cult could secretly direct the campaign, safely out of sight.[477]

If it seems impossible to accept the proposition that the priestly lines, who had been defeated by the Romans, could pull off such an incredible feat, remember that Josephus and the other representatives of the priestly lineage had been given extraordinary financial resources by the emperor whose very dynasty had been established with the help of those who had shown him to the hiding places of the vast treasures of the Temple. They enjoyed the favor of the imperial family, into which Josephus had been adopted, whose name he had taken, and whose very villa was now his own residence. Additionally, many of them had likely been placed in positions of authority in the Praetorian Guard, which became a crucial lever of power and one that would become the initial "beachhead" for the launch of the Sol Invictus institution.

Further, these priestly lines had the benefit of centuries of experience in the wedding of religious authority with political power. They had their own personal experience in wielding this power. Flavio Barbiero explains that they knew almost instinctively that control through religion required the supporting "symbiotic" relationship with political and economic power, and that Josephus and his co-conspirators would have made securing such power a top priority.[478] It is a pattern we will see played out again and again in history, right up to the present day.

In other words, Josephus and the other former leaders of Judea knew how to run an organization in which religious power was wedded to political power. We have also seen from the discussion in previous chapters that they had presided over a religious system whose sacred scriptures were esoteric in nature, scriptures which are now almost universally understood from an almost-exclusively literal perspective.

There is evidence in Barbiero's book which supports the conclusion that the priests were teaching a literal interpretation rather than an esoteric understanding of those scriptures even before the conquest of Judea by the Romans. The first chapters of Barbiero's *Secret Society of Moses* deals with evidence that the priestly lines may have altered some verses of the scriptures after returning from captivity in Babylon, in order to establish their lineage as descendants of Aaron (the brother of Moses) rather than as descendants of Moses himself.[479]

His argument is that, at the time of the return from captivity, the priest Ezra decreed that the priestly lineage would be reckoned through the *mother,* and that she must therefore be from the priestly lineage and not from outside of it if her descendants were to be reckoned as members of the bloodline.[480] This necessitated alteration of the scriptures to make the priestly lines descend from Aaron instead of Moses, because it was quite clear in the Pentateuch that Moses had taken a "Cushite" wife (for which he was criticized by his brother Aaron and his sister Miriam, in a famous incident). His descendents would not qualify under this later rule! Since they could not cover this incident up, the post-Babylon priestly families changed their lineage to that of Aaron, in Barbiero's theory.[481]

However, they would not have needed to have done so if these ancient stories of the early Israelites were understood in an esoteric sense. Barbiero himself treats them as literal. We have seen extensive evidence to suggest they were not literal, however. Moses himself, as we have seen, was probably an esoteric representation of the Nile, very much akin to Okeanos in Greek sacred tradition.

And yet the scriptural evidence Barbiero presents that shows that the scriptures were altered by Ezra and the other twenty-four priestly families after the return from Babylonian captivity is convincing. The alteration probably did take place, and perhaps for the very reason that Barbiero suggests. This indicates that the scriptures were not being taught esoterically after the Babylonian captivity, but rather that they were being taught literally. Perhaps the Babylonian captivity was the origin of this new literalism – it is difficult to say for certain (literalism may have been present even before Babylon). The evidence is very strong, however, that literalism was in place *after* Babylon.

It is very important to note that this fact does not mean that the priests themselves interpreted the scriptures in a literal sense – they may have retained the esoteric knowledge, while presenting a literal explanation to the masses.

If this was the case -- and the evidence suggests that it was -- then it makes sense that the institutions that the remnants of the priestly class established from their new position of influence at the center of the Roman Empire would share the same feature. The cult of Sol Invictus had seven grades or degrees, and only those above the third were initiated into the true meaning of the rites and symbols of the cult, according to lines written by the ancient Catholic bishop Porphyrius (AD 347 – AD 420). The life of Porphyrius spanned the period in which Sol Invictus reached the apparent peak of its influence, during which many emperors were participants, and even spanned the years during which Mithraism ostensibly left the scene, when paganism was abolished by the emperors with a series of decrees starting in AD 386.[482] It is only logical to assume that the esoteric understanding was revealed progressively, with those at the highest levels understanding the most but withholding some elucidation from those who were only beginning their journey at the lower levels of the organization. It would be those at the upper levels who made the real decisions about the implementation of the plan to eventually control the empire.

We have already seen evidence that Christianity has an esoteric understanding beyond the literal understanding that has been the only interpretation adamantly taught to the majority of its followers throughout the centuries; the reasons for this will be explored in greater depth later, when we discuss the origins of Christianity before Josephus.

If the priests of pre-conquest Judea knew the esoteric interpretations but taught primarily the literal interpretation, and if the upper levels of Sol Invictus Mithras knew the esoteric interpretations but withheld such information from those at the lower levels, then is it not logical to conclude that the leaders of hierarchical forms of historic Christianity also know the esoteric understanding, while providing a literal interpretation to those outside their inner circle?

Such a practice is the hallmark of institutions designed to control other people rather than to enlighten other people.

The actions of the priestly families who came to Rome with Titus after the fall of Jerusalem were designed to control. If Flavio Barbiero's theory is correct (and we will see even more evidence that it is correct, in the following chapter), then their actions were extraordinarily successful at gaining control – to the point that they had secured control over the office of emperor by the end of the fourth century, and established an institution that would wield an enormous amount of political and spiritual control worldwide for the next seventeen centuries.

It is worth pausing to consider what this tells us about the power of human consciousness. The system that the priestly families used to gain and retain control over the entire "western world" was primarily founded upon the selective concealment and revelation of the esoteric – revealing to a relatively tiny few, while concealing from the vast majority. It appears to have been the same pattern that these priestly families had been using to control one specific region (Judea, also spelled Judaea) for several hundred years since the return from Babylonian captivity in the sixth century BC. This form of power can be broadly categorized as "mind control."

Mind control uses the control of information in order to manipulate others and create outcomes, rather than using brute force. This information can take the form of words, images, symbols, and even the resonances and wavelengths created by physical structures and monuments and the dimensions of buildings. We have seen evidence that the ancient wisdom almost certainly incorporated such knowledge, in our previous examination of the symbology of the Gorgons, or the arrangement of Stonehenge.

If the priestly families that arrived in Rome with Josephus were privy to such ancient knowledge, such knowledge might have been even more important to the success of their plan than were the admittedly vast resources and privileges accorded to them by the new imperial family. The two factors together could go a long way towards explaining how they were able to accomplish the seemingly impossible feat of taking over the empire from within, through the institution of the twin engines of Mithraism and ecclesiastical Christianity.

The following chapter will examine the progress of their plan and its execution during the time of the Roman Empire and after its "fall," before leaving the ground covered by Flavio Barbiero to examine the evidence regarding the pre-Josephus origins and form of Christian thought, the evidence that at least some of those who attempted to preserve those pre-Josephus forms fled the increasing imposition of mind control, and the evidence that the adherents of the literal Christianity eventually tracked them down in ruthless campaigns many centuries later.

16

The rise of ecclesiastical Christianity

The conception of the Christ as *man* in his divine genius, or the God *in* man, opens at once the whole scripture to lucid and consistent intelligibility. It is indeed the "key" to any true grasp of the whole sense of that revered body of primeval literature. But the instant the concept is shifted to *a* divine man in an historical personage, dire confusion, entanglement in contradiction, ridiculous inconsistency and the eeriest "historical" nonsense are thrust into the structure.

[. . .]

It would seem as if St. Paul wrote with this cogent realization in mind when he fairly shrieks at us: "Know ye not your own selves how that Jesus Christ is within you?"

> Alvin Boyd Kuhn,
> *Who is this King of Glory?*[483]

The stage is now set.

We have seen the evidence presented by Flavio Barbiero that the arrival in Rome of several families of a lineage with long experience in the wedding of religious power and political power, and the granting of wealth and influence to members of those families (likely including positions of command over the imperial Praetorian Guard), enabled them to institute a secret esoteric organization – the cult of Sol Invictus Mithras – which would extend offers of membership to men in strategically-chosen fields (beginning with the Praetorian Guard, then spreading rapidly to the army at large, the bureaucrats in charge of the transportation and taxation of goods, and from there into many other influential groups as shown below) and eventually ensure that only members of the priestly families set the policy and occupied positions of greatest authority.

We will now briefly watch the unfolding of that plan through the centuries, as described in Flavio Barbiero's *Secret Society of Moses*. Note that for the remainder of the book, when discussing *literalistic, ecclesiastical, historical, orthodox,* or *"a-gnostic"* / *"anti-gnostic"* Christianity, these terms are used very broadly, to describe *all* of the Christian faiths whose leaders demand the interpretation of the scriptures which teaches an historical Jesus, rather than an esoteric understanding of the stories within. Literalistic churches, regardless of which branch of literalism into which they fall, typically see a divide between what they call Christianity and the sacred traditions of the rest of the world, rather than realizing that their scriptures, like those of almost every other sacred tradition the world over, are all primarily esoteric and that thus they should see one another as kin. The various differences within the literalistic Christian family are immaterial to this discussion (even though those differences may be quite real, quite bitterly disputed, and quite important to those within the literalistic family). For the most part, the arguments within Christianity since the end of the fourth century have really all been divisions within the literalistic family – nearly all members of which officially reject the gnostic or esoteric interpretation of the scriptures, meaning that they reject the interpretation in which the Christ is understood to refer to a divine principle in every man or woman, and not to an external historic personage.

One of the first and most important moves the priestly family undertook, in conjunction with their consolidation of power over the Praetorian Guard, appears to have been the consolidation of power over a scattered community of practitioners of the Christian faith. This would set in motion a chain of events whereby a new version of Christianity, one with a hierarchical structure under central control from Rome, would eventually become the predominant faith of the Roman Empire, and the vehicle of control whose leaders dictated who would be emperor (and later, after the "fall" of the empire, whose leaders guided the policy of the kings and nobles throughout western Europe).

Flavio Barbiero points to a letter written by the bishop of Rome, Clement, as the first instance in which the priestly family began to flex their power of control over the scattered community of Christians. This letter, called "The Letter to the Corinthians" or "The First Epistle of Clement" (not the same as the letters of Paul to the Corinthians included in the canonical New Testament) is believed to have been written in one of the final two years of the reign of the emperor Domitian, whom we have already met as the brother of and successor to Titus, whose reign stretched from AD 81 through his death in AD 96, and in whose reign the first known datable inscription in a mithraeum (also in Rome) was authored.[484]

It is likely that it took some time for the priestly families to gain a firm enough foothold after their arrival in Rome to begin to make their moves, but as we shall see the evidence is strong that Clement was a member of those priestly families who arrived from Judea after the fall of Jerusalem. By the reign of Domitian, the groundwork had apparently been laid down, and the members of the priestly family who had now reached positions of control over the Praetorian Guard and the community of Christians in Rome (as evidenced by the fact that one of their number was now the bishop of Rome) could begin to take decisive action.

The Letter to the Corinthians written by Clement of Rome in AD 95 or 96 is extremely significant, because it indicates the earliest known example in which a leader from one community of believers (and a leader who is not an apostle) demonstrates authority over another community of believers.

In the epistle, Clement chastises the Corinthian believers for removing their leadership (their presbyters or elders) without any evidence that those elders had committed acts of immorality. This action Clement calls "detestable and unholy sedition" in the translation of J. B. Lightfoot (1828 – 1889, Bishop of Durham in the Church of England)(1 Clement 1:1).[485]

In chapter 57 he commands those who "laid the foundation of the sedition" to submit to the elders and receive chastisement in order to keep their names on "God's roll," or else be cast out from "the flock of Christ" and from the hope of him (1 Clement 57:1-2). Elsewhere in the letter, Clement states that those "who do any thing contrary to the seemly ordinance of his will" (referring to God) "receive death as the penalty" (1 Clement

41:3). This may, of course, threaten spiritual death and damnation rather than a physical death penalty at the hands of the church, but it is clearly a threat of extreme and final sanctions for those who resist the will of the church leadership and hierarchy. Finally, as Flavio Barbiero points out, Clement states that he has sent "faithful and prudent men" to the Corinthians as his emissaries and "witnesses" to convey his great desire that those rebellious parties would "speedily return to peace" (1 Clement 63:3-4).[486]

The significance of this letter cannot be overstated. Flavio Barbiero notes that it marks the first time in history that one Christian community presumed to interfere with the decisions and governance of another. Early Christian communities were loose and independent entities, but Clement's letter changed that. He notes that Eusebius states in a surviving text that Clement's letter was read aloud in churches around the empire, a clear indication that the bishop of Rome was now seen as authoritative. It was a radical change.[487]

He then presents evidence that Clement was either a Romanized member of the Jewish families that came to Rome with Titus and Josephus, or a Jewish prisoner who had been sent to Rome with the apostle Paul in AD 63 or 64 and then set free.[488]

Barbiero argues that Christianity's steady rise in prominence and power began when Josephus and his fellows assumed their position of influence in the capitol of the empire, and began to use their two-pronged approach (the secret institution of the cult of Sol Invictus Mithras and the more open and public institution of Christianity) to further their plans. The rapidity with which Christianity became the state religion of the empire over the course of the subsequent centuries, he argues, becomes understandable when we realize that the families that had come from Jerusalem knew perhaps better than anyone else in the world how to organize and run a religion.[489]

After they had maneuvered into control over the hierarchy which they imposed upon the community of Christians, then the priestly families made membership in one of their family lines "a necessary and sufficient condition" for becoming a bishop or gaining access to membership in the ecclesiastic hierarchy of the church.[490] Flavio Barbiero cites numerous pieces of admittedly circumstantial evidence which all support this assertion.

The two-pronged approach using the two institutions that were now completely controlled by the priestly families would be used to gain access to all the important levers of power in the empire, even during the decades in which Christianity remained a small minority of the population. In spite of the rapidity of the dramatic transformation described above, the empire even as late as the reign of the emperor Diocletian (who ruled from AD 285 to AD 305, the year before Constantine would take the throne) was at least 80% pagan and the senate was composed of ancient local families who were also the heads of the pagan worship ceremonies and temples, and who stood as an important center of power that could oppose the emperor to a greater or lesser degree.[491]

The effectiveness of the twin institutions of Mithraism and Christianity in securing control over the levers of power, even while still in the minority, is evident in the plan to gain control of the Roman legions. The members of the upper ranks would be recruited into Mithraism, which was controlled at the higher grades of its own hierarchical structure by the family, and the rest of the army as well as the wives of the officers and leaders would be Christianized. Barbiero argues that it is not difficult to imagine how this would take place: Christian soldiers would be favored over non-Christian ones, and the members of the secret brotherhood of Mithras would support one another in every way.[492]

As their strategy progressed, the behind-the-scenes influence of the families became more and more pronounced, and their moves to gain the highest and most important levers of power more and more bold.

By the time about a century had passed (beginning perhaps around AD 180), Flavio Barbiero demonstrates that the Mithraic organization was appointing and deposing emperors almost at will, often through assassination. He writes that difficult emperors would be given Christian wives, in order to control them, as was done with Commodus through the concubine Marcia. Barbiero notes that among the thousands that Commodus murdered was not a single Christian, almost certainly due to the influence of Marcia, assisted by the prefect of the Praetorian Guard, Quintus Aemilius Laetus.[493]

In another fifty years, the first emperor to openly declare that he was a Christian would take the throne, the emperor Julius Philippus, in AD 244. He had been the head of the Praetorian Guard and was rumored to have poisoned the previous emperor (who had been descended from one of the emperors appointed by the Roman senate in one of the temporary setbacks for the behind-the-scenes machinations of Sol Invictus). Flavio Barbiero provides evidence that Julius Philipus was a member of the priestly families that had come from Judea – perhaps even a direct descendent of Josephus, in spite of the fact that he had been born in Bosra and bore the nickname "Philip the Arab."[494] He notes that by this time, the descendants of the priestly families were now employed in many important roles in the imperial administration, and were often posted to various provinces of the empire as bureaucrats or administrators.[495]

Although emperors under the control of the priestly lines initiated reforms to try to curb the power of the Roman senate, and to water down the control of the old patrician families who saw the senate as their stronghold, it was a long battle. However, Flavio Barbiero provides evidence that the old Italic senators who opposed the rise of Christianity (and the threat to their power that these new developments posed) never really reached a general awareness of the importance of Sol Invictus as the nerve center for the campaign against them. This fact demonstrates the strength of the "two-pronged" strategy initiated all the way back in the days of Josephus. They wasted their efforts in attacks against Christianity, which provided them "a well-identified target against which they could work out their frustrations" and which distracted them from the full understanding of their true enemy.[496]

In any event, the senate was steadily being infiltrated by Sol Invictus during these centuries, to the point that although it appeared to be largely "pagan" as opposed to Christian, it was increasingly coming under the influence of the priestly lines. Flavio Barbiero demonstrates that the high officials of all the various pagan dieties of the Roman Empire were also inductees at various levels into the cult of Sol Invictus Mithras, demonstrating that the seizure of control of the religious structures was proceeding along a similar strategic line to that used to infiltrate and gain control of the Roman legions.[497] Within fifty years of the death of Constantine, who finally declared Christianity the official religion of the state, the senate would vote to abolish paganism, in AD 383, and those who had been members of Sol Invictus slipped quite easily into Christianity, which was after all the public and open sister-vehicle of Mithraism, according to the Barbiero theory.

Readers are undoubtedly familiar with the importance of Constantine, who was proclaimed emperor by his troops in AD 306 and spent almost two decades in struggle for full control, which he gained in AD 324, and who then ruled through his death in AD 337. For the purposes of this overview of the priestly family thesis proposed by Flavio Barbiero, the declaration of Christianity as the religion of the empire by Constantine in AD 324 was of course a landmark event which demonstrated the effectiveness of the strategy employed by those displaced masters of an esoteric tradition. Their strategy of using a clandestine secret society (Sol Invictus) with an external and openly-operating popular religion (Christianity) had successfully captured the principle organs of power that led them inexorably to control of the empire itself. It was a revolution that was largely accomplished without external force of arms (although violence on varying scales had been used throughout the campaign). Instead of fighting pitched battles, the priestly families who had been vanquished in Judea used a sophisticated form of political and religious "re-patterning" to take over their erstwhile conquerors from within.

It was as if the Roman Empire had swallowed a micro-organism, or a spore, and that tiny organism or that tiny seed had propagated and spread and "gone viral," until it took over the entire beast that had previously swallowed it up.

But Flavio Barbiero explains that this decision to make Christianity the religion of the state did not really originate from Constantine, nor was it made because Christianity was now the majority religion in the empire (it decidedly still was not). He believes the institution of Sol Invictus, that shadow government behind the throne, took this step as a response to the actions of Diocletian, the emperor who had ruled up until AD 305 (just before Constantine was proclaimed emperor by his troops).

Diocletian had established a system known as the "tetrarchy," wherein the empire would be split between two emperors, east and west, and each would appoint a "caesar" who was designated to succeed him. Barbiero argues that this system appeared unwieldy (and it was), but it had one real purpose, and at this it succeeded brilliantly for a time: it prevented the apparatus of Sol Invictus from appointing a rival emperor in another part of the empire when they wanted to take down the current emperor (something they had done several times in the past).

He explains, "Each of the four colleagues – all from the same geographical area, Pannonia, tied to each other by bonds of personal loyalty and committed to reciprocal support – was able to control the Mithraic organization within his own territory, thereby making it impossible to form coalitions capable of standing up to them at the same time."[498] However, the system devolved into chaos when Diocletian's "caesar" G. Galerius Valerius began a series of bloody purges against Christians – probably because he had been raised by a mother to hate Christians, because she herself had once been slighted by some Christian noblewomen.[499]

Barbiero writes that Diocletian's strategy for breaking free of the grip of the Sol Invictus *pater patrum* took the secret organization by surprise, and caused them to adopt a radical new policy: the decision to govern through their public vehicle of Christianity, and to take steps to make it the official religion of the state.[500] This would happen in the reign of the successor to Diocletian, Constantine, who maneuvered his way into power during the violent and turbulent period at the end of Diocletian's tetrarchy. He was a member of the priestly line, and no doubt chosen by them to implement the next phase of their longrunning strategy.

Constantine was by no means the first emperor to have come from the Jewish priestly family line (although Barbiero demonstrates that Constantine did indeed come from those bloodlines).[501] However, Barbiero argues that just prior to Constantine, those in control of Sol Invictus had decided that emperors would thenceforth only come from those families.[502] He believes they made this move in order to prevent the kind of out-of-control situation that Diocletian had created (neither Diocletian nor his bloodthirsty "caesar" Galerius Valerius were of the priestly line).[503]

Not only that, but Barbiero points to evidence which strongly suggests that with Constantine, emperors from that point on would only be chosen from one specific line of the priestly family, to eliminate as much as possible the costly infighting that had been going on between the different branches as they jockeyed for power.[504] That family would be the Gens Flavia.

Barbiero demonstrates that after this decision had been made, "The presence of this name became almost an obsession from then on among the members of the imperial families, starting, obviously, with Constantine."[505] He argues that this probably indicates that the family line which had won this pre-eminence was that to which Josephus Flavius belonged. Long ago, Josephus himself had started out his autobiography by declaring that he was descended "not simply from priests, but from the first of the twenty-four priestly classes – itself a mark of distinction – and, within this class, from the most illustrious tribe."[506]

Significantly, Flavio Barbiero is able to cite several instances, after that decision to make the office of emperor the exclusive domain of one lineage, in which marriage to a woman from the Gens Flavia was apparently sought out by powerful men not eligible themselves in order to produce an heir who could be a contender for the throne. He notes that this significant and historically-provable piece of evidence regarding the leaders of Rome clearly links to the custom of the Jews (in which priestly status was inherited through the mother, a tradition going back at least to Ezra and one still observed to this day).[507]

Clearly, there are many different types of evidence which appear to confirm the priestly family theory of Flavio Barbiero from multiple directions. We will continue forward in history with his theory in order to encounter a few more powerful forms of evidence, before tying it in to the arguments we have been building in the earlier chapters and examining its profound ramifications.

Once the Christian church, with its hierarchical structure completely under the control of the priestly lines (who had in fact created the hierarchical structure on the model they brought with them from Jerusalem), was secure enough to enable it to be united openly to the political power of the empire – as it was after Constantine – the old underground Mithraic vehicle was no longer needed. The supreme head of the Mithraic organization had always been known as the *pater patrum* ("father of fathers"), or the *pa-pa* for short.[508] He was the highest of those who held the highest grade in the order (the degrees in Mithraism were seven in number, beginning at the bottom with Raven and proceeding to Occult, Soldier, Lion, Persian, Courier of the Sun, and finally Father or *Pater*). The *pater patrum* was the "Father of the Fathers," the head of the Mithraic gathering that met in the Vatican grotto in Rome.[509]

It is significant that Constantine had the basilica of St. Peter built over this grotto in AD 322. It is significant because, now that Christianity was coming into its own, the power structures of Sol Invictus Mithras and of hierarchical Christianity, which had been nominally separate, were going to be united. Flavio Barbiero argues that the fact that the basilica of St. Peter is co-located with the old Mithraic Vatican grotto (called the Phrygianum), the fact that upon the death of the last *pater patrum* of the cult of Mithras, named Vectius or Vettius Agorius Praetextatus, the cave was taken over by the Christian bishop of Rome Syricius, who adopted the *pater patrum* title for the first time in Christian history, the fact that he wore the same clothing and sat on the same Mithraic throne which is today known as the throne of St. Peter and which still has Mithraic designs engraved upon it – all establish the validity of his thesis that during this period in the fourth century Christianity took over from Sol Invictus as the vehicle through which the family would henceforth steer their policy.[510]

There would be some continued struggles and false starts as the vision was consolidated and the new situation settled out. One of these was the reign of the emperor Julian, the grandson of Constantine, whose reign began in AD 361 and followed immediately after those of Constantine's sons. Flavio Barbiero notes that Julian (nicknamed the Apostate) actually provides still further support for his thesis, because even though Julian renounced Christianity and attempted to revive Sol Invictus, he never persecuted the Christian church or its bishops.[512] It may be, Barbiero theorizes, that Julian wanted to create a syncretistic blend which would unite pagans and Christians together.

But that was not the direction that the leaders of the Christian church, who now were appointing and replacing emperors in much the same way that Sol Invictus had done in the past, wanted to go. Julian received a spear in the back under mysterious circumstances while fighting the Persians; it was portrayed as an accident.[513]

Thus the changeover from Sol Invictus Mithras was not entirely without incident. The institution itself continued on until AD 396, when it was formally dismantled. However, Flavio Barbiero explains that even then it did not disappear completely – it only changed its form, and retreated into the background, no longer the "kingmaker" that it had been before. In order to avoid the new edicts against pagan expression in a Roman Empire that was now officially Christian, Barbiero believes that the old Mithraic fraternity adopted a new name for its central deity: the Great Architect of the Universe, a title used among the Pythagoreans.[514]

This connection highlights the likelihood that the Masonic organizations which would arise in later centuries were continuations in slightly modified form of the institution of Sol Invictus, undoubtedly connected to the traditions of the priestly families who were relocated to Rome after the fall of the Temple, and supremely concerned with the building of a spiritual Temple in its place, and Flavio Barbiero presents numerous lines of evidence to support this general theory throughout his work.

Part III

As the discussion above indicates in numerous places, the Roman senate, once the stronghold of the old Italic families, had slowly been infiltrated over the centuries after Josephus by members of the priestly lines. Entrance into the Roman equestrian class (whose members were known as *equites*) had long been based on a property threshold, and it is not unreasonable to assume that many of the relocated priestly families who had been given property during the reigns of Vespasian and Titus had entered the order of equites. In the second century, when the priestly families began having more and more control over the appointment of emperors, entrance to the equestrian class was increasingly open to those who had distinguished themselves in military service – career military officers, the very institution that was under increasingly tight control by Sol Invictus and the priestly lines. As a result, the senate was increasingly composed of descendants of the priestly class and by members of the cult of Mithras (or both).

During the reign of Constantine, another very important event took place – the creation of a new capitol city, Constantinople. Again, the perspective which Flavio Barbiero sheds on this decision in light of the priestly family theory is somewhat different from that of conventional historians. Under Flavio Barbiero's theory, the declaration by Constantine of Christianity as the state religion was, as we have seen, the result of a decision among the leaders of the conspiracy's leaders to rule through the institution of the church rather than through the institution of Sol Invictus.

This decision, forced upon them by Diocletian's strategy to break free of the control of the Sol Invictus organization, did entail some risks. For one thing, the power center of the church was more visible than that of Sol Invictus, and it was located in Rome as was the emperor they wished to control. So, they came up with a brilliant plan – move the emperor out of Rome, which would then become the sole jurisdiction of the church.[515]

As Flavio Barbiero explains, this decision made inevitable the eventual dissolution of the Roman Empire itself, which would take place over the next hundred and fifty years.[516] In the west, the church (controlled by the families we have been following since Josephus) became more and more powerful and autonomous from the emperor, and in the east, Barbiero explains, the families would find their designs stymied repeatedly by the power of the imperial office in Constantinople (to which they continually lost out, because the center of the priestly bloodline's power, the Christian church centered in Rome, was far away while the new seat of the emperor and all its supporting infrastructure was now located in the east).[517]

Less than sixty years after the death of Constantine, in AD 395, the empire was officially divided east and west between the two sons of the emperor Theodosius. It would never be united again.

However, rather than seeing this end of the empire as a setback for the priestly families, it is perhaps better to view it as the final emergence of those families into their full power and autonomy. To return to the metaphor above in which we saw that the Roman Empire was like a larger animal or insect that eats a smaller organism, only to have that organism grow and multiply inside of it and take it over from within, the expulsion of the emperor from Rome and the eventual split and then further fragmentation of the empire was a sign that the parasite had grown to adulthood and was now tossing aside the husk of the former host, which was no longer needed.

In the theory of Flavio Barbiero, the end of the imperial office did not weaken the priestly families at all: far from it. Instead, when western Europe was divided among various apparently independent barbarian kingdoms, the church of Rome with its network of bishops was more in charge than ever, freed from the destabilizing counter-force of charismatic or overly ambitious occupants of the imperial office.[518]

The barbarians to which he refers had increasingly supplied much of the "muscle" of the Roman legions during the third century, when large numbers of natives of the northern regions (and other far-flung territories of the empire) were needed to fill the ranks of the legions. As the class of small free farmers, from which Rome had traditionally drawn its legionnaires, shrunk to the point of disappearing (as wealthy families, senators, and the clergy came to dominate larger and larger swathes of land), these "barbarians" were necessary to sustain Roman military might. Flavio Barbiero points out that many of them rose to positions of high rank, and some even married members of the Gens Flavia, so that their sons could be eligible to become emperor or to enter the church hierarchy.[519]

After the split of the empire in two, with two emperors East and West, Barbiero notes that in light of the conditions just described, the west had devolved into a bloodbath of successive battles over who would occupy the imperial throne.[520] The leaders of the Roman church and the Roman senate in the west came up with a novel solution: they decided to abolish the imperial office in the west, and grant the senate in the East the right to appoint the sole emperor themselves, without the previously-required ratification of the western senate as well.[521] This would put an end to the nonstop battles to appoint short-lived and ineffectual emperors, and leave the clergy and the wealthy landowners to consolidate their power in peace. Without an imperial office to fight over, the barbarian armies became a source of stability, instead of a threat.

This means, Barbiero points out, that "the so-called fall of the Western Empire should be wholly attributed to the Western priestly family, and not to the barbarians."[522] The priestly families were happy to free themselves of the emperor, and later to let the west disintegrate into a patchwork of local barbarian sovereigns at the head of their own armies of professional warriors.[523] Under this arrangement, the great landowners, civil servants, and the Catholic church itself all came from the wealthy and powerful priestly families.[524] The landowners supplied the food that kept the barbarian kings and their warriors alive, and the barbarians provided the defense. The hierarchy of the Church called the shots when necessary, able to exert its influence over the local leaders at least as effectively as it had been able to do so over the centralized emperor in the past.

"Thus in practice the West, although administratively divided, was more united than ever under the church of Rome," Flavio Barbiero writes. "None of the new states saw themselves as independent political and territorial entities. Instead, they continued for centuries to consider themselves as autonomous entities within a single Christian empire."[525] All these kingdoms in the west paid a tax to Rome, while the lands of the church wherever they were located remained exempt from any local taxation (significantly, one of the privileges which Josephus boasted of receiving from the imperial family was that of tax-exemption on his lands).[526]

The privileges of the priestly lineage became even more pronounced. In order to ascend into positions of real power in the hierarchy of the church, one had to be a member of the priestly family lines. The royalty and aristocracy of the various kingdoms into which the western empire eventually fragmented were likewise tied to the ancient lines. We have already noted that vast landholdings were consolidated into the hands of the wealthy senatorial families (who were almost entirely from the priestly lines by the end of the empire) and the Church. It was this situation, in fact, which led these landowners to decide to abolish the office of emperor in the western empire in order to stop the squabbling. These great landowners became the nobility of the Middle Ages.

Certainly these lines intermarried with the "barbarians" who also made up the ranks of the warrior classes, but as we have already seen, there was an understanding from the outset that marriage of a daughter of one of the priestly lines conferred upon the children all the ancient privilege of the mother's bloodline, and Flavio Barbiero demonstrates that the nobility and royalty of all the houses of Europe – from England to France to Spain and so on – can be traced to the priestly families.

One of the most startling and powerful veins of evidence supporting Barbiero's theory is the heraldry displayed by the nobility and royalty of Europe. He explains that later, during the Middle Ages, the unveiling of heraldic symbols by every noble house across the breadth of Europe between the years 1100 and 1200 would be very difficult to explain, unless all of those noble families had known the symbols for centuries. If the system were a new innovation in the twelfth century, he argues, we would expect vicious haggling over who was entitled to use what symbols, or who was displaying them improperly, but this was very rare: instead, all the noble families seemed to know exactly what symbols they belonged to, and to be able to recognize the symbols of any other noble house, regardless of how obscure that house might seem to outsiders.[527]

Barbiero demonstrates further that almost all the well-known symbols used in their heraldry indicate an origin that points back to the tribes of ancient Israel or the symbology of the Temple, or occasionally from the symbology of Sol Invictus – a clear and powerful confirmation of the priestly families theory.[528] He also demonstrates that the coats of arms of the Popes are replete with symbology of the same distinctive type.[529] "The chance that it is all coincidence must be considered remote," he concludes.[530]

To return now to the thesis of this book and tie in what we have learned, we can now begin to answer the question of what happened to the ancient shamanic wisdom, and how it was conquered in "the west" by a literalizing Christianity, which set to work stamping it out. Leaving aside further examination of the direct evidence provided by Flavio Barbiero, we will begin a more detailed exploration of the state of Christian thought before the arrival of Josephus in Rome.

It will be quite apparent that the events described in this chapter have everything to do with the deliberate suppression of the esoteric knowledge, a suppression that goes on to this day. In light of the stunning conquest of the Roman Empire from the inside by a group of priestly families who were apparently adept at keeping esoteric understanding from the masses, we can begin to see that those who wish to control others (and the founders of historic, hierarchical Christianity can clearly be placed in that category, if Barbiero's theory is correct, and the evidence seems to indicate that he is) can successfully use what may properly be termed "techniques of mind control" – often backed up, it is true, by violence and a callous disregard for human life – to exert tremendous influence over the lives of huge numbers of people.

And, while violence was certainly used, it must be pointed out that the astonishing reversal by which the captured families who had been in charge of the smoldering Temple in Jerusalem became the emperors of Rome and completely replaced the empire's religious and political structure was not accomplished primarily by violence alone. No amount of physical force that they could have mustered could have propelled them to the ultimate victory that they achieved. Their primary tool was mind control, exercised through hierarchical religious structures, backed up when necessary by ruthless acts of murder.

17

The Egyptian roots of Christianity

But the sheer fact that even amid the murks of ignorance and superstition the mere ghost, shell, husk and shadow of Egypt's wisdom inspired religious piety to extremes of faith and zealotry is singular attestation to its original power and majesty. Only by acknowledging and regaining its parenthood in that sublime pagan source will Christianity rise at last to its true nobility and splendor.

Alvin Boyd Kuhn,
Who is this King of Glory?[531]

Armed with the theory of Flavio Barbiero, we can now explore the origins of Christianity and see how his theory enables us to bridge the theories of other analysts such as Freke & Gandy and Joseph Atwill. We will also see how his theory, plus an understanding of the path Christianity may have been following prior to the arrival of Josephus in Rome, can shed light on the larger issue we have been exploring, which is the theory that ancient sacred traditions from all around the world evince understanding of the holographic universe model and of shamanic technique, but that something happened to that understanding at some point in antiquity.

Barbiero himself does not delve deeply into the origins of Christianity. We have seen that his theory does shed light on Clement's Letter to the Corinthians (the First Epistle of Clement) as the first time that the bishop of Rome began to exercise authority over other communities of Christian practitioners, an important piece of evidence supporting the thesis that the arrival of the priestly lines in Rome unleashed a deliberate new strategy which would use a new hierarchical Church to take control of the Roman Empire and, after tossing aside its husk, western Europe.

However, in general his book treats the figures of the Old and New Testaments as literal figures, including Moses and Aaron and David in the Old Testament and Jesus and the apostles in the New Testament. We have explored extensive evidence to support the argument that all of these figures are celestial metaphors, not actual historical human figures.

There is one New Testament figure, however, who probably did exist as a historical figure, and that figure is Paul. Evidence suggests that at least some of the epistles of Paul were written prior to the destruction of Jerusalem, perhaps as early as AD 50. This suggests that some form of Christianity existed prior to the arrival of the priestly families in Jerusalem and makes it extremely difficult to argue that Christianity was a whole-cloth invention of Josephus or any of his associates upon their arrival in Rome.

The fact of Paul's early letters, however, does not preclude the possibility that Christianity was changed in some way – perhaps in profound ways – by Josephus and the priestly families in the years following the destruction of the Temple and their arrival in Rome (and, as we have seen, the First Epistle of Clement argues that it was).

Our old acquaintance Robert Taylor argues that Paul himself may also be a celestial figure, bearing as he does two very suspiciously celestial names. We are told in the book of Acts that he had been known first as Saul, suspiciously close to *Sol* the sun, as Robert Taylor discusses in *Devil's Pulpit*.[532] His name was then, upon his conversion, changed to Paul, which Robert Taylor argues looks suspiciously like *Pol* or *Pollux*, as well as *Apollo*.[533]

However, in *The Jesus Mysteries*, Timothy Freke and Peter Gandy present evidence that while the earliest letters of Paul were penned in the years between AD 50 and AD 60, the gospel accounts that were later incorporated into the New Testament canon were not written until after the fall of the Temple (sometime between the years AD 70 and AD 135), and the book of the Acts of the Apostles was written even later than that, sometime between the years AD 150 and AD 177.[534]

It is quite possible, then, that the familiar details of Paul's "life" are a later invention, having little or nothing to do with the author of the epistles to the Galatians, Ephesians, and Colossians in the New Testament. If so, then the device of having his name change from Saul to Paul could have been added much later, perhaps over a hundred years after his letters were actually written.

The "name change" itself is actually not described in great detail in Acts. During the entire description of the "Road to Damascus experience" (Acts 9), when he is cast down to the ground and blinded, Saul is referred to by the name Saul only. It is only in Acts 13 verse 9 that we are told that Saul is "also Paul."

The likelihood that Acts was written long after the life of the actual author of the Pauline epistles, and embellished with solar-astrological metaphors (including the name change from Saul to Paul) is made more likely by several other celestial metaphors embedded in the "Road to Damascus" story from Acts 9.

For example, although the text of Acts 9 says nothing about a horse, the event in which Saul is cast to the ground by the Lord is often described as if he had been thrown to earth from his horse. Robert Taylor points out that if he had been on a horse, there would have been no reason for him to have had to have been led by the hand (implying that he was led *on foot*) the rest of the way into Damascus.[535] "Yet no piece of statuary," declares Robert Taylor, "no ancient entablature, no antique painting in the world, representing this allegorical conversion, omits to give the same prominence to the figure of the horse, which the horse bears in the figure of the Sagittarius of November."[536]

This is because, he argues, Saul represents the zodiac constellation of Sagittarius the Archer, who is depicted as a centaur shooting a bow (for the constellation resembles such a figure, as we have already seen). Sagittarius is located at the very bottom of the zodiac wheel we have used in previous chapters: the December (winter) solstice follows the end of Sagittarius, at the handoff point with Capricorn the Goat. It is thus in Sagittarius that the sun is "cast down" to the lowest point, just as we see Saul to be in Acts 9:4.

Saul and Sagittarius are thus the "persecutor" of the sign directly opposite on the zodiac wheel, the Twins of Gemini. At the end of Gemini, at the point of their handoff to Cancer, lies the June (summer) solstice. In the Old Testament version of the exact same relationship between Sagittarius and Gemini, Robert Taylor tells us, Saul persecuted the "twins" David and Jonathan. In the New Testament book of Acts (obviously written by someone with a profound understanding of the Old Testament stories and their esoteric symbology) Saul is paired with Paul, one being the "preconversion" version of the man (the persecutor Saul, linked to Sagittarius) and the other being the "converted" version (Paul, whose name links him to Castor and Pollux, the Twins of Gemini).

Robert Taylor explains:

> And Saul and Paul are one and the same persons, only in the same sense as the Sun of November is the same as the sun of May. Only in different characters: Saul before his conversion, being the November sun, in the sign of Sagittarius, where you see the Great Persecutor, with his bow and arrow, playing havoc with vegetable nature, stripping the trees of their foliage, riding down to Damascus, and on the high road to hell and Tommy – that is, to St. Thomas's day, which is the 21st of December, the lowest point of the sun's declension; and, consequently, the lowest pit of hell.[537]

Taylor also argues that the name *Saul* relates to the Hebrew word Sheol, which represents the pit or Hades, for Saul/Sheol is associated with the lowest point on the zodiac wheel, allegorized as Hell to summer's Heaven, just as in other places it is allegorized as Egypt to summer's Promised Land, and many other manifestations of the same pattern.[538]

In light of all this discussion, it is difficult to know whether the epistles attributed to "Paul" were actually written by someone who answered to that actual name, or if -- like the epistles and gospels attributed to apostles who were almost certainly representations of zodiac signs such as Peter, who brings to life the sign of Aries in the gospel accounts -- these are "stage names." Nevertheless, for lack of another name by which to call the author of the early epistles, we shall call him by the name he gives himself in those epistles, which is Paul.

As we have already seen in brief and will now examine in more detail, Freke and Gandy present evidence that the Paul who wrote the early epistles, decades before the canonical gospels were written and possibly a century or more before the book of Acts was written (Acts is not quoted by any early Christian authorities prior to AD 177), may not have believed in a literal, historical Jesus, but may instead have been a gnostic, putting forth a gnostic understanding of the Christ in his letters.[539]

Additionally, as previously stated, Gerald Massey almost a hundred years earlier had maintained the same argument. In an essay entitled *Paul the Gnostic opponent of Peter, not an Apostle of Historic Christianity*, Massey presents numerous powerful arguments from Paul's own letters to support the assertion that Paul taught an understanding of Christ which was dramatically different from those who advanced a literal, historic understanding (far different, in other words, from the literal doctrines which were enforced by the hierarchical church which began to take form after the arrival of Josephus and his cohort in Rome).[540]

Massey argues that although later proponents of the literal version of Christianity inserted passages to make it look as though the author of those early epistles taught a literal and historical Jesus, many other passages in those same letters teach something entirely the opposite. Massey asks which is more likely, that a later literalist forger would add interpolations supporting literalism, or that a later gnostic forger somehow inserted a bunch of gnostic teachings into the letters of a literalist Paul? To ask the question is to answer it: since the Church that compiled and approved the canon taught a literalist dogma, and since the literalists "won out" in the end, it is far more likely that later literalist censors added literalist interpolations into an originally gnostic epistle than that some gnostic forger snuck in gnostic doctrines at a later date.[541]

Massey presents numerous pieces of evidence to support his thesis. One of the most important of these is Paul's description of his own awakened awareness of the Christ in the first chapter of the epistle to the Galatians. There, Paul declares:

> [15] But when it pleased God, who separated me from my mother's womb, and called *me* by his grace,
> [16] To reveal his Son in me, that I might preach him among the heathen; immediately I conferred not with flesh and blood:
> [17] Neither went I up to Jerusalem to them which were apostles before me; but I went into Arabia, and returned again unto Damascus.

Gerald Massey points out that this account from Paul himself is quite different from what is given in the book of Acts (which, as we have seen, was probably written more than a hundred years later than early epistles such as Galatians, and which appears to have been written to fit an astro-theological model by someone intimately familiar with the pattern used in the Old Testament). The revelation of the Son "in me," Massey argues, "is totally antipodal" to the "apparition of Jesus of Nazareth outside of him!"[542] It is, as Massey says, "the Christ of the Gnosis."[543]

Further, in this passage we can see Paul making a very strong point of the fact that this experience was a personal experience, and one not mediated by anybody else. Paul offers the example of his own awakened perception of the Christ in him as support for the larger argument he is making to the Galatians, that he must answer only to God and not try to please men. He offers this example as he persuades them not to follow a gospel other than what they received from him – apparently the Galatians are being swayed by the authority of some others who came behind Paul preaching something different, and are being swayed by their desire to please them. So, as a supporting argument, he explains that he himself did not confer with "flesh and blood" but went into Arabia, apparently to commune alone.

So this passage shows Paul arguing for two things, which are connected: for an internal Christ ("his son in me") and for the individual's responsibility to follow this Christ on his or her own, not conferring with flesh and blood and not seeking to please men. In the verses which come immediately before those just cited, Paul writes "do I seek to please men?" and "the gospel which was preached of me is not after man. For I neither received it of man, neither was I taught it" (Galatians 1:10-12).

This again conflicts with the story told in the later book of Acts, where Paul is led to Damascus by "the men which journeyed with him," where God sends "a certain disciple at Damascus, named Ananias" expressly to minister to Paul, who has been struck blind by his Damascus Road experience (Acts 9:7-17). The seventeenth verse of Acts 9 implies that it is only through Ananias that Paul receives not only his vision again, but also the filling of the Holy Ghost. Ananias tells Paul, or Saul as he calls him, that Jesus has sent Ananias to him so that he might receive his sight and "be filled with the Holy Ghost."

The passage then goes on to say that Saul "was baptized" and that he stayed a certain number of days with the disciples that were in Damascus! (Acts 9:18-19). This account appears to be diametrically opposed to the vigorous argument Paul himself is making in Galatians 1, that once the Son was revealed *in him*, Paul did *not* confer with flesh and blood but went off by himself into the desert of Arabia, whereas the account in Acts has Paul receiving his sight back through the mediation of Ananias, the filling of the Holy Ghost through the mediation of Ananias, his baptism at the hands of other disciples in Damascus, and additional fellowship for some number of days in the company of other disciples in Damascus! Furthermore, the Acts account has Paul (or Saul) being led by the hand to Damascus after his Damascus Road experience, whereas his own account in Galatians says he went alone to Arabia *before* returning to Damascus.

These inconsistencies give strong support to Massey's argument that the author of the early epistles is teaching a gnostic Christ and a personal path to gnosis that is not under the authority of "flesh and blood," and that a later hand added new material to depict an external, literal, and historic Christ and a path of discipleship where the mediation of others is a necessary component.

Massey argues that the "other gospel" which Paul is imploring the Galatians to reject as different from that which he had preached among them is actually none other than the gospel of a literal, historical Jesus as opposed to the Christ within![544] While this may seem too difficult to accept by those who have only ever been taught that Paul championed the same things that the teachers of the literal, historical version of Christianity teach, Massey backs up this seemingly astonishing argument with more evidence from the epistles themselves.

Writing in section 8 of the same essay, Massey declares this about the "other gospel" of which Paul warns the Galatians in his epistle:

> We know what their gospel was, because it has come down to us in the doctrines and dogmas of historic Christianity. It was the gospel of the literalisers of mythology [that is, those who teach as literal the metaphorical and esoteric Old and New Testament events which we have seen are almost certainly reflections of celestial astronomical events][. . .] Theirs was that *other* gospel with its doctrines of delusion, against which Paul waged continual warfare. For, *another Jesus, another Spirit,* and *another gospel* were being preached by these pre-eminent apostles who were the opponents of Paul. He warns the Corinthians against those "pre-eminent apostles," whom he calls false prophets, deceitful workers, and ministers of Satan, who came among them to preach "*another Jesus*" whom he did not preach, and a different gospel from that which they had received from him. To the Galatians he says: "*If any man preacheth unto you any gospel other than that which ye received, let him be damned;*" or let him be Anathema. He chides them: "*O, foolish Galatians, who did bewitch you? Are ye so foolish: having begun in*

the Spirit, are ye perfected in the flesh?" That is, in the gospel of the Christ made flesh, the gospel to those who were at enmity with him, who followed on his track like Satan sowing tares by night to choke the seed of the spiritual gospel which Paul had so painfully sown, and who, as he intimates to the Thessalonians, were quite capable of forging epistles in his name to deceive his followers.[545]

In other words, Massey argues that Paul's warning against "the flesh" is a warning against a gospel that substitutes literal and historical events for the spiritual and esoteric truths that they should be focusing on instead. It is like the famous Buddhist saying, made even more famous by Bruce Lee in the opening scenes of *Enter the Dragon* (1973), in which he says: "It is like a finger, pointing a way to the moon: *Don't* concentrate on the finger, or you will miss all that heavenly glory."[546]

One of the most important insights offered by Massey in this essay concerns the fact that Paul explicitly refers to his own ecstatic experience when he writes to the Corinthians. Massey explains:

> [. . .] Paul, on his own testimony, was an abnormal Seer, subject to the conditions of trance. He could not remember if certain experiences occurred to him in the body or out of it! This trance condition was the origin and source of his revelations, the heart of his mystery, his infirmity in which he gloried – in short, his "thorn in the flesh." He shows the Corinthians that his abnormal condition, ecstasy, illness, madness (or what not), was a phase of spiritual intercourse in which he was divinely insane – insane on behalf of God – but that he was rational enough in his relationship to them. [. . .]
>
> Being in the trance condition, or in Christ, as he calls it, he was caught up to the third heaven, and could not determine whether he was in the body or out of the body.[547]

The passage Massey is discussing can be found in 2 Corinthians chapter 12. If Massey's interpretation of the state Paul describes is correct, and the apostle is describing an ecstatic experience (which the text itself seems to support), then Paul's "visions and revelations" (2 Cor 12:1) have more in common with the mysteries – and with the out-of-body travel described in the Pyramid Texts of Egypt – than with the literal Christianity that was built in the centuries following.

In a different essay, entitled *Man in search of his soul during 50,000 years, and how he found it!* Gerald Massey elaborates further on the importance of this ecstatic experience. He explains that the word *gnosis* means knowing, not merely believing. It was the actual experience of the other world that gave such knowledge – not mere doctrinal belief. In section 17 of that essay, Massey writes:

> "By means of wisdom," says the wise man in the Apocrypha, "I shall attain immortality;" and "to be allied into Wisdom is immortality." To *know* was salvation. Acquiring this wisdom is described in Revelation as eating a little book on purpose to be in the spirit – or be born again in the spirit, or in the Christ, as Paul has it – or to prophesy, or to know how to be entranced, and enter

spirit-world as a spirit, for that is the ultimate fact. Irenæus says of the Gnostics: "They affirm that the Inner and Spiritual man is redeemed by means of knowledge, and that they, having acquired the knowledge of all things, stand in need of nothing else, for this is the true redemption," hence they repudiated the Christian Salvation by faith (Irenæus, B. I., chap. Xxi. 4). "The souls which possessed the saving seed of Wisdom were considered superior to all others, and the Gnostics held these to be the souls of prophets, kings, and priests, who were consequently endowed with a nature loftily transcendent. They maintain that those who have attained to perfect knowledge must of necessity be regenerated into that power which is above all." "For it is otherwise impossible to find entrance within the Pleroma" (Irenæus, B. I., chap. Xxi. 2). In our day such persons are sometimes called Mediums or Sensitives; in India they are Adepts in the most hidden mysteries. But this Gnosis by which the deceased in the Ritual [scholars of Massey's period referred to the Egyptian Book of the Dead as "*the Ritual*"] prevailed over the destroyers of form, the extinguishers of breath, eclipsers of the astral shade, or the stealers of memory – for these are among the devourers named – this gnosis of redemption and salvation, the gnosis of enduring life, was not merely information or knowledge in our modern sense. It was the gnosis of the mysteries, and all that was therein represented. The ancient wisdom (unlike the modern) included a knowledge of trance-conditions, from which was derived the Egyptian doctrine of spiritual transformation. This passed on into the Christian doctrine of conversion, and then the fundamental facts were lost sight of, or cast out and done with.[548]

This insight has profound implications, and Massey's observation sheds light on all that we have been examining thus far. Massey is saying that the concept of gnosis refers to knowledge that comes only from personal experience, and specifically the experience of ecstasy. This experience of ecstasy – "to know how to be entranced," Massey calls it – is identical to that described in the most ancient Egyptian texts, and to that experienced by the participants in the mysteries. It was taught by the Christian gnostics – of whom the author of the letters to the Galatians and Corinthians clearly was one – but then it was subtly altered by those who formulated what we know today as "the Christian doctrine," and in the process "the fundamental facts were lost sight of, or cast out and done with."

Based on this profound insight, and informed by the theory of Flavio Barbiero (a theory that is supported by a wide array of historical evidence), we can now begin to trace out a possible explanation of what happened.

- An ancient culture with advanced scientific and spiritual understanding creates a world-wide grid of megalithic sites, positioned along natural energy lines. These sites are associated with out-of-body travel, and possibly with actual physical travel as well.
- For reasons that remain unclear, the ancient predecessor civilization is lost or destroyed, but somehow bequeaths remnants of its knowledge to ancient cultures including that of ancient Egypt, where some of the earliest written records extant today describe deliberate ecstatic experience. The presence of these ancient texts marks the boundary between what we know of today as "history" and the previous time, which is still largely unknown and which we

can only describe as "pre-history," even though numerous monuments remain from the time of "pre-history" and attest to the sophistication of their builders.

- The knowledge of the deliberate ecstatic experience continues to be practiced in the mysteries. The knowledge of the "other realm" or other world evinces an understanding of a model of the universe akin to the "holographic universe" model proposed in the twentieth century by certain theoretical physicists (including David Bohm).

- At the same time, various ancient texts display an understanding of such a universe, using different metaphors to describe it. Today we call these "myths." All of them can be thought of as a "finger, pointing a way to the moon." Despite their superficial differences, they all point to a model of the universe and of human experience that is holographic and shamanic (ecstatic). Among the ancient sacred traditions following this pattern are the "myths" of ancient Egypt, ancient Sumer and Babylon, ancient Greece, and the events in the Pentateuch. In other parts of the world, the same pattern can be seen in the Norse myths, and in the sacred traditions of the Maya, Inca, Aztec, and of the tribes of North America and the Polynesians of the Pacific Ocean.

- The region known later as Judea was originally a part of Egypt, although its location meant that it would be fought over and conquered by various other kingdoms in the ancient world (including the Assyrians and the Babylonians). Nevertheless, the culture there was essentially Egyptian and the sacred traditions followed the same pattern as those of ancient Egypt. In fact, it is very likely that the priests in Judea who guarded the sacred texts of the Old Testament and administered the Temple system were originally Egyptian.

- The priests in Judea understood the metaphorical nature of the stories of the tribes of Israel, but taught a literal interpretation of them and concealed their metaphorical nature from the people. This situation may have started during the Babylonian captivity (approximately 597 BC - 515 BC).

- Prior to the Roman campaigns in Judea of AD 66 – AD 70, a Pharisee whom we know as Paul revealed aspects of the hidden "inner mysteries" to people other than the priests in the inner circle. He wrote a series of letters describing these inner mysteries, which was a horrifying development to the priestly families who did not want them revealed to the masses.

- During the Roman campaigns of AD 66 – AD70, a priest from a prominent family named Josephus surrendered to Vespasian and promised him the vast wealth of the Temple at Jerusalem in exchange for his safety. After the fall of the Temple, he made good on this promise, and was rewarded with a position of power and influence in Rome.

- After Josephus and other surviving members of the priestly families came to Rome, they undertook to "literalize" the inner-mystery teachings that gnostics such as Paul had revealed. Narratives that became the four gospels were written after AD 70, to give a historical context to what had been an essentially gnostic concept (a gnostic concept that was directly connected to the ancient Egyptian ritual, and to the mysteries). It is also possible that these gospels were selected from a variety of gnostic texts as the "least gnostic" and easiest to canonize by those wishing to push the literalist interpretation. Either way, these gospels followed the same astronomical and metaphorical patterns that are found in the Old Testament, patterns the priestly families understood intimately. Later still, the book of Acts was written to further historicize and literalize the apostles and to give a back-story to Paul and his "conversion" that is completely different from his own testimony in his letters.

- At the same time, the surviving priestly families in Rome begin to build a "spiritual Temple" through the institution of the Mithraic Mysteries. These mysteries embody many of the hidden teachings and symbols whose inner meanings the priestly families had kept secret for centuries. The priestly families used a two-pronged approach to spread their influence to the most important power centers of the Roman Empire. This approach consisted of the use of the Mithraic Mysteries as a secret, underground network that guided the expansion, and the use of literal Christianity as the more open and popular manifestation of the same metaphors and symbols. Only the external and non-esoteric interpretations would be shared with the masses.

- Not long after the priestly families came to Rome, they began to exert their influence over the other groups of Christians around the empire, eventually imposing a hierarchy centered in Rome upon what previously had been a non-hierarchical and largely gnostic phenomenon.

- When the hierarchy became strong enough, all gnostic interpretations were stamped out. When the order was coming down through the church hierarchy to destroy all gnostic texts, some gnostic Christians near Alexandria took a library full of texts that they could not bear to destroy and buried it in the talus at the base of a cliff near present-day Nag Hammadi, in Egypt. Perhaps they intended to come back for them later, but apparently they never had the opportunity. These texts were found in 1947, and provide an invaluable source of evidence which tends to support the outline suggested above.

- Subsequently, the holographic and shamanic understanding was ruthlessly stamped out. When the priestly families gained control of the entire Roman Empire, they set out to suppress the shamanic and holographic throughout the reaches of the empire. The library at Alexandria, no doubt a repository of many ancient texts that could throw light on the historical events described above and that point to interpretations that are shamanic and holographic rather than literal, was destroyed and its texts either burned or seized by the church so that no one but those in the most inner circles could ever have access to them.

- In the following centuries, this pattern would continue worldwide, to every place that the influence of the enemies of the shamanic and holographic could reach with the force of arms. There is evidence to suggest that it continues to this day.

- Shamanic culture and knowledge remained in parts of the world where the combined forces of the church and "western" arms had not yet come to dominate. These parts of the world originally included almost everything outside of western Europe, including Africa, India, Tibet, China, and other "eastern" lands, eastern Europe, the steppes of Russia and Siberia and other lands in the far north, all of North, Central, and South America, the Pacific islands, and Australia. The church and the west would later wage campaigns of violent conquest and oppression in most of these areas, campaigns which included the deliberate destruction of the shamanic knowledge.

This timeline incorporates many of the concepts we have examined in previous chapters, which all now begin to come together. One of the more striking claims of the theory outlined above is the idea that the priests administering the astro-theological sacred texts of the Old Testament were originally Egyptian. We have already touched on some of the evidence that suggests this possibility, and we will now explore the idea in a little greater depth.

First, we have already spent considerable time examining together the evidence that the texts describing the wanderings of the tribes of the children of Israel, the personage of Moses, the adventures of characters such as Samson, the story of Adam and Eve and the serpent in the Garden, and the lives and deeds of the patriarchs Abraham, Isaac and Jacob are not intended to be understood as describing literal, historical, human figures. These individuals and groups are metaphorical representations of the motions of the sun, moon, visible planets, and constellations, operating as part of a very coherent esoteric system that incorporates sophisticated astronomical understanding as well as sophisticated cosmological understanding – including an understanding of the "holographic" model of the universe that was not proposed in "modern scientific" terminology until the era of quantum physics.

If Abraham represents a celestial body (most likely the planet Saturn), and the tribes of Israel represent groupings or "tribes" of stars (almost certainly the twelve zodiac constellations, with Judah representing Leo, and so forth), then the entire "timeline" of "history" which stretches back to the events described in the Pentateuch and treats them as literal and historical events rather than metaphorical allegories and pointers is potentially completely wrong! We have already seen evidence that even the youthful David and his companion Jonathan (the son of Saul – or "*sol*") were celestial figures (the Twins of Gemini).

If the people occupying the Holy Land during early antiquity (stretching back to 1000 BC and even earlier) were not descended from literal individuals named Judah, or Reuben, or Issachar, or Benjamin, then who were they?

It is very likely that they were Egyptians.

The Egyptians were star-gazers par excellence. They possessed an extremely advanced science of the celestial mechanisms – and of human consciousness. They possessed a mythology that followed the same pattern of allegorizing the motions of the sun, moon, planets and stars to impart profound esoteric knowledge about the condition of mankind in the universe. We have already seen very clear connections that the horned Moses and the horned Okeanos almost certainly descend from or relat to the personification of the "horned" Nile River. We will see more connections presently. Finally, there appear to be powerful parallels between very ancient Egyptian sacred traditions and the Christos-Messiah tradition, connections which writers such as Gerald Massey and later Alvin Boyd Kuhn examine in great detail.

There is historical support for the view that the section of the Levant that we know as the Holy Land was part of Egypt in very ancient times (although it was fought over and at times successfully invaded, and its inhabitants carted off to slavery). It is possible that its inhabitants enjoyed some degree of independence or autonomy from the central authority in Egypt, a level of autonomy which may have waxed and waned and eventually at some point in time become complete separation and independence.

For example, discussing the extent to which the Levant was controlled by Egyptian kings during the 15th Dynasty (the so-called "Hyksos Dynasty," which included the reign of the Hyksos king Apophis from approximately 1590 BC to 1550 BC) from approximately 1650

BC to 1550 BC, the *HarperCollins Atlas of the Bible* (edited by James B. Pritchard, Emeritus Professor of the University of Pennsylvania and assisted by over forty other contributors and scholars, archaeologists, and museum curators) avers:

> Certainly king Apophis was termed 'Ruler of Retenu' by his opponent Kamosis of Thebes; this could imply rule of part of Palestine. The distribution of Hyksos royal scarab-seals in Canaan, plus a broken stone lintel with remains of royal titles of about this age from near Yibna, would combine to suggest a sphere of direct rule as far north as Joppa, and reaching along the western foothills of Canaan from Gezer to T. Beit Mirsim. Stray finds would extend communication as far as Jericho and Carmel.[549]

The map accompanying the discussion just cited shows that archaeologists have uncovered scarabs bearing Hyksos names at Sharuhen (Tel el-Far'ah), Tel Beit Mirsim, Lachish, Tel es-Safi Gezer, Jericho, and Tel Shiqmona – all locations in the ancient land of Israel.[550]

Yet further, we can pick up the tools given to us by Flavio Barbiero's new theory and use them to examine the possibility that the priests of Judea were descended from priests of Egypt. If Barbiero's theory is correct, the priests of the Christian church in the west down through the Middle Ages and into the start of modern times were descended from the priests of Judea – from the families of Josephus and the other priestly families whose members he was able to save by his actions in forming an alliance with Vespasian (and giving Vespasian and Titus access to the buried treasures of the Temple). If Barbiero's theory is correct, the nobility of Europe is largely descended from those families as well. Under his theory, the male descendants of those family lines could choose between two fairly comfortable options during the centuries after they discarded the Roman Empire – they could go into the clergy and become priests and bishops and some of them could become popes, or they could enjoy secular life as nobles in possession of great parcels of land, and could marry and have children (which was forbidden to the priesthood).

If his theory is correct, then many of the noble and royal families of Europe are descended from those priestly families. And indeed, the fact that those families all unfurled coats of arms all across Europe at roughly the same point in time during the Middle Ages, coats of arms which bore symbols which relate to the Old Testament tribes of Israel, their zodiac or celestial counterparts, and the symbology of the Temple of Jerusalem (including lions, towers, palm trees, lilies, harps, eagles, etc.) is a very important and powerful piece of evidence which supports Flavio Barbiero's assertions.[551]

If, then, those priests of Judea were descended not from literal "tribes of Israel" who themselves were descended from a literal Chaldean or Mesopotamian nomad (Abraham, who supposedly came to Canaan out of Ur of the Chaldees, but who more likely represents a celestial body, with the division between Ur and Canaan probably depicting yet another manifestation of the two halves of the zodiac wheel, just as does the battle between Greece and Troy) but rather from priests of Egypt – then that means that the noble families of western Europe, and those selected to be leaders of the Church of Rome through the Middle Ages and into modern times are also descended from Egyptians!

This is a rather astonishing assertion, especially as modern students learning about the great ancient civilization of Egypt are often given textbooks which contain drawings of Egyptians whose physical characteristics look nothing like those of the typical kings and queens and nobles of western Europe. However, as we will discuss a bit more below, the ancient Egyptians were extremely concerned with creating mummies that would preserve as accurately as possible the physical characteristics of the individual in life, including his or her facial features. Many of these mummies which have survived to the modern era are badly ravaged by the actions of time, or the depredations of ancient tomb robbers, or the misguided actions taken by the archaeologists and Egyptologists and museum curators of the eighteenth and nineteenth and even early twentieth centuries, whose attempts to preserve or protect the mummies did more harm than good.

However, some of those ancient mummies are remarkably well-preserved, and one of the most astonishingly well-preserved is the mummy of the famous pharaoh Seti I, also known by the name Maat-Men-Ra. He reigned from about 1290 BC (some scholars think he came to power slightly later) until his death in 1279 BC. He was the son of Rameses I and the father of Rameses II (the pharaoh whom most literalists believe was in power when the Exodus led by a literal Moses took place). A photograph of the very well-preserved head of his mummy is shown below, and it is quite clear that his features could easily be those of a royal or noble European.

http://en.wikipedia.org/wiki/File:Pharaoh_Seti_I_-_His_mummy_
_by_Emil_Brugsch_(1842-1930).jpg
SETI I, MEN-MAAT-RE or MAAT-MEN-RA

It has also been discussed in my previous book that the mummy of his son, Rameses II, has reddish-blond hair to this day, and that scientists in the twentieth century conducted experiments to determine that this was Rameses II's original hair color (it was not dyed, in other words).[552]

These observations are in no way offered as some sort of support for any theory of racial superiority of one branch of the human family. Sadly, some in recent centuries have made the supposed "race" of the ancient Egyptians into an argument for the ancient accomplishments of one race versus another. These arguments are reprehensible (not to mention the fact that they focus on the physical matter of our temporary incarnation, rather than the divine spark of the hidden god, common to all humanity, upon which we should primarily focus). The physical features of ancient Egyptians such as Seti I or his son Rameses II are only mentioned because, due to the state of preservation of their mummies for over three thousand years, they offer startling supporting evidence for the possibility that the origins of the ancestors of the priestly families who resisted the Roman invaders in the time of Vespasian and Titus, and who were eventually taken to Rome after the fall of the Temple, were Egyptians, and that their esoteric system originated from the esoteric systems of Egypt.

These facts tend to support the theory of Flavio Barbiero, and to support the assertion that the "children of Israel" who lived in the Promised Land (but who were not descended from constellations or other celestial personages) were Egyptians.

Turning to the evidence in the sacred texts of the Old Testament, there is plenty of evidence to support the conclusion that the people of ancient Israel, their priests and their theology, were Egyptian in origin.

First, it can be shown that much of the theology of the Old Testament is solar in nature – the fact that the twelve "tribes" of zodiac stars feature so prominently already testifies to this fact. The Egyptians were, of course, well known for their deep reverence for the sun and for the central position it occupied in their religious sensibility. But the ancient Hebrew theology was not merely solar – it was deeply solar and lunar, and as it turns out the Egyptian theology was solar and lunar as well. We can see a clear indication of the joint solar-lunar aspect of Hebrew theology, for instance, in the calculations used to determine the date of Passover, which involve both a full moon (a lunar event) and the March equinox (a solar event).

As Ralph Ellis (whom we met in a previous chapter and whose arguments that the Israelites were actually Egyptians are very important, even if he does accept the literality and historicity of characters such as Abraham and Moses) has pointed out, one of the Egyptian names for the disc of the sun or one aspect of the divine principle as manifested in the sun was the Aten.[553] As for the moon, it was associated with the supremely important god Thoth, giver of wisdom and sacred writing and the god of magic. The Egyptian name for Thoth has more recently been written in Roman letters as Tehuty or Djeheuti, which is probably closer to the way the ancient Egyptians referred to this ibis-headed Moon god (incidentally, the Arabic names Daud, Daudi and Dodi, as well as the familiar Biblical name David, all probably descend from and refer to the name of this god Thoth/Tehuty/Djeheuti).

To show how likely it is that the sacred Hebrew scriptures came from Egypt, Ralph Ellis has pointed out that the Old Testament names for God include of course the most sacred name of the tetragrammaton (the four letters which are sometimes spelled out as Yahweh in modern translations and Jehovah in older translations), and the ancient title Adonai, which means "lord" (and which is related to the name of the youth Adonis, beloved by Aphrodite in Greek myth). Ellis argues that the name Yahweh or Jehovah is linguistically related to the name Tehuty or Djeheuti (a moon deity), and that the name Adonai is linguistically derived from the Egyptian name Aten (the sun disc). He puts this argument forward in an essay called "Mt Sinai discovered," as well as in some of his books.[554]

Gerald Massey conducts a detailed analysis of the lunar-derived symbolism in the mythology of ancient Egypt and its transference into the scriptures of the Old and New Testaments in his fascinating study *Luniolatry, Ancient and Modern*. In it he traces the numerous symbolic patterns which arise from the moon's cycles and transformations. Among these was of course a cycle of death and rebirth each month which is every bit as powerful as that of the sun in its own annual cycle. He says of the moon, which waxes again to full after waning away to nothing at the time of new moon: "The re-arising and transforming orb at last proclaimed that even as it did not die out altoghether, but was renewed from some hidden spring or source of light, so was it with the human race, who were likewise renewed to re-live on hereafter like the moon."[555]

In that essay, Massey traces out patterns of "trinities" that arise from the monthly cycle of the Moon. One of these is that of the goddess, the dying god, and their powerful and potent son, born from their union. The goddess is the full moon in all its glory, and the dying god is the waning moon as it declines towards darkness. But, the dying god is destined to rise again in the prepotent child, the personification of the sharp-horned waxing crescent moon who arrives after the darkness of the new moon, and grows more and more powerful: the son who avenges the death of his father.[556] This pattern is very clearly evident in the Isis-Osiris-Horus mythos, where Isis is of course the goddess, Osiris is the dying declining god, and Horus is the powerful child-god.

That Osiris is not only an astral god (associated with Orion) but also has a lunar component which corresponds to the trinity outlined above and identified by Massey is evident from the fact that in his death he is cut into *fourteen* pieces by Set and his henchmen, as Massey points out in *Luniolatry*.[557] The cycle of the moon is traditionally twenty-eight days – the death of Osiris is by this symbolism identified with the declining part of the monthly cycle, according to Massey. The fact that the last of the fourteen dismembered pieces of Osiris was never found is not mentioned in this essay by Massey, but this fact could be further support for his argument, as the final day of the moon's waning cycle brings it to the new moon, when the moon cannot be seen as its illuminated side is completely turned towards the sun and the moon passes between the sun and the earth.

Elsewhere, in his book *The Hebrew and Other Creations Fundamentally Explained*, Gerald Massey elaborates more fully on the lunar cycle and its allegorization in mythology around the world. The struggle between the power of light and darkness that is seen in the cycle of the Moon is described as mortal combat, often in the form of a wrestling match, in which the power of light may seem to be winning, growing stronger and stronger, until he is about to finish off his opponent for good, but at the last moment the opponent representing darkness delivers a blow which wounds or maims the other, usually either in the joint of the knee or the hip. This wound causes the champion of light to cease growing stronger and actually to become maimed (and after that apparent triumph of the light, the moon will begin to decline again towards darkness).[558]

Massey sees this pattern in operation in the Egyptian mythos of the struggle between Osiris and Set, as well as in the Old Testament episodes of Cain and Abel, Esau and Jacob, Jacob "wrestling all night with the power called an angel," and in the New Testament twinning of Jesus and John the Baptist (in *Luniolatry*, Massey points to the well-known verse in which John, the darker twin of Jesus, the wild-man of the desert who dresses in hairy garments and thus takes the form of the "hairy twin" like Esau, declares of Jesus "He must increase, but I must decrease," John 3:30).[559] These connections argue for the possibility of a connection between the esoteric legends of ancient Egypt and those in the Old Testament.

We have also already seen some evidence that further Old Testament scriptural support for the idea that the ancient Hebrews were Egyptian may also be found in the story of Moses and the Israelites at Mt. Sinai, according to Ralph Ellis. In his essay, "Mt. Sinai Discovered," Mr. Ellis points out that the description of the events that took place around "Mt. Sinai" during the Exodus share some striking features which are difficult to understand, if this mount is truly a huge natural geological feature the way it is usually portrayed or imagined by readers of the texts.[560]

For example, in Exodus 19 verses 12 and 13, The LORD tells Moses that when Moses goes up to commune with God, the people are not to enter the mount, nor even reach out a hand to touch it. In fact, some sort of boundary is directed to be placed around the mount itself, "round about" or all the way around it. The text itself reads:

> [12] And thou shalt set bounds unto the people round about, saying, Take heed to yourselves, *that ye* go *not* up into the mount, or touch the border of it: whosoever toucheth the mount shall be surely put to death;
> [13] There shall not an hand touch it, but he shall surely be stoned, or shot through; whether *it be* beast or man, it shall not live: when the trumpet soundeth long, they shall come up to the mount.

What kind of "real" (that is to say, geological) mountain can have "bounds" set up all around it, so that people can come up to it but are prevented from touching it? For that matter, of what mountain can it be said that anyone who puts out a hand to touch it must be put to death? How would the people know where the mountain began and where they must not put out their hand to touch it, on pain of death? Most mountains are both too massive to easily ring with some kind of boundary, or to know exactly where the "mountain" itself begins so that a prohibition on touching "the mountain" could be enforced.

Ralph Ellis points out:

> Here we have a peculiar description of a mountiain that one cannot touch the borders of, as though the base of the mountain was more like a cliff than a gentle ascent. This mountain also appears to be small enough to cordon off, so that the

people cannot get close enough to touch it. In this case, Mt. Sinai must be relatively small, as mountains go, and thrust itself rather dramatically out of the surrounding plains.[561]

He also notes that the texts describing the encounter on Mt. Sinai consistently describe Moses as going into the mount, such as in Exodus 24:12 when the LORD tells Moses "Come up to me into the mount, and be there: and I will give thee tables of stone, and a law, and commandments which I have written; that thou mayest teach them."[562] The preposition "into" is used again in Exodus 24:18, and the preposition "in" is used in Exodus 34:32 and Leviticus 26:46 to describe the commandment which the LORD had spoken with Moses "in mount Sinai." It should be pointed out that there are also verses in which the LORD commands Moses to come up to the top of Mt. Sinai, and sometimes to bring Aaron with him to the top as well, such as Exodus 19:20 and 24.

Ellis argues that the mount being described, at the base of which the people were ordered to assemble but which was to be ringed about by bounds to prevent any from laying a hand upon it, that mount into which Moses would go to commune with the LORD (and, we might add, upon the summit of which he and occasionally he and Aaron would stand to meet with God) was none other than the Great Pyramid of Giza!

He writes:

> While the description of a natural mountain would agree with very few of these points, the Great Pyramid of Giza fulfills each and every one of them. The Great Pyramid is both sharp and steep, it contains a steeply inclined passageway that terminates in a rough cavern, it resides on the edge of the desert and it also rises very suddenly from the surrounding pavement area. As mountains go the Great Pyramid is rather small and easy to cordon off, yet it is also the tallest pyramid in Egypt.[563]

These arguments are very compelling, and Ellis bolsters them with additional arguments based on other texts and aspects of ancient Giza. If the events describing the encounter of Moses with God at Mt. Sinai are not actually describing events that took place around some geological massif in the middle of the Sinai peninsula but rather at Giza at the base of the Great Pyramid, this is yet more evidence which argues for the idea that the Israelites came out of Egypt and brought an Egyptian mythos-system with them.

Note also that this compelling analysis by Ellis does not necessarily establish that Moses, Aaron and Miriam and the events of the Exodus were literal historical persons and events either. It is quite possible to argue that the events described in the Pentateuch were metaphorical representations of heavenly dramas, and to argue that the priests of ancient Egypt would enact these dramas on earth – possibly at Giza and possibly around the base of the Great Pyramid.

Based on the extent and variety of evidence discussed above, there appear to be ample grounds for concluding that the priestly lines from which Josephus was descended were in possession of scriptures and wisdom which had their origins in Egypt, and which still contained strong traces of their Egyptian origins (although they were being applied to the spiritual needs of Egyptians who were now living in the land of Canaan).

But if all this is accepted as a likely premise, then where did Paul (a priest of the line of Benjamin and a former Pharisee, by his own declaration in his letters) get tuned in to what seems to be a completely different mythos, the doctrines of the Christ? Once again, it is through an observation recorded in the analysis of the perceptive Gerald Massey which provides an important clue – a clue which really leads to a complete paradigm-shift in the understanding of the relationship between the Old Testament and the New.

In section 18 of his essay *Paul the Gnostic Opponent of Peter, not an Apostle of Historic Christianity*, Massey writes:

> It is impossible to comprehend the mystery of Paul's Christ without a fundamental knowledge of the Messianic mystery that had been from the Beginning. This was his mystery, which he would not make so much of if he had started with what are held to be plain historical gospel truths. He spoke the *"Wisdom of God in a mystery that hath been hidden; which God foreordained before the worlds unto our glory."* The *"mystery which is Christ in you."* His was the *"revelation of the mystery which hath been kept in silence through times eternal."* The fact is that Paul was a publisher of the ancient mysteries; that was why his enemies strove to kill him! He openly promulgated the Gnosis which had always been kept secret.[564]

This is a truly astonishing new concept! Massey is averring that the doctrines of the Christ are just as ancient as all the Old Testament doctrines we have just been dealing with, but that the doctrines of the Christ were secret – they were Mystery, and they were kept by the priests but not disseminated to the uninitiated. It was, as Massey says, "the Messianic mystery that had been from the Beginning." In Romans 16:25, it is called (in a passage quoted by Massey in the third of the three scriptural texts which he puts in italics in the section above) "the revelation of the mystery which was kept secret since the world began."

If this paradigm-shifting theory proposed by Massey is correct, then it sheds new light on the efforts of Josephus and the priestly families after they arrived in Rome under the good graces of the emperor. By fashioning a new, authoritarian, and literal-historical (and above all a-gnostic or anti-gnostic) Christianity, they were attempting to repair the damage or contain the breach of a secret which they had guarded zealously "since the world began."

This proposal appears to fit the historical evidence we have been examining and discussing, and to fit it "to a T." Is there further evidence in ancient scripture which supports the idea that the Christ mythos is extremely ancient, and that it was known in ancient Egypt in remote antiquity? Indeed there is.

The idea that the teachings which eventually became literal and historic Christianity (teaching a literal and historic Christ) came from priests who were following the essential teachings of ancient Egypt has significant support in the New Testament doctrines themselves. Evidence can also be seen in Egyptian theology manifested in extremely ancient texts, including the Pyramid Texts and the Egyptian Book of the Dead, which show that the secret doctrines Paul proclaimed existed millennia before "AD 33."

Following the decipherment of the hieroglyphic and grammatical system of ancient Egypt by Jean-François Champollion in 1822, scholars for the first time in centuries could examine the contents of texts that had been effectively silent since the fourth century AD (the same time period, significantly enough, that Christianity was declared the official religion of the Roman Empire). Gerald Massey, who lived from 1828 to 1907, learned the system of Egyptian hieroglyphics and became a member of one of the earliest generations of modern scholars to explore the contents of the ancient texts.

What he found there showed that the ancient Egyptians had a version of the Christ story long before the gospels were written, and long before the time of Tiberius Caesar in which the timeline of the gospels is supposed to have begun. Perhaps it should not be too surprising that the first scholar to discuss this aspect of the ancient texts of Egypt should have been a self-taught "amateur" Egyptologist, rather than a formal member of academia. If the theory outlined above is correct, it is quite possible that the agents of the organization that suppressed the ancient wisdom through the ages since the time of Josephus maintain control over the universities of "the west" and the subjects that can and cannot be countenanced in academe.

In *Man in search of his soul during fifty thousand years, and how he found it!*, Massey outlines the essentially Egyptian nature of the gospel story. Later authors, such as Alvin Boyd Kuhn (who lived from 1880 to 1963) would explore the details of the connection in even greater depth. On this subject, Massey states:

> To "karas," in Egyptian, is to anoint, embalm, or make the mummy; and the type of preservation so made was called the Karast or Christ. Such, I maintain, is the Egyptian origin of the Christ called the Anointed in Greek. The one who transformed and rose again from the dead, designated the Karast or Christ, was represented both by the prepared and preserved mummy, and by the carven image, which was the likeness of a dead man. Moreover, this was the original Christ, whose vesture was without seam. In making the perfect mummy type of continuity or immortality the body had to be bound up in the ketu or woof, a seamless robe, or a bandage without a seam. No matter how long this might be – and some swathes have been unrolled that were 1000 yards in length – it was woven without a seam. This, I repeat, was the seamless robe of the mystical Christ, which re-appears as the coat, coating, or chiton (cf. ketu, Eg. Woof) of the Christ according to John. [. . .]

> We can trace the Karast or Mummy-Christ of Egypt a little further. When he transformed in the underworld, spirtualised or obtained a soul in the stars of heaven, he rose on the horizon as or in the constellation Orion – that is, the star of Horus, the Karast, or Christ. Hence Orion is named the Sahu, or constellation of the mummy who has transformed and ascended into heaven from the Mount of the Equinox, at the end of forty days, as the starry image of life to come, the typical Saviour of men. And Orion must have represented the risen Horus, the karast or Christ, at least 6000 years ago! This Christ is said to come forth sound, with no limb missing and not a bone broken, because the deceased was reconstituted in accordance with the physical imagery. And by aid of this Corporeal Christ of Egypt we can understand why the risen Christ of the Gospels is made to demonstrate that he is not a spirit or bodiless ghost, as the disciples

thought, but is in possession of the flesh and bones of the properly preserved corpse.[565]

Later, in *Ancient Egypt the Light of the World*, the last text Massey would publish, appearing in 1907, the year of his death, Massey would elaborate on this connection in far greater depth and detail.

He explains that the legend of Osiris forms a very clear pattern which can be seen to have direct parallels in the language and symbols and events of the gospels. Osiris is the god who suffers and dies, only to rise again and to be transformed. He is the personification of the aspect of the suffering god, who gives himself for the life of the entire world. Massey writes:

> An essential element in Egyptian religion was human sympathy with the suffering god, or the power in nature which gave itself, whether as herself or himself, as a living sacrifice, to bring the elements of life to man in light, in water, air, vegetation, fruit, roots, grain, and all things edible.[566]

In the chapter in Massey's *Ancient Egypt the Light of the World* entitled *Book 4: Egyptian Book of the Dead and the Mysteries of Amenta*, Massey plumbs the mysteries of the Book of the Dead (or the *Book of the Going Forth by Day*, as it is more often called today, and which Massey argues could in its entirety be properly called "The Ritual of the Resurrection") and finds very clear parallels to the events and symbols and sayings of the New Testament.

He notes that in the various texts which make up the Book of the Dead, the deceased is referred to as "the Osiris," and specifically declares that he is united with Osiris in his journey through the underworld from western horizon to eastern horizon (the same journey the "deceased" sun makes each night before being reborn into the heavens at daybreak the next day).[567]

Examples of the texts referring to the deceased as "the Osiris" can be found throughout the Egyptian Book of the Dead.

Already we can see a parallel with the larger theme this book has been arguing about identifying the individual (who in himself or herself is a microcosm) with the infinite of the macrocosm. In "putting on" the Osiris or donning the identity of the Osiris, the soul in the Egyptian theology is putting on the principal aspect of the god: the suffering one who died and who rises again. It goes without saying that this concept has clear parallels in the understanding of the Christ articulated by Paul in his letters, such as the statement in Galatians 3:27 in which he proclaims: "For as many of you as have been baptized into Christ have put on Christ."

In his identification with Osiris, the soul is hoping to repeat the transformation of Osiris, who is very distinctly depicted as an inert mummy lying supine in the form of one who has been laid to rest, and also as an erect risen mummy who is now identified with the Djed column (or, as earlier translators called it, the *Tet* column or the *Tat* pillar as Massey calls it), which is also called the "backbone" of Osiris and which supports the heavens.

Here we can see numerous parallels to the esoteric concepts we have been discussing, such as the importance of the spine that supports the dome of heaven which in the microcosm is contained within the human skull. The Djed column, Massey explains, is also the solstitial column, which ascends from its bottom at the winter solstice to its summit at the summer solstice.[568] The reader may recall from our examination of the astro-theological symbology of the New Testament that Philip, whose name means "lover of the horse" and whom Robert Taylor identifies with the zodiac constellation of Sagittarius, was according to ancient Christian tradition hanged against a pillar, and that the church of Philadelphia in the book of the Revelation is given the promise by the Christ: "him that overcometh will I make a pillar in the temple of my God" (Revelation 3:13). These pillars are one and the same pillar: the vertical column which runs on our circle of the zodiac between the winter solstice (at the base) to the summer solstice (at the top of the pillar).

Thus the two forms of Osiris, lying inert and rising to the erect or vertical position reflect the journey of the sun, which at the winter solstice begins to "go back up" from the depth that it has reached on its lowest day. Osiris can be thought of in some ways as equinoctial (lying flat) and soltistial (erect), and the identification of the soul with the principle of Osiris figures its journey through death to glory.

"In the mythos," writes Gerald Massey, "the *tat* is a type of the sun in the winter solstice that has the power of returning from the lowest depth and thus completing the eternal road. In the eschatology it is the god in person as Ptah-Sekeri or Osiris, the backbone and support of the universe. Horus erecting the *tat* in Sekhem was raising Osiris from the sepulchre, the father re-erected as the son in the typical resurrection and continuity of the human spirit in the after life."[569] This Tat or Djed column, he says, was "a figure of stability that was to be eternal."[570]

Djed-column, Papyrus of Ani, with Isis and Nephthys.
http://upload.wikimedia.org/wikipedia/commons/e/e5/Totenbuch.jpg

We can already see that this ancient mystery prefigures the Christ, the dying and resurrected. The portrayal of Osiris in the form of an inert mummy and as an erect risen mummy exactly parallels the portrayal of Christ as the *Corpus Christi* and as the resurrected savior in later Christian symbology and ritual, as Massey explains throughout his examination of the doctrine of the soul's journey.[571]

All of this discussion reveals that the teachings which Paul revealed in his letters had roots stretching back thousands of years into antiquity before he wrote those epistles, and that the parallels are so clear as to be instantly recognizable. The image of the Djed column above, which is being adored by the goddesses Isis and Nephthys (who, we will see shortly, are directly identifiable as the two Marys of the New Testament who often accompany the Christ and who are often depicted at the base of the Cross of the Crucifixion), is from the beautiful Papyrus of Ani (containing a version of the Book of the Dead), a scribe and priest in the reign of Seti I, whose mummy we saw above and who died in 1279 BC (thirteen long centuries before the birth of Paul).

In a very real sense, then, the imagery of the Christ who comes to earth and is incarnated in a body, and who dies and rises again glorified is the secret mystery of the ancient Ritual. The travel through the netherworld was in the pattern of the sun, who sinks below the western horizon each evening and in doing so, as Massey says, "was buried as a body (or mummy) in the nether world of Amenta."[572] It thus perfectly illustrates the teaching, which we have examined before, of the fiery spirit being "incarnated" in massy earth, or clay, which is a picture of every human soul during its journey in this life.

In fact, as has already been expounded at some length, the later author Alvin Boyd Kuhn, who drew heavily on the analysis of Massey in his own examination of the ancient Egyptian roots of the Christ Mystery, wrote that Massey committed a profound error in his analysis of the Book of the Dead, in that Kuhn believes the text is *primarily* referring to our incarnated state in this life, which is metaphorically speaking the realm of the dead and the realm of the underworld. Kuhn in numerous places takes pains to make clear his very high opinion of Massey, calling him at one point "the profoundest and most discriminating of Egyptologists."[573] However, in Massey's identification of Amenta as an otherworldly netherworld, traversed only by the souls of men and women after the death of the body, he believes that Massey is guilty of a sort of "literalizing" error – taking metaphorical language (language meant to be understood allegorically and spiritually) and reading it as describing a literal place.

Alvin Boyd Kuhn, in contrast, believes that Amenta describes this world through which we are all traveling during the life of the body, and that all the travails of the soul described in the Book of the Dead refer to soul-work that goes on in this incarnation, when we are incarnated like mummies in the flesh of matter. Kuhn provides extended discussion bolstered by evidence and logical argument to establish this position, most notably in his 1940 text *Lost Light: An Interpretation of Ancient Scriptures.*

In fact, he avers that all "netherworlds" in myth refer not to some literal subterranean or post-mortem place, but to this world which we are experiencing right now, through which the soul must toil as a being of fire and light who has been immersed (and almost drowned completely) in a body of water and mud, the red clay of Adam or

Edom. In the five hundred-plus pages of *Lost Light* and in the four hundred-plus pages of its companion and sequel *Who is this King of Glory*, Alvin Boyd Kuhn lays out example after example to establish the undeniable conclusion that ancient Egyptian sacred symbology was ingeniously crafted to depict this truth of the soul's descent into the world of matter – which is a world of the dead, when compared to the spirit realm – and the necessity of reminding it during this sojourn of its divine origin, of the Christ within, and of its own eternal nature and its eventual return to the spiritual – a process that takes place over and over until the spirit's work is done and having "mastered all its mundane instruction" its "descent into the tombs of bodies will be at an end at last" and it will remain forever in the blessed realms.[574]

He then shows that this ingenious ancient Egyptian symbology is at the heart of the teachings of the Old and New Testaments as well, and the key to their proper interpretations. The mistaking or deliberate obscuration of their teachings has been a "crushing weight upon the happy spirit of humanity" for at least sixteen centuries, Kuhn says, "and rectification of such misconstruction is urgently needed."[575]

In *Lost Light*, Kuhn provides his own analysis of the Book of the Dead (or "the Ritual"), in light of this interpretation:

> In the Egyptian Ritual the soul rejoices in life, shouting, "He hath given me the *beautiful* Amenta, through which *the living* pass from *death* to life." Amenta is this world, and the soul is pictured as running through cycles of descent from life to "death" and back again. The same sequence is set forth in the third chapter of Revelation: "I am he that *liveth* and was *dead*, and behold I am *alive* for evermore!" The Law precipitates us from the life above to the "death" down here, but lifts us up again.[576]

He explains that the Law to which he is referring – and to which the gnostic Paul (whom Kuhn sometimes calls "the Mystery initiate") refers – is "that cosmic impulsion which draws all spiritual entities down from the heights into the coils of matter in incarnation. It is the ever-revolving Wheel of Birth and Death, the Cyclic Law, the Cycle of Necessity. As every cycle of embodiment runs through seven sub-cycles or stages, it is the seven-coiled serpent of Genesis that encircles man in its folds."[577]

In the tomb of the body, Kuhn explains, the soul is imprisoned, and the animalistic demons the soul encounters in the Amenta described in the Book of the Dead are figures of "the menace to the soul of its subjection to the constant beat upon it of its animal propensities, since it had taken residence in the very bodies of the lower creatures" in its incarnated form here in this world.[578] "In a measure detached, it was yet not immune to being drawn down into ever deeper alliance with the carnal nature" – in other words, of having its spiritual nature "swallowed up" or devoured by the animal passions figured in the various "dragons, serpents, crocodiles, dogs, lions, bears, etc." who lie in wait, according to the Book of the Dead, in the "underworld" (this world, this incarnation) to devour the unfortunate spirit being and make it forget its spiritual nature altogether.[579]

Kuhn provides extended discussion to establish the thesis that the entrance of the soul into the body corresponds to the descent of Osiris into mummy-form in Amenta, where the god is "rendered lifeless by his suffocation in the body of matter."[580] But the Egyptian theology taught that the sojourn in the tomb of the body – in the land of the dead, or the Amenta – is not permanent: "Horus, Ptah, Anup, Ra and others of the savior gods would come in due time to awaken the sleepers 'in their sepulchres,' open the gates and guide the souls out into the light of the upper regions once more."[581] This analysis gives a whole new meaning to the constant reference to the soul as "the Osiris" in the Book of the Dead.

Kuhn's interpretation is a paradigm-shifting new perspective as profound as Massey's insight that Paul was articulating an ancient mystery in his letters and one which the literalists wanted to cover up, and Kuhn's theory accords very well with this assertion of Massey's and helps to illuminate the rise of a hierarchical and authoritarian church which allowed only a literal and historic interpretation to be taught to the masses and which actively stamped out the public teaching and explication of all gnostic or esoteric interpretations (while likely retaining these secrets within the priestly family lines, discussed in private among the inner circles).

After showing how this interpretation unlocks the often-perplexing passages of the Book of the Dead, and makes them make perfect sense when viewed in light of this new perspective, Alvin Boyd Kuhn then does the same for the scriptures of the Old and New Testaments, revealing both their essentially Egyptian origin and their essentially esoteric nature.

Among the beautiful verses of Isaiah 53, very well-known for their majestic description of the incarnation of the "man of sorrows" and which are often seen by those who advocate a literal interpretation as a clear prophecy of the later arrival of an historic and literal Christ, there is a verse which poses difficult problems for interpretations other than those informed by Kuhn's theory – interpretations which force upon the verse "mutilation and sheer nonsense" in his opinion.[582] That verse is Isaiah 53:9, wherein it is said of the one being described "And he made his grave with the wicked, and with the rich in his death [and the gloss tells us that the original Hebrew says "in his *deaths*," plural]."

This verse provides a king-sized problem for those who believe the "prophesies" of Isaiah 53 are referring to the coming of a literal and historic Christ centuries later. If the verse is intended to refer to a literal and historic Christ, the use of the plural is seriously upsetting to those whose doctrinal position is that the Christ came and died only once. How could it refer to a savior who comes "once for all" if the original Hebrew says he made his grave with the wicked and with the rich in his *deaths*? But if, as Kuhn avers, each incarnation of a human soul was seen as a "death" (in which the divine soul or "the Christ" becomes "the Osiris," enfleshed in mirey matter, like the spirit-fire of the sun ploughing through the cold earth each night), then the verse makes perfect sense.

All that is required is the shift of perspective to one which sees our physical body as a "tomb" for the spiritual and fiery entity of the soul, and which thus sees each life or each incarnation as a "death."

Of this verse and specifically its use of the word "deaths," Kuhn says:

> Here is invincible evidence that the word carries the connotation of "incarnations," for in no other possible sense can "death" be rationally considered in the plural number. In one incarnation the Christ soul is cast

among the wicked; in another among the rich. This is a common affirmation of most Oriental texts. And his body is his grave.[583]

Moving to the New Testament, Kuhn shows that there as well the texts support his assertion that the Bible, like the ancient Egyptian Ritual thousands of years before it, teaches multiple incarnations of the soul into the "death" of this life, and eventual transcendence of the cycle of incarnations when the soul's work here in "Amenta" is done.

For instance, in a verse which has caused endless confusion and disputation, 1 Peter 4:6, we are told that "the Gospel is preached also to them that are dead," a verse which gives much less difficulty if it is understood that this world itself is the "underworld" spoken of in sacred traditions and that those currently sojourning in it are referred to as the dead.

Alvin Boyd Kuhn adds substantially to the discussion of the "Tat cross" (the Djed column) introduced above by Gerald Massey, demonstrating that this symbology was central to the Egyptian esoteric system as well as to the New Testament. Kuhn writes:

> One of the rites of the resurrection was the "erecting of the Tat," or setting the Tat cross or the mummy upright on its feet. In addition to the imagery of death in all its forms to type our spiritually defunct condition here, there was employed also the idea of an entire reversal of position to portray the true state of the soul in its untoward predicament. We are heavenly spirits turned upside down here on earth! Earth reverses heavenly lines of motion. It reflects the pattern of things in the mount, but inverted. The highest symbols of heaven therefore fall at the very bottom of earthly tracing. [. . .]
>
> Man's lower nature, as seen in any diagram, is composed of the elements of earth and water, his higher nature of fire and air. Any time either of the upper two is crossed with either of the two lower, there is a rough symbol of incarnation, or combination of the divine with the human.[584]

Thus, in Kuhn's interpretation of the symbology, the cross always stands for the incarnation of the spirit, the "crossing" of the higher spiritual elements of air and fire with the lower material elements of earth and water: the human condition. The creation of the mummy, as Kuhn explains in an entire amazing chapter, was a complex symbolizing of this fact of the human condition.[585] The "Tat cross" (what we today usually refer to as the Djed column) was a symbol of the same thing. That is why it was also called the "backbone of Osiris" (we are, in a sense, each "an Osiris," the god who has been entombed in earth, the sun on its underworld journey, which it begins after crossing the airy realm of the sky and encounters the western horizon, to toil through the clay until it rises again in the east). Thus the mummy laid upon its back, or the Tat cross "cast down" represents our incarnational earthly sojourn, while the mummy raised to its feet, and the Tat cross or Djed column stood back upright represents the realization of our true spiritual self, our fiery divine spark within, and its ultimate destiny in the upper realms, freed at last from the cycle of incarnation (having learned all its lessons here in the earthly "vale of tears").

Kuhn elaborates still further on this theme, in words that clearly show the connection to the symbology of the Cross in the New Testament:

The Logia and Revelation both yield data on the theme of fire. At the first angel's trumpet message there ascended on earth a hail of fire which was scattered from the Altar of Fire before the throne. "And the hail of the fire was mingled with the blood of the Lamb; these were cast upon earth to consume away its evil." Horus had said that he came to put an end to evil. At the second angel's blast lightning flashed forth and *went down into the sea*, which it changed into blood. We have seen that a hail of stars or sparks over the earth was the typical figuration of the descent of the bright deities. The Egyptian ceremony of flinging a blazing cross into the Nile conveys the same connotation. The deities in incarnation were styled by the Greeks water-nymphs. A fiery cross thrust into water carried the purport of the sacrificial act of incarnation. A fiery serpent on the cross is a kindred element.[586]

All these symbols and stories esoterically convey to the incarnated man or woman, in his or her drugged condition of amnesia, the true state of affairs: he or she is a divine being, plunged for a time into the mirey clay, destined for a higher purpose. Metaphorically speaking, he or she is a star that has gone below the horizon. But one day, the soul will have fashioned through its incarnational cycles the fiery spirit body that will no longer need to be incarnated. The soul will join those souls that have transcended the incarnational cycle. This is metaphorically typed by the stars that never plunge below the horizon, which the ancient Egyptians called "the undying stars," the "imperishable stars," the "never-setting stars." Kuhn shows that this realm was to the Egyptians the heavenly Jerusalem:

> This was the Mount of Jerusalem, the Aarru-Salem, or Aarru-Hetep, the mount of eternal peace. In escaping from Egypt or Amenta, the goal of refuge is the Mount of Peace, as every religion on earth has attested. As spirits, not human marching columns, the children of Israel, after crossing the swampy Reed Sea of this life, are led to the celestial land flowing with milk and honey. Here the Eridanus emptied its stream of purifying water. This heavenly home was located and dramatized as the circumpolar paradise, the homeland of exiles and captives. [...]

> There the risen spirit becomes one of the glorious stars that nevermore shall set in ocean's or in earth's depths. "A divine domain hath been constructed for me: I know the name of it; the name of it is the garden of Aarru" (Ch. 109, Renouf).[587]

To explain the method by which the ancient systems said that the soul attains to this condition, Dr. Kuhn tackles some of the weightiest chapters of Romans and shows that this esoteric understanding resolves perplexing passages and verses in a most satisfactory way. His analysis of Romans 7, another Biblical text which has given rise to contentious disagreement among theologians of different persuasions, provides strong evidence for his interpretation. In Romans 7 verses 7 through 12, Paul writes:

> 7 What shall we say then? Is the law sin? God forbid. Nay, I had not known sin, but by the law: for I had not known lust, except the law had said, Thou shalt not covet.
> 8 But sin, taking occasion by the commandment, wrought in me all manner of concupiscence. For without the law sin was dead.

⁹ For I was alive without the law once: but when the commandment came, sin revived, and I died.

¹⁰ And the commandment, which *was ordained* to life, I found *to be* unto death.

¹¹ For sin, taking occasion by the commandment, deceived me, and by it slew *me.*

¹² Wherefore the law is holy, and the commandment holy, and just, and good.

These verses, along with the rest of Romans 7, have been interpreted in various different ways, but outside of the understanding offered by Kuhn, certain aspects of what Paul is trying to teach here are difficult to reconcile.

In particular, what does Paul mean when he said he "was alive without the law once"? Orthodox explanations typically argue that, until one knows the law, one cannot sin, and that before one is converted to Christianity one does not know the law and thus is not even aware of his sinfulness. But as Paul was raised (as he says elsewhere in Philippians 3:5) a "Hebrew of the Hebrews; as touching the law, a Pharisee," he would certainly have known about the law if we follow most conventional interpretations. In other words, it is possible to argue that he was not aware of his own sinfulness, but it seems exceedingly strange for Paul to describe that condition, especially in his own case, as being "alive without the law once." What is he talking about?

Alvin Boyd Kuhn's analysis of the scriptures solves the dilemma and sheds a completely new light on Paul's Romans 7 discussion of the concepts of "sin" and "death." In his analysis, the soul comes down from the spirit realms into the earthly realm of animate matter, where the human being is an altogether unique mixture of animal and spiritual. This mixture, incidentally, is the reason for the appearance throughout mythology of so many "twins," one of whom is divine and one of whom is mortal.[588] In Kuhn's analysis, these twins are a figure of the human condition – the divine spark submerged in the animal matter of corporeality. For this reason, the twin who represents the animal nature is often exceedingly hairy (such as Enkidu in the twinning of Gilgamesh and Enkidu in the ancient texts of Sumer and Babylon, or Esau in the twinning of Jacob and Esau in the Bible).

The descent of the divine spark into the corporeal nature is depicted in the esoteric literature as a kind of death, as we have already seen. And, according to a passage we have already cited, in Kuhn's theory the concept of "the Law" is the "cosmic impulsion" or force which sends souls down into the "underworld" of this existence, to work out their transformation.[589]

With this understanding , we can make better sense of Paul's discussion in Romans 7, including the difficult verses in Romans 7:7-12. Alvin Boyd Kuhn writes:

> Neither as animal below our status nor as angel above it can man sin. For the animal is not spiritually conscious and hence not morally culpable. And the angel is under no temptation or motivation from the sensual nature, which alone urges to "sin." Only when the Law links the soul to animal flesh does sin become possible. *Romans* (7:7) expressly declares: "Nay, I had not known sin, but by the law . . . For without the law sin was dead." Paul even says that at one time he lived without the law himself; this was before "the command" came to him. And what was this command? Again theology has missed rational sense

because it has lost ancient cosmologies and anthropologies. *The "command" was the Demiurgus' order to incarnate.* It is found in the *Timaeus* of Plato and Proclus' work on Plato's theology. Then the Apostle states the entire case with such clarity that only purblind benightedness of mind could miss it: "When the command came home to me, *sin sprang to life,* and I *died;* . . ." He means to say that sin sprang to life *as* he died, i.e., incarnated. And then he adds the crowning utterance on this matter to be found in all sacred literature: *"the command that meant life proved death to me."* He explains further: "The command gave an impulse to sin, sin beguiled me and used the command to *kill me."* And he proceeds to defend the entire procedure of nature and life against the unwarranted imputations of its being all an evil miscarriage of beneficence: "So the Law at any rate is holy, the command is holy, just and for our good. Then did what was meant for my good prove fatal to me? Never. It was sin; sin resulted in death for me *to make use of this good thing."* [590]

The final verse Alvin Boyd Kuhn is quoting here is Romans 7:13, in which Paul in the King James Translation says sin was "working death in me by that which is good," and which Kuhn suggests means that sin and death in this incarnation are altogether a "good thing" because it is through these incarnations that the soul is transformed and eventually transcends the cycle of incarnations.

Just before this explication, Kuhn opined that sin takes its place alongside what the esoteric texts refer to as "death" (that is, incarnation) as a natural part of the whole experience. He writes, "Sin is just the soul's condition of immersion or entanglement in the nature of the flesh. And happily much of its gruesome and morbid taint by the theological mind can be dismissed as a mistaken and needless gesture of ignorant pietism." [591] By this Kuhn no doubt meant the kinds of pietistic injunctions which arose from literalistic interpretations of what are supposed to have been metaphorical or symbolical stories (pietistic injunctions which were followed by and enforced upon by a much larger segment of the population back in the nineteenth century when Kuhn grew up than they is the case today), rather than injunctions against actual violations of natural law of the kind that the soul in the Book of the Dead disavows in its "negative confessions" in the Hall of Two Truths (the Judgment Hall).

Following his explication of this passage from Romans 7, Kuhn avers: "In this light it may be seen that the whole lugubrious posture of theology as to 'sin' and 'death' as its penalty, might be metamorphosed into an understanding of the natural and beneficent character of all such things in the drama." [592] It is at this point that he opines: "Ancient meaning has miscarried, with crushing weight upon the happy spirit of humanity; and rectification of such misconstruction is urgently needed."

And he is right.

The "crushing weight upon the happy spirit of humanity" which has come from the deliberate or accidental misreading of texts that are meant to explain a system of incarnation and reincarnation (if Kuhn is right and that is what they teach) has had atrocious consequences. It must include the crushing guilt inflicted by pietistic teachings derived from the literal reading of Old Testament texts, but even more so the fear of eternal hellfire and damnation for relatives, loved ones, friends, and even strangers who have not "accepted the gospel" as it has been taught by a literalistic and anti-gnostic church for seventeen centuries, as well as the horrendous wars and slaughter and violence that have been unleashed by literal misinterpretations and deliberate scripture-twisting, and that have been inflicted by groups holding one interpretation versus another and who are willing to torture or kill those who disagree with their interpretation.

Whether or not the actual progress of the human soul follows the incarnations described under the theory of Alvin Boyd Kuhn is not really the question at hand here. The real question is whether such a system is what is being taught in the scriptures of the Old Testament and New Testament, and in the sacred texts of ancient Egypt (and other ancient sacred traditions around the world). The interpretation offered by Kuhn seems to fit those texts very well, and to unlock certain aspects which are difficult to explain otherwise. Whether or not one believes or buys into the system explained in those texts is another matter: what matters is the clear parallel between the system of ancient Egypt and that found in the Bible (both Old and New Testaments).

The analysis of Alvin Boyd Kuhn and of Gerald Massey before him provide strong supporting evidence for the thesis that the priestly lines of Judea and the theology and esoteric system they followed were in some way descended from the civilization of ancient Egypt.

This is the system that saw every soul as an incarnation of "the Osiris," entombed in massy clay. But, by a secret and mysterious doctrine that is outlined in the texts of the Book of the Dead (albeit in language that is difficult and very symbolical, and which may indeed have concealed the very heart of the teaching from those not possessing the key to their interpretation), the massy clay carried within it the hidden divinity of the Christ. Through the anointing of the mummy, which is what Gerald Massey discusses in his examination of the "karast," and the transformations and transfigurations described in the Book of the Dead and other ancient Egyptian texts (and, using different language, the texts of the Old and New Testaments as well), "the Osiris" could become the transfigured, resurrected Horus.

This is the secret doctrine, the "mystery which was kept secret since the world began," which Paul was revealing and teaching to the Romans, and the Galatians, and the Corinthians in his letters. It came from Egypt, and was no doubt known and taught within the priestly lines for many centuries before the time of Vespasian's Roman campaigns (and perhaps it was taught and known more openly among the people in previous times, if it was later decided to keep it secret and replace it with literal interpretations of the Old Testament texts).

This is the secret which the literalistic or anti-gnostic church, as it grew in power, opposed. And, when its power reached a point where it could inflict its will at the point of a sword, it began the process of crushing the esoteric understanding of the Christ and the scriptures. With the theory of Flavio Barbiero and the benefit of access to the Copper Scroll found among the Dead Sea Scrolls, as well as the benefit of access to the Gnostic Nag Hammadi texts (vital pieces of information which were unavailable during the lives of Gerald Massey and Alvin Boyd Kuhn), we can gain greater insight into the historical events which may have led to the obfuscation of the esoteric side of the sacred scriptures, and the imposition of a literalistic and historical regime which has lasted for more than 1700 years, and which still exerts tremendous influence (sometimes at the "point of a sword") even today.

18

The literalists against the esoteric

It is by no means an unwarranted assertion to hint that the hostile attitude toward esotericism has been an item in the policy of a great conspiracy, operative ever since the third century, to diminish the influence of pagan teachings. Evidence to support such a forthright statement is not wanting, although, as Sir Gilbert Murray has noted, most of the evidence supporting the pagan side has been destroyed by the Christians.

Alvin Boyd Kuhn,
Who is this King of Glory?[593]

We have now examined abundant evidence which strongly supports the following conclusions:

- The scriptures of both the Old and New Testament are founded upon celestial allegories, ingeniously incorporating allegories relating to the human body at the same time, likely designed to impart profound esoteric teachings regarding the nature of the universe and the nature of human existence.
- The esoteric teachings, and the system of celestial allegories and human body allegories used, indicate that the scriptures of the Old and New Testaments are close kin to the ancient wisdom imparted to humanity in the sacred texts and traditions of ancient Egypt, ancient Greece, and many other traditions found the world over. It is only the later literalist tradition which teaches that the scriptures of the Old and New Testaments are literal and historical; upon this teaching, literalists assert a clean break between the Old and New Testament scriptures and the scriptures and traditions found the world over, but this is a false teaching based upon a mistaken or deliberately deceitful reading of the texts.
- The scriptures of the Old and New Testament show signs of being related to the ancient mythological esoteric system of ancient Egypt. Their message appears to have included an understanding of the universe that was what we today might call "holographic," composed of an explicate, unfolded and apparently material projection which unfolds from and depends upon an interpenetrating, hidden, implicate spirit realm or seed realm, the Duat or the shamanic realm. Their message also appears to have included an understanding of the human condition of each man or woman as that of a spiritual being, incarnate in material form in order to have certain experiences and learn and do certain things, but descended from the spiritual realm and returning to it bearing the benefits of the experiences, actions, and learning acquired in each physical sojourn, and perhaps destined to one day transcend the cycle of incarnation, through the accumulated experiences, actions, and learning acquired in their material lives.
- The scriptures of the world, along with other forms evidence, all convey a view of the nature of the universe and of human existence implying the

possibility and even the importance and necessity of various forms of shamanic travel or contact with the spirit realm or hidden realm or implicate realm. Such shamanic practice took various forms in various different times and different cultures. It appears to have been related to helping others, just as shamanic activity is often related to solving problems or medical issues or otherwise helping other individuals or the entire community in modern accounts of shamanic practice. It appears also to have been related to gaining knowledge which cannot be attained in other ways – including knowledge of the secret properties of plants, knowledge of medical technique, knowledge of a spiritual nature, knowledge of the natural energy of the earth and its "dragon paths," and possibly knowledge of an advanced technical and scientific nature, related to the manipulation of objects or even to the levitation of heavy objects and forms of physical travel long forgotten today, as well as many other important subjects. Even the author we know as Paul attests in his writings to out-of-body experiences which may be described as shamanic in nature.

- The end of such a worldview in the west, and its attendant "shamanic-holographic" rituals and techniques, appears to closely coincide with the rise of the literalist-historicist interpretation of those scriptures chosen to be included in the Old and New Testaments, as well as the suppression of other contemporary texts such as those buried at Nag Hammadi. Specifically, the end of such a worldview, and the suppression and marginalization of the writings of those who would propagate or defend that worldview, corresponded to the rise of ecclesiastical, literalist Christianity. The evidence strongly suggests that the rise of ecclesiastical, literalist Christianity followed directly from the conquest of Jerusalem by the Romans and the "ransom of Josephus," after which a number of powerful priestly families were spared by Vespasian and Titus and were brought back to Rome, where they were given wealth and privilege.

We can now begin to examine some of the historical evidence that haof events that have taken place since the events described to this point, to see that the actions of the Christian church – and the actions of the nobles and royals who have ruled western Europe since the fall of the western empire and who must be descended from those priestly lines saved by Josephus – provide even further evidence to support the already well-supported conclusions listed above. Specifically, we can see evidence of a deliberate, concerted, centuries-long war on esotericism, on gnosticism, and on shamanism. It is both a violent war, involving murder and even genocide, and it is a "consciousness war," involving mind control and reprehensible techniques designed to keep people in ignorance of the truth, to deny them access to shamanic techniques and knowledge, to deny them access to the teachings about human nature as essentially divinity incarnated, and to get men and women to passively and even happily accept and acquiesce to the designs of those who manipulate, suppress, and imprison them.

One of the first things which the literalists did as part of this campaign was to assert their right to declare which texts and teachings would be countenanced, and which were too overtly gnostic and had to be suppressed. We can see plain evidence of this suppression of thought and discourse through the suppression of texts and teachings in at least two ancient sources of evidence: the letter of Athanasius listing the New Testament canon, and the library of texts unearthed at Nag Hammadi in the twentieth century, buried since antiquity.

Both of these pieces of historical evidence demonstrate the same pattern by the literalist Christian hierarchy during the century in which Christianity became the appointed state religion of the empire: the pattern of the control of thought through the sharp delineation between what discourse is acceptable and what is not. This pattern would continue for the next sixteen centuries in various forms, and it continues today in this seventeenth century since the watershed fourth century AD.

The campaign against opponents of literalist doctrine had been ongoing in the centuries leading up to the fourth century. The second and third centuries saw the rise of literalist "apologists" and polemicists who railed against "heresies" – and their targets seem to have been primarily gnostic in nature. Among the attackers of the esoteric understanding of Christianity from this period were Justin Martyr (AD 100 – AD 165), Irenaeus (AD 130 – AD 202), and Tertullian (AD 160 – AD 225), all of whom wrote tracts in support of literalist understandings of Christianity, in support of the hierarchy of the church, and specifically against heresies, the most frequent heretical target being the gnostics. These works are all evidence of a concerted effort to establish literalist Christianity (which in light of the theory we are examining was a deliberate creation by the leaders of a conspiracy to take control of the Roman Empire, using the twin engines of Mithraism and literalist historicist Christianity).

During the second century, several strongly esoteric (and sometimes openly gnostic) Christian teachers were as prominent or even more prominent than the literalists who opposed them, esoteric thinkers including: Valentinus (AD 100 to AD 175); Basilides (dates of birth and death not certain but he was probably active in Alexandria from AD 117 to AD 138); Clement of Alexandria, who lived from approximately AD 150 to AD 215 (not to be confused with the earlier Clement of Rome, who wrote the letter to the body of Christians at Corinth in AD 95 or 96, which was earlier discussed as the first evidence of the sudden importance of the Christian hierarchy being established in Rome after the arrival of the priestly families led by Josephus); and Origen (AD 184 to AD 253), whose teaching was extremely influential, and widely accepted among Christian circles during the second and third century, before the triumph of literalism towards the end of the third and especially the fourth century.

Alvin Boyd Kuhn notes that the later excommunication of the once profoundly-influential Origen by the now solidly-literalist church, 299 years after his death, is clear evidence "that Christianity had been radically transmogrified within a few hundred years after its inception."[594]

Some of the most powerful evidence of deliberate suppression of the esoteric, evidence which only came to light in the middle of the last century, are the scrolls found at the foot of a cliff near the little modern village of Nag Hammadi in Egypt, just north of the ancient city of Luxor, introduced as evidence in some of the previous chapters' discussions.

We have already examined some of the reasons Marvin Meyer, author of the 2005 study of the texts entitled *The Gnostic Discoveries: The Impact of the Nag Hammadi Library*, believes that those who buried the texts at the base of a cliff after sealing them in a large jar were hiding them from those who wanted to suppress or even destroy them. He provides evidence that the texts may have been buried upon the publication of the Festal Letter of Athanasius, Archbishop of Alexandria, in AD 367 (also known as the 39th Festal Letter).

Meyer explains that the very fact that the texts were buried in a manner meant to protect them indicates the desire by the community that had been using the texts to preserve the texts, and not simply to dispose of or destroy them. He also notes that "the scribal notes in the texts themselves are pious and not heresiological in their perspectives."[595] In other words, the notes are most decidedly *not* from the perspective of one who saw these texts as heretical. But, Meyer explains, in AD 367, Athanasius the archbishop of Alexandria, "soon to be acclaimed the champion of orthodox Christianity, wrote a festal letter to be read in the churches of Egypt."[596] Meyer goes on:

> Among other things, the letter addresses the issue of the canon, of what books should be considered authoritative and inspired and thus included in the Bible. In his festal letter Athanasius lists what he as archbishop believes to be the canonical books of the Christian scriptures, and his list may be the first ever to include the twenty-seven books of the New Testament that eventually were used in most churches. Later Jerome opted for the same twenty-seven books in his Latin translation of the Bible, the Vulgate.[597]

The letter condemns heretics and heretical texts. Meyer surmises that the Nag Hammadi texts may have been buried beneath the cliff at that time, since many clues in the texts themselves point to a date of around the middle of the fourth century for their time of inscription and use.[598]

Among these clues are the form of writing and language used, and – perhaps most useful – the "cartonnage" or scrap papyrus that was recycled into the durable covers for the various the Nag Hammadi codices. These scraps of old documents were pasted on the inside of the soft leather covers around the codices, in order to make the leather stiffer and to turn them, in effect, from "softback" books into "hardback" books.[599] Although the texts themselves could have been in use prior to the operation of pasting cartonnage into their covers, they most likely were not written *afterwards*. Scholars have examined the writing on these old, recycled pieces of papyrus and found references to dates or events that show that the cartonnage came from the middle of the fourth century (since they obviously could not have contained writing about events in the future).

Meyer explains that, "In the cartonnage there are dates in the middle of the fourth century and just before, and names suggesting monks and locations around Pbow and Šeneset (Chenoboskia)."[600] Thus, the Nag Hammadi codices probably date to the period of the mid-fourth century (mid-300s AD; remember that the "first century AD" contained the years up to 100 AD, from AD 1 through AD 99, and so the second century contained years beginning with AD 100 and going through AD 199, and so on, such that the fourth century would contain years beginning with AD 300 and going on to AD 399).

Among the Nag Hammadi texts is a group that are characterized as "Valentinian" in style and content, after Valentinus the important Christian gnostic teacher of Alexandria and Rome mentioned above (he lived from about AD 100 to AD 175). At least one of the texts in the Nag Hammadi collection was probably authored by Valentinus, the text known as the Gospel of Truth, found in Codex I of the group and in fragmentary form in Codex XII, (Codex XII was partially destroyed in the twentieth century).[601]

The simple fact that the community of adherents who treasured these texts, who studied them and wrote margin notes in them, and who buried them carefully next to a large boulder beneath the cliffs of the Jabal al-Tarif in hopes (apparently) of someday going back to retrieve them felt it was necessary to include Valentinian texts in the group shows that by the latter half of the fourth century the pressure from the "orthodox" faction – which was rapidly consolidating power – was becoming intense against those caught in possession of "heretical" texts. The rest of the texts in the Nag Hammadi library are also of an esoteric nature, from various gnostic and Hermetic perspectives and schools of interpretation. None of them are "orthodox" in nature.

As we already saw during the examination of the outlines of Flavio Barbiero's theory, it was during the fourth century AD that the priestly family was taking major steps to consolidate power over the empire. Constantine was declared emperor in AD 306, and had declared Christianity the official religion in AD 324. Constantine's successors Valentinian, Gratian, Magnus Maximus, and Theodosius, in Barbiero's analysis, "dealt the fatal blow to paganism and what little still remained of the ancient Roman senatorial aristocracy."[602] In AD 380, the emperor Theodosius published an edict obliging all Christians throughout the empire to profess faith in the bishop of Rome.[603] And, Barbiero explains, "In 392, he promulgated a decree that outlawed paganism, forbidding any manifestations of pagan cults, including the Olympic games, which were held in honor of Zeus."[604]

Of this period of Roman history, Barbiero summarizes:

> It is clear that in the course of the second century AD, without realizing it, paganism had lost all control over Roman society, which had passed into the hands of the esoteric organization of Sol Invictus Mithras. Throughout the third century, Sol Invictus created and got rid of emperors at its pleasure. Only Diocletian managed for a while to evade its will with the system of the tetrarchy, but he never succeeded in denting its power. On the contrary, he determined a radical shift in Sol Invictus policy, with its consequent choice of forced Christianization of the whole of Roman society.[605]

During the fourth century, this forced Christianization was put into place, and the form of Christianity that would be privileged would be the literalist, historicist, anti-gnostic, hierarchical form, with power centralized in the bishop of Rome. All other forms would be marginalized, and eventually obliterated or driven underground. Meyer tells us that "from the fourth century on," Valentinian Christians were "subjected to a series of edicts and attacks, and late in the fourth century a mob of angry Christians burned down a Valentinian chapel on the banks of the Euphrates River."[606]

During the rule of the emperor Theodosius, the Patriarch Theophilus of Alexandria closed all the pagan temples of Alexandria, and at least some of them were destroyed, including the Serapeum, which housed large numbers of texts of the famous ancient library of Alexandria. Theophilus built a Christian church on the site of the old Serapeum.

In AD 415 occurred the infamous murder of the accomplished Neoplatonist scholar Hypatia at the hands of a mob of Christian monks. Some sources believe that Hypatia, who was the head of the Platonist school at Alexandria, was the last Head Librarian of the great library of Alexandria. Her death is often conflated, rightly or wrongly, with the final destruction of the library of Alexandria. In any event, her murder is widely seen as one of the signs heralding the destruction of the wisdom of antiquity and the descent into the Dark Ages.

After the reign of Theodosius, as discussed previously, the office of emperor was divided between his two sons, with one ruling in the east and one in the west. The seat of the emperor had already been moved to Constantinople, a move which Flavio Barbiero's theory interprets as being necessary to further increase the power of the priestly family's rule through the ascendant power of the Church of Rome and its leader, the bishop of Rome (who, as noted already, after the end of the institution of Mithraism assumed the title of *Pater Patrum*, shortened to *PaPa*: the Pope).

Not long after, as we have already seen, the power of the Church (controlled by the priestly lines) would become dominant in the west and the office of emperor and the trappings of empire would dissolve. In the east, the emperor at Constantinople would become more powerful and the power of the church as an independent entity capable of dictating policy or of controlling the eastern Roman Emperor would wane.

These events are widely known to history, and have been the subject of voluminous study and commentary by scholars through the centuries.

Less well known, however, and in fact actively suppressed by academia through the years is the body of evidence suggesting that some adherents to philosophies and belief systems that were being increasingly persecuted during the second and third centuries fled the scene altogether. There is an enormous amount of evidence which suggests that some of these, fleeing persecution and perhaps even fleeing for their lives in those early centuries of consolidation of power by the literalist church centered in Rome, actually came to the Americas.

We will examine some of that evidence here, although there is so much of it that several more volumes dedicated to that subject alone would be necessary to properly address it all. Perhaps the most telling evidence that such an evacuation to the New World took place might be the behavior towards the inhabitants and civilizations of "the New World" by the Europeans when they were finally able to cross the oceans again: they immediately began to slaughter them with extreme prejudice, and forcibly converted them to literalist Christianity.

This behavior strongly suggests that the families in charge of the consolidation of power during the third and fourth centuries within the literalist church centered in Rome knew of the escape of "heretics" who were in possession of the ancient esoteric wisdom that the leaders of the families had decided to stamp out, and that they nursed a desire for revenge against those escapees down through the centuries. The descendants of those priestly families, still in control of the hierarchical and literalist western church, and still in control of the fragmented nation-states of Europe that had arisen after the church threw off the shell of the Roman Empire, eventually found it expedient to cross the oceans in pursuit of new lands, and to punish the descendants of those who had escaped – as well as the members of the shamanic Native American cultures they encountered there as well.

Part III

That episode, and one which came earlier – the Crusades to retake the "Holy Land" and the site of the Temple of Jerusalem which had been wrested from their ancestors during the campaigns of Vespasian and his son Titus – constitute strong evidence in support of the "priestly families" theory of Flavio Barbiero, and in support of the theory that these families have been waging a war of suppression and extermination against the shamanic-holographic teachings of the world's "non-western" cultures.

Both the Crusades and the treatment of the people of the Americas will be examined in subsequent chapters for the light they can shed on the history of the campaign of deliberate suppression of the ancient wisdom, and its continuation into the modern age.

19
Escape to Atlantis?

We have reason to believe that good maps of the St. Lawrence River were available in Europe before Columbus sailed in 1492. In Fig. 34 we see a map of the river and the islands near its mouth that the mapmaker Martin Behaim placed on a globe he made and completed before Columbus returned from his first voyage. Columbus was not an ignorant mariner, as some people seem to imagine. He was quite at home in Latin, which indicated some education, and he was a cartographer by trade. It is known that he traveled widely in Europe, always on the lookout for maps. His voyage was not a sudden inspiration; it was a deeply settled objective, one followed with perseverance for many years, and it required, above all, maps. The historian Las Casas said that Columbus had a world map, which he showed to King Ferdinand and Queen Isabella, and which, apparently, convinced them that they should back Columbus.

Charles H. Hapgood,
Maps of the Ancient Sea Kings.[607]

There is ancient textual evidence suggesting awareness of and even detailed knowledge about the Americas. Diodorus Siculus, one of the most respected historians of antiquity, was a Greek historian who lived in Sicily, and published an exhaustive forty-volume "universal history," which he called the *Bibliotheca historica,* or the "Historical Library." They were probably written between the years 60 BC and 30 BC. Of the forty books in the *Bibliotheca historica,* only books 1 through 5 and 11 through 20 survive today.[608]

In Book 5, chapter 19 begins with two lengthy sections describing in detail a vast "island" located far to the west of the Pillars of Hercules across the Atlantic Ocean, which matches in all its details the massive continents of the Americas.

Diodorus relates:

> [1]But now that we have discussed what relates to the islands which lie within the Pillars of Heracles, we shall give an account of those which are in the ocean. For there lies out in the deep off Libya an island of considerable size, and situated as it is in the ocean it is distant from Libya a voyage of a number of days to the west. Its land is fruitful, much of it being mountainous and not a little being a level plain of surpassing beauty. [2]Through it flow navigable rivers which are used for irrigation, and the island contains many parks planted with trees of every variety and gardens in great multitudes which are traversed by streams of sweet water; on it also are private villas of costly construction, and throughout the gardens banqueting houses have been constructed in a setting of flowers, and in them the inhabitants pass their time during the summer season, since the land supplies in abundance everything which contributes to enjoyment and luxury. [3]The mountainous part of the island is covered with dense thickets of great extent and with fruit-trees of every variety, and, inviting men to life among the mountains, it has cozy glens and springs in great number. In a word, this island

is supplied with springs of sweet water which not only makes the use of it enjoyable for those who pass their life there but also contribute to the health and vigour of their bodies. ⁴There is also excellent hunting of every manner of beast and wild animal, and the inhabitants, being well supplied with this game at their feasts, lack of nothing which pertains to luxury and extravagance; for in fact the sea which washes the shore of the island contains a multitude of fish, since the character of the ocean is such that it abounds throughout its extent with fish of every variety. ⁵And, speaking generally, the climate of the island is so mild that it produces in abundance the fruits of the trees and the other seasonal fruits for the larger part of the year, so that it would appear that the island, because of its exceptional felicity, were a dwelling-place of a race of gods and not of men.[609]

As the ancients were accustomed to referring to the continent of Africa as "Libya," the account in Diodorus' work of this land lying "distant from Libya a voyage of a number of days to the west" and which he describes in such terms is almost certainly the continent of either North or South America (or both). Those who have grown up and spent their entire lives in this land can certainly attest to the fact that the Diodorus' description matches their experience exceedingly well, from the abundance of the beasts and wild animals, the springs which "contribute to [. . .] health and vigour" and the ocean which washes the shore and which produces "fish of every variety."

In his book *Discovery of Ancient America*, David Allen Deal notes that this land described by Diodorus was apparently known to the Greeks in the time of Plato as well.[610] In *Timaeus*, Plato writes of "a mighty power which unprovoked made an expedition against the whole of Europe and Asia," and to which the city of Athens "before the great deluge of all" put an end. Speaking through Socrates, Plato recounts the description given by an extremely aged priest of Egypt to the Athenian Solon:

> This power came forth out of the Atlantic Ocean, for in those days the Atlantic was navigable, and there was an island situated in front of the straits which are by you called the Pillars of Heracles. The island was larger than Libya and Asia put together and was the way to other islands, and from these you might pass to the whole of the opposite continent which surrounded the true ocean, for this sea which is within the Straits of Heracles is only a harbor, having a narrow entrance, but that other is a real sea, and the land surrounding it on every side may be most truly called a boundless continent.[611]

To this mighty "island," larger than Libya and Asia put together, the *Timaeus* gives the famous name *Atlantis*, and indeed Plato's work is one of the only places in all of ancient literature where that name is found.

While the Egyptian priest apparently told Solon that Atlantis sank into the ocean after "violent earthquakes and floods," it is certainly possible that the lost island continent, for which so many minds have searched in the centuries thereafter, was never lost at all – and that hundreds of millions of people are living on Atlantis right now, in North or South America. This possibility has been raised by many analysts in the past, although conventional academics reflexively reject it. Henriette Mertz, discussed below, published a book in 1976 entitled *Atlantis: Dwelling-place of the Gods* which forwarded such a theory.

The fact that Atlantis is described as being the way from which one could reach "other islands" makes it tempting to believe that the ancient Egyptian priest was here talking about the islands of the mighty Pacific, especially since he declares that from those islands one might pass all the way to "the opposite continent" – the other edge of the world, the easterly coast of Asia.

This story in Plato's *Timaeus,* and the later confirmation in the history of Diodorus, provides very solid evidence that the ancients knew about the existence of the Americas, and that they had in fact visited them and returned with good and accurate descriptions of those lands, and even of the great ocean further west of the Americas, the Pacific Ocean and its myriad islands – the islands we now call Polynesia.

It is also significant to note that Plato's account puts the original description of the far-off island of Atlantis in the mouth of one of the priests of Egypt, one "of a very great age," who begins his account to Solon by rebuking the Athenian and telling him that "you Hellenes are never anything but children, and there is not an old man among you," by which, the priest explains, he means that, in contrast with the civilization of ancient Egypt, "there is no old opinion handed down among you by ancient tradition, nor any science which is hoary with age."[612] Plato is here letting us know that the Egyptians were possessed of knowledge that was far more ancient than that of the ancient Greeks (at least in their own opinion), and also that the Egyptians were the ones who were aware of the continent of Atlantis before the Greeks ever told of it.

But why would Plato (or the Egyptian priest) have told us that Atlantis sank beneath the waves in a single night and day, if Atlantis was actually their name for the American continents? David Allen Deal gives us an excellent answer, based on his analysis of the next paragraph in the account of Diodorus from Book 5 section 20 (following immediately after section 19, cited above).

In that next paragraph, which David Allen Deal cites on pages 47-48, Diodorus tells us that the island west of Libya he described was originally discovered by Phoenicians (those outstanding sailors of the ancient world, whose cities of Sidon, Byblos and Tyre were along the coastline of modern Lebanon and whose colonies stretched across the southern Mediterranean coast of north Africa and included Carthage, Cadiz in Spain and Tingis at modern Tangier near the straits of Gibraltar), and that when they first discovered it, the land's felicity and nature impressed them so much that "they caused it to be known to all men."[613] However, Diodorus goes on to tell us that the Carthaginians prevented anyone from sailing there, "partly out of concern lest many inhabitants of Carthage should remove there because of the excellence of the island, and partly in order to have ready in it a place in which to seek refuge against an incalculable turn of fortune, in case some total disaster should overtake Carthage."[614]

Perhaps it was from the Phoenicians that the priests of Egypt described in Plato learned of that happy land far to the west. In any event, it seems that those who knew of it had a very good reason for keeping its location something of a secret: the far continent could serve as a place of escape, in the event of "some total disaster."

Could it be that certain ancients from the region of Egypt considered the events of the third and fourth centuries AD, during which the literalist faith was being set up as the religion of the empire and during which all "non-canonical" texts were being banned, to have qualified as "some total disaster"? Is it conceivable that some numbers of them sought passage to the New World on ships crewed by mariners from the north coast of Africa who were still able to make the voyage?

The idea may seem to be ridiculous to those whose upbringing has included years or even decades in the educational structure of the modern "west," and it may strike even fair-minded readers as being at the very least highly speculative – except for the fact that numerous pieces of archaeological evidence support the assertion that sailors from the Mediterranean had been visiting the shores of North and South America for centuries (as the accounts of Plato and Diodorus Siculus appear to indicate), and that while many of these archaeological artifacts contain writing that is Phoenician or Libyan, some of them are in Hebrew, some of them contain Egyptian writing and concepts, and some of them even appear to reflect gnostic Christian iconography and religious doctrines!

In *America BC: Ancient Settlers in the New World*, published in 1976, Harvard professor Barry Fell documents numerous examples of ancient Phoenician, Iberian, and Libyan texts found inscribed on large rocks and stone monuments throughout the New World. In addition to these writing systems, he also identifies evidence of an "Egyptian presence."

One such piece of evidence for an Egyptian presence in the New World which is extremely difficult to explain away is the celebrated case of the "Mi'kmaq hieroglyphs." Written systems for conveying language were extremely rare among the Native American tribes of North America. A notable exception, however, was the written language of the Mi'kmaq people (sometimes spelled "Micmac" in older texts, the name of this people is more commonly spelled *Mi'kmaq* today, with the sound *mi* representing the definite article in their language, and the full word *Mi'kmaq* indicating "the Family" or "the People").

The Mi'kmaq written language, which contains remarkable similarities to ancient Egyptian hieroglyphics, was preserved in extensive records made by a French missionary named Pierre Maillard (1710 – 1762). The fact that many symbols in this writing system resemble so strongly the sacred hieroglyphs of ancient Egypt causes proponents of the isolationist view (which dominates conventional academia) varying levels of discomfort, frustration, and defensive behavior, usually manifesting itself in the form of scornful criticism of anyone who suggests there may have been some ancient connection between citizens of ancient Egypt and the Indians of the Americas.

If the Mi'kmaq script were the only isolated data point suggesting ancient contact across the great oceans, then such skepticism would perhaps be warranted. However, it is only one of hundreds and perhaps thousands of other pieces of evidence which make the possibility of ancient trans-oceanic contact a certainty.

Among these are certain similarities of proportion between the pyramids of Central America and the pyramids of Giza, for instance. The base perimeter of the Great Pyramid of Giza in Egypt and the base perimeter of the Pyramid of the Sun at Teotihuacan in Mexico, for example, are remarkably close. Further, and more difficult to explain away, is the fact that the height of each of these pyramids is related to the base perimeter by a factor of pi. For the Great Pyramid, two pi times the height yields the perimeter of the base, while for the Pyramid of the Sun in Mexico, four pi times the height yields the perimeter of the base.

Numerous researchers in addition to Barry Fell have proposed that the ancient Phoenicians, Chinese, Africans, Norsemen and Celts may all have had the capability and inclination to cross the Atlantic and Pacific, and may have done so somewhat regularly. In *Before Columbus: New History of Celtic, Egyptian, Phoenician, Viking, Black African and Asian Contacts and Impacts in the Americas Before 1492* (published in 1980), author Samuel D. Marble has suggested that the Egyptians (with their superior knowledge of the stars and of the size and shape of the earth) may have joined forces with the Phoenicians (with their superior capabilities as shipbuilders and mariners) in a sort of happy marriage, "a partnership that benefited both people, and in this case that benefit was substantial."[615]

If there were Egyptians present on Phoenician voyages of discovery and trade with the Americas, it is entirely possible that the hieroglyphs of the Mi'kmaq, whose territory included the excellent sea-landings of Nova Scotia, were influenced by these ancient voyagers. If the Mi'kmaq hieroglyphs do indeed have an Egyptian influence, it would validate the account of Plato which suggests that the ancient Egyptians were aware of the vast continents lying across the Atlantic.

Professor Fell published some persuasive side-by-side analyses of the Mi'kmaq writing system with that of the ancient Egyptians in *America BC*. There, he illustrates the hieroglyphs recorded by the eighteenth-century missionary Father Maillard next to the hieroglyphs he maintains would be the Egyptian counterparts to the same words.[616]

Those who oppose the idea that ancient civilizations could cross the deep oceans argue that Father Maillard must have invented this writing system for the Mi'kmaq, in order to enable them to record the doctrines of Christianity. Why he would use ancient Egyptian hieroglyphs rather than the Latin alphabet is a bit of a problem for this theory; it is usually asserted that this writing system was introduced by the missionaries or that they modified an existing Mi'kmaq system of writing and deliberately made it look Egyptian because Egyptian hieroglyphs were all the rage during the seventeenth and eighteenth centuries (although they would not be translated successfully until the famous deciphering of the Rosetta Stone in the nineteenth century by Champollion in 1822).

This explanation, it must be noted, is completely speculative: there is no direct evidence that Maillard "invented" a system of writing based on Egyptian symbols and gave it to the Mi'kmaq. He himself never claimed to have done so. This explanation was dreamed up by detractors based on their prior assumption that Egyptians could not possibly have crossed the oceans during the time in antiquity in which hieroglyphs were still used and understood.

Further, closer examination of the Mi'kmaq writing recorded by Maillard provides powerful evidence against the theory that the writing system was introduced by missionaries after the time of Columbus. For example, one collection of Mi'kmaq writing that had been preserved by Father Maillard and published in a German book in 1880 shows the Mi'kmaq version of the Lord's Prayer (taught to them by the missionaries). As you can see from the transcript below, the word "name" (in the phrase "hallowed by thy name") is represented by a Mi'kmaq symbol that is extremely suggestive of the ancient Egyptian symbol for a name, which is the symbol known as a "cartouche." The Mi'kmaq symbol for "name" can be found about midway through the first line, and is in the shape of an oblong angular "box" with two triangular "fins."

This similarity is extremely problematic, because it is well known that the feat of deciphering the Rosetta Stone rested upon the insight by Champollion that these cartouches contained royal names, as well as his breakthrough discovery that the individual hieroglyphs could play a dual role in representing both individual phonetic sounds in one usage and an entire word in another usage.

To suggest that Maillard, who died in 1762, had known that cartouches represented the concept of a "name" is speculative beyond belief, and implies that this missionary priest, who spent the bulk of his adult life in remote woodlands ministering his faith to Native Americans and who had never been to Egypt nor shown any evidence of interest in deciphering the mystery that had puzzled linguists for centuries, had somehow found time to crack the Egyptian code before Champollion did, but had kept his understanding of it a secret.

In the end, it does not really matter whether one is convinced by the evidence of ancient contact present in Mi'kmaq script. One piece of evidence, on its own, can be explained away as an incredible coincidence. The important perspective to adopt when examining such evidence is the understanding that each such clue is "one data point." When viewed in conjunction with other data points found in the Americas which point to ancient contact, the Mi'kmaq writing system helps paint the picture and contribute to a pattern that tends to confirm the theory being put forward here.

Another data point is the so-called Davenport Stele or Davenport Calendar tablet, which was unearthed in a mound in Iowa in 1874 and which was discussed in my previous book, as well as being analyzed at some length in Barry Fell's *America BC*.[617] The tablet contains inscriptions in hieratic, a form of "shorthand" used on some inscriptions in place of the formal sacred Egyptian hieroglyphs. It also contains inscriptions in two other ancient scripts, neither of which, according to Fell, had been deciphered by modern scholars at the time of the tablet's discovery.

Nevertheless, academicians immediately declared it to be a fake. Does this hastiness, all too typical of the academic response whenever a piece of evidence revealing ancient contact between the continents, reveal a "sinister design," rather than simple "stupidity"? In other words, can we say along with Shakespeare's Queen Gertrude, "The lady protests too much, methinks"? (*Hamlet* III, 3, 210).

Is it possible that there is a conspiracy to suppress the evidence of ancient contact because such information could lead to the uncovering of the truth about the overthrow of the universal ancient system of esoteric wisdom and its replacement by a counterfeit literalist interpretation that absolutely does not fit the texts which supposedly support it? Information that could lead to the unraveling of the entire power structure that was built upon that supplanting of the ancient system, by families whose descendants would become the heads of the powerful hierarchical church and who would become the kings and nobles of all the countries of Europe?

While such a conspiracy to suppress the evidence may seem somewhat farfetched to the reader at this point, the evidence that supports such a possibility will pile up the further forward we go in history, as we continue our pursuit of the ramifications of that ancient overthrow of the shamanic and holographic wisdom. And there are far more examples of such evidence than will be dealt with in this volume.

A important aspect of the Davenport Stele is the fact that it depicts a curious drawing centered around a structure which Fell identifies as a Djed pillar.[618] On either side of the pillar are shown human figures linked in a human chain, under a symbol of the moon on one side and the sun on the other. As discussed in my previous book, the drawing is very reminiscent of other depictions of the "tug of war" between the forces of light and dark, or the turning of the central pillar of the heavens that is known as the "churning of the sea of milk" in Hindu symbology.[619]

The stele is rather hastily drawn, and the resemblance to a Djed column is not perfect, but it is certainly possible that this is what the tablet represents. The point is that such a diagram seems a most unlikely subject for a forger to select. Even if a forger were aware of the esoteric symbology of the Djed column, it would seem that he or she would depict the Djed more carefully, if that is indeed what the forger had been aiming at. However, the hasty Djed column on the Davenport tablet suggests that its designer, and those who were the tablet's "target audience," would have been familiar enough with the concept of the Djed column that a kind of "shorthand" depiction of the Djed was enough. This in itself argues against the Davenport tablet being a forgery, and argues that it is another piece of evidence that Egyptians visited the New World during antiquity.

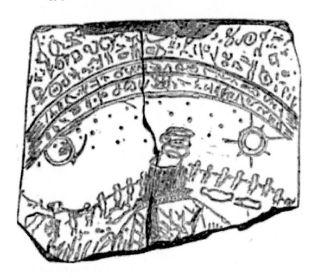

Other evidence that the Egyptians were in contact with the New World includes the presence of tobacco fragments in the mummy of Rameses II, the son of Seti I. Fragments of tobacco were discovered among the wrappings of the mummy in 1976 by a French scientist, Dr. Michelle Lescot of the Natural History Museum in Paris. Anther researcher, Dr. Svetlana Balabanova of the Institute of Forensic Medicine in Ulm, Germany, documented traces of both nicotine and cocaine in the tissues of multiple different mummies.[620]

It is generally agreed that tobacco and coca are New World plants, unknown to Old World civilizations prior to AD 1492. Detection of tobacco and coca in ancient Egyptian mummies implies extremely ancient contact across the oceans, and more than merely chance contact also. It is one thing to admit the possibility that a random Mediterranean ship was somehow blown off course, made it to the New World, and somehow returned safely, but the detection of tobacco derivatives and coca derivatives in the tissues and hair follicles of ancient mummies indicates familiarity and ongoing use – perhaps even ritual use (perhaps even for shamanic purposes). Such use suggests deliberate, ongoing, long-term trans-oceanic travel and trafficking in such substances.

The theory that the tobacco fragments in the mummy of Rameses II could have been accidentally dropped there from the cigar or pipe of a nineteenth century archaeologist was later weakened by the discovery of further tobacco inside the abdomen section of the mummy, an area that had been previously undisturbed. Nevertheless, many skeptics continue to maintain that any evidence of tobacco products in the Rameses II mummy must have been introduced later.

The Rameses II mummy also contains evidence of cannabis, which was in fact known in the Old World, although not generally associated with the region and culture of ancient Egypt. Strangely nobody seems to be coming forward with arguments that nineteenth century archaeologists accidentally dropped cannabis into the Rameses II mummy. The presence of this drug may indicate use of reactive plants in some type of shamanic ritual practice among the ancient Egyptians as well.

The presence of these substances (coca and tobacco) constitute further data points of evidence arguing that ancient Egypt was aware of the existence of the New World long before (over a thousand years before) the fall of the Temple in Jerusalem. It is therefore not unreasonable to suggest that some persecuted communities within the Roman Empire in later centuries might have found a way to escape the religious repression that accompanied the rise of the literalist Christian Church during the second, third, or fourth centuries AD by sailing to the Americas.

These are just a few of literally hundreds or even thousands of other data points which strongly point to the possibility of ancient Old World contact prior to (and after) the time period we are examining. Some of this evidence includes:

- The unanimous testimony from miners who started mining copper in the upper peninsula of Michigan the 1860s of the presence of extensive ancient mining pits, some of which had clearly been worked many centuries before, as pieces of native copper inside had been turned into the carbonate form by the passage of time. While it is possible that the Native Americans of the region or their remote ancestors were responsible for these major copper mining operations, it is also possible that visitors from the Old World were responsible for removing enormous amounts of New World copper from the region, perhaps as early as the dawn of the Bronze Age. Dr. Reinoud M. de Jonge and Jay Stuart Wakefield have written an entire book, entitled *Rocks and Rows*, which examines the evidence based upon analysis of the content and makeup of ancient copper from European relics, evidence which strongly suggests that the ancients had access to the extremely pure copper of Michigan's upper peninsula, which is of a purity found nowhere else on earth.[621]
- Artifacts containing inscriptions in Phoenician, Ogham, and other European writing systems that have been found in the Americas.[622]
- Numerous statues and figurines from pre-Columbian Mesoamerican civilizations accurately depicting individuals with distinctly European, African, and Asian features, often rendered with a tremendous degree of artistic talent.[623]
- The "Calixtlahuaca head," discovered in 1933 underneath two undisturbed cemented floors predating the Aztec period at Calixtlahuaca, and depicting a head with clearly European features done in a style of sculpture that has been described as "unquestionably" Roman in origin by professional scholars.[624]
- The discovery in 1982 of over two hundred broken amphoras (a type of two-handled clay jar used by the Canaanites, Phoenicians, Greeks and Romans to ship wine, olive oil, fish sauce, and other goods) littering the bottom of Guanabara Bay outside of Rio de Janeiro, Brazil, amphoras which Professor Elizabeth Lyding Will (1924 – 2009), one of the world's foremost authorities on amphoras, believed to exhibit characteristics indicating a date of the third century AD.[625]

- Statues of lions and "bearded jaguars" found guarding portals in pre-Columbian Mesoamerican architecture, when maned lions are unknown in the Americas.[626]
- The research of Professors John L. Sorenson and Carl L. Johannessen of Brigham Young University and University of Oregon at Eugene (respectively), who in a paper entitled "Scientific Evidence for Pre-Columbian Transoceanic Voyages to and from the Americas" discuss evidence from ninety-eight species of plants which are native to either the Old World or the New for which the authors found decisive evidence of pre-Columbian transport across the oceans, including for example jimson weed (native to North America but apparently transported to both Europe and Asia prior to 1492), marigolds (also native to the New World and found in China and India), sarsaparilla (native to the Old World, found in Central America), and certain breeds of cotton from the Old World found in South America, as well various infectious organisms, twenty-one species of micro-predators and six other species of fauna, with distributions that "could not have been due merely to natural transfer mechanisms" nor migrations across the Bering Strait, and taken together indicating "a considerable number of transoceanic voyages in both directions across both major oceans" between the 7th millennium BC and the European age of discovery.[627]
- The presence of hundreds of mummies unearthed in New World locations including Peru, many of which have red, blond, or auburn hair, some of it wavy, and all of it very unlike the hair that is characteristic of the native peoples of the continent.[628]

This extensive evidence (and there is plenty more) indicates that the existence of the New World, and the techniques to get there, were well known to ancient civilizations (although the secrets may have been rather more closely guarded during some periods than others). The evidence above probably spans many centuries if not millennia of ancient transoceanic travel, exploration, and settlement.

All of it is important for the theory that refugees from parts of the Roman Empire, or from regions threatened by the Roman Empire, may have fled to the Americas during the second, third and possibly fourth centuries BC, as the hierarchical and literal version of Christianity was asserting its orthodoxy over all alternatives, and was tightening its grip on political power during the reigns of Constantine, Theodosius and others, because taken in its entirety it helps to establish the knowledge of the New World as a potential avenue of escape.

However, some of the most intriguing evidence, evidence which may directly confirm the presence of non-orthodox Egyptian Christians in the New World, was discovered in Michigan in the form of thousands (actually, tens of thousands) of tablets containing somewhat crudely-drawn representations of religious themes, as well as a curious writing system that seems to have been an adaptation of Hebrew lettering.

The theological concepts depicted on these tablets, discovered in the 1800s, are quite different from anything taught by any "orthodox" church since the time of the disputes over the Arian "heresy," which raged during the time of Constantine. Such theological concepts seem to be extremely unlikely subjects for some hoaxer in the 1800s to have decided to carve into tens of thousands of clay tablets, but they provide startling confirmation, if authentic, of the theory being put forward in this book regarding the suppression of ancient esoteric sacred traditions.

Before embarking upon a discussion of this particular piece of evidence, a few cautions are in order. The Michigan tablets and associated relics found in Michigan during the nineteenth century, according to the conventional literature and the consensus opinion, have been "thoroughly debunked." They are now almost universally viewed as a forgery, the work of one or at the most a few unscrupulous individuals working in their toolsheds during the late nineteenth and early twentieth centuries in order to deceive the public and gain some pecuniary reward through the sale of fabricated "antiquities."

Various arguments are put forward as conclusive proof that these tablets and associated artifacts are fraudulent. These arguments include assertions that the writing systems on the tablets consist of symbols from multiple different ancient writing systems that were known by the time of the nineteenth century and reproduced in various books, some of which were owned by those who "found" the artifacts. Skeptical professors as early as the late eighteen hundreds called the markings on the Michigan relics "a horrible mixture of Phoenician, Egyptian and ancient Greek characters taken at random from a comparative table of alphabets such as is found at the back of Webster's Dictionary."[629]

Other lines of argument used by those who believe the Michigan relics to be a massive fraud include the generally inelegant nature of the drawings on the tablets, the fact that some of the supposedly ancient tablets display evidence of perspective (which was not "invented" until the Renaissance), the fact that copper pieces in the collection were smelted using techniques that the ancients were not known to have mastered, and a sworn statement by the daughter-in-law of one of the main "discoverers" of the artifact that her father-in-law had made them himself (a sworn statement she did not give until after both he and her mother had died).

While these are formidable arguments, there are countervailing arguments which need to be considered before the Michigan relics are completely disregarded as potentially important evidence from antiquity. Before considering some of those counter-arguments, a few points need to be clarified at the outset.

First, and perhaps most importantly, the Michigan relics are by no means the only evidence of ancient trans-oceanic contact with the Americas. As we have already seen, there is a tremendous amount of evidence which supports the conclusion that ancient civilizations from Europe, Africa and Asia almost certainly visited the shores of the Americas, some of them doing so on a regular basis during some periods of antiquity. Even if all of the Michigan relics were conclusively shown to be complete forgeries, it is far more difficult to argue that all the ancient amphoras found on the bottom of Guanabara Bay in Brazil are forgeries, or that all of the red-haired, blond-haired, and auburn-haired mummies found in Peru are somehow forgeries!

Second, it is important to point out that it is certainly possible that some of the relics brought out by individuals in the late nineteenth century and early twentieth century in connection with the Michigan artifacts were forgeries, even if all of them are not. It is quite possible that authentic relics were found and that during the wave of enthusiasm over these relics some unscrupulous individuals took it upon themselves to manufacture fraudulent relics for pecuniary or other reasons. While I am not convinced that this necessarily took place, it is certainly possible that it did, and it could explain testimonies of forgery or evidence of supposedly "modern copper" among the relics. However, it is also possible that the "testimonies" of forgery were coerced or influenced by other motives, and it is also possible that findings that the copper was smelted by "modern" methods were similarly motivated by those with an interest in suppressing the Michigan relics, or those who are ignorant of the capabilities of ancient smelters.

Third, discussion of these tablets (and the question of ancient trans-Atlantic contact in general) is in no way intended to disparage or denigrate the culture of the Native Americans. Some allege that any discussion of ancient trans-oceanic contact is motivated by racism, and while it is possible that some of it is or has been in the past, that by no means implies that all such investigation is fueled by such motives, or even that the majority of it is fueled by such motives. If trans-oceanic ancient contact in fact took place, then that contact is a fact of history and while some may hasten to import agendas of one sort or another into the discussion of the ramifications of this historical fact, this regrettable development tells us more about the failings of the moderns who do so than it does about anyone else.

Fourthly, the theory that we have been building throughout the book so far in no way stands or falls on the authenticity of the Michigan relics alone. The Michigan relics if authentic constitute an interesting and dramatic piece of supporting evidence for the theory that the ancient wisdom was deliberately and violently suppressed during the second and third centuries (and ever since), by the descendants of the Judaic priestly lines after the fall of Jerusalem operating a hierarchical and literal form of Christianity based in Rome. If the Michigan relics are a fraud, then they really have no bearing on the theory and can be disregarded. However, the dogmatism with which they have been declared to be "obvious forgeries" should raise a hint of suspicion, especially in light of the evidence discussed below.

Finally, I should make clear that I am not nor have I ever been a member of the "Church of Jesus Christ of Latter Day Saints" or the Mormons, nor have I ever subscribed to any of their specific theories about ancient cultures in the Americas. Mention of this point is necessitated by the fact that for some time the LDS church enthusiastically supported the Michigan relics as support for their doctrines, although that position has changed and the current official position, I believe, is that the Michigan relics are forgeries. My willingness to entertain the possibility that some or even all of these artifacts might be authentic ancient evidence is not motivated by a desire to promote any specific religious doctrine (especially not any doctrine based on literal interpretations of any scriptures or the belief in a literal and historical Christ), but rather by the belief that *any and all* evidence about mankind's ancient past, and the events that brought mankind to the present situation, should be examined.

In 1986, a book entitled *The Mystic Symbol: Mark of the Michigan Mound Builders* by Henriette Mertz (1898 – 1985) was published, examining the tablets and the debate over their authenticity, as well as advancing some theories as to their origin. Mertz had been a codebreaker during the Second World War, and brought her own considerable experience and insight to bear on the question of whether the markings on the stones, which appear to be in a unique writing system (one probably made up in order to be a code known only among the community that made the tablets), were the work of a forger or not.

Citing specific examples from the thousands of Michigan tablets, Mertz demonstrates that there is no evidence that the writing on the plates is the work of a forger, and ample evidence that it is not.

She explains that, "Each individual's writing has certain unmistakable characteristics peculiar to himself."[630] Examining the clay plates, she finds great diversity of hands, with no evidence of "tell-tale" quirks that would indicate that one forger had created a large number of them at all. In fact, she concludes that the artifacts were written by many different hands – no two alike.[631]

First she examines the question of the instruments used to make the markings themselves. There are two types of writing employed on the tablets, and finds that: "Two dissimilar methods of incising appear on these plates – first by carving direct on copper, slate or stone and second by stamping on wet clay."[632]

Of the stamped markings, close examination reveals that not only were the markings stamped with pre-fabricated die-stamps, but the various plates indicate stamping by different die-sets: "no two have like letters of the same size or thickness which indicates that many sets of die-stamps had been employed and in all probability many more plates must once have existed – for labor in casting die-stamps would imply more uses than one."[633]

This fact is extremely damaging to the forgery hypothesis: if a forger were indeed to go to the great length of casting stamps in metal or carving them out of sandstone or other sedimentary rocks, would he or she really go to the extreme of manufacturing multiple duplicate sets, as if creating a wide variety of different "fonts" to be used on the different "forged" tablets, never using the same metal font set twice? Such a suggestion stretches credulity: what sort of cost-benefit analysis would justify the tremendous time and effort (and expense) necessary for such a detail on the part of a forger?

Turning to the handwritten markings, Henriette Mertz notes that most of the tablets were inscribed with "a very sharp instrument – probably of copper – and applied direct to slate, copper, or hard granite."[634] Here again, she finds that the instruments themselves varied considerably from tablet to tablet. Some left fine, delicate lines, while others left much broader tracks. The "handwriting" varies dramatically from plate to plate, indicating different individuals wrote them, but in each and every case, the writing indicates that the hand doing the inscribing was sure of what it wrote, and fluent with the lettering system being employed. There is no hesitation or pausing indicated in the carving, as there would be if a forger were copying out of a book.[635]

The samples she gives from the tablets themselves inspire an appreciation for the individuality of the writers of these very foreign markings, markings which have a certain beauty and symmetry all their own. We have to agree with her when she says that the samples she gives "are superb examples of fluent writing by different trained hands neither having hesitation, puddle or error."[636]

Mertz points out further evidence that the writing on the tablets is not the work of a forger:

Many of these Michigan tablets read from right to left – a customary practice anciently in certain areas and at certain periods of time. If one believes he could copy characters with sufficient éclat and not be detected, let him try writing them backward as is done here – a matter where no dictionary table would guide him. Some plates read from left to right, some from right to left but others read boustrophedon – up one line and down the next, one line from right to left, the next line from left to right – quirks that only one with long familiarity in writing a language would understand.[637]

Finally, she notes that the writing system also contains birds and animals and other symbols characteristic of Egyptian hieroglyphs, and that these symbols had to face into the direction that the line was intended to be read. Not only do the Michigan tablets have these symbols employed properly every time, but again there are clear differences between tablets in the way that hieroglyphic symbols were drawn. While a forger would be likely to draw a bird-hieroglyph roughly the same way every time, the writers of the various Michigan tablets again display great individuality, while still clearly drawing the same hieroglyph – just as writers today may use the same general system of cursive writing but display great individuality in the formation of particular letters, with wide variance between one writer and the next.

Below is a sampling of a bird hieroglyph whose shape varies widely from one Michigan tablet to another (while maintaining integrity of form when it appears multiple times on the same plate).

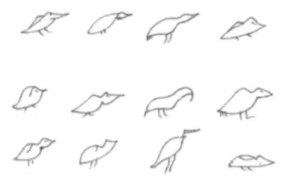

In the above picture, which is an approximate reproduction of that shown in Figure 16 on page 120 of *The Mystic Symbol*, we can see that the same hieroglyphic symbol may be intelligibly rendered in a wide variety of forms by different people, who have each cultivated a different "hand" during their educations and later "scribing" careers. For instance, in the diagrams above, note the wide variance in body shape for the birds, and yet each has a distinctly "hump-backed" shape, which is sometimes rendered as a smooth dome and sometimes in a more angular fashion.

In two of the images (those on either end of the top line), the "wing" feature of the bird is created by adding a sort of "triangle" to the top of the body-shape, but more commonly this "wing" is denoted by a simple curved line drawn so that it extends down into the body region behind the head, such as we see in the two birds on the extreme left of the lower two rows. In the "mouse-like" version of the bird seen at the far right of the bottom row, the "wing" feature curves back up to meet the boundary line of the body shape. Even more commonly, the "wing" feature is left out entirely.

The shapes of the heads also vary widely, but a pointed "beak" is always evident. The shape of the feet (or, more precisely, the legs of the bird) also varies widely, as does their length. In two of the images, three small "feathers" are indicated by short parallel lines at the bottom of the bird's tail, but in most cases these are absent. Similarly, some scribes place an eye on their birds, but most leave this feature out as well.

Clearly, these are individuals who have gone to different "schools" of writing, through which certain common features were emphasized but which permitted a fairly wide range of form to convey the meaning. Would a forger really be expected to display such wide variance? Would he or she (and his or her possible compatriots in the act of forgery) not hew more closely to whatever original standard they were attempting to duplicate? Would forgers really permit such wide deviation from their model text, in an attempt to duplicate a huge community of writers who each displayed very unique "hands" containing common elements, some of which (like the small tailfeathers) seem to have been emphasized in some "schools" of writing but not in others?

If so, then it was an extremely sophisticated and thoughtful mastermind who concocted this forgery. The extent of the planning we are expected to accept goes well beyond credibility. A far more simple and far more likely explanation is that these tablets were actually inscribed by different people who had learned a writing system that is very different than that used today, a writing system that utilized both abstract symbols and hieroglyphic elements, which could be written from left to right, but was more commonly written from right to left, and was occasionally written boustrophedon ("as the ox plows," with one line being from right to left and the next line below it from left to right, the way an ox-drawn plow would go back and forth across a field). The weight of the evidence seems to point rather clearly to the conclusion that these tablets, whatever they represent, are not the work of a forger.

At the end of her chapter on forgery (which should be read in its entirety by any who are not yet convinced that these tablets are not the work of a nineteenth-century forger), Henriette Mertz concludes:

> Where any written document is put in question, and one man stands accused of forgery, professional analysts instantly spot one outstanding characteristic appearing on the questioned specimen – as for example the foreign letter "X" on the Lindbergh ransom notes. A like analysis of inscriptions on the Michigan artifacts indicated that these writings stemmed from many hands – no single outstanding characteristic of one individual hand stood out. If each tablet had been written by a different hand as appears on these specimens, forgery by one person is obviously untenable. It must be borne in mind that self-appointed "experts" had passed on this question of forgery and sale of fraudulent material – a criminal act – without themselves having been trained in the law of detection or analysis. Little credence can normally be given to this type of opinion – for it is recognizable only as opinion and carries little or no weight unless supported by factual evidence.

Question raised by this chapter was – Did one man alone forge each and every artifact comprising this vast collection of some 3,000 pieces? During the long heated controversy, the academic world would have us so believe and isolated one man charging him with the perpetration of forgery and manufacture and sale of fraudulent material. No proofs were ever offered nor was the man brought to trial. Most of this inscribed matter has now been destroyed as a result.[638]

Again, the haste and impropriety with which the academic world passed rapid and unanimous judgment upon the Michigan tablets, and declared them to be fraudulent, itself raises the question of sinister intent. What is it that the people controlling the factories of thought and opinion in "the west" are so afraid to have examined in the clear light of day? What so dangerous that artifacts and evidence which could shed light upon it must be destroyed outright, rather than preserved and examined and debated?

The previous chapters have presented evidence which allows us to formulate a broad theory, a theory which provides a compelling answer to that question. The ruling families who staged a slow-motion coup to gain power over the Roman Empire and to implement a hierarchical ecclesiology that supplanted the ancient esoteric knowledge with a deliberately fraudulent literalist interpretation knew that some groups of gnostics escaped – to the New World. The evidence of that escape might provide a pointer to the evidence of the larger coup – the coup that robbed the west of its ancient birthright and struck a decisive blow in a war against consciousness. Because that war continues to this day, there are powerful forces with a vested interest in ensuring that the truth about the conspiracy of Josephus never comes to light.

Let us now turn to the contents of the tablets themselves, where we may find striking confirmation of that theory.

David Allen Deal has published numerous articles and essays analyzing the marks and drawings on the tablets. Some of these are included at the end of *The Mystic Symbol*. His translations and interpretations point to the conclusion that the tablets exhibit doctrines that are very different from the orthodox views that the western Church enforces, and that it has enforced for the past sixteen or seventeen centuries. The doctrines instead show clear harmonies with gnostic and Arian "heresies" that were persecuted by the "orthodox" hierarchy from the third and fourth centuries forward, but which are still recognizable among the doctrines of the Coptic Church in Egypt to this day.

The writing on the tablets appears to fall into at least three broad family-groupings. There are inscriptions that are written in Egyptian hieroglyphics. An example of such an inscription can be seen in the sketch of part of the inscription of a tablet below (a photographic plate of the original tablet, along with discussion of its contents and a possible translation, can be found in David Allen Deal's essay, "Michigan-Egyptian Hieroglyphics," found in *The Mystic Symbol* pages 206-208):

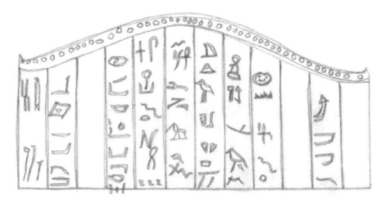

Secondly, there are inscriptions that are written in systems that appear to either be Hebrew or to be based on it, including the peculiar form of "Michigan cuneiform" evident in many of the tablets, which David Allen Deal demonstrates to have been based quite clearly on the Hebrew lettering system and which he believes may have been altered in order to make it more private by the groups that sought refuge in North America.[639]

Finally, there is a form of lettering which has been called the "toothbrush" style, consisting of letters composed of vertical lines with a variety of smaller angular lines coming off of them, much like our letter "K" (in fact, David Allen Deal demonstrates that one of them probably did stand for the letter "K" and was used as a shorthand for "*Kurios*" or "Lord").[640] Some of these resemble a "K" with multiple, parallel short lines coming off of the single vertical stroke, and they come off of one side only but can face to either the left or the right. The shorter parallel strokes can come off at an angle, either up or down (as do the strokes on our letter "K") or they can be perpendicular to the vertical stroke. It has not been successfully translated to date. An example of a tablet containing primarily this type of "toothbrush" writing is shown below:

In the Michigan tablets, more than one writing system is almost always present on a single tablet. Even the tablet above, which contains almost entirely "toothbrush" inscriptions, displays at the very top a scroll-like or tablet-like shape containing three "cuneiform" symbols: from left to right a single vertical stroke, an "H-shaped" symbol of two vertical strokes with a horizontal crossbar, and a diagonally-inclined vertical stroke.

This symbol is characteristic of all the Michigan tablets, and has been the target for some ridicule by debunkers, who see it as a clumsy attempt to import the Constantinian "I.H.S." inscription. This grouping is that which Henriette Mertz called "The Mystic Symbol" and which gave her the title for her book on the tablets. However, David Allen Deal has convincingly argued that this grouping of three symbols may well stand for YHW, the name of the deity, or a gnostic name for a deific power.[641] In fact, he points to evidence that these letters are used in a manner consistent with the more gnostic doctrines contained in the Pistis Sophia, an ancient text often attributed either to the gnostics Valentinus or Basilides, although their authorship is by no means certain, and which had been translated into English in the late 1800s, as well as to the doctrines found in the Nag Hammadi texts which would not be discovered until well after the supposed forgery took place.[642] In ancient gnostic literature, there was a greater YHW and a lesser YHW, two distinct entities, and the lesser proceeded from the greater. The greater corresponds to the Father, and the lesser to the Son, but there is also an elder brother to the lesser, who is known as Samma-El or the Son of the Left Hand, a completely distinct entity from the lesser YHW of the Son of the Right Hand (at least, presented as distinct in the ancient gnostic literature, which – like other ancient sacred texts – is almost certainly meant to be read in an esoteric manner and not in a literal).[643]

In an essay entitled "The Mystic Symbol Demystified" Deal explains:

> The Copts, worshiped a most high deity, called by them, "yao" or "the greater yao," as opposed to the "lesser yao," or "little yao, sabboath the good, son the the right hand [sic]," who was an angelic personage, just under the throne of the father and most high YHW (greater yao). The opposing force was led by "Samma-el" the evil "son of the left hand." Samma-el is a Jewish title for Satan, acquired by the Copts via a direct biblical connection with the Jews. The lesser Yahweh, (the angel Yahweh) also called "Metatron" in the "Book of Enoch," is also well-attested to among the Jewish rabbinical sources. He is called the "lesser YHWH (Yahweh)," and the use of this term acknowledges the existence of a greater YHWH (Yahweh) the father, who is above all. These concepts are inscribed all over these Michigan tablets. In many cases we see the hierarchy of heaven displayed at the top of the tablets, wherein we see a central figure, usually only a body and hands, with the face obscured (who is the father Yahweh). And sometimes he is only a light with rays emanating. Immediately below we see the two angels of the presence, the one on the right hand of the throne and the one on the left hand side.[644]

In his suggested decipherment of a tablet seen in plate 12 on page 98 of *The Mystic Symbol*, David Allen Deal argues that these three different entities are being depicted, and that the son of the right hand and the son of the left hand are being contrasted. In the drawing of the tablet shown below, we can see that it is divided into three basic sections: two of these at the tablet's top and bottom contain writing, and the central panel contains a scene featuring a bearded figure seated in the center, with a figure to his right (viewer's left) kneeling and presenting an infant, and a figure to his left (viewer's right) walking away towards the edge of the tablet:

We can see quite clearly from this drawing of the tablet that the inscriptions on this particular tablet fall into all three categories of writing system described previously.

There is the evidence of some hieroglyphics (particularly in the bottom section of the tablet, where a bird-like figure is seen towards the right edge as we look at the tablet, above the chipped off corner, and there is another bird-like figure near the top center of the bottom section, next to a serpent-like figure).

There is evidence of the "Michigan cuneiform," which David Allen Deal argues has parallels to Hebrew lettering and which he deciphers in his analysis of this tablet (examples of the cuneiform lettering system can be seen in the top section and in the bottom section – the "I H /" pattern being evident at the very top center of the tablet, as well as near the top edge of the bottom section, just right of center as we look at the tablet).

Finally, there is extensive use of the "toothbrush style" lettering, again found in both the top and bottom sections.

While the toothbrush lettering has yet to be decoded, David Allen Deal has suggested that the "Michigan cuneiform" is clearly related to the Hebrew lettering system, and in a table in his essay "The Mystic Symbol Demystified" he shows its similarity to square Hebrew as well as the relationship to the earlier "round" paleo-Hebrew and to the Greek and Roman alphabets.[645]

Beginning at the top of the tablet shown above, Deal points to the ubiquitous I H / symbol, and notes that just below it is a glyph resembling two hands, with a "V-shaped" channel cut between them – possibly suggesting a choice between two pathways, the "right-hand" and the "left-hand" pathway.[646]

This interpretation is supported by the fact that the tablet contains more than one instance of a hieroglyphic symbol which is identified in the venerable *An Egyptian Hieroglyphic Dictionary* of Sir E. A. Wallis Budge as meaning "heavens" and "rulership," along with two vertical strokes either to the right (as we look at it) or to the left. These signs are used in context on this and other tablets to mean "son of the right hand" or "son of the left hand," respectively – and more broadly to indicate the "way of the right hand" and the "way of the left hand."[647]

To support this broad interpretation of them, Deal points out that these same symbols appear on another tablet (photographic plate 22 on page 143 of *The Mystic Symbol*) showing Cain killing Abel with a "son of the left hand" symbol, and on that same tablet showing Adam and Eve taking the fruit from the tree again with a "son of the left hand" symbol, and again on that same tablet showing Abraham's sacrifice of Isaac along with the appearing angel and ram in the thicket and a "son of the right hand" symbol.[648]

In the drawing of the tablet below, some of the symbols discussed in David Allen Deal's decipherment of the tablet are indicated by boxes with letters. The box marked "A." shows the I H / symbol, as well as the two "hands" symbol which Deal suggests mean that YHW has created "two paths."

The box marked "B." shows the "son of the right hand" symbol (the "throne" or "vault of heaven" symbol, with two vertical strokes to the right of the symbol as we look at it), as well as a shepherd's crook. Similarly, the box marked "C." shows the "son of the left hand" symbol, with another throne or vault of heaven symbol but with vertical strokes to the left, along with a shepherd's crook facing the opposite direction from that in box "B."

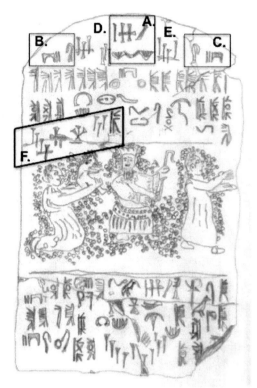

Between the boxes marked "A." and those marked "B." and "C." on either side of it are some examples of the "cuneiform" writing. Marked by the letter "D." in my drawing, and located on the side corresponding to the "son of the right hand" symbol (the viewer's left) are lines which Deal believes are the two letters "D" and "Q," written from right to left.

The first letter which he sees as a "D" consists of three vertical lines, the middle one elevated. Deal's "comparison of alphabets" table on page 175 of the Mertz book shows that both the ancient Greek alphabet and paleo-Hebrew depicted the letter "D" as a triangle (the Greek letter *delta*), and argues that the "Michigan cuneiform" indicated this triangular shape with these three vertical strokes in a triangular pattern.

To the left of that letter is another with three vertical strokes, this time with the middle stroke made lower than the two flanking strokes, and with a fourth horizontal stroke crossing through all three of them. Deal's table of alphabets shows that this corresponds to a hard "Q" sound and was indicated in paleo-Hebrew by a circle divided by a vertical line that extended down beyond the lower edge of the circle, making a kind of "double-P" shape. The later square Hebrew would replace this symbol with a mark that was more like a "single P." The cuneiform version can be seen to be related to the earlier "double-P" shape, but much easier to draw when carving, since it consists only of lines.

Deal translates this word "DQ" as indicating the Hebrew word "daq" (vowels are omitted, as they were in many ancient inscriptions and texts, including ancient Hebrew texts). This word, Deal says, means "small," "younger," and "bruised."[649]

On the other side, corresponding to the "son of the left hand" symbol and marked in my drawing by the letter "E." are more cuneiform strokes, which David Allen Deal interprets as indicating three letters. Reading again from right to left, there is a single vertical stroke, followed by a letter consisting of two vertical strokes connected or crossed near their base by a horizontal stroke (the leftmost vertical stroke being higher than the right stroke), followed by another single vertical stroke. Deal translates the single vertical stroke as indicating our "W" sound (the square Hebrew symbol for this sound is very similar), and the letter consisting of two vertical strokes crossed by a horizontal stroke as indicating a "Kh" sound (the square Hebrew symbol for this sound resembles the Greek letter *pi*, which is also two vertical strokes crossed – this time at the top – by a horizontal stroke).

Deal translates this word, "W-Kh-W," as the Hebrew word for "elder."[650] This personage Deal identifies as "the elder brother, typified by such biblical stories as Cain and Abel, Jacob & Esau, Isaack & Ishmael, Mannaseh & Ephraim."[651] We will examine this important assertion in a moment. Before going further, however, it is important to point out that the fact that these symbols actually spell out Hebrew words seriously undermines the smug assertion by conventional "debunkers" that an unsophisticated forger simply copied a mish-mash of symbols out of the back of a dictionary!

One other translated inscription is very significant, indicated by the group of symbols in the box marked "F." Again reading from right to left, David Allen Deal first suggests that the large symbol in "toothbrush" lettering resembling a "K" and positioned almost over the head of the enthroned figure wearing a crown in the drawing below may be a shorthand indicator for the word "*Kurios*" or "Lord."[652] Continuing from that large "K" and reading from right to left, we encounter "Michigan cuneiform" letters as follows:

- three vertical strokes, with the center one lower than the outer flanking strokes.
- three strokes arranged such that the center stroke is vertical and the flanking strokes come together with the center stroke at the base, such that they resemble a downward-pointing arrowhead, or a "W" made with only three straight lines.
- two vertical strokes, with the left one higher, and these are crossed by a horizontal stroke (we have already encountered this letter, in the word for "elder" and seen that it represents the sound "Kh").
- another "Kh" letter identical to the one just described.
- two vertical strokes, with the one on the viewer's left higher than that on the right.

Deal shows that the first letter described above, the three vertical strokes with the center stroke lower, is an "M," and it resembles a Greek "M," a Roman "M," and a paleo-Hebrew "M" (see his table on page 175 of the Mertz book). The second letter, with three strokes arranged like a downward-facing arrow, is an "S" and it resembles very closely the square Hebrew letter "S" as well as the original Greek capital *sigma*. After that comes the letter we have already seen to represent "Kh." These three letters, M-S-Kh, represent the word "MeShiaKh" or "Messiah," according to David Allen Deal.[653]

The next two letters are a different word: Kh-N (the two vertical strokes of the final letter described above are the letter "N," and like the letter "M" the resemblance to the Greek and Roman and paleo-Hebrew "N" is quite evident from the table Deal presents on page 175). Deal argues that these two letters indicate the Hebrew word "*Khun*," or "precious."[654]

All of these inscriptions appear to comment upon the drawing below, in which a seated crowned bearded figure is in the center, and on the viewer's left (to the crowned figure's right) an infant is being presented by a kneeling figure, while on the viewer's right (to the crowned figure's left) another figure is exiting the scene.

Above the infant are the words "Messiah" and "precious" and (higher up) the symbol for "son of the right hand." Above the central seated enthroned figure with the crown is the symbol that Deal thinks may be a large "K" representing "*Kurios*," and higher up the I H / symbol as well as the glyph resembling two hands, which may mean "choose between the right-hand and left-hand way." Finally, above the figure who is leaving the presence of the seated figure is the word "elder" and (higher up) the symbol for "son of the left hand."

The implication is that the infant is the Messiah and the son of the right hand, and the figure leaving is the elder brother and the son of the left hand. However, the idea that Christ (the Messiah) has an "elder brother" is hardly "orthodox" theology! In fact, the suggestion will strike anyone who has been raised in almost any of the Christian traditions prevalent in the west as very difficult to accept – especially when it is suggested that this "elder brother of Christ" is the Adversary, that is to say Satan. What forger in the midwest of the United States of America in the nineteenth century would decide to depict such a doctrine? The idea would have been absolutely anathema to the religious sensibilities that predominated in that period of time. So-called "debunkers" who want to pin the fabrication of these tablets on unsophisticated forgers will have to explain how and why they came up with such a foreign theological concept!

However foreign this concept is to traditional orthodox Christianity as it has survived into modern times, the doctrine actually has very ancient roots – stretching back, in fact, to the contendings of Set and Horus in ancient Egyptian mythology. In that mythos, Set plays the part of the Adversary, and Horus is the child-redeemer who struggles against and finally overcomes Set and avenges Osiris.

While Set is actually the brother of Osiris, rather than of Horus, he is also portrayed as the twin to Horus, his opposite and countervailing nemesis. Alvin Boyd Kuhn writes: "Sut (Satan), the twin of Horus, is portrayed imprisoning his brother, the soul of light, in the realm of darkness. He is called 'the power of darkness'."[655]

Later, in the same work, Kuhn presents evidence arguing that Satan and Jesus are twins in the same way that Horus and Set were twins in the Egyptian allegory. The parallel should not come as a surprise, if we accept the previous argument that the priests of Jerusalem who were conquered by Vespasian and Titus were actually descended from Egyptians, and that their sacred texts – and the aspects of the Messiah tradition which would later be taught by Paul – were closely related to those of Egypt.

He explains himself by noting that in Revelation 22:16, the risen Jesus says "I am [. . .] the bright and morning star," but that this title very much resembles that of Lucifer, who in Isaiah 14:12 is called the "son of the morning" and whose name indicates that he is a light-giving being, and whose fall is associated with the fall of stars in Revelation 8:12. Kuhn writes:

> The descending god was the Light-bringer, Lucifer, the bright and morning star, which is precisely the character assumed by the Jesus of the Biblical Revelation!

> The Christian devil, the hated serpent of evil, Satan, is Lucifer, the god of light on earth, Prometheus, the "benefactor of mankind," – "the god" himself.
>
> Indoctrinated orthodoxy may rise to protest the identification. Some ghastly mistake will be alleged in the philology. It will be in vain. Erudite theology has at times perhaps known the truth, but has kept an advised silence. The general mind has lost the key to the mystery. By dropping the name Lucifer and clinging to that of Satan alone, the mischief has been bred and perpetuated. That Satan and Jesus are identical is as true as that Sut and Horus in Egypt are twins! The god and devil are kindred. They are full brothers. Their mother is one. They are the two aspects or manifestions of the same force.[656]

Again, such suggestions are absolutely repugnant to orthodox theology as it has been taught for these past seventeen centuries. Even when the church underwent violent divisions, such as that between the Catholic Church and the Reformers led by Luther and later Calvin and other theologians, the idea that Satan and Jesus could be considered brothers was never entertained for an instant. And yet it was present in some aspects of gnosticism prior to the ejection of gnostic texts and gnostic teachers and the hardening of orthodoxy that took place during the second, third, and fourth centuries AD.

The fact that aspects of this doctrine show up in many places in the Michigan tablets is, as David Allen Deal makes clear, a very strong piece of evidence supporting the possibility that they may be the authentic relics of escapees from the persecution of those centuries. The possibility that a late nineteenth-century forger would dream to incorporate such doctrines in his forgeries flies in the face of Occam's proverbial razor. It is *perhaps* remotely possible, but the reasoning that would go into explaining such a choice is very difficult to imagine, and must be convoluted in the extreme. Conventional "debunkers" don't even try – they conveniently ignore the clear presence of the "son of the right hand" and "son of the left hand" theology present in so many of the relics, relics which were clearly in the public eye long before the discovery of the Nag Hammadi texts and the trove of information about gnostic doctrine that they provide modern scholars – information which appears to vindicate these tablets.

Note that one does not have to accept the doctrine that Jesus and Satan were brothers in order to accept the fact that it was anciently taught and anciently accepted by some groups (although not by those groups which would later enforce their "orthodoxy" on the church at large). Those who insist upon seeing the scriptures as literal and historical might be expected to have a violent negative reaction to the suggestion; those who see them as metaphorical stories teaching profound truths might be less apt to be repulsed by this doctrine and to instead ask what esoteric insights it was intended to convey.

And, whether one personally takes the literal or the esoteric position is actually immaterial when it comes to observing the clear fact that the doctrine is abundantly present in the Michigan tablets.

Robert Taylor, with whose astronomical explications of scriptures we are already now quite familiar, has much to say on the subject of the relation between Jesus and Satan. In a chapter entitled "The Devil" in his *Astronomico-Theological Lectures*, he explains that the title of "The Adversary" given to Satan can be understood in its most literal meaning to be describing his *location* in relation to someone else: *ad+verso*. His title indicates that he stands "across from" or "on the side against." This fact, Taylor says, "is the key that unlocks the whole mystery":

> For, as the sun passes successively through every degree of these twelve signs of the Zodiac – the sign at which the sun, at any given time, is found to be, is for *that* season or time, the Supreme God: and the directly opposite sign is the *accuser*, the adversary, or the *Devil*: so that they are each of them both God and Devil in their turns.[657]

Taylor is saying that as the sun moved through the zodiac wheel, whatever sign it occupied had an adversary sign standing directly opposite to it. We can easily envision this by returning to our now-familiar diagram:

The "adversary" of Cancer, then, would be Capricorn. The "adversary" of Taurus would be Scorpio. The "adversary" of Leo would be Sagittarius, and so forth. Note that the motion of the sun as it moves through the successive signs causes the "adversary" to move at the same pace; put another way we could say that the rise of one sign thrusts down the other, or that the motion of the one causes an equal and opposite reaction in the motion of the other. We have already encountered this concept, the reader may recall, in the esoteric interpretation of Saul (before he becomes Paul) as the "persecutor" of Christ, and Saul's being thrown down from his horse (since Sagittarius is the "adversary" sign opposite the sun's exaltation in the place of summer solstice).

Robert Taylor continues: "The Prince of Darkness is, of course, the adversary of the Prince of Light, and consequently persecutes or follows after him, as the night must follow the day, and the cold and cheerless reign of winter succeeds the summer."[658]

With this in mind, could we not allegorize this relationship as two brothers, one of whose rising causes the fall of the other? And what do we see depicted in the Michigan tablet above? The arrival of one brother (the child) causing the departure of the other (the elder brother). Gnostics, who see the story in this light, would probably have no problem with it. Literalists, who want the scriptures to tell a literal and historical story, would have a serious problem with the suggestion that Jesus and Satan are brothers (and not just brothers in some tellings, but twins!).

The fact that the Michigan tablet depicts this exact esoteric truth, in quite unmistakable imagery, poses a king-sized problem for those who want to claim they are the work of a forger. If so, then the forger understood intimately the esoteric concept just outlined, a concept so foreign to western culture that the very mention of it was enough to get the Reverend Robert Taylor, in the very same nineteenth century, defrocked and thrown into prison for years.

It is a concept so foreign to western civilization these past seventeen centuries that, even now, writing in the twenty-first century, most people will have never even heard of this idea, and the mention of these concepts in print will cause serious emotional reactions in some readers, and probably some level of criticism from those who don't wish to consider these concepts, even though considering them is an important part of the examination of the possible authenticity of something which may be a crucial archaeological discovery with enormous implications for the history of North America – and the history of the world.

There are many other aspects of the Michigan tablets which argue strongly for their authenticity. David Allen Deal has demonstrated that tablets containing calendars clearly indicate that the designers worshiped and kept their sabbath on the *seventh* day of the week, rather than on the *first* day of the week as had been the tradition in most of Christendom since the order of Constantine.[659] Again, in a nineteenth-century America that had laws prohibiting the sale of alcohol (and a host of other activities) on Sundays, in a time in which common people regularly referred to Sunday as either "the Sabbath" or the "Lord's Day" in day-to-day speech, why would a forger do that, and where would he get the idea to do so?

In addition to tablets which show aspects of Christian iconography (including some showing crucifixes with a Christ-figure on them, and some depicting a manger-scene with baby-bundle, holy star, and a kneeling donkey), albeit with details that reveal a doctrine very different than that which came down through history as "orthodox," Henriette Mertz has also pointed to tablets which show Egyptian deities, including Horus and Isis.[660] This mixture of iconography is quite unexpected, and again appears to argue against a forger: would a nineteenth-century hoaxer, trying to pass tablets off as authentic, include a mix that had both imagery of figures on crosses and imagery with direct parallels to Egyptian scenes of the adoration of Osiris, Isis, or Horus?[661]

The clay tablet depicted below shares a distinctive shape with other such small tablets found in Michigan, as well as others found in Ohio, Wisconsin, Kentucky, Indiana, and Illinois. They typically have a hole drilled near the top center of the seal, and are sometimes referred to as "banner-stones."

This one, from Michigan, contains a scene scratched into the clay depicting a robed figure with a high hat presenting a large flowering lotus-plant floating over a vertical pillar, his hands upraised in a gesture of adoration or praise, while on the other half of the same side of the tablet is a scene of a hawk on a throne, a female figure, and some written symbols below (this is a drawing of the seal photographed in plate 8 on page 82 of *The Mystic Symbol*).

Henriette Mertz believes that these small clay tablets (she calls them "clay seals") were placed in the right hand of the deceased at their burial, as a sort of "passport" to the next world.[662] She notes their similarity to the Minoan "double-axe" shape found on Crete, and points out that the first such seal found in Michigan was recorded in 1907 – two full years before Sir Arthur Evans first published results of his excavations at Knossos (which also took place in 1907, but whose report was not published for two more years; it is of course possible to argue that Evans somehow communicated this knowledge to the Michigan "forgers," but such a theory is almost beyond ridiculous to suggest – he would not take time prior to publishing his important discoveries to cook up an obscure hoax in Michigan which no one would even be able to understand, based on discoveries which had not yet been made public).[663]

In *Lost Light*, Alvin Boyd Kuhn discusses the ancient symbolism of the axe, providing evidence that the ancient wisdom used the axe as one of the standard metaphors for the sun, which "cleaved" through the sky each day like an axe:

> The ax, as in the Roman *fasces*, was a symbol of the sun, because in making its transit through the earth and water of fleshly life it was known as the divider or cleaver of the way. It cleft a passage for itself through the lower elements, dried up the water by its fiery potency and crossed on dry land.[664]

Kuhn argues that all of the ancient sacred traditions involving the crossing of a body of water (such as the crossing of the Red Sea by the Israelites, the crossing of the Styx by the soul of the dead in ancient Greek myth, or the crossing of the soul in the underworld in the Book of the Dead in the solar bark along with Horus journeying at night from the western horizon of the setting sun towards the eastern horizon of the rising sun) were all representative of the soul coming down from the spirit realm and incarnating in the fleshly (watery) body of this life, as were sacred traditions of submergence in the water including baptism.[665] Hence, the symbol of the axe would be an appropriate medallion for inclusion in the burial (recall that in ancient times, baptism among early Christians was often done immediately before death).

When the soul reached the eastern shore, the point of rebirth and the exit from the "underworld" of incarnation, Kuhn says that "a plate of *tahn* was given each disembarking sailor, as a type or protection and salvation. This matched the 'eye of Horus' and the white stone given to the redeemed in *Revelation.*"[666]

This observation is extremely significant, in light of these axe-shaped "clay seals" or badges which allegedly came from mounds throughout Michigan, Wisconsin, Ohio, Kentucky, Indiana and Illinois (which Kuhn does not discuss). The seal was given at the *end* of the voyage through this life (the underworld), when the soul had reached the eastern horizon (as we have seen, Kuhn avers that this life was typified in ancient legend by the long passage through water in the underworld). That is to say, the seal was given at the conclusion of the voyage – and it is thus not surprising to find them clutched in the hands of the dead in burials (Mertz provides evidence that the custom of burying a certificate of salvation in the right hand of the dead was common in some places, such as Russia, right up through the end of the nineteenth century).

Kuhn's analysis points us to the probability that these seals were representative of the "Eye of Horus" – the sun god in his triumphant state, the god of the Two Horizons, where he rises out of the underworld of Osiris into the daytime heavens. We find that the seals found in mounds in America were in the form of a double-axe, and we see that Kuhn argues that the axe was an ancient symbol representative of the sun. Thus, these seals are akin to the "Eye of Horus" given to the sailor at the end of his watery journey – that is, placed in the hand of the corpse in burial, to signify the end of the journey through the underworld, that journey being *this incarnated life.*

We have seen that seals in this shape were found in North America two years before the double-axe motif of Knossos was even described by modern scholars. How did the supposed "hoaxer" get *so many details* right? How did the hoaxer hit on the double-axe shape? Did the hoaxer know that the axe-shape typified the "cleaver" of the sun, and that sailors at the end of their incarnational voyage would be buried with the "Eye of Horus" in Egypt (which is represented in the New Testament book of the *Revelation* by the "white stone" which would be given to "him that overcometh," Rev 2:17)? How sophisticated and subtle this supposed hoaxer must have been, to have anticipated so many details!

With connections like these, the hoaxer hypothesis becomes more and more difficult to maintain. And those are just some of the connections raised by the *shape* of these North American relics; let us now examine the *content* of the drawing, and see that it too has clear and obvious connections to ancient Eygptian iconography and sacred tradition (connections which a forger would be very unlikely to want to include among relics supposedly coming from an early Christian community that wandered to North America, unless the forger was well versed in the very different kinds of beliefs that Alexandrians comfortable with gnostic Christian doctrines might have held – a very remote possibility, bordering on the outrageous).

Below is a drawing of a scene from an Egyptian tomb painting showing the "adoration of Horus-Osiris and Isis." Note the elements that this scene has in common with the scene in the clay seal found in Michigan: the lotus is depicted as floating in the air above a column (in this case, one that has similarities in shape to the Djed-column), the figure giving worship has his hands positioned in a characteristic posture of adoration seen very frequently in ancient Egyptian artwork, the Horus-Osiris figure (he wears the single crown of Osiris but has the head of Horus) is seated upon a throne with clear similarities to that in the clay seal, and a figure who may be identified as Isis is present in each scene.

Similar scenes depicting figures adoring Horus or Osiris and featuring the floating lotus over a pillar are not uncommon. In the Louvre, there is a fine example on the stele known as the "Harpist's Stele" from the 3d Intermediate Period (1069 BC – 664 BC), where a kneeling figure before the lotus-and-pillar has his hands upraised in a similar fashion to the adoration of Isis and Osiris, but he is playing a harp as he gives worship to the gods. There is another stele in the Louvre from the Ptolemaic period depicting Cleopatra making an offering to Isis, dated 51 BC, and it also contains the lotus over the pillar, with the Cleopatra-figure raising arms in the same characteristic gesture of adoration or praise.

Again, the presence of artifacts among the Michigan finds containing such clearly Egyptian iconography raises the possibility that these relics were the product of a community of refugees from Alexandria or Roman Egypt, with gnostic doctrines that had no problems with the use of iconography that at times appears to be what we think of today as "Biblical" and at times is clearly descended from the iconography of ancient Egypt. Which is the better explanation: that they are the product of a prolific nineteenth-century forger who couldn't make up his mind and decided to portray a random jumble of iconographies, or that they came from a community who fled to the New World in the decades *before* the Christian canon was decreed by the hierarchical church authorities, and who were comfortable with the use of symbolism from both gnostic-Christian and ancient

Egyptian (and possibly from mystery school) sources? Because the ancients saw these symbols as representative of deeper truths, they would not be concerned by the kind of literalist worries that believers in later centuries (including the nineteenth century) would have over such depictions.

David Allen Deal has also analyzed another calendar tablet in great detail and found evidence that its designer witnessed a total solar eclipse in which a meteor shower was visible during totality. The calendar itself has a marker on its circular calendar wheel to indicate the month of the year in which the eclipse took place. Deal presents compelling arguments that the tablet commemorates a total eclipse whose path of totality passed over the location in which the artifact was found, on the date we would call July 27, AD 352.[667] He needed computer software in order to pinpoint a solar eclipse that would have passed over the correct site in the correct month as indicated on the tablet: how would a forger in the late 1800s have been able to have known such information?

These pieces of evidence, in addition to all the evidence discussed so far, argue strongly for a reconsideration of the too-hasty dismissal and condemnation of the Michigan tablets.

However, it must be asserted yet again that these tablets are by no means the only evidence for ancient trans-oceanic contact, nor are they even the best such evidence. They are, however, unique in their preservation of some theological details which may be very important clues supporting the larger thesis of the complete suppression of the gnostic or esoteric sacred traditions by the literalist conspiracy in the second, third, and fourth centuries (a literalist conspiracy that was the product of priestly families who had escaped the destruction of the Temple). Not only do these tablets (if authentic) help to confirm that theory, but they also would confirm that some esoteric adherents (almost certainly from Egypt, perhaps from Alexandria) escaped to the New World during those centuries in which the vise of Roman orthodoxy was tightening (probably around the same time that others were burying texts beneath the cliffs of the Jabal al-Tarif near modern-day Nag Hammadi).

Even if we set aside the Michigan tablets completely, there is still the troubling fact that an entire US state has a name which linguistically has direct parallels to the sacred name of the Old Testament deity. That state, of course, is *Iowa* (a clear linguistic parallel to Yahweh or Jehovah), and that region was given that name from the name of the Native American people who lived in that region prior to and after the arrival of Europeans. David Allen Deal calls attention to this important piece of evidence and notes as well that in *The Book of the Hopi*, Frank Waters reports that the Hopi people used the name "Ta-IOWA" in their worship of the Great God as well.[668]

Deal also notes that the Leni Lenape or Delaware people had a name for a legendary people who had lived in the Ohio Valley in some extremely ancient time. The name that they had for these people, as recorded by missionary John Heckewelder (1743 – 1823) was the "Allegheny" people, or the "Tallegewi." David Allen Deal notes that the name "Tallegewi" is extremely significant when examined in light of the Hebrew language, where the word "*Tel*" means a mound or hill (as in "Tel Aviv") and the word "Gewi" means "nations" or "peoples" (as in the term "Goyim"). Thus, the word "Tallegewi" means "mound nations" or "mound peoples" – or, as they were called in nineteenth century America when many of the ancient mounds still stood, the "Mound Builders."[669]

These facts are much more difficult to dismiss than are the Michigan tablets, which unfortunately have been so ridiculed that most conventional scholars would not dare to examine them seriously today (for fear of destroying their own academic reputation). But the linguistic parallels are indisputable. The existence of words such as "Iowa" and "Tallegewi" – both in recorded use long before the supposed arrival of the Michigan forger – provide powerful support for the possibility that a community of esoteric refugees, with familiarity in the use of hieroglyphics and an additional alphabet patterned on the Hebrew writing systems, as well as familiarity with the Hebrew language, could have arrived in the center of the North American continent in ancient times.

There is another enormous category of supporting evidence for the theory that some members of the gnostic resistance against the empire fled to the New World. It will be saved until its rightful place on the chronological timeline, after we examine the Crusades. That category of evidence, however, can be mentioned now, and it is: the ferocity with which the Native Americans were set upon by the representatives of the "orthodox" doctrines and teachings, centuries later, and the fanaticism with which their shamanic world-view was deliberately indoctrinated out of their children in the centuries following the arrival of the European descendents of the empire, an indoctrination which continued right up until the present day.

20

Crusades and genocides

My Dad took me to his Dad, my grandfather, who was an Indian doctor. I told him I was hurting in the chest; it hurt most in the left bottom lung. Grandfather kept his finger there on my chest and he chanted, then he sucked on my chest where it hurt the most. He spat out three times, into a bowl, and each time it was pitch black stuff he spat. I remember so well watching him: three times, pitch black stuff into that bowl, a mouth-full each time. Then he said, "You're going to live, son." Over the next few days I got hungry again, I started playing, and I got well. I was the only kid who survived from a bunch of us who were given TB by Pitts. He fed us this poisoned food to kill us. *That Principal wanted me to die. He had his orders to feed us this food that was contaminated with TB, and sure enough I was the only one of that group to survive*, thanks to my Grandfather.

> Testimony of Willie Sport, 75, given to
> (Rev.) Kevin Annett on March 28, 1998.
> *Hidden No Longer: Genocide in Canada, Past
> and Present.*[670]

Now that we have explored some of the abundant evidence supporting the theory that refugees fled to the New World to escape the clutches of an intolerant, hierarchical, literalist and anti-gnostic church, a church that had become increasingly intertwined in the power structures of the Roman Army, the Praetorian Guard, and eventually the offices of the Emperor and even the Senate of Rome, we can look back on the record of history since that time with a completely different perspective. There is no aspect of world history that is not radically changed by this new perspective.

This understanding of world history explains the oppression by the nobles of the serfs of Europe for centuries, and it explains much of the warfare and bloodshed among European powers on that continent, and which later expanded to other continents as well, beginning primarily with the Crusades of AD 1096 – AD 1192. In this chapter, we will explore the evidence which suggests that in their quest to keep all the knowledge of the ancient wisdom to themselves, the literalist religious powers (aided by the political and economic muscle controlled by the European families descended from those original priestly families) embarked on a campaign of destruction against shamanic cultures the world over, a campaign which continues to this day. In the brief examination of this subject presented here, we will primarily examine the evidence surrounding the Crusades and that surrounding the invasion of North and South America and the brutal extermination and oppression of the indigenous nations who live there.

From their precarious escape to Rome, the priestly families who were led by Josephus had first conquered the Roman Empire, and then discarded it. They then consolidated their power over the rest of western Europe in the centuries that followed, installing members of their families in all the positions of secular power, and backing it up with their absolute control over the religious structure of the church.

During those centuries, access to the ancient wisdom was severely restricted. Most of the population could not read or write: that was a skill that was primarily the prerogative of the clergy and some nobles. Access to the ancient scriptures was likewise restricted: it was forbidden to translate the scriptures of the Old and New Testaments into the "vulgar languages" of the people. Through this tactic, the odds that someone outside of the tightly controlled circles of religious power might on his or her own examine the scriptures themselves and see that they were completely composed of metaphors pointing to esoteric truths about our condition in this life were kept to a minimum.

The theory of Flavio Barbiero argues that after the successful infiltration of the most important power structures of the Roman Empire by Sol Invictus Mithraism, and the establishment of the hierarchical Christian church centered in Rome, those now controlling the levers of power set about consolidating their grip on western Europe through the institution of the feudal societal structures that characterized the Middle Ages.

During the fifth century, the Empire began to dissolve, until about a hundred years after Theodosius it dissolved altogether in the west. In the last years of the fourth century, the empire had been split into east and west upon the death of Theodosius. The emperor Theodosius (AD 347 – AD 395) reigned from AD 379 until his death in 395, and issued decrees that made the Christian doctrines articulated in the Nicene Creed the official religion of the empire. The Council of Nicaea in AD 325 had effectively declared as heretical all alternative doctrines, especially those of Arius of Alexandria, who was declared a heretic and banished by the majority. The main precepts of Nicea still form the bedrock of what is considered "orthodox" by most Catholic and Protestant theologians in the west today.

Upon his death, Theodosius appointed his two sons emperors, one in the east and one in the west. Less than a hundred years later, in order to put an end to the destructive and destabilizing battles over who would become emperor in the west, the barbarian general Odoacer (AD 433 – AD 493), with the full support of the Roman Senate, declared that there would no longer be an emperor in the west.

Flavio Barbiero writes that "the imperial office died without trauma," leaving a west which may have appeared to have been divided but which was actually united more powerfully by the church and the concept of "Christendom" than it had been under the emperors.[671]

Although the remnants of the western empire appeared to be divided, in reality it was more united than ever. This fact is attested to not only by Flavio Barbiero but by many other historians who have described the situation after the fall of Rome. Western Europe was united in that the new kingdoms that arose in the wake of the dissolution of the western empire all saw themselves as members of "Christendom." Flavio Barbiero is only repeating the statements of most conventional historians when he says that the new kingdoms did not really see themselves as completely independent states but rather as self-directed entities operating within "a single Christian empire."[672] He summarizes the situation by saying that "in practice the West, although administratively divided, was more united than ever under the church of Rome."[673]

In her comprehensive examination of the first three Crusades, published in 1966 well before Flavio Barbiero's theory was published, Zoé Oldenbourg makes very much the same sort of observation regarding the situation in western Europe during the centuries following the "fall" of the western empire and leading up to the Crusades:

> The common man in the Middle Ages was a Christian in the same way as a twentieth-century man is an Englishman or a Frenchman, a worker, a peasant, or a city dweller. In Russian, for example, the word "peasant" means literally "Christian," and the distinction existing between the two ideas in the present-day language is a later development. This etymological synthesis corresponds to an attitude that was more or less general in the Middle Ages. Men thought of themselves first and foremost as religious beings, members of a community of the faithful.[674]

The evidence from the period shows that, while there were differences in language, in dress, and in culture between them, the different fiefdoms and kingdoms of western Europe did function as a single "pond" in which the nobility and the clergy could swim freely and at will, largely above the law and above the ties that bound the peasants to one specific locale. A nobleman from one part of Europe could be installed in a dukedom or baronetcy completely on the other side of the continent, and the peasants could do nothing to object. This sort of situation took place quite frequently.

Flavio Barbiero asserts that throughout the Middle Ages, the priestly families continued to maintain complete control over the ownership of land, the civil service, and – most importantly – the institutions of religion. It is true that during the waning years of the western empire, the "barbarians" including the Germanic tribes, the Franks, the Vandals, the Bastamae, the Alamanni, the Visigoths, the Swabians, the Alans, the Sarmatians, and a host of others had been incorporated into the armies of Rome, until the western empire depended almost entirely upon these barbarian "foederati" for its military needs. The western empire (and the families that were now controlling its fate) found this to be an excellent arrangement for the most part – the barbarians made an extremely effective military, and for less cost or trouble than they would incur by doing it themselves or compensating Roman citizens to do it. In return, the barbarians were awarded property and privileges, and were subjected to conversion to the faith of the centralized church.

While many historians (including Zoé Oldenbourg) believe that the nobility that came to rule the various kingdoms and fiefdoms of western Europe was largely descended from these barbarians, Flavio Barbiero argues differently. He presents compelling evidence that Charlemagne was very clearly descended from the priestly families who traced their lineage back to the days before the Roman conquest, and that after Charlemagne's consolidation of control over most of western Europe, he promptly installed his own selections as the nobility who would rule over every conquered vassal state, and that these were chosen from the small pool of families of the priestly lines.

FlavioBarbiero points out the significant fact that Charlemagne's grandfather, Charles Martel (c. AD 688 – AD 741), took a moniker with ancient connections to the name of the founder of the Hasmonean dynasty which had ruled Judea and from whom Josephus claimed direct descent: Judas Maccabeus, whose name means "Judas the Hammer." Charles Martel was the father of Pepin III (AD 714 – 768, known as "Pepin the Short"), who was the father of Charlemagne, and Pepin III introduced the practice of paying tithes to the church immediately upon becoming King of the Franks in 752, a practice which would remain in effect for almost the next thousand years.[675]

Charlemagne expanded his kingdom by a series of campaigns to the south, east, and north, to eventually cover much of Europe. In a section of his book entitled "Judaic Aspects of the Carolingian Kingdom," Flavio Barbiero demonstrates distinct parallels between the kingdom presided over by Charlemagne and the glory days of the priestly families before the conquest of Jerusalem by the Romans.

He begins the section by saying, "It seems clear that the Carolingians and the whole clerical and non-clerical nobility behind them strived to reproduce in every detail the reality of the Jerusalem of the Hasmoneans."[676] In addition to the payment of the tithe, which mirrored exactly the tithe which had been due to the Temple of Jerusalem in ancient times. Barbiero highlights further similarities: Charlemagne compared himself to the Old Testament King Josiah of Judah; he considered himself a king and a priest simultaneously (in much the same manner as Josiah); he encouraged his portrayal as a "new David, triumphant over the enemies of Israel," and in that role would forcefully impose the Christian faith on conquered Germans, Slavs, Magyars, and others, and was not above committing mass extermination in order to coerce the survivors into accepting the faith; he encouraged his soldiers to fast before battle, and they would commence the attack by singing in unison the *Kyrie eleison*; and in addition to all of the above, Charlemagne was fond of calling himself the "chief of the new chosen people."[677]

Barbiero points out that in the kingdom of Charlemagne, "the territorial, ethnic, political, and administrative subdivisions had no relevance and varied continuously without in any way damaging the united nature of the Christian world."[678] He describes Charlemagne's method for governing, and his criteria for emplacing nobles throughout his new empire, appointing nobles to conquered territories without any regard to national origin or even native language, so long as the new local nobility came from the lineage of the priestly families. He writes:

> Each vassal, of course, immediately adopted the vernacular spoken by the population subjugated to him, which makes it extremely difficult to establish the true origins of his family. At one time, for example, historians believed the various princes, dukes, marquises, and barons who governed Germany came from the local populations, which is not at all true. Today, even the most nationalistic historians acknowledge that the whole German nobility derives from a class of military officers and royal functionaries installed by the Carolingians and often tied to them by bonds of blood. Further, they have descended from the same restricted group.[679]

Barbiero cites research from German historian Gerd Tallenbach and others to support his assertion that the same situation prevailed throughout the various regions that composed Charlemagne's empire, and that compose most of the states of modern Europe today.

He also presents evidence that the institution of Freemasonry existed throughout the Middle Ages – being fully in force by the time of Charlemagne – and that it was used as a powerful tool to both perpetuate the identity of the priestly family lines, and to stoke a burning desire in each member of those lines to one day recapture the place that had been taken from them so long ago: the site of their Temple, the city of Jerusalem.

As well, it may have preserved the esoteric knowledge that was denied to the masses, and may have served as a secret or shadow power structure through which important decisions could be made, fulfilling the same role that the society of Sol Invictus Mithras had played during the Roman Empire.

In fact, Barbiero shows that Masonry *is* essentially the cult of Sol Invictus Mithras, but with Mithras removed and replaced by the Great Architect of the Universe. Between their exclusive control of the institutions of royalty and nobility, the institution of the church, and the secret institution of Freemasonry, the families had almost total control of western Europe.

Explaining the connections between Mithraism and Masonry (and Catholicism and the rituals important to the royal and noble families of Europe), Bariero demonstrates that while the name of Mithras himself was now omitted, the reverence of the sun permeated Christian religion (as it does to this day): the feast days were connected with the annual solar cycle, the first day of the week ("the day of the sun") became "the day of the Lord," and Christmas (connected to the winter solstice) became the most important holy feast day of the year, reserved from the most important political rituals, including the baptism of Clodeveus and the crowning of both Pepin the Short and Charlemagne himself.[680]

And while Charlemagne had never conquered the islands of Britain, Barbiero shows conclusively that those islands had been the almost exclusive domain of the priestly families from very early in the days of the empire, and still are today.

Once their domains were firmly in hand, with the institutions that would ensure continuity of power under their absolute control, the priestly families of Europe could at last turn their attention to a dream that, as Flavio Barbiero puts it, "they had been harboring for a thousand years in the secret of their 'lodges': to regain possession of Jerusalem from which they had been driven out."[681]

That is to say, they began to plan the Crusades.

He shows that the conventional explanations for the sudden fervor that launched the Crusades all have serious problems. The trip to the Holy Land was extremely costly and extremely risky, one that entailed nearly a year of planning and preparation even for the wealthiest of nobles and kings, one that ruined many of them and led to the death of thousands of knights, and for what? Flavio Barbiero points out that Rome was really the center of Christianity, not Jerusalem, and that although the holiest sites of the gospels (if we take them literally) were found in and around Jerusalem, all of those sites were actually open to pilgrims and maintained by the various ecclesiastical hierarchies who were allowed to operate them freely.

He concludes that the religious motivation was almost certainly "only a pretext, officially proclaimed before the population in order to mask motivations of a quite different nature."[682] The real reason, he proposes, is that the families who now controlled Europe and the church saw Jerusalem as a family possession that was theirs by right: it had been "the cradle of their origins," and for a thousand years the male members of the priestly families had been steeped in the secret rituals of the princes and priests of Jerusalem, through the institution of Freemasonry, through which the idea that Jerusalem was the Holy City which belonged to their family "by divine right was drummed into them from the first moment they entered a Masonic lodge and was repeated continually as they gradually advanced in the hierarchy of the organization."[683]

The reader can decide which theory for the Crusades is more convincing – that they were the product of some sort of mass outpouring of religious fervor that simultaneously gripped Europe from the highest king to the lowest peasant, or that the "crème de la crème of nobility: dukes, counts, barons, and at least six kings and two emperors put their kingdoms and their own lives at stake [. . .] because Jerusalem was always considered a common possession" of the priestly families, who had patiently gathered their strength and bided their time until they could march back in force to seize what they believed belonged to them by right.[684]

The implications of this theory are staggering, if we stop here and let the import fully sink in. The Crusades did not have to happen: the holy sites were already under the care of Christian caretakers, and reasonably open to any pilgrims who wished to visit them. Thousands of peasants marched to their death, and waves of knights invaded and slaughtered, under a pretext that covered up a purpose that was unstated then – and that has remained unstated in the centuries since.

In this disastrous event, we see the true character of the leadership of these priestly families: their willingness to cover their true intentions with a "noble lie," their complete disregard for the collateral damage they need to inflict in order to pursue their own selfish agenda, their overweening pride which drives them to avenge every wrong even if they have to plot for centuries in order to avenge, their secrecy, their ruthlessness, their cunning. These characteristics can be seen again and again, if we examine the history of the world since the Crusades in light of the theory we have been developing.

But we did not need the Crusades to reach these conclusions about the ruthlessness and the selfishness of the leaders of this centuries-long conspiracy. We need only consider the incontestable fact that the descendants of Josephus established the hierarchical, ecclesiastical Christian church that deliberately suppressed the esoteric ancient wisdom that was mankind's common heritage prior to that time. They had the light of the knowledge of ancient Egypt, and they deliberately hid it under a bushel of literalism – a literalism which their very scriptures plainly do not support. They have continued to hide it to this day, and to persecute those who attempt to share it with any outside of their circles, just as they did with Paul, whose esoteric and gnostic teachings they perjured and twisted and eventually co-opted into their own literalistic system.

Not only did they withhold this teaching from the masses who came to literalist Christianity in search of answers (or, as was more common in history, because they were driven into the fold of Christianity by the armed representatives of the political power of the Roman Empire and of the later nobility and royalty of Europe), but they also set out to seize the texts attesting to the ancient wisdom and keep those texts and that wisdom for themselves, and to destroy ancient sacred texts as necessary in order to cover up their own misdeeds or to prevent the ancient wisdom from being understood by anyone outside of their clerical circles.

We can see this repulsive agenda in full action when the states of western Europe finally developed vessels capable of taking soldiers and horses across the Atlantic again, after long centuries of isolation between the continents. The slaughter that the Europeans perpetrated upon the peoples of the Americas, beginning with the Inca and the Maya, was genocidal. In addition to the slaughter, the Europeans also gathered up the sacred texts of those people – filled with priceless ancient wisdom and (no doubt) also clues that could shed invaluable light on the refugees who had fled the growing strength of the Christian church centuries before – and put them to the torch.

In the brutal massacres that the conquistadors carried out, we can see the cold-blooded thirst for vengeance, vengeance that can wait for centuries, that characterizes the leadership of these families. It is of a pattern with the Crusades. There is sufficient evidence to conclude that the elite of Europe *knew* of the existence of the Americas before Columbus took his voyage – that Columbus had maps showing him in general terms how far he would have to go and what he would find.

That Columbus did have some sort of map is an established fact, but most conventional historians believe it was merely a vague and inaccurate map that omitted the New World entirely. In his important 1966 book *Maps of the Ancient Sea Kings: Evidence of Advanced Civilization in the Ice Age*, Charles Hapgood presents arguments showing that Columbus may have had a "portolan" map showing all or part of the regions depicted on the Piri Re'is map that dates to 1513 and contains inscriptions which specifically sate that parts of it were based on maps made by Columbus.

However, Hapgood demonstrates that Columbus apparently misunderstood his own portolan map, because the portolan maps are based on an arcane ancient mapmaking convention which uses trigonometric projections and can have multiple "norths" on the same map – something that threw Columbus off and caused him to miscalculate the distance he would have to travel to reach the Caribbean drawn on his map (which he thought was actually depicting part of Asia). In other words, Columbus had maps that were far more detailed than the maps conventional historians believe that he had, but he misunderstood them to the extent that he miscalculated the distance of his voyage (nearly leading to a mutiny by his crew when the crossing took longer than he said it would) and to the extent that he thought the excellent depiction of the east coast of the Americas on his map was actually a depiction of the east coast of Asia.[685]

However, the existence during the time of Columbus of sophisticated portolan maps that far surpassed in accuracy and knowledge of the shape and location of the Americas cannot be denied, and even though the ability to draw such maps had long ago been lost to the west, their existence and the fact that Columbus most likely had one of them (remember that he was sponsored by royalty – that is to say, members of the ancient bloodlines) suggests the possibility that Columbus was sent on his mission by people who had a pretty good idea of what he was going to encounter.

The fact of Columbus' foreknowledge of the distance to the Americas (even if he himself thought he was going to the East Indies), and the fact of the bloodbath perpetrated by the conquistadors upon the Mesoamericans (the extent of which is known to us today by their own admission and by the records kept by the priests who accompanied the soldiers), go a long way towards establishing the hypothesis that the havoc unleashed upon the inhabitants of the New World was planned beforehand.

To accomplish their objectives, the leaders standing behind the levers of power at the highest level have repeatedly shown themselves to be willing to kill thousands, and they will order the slaughter of women and children just as willingly as they will order the death of men of military age.

At the end of 2012, as the celebrated Maya Long Count was drawing to a close (or a restart), I wrote that the fact that there is so much confusion and debate over the meaning of the count and the question of what the ancient Maya might have been anticipating with the count should have caused moderns to ask, "Why exactly *is* there so much confusion about this whole subject?"

The answer to that largely unanswered question, I proposed, was the heartbreaking answer: the reason that so little is known about this ancient civilization and what they thought is that *their records were cruelly and deliberately and almost completely destroyed by violent men.*[686]

You can read the heart-rending account in the words of one of those responsible for the destruction of those records, the Franciscan friar Diego de Landa (later a Bishop), in his own sixteenth-century account entitled *Yucatan Before and After the Conquest.* Translator William Gates wrote in 1937 in an introduction to that text:

> It is perhaps not too strong a statement to make, that ninety-nine percent of what we today know of the Mayas, we know as the result either of what Landa has told us in the pages that follow, or have learned in the use and study of what he told. [...]

> If ninety-nine hundredths of our present knowledge is at base derived from what he told us, it is an equally safe statement that at that Auto de fé of '62, he burned ninety-nine times as much knowledge of Maya history and sciences as he has given us in his book.[687]

By "that Auto de fé of '62," Gates means the year 1562, just over four hundred fifty years ago now, when Landa and his forces tortured many Maya to death as part of his efforts to subdue and convert them. An *Auto de fé* ("Act of faith"), of course, is an Inquisition – a sanctioned tool of the church to use physical violence of the most brutal kind against those who do not yet accept their literalist faith and their ecclesiastical hierarchy, in an attempt to bend them into acceptance of it through the application of pain and ultimately the threat of death.

During the same year, 1562, Landa admits to destroying a great number of the Maya texts. In Section 41 (entitled "Cycle of the Mayas. Their Writings.") of his *Yucatan Before and After the Conquest* (the chapters were probably divided and numbered later by someone other than Landa), Diego de Landa describes some details of the Maya calendar cycles, and then adds these terrible words:

> These people also used certain characters or letters, with which they wrote in their books about the antiquities and their sciences; with these, and with figures, and certain signs in the figures, they understood their matters, made them known, and taught them. We found a great number of books in these letters, and since they contained nothing but superstitions and falsehoods of the devil we

burned them all, which they took most grievously, and which gave them great pain.[688]

In his book *Fingerprints of the Gods*, Graham Hancock writes of the above statement, "Not only the 'natives' should have felt this pain but anyone and everyone – then and now – who would like to know the truth about the past."[689] On the same page, Mr. Hancock also describes similar depredations, such as those of Juan de Zumárraga, who in November of 1530 "burned a Christianized Aztec aristocrat at the stake for having allegedly reverted to worship of the 'rain-god' and later, in the market-place at Texcoco, built a vast bonfire of astronomical documents, paintings, manuscripts and hieroglyphic texts which the conquistadores had forcibly extracted from the Aztecs during the previous eleven years."[690]

How far could these ancient texts have gone towards shedding light upon the thinking of those who created the Long Count and who had been diligently keeping it so many centuries before the invasion of their land by these violent Christian intruders!

How much more might the Maya themselves have been able to tell us today if so many of their ancestors had not been horribly murdered *en masse* and their culture forcibly erased at the point of a sword!

In section 15 of his *Yucatan Before and After the Conquest*, Diego de Landa offers some samples of the atrocities that were perpetrated upon the Maya by the invading forces:

> I, Diego de Landa, say that I saw a great tree near the village upon the branches of which a captain had hung many women, with their infant children hung from their feet. At this town, and another two leagues away called Verey, they hung two Indian women, one a maiden and the other recently married, for no other crime than their beauty, and because of fearing a disturbance among the soldiers on their account; also further to cause the Indians to believe the Spaniards indifferent to their women. The memory of these two is kept both among the Indians and Spaniards on account of their great beauty and the cruelty with which they were killed. The Indians of the provinces of Cochuah and Chetumal rose, and the Spaniards so pacified them that from being the most settled and populous it became the most wretched of the whole country. Unheard-of cruelties were inflicted, cutting off their noses, hands, arms and legs, and the breasts of their women; throwing them into deep water with gourds tied to their feet, thrusting the children with spears because they could not go as fast as their mothers. If some of those who had been put in chains feel sick or could not keep up with the rest, they would cut off their heads among the rest rather than stop to unfasten them. They also kept great numbers of women and men captive in their service, with similar treatment.[691]

These genocidal accounts record some of the darkest chapters in human history, some of the worst demonstrations of man's inhumanity to man and some of the most execrable deeds that have ever been perpetrated by men against their fellow beings. We must ask what prompted such barbarity and fiendish behavior, and who ordered it? Was it simply an outpouring of viciousness by the soldiers of the conquistadors, or was there some kind of standing order that had been given to the leaders of the expedition, before they ever left the shores of Europe? The wholesale destruction of the written texts of the Maya, the constant accompaniment of the priests in the entire procedure, and the careful recording of the results (again by the priests) suggests that something more was at work here.

What it suggests is that the conquest of the so-called "New World" was a deliberate campaign of revenge upon those who had harbored the refugees from the rising power of the literalist church so many centuries before. It was also a campaign of deliberate destruction of one of the repositories of the ancient wisdom which had escaped the destruction meted out to such texts in the Old World. As Graham Hancock declared in the quotation above, this deliberate destruction of the Maya texts robbed not just the Maya but all the people of the earth of the benefits of that stream of the ancient wisdom. This crime is part of a larger pattern: the literalist church in all its permutations has done something similar to the scriptures of the Bible as well, by deliberately imposing an anti-esoteric interpretation on them, and it obviously did something similar to many other texts of all descriptions during the third and fourth centuries in Europe and Africa, as evidenced by the buried library of texts at Nag Hammadi and by the destruction of the trove of texts at the Library of Alexandria.

Lest it be argued that the barbarity displayed in Mesoamerica and again in South America was somehow unique to just one period of literalist Christian history, and cannot be said to be characteristic of the *modus operandi* of the ancient priestly families who had long ago consolidated their power over first the Roman Empire and then all of western Europe, the reader is invited to examine in detail the history of the empire from the days of the Vespasians onward as recounted in Flavio Barbiero's book. During the centuries that the families were slowly gaining power through the institution of their secretive Sol Invictus Mithras cult, assassinations were common and the lifespan of an emperor after taking the throne was seldom more than a few years – and was often only a few weeks or months. Often these assassinations took place at the hands of the Praetorian Guard, or at the hands of the army itself, both institutions which historical evidence shows to have been the most heavily-infiltrated by the Mithras cult. If Barbiero's theory is correct, it was the leadership of the priestly family lines that ordered these violent removals from office through assassination during the period prior to their decision to jettison the trappings of the Roman Empire altogether.

Or, examine the record of the Crusades. Or the record of Charlemagne's conquest, and his campaign to forcibly convert everyone within the reach of his domain to ecclesiastical Christianity, accompanied by massacres as necessary to prove the point and eliminate opposition. Or the record of the Inquisition, which was turned against Europeans with just as much ferocity as it was used against the Mesoamericans.

Finally, the record of the campaigns against the indigenous nations of North America can be examined, campaigns which continued for more than three centuries after the atrocities described by Diego de Landa. The Native Americans in North America were reconnoitered extensively by the Jesuits during the initial centuries prior to the US Declaration of Independence, their lands were stolen from them through the force of arms, the invading generals sometimes deliberately used biological warfare such as the infamous example of blankets taken from smallpox victims in hospitals and given to indigenous tribes in order to infect them, and huge numbers of people were sometimes displaced in massive death marches such as the infamous "Trail of Tears," the name given to the forced relocation of the Cherokee, Creek, Seminole, Chickasaw and Choctaw nations during which many thousands died of starvation, disease, and exposure to the freezing temperatures, swamps, and rain or snow without adequate shelter or clothing. Across the continent and especially in the plains those warriors who tried to resist were eventually ground down by sheer force of numbers and the technological advantages their industrialized opponents could bring against them. These resisting warriors were additionally tormented by the knowledge that their noncombatant friends and family members were being rounded up and imprisoned in concentration camps known as "reservations," and finally their children were forcibly educated in schools which were often run by representatives of the literalist Christian religion (whether Catholic or Protestant).

There, the children were forbidden to use the language of their people, they were forced to learn the Christian religion and told that their beliefs were idolatrous and heathenish, and in many cases they were deliberately exposed to horrendous conditions and denied humane medical treatment as a matter of policy, as researchers such as Kevin Annett have documented.

Kevin Daniel Annett was a former minister in the United Church of Canada, who in 2001 published a book entitled *Hidden from History: The Canadian Holocaust*, which has been allowed to go out of print after two editions and has not been reprinted in a third edition, but which Annett has republished for free on the web as *Hidden No Longer: Genocide in Canada, Past and Present* (An Updated New Edition of *Hidden from History: The Canadian Holocaust*, 3rd Edition). It can be found in its entirety, for example, on scribd.com. It documents the death of more than fifty thousand First Nations people, most of them children and adolescents, in the residential schools over the course of a century – going right into the twentieth century – due to deliberate exposure to disease, the withholding of medical attention, and the violence of brutal rape, beating, and outright murder.

Annett writes:

> At the risk of being misunderstood, I would venture to call this battle a spiritual one, for behind the beguiling appearance of things lies an older and untold story about how it is that we came to conquer, mutilate and destroy one another, again and again: and the unseen forces that are responsible.
>
> In 1987, a defrocked priest named Fidel who labored among Mayan refugees, and who was eventually killed by a landowner's gunman in Chiapas, Mexico, told me that, like him, I would one day have to choose between Christ and the church; and that in that choice, whenever I was confused, I should simply go to the poorest child and ask her what I should do.[692]

He describes how in 1886, Canada banned all west coast traditional native ceremonies, and outlawed the use of indigenous languages and the celebration of the potlatch ceremony. Then, in 1889, the federal Department of Indian Affairs was established in Canada, which created "industrial schools" run by Catholic and Protestant churches, into which all native children across Canada were forcibly removed. No more than two years later, the first report by a doctor was submitted to the government of Canada, alleging massive death among the imprisoned population of native children at these schools, due to untreated tuberculosis (tuberculosis that was apparently encouraged to run wild among the children, because infected children were not segregated but deliberately left among healthy children in order to infect them as well, as many eyewitness accounts and even published photographs testify).[693]

He also documents deliberate introduction of smallpox among children of the native peoples, a practice that is known to have been going on for centuries. Kevin Annett's award-winning film documentary on the same subject, entitled *Unrepentant* (also available on the web), shows letters from early British officers who describe this policy of deliberately giving blankets taken from smallpox victims in hospitals to unsuspecting members of the Mi'kmaq people in Nova Scotia in the 1700s (the same nation with the unique writing containing strong parallels to Egyptian hieroglyphics).[694]

That film contains heartbreaking interviews with survivors of the residential schools, men and women who saw their friends beaten, abused, and murdered, and who themselves were tortured both physically and mentally by the members of the church organizations into whose hands the Canadian government had forced them through legislation, backed up by the actions of the Royal Canadian Mounted Police.

In Annett's book, he provides massive amounts of evidence to establish that these demonic practices did indeed take place – that in fact they continued well into the 1980s, and that the Canadian federal government was clearly complicit in these crimes and continues to act in concert with the churches in question to cover up the genocide.

The book cites reports of physicians who toured the schools and were shocked at the cases of rampant and untreated tuberculosis, beginning with the report of Dr. George Turner Orton (1837 – 1901) in 1891.[695] Subsequent reports from Dr. Peter Henderson Bryce (1853 – 1932), the Chief Medical Officer for the federal Department of Indian Affairs, who toured the boarding schools nationwide, provided evidence that over half of the children – nationwide – were dying of deliberately induced and untreated tuberculosis.[696] A photocopy of a page of data from one of Dr. Bryce's actual reports is presented in Annett's book.[697] In one of his reports, submitted in 1907, and entitled *Report on the Indian Schools of Manitoba and the North-West Territories*, Dr. Bryce states: "conditions are being deliberately created to spread infectious disease."[698] Far from addressing the problem, the Canadian government banned further inspection by outside medical officials in 1919.[699] Deaths from tuberculosis rose sharply after that.[700]

Annett presents primary documents written and signed by school officials or by doctors, revealing a policy of admitting children with tuberculosis, as well as documents declaring that there are two standards of medical care regarding children at the Indian schools and "children of the white schools."[701]

Survivors of the boarding schools who had been there in the 1950s, 1960s, and 1970s go on record in the movie *Unrepentant* to describe their own experiences of being forced to play with and even sleep in the same beds with other children who were exhibiting symptoms of advanced tuberculosis. Kevin Annett provides photographic evidence in both his books and that movie to support these testimonies. Dr. Bryce was writing about it at the turn of the century, was sending letters to the government officials who should have been responsible for addressing the problem (had they desired to stop it), and the evidence shows that this murderous practice was still in full force well into the closing decades of the twentieth century.

In 1928, Alberta passed the Sexual Sterilization Act, allowing (as Annett describes it) "any inmate of an Indian residential school to be involuntarily sterilized at the decision of the Principal: a church employee."[702] Five years later, an identical law would be passed in British Columbia, and three sterilization centers would be established at hospitals located in heavily-populated native communities.[703] Survivor testimonies in Annett's book and in the movie recount involuntary sterilization operations, the deliberate radiation of childrens' pelvic regions with X-ray machines for long periods of time in order to render them sterile, a policy of sterilizing children whose scores were *too high* on intelligence tests, a policy of sterilizing women marrying into the bloodlines of the chiefs of the First Nations tribes, the importation of white Canadian prostitutes to encourage them to have children with traditional First Nations men especially chiefs in order to confuse the traditional bloodlines, and the complicity of doctors and government representatives in this longrunning policy (some of the survivors recount deliberate sterilization procedures taking place as recently as the 1980s).[704]

Kevin Annett even documents evidence that German scientists came to the schools to perform various medical experiments on the children (involuntary experiments, of course), both in the years immediately prior to World War II and – even more tellingly – in the years after the war was supposedly over.[705] Included in his book are references to eyewitnesses who claim to have seen the Nazi SS identification tattoo (with ID number) of one of those in charge of horrendous medical experiments that went on in Canada in the 1950s.[706]

Kevin Annett's careful documentation of these atrocities is critically important, both for the bringing to light of the longstanding and deliberate campaign of violence and torture (physical and mental) against the indigenous people of Canada, and their efforts to have these crimes acknowledged and addressed, but also for the light that his analysis sheds on the pattern and tactics used by the perpetrators of this genocide. One of the most important points that his work reveals is the fact that this deliberate campaign cannot be laid at the feet of any single branch of the western literalist Christian church: different branches were equally complicit. Nor can the blame be laid at the doorstep of the church alone: those in political power clearly directed policy, passing laws and providing the force of arms to enforce the policy (including a long history of enforcement and complicity by the Royal Canadian Mounted Police). The court system is guilty as well, enforcing legal policies such as the criminal fiction that the children seized and incarcerated in these schools were under the legal guardianship of the principal of the school and no longer under the guardianship of their parents (the fact that parents were forced or tricked into signing documents declaring such guardianship in no way makes such kidnaping "legal" or legitimate).[707]

Further, Annett's work reveals a clear connection between the genocidal policies he documents in Canada and those which have taken place in the wider world. The sterilization practices he documents that took place in Canada he shows to have been related to sterilization and eugenics campaigns elsewhere in the world during the twentieth century, including in the United States – against "undesirables" of various ethnicities but also deliberately against Native Americans. He cites evidence that "since

1970, over one-third of native women living on reserves in the western United States have undergone some form of sterilization, either chemically, in vaccines, or through direct tubal ligation."[708] The connections between the involuntary medical experimentation perpetrated upon the First Nations children incarcerated in the schools *before and after* World War II and the atrocities committed by the Nazis at concentration camps during the Second World War are chilling, as is the evidence that some of the same perpetrators of these atrocities may have moved easily back and forth across the Atlantic and between the governments of Germany and the governments of the nations of North America both before and after the war.

The evidence documented by Kevin Annett should spark outrage and action among every human being who learns of it, for the sake of the indigenous people who were subjected to these crimes. The evidence he documents is also important for the support it provides to the larger thesis of history that has been developed based upon the evidence we have examined thus far. According to that theory, the families who "conquered" the Roman Empire from within placed themselves in charge of *both* the religious institution of the literalist hierarchical Christian church, *and* the power centers of political and economic control (the "noble" fiefdoms and the lands that represented political and economic power during the feudal period, which translated into political control over the countries of Europe and access to the wealth of Europe after feudalism transitioned into mercantilism and later versions of socialism and other corrupted forms of economic control and coercion). It is not merely "the church" which is guilty in this conspiracy – although it most certainly is guilty – but also the "nobility" and "royalty" in control of the enforcing mechanisms of violence (the police, military, and court systems) and the mechanisms of establishing and directing policy.

In light of the theory that has been put forward in this book and supported by historical evidence stretching back to the Roman Empire, does it seem to be more than coincidence that representatives of the Christian church (in this case, both Catholic and Protestant) were put in charge of these internment centers by the representatives of the Crown? Is it any wonder that these atrocities were perpetrated primarily by agents of those churches? And is it any wonder that they are being vigorously and criminally covered up to this day by both the churches and their enablers in government? The undeniable connection between literalist Christian churches and the pitiless slaughter of the native peoples of North America is powerful supporting evidence for the paradigm that has been argued throughout this book.

The sickening connection between the atrocities of the Nazis and those documented in Annett's book and movie do not appear to be mere coincidence, particularly because he provides evidence that some of the perpetrators of these atrocities appear to have moved freely between Europe and Canada both before and after the war. This connection invites further examination of twentieth century wars in light of the "church and nobility" thesis.

We have already seen evidence that the majority of those who marched off to their deaths in the Crusades (and even some of those who perpetrated atrocities in Palestine during the Crusades) were unaware of the real purpose behind the Crusades. If Flavio Barbiero is correct, and the evidence strongly indicates that he is, then the real purpose of the Crusades stemmed from the desire to gain greater control of those sites taken from the priestly lines by the armies of Vespasian and Titus, and possibly of ancient treasures and secrets that the descendents of those families thought might still be found there. Those outside of the circles in which this true purpose was discussed – most likely the majority of those who went to Palestine from Europe – went in ignorance of the true purpose. To what extent can we ask did the majority of those who participated in the wars of the twentieth century do so in ignorance of the root motives behind those wars as well? The apparent cooperation at some level (perhaps a primarily secret level) between governments who had fought on both sides of the Second World War indicated by some of the evidence uncovered by Kevin Annett raises questions about the complicity of some branches of the Christian church in the orchestration of that catastrophe. The genocides which have accompanied other wars since the Second World War – including the wars in Vietnam and the surrounding regions of Indochina, the wars in Central and South America, and others – raise questions as to what degree the genocide documented by Kevin Annett against the indigenous peoples of Canada may be found to conform to patterns of genocide in Cambodia and Vietnam and Peru and Africa and China and Eastern Europe and regions formerly conquered by Russia or incorporated into the former Soviet Union, and many other parts of the world during the second half of the twentieth century.

As a former minister of the United Church of Canada – and one who has gone through the difficult ordeal of realizing that the literalist religion he once believed to be true may in fact be a creation of tyrants and deceivers during the first through fourth centuries AD – Kevin Annett does not miss the importance of the Christianity connection. In fact, he examines the issue in depth, and concludes that the Christian religion itself is inherently bloodthirsty, based on conquest and bloody sacrifice and equating both of those activities with salvation. In his book, he only goes back to Constantine, whom he believes to be responsible for the creation of the Christian religion, and appears to be as yet unaware of the thesis of Flavio Barbiero or the arguments discussed in this book. It is possible that, were he to examine this evidence, he might conclude that it is the rigid *literalist* interpretation that is the real root of the pathological behavior.

Kevin Annett insightfully connects the atrocities perpetrated in Canada against the native peoples to the Crusades, and notes that the same shared theological foundation can be seen to have animated both man-made catastrophes. In *Hidden No Longer*, he writes:

> Obviously, in a culture that makes ritual cleanliness and sacredness inseparable from ritual killing and sacrifice, *murder and divine action will also be indistinguishable*. And whatever is pure and innocent will be a candidate for extermination.

> The fact that Christianity created an enormous substitute sacrifice in the symbol of Jesus Christ did not diminish the power and hold of this concept of equating spiritual purification with killing. For, indeed, with the further substitution of the Catholic Church for Christ, and the equating of the one with the other, the practice of making oneself or one's people "holy" through the slaughter of others reached new heights.

> The most blatant example of this was expressed in the papal doctrine of "indulgence," which arose on the eve of the first Crusades in 1095. Pope Urban declared that any act of violence, murder or conquest committed by those in the service of "God" – that is, the church – restored the perpetrator to a state of

"original grace" and freed him of all of his sins. As in Hebrew beliefs, one was sanctified through the sacrificial killing of others.[709]

But, while agreeing wholeheartedly with Kevin Annett on a profound connection between the Crusades and the later slaughter of the peoples of the Americas -- including those of Central, South, and North America – we should ask if it is truly the presence of a "sacrificed god" (such as the crucified Christ represents) that is the culprit at the heart of the problem. In fact, as Alvin Boyd Kuhn and Gerald Massey and a host of others have amply demonstrated, the motif of the sacrificed god is recurrent throughout sacred traditions around the world. Dionysus was a sacrificed god, as was Osiris, as was Balder among the Norse myth-cycle, as well as the great god Odin, and we could continue into the sacred traditions of the Vedas and all the various shamanic traditions of Asia and even the Americas. There are even self-sacrificing gods among the Maya pantheon.

The fatal difference, I would argue, is in the *literalist* acceptance of the sacred scriptures. If one takes the stories of the Israelite conquests in the Old Testament as literal history, one is far more prone to see them as justification for current "holy wars" of conquest and extermination than would be the case if one realizes that they were always intended to describe the motions of the sun, moon and planets through the twelve "tribes" of zodiac stars, and to point to the esoteric truths which are contained therein. If one takes the New Testament gospel stories as literal truth (as ecclesiastical Christianity has forced its adherents to do for seventeen centuries, often enforced by the threat of imprisonment, torture, and death) then one is far more prone to follow demagogic calls to liberate the birthplace of Christ in a "Holy Crusade" than would be the case if one had been taught that the gospel stories are representative myths selected from a raft of esoteric texts which used the motions of the sun, moon, and planets among the twelve houses of the zodiac to teach profound truths about human existence in a "holographic" universe.

In other words, it was not simply the violence present in the Hebrew Old Testament or the Greek New Testament that led to the Crusades and the residential schools – there is plenty of violence among the Greek myths and the Egyptian myths and so on around the world. The difference appears to lie with the crucial point in history at which an aggressive military machine – the Roman Empire – swallowed up the Temple of Jerusalem, and in doing so ingested the unrepentant representatives of a line of successful manipulators of the sacred truths, men who knew how to use the weapons of consciousness and what we might call "anti-consciousness," men who made it their policy to keep the esoteric truths to themselves while stamping out the knowledge of the esoteric everywhere else and enforcing a rigid, barren, murderous literalism on everyone outside of their inner circles.

These families then worked to take over that mighty empire from the inside, beginning with the Praetorian Guard and the army, but also targeting the institutions in control of the critical nodes of its economic power. When they succeeded in at last securing the very head of the entire machine, they kept that control through the use of a hierarchical institution of literalist Christianity. With the engines of military might and economic wealth in their control, they could then use this vast machine to stamp out esotericism, beginning within the boundaries of empire itself, such as among the gnostics of Alexandria, and other places where "heretical" challenges to the literalist cult presented pockets of resistance to the literalist dogma.

Later, they stamped out the Druidic traditions of western Europe and the British Isles. Eventually, they would not even need the trappings of the empire, and cast it off, while retaining their ability to muster military armies to accomplish the long-standing goals of their ancient families (including the invasion of Jerusalem during the Crusades). These families appear to have been able to weather even the violent division of the western church during the protestant reformation. Some descendants of the ancient families, such as the royalty of England, and the kingdoms of Scandinavia, would become Protestant, and others would remain Catholic. Their willingness to use violence to further their ends does not seem to have suffered either way.

There is abundant evidence that possessors of the esoteric knowledge crossed the oceans to escape the rising ecclesiastical power of those very families, probably during the fourth century. The level to which they may have co-existed with the people who were already there is now almost impossible to say. Certainly there would have been examples of mutual co-operation, co-existence, and perhaps even intermarriage and eventual cultural intermingling. No doubt there were also examples of violent interchange. But there is no doubt that some religious contact took place, as evidenced by the survival of the holy name Taiowa among the Hopi and in the name of the state of Iowa to this day.[710]

When the avenging forces of the church arrived on the shores of the New World beginning in the 1500s, they may not necessarily have commenced killing the native peoples out of the delusion that these were all descendants of those who escaped their clutches in the early centuries of the Roman Empire. However, they certainly may have known that some did escape. It is undeniable that the peoples of the Americas were in possession of shamanic knowledge and aspects of the ancient traditions that the literalists wanted stamped out. The texts of the Maya and other great Mesoamerican civilizations may well have contained incontestable evidence pointing to the fact that the ancient sacred traditions were all very similar, and that the Old and New Testaments are of a piece with the ancient sacred traditions and like them are meant to be understood esoterically. Those texts would also (in all likelihood) have confirmed a connection between the traditions of ancient Egypt and other Mediterranean civilizations and the Mesoamericans. The oral traditions of the North American tribes, such as those of the Hopi, appear to confirm such a connection, as do some of the surviving stele and the one surviving Maya creation epic, the *Popol Vuh*.

The *Popol Vuh* is a Maya sacred text preserved through the efforts of a Dominican friar named Francisco Ximenez, a text he preserved by hand in a manuscript he wrote in 1701. It contains a creation account, a flood account, and the account of two Hero Twins named Hunahpu and Xbalanque.

The fact that much of the narrative of the *Popol Vuh* concerns two heroic twins who descend to the underworld as part of their adventures immediately brings to mind the epic of Gilgamesh (in which Gilgamesh and his "hairy twin" Enkidu also go on a series of adventures, including a trip to the underworld by Gilgamesh to try to rescue Enkidu), as well as the well-known myths of Castor and Pollux, the hero-twins of Greek and Roman mythology, in which Castor is human and Pollux divine, and immortal Pollux must go to the underworld to retrieve his mortal brother.

The fact that the Gilgamesh series also features a flood narrative, as does the *Popol Vuh*, is another important similarity.

Even more significant is the fact that, in the *Popol Vuh*, there is a deity named "Gucumatz" (as transcribed by Francisco Ximenez when he preserved the text).[711] While Gucumatz in the *Popol Vuh* is not one of the twins (he is one of the creator deities, and his name means Quetzal Serpent), the linguistic similarity to the name "Gilgamesh" is striking, and difficult to dismiss as a simple coincidence (especially given the other similarities in the content of the epics). Henriette Mertz calls attention to this similarity in *The Mystic Symbol*.[712]

Any student of the night sky, and of the work of Giorgio de Santillana and Hertha von Dechend, will be suspicious of the possibility that prominent mythological twins may have a celestial component, and it appears quite likely that the Hero Twins of the *Popol Vuh* represent the celestial twins of Gemini in some way.

For example, in the important stelae found at Izapa in modern-day Chiapas, Mexico, the Hero Twins are depicted in activities and orientations that strongly suggest a celestial component. In the stele shown below, Izapa Stele 25, scholars have asserted that the carvings represent the Hero Twins in the act of "shooting a perched demon bird with a blow-gun."

The presence of a bird on a stick next to a depiction of mythological twins is very significant: it should immediately call to mind the scene from the "Panel of the Wounded

Man" at the cave of Lascaux, in France. There, the "Wounded Man" may well represent the constellation Gemini in between Taurus (depicted as a charging bull in the cave-painting) and Leo (depicted as a wooly rhino, but with a tail hooked in a curve that strongly suggests the "coat-hanger" front stars of the zodiac constellation Leo).

There is a prominent bird on a stick depicted nearby in that panel in the caves of Lascaux. William Glyn-Jones, whose insightful analysis deciphered the similarity between the inclined "Wounded Man" and the constellation Gemini, as well as the similarity of the rhino tail to the front of Leo (and the similarity of the charging bull to Taurus, which is fairly obvious), has presented a compelling argument that the "Wounded Man" may well be associated with the ancient Indo-European myth of Yima, also known as Ymir, or Yama, who is associated with Saturn/Kronos in de Santillana's and von Dechend's *Hamlet's Mill*.[713] Glyn-jones also notes that there is a "bird-on-pole" image in the famous Dendera Zodiac, in this case a Horus-falcon perched on a vertical scepter. The connections between Egypt, Lascaux, and the Maya stelae at Izapa are remarkable and significant.

We have already seen that the Twins, like Saturn, are associated with a lost "Golden Age," the precessional age when Orion (also associated with Saturn, and with Osiris) who is quite close to the Twins in the sky, rose with the March equinoctial sunrise that signaled the rebirth of the year, the rebirth of the sun, and the rebirth of the human soul. The Age of Gemini was the age immediately prior to Age of Taurus. When the motion of precession "delayed" the heavens enough that Orion no longer rose in time for the March equinox, but the preceding zodiacal constellation of Taurus was there in his place, it was allegorized in the ancient myths of Egypt that Set (associated with the red star Aldebaran in Taurus) had "drowned" his brother Osiris (Orion, the rightful ruler).

We have seen how his same precessional usurpation is behind the legends of the castration (or "wounding") of Saturn/Kronos, as well as a host of other lame or wounded figures in ancient mythology (including Hephaestos in Greek myth, and Jacob-Israel in the Old Testament, who is wounded in the "hollow of his thigh" while wrestling with the angel of God at Peniel in Genesis 32:24-42, and who is of course a Hero Twin, along with his "hairy" brother Esau).

The obvious connections between the twin-legends across cultures – and across the oceans to the Maya – are clear evidence that the theory being presented here in this book (of an ancient unity of esoteric knowledge, overthrown by a violent usurping literalist contagion originating in Rome following the conquest of Jerusalem) is on the right track. Some of the details of the theory presented so far may later prove to be misinterpreted or misunderstood, but there seems to be enough evidence to say that the general outlines are painting a picture that is close to the truth.

Lest some argue that the correlation suggested between the Hero Twins of the Maya *Popol Vuh* with the bird-on-a-pole imagery found in the Old World caves of Lascaux is too much of a stretch, we can examine for further support the stele shown below, also from Izapa and known as Stele 2.

Here, scholars have identified the Hero Twins again, this time flanking a figure which is described as a "steeply descending bird impersonator." While that may be a literal enough description of the central figure in this stele, since it does clearly have human features such as human legs in addition to its bird-like wings, it may be a misnomer to call it "steeply descending." After all, it appears to be in a kneeling posture (albeit inverted on the stele).

In fact, the kneeling posture of the bird-man figure in this stele recalls quite strongly the image of Isis kneeling with outstretched bird-wings, found throughout ancient Egypt (such as the image from the tomb of Seti I depicted below). It should also be noted that this depiction of Isis bears a striking resemblance to the stars of the celestial Swan who flies "downward" in the Milky Way towards the horizon (for viewers in the northern hemisphere), the beautiful constellation Cygnus.

Isis, of course, disguised herself as a bird and flew around the tree in which Osiris was entombed after he was slain, an event with many echoes in other mythologies. Author Andrew Collins believes that Isis is closely associated with the constellation Cygnus, and explores the importance of Cygnus extensively in *The Cygnus Mystery: Unlocking the Ancient Secret of Life's Origin in the Cosmos*. In the heavens, Cygnus is flying in the Milky Way downwards towards another majestic bird, Aquila the Eagle, who is flying upwards in the Milky Way towards Cygnus. There are many echoes of these figures throughout mythology, such as in the swan-suits or swan wings found in various aspects of Norse mythology, including among the Valkyries and the hawk-suits and hawk wings used by Freya and her brother Frey, or the flight of Daedelus and his son Icarus using bird-like wings (a flight in which one of the two plunged to earth because he flew too high, just as the constellation of Cygnus which is "above" Aquila in the sky appears to be plummeting earthward).

If the above figure from the ancient Maya Stele 2, which is strongly reminiscent of the kneeling depiction of winged Isis in ancient Egyptian iconography, also represents the constellation Cygnus, then it could explain the reason that its head is pointing downward towards the tree (which could be a World-Tree like Yggdrasil of Norse mythology, which had an Eagle in it just as the Milky Way does). Note that the Twins are located at the far end of the Milky Way from the Eagle and the Swan, and that the Swan is flying away from the end of the Milky Way where the Twins are located.

All of this evidence is strong confirmation that the native peoples of the Americas were anciently visited by other ancient civilizations from across the oceans, and that there was cultural diffusion of many aspects of sacred iconography and (probably) esoteric meaning across the oceans as well.

The motive for destroying the evidence of this ancient esoteric knowledge, and for continuing to suppress and deny and deliberately misinterpret that evidence to this day, would seem to be strongest among those with a vested interest in the system built upon the literalist creed. It is their belief system that is most threatened by the evidence that all the sacred traditions (including those underlying the scriptures that they co-opted for their literalist system) shared a rich and profound esoteric ancient wisdom. Their system of religious mind control, while capable of taking on new forms over the centuries as exigencies demanded (morphing into protestantism when necessary, or downplaying some aspects of "literal" interpretation of the Bible, while still teaching doctrines based on a historical Jesus rather than a gnostic Christ-force in every man and woman), would be threatened by such a revelation. Their legitimacy would be even more threatened by the revelation that their policy over the years had included the deliberate destruction of textual and archaeological evidence, as well as the torture, enslavement, and murder of individuals and entire cultures, in order to maintain their system of mental and spiritual misdirection.

This chapter has touched on some of the evidence of a deliberate campaign of genocidal extermination that has gone on for centuries, and that stretches right up to this day. The last native residential schools in Canada did not close until 1995 – do we really believe that all those who implemented the horrendous policies documented by Kevin Annett and others, and which individuals at high levels of authority inside the government and the various churches involved continue to obfuscate and cover up, have now simply abandoned policies of this nature?

No.

The connection Kevin Annett demonstrates between the Crusades and the Canadian genocide is significant, in that it demonstrates that the policies of these families has not been derailed in all the centuries intervening. In fact, other cultures around the world which are heirs to the ancient esoteric traditions and which were not originally conquered by the Roman Empire, in places such as China or Vietnam or Tibet or India or Hawaii or New Zealand or Australia or Africa, can each provide examples stretching right up to the modern era of similarly genocidal policies implemented to stamp out old cultures and old religious traditions or shamanic practices, examples which are similarly horrific and which in every case can be demonstrated to contain a common denominator of manipulation by the European powers most closely associated with the ancient priestly family lines, family lines whose influence has clearly crossed the oceans and come to control the policies of both Canada and the United States as evidenced by the official policies of eugenics and genocide perpetrated by both governments in the past.

It is a war on the shamanic, on the esoteric, on the "holographic," and it is a war that has been raging – carried out by enemies of human consciousness – since at least the time of Josephus.

We will conclude with a final chapter examining the profound ramifications of this theory of human history, and exploring the possible reasons that this war has been able to have been waged for so long and with such devastating effect on the individual's quest to achieve consciousness and enlightenment.

21

Conclusion

Such a carrier and preserver of values was the Atmic spark, described by Heraclitus as "a portion of cosmic Fire, imprisoned in a body of earth and water." It was on earth to trace its line of progress through the ranges of the elements and the kingdoms, harvesting its varied experiences at the end of each cycle. It was described by Greek philosophy as "more ancient than the body," because it had run the cycle of incarnations in many bodies, donning and doffing them as garments of contact with lower worlds, so that it might treasure up the powers of all life garnered in experience in every form of it. The mutual relation of soul to body in each of its incarnate periods is the nub of the ancient philosophy, and the core of all Biblical meaning. As the Egyptian Book of the Dead most majestically phrases it, the soul, projecting itself into one physical embodiment after another, "steppeth onward through eternity."[714]

Mt. Olympus of the Greeks was identical with Mount Hetep of the Egyptians. Hence the Kimmerians of Homer may possibly be identified with the Egyptian Khemi, or Akhemu, the dwellers in the northern heaven, as never-setting stars or spirits of the glorified, the Khus or Khuti.[715]

Alvin Boyd Kuhn, *Lost Light.*

As we step back and survey the full sweep of the ground we have covered, the view is somewhat breathtaking.

We have seen evidence that the ancients appear to have envisioned the cosmos as being holographic in nature, with our familiar "material" universe corresponding to the holographic projection, and the "other world" (the spiritual realm, the Duat, the seed world, the realm of the gods) corresponding to the holographic medium.

Additionally, their art and monuments demonstrate an awareness that this seemingly material realm is made up of waves of energy, "petrified" into materiality (a message that may be incorporated into the design of Stonehenge, as well as into the iconography of the Gorgons – who petrify men into stone with their gaze – and in other cymatic-like art including the "Green Man" images). In a sense, this demonstrates their knowledge that what *appears* to be static and solid is actually only static and solid in an illusory sense.

This awareness, then, appears to be integral to their apparent ability to transcend the static – to journey to the "other world" – through techniques of ecstasy (*ex stasis*). We have seen evidence that ancient sacred scriptures and traditions appear to demonstrate knowledge of the ability to transcend the boundary between these two realms.

This knowledge may be evident in the Pyramid Texts – among the oldest extant texts in human history. It is also evident in aspects of the mysteries, which flourished in the ancient world all the way up until the advent of literalist Christianity. The techniques of ecstasy appear to have survived in shamanism, which continued into the modern era in parts of the world that were outside the boundaries of the western Roman Empire (which later became western Europe).

We examined evidence that the sacred scriptures of the world communicate this "shamanic" or "holographic" worldview, and that they are united in communicating their message esoterically – that is, they do it through symbology and metaphors which appeal directly to the intuition, rather than trying to convey these truths through the "discriminating" or "logical" left brain, which is inherently unable to grasp such concepts.

This esoteric and shamanic-holographic message was embodied in the mythos of ancient Egypt, ancient Greece, and numerous other sacred traditions the world over – so widely spread and so consistently similar that they appear to be the legacy of some now-forgotten extremely ancient and extremely sophisticated civilization or people. These traditions were not intended to be taken literally – but the fact that they were not literal does not imply that they were not conveying *the truth*. It is quite possible that the ancients believed they were conveying profound truth, without demanding that the stories themselves be taken as literal (if miraculous) history. Similarly, the personalities in those stories – the gods and demons and monsters and heroes – may have represented very real powers, principles, and aspects of the universe and of the human condition, without being mistaken for literal beings whom one could physically meet, if only they had the right kind of "faith."

In fact, we saw that the ancient scriptures that have been twisted into modern literalist dogma by ecclesiastical Christianity over the past seventeen centuries quite clearly fall into the same category, and have everything in common with the other ancient esoteric traditions of the world. Like the others, they are composed of sophisticated astro-theological metaphors, with clear parallels between the stories of the Old Testament tribes of Israel or the New Testament accounts of Jesus and his twelve apostles and the motions of the sun, moon, and planets through the twelve houses of the zodiac.

Some may object that even if the evidence that the Old and New Testament scriptures were not intended to be taken literally, the fact that so many now do take them literally, and find so much comfort and meaning from the literalist interpretation, argues that they should not be disabused of the literalist interpretation that they have been taught. This argument seems to have some merit on its surface, but upon closer examination can be shown to have tremendous moral problems. First, it argues that teaching something we know to be a lie is better than teaching what we believe to be the truth. Those who came to believe the literal interpretation were presumably taught it either as children, before they were old enough to know better and (wrongly) trusting those who were teaching it to them to tell the truth, or they came to belief in these literal misinterpretations as adults, when they were genuinely seeking for answers and were given a substitute in place of the real thing.

It may be one thing to teach a simpler version to the very young in the understanding that when they are old enough (certainly by the age of twelve or thirteen, at which age in ancient times and in traditional cultures children were typically initiated into adulthood), they will be allowed to wrestle with the full truth, but clearly that is not the methodology that has been in place these past nearly seventeen centuries. Perhaps in some inner circles it is done, but for the most part, those seeking knowledge are intentionally being given a falsehood instead. This creates a situation in which some are judged worthy to be told the truth, while others are condemned (perhaps "for their own good," in someone's opinion) to be given an illusion which they are expected to live with for life.

Who presumes to decide who will be taught the truth and who will be given a known deception? Such a question exposes the inescapable fact that maintaining the position that some people should just be given a literalist deception because "they can't handle the truth" creates two classes of people, and is inherently elitist. It leads to the repulsive belief that some human beings have more worth than others. It can be argued that such a mindset can lead to the medieval belief that some men and women are born to be nobles and others born to be serfs, or to the Nazi belief that some men and women can be imprisoned, tortured, experimented upon, and executed with impunity, because some human beings have more worth than others. It can in fact be argued that the evidence of history shows that the literalist church was connected to both of those institutions, as well as to the massacre of Native Americans in North, Central and South America in massive numbers, which are also manifestations of the same repulsive mindset that some human lives have more worth than others.

On the other hand, the alternative perspective on the ancient shared wisdom of mankind – with the scriptures of the Bible taking their place alongside all the other sacred texts and traditions of the world – has incredibly liberating potential. It frees us from many of the most oppressive aspects of the literalist paradigm that have dominated "the west" for so long – from the fear of a literal hell and a literal devil, and from the ultimatum of placing faith in a literal Jesus or suffering eternal damnation (along with the teaching that any now-deceased relatives who did not respond rightly to that same ultimatum are now suffering eternal hellfire). This threat of damnation can now be seen to be based upon a literalist misinterpretation of the lower half of the zodiac wheel, which in turn conveys the exalted esoteric truth that like the sun, moon, planets and stars of the zodiac, we incarnate souls have come down to the "underworld" below the horizon, for a very real purpose, but we are destined to return again to the spiritual realm whose reality we are prone to forget in our amnesiac state.

The threat of damnation has been wielded mercilessly against individuals and entire cultures, as a form of mind control to coerce them into compliance with ecclesiastical "authorities," whose authority is itself based upon an historical deception. Can we justify the continuation of such mental violence based upon the argument that some people now find it (and the rest of the literalist misinterpretation that surrounds it) to be comforting? Such an argument is akin to saying that hostages suffering from the "Stockholm syndrome" should not be told how to escape from their captors, because they are obviously happier in captivity than they would be in freedom.

If we know of a door that leads out of the literalist prison, we should show it to those trapped inside, even if they choose not to open it (that choice, of course, must be up to them). But to say, "Let's not tell them of the existence of that door – it might upset them" is really no form of compassion at all.

And, as even St. Augustine the early literalist champion and bishop of the church (who nevertheless had been heavily steeped in Platonism in his early adulthood and still carried much of Platonism's philosophy into his Christian arguments) argued in *City of God*, Book XI and Chapter 27: "If proof be needed how much human nature loves to know and hates to be mistaken, recall that there is not a man who would not rather be sad but sane than glad but mad."[716]

But to know the truth – or at least to continue to pursue it as best we can – is in fact incredibly liberating. It is, in fact, arguably one of the primary things we are designed to do in this world. It also opens to us incredible new possibilities, through the exploration of the techniques of ecstasy, which themselves may in part account for the advanced technologies apparently possessed by the ancients, whose knowledge of plant medicine, megalithic engineering, even perhaps levitation and travel along the earth-energy "ley lines" of our terrestrial globe, seem to defy explanation via the methodologies with which we make technological advances today.

For these reasons, the argument that we should – out of some kind of sentimental affection for the cultural accretions of seventeen centuries of misguided literalism – suppress what anyone can see to be the clear allegorical nature of the ancient scriptures simply cannot be accepted. The comfort and beauty and goodness that millions *have* undeniably found in the literalist paradigm, and any good that has in fact come from its tenets, only go to prove the unbelievable power and beneficence of the authentic article, if even its *counterfeit* can command such a response. But to paternalistically decide who is allowed to be shown the real meaning behind the ingenious ancient system of metaphor, and who is not worthy to have their questions about the nature of their own human existence answered honestly, is the worst kind of elitism.

Such elitism, we have seen, was clearly at work during the Crusades, and such elitism was behind the atrocities of the eugenicists and exterminators of the Third Reich. It is long past time to reject such elitism, and to pull down the veil of pious legitimacy with which it cloaks its evil deeds, and expose its hideous countenance for all to see. Such elitist thinking ultimately leads to the belief that some men and women can treat other men and women as insects, to be swept aside or killed whenever convenient or "necessary." It is a denial of the inner divinity and thus infinite worth of every human being – can it be a mere coincidence that the stamping out of the esoteric teachings of the ancient scriptures was an identical rejection of their teaching of the same inner divinity in each man and woman, which we forget upon each successive incarnation in this material realm? Is it not evident from the record of history that those who have perpetrated this suppression of the ancient teaching these past seventeen centuries are the same ones who propagate the elitist lie and who have unblinkingly ordered the slaughter of millions of innocents, and who have employed lies and mind control to keep the "uninitiated" in ignorance and even in slavery and conditions of degradation?

Can anyone deny that such a mindset lies behind the decades of abuse documented by Kevin Annett and the survivors of the residential schools in Canada? Can anyone deny that such a mindset lies behind the massive spraying of chemicals from jets over populated areas for "geoengineering" or some other unannounced and undebated purpose? Can anyone deny that such a mindset lies behind staged terror events to manipulate the populace into accepting greater restrictions of their natural-law freedoms at home, and accepting murderous wars abroad? Can anyone deny that such a mindset lies behind the decisions of those who unilaterally choose to introduce fluoride into the public water supply, which millions use for drinking, cooking, and bathing, and watering their gardens or their sprouts? Can anyone deny that such a mindset lies behind the laws prohibiting the growing of, possession of, or use of various plants and mushrooms, for peaceful use of whatever kind, but especially for medicinal use in the case of the new aggressive bans on the use or possession of traditional herbs and plants being enacted in many parts of Europe? Can anyone deny that such a mindset lies behind the massive introduction of genetically modified food-crops into the food chain, and the suppression of studies raising questions about the safety of such genetic material or the possibility that such foods and the genetic "triggers" engineered into those foods could wreak havoc on the symbiotic bacteria inside the human organism, or even upon the genetic material of the man, woman, or child who eats that food? All of these crimes – and they are crimes – share a common element of elitist thinking by those who have implemented them and those who defend them. All of them, and many more like them, demonstrate the moral bankruptcy of the elitist position. Each of them, by itself, should be enough to cause men and women to wake up and reject the elitist fallacy. Taken together, they demonstrate that the hour is very late, and the urgency of the need for each of us to cast aside, like Theoden in the *Lord of the Rings*, the spells and illusions of the Sarumans and the Wormtongues, is very dire.

It really is no act of hyperbole to cast the struggle in such epic terms. The battle against consciousness is very real, and the battle has gone quite well for the enemies of consciousness for at least seventeen hundred years. We have already seen compelling evidence which suggests that the ancient shared esoteric wisdom of mankind was deliberately targeted by a malevolent force, one which we can trace back at least as far as the arrival of Josephus and a handful of ancient priestly families from the land of Judea, after the conquest of Jerusalem by the Roman generals Vespasian and Titus (who later became emperors). While the struggle to suppress the ancient wisdom may stretch back further into antiquity than that event, it is evident that after the arrival of Josephus and his cohorts in Rome, the last open vestiges of the ancient wisdom began to disappear in the part of the world that would come to be known as "the west" – a part of the world whose representatives to this day appear to be engaged in the destruction of the vestiges of the ancient wisdom wherever they can be found.

We have seen evidence suggesting that the esoteric, gnostic teachings embodied in the early letters of Paul may well have had their roots in esoteric Egyptian teachings dating to thousands of years before the life of Paul and his contemporary Josephus, and that the priestly families (who were probably descendants of Egyptians in the land of Judea, which had always been an on-again, off-again possession of Egypt, and whose Old Testament scriptures probably came right out of Egypt) decided to "contain" the doctrines Paul and the gnostics were teaching by putting a literalist spin on them and turning the esoteric truths of the Christ into a historical account of a literal son of God, replacing the gnostic message of the divinity in every incarnated soul (what Paul called "the Christ in you") with the new literalist message that deity was restricted to the literal Jesus who came, and who was divine on their behalf.

These priestly families apparently used a two-pronged method of gaining control over the empire, using the more secretive, more exclusive, and more esoteric cadre of the men invited into the Sol Invictus cult to guide policy, while at the same time influencing the masses in the more inclusive, more open, and more literalistic religion of Christianity. Due to events that came to a head during the tumultuous period immediately preceding the triumph of Constantine, this policy was later jettisoned and Christianity became the primary tool for exercising control over the institutions of empire. The Sol Invictus cult withered away in the decades that followed, lingering on longer in some parts of the empire than others, but many of its traditions and teachings continued in the secret societies that became Freemasonry.

Finally, we saw evidence that these families ultimately gained control of Europe, and with their power secure began to launch campaigns to stamp out the ancient traditions around the world, beginning within western Europe but continuing through the centuries to include the Americas – a campaign that appears to have continued right up to the present day. It must rank as one of the largest and most destructive deceptions in human history.

The idea that such a "conspiracy" could have gone on for so long gives one pause. It is almost incredible. How could this campaign to promote "literalism" and suppress "esotericism" be so long-lived? Can we really imagine family lines, even if they are incredibly tightly-run and motivated by the desire to preserve their positions of privilege and power, that can carry on such a deception for going on seventeen hundred years? We can all probably think of specific wealthy families in the modern period, perhaps families where an extraordinary businessman built a strong business during his life, in which the children or (at the latest) the grandchildren eventually lost interest in the business, and let all that the founder of the family's wealth had built eventually crumble. How can we envision families who are able to preserve their vision for seventeen centuries, through vast changes in culture, even changes in language, and economics, and political landscape? It seems absurd.

Furthermore, we must ask, what could possibly be so important about the somewhat arcane distinction between esotericism and literalism? Why would these families, and the institutions they built, pledge themselves to keep the esoteric secrets to themselves, and foist literalism on others – going to such lengths as to track down and exterminate those who tried to smuggle esoteric beliefs across the oceans to the New World, going to such lengths that the esoteric communities of Egypt felt they needed to bury their esoteric texts in sealed pots at the foot of mountain cliffs in order to save them for posterity?

To ask such a question is to suggest the answer. There must be something incredibly important about the topic we are discussing, about the knowledge of the "holographic universe" and the true interpretation of the ancient scriptures of mankind. For, as difficult to believe as it may seem, the evidence suggests that the above description is exactly what *did* happen in the centuries since Josephus and his peers arrived in Rome.

If so, then the campaign to impose literalism and stamp out esotericism must somehow be incredibly important *in reality* (or at least, be perceived to be incredibly important to those involved in the campaign). From our vantage point at the end of all the discussion that has taken place so far, we can begin to see why that might be. If the universe is, in fact, holographic in nature, composed of an implicate (hidden) order and an explicate (evident) order, then there *really is*, in some sense, a hidden pattern or "holographic medium" which contains the "seed" form of everything that works itself out in the material realm with which we are most familiar and in which we perceive ourselves to dwell.

If so, then everything in this material realm is really a manifestation of an idea, a Platonic *form*, a datum in the underlying implicate order. In that sense, then, the material world and its contents are, in fashion, *symbols* for the deeper truths or *types* that they are manifesting in this plane of existence, in exactly the same way that the Egyptian *neters* (gods and goddesses) such as Osiris or Horus or Isis were themselves symbolic embodiments and expressions of the very real principles and truths which they stood for (truths as real as the latent power that sleeps in the seed, entombed in the earth like Osiris, or the rejuvenating power that awakens inside the seed to force its root to shoot down deep into the earth and its first sprout to push upward through the soil to burst into the sunlit day, like Horus-of-the-two-horizons, soaring upward into the blazing sky).

In other words, this material realm is a form of "thinging" (in the expression of Gerald Massey) the deeper truths and patterns of the implicate realm.[717] And, because they are intimately connected (connected so intimately that human consciousness can actually cross the boundary between the "realms," the way the ancient pharaohs and modern-era shamans could apparently do, because the two realms are not actually separate at all), changes made in one side of the implicate/explicate orders can impact reality in the other.

Again, we find that the observations of modern quantum physics appear to support this conclusion in every way. In the foundational experiments of quantum theory, particles are seen to enter a state of "superposition," in which a particle is actually in some sense existing in the world of *pure potentiality*: it is neither in one state nor the other (wave or particle), neither in one box or the other in two box-pairs, but simultaneously in *both* states or both boxes *at the same time*. Such particles are, in a very real sense, in the implicate realm and not in our material realm . . . until a consciousness intervenes, and then they manifest in the explicate realm in *either* the form of a wave or a particle, in *either* one box or the other but not both. In some way which physicists still do not fully comprehend (and which our discriminating, dividing, distinguishing, logical left-brain thinking cannot possibly grasp), the particle crosses from the hidden realm of potentiality to the manifest realm of materiality when consciousness enters the picture. Thus, in some way, consciousness itself is the bridge between the implicate and the explicate orders.

If this is the case, then knowledge of the existence of the implicate order, and the ability of one realm to influence the other, might be an extremely powerful piece of knowledge indeed, and keeping it from others might be seen as a critical advantage to those who had the secret and wanted to use it to their advantage at the expense of those who did not.

The ancient esoteric wisdom quite clearly taught that what goes on "here below" reflects what takes place in the "heavenly realms." Just as each individual man or woman was an embodiment of the endless cosmos, a microcosm reflecting the zodiac signs from head to toe, and containing an infinity within the vaulted dome of his or her own skull, the ancient builders appeared to have patterned the very landscape after the heavenly pattern, making Egypt's Nile into a reflection of the celestial band of the Milky Way, and placing monuments along its either side to reflect the constellations (including Orion, as Robert Bauval and Graham Hancock have famously argued since the early 1990s). Why would they go to such trouble, if not because they believed that what they did here in the material realm had an impact there in the heavenly realm as well – on the other side of the illusory boundary between the explicate and the implicate order!

In this explanation, we possibly perceive the answer to the troubling question of why the powers that be seem to be happy to promote the modern secular Darwinian materialistic paradigm in their universities, when for so many centuries they appeared to offer only belief-systems based on a historical-literal Biblical understanding (even if not always so literal as some of the protestant fundamentalists whose extremely strict literalism arose partly in response to the pressures of the Darwinian paradigm's ascendency in the second half of the nineteenth century). The answer may lie in the fact that both systems, the modern aggressive form of materialism and the literalist anti-gnostic interpretation of Christianity that is based on a personal Jesus, both point their followers away from the existence of a holographic-shamanic universe, and away from the teaching that men and women have divinity within themselves. Neither the follower of anti-gnostic, anti-esoteric Christianity nor the die-hard materialist is likely to discover the secret of the existence of the implicate realm, or delve into the shamanic consciousness that enables one to bridge the two realms, and the truth that changes in one realm influence the other, since both realms are really connected.

By denying the existence or at least the importance of the Duat-realm, these teachers of falsehood are denying the common heritage of humanity. We have already very briefly touched upon the possibility that we see into the world of potentiality when we go into a dream-state, something we do every time we sleep, usually once for every complete turn of the earth on its axis.

That the dream-state is related to the implicate realm, the seed world, is indicated by the many instances in ancient sacred writings where human characters are visited by gods in their dreams, or are otherwise given important messages while in a dream-state, messages which help them to bring something important to pass here in the material world. Greek myth is replete with such examples, as is Norse myth, and ancient Egyptian myth, and of course so is the Bible as well. Such instances represent the movement of the "seed" idea from the realm of potentiality across the boundary of consciousness into the realm of manifestation or materiality.

They can be seen as a working-out on a human scale of the same principle that we see at work on the sub-atomic level in quantum experiments. The idea which comes across in the dream is moving out of the world of pure potentiality, and when the person acts on that idea and brings it to pass, it crosses into the world of actuality. In the dream-world, it can be said to be in "super-position," neither in one state or the other, just as a quantum can be in super-position prior to being encountered by a consciousness. When it crosses from the world of the unconscious to the conscious, the particle manifests in a single state (as a particle or a wave, or in this box or that box of a specific box-pair). It has gone from a condition of *ex stasis* to a single state. Thus particles in superposition are in a state of ecstasy! When they come into contact with consciousness, they leave that condition and manifest in a state (they become more "static" and can be found in this box or that box, or described as a wave or a particle). Similarly, the dream crosses into actuality through the door of consciousness. It moves from the unconscious into the conscious, through the door of the dream-state. It is also highly significant that the word that the Australian aboriginal people use to describe the "other world," the world of the implicate order, is "Dreamtime."

We have also seen that out-of-body experiences and near-death experiences share characteristics with the journeys described by shamans the world over. They often involve a "tunnel" and the experience of floating or flying, as well as the experience of feeling the consciousness depart from the body and travel on its own in a disembodied (we might say an "ex-static") condition. Like the dream-state which we visit every night, OBEs and NDEs almost certainly represent a crossing-over of the consciousness into the world of the implicate order. These experiences, in fact, appear to be more common than we are generally led to believe.

If shamanic travel to this other realm was used by the ancients to seek out knowledge that could not be learned by any other method, then shutting the door on the other realm (or hiding the door, while denying or obscuring the existence and importance of that other realm) becomes a deeply misanthropic act. Jeremy Naydler has shown evidence that the secret rites of the pharaohs inside their pyramid chambers involved a journey to the other realm that, it was believed, would provide renewal and regeneration to the entire kingdom. If so, then the loss of this ancient knowledge, which was described in all the ancient sacred texts of humanity, and the substitution of a literalistic and anti-esoteric religion in its place represents a coup of catastrophic proportions.

We have also seen evidence that the perpetrators of this coup used their power to systematically destroy the cultures who retained this ancient heritage. The deliberate massacre of North American Indian peoples, whose culture was at one time deeply shamanic, may be one of the most recent and most obvious examples of this hideous centuries-long process, along with perhaps the genocidal wars of the twentieth century.

The fact that the atrocities documented by Kevin Annett and by survivors of that genocide continued right up into the final decades of the twentieth century indicates that the legacy of the priestly family lines who had seized control of the entire Roman Empire by the close of the fourth century is alive and well today, and entrenched in positions of tremendous political power. The evidence presented by Annett and the survivors who describe medical experimentation before and after World War II by German doctors, and deliberate sterilization of children by surgical operations or by exposure to X-rays (which survivors describe as taking place into the 1980s), suggests a chilling connection between the perpetrators of the Canadian residential-school atrocities and the perpetrators of similar horrific acts during the Second World War in Europe.

This evidence suggests some kind of a trans-national conspiracy, one which moves fluidly across boundaries and even between states that were ostensibly fighting on opposite sides during major wars. And yet such a trans-national character is exactly in keeping with the historical evidence provided by Flavio Barbiero going all the way back to the earliest institution of the Sol Invictus cult. He has provided extensive evidence that the Sol Invictus society acted as a "shadow government," a power behind the throne, controlled at the top by men who were carefully selected for their ability, and always selected because of their membership in the proper families. We saw that during the reign of Charlemagne, nobles were given control of fiefdoms across Europe without regard to their region of origin, but rather based upon their family credentials. This means that these families operated as a trans-national entity, with loyalty to their own blood rather than loyalty to the people of the country in which they ruled. This trans-national character parallels the situation that Kevin Annett's investigations have brought to light, in which German doctors under the umbrella of "the church" moved freely between Germany and Canada to perform their dark experiments and crimes.

Flavio Barbiero has provided evidence that even after the specific aspects of the Sol Invictus symbology disappeared, Freemasonry served a similar function, by inculcating the goals and traditions of the noble equestrian class (descended from the priestly lines) among the male descendants of those families who by the Middle Ages had been ensconced in positions of power across western Europe. Barbiero shows that Charlemagne, very likely a descendent of those families based on his descent from kings who took the moniker "Martel" or "the Hammer," is credited with the establishment of Freemasonry in Europe by the Cooke Manuscript, an important Masonic document which was probably written between 1410 and 1440, and even then was probably transcribed from a much older document.[718]

Barbiero also points to the fact that "every year, at the beginning of the summer, Charlemagne convened a general meeting of his great nobles, ecclesiastics, military chiefs, and functionaries (a few hundred people, all belonging to families of priestly origin) to discuss matters of state."[719] This trans-national gathering (attendance at which was determined by membership in the right family lines) clearly shows the modus operandi of these families, and their trans-national character. There is evidence that similar trans-national gatherings take place every year to the present day.

Again, we must return to the question of how and why this conspiracy against humanity has gone on for so many centuries, and how its perpetrators have been able to maintain their malevolent vision through so many generations (keeping the true meaning of the scriptures hidden from humanity, teaching a false literal interpretation to those seeking enlightenment, exterminating native peoples and those with shamanic traditions, launching family wars of conquest such as the Crusades, and inflicting deliberate physical suffering through horrific medical experiments and the deliberate introduction of infectious diseases). All these actions justify the term "malevolent" to describe their overarching vision.

First, we can speculate that the incentive of retaining power and wealth would provide strong motivation for each older generation to transmit the family secrets to the next generation. If Freemasonry was originally used to initiate the younger generation into the secrets of the family (using a hierarchical structure, so that the most promising could be successively taught more information while the less promising could be left at lower levels of insight), that would be a powerful method of perpetuating the identity and goals of the group. Also, we can surmise that the sheer instinct of self-preservation would dictate that the families might fight within themselves for supremacy from time to time, but that they would instinctively unite when faced with a challenge from outside.

However, as powerful as these mechanisms might be for preserving the vision of the family lines through the centuries, the sheer enormity of the number of centuries involved suggests that something even more powerful is at work. Another possibility is that the knowledge of the ability to enter the implicate realm, and of the value of doing so, has enabled those at the top of the proposed trans-national conspiracy to gain greater insight into the political moves that needed to be taken down through the centuries. Access to what we might call "supernatural" or at least "super-material" guidance might help to explain the longevity of the conspiracy, far beyond the number of years that even the most successful of human institutions generally can achieve through what we might characterize as "naturalistic" methods.

Finally, and this suggestion will no doubt be even more controversial than the assertions that have been made thus far, this last point also brings up the possibility of some kind of co-operation from entities that exist in the non-material realm – that is to say, there might be some kind of "demonic element" at work that would help to explain the remarkable continuity of purpose over the course of seventeen centuries. Whether we label these entities by the term "demon" or by some other appellation, the possibility it seems must at least be entertained that non-material entities are directing some of the actions that we see documented in the historical record.

What other word than "demonic" is more appropriate to describe the turning of X-ray machines onto the pelvic regions of young Indian boys and girls in the native schools, in order to deliberately sterilize them? What other word is appropriate to describe the repeated rape of children? What other word is appropriate to describe the atrocities of the Nazis? What other word is appropriate to describe the actions of the conquistadors upon their arrival in the land of the Maya or the Inca?

Alvin Boyd Kuhn demonstrates that the suggestion of the existence of malevolent spiritual entities is present in the ancient mythologies which suggest that souls come down and incarnate in this material realm in order *to hide* – from whom or from what is not exactly clear. In *Lost Light*, Kuhn explores this idea:

> If the descent was in partial degree a karmic punishment for sin, an enforced expiation of evolutionary dereliction in past cycles, as is hinted in Greek philosophy, it was also pictured as a seeking of refuge or a hiding for safety. Some contingency or crisis in celestial affairs, not fully divulged, made it both obligatory and advantageous for the angel hosts to flee heaven and find on earth, or in "Egypt," an escape from danger involved in some evolutionary impasse. It is not customary to think of hell as a haven, but certain implications in the old theology require us to do just that. At all events the legend of the hiding away of the young divine heroes is too general to be without deep significance. [. . .] The child Jesus had to be hidden away from danger in "Egypt"! The Old Testament Joseph went down to "Egypt" to be saved from danger. Jotham preserved his life from his murderous brother Abimelech by hiding. Saul was found in hiding among the baggage when he was chosen to be king in Israel. In Egypt, Bulo, the nurse, concealed Horus, the analogue of Jesus, in Sekhem, "the hidden shrine and shut place," – our earth. Horus' birth was in a secret place. A similar legend is related of the mythical Sargon in the cuneiform tablets. He says: "My mother, the Princess, conceived me; in a secret place she brought me forth." The supreme Egyptian sun-god, the mighty spiritual divinity Ra, says to the earth: "I have hidden you." He says that in the "Egypt" of this lower world he had prepared a secret and mysterious dwelling for his children. This divine dwelling created by Ra as the place of protection for the elect, is called "the Retreat."[720]

If souls in this world are in some way (which is not entirely clear) hiding from something in the other world, then this situation might explain the sustained campaign described in the foregoing chapter, and the eagerness of some entities to keep the true situation from being widely known by the children of men. If those who are bent on keeping the secrets of the ancient wisdom to themselves, and giving to the rest of us a counterfeit literalism in its place, are in fact in contact with malevolent entities in another dimension of reality, then the malevolence of those entities might explain the pattern we find of deliberate inflicting of suffering (documented by the survivors of the residential schools, for example, who underwent repeated rape as children, or who saw the deliberate introduction of infectious diseases which kill slowly accompanied by great bodily suffering).

It is a fact that in Tibetan, Chinese, Thai, Burmese, Indian and Japanese traditional religions, entities described as "hungry ghosts" exist, spirits which are afflicted with insatiable hunger. They are sometimes given food-offerings – suggesting that they can somehow feed off of things here in the material realm, although those traditions are fairly unanimous in stating that the ghosts are never satisfied, and that nothing they can take in can assuage their enormous appetites.

Normally invisible to the human eye, these hungry ghosts can sometimes be seen by the living when a man or woman enters into altered states of consciousness. This suggests that these traditions are indicating that those who can see across the boundary to the other realm can perceive these entities, and perhaps communicate with them.

Is it possible that the deliberate, centuries-long campaign to keep human beings in ignorance about the ancient wisdom is somehow directed (or at least partially influenced) by beings that possess a hatred towards the souls who have come here to this material realm for refuge? Is it possible that the almost unspeakable atrocities carried out against men and women – and, worse, against children – down through the ages (including in the massacres of the Mesoamericans described in the accounts of Diego de Landa, among others) create an energy of suffering that malevolent beings somehow crave for their insatiable appetites?

These possibilities, while horrible to contemplate, demand further investigation, in light of the historical evidence.

What *is* certain is that, if the hidden realm and the material realm are intimately connected, and if what goes on in one can profoundly influence realities in the other, then we need to wake up to that fact, despite the concerted efforts of those who would keep us asleep. If this world is a symbolic manifestation of ideas and forms found in the seed-world, then perhaps our actions here can have karmic impact there. Conversely, perhaps it will take re-learning the techniques of ecstasy which have been deliberately stamped out, so that individuals can undertake shamanic journeys to address aspects of the "holographic film" that are causing problems here in the world of the "holographic projection."

At the very least, the information discussed in this book should cause us to reassess the sacred traditions of all humanity, from the Vedas to the Egyptian Book of the Dead, from the Tao Teh Ching to the gnostic gospels, from the Gilgamesh series to the Popol Vuh, from the legends of the peoples of the Pacific islands to the traditions of the Native American tribes and nations, from the Greek myths to those of the Australian aboriginal peoples, from the Norse myths to the stories passed down among the shamanic peoples of Asia, and on and on, up through those texts which were selected for inclusion in the Old and New Testaments. Far from being the primitive accretions of unscientific attempts to explain the natural phenomena, as we have been generally taught to believe, these sacred traditions all contain sophisticated truths about our holographic universe, and our place in it as we traverse this material part of our existence.

Conclusion

The information discussed here should also help to awaken us to the spiritual war that appears to be going on all around us, and which the evidence suggests has been raging down through the millennia: a battle between the forces of consciousness and anti-consciousness, between those who desire to inform us of the true nature of things (among whom we must include those who gave us all these scriptures in the first place) and those who desire to deny this knowledge to mankind and keep men and women in ignorance of their true inheritance.

Finally, these revelations should spur us to action, to stand for truth and against falsehood, and to do whatever we can, with the talents we have been given and the position in which we have been placed by circumstance or by training or by life experience, to expose and to thwart those whose goal it is to deliberately cause human suffering, and to seek ways of bringing them to justice where murder and other crimes can be proven. We must wake up to the fact that the atrocities committed against entire peoples are not just events of past history, safely removed from us by the intervening buffer of decades or centuries. We should now be aware that malevolent acts against children and adults are being carried out under the protective aegis of the very institutions which many turn to for protection and aid – including the institutions of federal governments and trans-national churches, even in "civilized" countries which are seemingly at peace and not undergoing any sort of violent revolution or civil war. The common duty of natural law, which compels us to protect ourselves from physical violence but also to protect our neighbor if he or she is threatened with physical violence, demands that we become aware of such atrocities taking place around us and take action to stop them, as well as that we take up the cause of those who have already suffered such atrocities (such as the victims of the residential schools) and demand that the crimes they have suffered be atoned for by the perpetrators.

Far from making us feel helpless, however, the subjects addressed in this book should give us hope: hope that we as human beings are far more than we have been taught to believe by the purveyors of materialistic secularism or by the purveyors of a dead literalism. We are in fact incarnations of a divine and immortal fire temporarily encased in a body of earth and water, possessors of a Christ element, of a Horus principle which – although entombed in the underworld material realm of Osiris, like the sun on its dark night journey after dropping below the western horizon to toil its way back to the east – will one day burst forth on the eastern horizon to sail upwards like a fiery falcon, freed again of the mirey clay.

And, even while we are here in this material life, we have access to the world of pure potentiality – the realm of the Duat, the realm of the shamanic, the realm of the implicate order – and we can access this realm through the gateway of our consciousness, just as the quantum experiments of modern physics confirm. The texts bequeathed to us by our ancient ancestors tell us that we can dream we can make into reality. We can in fact be co-creators of this cosmos even while we are here in this incarnation, for we are each one of us a microcosm of that cosmos, and reflect and contain the entire infinity of the macrocosm within our human frame.

Armed with such knowledge, we are each one of us more than a match for all those who have chosen to pursue deeds of darkness, and to peddle lies when they could be serving the truth.

THE END

End Notes

1. Massey, Gerald. *Man in search of his soul during fifty thousand years, and how he found it!* <www.gerald-massey.org.uk/massey/dpr_08_man_in_search.htm> Accessed 01/26/2014.

2. Kuhn, Alvin Boyd. *Who is this King of Glory? A Critical Study of the Christos-Messiah Tradition.* <www.scribd.cm/mobile/doc/27243209> Accessed 01/26/2014. Page 29 in the original pagination as noted in the online edition.

3. Massey, Gerald. *The Natural Genesis: or Second Part of a Book of the Beginnings, Containing an Attempt to Recover and Reconstitute the Lost Origins of the Myths and Mysteries, Types and Symbols, Religion and Language, with Egypt for the Mouthpiece and Africa as the Birthplace.* 1887. <www.masseiana.org/ngbk0.htm> Accessed 01/26/2014. Page 14 in the original pagination as noted in the online edition.

4. Aristotle. *Metaphysics.* Book XII, part 8. Translation by W. D. Ross. <http://classics.mit.edu/Aristotle/metaphysics.12.xii.html> accessed 01/24/2014.

5. De Santillana, Giorgio and Hertha von Dechend. *Hamlet's Mill: An Essay on Myth and the Frame of Time.* Boston: Godine, 1977. Page 4.

6. *Hamlet's Mill,* 177.

7. Odyssey, Homer. VIII. 301-328.

8. *Hamlet's Mill,* 165.

9. *Hamlet's Mill,* 166.

10. *Ibid.*

11. *Ibid.*

12. *Hamlet's Mill,* 167.

13. Rey, H. A. *The Stars: A New Way to See Them,* 29th Printing. Boston: Houghton-Mifflin, 1952. Page 44.

14. *Hamlet's Mill,* 423-424.

15. *Hamlet's Mill,* 243-244.

16. *Hamlet's Mill,* 295.

17. *Hamlet's Mill,* 424.

18. *Who is this King of Glory,* 115.

19. *Red Ice Radio,* interview with John Anthony West, December 2008. 00:08:45. <www.youtube.com/watch?v=smFCj-okLBE> Accessed 01/26/2014.

20. Kuhn, Alvin Boyd. *Lost Light: An Interpretation of Ancient Scriptures.* <www.scribd.com/mobile/doc/98330788#fullscreen> Accessed 01/26/2014. Pages 79-80 in the original pagination. Emphasis in the original.

21. *Who is this King of Glory,* 29-30.

22. Talbot, Michael. *The Holographic Universe.* New York: HarperCollins, 1991. Edition cited is the HarperPerennial paperback edition, published in 1992. Pages 14-17.

23. Schwaller de Lubicz, R. A. *Sacred Science: The King of Pharaonic Theocracy.* Originally published in French under the title *Le Roi de la théocratie Pharaonique* by Flammarion in 1961. English Translation by André and Goldian VandenBroeck, 1982. Rochester, Vermont: Inner Traditions, 1988 (first Quality Paperback edition). Page 170. This is how Schwaller translates the third dictum of *The Emerald Tablet.*

24. Schwaller de Lubicz, R. A. *Esoterism & Symbol.* Originally published in French under the title *Propos sur Esotérisme et Symbole by La Colombe,* Editions du Vieux Colombier in 1960. English translation by André and Goldian VandenBroeck, 1985. Rochester, Vermont: Inner Traditions, 1985. Page 9.

25. *Esoterism & Symbol*, 13-14.
26. *Sacred Science*, 120.
27. *Esoterism & Symbol*, 1, 3.
28. *Esoterism & Symbol*, 75.
29. West, John Anthony. *Serpent in the Sky: the High Wisdom of Ancient Egypt*. New York: Julian Press, 1979. 1987 edition. Page 45.
30. *Sacred Science*, 151.
31. *Serpent in the Sky*, 47.
32. Rosenblum, Bruce and Fred Kuttner. *Quantum Enigma: Physics Encounters Consciousness*. Second Edition. Oxford: Oxford UP, 2011. Page 7.
33. *Quantum Enigma*: 95-96.
34. *Lost Light*, 71-72.
35. *Lost Light*, 53.
36. *Lost Light*, 72.
37. Freeman, Gordon. *Hidden Stonehenge: Ancient Temple in North America Reveals the Key to Ancient Wonders*. London: Watkins, 2012. Pages 64-68. In this vitally important book, Professor Gordon Freeman explores the alignments of ancient stone sites, especially Ómahkiyáahkóhtóohp and Stonehenge, with a level of rigor and detail not found in previous works on Stonehenge (and for the first time in print for Ómahkiyáahkóhtóohp), and he also proposes additional more precise nomenclature for the annual solar cyclical days, including Equalday/Night and Sun Zenith Midaltitude, or SZM (which he pronounces *zem*).
38. Burgoyne, Thomas. *The Light of Egypt, or The Science of the Soul and the Stars, volume 2*, first published in 1900. <www.scribd.com/mobile/doc/140002292> Accessed 01/28/2014. Pages 7 - 9.
39. Taylor, Robert. *The Astronomico-Theological Lectures of the Rev. Robert Taylor, B.A.* New York: Calvin Blanchard, 1857. Page 130. Later, on page 233 of the same work, Robert Taylor provides a footnote in which he cites his source for the assertion that Israel is the ancient Phœnician name for the far planet Saturn. He cites Eusebius (a fourth-century Christian polemicist), who actually says several times that Kronos was called "El" or "Elus" by the Phœnicians and that he was deified as the planet Saturn: Eusebius. *Praeparatio Evangelica*, Book I, chapters 9 and 10 and also Book IV chapters 15 and 16.
40. See for example *Lost Light* page 448 for discussion of "Horus of the Two Horizons," and *Lost Light* pages 110, 173, and 196 for discussion of Osiris as "the sun in Amenta" (the underworld – that is to say: this material world).
41. *Hamlet's Mill*, 177.
42. Taylor, Robert. *The Devil's Pulpit: or Astro-Theological Sermons by the Rev. Robert Taylor, B. A.* New York: Calvin Blanchard, 1857. Pages 303-304.
43. *Astronomico-Theological Lectures*, 157.
44. *Astronomico-Theological Lectures*, 157-158.
45. See for instance his argument in *Lost Light*, 218-219.
46. *Hamlet's Mill*, 58.
47. *Hamlet's Mill*, 62-63.
48. *Astrononico-Theological Lectures*, 184.
49. Hyginus, *Astronomica*. II:29. Translated by Mary Grant. <www.theoi.com/Text/HyginusAstronomica2.html> Accessed 01/30/2014.
50. See for instance *Hamlet's Mill*, pages 222-223.
51. *Hamlet's Mill*, 63.

52. Plutarch. *Moralia*. Online edition of the Loeb Classical Library edition, 1957.
<www.penelope.uchicago.edu/Thayer/E/Roman/Texts/Plutarch/Moralia/Intelligence_of_Animals*/B.html> Accessed 01/31/2014.
53. Clement of Alexandria. *Paedogogus*. Book III, chapter 1.
<www.newadvent.org/fathers/02093.htm> Accessed 02/01/2014.
54. *Lost Light*, 422.
55. *Lost Light*, 424.
56. *Astronomico-Theological Lectures*, 209.
57. *Astronomico-Theological Lectures*, 195-196.
58. *Astronomico-Theological Lectures*, 195.
59. Eusebius, *Praeparatio Evangelica* Book I, and Tacitus *Histories* Book V.
60. *Astronomico-Theological Lectures*, 221-222.
61. *Hamlet's Mill*, 135-136.
62. *Hamlet's Mill*, 135.
63. *Astronomico-Theological Lectures*, 203.
64. *Ibid.*
65. *Astronomico-Theological Lectures*, 202.
66. *Ibid.*
67. *Astronomico-Theological Lectures*, 199.
68. *Ibid.*
69. *Ibid.*
70. Best, Elsdon. *The Astronomical Knowledge of the Maori, Genuine and Empirical: Including Data concerning their Systems of Astrogeny, Astrolatry, and Natural Astrology, with Notes on certain other Natural Phenomena*. Wellington: Dominion Museum, 1922. Page 3.
<www.nzetc.victoria.ac.nz/tm/scholarly/tei-BesAstro-t1-body-d1-d1a.html> Accessed 02/01/2014.
71. *Astronomical Knowledge of the Maori*, 12.
72. *Astronomical Knowledge of the Maori*, 36.
73. *Astronomical Knowledge of the Maori*, 35-36.
74. *Astronomical Knowledge of the Maori*, 36.
75. *Astronomico-Theological Lectures*, 83-84.
76. See for example *Hamlet's Mill*, 146.
77. *Hamlet's Mill*, 46.
78. *Hamlet's Mill*, 270.
79. *Hamlet's Mill*, 222.
80. *Hamlet's Mill*, 319.
81. *Astronomico-Theological Lectures*, 69.
82. *Hamlet's Mill*, 222.
83. *Ibid.*
84. *Ibid.*
85. *Astronomico-Theological Lectures*, 198.
86. *Astronomico-Theological Lectures*, 198-199.
87. *Devil's Pulpit*, 86.
88. *Lost Light*, 112-113.
89. *Lost Light*, 113.
90. *Astronomico-Theological Lectures*, 360.
91. *Astronomico-Theological Lectures*, 344-345.
92. *Astronomico-Theological Lectures*, 345-346.
93. *Astronomico-Theological Lectures*, 351.

94. *Astronomico-Theological Lectures,* 345.

95. *Astronomico-Theological Lectures,* 351-352.

96. *Ibid.*

97. *Orphic Hymns.* <www.sacred-texts.com/cla/hoo/hoo49.htm> Accessed 02/01/2014.

98. *Orphic Hymns.* <www.sacred-texts.com/cla/hoo/hoo34.htm> Accessed 02/01/2014.

99. Mathisen, David Warner. *The Mathisen Corollary: Connecting a Global Flood with the Mystery of Mankind's Ancient Past.* Paso Robles, CA: Beowulf Books, 2011. Pages 57-66.

100. *Astronomico-Theological Lectures,* 131.

101. *Astronomico-Theological Lectures,* 393-394.

102. *Astronomico-Theological Lectures,* 394.

103. *Astronomico-Theological Lectures,* 309.

104. *Astronomico-Theological Lectures,* 294.

105. *Astronomico-Theological Lectures,* 300-302.

106. *Astronomico-Theological Lectures,* 304.

107. *Astronomico-Theological Lectures,* 306.

108. All of the specific discussion of the zodiac connections for the children of Israel can be found in *Astronomico-Theological Lectures,* pages 303-309.

109. *Lost Light,* 128.

110. *Lost Light,* 24. Emphasis in the original.

111. *Devil's Pulpit,* 89.

112. *Devil's Pulpit,* 94.

113. *Devil's Pulpit,* 93-94.

114. *Hamlet's Mill,* 266.

115. *Hamlet's Mill,* 419.

116. *Hamlet's Mill,* 270.

117. *Ibid.*

118. *Devil's Pulpit,* 42-45. All italics in the original.

119. *Devil's Pulpit,* 134.

120. *Devil's Pulpit,* 42.

121. *Devil's Pulpit,* 86.

122. See for example *Mathisen Corollary,* pages 94-108.

123. See for example *Hamlet's Mill,* pages 140 and also 159.

124. *Devil's Pulpit,* 157.

125. *Devil's Pulpit,* pages 186-188.

126. *Devil's Pulpit,* 199.

127. Taylor, Robert. "On the Transfiguration of Jesus," sermon given on December 6, 1829 and published in Robert Carlile's periodical, *The Lion,* number 24, volume 4, December 11, 1829, pages 754-768 of that volume. In *The Lion, Volume IV: From July 3, to Decenbver 25, 1829.* London: Richard Carlile, 1829. Available online on <books.google.com> Accessed 02/02/2014.

128. "On the Transfiguration of Jesus," 766.

129. *Ibid.*

130. "On the Transfiguration of Jesus," 768.

131. *The Stars: A New Way to See Them,* 50.

132. *Devil's Pulpit,* 228-232.

133. *Devil's Pulpit,* 138-139.

134. *Devil's Pulpit,* 311.

135. *Devil's Pulpit,* 91-93.

136. *Devil's Pulpit,* 93.

137. *Devil's Pulpit*, 92.

138. *Ibid.*

139. *Devil's Pulpit*, 314.

140. *Devil's Pulpit*, 92.

141. *Devil's Pulpit*, 92-93.

142. *Devil's Pulpit*, 93.

143. *Ibid.*

144. *Devil's Pulpit*, 231-232.

145. *Devil's Pulpit*, 219.

146. *Devil's Pulpit*, 272.

147. *Devil's Pulpit*, 218.

148. *Ibid.*

149. *Devil's Pulpit*, 220.

150. *Devil's Pulpit*, 154-155 as well as 219.

151. *Devil's Pulpit*, 155.

152. Plato. *Phaedo*, in *Collected Dialogues of Plato, including the Letters.* Edited by Edith Hamilton and Huntington Cairns. Princeton, NJ: Princeton UP, 1961. Translated by Hugh Tredennick. Pages 40-98. Quotation is on page 98.

153. *Mathisen Corollary*, 212-216.

154. *Hamlet's Mill*, 140. Here, the authors write: "It should be stated right now that *'fire'* is *actually a great circle reaching from the NorthPole of the celestial sphere to its South Pole*," (italics in original). This is the great equinoctial colure, depicted in ancient myth from around the globe as a great arc of fire (since it is the path of the sun).

155. *Quantum Enigma*, 221.

156. *Astronomico-Theological Lectures*, 298-299.

157. *Lost Light*, 71-72.

158. *Lost Light*, 113.

159. Kuhn, Alvin Boyd. *The Esoteric Structure of the Alphabet and Its Hidden Mystical Language.* Kessinger Publishing's Rare Reprints. Page 20.

160. See for example *Mathisen Corollary*, 144.

161. *Mathisen Corollary*, 172-176.

162. Hancock, Graham and Santha Faiia. *Heaven's Mirror: Quest for the Lost Civilization.* New York: Crown, 1998. Page 254.

163. *Ibid.*

164. *Hamlet's Mill*, 162. Also discussed in *Mathisen Corollary*, 159.

165. Farrell, Joseph P. and F. Scott De Hart. *Grid of the Gods: The Aftermath of the Cosmic War and the Physics of the Pyramid Peoples.* Kempton, Illinois: Adventures Unlimited, 2011. Pages 63-64.

166. *Holographic Universe*, 14.

167. *Ibid.*

168. *Holographic Universe*, 16-17.

169. Waller, Steven J. "Stonehenge-like Auditory Illusion Evoked by Interference Pattern," popular version of paper 2aAAa9, presented November 01, 2011 to the 162nd Acoustical Society of America meeting in San Diego, California. <www.acoustics.org/press/162nd/Waller_2aAAa9.html> Accessed 02/04/2014.

170. *Ibid.*

171. *Hidden Stonehenge*, 175.

172. *Hidden Stonehenge*, 65.

173. *Hidden Stonehenge*, 116.

174. *Hidden Stonehenge*, 317. The image of the Stonehenge plan with conventional numbering for the stones can be found at:
<http://commons.wikimedia.or/wiki/File:Stone_Plan.jpg> Accessed 02/08/2014.
175. *Hidden Stonehenge*, 122-124.
176. *Hidden Stonehenge*, 180.
177. Ovid. *Metamorphoses*. Translated by Charles Martin. New York: Norton, 2004. Pages 155-156.
178. *Serpent in the Sky*, 79.
179. Cowan, David. *Ley Lines and Earth Energies: A Groundbreaking Exploration of the Earth's Natural Energy and How it Affects Our Health*. Kempton, Illinois: Adventures Unlimited, 2003. Page 224.
180. *Ibid.*
181. *Lost Light*, 414-415.
182. Eliade, Mircea. *Shamanism: Archaic Techniques of Ecstasy*. Originally published in French under the title *Le Chamanisme et les techniques archaïques de l'extase* by Librarie Payot: Paris, 1951. English translation by Willard R. Trask. Princeton, NJ: Princeton UP, 1964. First Princeton / Bollingen paperback edition, 1972. Page 259.
183. Susskind, Leonard. *The World as Hologram*. Delivered at the University of Toronto, 06/28/2011. Lecture.
<http://m.youtube.com/watch?v=2DII3Hfh9tY> Accessed 02/08/2014.
184. *World as Hologram*, (0:01:38).
185. *World as Hologram*, (0:02:03).
186. *World as Hologram*, (0:02:36).
187. *World as Hologram*, (0:18:56).
188. *World as Hologram*, (0:40:00).
189. *World as Hologram*, (0:44:03).
190. Described by David Icke in various books and presentations, for example in *Remember Who You Are: Remember Who You Are and Where You Came From*, David Icke Books, 2012, in the entire second chapter (entitled "The 'world' is in your 'head'").
191. Carter, Chris. *Science and the Near-Death Experience: How Consciousness Survives Death*. Rochester, Vermont: Inner Traditions, 2010. Page 221.
192. Sabom, Michael. *Light & Death: One Doctor's Fascinating Account of Near-Death Experiences*. Grand Rapids, Michigan: Zondervan, 1998. Page 43. Cited in *Science and the Near-Death Experience*, Pages 223-224.
193. *Science and the Near-Death Experience*, 223.
194. *Shamanism*, 259.
195. *Shamanism*, 234.
196. *Shamanism*, 142.
197. *Light & Death*, 44.
198. *Lost Light*, 360.
199. *Esoteric Structure of the Alphabet*, 20.
200. *Ibid.*
201. *Esoteric Structure of the Alphabet*, 5.
202. *Esoteric Structure of the Alphabet*, 21.
203. *Esoteric Structure of the Alphabet*, 23.
204. *Esoteric Structure of the Alphabet*, 18.
205. *Esoteric Structure of the Alphabet*, 23.
206. Vettius Valens. *Anthologies*. Translated by Mark Riley and published in its entirety online in December, 2010.

<www.csus.edu/indiv/r/rileymt/Vettius%20Valens%20entire.pdf> Accessed 02/09/2014. All quotations from page 48.

207. Waters, Frank and Oswald White Bear Fredericks. *Book of the Hopi*. New York: Penguin, 1963. Pages 9-10.

208. *Hamlet's Mill*, 189.

209. *Ibid*.

210. *Hamlet's Mill*, 190-191.

211. *Orphic Hymn LXXXII: To Ocean*. Translated Thomas Taylor. <www.sacred-texts.com/cla/hoo/hoo87.htm> Accessed 02/09/2014.

212. *Hamlet's Mill*, footnote on page 191.

213. Bauval, Robert and Graham Hancock. *Keeper of Genesis: A Quest for the Hidden Legacy of Mankind*. London: Heinemann, 1996. Pages 138-139.

214. Hall, Manly P. *Occult Anatomy of Man & Occult Masonry*. Los Angeles, California: Philosophical Research Society, 1997 edition. Page 12.

215. *Esoteric Structure of the Alphabet*, 20.

216. *Esoteric Structure of the Alphabet*, 23-24.

217. *Esoteric Structure of the Alphabet*, 34.

218. See for example *Mathisen Corollary*, 212.

219. *Metamorphoses*, 103.

220. *Ibid*.

221. *Ibid*.

222. *Metamorphoses*, 104.

223. *Metamorphoses*, xiii.

224. *Metamorphoses*, 527.

225. Smallstorm, Sofia. *9/11 Mysteries, Chemtrails, Nanotechnology & the Artificial Environment*. Interview on *Red Ice Radio*, 07/02/2009. Hour 1. <www.redicemembers.com/secure/radio/program.php?id=276> Accessed 02/11/2014. (0:07:40).

226. *Hamlet's Mill*, 122.

227. *Holographic Universe*, 244-245.

228. *Holographic Universe*, 242.

229. *Science and the Near-Death Experience*, 229.

230. Fenwick, Peter and Elizabeth Fenwick. *The Truth in the Light: Investigation of Over 300 Near Death Experiences*. Headline Books: London, 1995. Pages 200 and 134, cited in *Science and the Near-Death Experience*, Pages 124 and 125.

231. *Holographic Universe*, 257.

232. *Holographic Universe*, 232-233.

233. *Holographic Universe*, 230.

234. *Holographic Universe*, 234.

235. *Ibid*.

236. Naydler, Jeremy. *Shamanic Wisdom in the Pyramid Texts: The Mystical Tradition of Ancient Egypt*. Rochester, Vermont: Inner Traditions, 2005. Page 120.

237. See for example the captions to the series of illustrations found in *Hamlet's Mill* between pages 290 and 291 (the illustration pages are not numbered).

238. *Shamanic Wisdom in the Pyramid Texts*, 91-94.

239. *Shamanic Wisdom in the Pyramid Texts*, 95.

240. *Ibid*.

241. *Shamanic Wisdom in the Pyramid Texts*, 95-105.

242. *Shamanic Wisdom in the Pyramid Texts*, 82-83.

243. Allen, James P. and Peter Der Manuelian. *Ancient Egyptian Pyramid Texts. Writings from the Ancient World Series*, Book 23. Atlanta: Society of Biblical Literature, 2005. Page 15.

244. *Shamanic Wisdom in the Pyramid Texts*, 152-153.

245. *Pyramid Texts Online*, copyright 2002-2013 by Vincent Brown. <www.pyramidtextsonline.com> Accessed 02/15/2014.

246. *Shamanic Wisdom in the Pyramid Texts*, 165.

247. *Shamanic Wisdom in the Pyramid Texts*, 160-161.

248. *Serpent in the Sky*, 147.

249. *Serpent in the Sky*, 14.

250. *Shamanic Wisdom in the Pyramid Texts*, 166-167.

251. *Shamanic Wisdom in the Pyramid Texts*, 160.

252. *Shamanic Wisdom in the Pyramid Texts*, 161-162.

253. *Shamanic Wisdom in the Pyramid Texts*, 166.

254. *Ibid.*

255. *Shamanic Wisdom in the Pyramid Texts*, 188.

256. *Shamanic Wisdom in the Pyramid Texts*, 191-192.

257. *Shamanic Wisdom in the Pyramid Texts*, 192.

258. *Shamanic Wisdom in the Pyramid Texts*, 196.

259. *Lost Light*, 191: "In every ancient system of cosmology this globe is the lowest of all planetary spheres. There can be no other hell, Tartarus, Avernus or Orcus, Sheol or Tophet below it. It is that darksome limbo where the Styx, the Phlegethon, the river of Lethe and other murky streams run their sluggish courses through the life of mortals."

260. *Lost Light*, 224.

261. *Shamanic Wisdom in the Pyramid Texts*, 166.

262. *Shamanic Wisdom in the Pyramid Texts*, 201.

263. *Shamanic Wisdom in the Pyramid Texts*, 202.

264. *Shamanic Wisdom in the Pyramid Texts*, 203-204.

265. *Shamanic Wisdom in the Pyramid Texts*, 210.

266. *Ibid.*

267. *Pyramid Texts Online*, Sarcophagus Chamber, East Wall Hieroglyphs. <www.pyramidtextsonline.com/sarceast.html> Accessed 02/15/2014.

268. *Shamanic Wisdom in the Pyramid Texts*, 219.

269. Wyatt, Lucy. *Approaching Chaos: Can an Ancient Archetype Save 21st Century Civilization.* Winchester: O Books, 2010. See for example page 147.

270. *Shamanic Wisdom in the Pyramid Texts*, 85.

271. *Shamanic Wisdom in the Pyramid Texts*, 56. With an endnote directing the reader to Utterances 317, 403, and 409.

272. *Shamanic Wisdom in the Pyramid Texts*, 85.

273. Wyatt asserts that "it was the pharaoh's responsibility as the people's earthly representative to undertake the potentially sacrificial role of performing rituals on their behalf" on page 185 of *Approaching Chaos*.

274. *Shamanism*, 303.

275. *Approaching Chaos*, 182-183. Bracketed page references are in the original quotation and refer to passages in Jeremy Narby's *The Cosmic Serpent: DNA and the Origins of Knowledge.* New York: PenguinPutnam, 1999.

276. Wyatt, Lucy. "Megaliths, Shamen & the City Builders – the hidden connections." <www.grahamhancock.com/forum/WyattL1.php> Accessed 02/16/2015.

277. See for example *Shamanism*, pages 168, 257-258, 351-352, and 461-462.

278. See for example discussions in *Shamanic Wisdom in the Pyramid Texts* on pages 183-184, and especially endnote 36 on page 392. There, Naydler explains:

> The Dwat is described as "at the place where Orion is" in utt. 437, §802 and utt. 610, §1717. Since Orion is the principal southern constellation, the Dwat was evidently regarded as having a southern location. Orion was also the stellar manifestation of the god Osiris, the Lord of the Dwat. See Sellers, *The Death of Gods*, 39 f. See also James P. Allen, "The Cosmology of the Pyramid Texts," 21 ff. According to Allen, although the celestial location of the Dwat is at the southeastern rim of the sky, the entrance to the Dwat is at the opposite end of the sky, in the northwest. See also cha. 7, n. 54, in this book. [The note referred to in the final sentence can be found on page 400 of *Shamanic Wisdom in the Pyramid Texts*].

279. *Shamanic Wisdom in the Pyramid Texts*, 83-84.
280. *Holographic Universe*, 46-47.
281. *Shamanism*, 581.
282. *Shamanic Wisdom in the Pyramid Texts*, 83-84, and *Lost Light*, 423.
283. See for example *Lost Light*, 117.
284. *Who is this King of Glory*, 5.
285. *Devil's Pulpit*, 157.
286. Ellis, Ralph. *Jesus, Last of the Pharaohs*. Revised 2nd Edition. Padstow: T. J. International, 2001. Page 39.
287. *Jesus, Last of the Pharaohs*, 46.
288. *Jesus, Last of the Pharaohs*, 37.
289. *Jesus, Last of the Pharaohs*, 29.
290. Ellis, Ralph. *Tempest & Exodus: The biblical exodus inscribed on an ancient Egyptian stele*. Kempton, Illinois: Adventures Unlimited, 2001. His discussion of the connection between the Giza pyramids and the mountains of the Old Testament (and in particular between the Great Pyramid and Mt. Sinai) begins on page 68 and following.
291. Josephus *Antiquities*, quoted in *Jesus, Last of the Pharaohs*, 6.
292. *Jesus, Last of the Pharaohs*, 6.
293. *Ibid*.
294. *Jesus, Last of the Pharaohs*, 31.
295. *Jesus, Last of the Pharaohs*, 33.
296. *Jesus, Last of the Pharaohs*, 49.
297. Josephus (Titus Flavius Josephus). *Antiquities of the Jews*. Translated by William Whiston (1667 – 1752). Book I, Chapter 8, Section 2. <www.gutenberg.org/files/2848/2848-h/2848-h.htm> Accessed 02/16/2014.
298. The description of the events on Mount Moriah and the "sacrifice" of Isaac are treated by Josephus in *Antiquities* Book I, Chapter 13. The declaration that Isaac was twenty-five years of age at the time is found in Book I, Chapter 13, Section 2.
299. *Jesus, Last of the Pharaohs*, 50.
300. *Jesus, Last of the Pharaohs*, 51.
301. *Jesus, Last of the Pharaohs*, 30.
302. *Astronomico-Theological Lectures*, 217. Italics in the original.
303. *Astronomico-Theological Lectures*, 217-218.
304. *Astronomico-Theological Lectures*, 235-236.

305. *Antiquities*, Book I, Chapter 7, Section 1.

306. Sellers, Jane B. *Death of Gods in Ancient Egypt: A Study of the Threshold of Myth and the Frame of Time*. Lexington, Kentucky: Lulu Books, 1992. Revised edition, 2007. Pages 86-88. Also discussed at length in *Mathisen Corollary*, 91-124, with quotations from Jane B. Sellers.

307. *Lost Light*, 13-14.

308. *Lost Light*, 14.

309. *Lost Light*, 15.

310. *Lost Light*, 14.

311. *Lost Light*, 15.

312. *Lost Light*, 16.

313. Michell, John. *New View Over Atlantis*. First US Edition. San Francisco: Harper & Row, 1983. Page 162.

314. *New View Over Atlantis*, 83.

315. *New View Over Atlantis*, 204.

316. *New View Over Atlantis*, 204-205.

317. *New View Over Atlantis*, 205.

318. Alison, Jim. *The Prehistoric Alignment of World Wonders: A New Look at an Old Design*. <http://home.hiwaay.net/%7Ejalison/index.html> Accessed 02/16/2014.

319. *Ibid.*

320. Hancock, Graham and Santha Faiia. *Heaven's Mirror: Quest for the Lost Civilization*. Crown Publishers: New York, 1998. See for example page 254.

321. Heyerdahl, Thor. *Easter Island: The Mystery Solved*. New York: Random House, 1989. See for example pages 82, 85, and 101.

322. *Grid of the Gods*, 23-25.

323. *Grid of the Gods*, 124.

324. *Grid of the Gods*, 125-126.

325. *New View Over Atlantis*, 203.

326. *Serpent in the Sky*, 197.

327. *Ibid.*

328. *Shamanic Wisdom in the Pyramid Texts*, 69.

329. *Shamanic Wisdom in the Pyramid Texts*, 317.

330. *Approaching Chaos*, 182.

331. *Holographic Universe*, 235.

332. *Holographic Universe*, 236.

333. *Holographic Universe*, 267.

334. See for example *Science and the Near-Death Experience*, 208-210.

335. See for example *Lost Light*, 261-262.

336. See for example *Lost Light*, 147, 277, 334, 515.

337. *Lost Light*, 281.

338. Bowden, Hugh. *Mystery Cults of the Ancient World*. Princeton, NJ: Princeton UP, 2010. Page 14.

339. *Mystery Cults of the Ancient World*, 15.

340. *Mystery Cults of the Ancient World*, 16-17.

341. *Mystery Cults of the Ancient World*, 17.

342. *Who is this King of Glory*, 50.

343. Burkert, Water. *Ancient Mystery Cults*. Cambridge, Massachusetts: Harvard UP, 1987. Pages 3-4.

344. *Ancient Mystery Cults*, 63.

345. *Ibid.*

346. *Ibid.*

347. *Ancient Mystery Cults*, 62-66.

348. *Ancient Mystery Cults*, 65-66.

349. *Ancient Mystery Cults*, 66.

350. *Ibid.*

351. See for example *Hamlet's Mill*, 56ff.

352. See for example *Hamlet's Mill*, 430. The authors of *Hamlet's Mill* are not extraordinarily straightforward in the explication of the thesis that underlies their choice of title for their book, but in the passage at the top of 430 they clearly associate Hamlet (or "Amlethus") with Horus ("nephew of Seth" or Set), and with other "nephew heros" who must avenge their father's murder at the hands of their father's brother – the clear pattern of the Horus-Osiris-Set myth of ancient Egypt.

353. See for example *Astronomico-Theological Lectures*, 331-337.

354. Discussed in an entire chapter in *Hamlet's Mill* entitled "The Great Pan is Dead," found on pages 275-287.

355. Discussed in an entire chapter in *Hamlet's Mill* entitled "The Fall of Phaethon," found on pages 250-262.

356. See for example *Hamlet's Mill*, 258.

357. *Hamlet's Mill*, 259.

358. *Hamlet's Mill*, 258.

359. See for example *Hamlet's Mill* 133, 139, and 381.

360. *Hamlet's Mill*, 129 and 135.

361. *Hamlet's Mill*, 258-259.

362. See for example *Hamlet's Mill* 275-287, especially 283-285.

363. See for example *Lost Light* 192, and especially 404, 425, and 506, as well as 260-262, and 550.

364. *Lost Light*, 425.

365. *Lost Light*, 260-261.

366. For discussions of Arthur as a type of Kronos-Saturn asleep in Ogygia, see for example *Hamlet's Mill*, 34 and 46.

367. *Hamlet's Mill*, 283-285.

368. Crinagoras. *Greek Anthologies*, 11.42. Cited in *Mystery Cults of the Ancient World*, 26.

369. Sophocles. *Triptolemos*, fragment 837. Cited in *Mystery Cults of the Ancient World*, 47.

370. Plutarch, fragment 168. Cited in *Mystery Cults of the Ancient World*, 40.

371. Plato. *Phaedrus*, 250b-c. Cited in *Mystery Cults of the Ancient World*, 215.

372. See for example *Shamanism* 12, 24, 73, 91, 168, 171, 173, 200-203, 221, 224, 232, 235, 239, 291, 511 and numerous other places throughout the text (too numerous to list).

373. See for example *Shamanism* 19, 81.

374. *Mystery Cults of the Ancient World*, 43.

375. McKenna, Terence. *Food of the Gods: The Search for the Original Tree of Knowledge. A Radical History of Plants, Drugs, and Human Evolution.* New York: Bantam, 1992. Trade paperback edition, 1993. Page 133.

376. *Food of the Gods*, 125-127.

377. *Food of the Gods*, 76.

378. *Approaching Chaos*, 178-179.

379. *Approaching Chaos*, 178, 190-200.

380. *Approaching Chaos*, 169-171.

381. *Approaching Chaos*, 170.

382. *Approaching Chaos*, 171-177.

383. *Who is this King of Glory*, 78.

384. *Mystery Cults of the Ancient World*, 340-345.

385. *Mystery Cults of the Ancient World*, 23.

386. *Mystery Cults of the Ancient World*, 74.

387. *Who is this King of Glory*, 9.

388. Freke, Timothy and Peter Gandy. *The Jesus Mysteries: Was the "Original Jesus" a Pagan God?* New York: Three Rivers Press, 1999. Page 204.

389. See for example *The Jesus Mysteries*, 48-52, 92-93.

390. *Jesus Mysteries*, 9-10.

391. *Jesus Mysteries*, 4.

392. Meyer, Marvin. *The Gnostic Discoveries: The Impact of the Nag Hammadi Library.* New York: HarperCollins, 2005. Pages 48-52.

393. *Gnostic Discoveries*, 1-6.

394. *Gnostic Discoveries*, 30-31.

395. Athanasius, Festal Letter 39 (AD 367). From an online version of *Select Writings and Letters of Athanasius, Bishop of Alexandria: Edited, with Prolegomena, Indices, and Tables, by Archbald Robertson, Principal of Bishop Hatfield's Hall, Durham, Late Fellow of Trinity College, Oxford.* <http://www.ntslibrary.com/PDF%20Books/Athanasius%20Select%20Writtings%20and %20Letters.pdf> Accessed 02/16/2014. page 1290. This edition was edited (as indicated in the title) by Archibald Robertson (1853 – 1931). It states that "The principal English Translations are those in the 'Library of the Fathers.' Of these, those edited or translated by Newman are incorporated in this volume" (16).

396. But see Michael J. Kruger, *The Question of Canon*, as well as his blog entitled *canon fodder*, particularly "10 Misconceptions about the NT Canon: #10: Athanasius' Festal Letter (367 A. D.) is the First Complete List of New Testament Books." 12/11/2012. <www.michaeljkruger.com/10-misconceptions -about-the-nt-canon-10-athanasius-festal=letter-367-a-d-is-the-first-complete-list-of-new-testament-books/> Accessed 02/21/2014. In which Kruger argues that Origen at least appears to have had a 27-book New Testament a hundred years prior to Athanasius.

397. *Jesus Mysteries*, 119.

398. *Jesus Mysteries*, 122.

399. *Jesus Mysteries*, 127-128.

400. *Jesus Mysteries*, 127.

401. *Jesus Mysteries*, 127-128.

402. *Jesus Mysteries*, 128.

403. *Jesus Mysteries*, 129.

404. *Jesus Mysteries*, 159.

405. *Ibid.*

406. *Jesus Mysteries*, 160.

407. *Jesus Mysteries*, 151.

408. *Jesus Mysteries*, 154.

409. *Jesus Mysteries*, 156.

410. *Jesus Mysteries*, 200-202.

411. *Jesus Mysteries*, 213.

412. *Ibid.*

413. Atwill, Joseph. *Caesar's Messiah: The Roman Conspiracy to Invent Jesus.* Berkeley, California: Ulysses Press, 2005. Pages 35-37.

414. *Caesar's Messiah*, 36.

415. These events and Biblical parallels are detailed at length throughout *Caesar's Messiah*, but see in particular the chapter entitled "The Typological Method" (pages 219-225) and in particular the table presented on page 221.

416. *Caesar's Messiah*, 166-167.

417. *Caesar's Messiah*, 170.

418. Josephus (Titus Flavius Josephus). *Life of Flavius Josephus*. Translated by William Whiston (1667 – 1752). <www.penelope.uchicago.edu/josephus/autobiog.html> Accessed 02/22/2014. Section 76.

419. *Jesus Mysteries*, 155.

420. *Ibid*.

421. Josephus (Titus Flavius Josephus). *War of the Jews*. Book III, Chapter 8, Section Translated by William Whiston (1667 – 1752). Book III, Chapter 8, Section 7. Available at <www.penelope.uchicago.edu/josephus/war-3.html> Accessed 02/22/2014.

422. Barbiero, Flavio. *The Secret Society of Moses: The Mosaic Bloodline and a Conspiracy Spanning Three Millennia*. Translated by Steve Smith. Rochester, Vermont: Inner Traditions, 2010. Page 107.

423. *Secret Society of Moses*, 108.

424. *War of the Jews*, Book II, Chapter 21, Section 3, cited in *Secret Society of Moses*, 108.

425. *Secret Society of Moses*, 108-109.

426. *Secret Society of Moses*, 109.

427. *Ibid*.

428. *War of the Jews*, Book VI, Chapter 6, Section 1, cited in *Secret Society of Moses*, 114.

429. *Secret Society of Moses*, 115.

430. *Secret Society of Moses*, 110-111.

431. *The Copper Scroll*. Translated by J. T. Milik (1922 – 2006). <umdrive.memphis.edu/jjsledge/public/Jewish%20Studies/04a%20-%20DSS%20Texts/Copper%20Scroll.pdf> Accessed 02/22/2014. For the *editio princeps*, see Józef Tadeusz Milik, *Discoveries in the Judaean Desert*: Volume III, Pages 199-302.

432. *Ibid*.

433. *Ibid*.

434. *Secret Society of Moses*, 111.

435. *Ibid*.

436. *Secret Society of Moses*, 112.

437. *Secret Society of Moses*, 107, 112, 115.

438. *Secret Society of Moses*, 112.

439. Ulansey, David. *The Origins of the Mithraic Mysteries: Cosmology and Salvation in the Ancient World*. New York: Oxford UP, 1989. Pages 102-103, 110.

440. *Secret Society of Moses*, 116.

441. *Secret Society of Moses*, 117.

442. *Secret Society of Moses*, 119.

443. *Secret Society of Moses*, 121.

444. *Secret Society of Moses*, 118.

445. See for example *Secret Society of Moses*, 175-180.

446. *Secret Society of Moses*, 319-324, 397-414.

447. *Mathisen Corollary*, 202-218.

448. *Secret Society of Moses*, 178.

449. *Secret Society of Moses*, 122.

450. *Secret Society of Moses*, 178.
451. *Secret Society of Moses*, 179.
452. *Origins of the Mithraic Mysteries*, 95-111.
453. *Origins of the Mithraic Mysteries*, 104.
454. See *The "Mithras" Liturgy from the Paris Codex*, edited and translated by Marvin W. Meyer. <www.hermetic.com/pgm/mithras-liturgy.html> Accessed 02/23/2014.
455. *Origins of the Mithraic Mysteries*, 105.
456. *Ibid.*
457. *Ibid.*
458. Palmer, Glenn. "Why the Shoulder?: A Study of the Placement of the Wound in the Mithraic Tauroctony." In *Mystic Cults in Magna Graecia*. Edited by Giovanni Casadio and Patricia A. Johnston. Austin, Texas: U of Texas Press, 2009. This essay is found as Chapter 17, Pages 314-323. Pages quoted: 319-320.
459. *Origins of the Mithraic Mysteries*, 103-105. For further discussion on the mechanism of precession which turns the entire "equinoctial colure" and with it the north and south celestial poles, see also *Mathisen Corollary*, 36-69.
460. "Why the Shoulder?" 317.
461. "Why the Shoulder?" 323, note 7.
462. *Secret Society of Moses*, 175.
463. *Secret Society of Moses*, 176.
464. *Ibid.*
465. *Ibid.*
466. *Secret Society of Moses*, 163.
467. *Secret Society of Moses*, 162.
468. *Secret Society of Moses*, 163.
469. *Secret Society of Moses*, 164.
470. *Ibid.*
471. *Secret Society of Moses*, 163, 241.
472. *Secret Society of Moses*, 160-161, 179-180.
473. *Secret Society of Moses*, 180.
474. *Secret Society of Moses*, 161.
475. *Secret Society of Moses*, 186.
476. *Secret Society of Moses*, 165.
477. *Ibid.*
478. *Secret Society of Moses*, 148.
479. *Secret Society of Moses*, 164.
480. *Ibid.*
481. *Ibid.*
482. *Secret Society of Moses*, 159, 237.
483. *Who is this King of Glory*, 13.
484. *Secret Society of Moses*, 126.
485. Clement of Rome. "First Epistle of Clement to the Corinthians." Translated by J. B. Lightfoot. <www.earlychristianwritings.com/text/1clement-lightfoot.html> Accessed 02/23/2014.
486. *Secret Society of Moses*, 126.
487. *Secret Society of Moses*, 126-127.
488. *Secret Society of Moses*, 130-131.
489. *Secret Society of Moses*, 136-137.
490. *Secret Society of Moses*, 167.

491. *Secret Society of Moses*, 233.
492. *Secret Society of Moses*, 180.
493. *Secret Society of Moses*, 186-187.
494. *Secret Society of Moses*, 191.
495. *Ibid*.
496. *Secret Society of Moses*, 192.
497. *Secret Society of Moses*, 236-239.
498. *Secret Society of Moses*, 200.
499. *Secret Society of Moses*, 201.
500. *Secret Society of Moses*, 314.
501. *Secret Society of Moses*, 206.
502. *Secret Society of Moses*, 205.
503. *Secret Society of Moses*, 314.
504. *Secret Society of Moses*, 207.
505. *Secret Society of Moses*, 210.
506. Josephus, *Life*, Section 1. Cited in *Secret Society of Moses*, 1.
507. *Secret Society of Moses*, 211.
508. *Secret Society of Moses*, 161, 316.
509. *Secret Society of Moses*, 161.
510. *Secret Society of Moses*, 163.
511. *Secret Society of Moses*, 214.
512. *Secret Society of Moses*, 220.
513. *Secret Society of Moses*, 221.
514. *Secret Society of Moses*, 317.
515. *Secret Society of Moses*, 229-230.
516. *Secret Society of Moses*, 230.
517. *Secret Society of Moses*, 231.
518. *Ibid*.
519. *Secret Society of Moses*, 249.
520. *Secret Society of Moses*, 256.
521. *Secret Society of Moses*, 257.
522. *Secret Society of Moses*, 260.
523. *Secret Society of Moses*, 264.
524. *Ibid*.
525. *Secret Society of Moses*, 265.
526. Josephus, *Life*, Section 76.
527. *Secret Society of Moses*, 357.
528. *Secret Society of Moses*, 359ff.
529. *Secret Society of Moses*, 390-392.
530. *Secret Society of Moses*, 392.
531. *Who is this King of Glory*, 5.
532. *Devil's Pulpit*, 102.
533. *Devil's Pulpit*, 103.
534. *Jesus Mysteries*, 155-156.
535. *Devil's Pulpit*, 104.
536. *Ibid*.
537. *Devil's Pulpit*, 102.
538. *Ibid*.
539. *Jesus Mysteries*, 150-154, 159 ff.

540. Massey, Gerald. *Paul the Gnostic opponent of Peter, not an Apostle of Historic Christianity.* <www.gerald-massey.org.uk/massey/dpr_02_paul_as_a_gnostic.htm> Accessed 02/23/2014.
541. *Paul the Gnostic opponent of Peter*, section 17.
542. *Paul the Gnostic opponent of Peter*, section 6.
543. *Ibid.*
544. *Paul the Gnostic opponent of Peter*, section 8.
545. *Ibid.*
546. *Enter the Dragon.* Dir. Robert Clouse. Golden Harvest, 1973. Film.
547. *Paul the Gnostic opponent of Peter*, section 24, section 26.
548. *Man in search of his soul during fifty thousand years*, section 17.
549. *HarperCollins Atlas of the Bible.* General Editor James. B. Pritchard. London: Times Books Ltd, 1987. Reprinted with Revisions 1989, This edition printed 1997 for Borders Group, Inc. Page 36.
550. *HarperCollins Atlas of the Bible*, 37.
551. *Secret Society of Moses*, 355-396.
552. *Mathisen Corollary*, 285-290. Tests conducted on the mummy of Rameses II indicate that his hair had been dyed with a henna solution to achieve its reddish color, but the same researchers who conducted those tests found that traces of the hair's original color could be found in the roots, indicating that Rameses had been red-haired prior to old age, when his hair turned white and when he apparently had it dyed to resemble its original natural color. See for example L. Balout, C. Roubet, and C. Desroches-Noblecourt, *La Momie de Ramsès II: Contribuion Scientifique à l'Égyptologie.* Paris: Editions Recherche sur les civilisations, 1985.
553. Ellis, Ralph. "Mt. Sinai Discovered." www.world-mysteries.com/gw_rellis2.htm> Accessed 02/24/2014.
554. *Ibid.*
555. Massey, Gerald. *Luniolatry, Ancient and Modern.* <www.gerald-massey.org.uk/massey/dpr_07_luniolatry.htm> Accessed 02/24/2014. Section 9.
556. *Luniolatry*, sections 16, 27, 29, and 36.
557. *Luniolatry*, section 13.
558. Massey, Gerald. *The Hebrew and Other Creations Fundamentally Explained.* <www.gerald-massey.org.uk/massey/dpr_05_hebrew_and_other.htm> Accessed 02/24/2014. See the discussion throughout. Massey also makes the same argument, in section 74. of this text, that we saw Ralph Ellis make in the passage connected to note 544. (above), that the Egyptian *Aten* and the Hebrew *Adonai* are linguistically identical.
559. *Luniolatry*, section 14.
560. "Mt. Sinai Discovered."
561. *Ibid.*
562. *Ibid.*
563. *Ibid.*
564. *Paul the Gnostic opponent of Peter*, section 18.
565. *Man in search of his soul during fifty thousand years*, sections 41-42.
566. Massey, Gerald. *Ancient Egypt the Light of the World: A Work of Reclamation and Restitution in Twelve Books.* Originally Two Volumes. London: T. Fisher Unwin, 1907. Online Edition Published in 2007 and available at <www.masseiana.org/aebk0.htm> Accessed 02/24/2014. Page 211.

567. *Ancient Egypt the Light of the World,* 215-216.
568. *Ancient Egypt the Light of the World,* 190.
569. *Ibid.*
570. *Ibid.*
571. See for example *Ancient Egypt the Light of the World,* 217-218.
572. *Ancient Egypt the Light of the World,* 189.
573. *Who is this King of Glory,* 65.
574. *Lost Light,* 174.
575. *Lost Light,* 173.
576. *Lost Light,* 174.
577. *Lost Light,* 172.
578. *Lost Light,* 170.
579. *Ibid.*
580. *Lost Light,* 169.
581. *Ibid.*
582. *Lost Light,* 173.
583. *Ibid.*
584. *Lost Light,* 268.
585. *Lost Light,* 176-209.
586. *Lost Light,* 306.
587. *Lost Light,* 589-590.
588. See for example *Lost Light* 309, 368, 370.
589. *Lost Light,* 172.
590. *Lost Light,* 172-173.
591. *Lost Light,* 172.
592. *Lost Light,* 173.
593. *Who is this King of Glory,* 78.
594. *Lost Light,* 43.
595. *The Gnostic Discoveries,* 30.
596. *Ibid.*
597. *The Gnostic Discoveries,* 31.
598. *The Gnostic Discoveries,* 29.
599. *The Gnostic Discoveries,* 28.
600. *The Gnostic Discoveries,* 29.
601. *The Gnostic Discoveries,* 120.
602. *Secret Society of Moses,* 216.
603. *Secret Society of Moses,* 217.
604. *Ibid.*
605. *Secret Society of Moses,* 218.
606. *The Gnostic Discoveries,* 118.
607. Hapgood, Charles H. *Maps of the Ancient Sea Kings: Evidence of Advanced Civilization in the Ice Age.* Originally published in 1966. New edition Kempton, Illinois: Adventures Unlimited, 1996. Page 59.
608. Based on the theory being built in the chapters up to this point, one must wonder what happened to those missing volumes of Diodorus Siculus, and what history they might have contained! How interesting that it is after Diodorus has introduced the idea of a mighty "island" lying some days west of Libya, in Book V, that the gap in his *Library of History* appears.

609. Diodorus Siculus. *The Library of History.* Online LacusCurtius version of the original Loeb Classical Library edition. Translation by C. H. Oldfather. Cambridge, Massachusetts: Harvard UP, 1933 – 1967.
<http://penelope.uchicago.edu/Thayer/E/Roman/Texts/Diodorus_Siculus/5B*.html> Accessed 02/26/2014. Book V, Chapter 19, lines 1-5.
610. Deal, David Allen. *Discovery of Ancient America.* Irvine, California: Kherem La Yah Press, 1984. Pages 46 ff.
611. Plato. *Timaeus.* In *The Collected Dialogues of Plato, Including the Letters* (1151-1211). Ed. Edith Hamilton and Huntington Cairns. Bollingen Series LXXI. Princeton, New Jersey: Princeton UP, 1963. (1151-1211). Sections 23-25 (Pages 1158-1160).
612. *Timaeus,* Section 22 (Page 1157).
613. *Library of History,* Book V, Chapter 20, line 3.
614. *Library of History,* Book V, Chapter 20, line 4.
615. Marble, Samuel D. *Before Columbus: New History of Celtic, Egyptian, Phoenician, Viking, Black African and Asian Contacts and Impacts in the Americas Before 1492.* Lancaster: Gazelle Book Services, 1980. Page 119.
616. Fell, Barry. *America B.C.: Ancient Settlers in the New World.* New York: Pocket Books, 1976. Pages 254-255, 258.
617. See *Mathisen Corollary,* 270-275 and *America B.C.,* 260-269.
618. *America B.C.,* 266-267.
619. *Mathisen Corollary,* 271.
620. Balabanova, Svetlana. *Detection of Nictotine and Cocaine in Ancient Human Remains from Different Locations out of America and an Archaeological Period Spans a Range from 9,000 BC to 700 AD.* Originally published in *Naturwissenschaften* 79: 358.
<www.migration-diffusion.info/pdfdownload.php?id=213&file=1>
Accessed 02/26/2014.
621. Wakefield, Jay Stuart and Reinoud M. De Jonge. *Rocks and Rows: Sailing Routes across the Atlantic and the Copper Trade.* Kirkland, Washington: MCS Inc., 2009.
622. *America B.C.*
623. See for example: "More evidence of ancient transcontinental contact in Central American sculpture." *Mathisen Corollary Blog,* 08/11/2011. Available at
<http://mathisencorollary.blogspot.com/2011/08/more-evidence-of-ancient.html>
Accessed 02/26/2014.
624. See for example: "The Calixtlahuaca head." *Mathisen Corollary Blog,* 09/17/2011. Available at <http://mathisencorollary.blogspot.com/2011/09/calixtlahuaca-head.html> Accessed 02/26/2014.
625. See for example: "The lowly amphora (and ancient contact across the oceans)." *Mathisen Corollary Blog,* 02/06/2012.
Available at <http://mathisencorollary.blogspot.com/2012/02/lowly-amphora-and-ancient-contact.html>
Accessed 02/26/2014.
626. See for example: "Why do lions guard gates around the world, even on continents that had no lions?" *Mathisen Corollary Blog,* 08/10/2011.
Available at <http://mathisencorollary.blogspot.com/2011/08/why-do-lions-guard-gates-around-world.html> Accessed 02/26/2014.
627. Sorenson, John L. and Carl L. Johannessen. "Scientific Evidence for Pre-Columbian Transoceanic Voyages to and from the Americas, part 1." 2001.
<http://publications.maxwellinstitute.byu.edu/fullscreen/?pub=1068&index=1>
Accessed 02/26/2014.

628. Doutré, Martin. "Nazca." *Ancient Celtic New Zealand Blog.* <www.celticnz.co/nz/Nazca/Nazca1.htm> Accessed 02/26/2014.

629. Mertz, Henriette. *The Mystic Symbol: Mark of the Michigan Mound Builders.* Originally published in Gaithersburg, Maryland: Global Books, 1986.   Republished Colfax, Wisconsin: Ancient American Magazine/Hayriver Press, 2004. Page 13.

630. *Mystic Symbol*, 112.

631. *Mystic Symbol*, 122.

632. *Mystic Symbol*, 113.

633. *Ibid.*

634. *Mystic Symbol*, 113-114.

635. *Mystic Symbol*, 114.

636. *Mystic Symbol*, 117.

637. *Ibid.*

638. *Mystic Symbol*, 122.

639. Deal, David Allen. "Complete Translation of a Michigan Clay Tablet." *The Mystic Symbol*, pages 176 – 190; he makes this assertion on page 185.

640. See for example "Complete Translation of a Michigan Clay Tablet," 181.

641. Deal, David Allen. "The Mystic Symbol Demystified." *The Mystic Symbol*, pages 168 – 175; see discussion on pages 169-170.

642. "Complete Translation of a Michigan Clay Tablet," 180.

643. "Mystic Symbol Demystified," 172-173.

644. "Mystic Symbol Demystified," 170.

645. "Mystic Symbol Demystified," 175.

646. "Complete Translation of a Michigan Clay Tablet," 178.

647. *Ibid.*

648. *Ibid.*

649. *Ibid.*

650. "Complete Translation of a Michigan Clay Tablet," 179.

651. *Ibid.*

652. "Complete Translation of a Michigan Clay Tablet," 182.

653. *Ibid.*

654. *Ibid.*

655. *Lost Light*, 154.

656. *Lost Light*, 333.

657. *Devil's Pulpit*, 70.

658. *Ibid.*

659. Deal, David Allen. "Michigan Sabbath Tablets." *Mystic Symbol*, pages 191-192.

660. *Mystic Symbol*, 82-91.

661. *Mystic Symbol*, 91.

662. *Mystic Symbol*, 74-75.

663. *Mystic Symbol*, 78-80.

664. *Lost Light*, 400.

665. *Ibid.*

666. *Lost Light*, 400-401.

667. Deal, David Allen. "Michigan solar eclipse tablets & Mound-builder city," *Mystic Symbol*, pages 193 – 205.

668. "Mystic Symbol Demystified," 170.

669. "Michigan Solar Eclipse Tablet & Mound Builder City," 193-194.

670. Annett, Kevin D. *Hidden No Longer: Genocide in Canada, Past and Present.* And Updated New Edition of *Hidden from History: The Canadian Holocaust* (3rd Edition). Occupied Territory of the Squamish Indigenous Nation: International Tribunal into Crimes of Church and State and The Friends and Relatives of the Disappeared, 2010. <www.scribd.com/mobile/doc/110817677> Accessed 02/28/2014. Pages 209-210.

671. *Secret Society of Moses*, 231.

672. *Secret Society of Moses*, 264.

673. *Ibid.*

674. Oldenbourg, Zoé. *The Crusades*. Translated from the French by Anne Carter. New York: Pantheon, 1966. Originally published in French as *Les Croisades*. Paris: Éditions Gallimard, 1965. Page 28.

675. *Secret Society of Moses*, 300.

676. *Ibid.*

677. *Ibid.*

678. *Secret Society of Moses*, 302.

679. *Secret Society of Moses*, 303.

680. *Secret Society of Moses*, 318.

681. *Secret Society of Moses*, 325.

682. *Secret Society of Moses*, 327.

683. *Ibid.*

684. *Secret Society of Moses*, 326.

685. *Maps of the Ancient Sea Kings*, 53-54.

686. "450 years." *Mathisen Corollary Blog.* Available at <http://mathisencorollary.blogspot.com/2012/12/450-years.html> Accessed 02/28/2014.

687. de Landa, Diego. *Yucatan Before and After the Conquest.* Translated, with notes, by William Gates. Baltimore, Maryland: Maya Society, 1937. <www.sacred-texts.com/nam/maya/ybac/ybac00.htm> Accessed 02/28/2014. Pages v – vi.

688. *Yucatan Before and After the Conquest*, 82.

689. *Fingerprints of the Gods*, 112.

690. *Ibid.*

691. *Yucatan Before and After the Conquest*, 25.

692. *Hidden No Longer*, 10-11.

693. *Hidden No Longer*, 12.

694. *Unrepentant.* Dir. Louie Lawless. 2006. Film. <http://m.youtube.com/watch?v=88k2imkGIFA> Accessed 03/01/2014.

695. *Hidden No Longer*, 13.

696. *Hidden No Longer*, 46, 60-62.

697. *Hidden No Longer*, 62.

698. *Hidden No Longer*, 69.

699. *Hidden No Longer*, 63.

700. *Ibid.*

701. *Hidden No Longer*, 71, 95-100.

702. *Hidden No Longer*, 14.

703. *Ibid.*

704. See for example *Hidden No Longer*, 102-105 and 110-116 as well as the film *Unrepentant.*

705. *Hidden No Longer*, 174.

706. *Hidden No Longer*, 175.

707. *Hidden No Longer*, 128-132.

708. *Hidden No Longer*, 114.

709. *Hidden No Longer*, 26-27.

710. As recounted by Frank Waters in the *Book of the Hopi*, page 5 and elsewhere; also discussed in *Mathisen Corollary*, 240.

711. See for example *The Popol Vuh: Mythic and Heroic Sagas of the Kichés of Central America*, translated by Lewis Spence, 1908.
Available online at <www.sacred-texts.com/nam/pvuheng.htm> Accessed 03/01/2014.

712. *Mystic Symbol*, 93.

713. Glyn-Jones, William. "Yima and his Bull: Gemini and Taurus in the Lascaux Caves." Published on the Graham Hancock website (www.grahamhancock.com), 01/28/2008.
<www.grahamhancock.com/forum/GlynJonesW1.php>
Accessed 03/01/2014. This article is a shorter version of a longer piece published as "The Lascaux Twin." Published in the *ELPHINofANGELAND* blog. Published on 05/26/2007.
<http://cuppalot.blogspot.com/2007/05/lascaux-twin.html>
Accessed 03/01/2014.

714. *Lost Light*, 41. The term "Atmic" in Kuhn's usage derives from the word *Atma* or "soul" (note the linguistic similarity to the Latin or Spanish *alma*, "soul").

715. *Lost Light*, 587.

716. Augustine of Hippo. *City of God*. An abridged version from the translation by Gerald G. Walsh, Demetrius B. Zema, Grace Monahan, and Daniel J. Honan. Edited by Vernon J. Bourke. Image Books: New York, 1958. Page 237.

717. See for example Massey's *Luniolatry*, section 2, in which he says: "Mythology was a primitive mode of *thinging* the early thought," and the discussion in Kuhn's *Lost Light*, page 42.

718. *Secret Society of Moses*, 320 and also footnote on 302.

719. *Secret Society of Moses*, footnote on 302.

720. *Lost Light*, 116-117.

Bibliography

Alison, Jim. *The Prehistoric Alignment of World Wonders: A New Look at an Old Design.* <http://home.hiwaay.net/%7Ejalison/index.html> Accessed 02/16/2014.

Allen, James P. and Peter Der Manuelian. *Ancient Egyptian Pyramid Texts. Writings from the Ancient World Series,* Book 23. Atlanta: Society of Biblical Literature, 2005.

Annett, Kevin D. *Hidden No Longer: Genocide in Canada, Past and Present.* And Updated New Edition of *Hidden from History: The Canadian Holocaust* (3rd Edition). Occupied Territory of the Squamish Indigenous Nation: International Tribunal into Crimes of Church and State and The Friends and Relatives of the Disappeared, 2010. <www.scribd.com/mobile/doc/110817677> Accessed 02/28/2014.

Aristotle. *Metaphysics.* Book XII, part 8. Translation by W. D. Ross. <http://classics.mit.edu/Aristotle/metaphysics.12.xii.html> Accessed 01/24/2014.

Athanasius, Festal Letter 39 (AD 367). From an online version of *Select Writings and Letters of Athanasius, Bishop of Alexandria: Edited, with Prolegomena, Indices, and Tables, by Archbald Robertson, Principal of Bishop Hatfield's Hall, Durham, Late Fellow of Trinity College, Oxford.* <http://www.ntslibrary.com/PDF%20Books/Athanasius%20Select%20Writtings%20and%20Letters.pdf> Accessed 02/16/2014.

Atwill, Joseph. *Caesar's Messiah: The Roman Conspiracy to Invent Jesus.* Berkeley, California: Ulysses Press, 2005.

Augustine of Hippo. *City of God.* An abridged version from the translation by Gerald G. Walsh, Demetrius B. Zema, Grace Monahan, and Daniel J. Honan. Edited by Vernon J. Bourke. Image Books: New York, 1958.

Balabanova, Svetlana. *Detection of Nictotine and Cocaine in Ancient Human Remains from Different Locations out of America and an Archaeological Period Spans a Range from 9,000 BC to 700 AD.* Originally published in *Naturwissenschaften* 79: 358. <www.migration-diffusion.info/pdfdownload.php?id=213&file=1> Accessed 02/26/2014.

Barbiero, Flavio. *The Secret Society of Moses: The Mosaic Bloodline and a Conspiracy Spanning Three Millennia.* Translated by Steve Smith. Rochester, Vermont: Inner Traditions, 2010.

Bauval, Robert and Graham Hancock. *Keeper of Genesis: A Quest for the Hidden Legacy of Mankind.* London: Heinemann, 1996.

Best, Elsdon. *The Astronomical Knowledge of the Maori, Genuine and Empirical: Including Data concerning their Systems of Astrogeny, Astrolatry, and Natural Astrology, with Notes on certain other Natural Phenomena.* Wellington: Dominion Museum, 1922. <www.nzetc.victoria.ac.nz/tm/scholarly/tei-BesAstro-t1-body-d1-d1a.html> Accessed 02/01/2014.

Bowden, Hugh. *Mystery Cults of the Ancient World.* Princeton, NJ: Princeton UP, 2010.

Burgoyne, Thomas. *The Light of Egypt, or The Science of the Soul and the Stars, volume 2*, first published in 1900.
<www.scribd.com/mobile/doc/140002292> Accessed 01/28/2014.

Burkert, Water. *Ancient Mystery Cults.* Cambridge, Massachusetts: Harvard UP, 1987.

Carter, Chris. *Science and the Afterlife Experience: Evidence for the Immortality of Consciousness.* Rochester, Vermont: Inner Traditions, 2012.

Carter, Chris. *Science and the Near-Death Experience: How Consciousness Survives Death.* Rochester, Vermont: Inner Traditions, 2010.

Clement of Alexandria. *Paedogogus.* Trans. William Wilson. From *Ante-Nicene Fathers*, volume 2. Ed. Alexander Roberts, james Donaldson, and A. Cleveland Coxe. Buggalo, New York: Christian Literature Publishing Co., 1885.
<www.newadvent.org/fathers/02093.htm> Accessed 02/01/2014.

Clement of Rome. "First Epistle of Clement to the Corinthians." Translated by J. B. Lightfoot. Available at <www.earlychristianwritings.com/text/1clement-lightfoot.html> Accessed 02/23/2014.

The Copper Scroll. Translated by J. T. Milik (1922 – 2006).
<umdrive.memphis.edu/jjsledge/public/Jewish%20Studies/04a%20-%20DSS%20Texts/Copper%20Scroll.pdf> Accessed 02/22/2014.
For the *editio princeps*, see Józef Tadeusz Milik, *Discoveries in the Judaean Desert*: Volume III, Pages 199-302.

Cowan, David. *Ley Lines and Earth Energies: A Groundbreaking Exploration of the Earth's Natural Energy and How it Affects Our Health.* Kempton, Illinois: Adventures Unlimited, 2003.

Deal, David Allen. "Complete Translation of a Michigan Clay Tablet." *The Mystic Symbol*, pages 176 – 190.

Deal, David Allen. *Discovery of Ancient America.* Irvine, California: Kherem La Yah Press, 1984.

Deal, David Allen. "Michigan solar eclipse tablets & Mound-builder city," *Mystic Symbol*, pages 193 – 205.

Deal, David Allen. "Michigan Sabbath Tablets." *Mystic Symbol*, pages 191-192.

Deal, David Allen. "The Mystic Symbol Demystified." *The Mystic Symbol*, pages 168 – 175.

de Landa, Diego. *Yucatan Before and After the Conquest.* Translated, with notes, by William Gates. Baltimore, Maryland: Maya Society, 1937.
<www.sacred-texts.com/nam/maya/ybac/ybac00.htm> Accessed 02/28/2014.

De Santillana, Giorgio and Hertha von Dechend. *Hamlet's Mill: An Essay on Myth and the Frame of Time*. Boston: Godine, 1977.

Diodorus Siculus. *The Library of History*. Online LacusCurtius version of the original Loeb Classical Library edition. Translation by C. H. Oldfather. Cambridge, Massachusetts: Harvard UP, 1933 – 1967.
<http://penelope.uchicago.edu/Thayer/E/Roman/Texts/Diodorus_Siculus/5B*.html> Accessed 02/26/2014.

Doutré, Martin. "Nazca." *Ancient Celtic New Zealand Blog*.
<www.celticnz.co/nz/Nazca/Nazca1.htm> Accessed 02/26/2014.

Eliade, Mircea. *Shamanism: Archaic Techniques of Ecstasy*. Originally published in French under the title *Le Chamanisme et les techniques archaïques de l'extase* by Librarie Payot: Paris, 1951. English translation by Willard R. Trask. Princeton, NJ: Princeton UP, 1964. First Princeton / Bollingen paperback edition, 1972.

Ellis, Ralph. *Jesus, Last of the Pharaohs*. Revised 2nd Edition. Padstow: T. J. International, 2001.

Ellis, Ralph. "Mt. Sinai Discovered."
www.world-mysteries.com/gw_rellis2.htm> Accessed 02/24/2014.

Ellis, Ralph. *Tempest & Exodus: The biblical exodus inscribed on an ancient Egyptian stele*. Kempton, Illinois: Adventures Unlimited, 2001.

Enter the Dragon. Dir. Robert Clouse. Golden Harvest, 1973. Film.

Farrell, Joseph P. and F. Scott De Hart. *Grid of the Gods: The Aftermath of the Cosmic War and the Physics of the Pyramid Peoples*. Kempton, Illinois: Adventures Unlimited, 2011.

Fell, Barry. *America B.C.: Ancient Settlers in the New World*. New York: Pocket Books, 1976.
Fenwick, Peter and Elizabeth Fenwick. *The Truth in the Light: Investigation of Over 300 Near Death Experiences*. Headline Books: London, 1995.

Freeman, Gordon. *Hidden Stonehenge: Ancient Temple in North America Reveals the Key to Ancient Wonders*. London: Watkins, 2012.

Freke, Timothy and Peter Gandy. *The Jesus Mysteries: Was the "Original Jesus" a Pagan God?* New York: Three Rivers Press, 1999.

Glyn-Jones, William. "Yima and his Bull: Gemini and Taurus in the Lascaux Caves." Published on the Graham Hancock website (www.grahamhancock.com), 01/28/2008. Available online at <www.grahamhancock.com/forum/GlynJonesW1.php> Accessed 03/01/2014. This article is a shorter version of a longer piece published as "The Lascaux Twin." Published in the *ELPHINofANGELAND* blog. Published on 05/26/2007. Available at <http://cuppalot.blogspot.com/2007/05/lascaux-twin.html> Accessed 03/01/2014.

Hall, Manly P. *Occult Anatomy of Man & Occult Masonry*. Los Angeles, California: Philosophical Research Society, 1997 edition.

Hancock, Graham and Santha Faiia. *Heaven's Mirror: Quest for the Lost Civilization*. New York: Crown, 1998.

Hapgood, Charles H. *Maps of the Ancient Sea Kings: Evidence of Advanced Civilization in the Ice Age*. Originally published in 1966. New edition Kempton, Illinois: Adventures Unlimited, 1996.

HarperCollins Atlas of the Bible. General Editor James. B. Pritchard. London: Times Books Ltd, 1987. Reprinted with Revisions 1989, This edition printed 1997 for Borders Group, Inc.

Heyerdahl, Thor. *Easter Island: The Mystery Solved*. New York: Random House, 1989.

Homer. Odyssey. Trans. Robert Fagles. New York: Penguin, 1996.

Hyginus, *Astronomica*. Translated by Mary Grant.
<www.theoi.com/Text/HyginusAstronomica2.html> Accessed 01/30/2014.

Josephus (Titus Flavius Josephus). *Antiquities of the Jews*.
Translated by William Whiston (1667 – 1752).
<www.gutenberg.org/files/2848/2848-h/2848-h.htm> Accessed 02/16/2014.

Josephus (Titus Flavius Josephus). *Life of Flavius Josephus*.
Translated by William Whiston (1667 – 1752).
<www.penelope.uchicago.edu/josephus/autobiog.html> Accessed 02/22/2014.

Michael J. Kruger, *The Question of Canon*, as well as his blog entitled *canon fodder*, particularly "10 Misconceptions about the NT Canon: #10: Athanasius' Festal Letter (367 A. D.) is the First Complete List of New Testament Books." 12/11/2012. <www.michaeljkruger.com/10-misconceptions -about-the-nt-canon-10-athanasius-festal=letter-367-a-d-is-the-first-complete-list-of-new-testament-books/> Accessed 02/21/2014.

The King's Speech. Dir. Tom Hooper. Momentum Pictures, 2010. Film.

Kuhn, Alvin Boyd. *The Esoteric Structure of the Alphabet and Its Hidden Mystical Language*. Kessinger Publishing's Rare Reprints.

Kuhn, Alvin Boyd. *Lost Light: An Interpretation of Ancient Scriptures*.
<www.scribd.com/mobile/doc/98330788#fullscreen> Accessed 01/26/2014.

Kuhn, Alvin Boyd. *Who is this King of Glory? A Critical Study of the Christos-Messiah Tradition*. <www.scribd.cm/mobile/doc/27243209> Accessed 01/26/2014.

Lemony Snicket's A Series of Unfortunate Events. Dir. Brad Silberling. Nickelodeon, 2004. Film.

Lion King. Dir. Roger Allers, Rob Minkoff. Walt Disney Pictures, 1994. Film.

Marble, Samuel D. *Before Columbus: New History of Celtic, Egyptian, Phoenician, Viking, Black African and Asian Contacts and Impacts in the Americas Before 1492*. Lancaster: Gazelle Book Services, 1980.

Massey, Gerald. *Ancient Egypt the Light of the World: A Work of Reclamation and Restitution in Twelve Books*. Originally Two Volumes. London: T. Fisher Unwin, 1907. Online Edition Published in 2007 and available at <www.masseiana.org/aebk0.htm> Accessed 02/24/2014.

Massey, Gerald. *The Hebrew and Other Creations Fundamentally Explained*. <www.gerald-massey.org.uk/massey/dpr_05_hebrew_and_other.htm> Accessed 02/24/2014.

Massey, Gerald. *Luniolatry, Ancient and Modern*. <www.gerald-massey.org.uk/massey/dpr_07_luniolatry.htm> Accessed 02/24/2014.

Massey, Gerald. *Man in search of his soul during fifty thousand years, and how he found it!* <www.gerald-massey.org.uk/massey/dpr_08_man_in_search.htm> Accessed 01/26/2014.

Massey, Gerald. *The Natural Genesis: or Second Part of a Book of the Beginnings, Containing an Attempt to Recover and Reconstitute the Lost Origins of the Myths and Mysteries, Types and Symbols, Religion and Language, with Egypt for the Mouthpiece and Africa as the Birthplace*. 1887. <www.masseiana.org/ngbk0.htm> Accessed 01/26/2014.

Massey, Gerald. *Paul the Gnostic opponent of Peter, not an Apostle of Historic Christianity*. <www.gerald-massey.org.uk/massey/dpr_02_paul_as_a_gnostic.htm> Accessed 02/23/2014.

Mathisen, David Warner. *The Mathisen Corollary: Connecting a Global Flood with the Mystery of Mankind's Ancient Past*. Paso Robles, CA: Beowulf Books, 2011.

The Matrix. Dir. Andy and Lana Wachowski. Warner Brothers, 1999. Film.

McKenna, Terence. *Food of the Gods: The Search for the Original Tree of Knowledge. A Radical History of Plants, Drugs, and Human Evolution*. New York: Bantam, 1992. Trade paperback edition, 1993.

Mertz, Henriette. *The Mystic Symbol: Mark of the Michigan Mound Builders*. Originally published in Gaithersburg, Maryland: Global Books, 1986. Republished Colfax, Wisconsin: Ancient American Magazine/Hayriver Press, 2004.

Meyer, Marvin. *The Gnostic Discoveries: The Impact of the Nag Hammadi Library*. New York: HarperCollins, 2005.

Michell, John. *New View Over Atlantis*. First US Edition. San Francisco: Harper & Row, 1983.

The "Mithras" Liturgy from the Paris Codex, edited and translated by Marvin W. Meyer. <www.hermetic.com/pgm/mithras-liturgy.html> Accessed 02/23/2014.

Naydler, Jeremy. *Shamanic Wisdom in the Pyramid Texts: The Mystical Tradition of Ancient Egypt*. Rochester, Vermont: Inner Traditions, 2005.

Oldenbourg, Zoé. *The Crusades*. Translated from the French by Anne Carter. New York: Pantheon, 1966. Originally published in French as *Les Croisades*. Paris: Éditions Gallimard, 1965.

Orphic Hymns. Translated Thomas Taylor. <www.sacred-texts.com/cla/hoo/hoo49.htm> Accessed 02/01/2014.

Ovid. *Metamorphoses*. Translated by Charles Martin. New York: Norton, 2004.

Palmer, Glenn. "Why the Shoulder?: A Study of the Placement of the Wound in the Mithraic Tauroctony." In *Mystic Cults in Magna Graecia*. Edited by Giovanni Casadio and Patricia A. Johnston. Austin, Texas: U of Texas Press, 2009. This essay is found as Chapter 17, Pages 314-323.

Plato. *Phaedo*, in *Collected Dialogues of Plato, including the Letters*. Edited by Edith Hamilton and Huntington Cairns. Princeton, NJ: Princeton UP, 1961. Translated by Hugh Tredennick. (40-98).

Plato. *Timaeus*. In *The Collected Dialogues of Plato, Including the Letters* (1151-1211). Ed. Edith Hamilton and Huntington Cairns. Bollingen Series LXXI. Princeton, New Jersey: Princeton UP, 1963. (1151-1211).

Plutarch. *Moralia*. Online edition of the Loeb Classical Library edition, 1957. <www.penelope.uchicago.edu/Thayer/E/Roman/Texts/Plutarch/Moralia/Intelligence_of_Animals*/B.html> Accessed 01/31/2014.

Pyramid Texts Online. <www.pyramidtextsonline.com> Accessed 02/15/2014.

Rey, H. A. *The Stars: A New Way to See Them*, 29th Printing. Boston: Houghton-Mifflin, 1952.

Rosenblum, Bruce and Fred Kuttner. *Quantum Enigma: Physics Encounters Consciousness*. Second Edition. Oxford: Oxford UP, 2011.

Sabom, Michael. *Light & Death: One Doctor's Fascinating Account of Near-Death Experiences*. Grand Rapids, Michigan: Zondervan, 1998.

Schwaller de Lubicz, R. A. *Esoterism & Symbol*. Originally published in French under the title *Propos sur Esotérisme et Symbole by La Colombe*, Editions du Vieux Colombier in 1960. English translation by André and Goldian VandenBroeck, 1985. Rochester, Vermont: Inner Traditions, 1985.

Schwaller de Lubicz, R. A. *Sacred Science: The King of Pharaonic Theocracy.* Originally published in French under the title *Le Roi de la théocratie Pharaonique* by Flammarion in 1961.

Sellers, Jane B. *Death of Gods in Ancient Egypt: A Study of the Threshold of Myth and the Frame of Time.* Lexington, Kentucky: Lulu Books, 1992.

Smallstorm, Sofia. *9/11 Mysteries, Chemtrails, Nanotechnology & the Artificial Environment.* Interview on *Red Ice Radio,* 07/02/2009. Hour 1. <www.redicemembers.com/secure/radio/program.php?id=276> Accessed 02/11/2014.

Sorenson, John L. and Carl L. Johannessen. "Scientific Evidence for Pre-Columbian Transoceanic Voyages to and from the Americas, part 1." 2001. <http://publications.maxwellinstitute.byu.edu/fullscreen/?pub=1068&index=1> Accessed 02/26/2014.

Susskind, Leonard. *The World as Hologram.* Delivered at the University of Toronto, 06/28/2011. Lecture. <http://m.youtube.com/watch?v=2DII3Hfh9tY> Accessed 02/08/2014.

Talbot, Michael. *The Holographic Universe.* New York: HarperCollins, 1991. Edition cited is the HarperPerennial paperback edition, published in 1992.

Taylor, Robert. *The Astronomico-Theological Lectures of the Rev. Robert Taylor, B.A.* New York: Calvin Blanchard, 1857.

Taylor, Robert. *The Devil's Pulpit: or Astro-Theological Sermons by the Rev. Robert Taylor, B. A.* New York: Calvin Blanchard, 1857.

Taylor, Robert. "On the Transfiguration of Jesus," sermon given on December 6, 1829 and published in Robert Carlile's periodical, *The Lion,* number 24, volume 4, December 11, 1829, pages 754-768 of that volume. In *The Lion, Volume IV: From July 3, to Decenbver 25, 1829.* London: Richard Carlile, 1829. Available online on <books.google.com> Accessed 02/02/2014.

Ulansey, David. *The Origins of the Mithraic Mysteries: Cosmology and Salvation in the Ancient World.* New York: Oxford UP, 1989.

Unrepentant. Dir. Louie Lawless. 2006. Film. <http://m.youtube.com/watch?v=88k2imkGIFA> Accessed 03/01/2014.

Vettius Valens. *Anthologies.* Translated by Mark Riley and published in its entirety online in December, 2010. <www.csus.edu/indiv/r/rileymt/Vettius%20Valens%20entire.pdf> Accessed 02/09/2014.

Wakefield, Jay Stuart and Reinoud M. De Jonge. *Rocks and Rows: Sailing Routes across the Atlantic and the Copper Trade.* Kirkland, Washington: MCS Inc., 2009.

Waller, Steven J. "Stonehenge-like Auditory Illusion Evoked by Interference Pattern," popular version of paper 2aAAa9, presented November 01, 2011 to the 162nd Acoustical Society of America meeting in San Diego, California.
<www.acoustics.org/press/162nd/Waller_2aAAa9.html> Accessed 02/04/2014.

Waters, Frank and Oswald White Bear Fredericks. *Book of the Hopi*. New York: Penguin, 1963.

West, John Anthony. *Serpent in the Sky: the High Wisdom of Ancient Egypt*. New York: Julian Press, 1979. 1987 edition.

Wyatt, Lucy. *Approaching Chaos: Can an Ancient Archetype Save 21st Century Civilization*. Winchester: O Books, 2010.

Wyatt, Lucy. "Megaliths, Shamen & the City Builders – the hidden connections." <www.grahamhancock.com/forum/WyattL1.php> Accessed 02/16/2015.

INDEX

Magyars, 337
Maillard, Pierre (1710-1762), 306-308
Man in search of his soul etc. (Massey), I, 285
Manasseh, 65
Manetho, 179
Manger, 66-67, 75-79, 328
Maori, 5, 49, 53-54
Maps of the Ancient Sea Kings (Hapgood), 303, 340
Marble, Samuel D., 307
March equinox, 29-31, 33, 37, 45-46, 49, 64, 67, 81, 83-84, 101, 147, 187, 189, 212-213, 227, 251, 280, 352
Marcion, 232
Marcus Aurelius. *See* Aurelius
Marduk, 5
Marigolds, 312
Mark, 85, 95, 186, 233-234
Mars, 2-4, 7, 42, 55-56, 137
Martin, Charles, 152
Mary, 60, 76, 78-80, 88-90, 135, 185, 207, 288
Mary Magdalene, 89
Masonry. *See* Freemasonry
Massey, Gerald (1828-1907), i, iii, 234, 270-274, 277, 281-282, 284-288, 290-291, 295, 349, 362
Materialism, 14, 105, 125, 130, 156, 219, 362-363, 368
Mathisen Corollary (book), 46, 81, 309
Mathisen Corollary Blog, 46
Matrilinearity, 254, 262, 266
Matrix, The (film), 128, 130
Matthew, 78, 81-85, 95, 186, 233-234
Maui, 5
Maya, 340-344, 349-350, 352-354, 366
Mayebra, 180
McKenna, Terence (1946-2000), 221-222
Mediterranean, i, 52, 114, 206, 305-306, 310, 350
Medusa, 114-116, 119-122, 176
"Megaliths, Shamanism, and the City-Builders" (Wyatt), 170
Mem (Hebrew letter), 148
Menelaus, 223-224, 228
Menorah, 240

Mercury, 3-4, 42, 55-56, 67, 137, 151
Mertz, Henriette (1898-1985), 304, 314-315, 317, 320, 328-330, 351
Messiah, 229, 234-235, 277, 324
Metamorphoses (Ovid), 114, 128, 151-152, 204
Metaphysics (Aristotle), 1
Metatron, 320
Mexico, 57, 306, 344, 351
Meyer, Marvin W., 230-231, 298-300
Mi'kmaq, 306-307, 309, 345
Michelangelo (1475-1564), 61, 143
Michell, John (1933-2009), 191-196
Michigan, Michigan relics, 311-320, 322-324, 326, 328-333
Micmac. *See* Mi'kmaq
Microcosm/macrocosm, 16-17, 41, 102-103, 124, 133-137, 139-140, 147-148, 150, 171, 176, 202-204, 216, 227, 286-287, 362, 368
Midsummer, 28-29
Midwinter, 28-29
Milik, Józef Tadeusz (1922-2006), 241-244
Milk and honey, 292
Milky Way, 9-13, 28, 53, 82, 140-141, 149-150, 354, 362
Milton, John (1608-1674), 15
Mind control, 153, 199, 256, 266-267, 294, 297, 355, 358-359
Minelauva, 44
Minoans, 7, 221, 329
Miriam, 60, 62-63, 254
Mithraeum, mithraea, 247-249, 252-253, 258
Mithraic grades, 249
Mithras Liturgy, 249
Mithras Sol Invictus, Mithraism, 75, 77, 95, 205-206, 245, 248-253, 255, 257, 259-260, 263-264, 300, 338, 343
Modes of religion, 202-204
Mog Ruith, 193
Monotheism, 187-188
Monroe, Robert (1915-1995), 199
Monumental architecture, 81, 104-105, 107-109, 113-114, 123, 140, 154, 174, 176, 192-193, 197, 222, 256, 274-275, 306, 356, 359, 362

Passover, 32, 93-94, 280
Pastoral letters, Pastoral epistles, 232, 238
Pater patrum, 253, 261, 263, 301
Patriarchs, 59, 64-65, 134, 182, 186, 277
Paul, 70, 232-234, 236, 238, 257-259, 268-273, 275-276, 284, 286, 288-290, 292-295, 297, 325, 327, 339, 360
Paul the Gnostic opponent of Peter (Massey), 270, 284
Paulicians, 232
Pbow, 299
Peleg, 50, 179
Pepi II (reign 2278 BC-2184 BC), 160
Pepin III (AD 714-AD 768), Pepin the Short, 336-338
Pepin the Short. *See* Pepin III
Pergamon, 208
Pergamos, 91
Perseus, 44-45, 116, 221
Persia, 54
Peru, 169, 194, 312-313
Peter, 84-85, 93-96, 233, 235, 263, 270, 291
Petrification, 114, 122-123, 176, 356
Phaeacia, 2, 54
Phaedo (Plato), 95, 374 (note 152)
Phaedrus (Plato), 218
Phaenomena, phenomena (heavenly), 14, 16, 26, 64, 72, 81, 84, 9, 100, 104, 187-188, 227, 367
Phaethon, 41, 56, 213-214
Pharaoh, 19, 60, 64, 158, 161, 165, 171, 179-182, 189, 219, 228, 279, 362, 364, 377 (note 273)
Pharisees, 201, 275, 284, 293
Philadelphia, 91, 287
Philae, 161
Philip (New Testament), 84, 91, 232
Philip the Arab. *See* Julius Philippus
Philip, Gospel of. *See* Gospel of Philip
Philistines, 5-8, 76
Philo of Byblos (c. AD 64-AD 141), 51
Phineas, 240-241
Phoenicians, 51-52, 305-307, 311, 313
Phrygia, 208
Phrygian cap, 95, 249

Phrygianum, 263
Pi, 306
Pietism, 294
Pillars of Heracles, Pillars of Hercules, 303-304
Pingala. *See* Ida and Pingala
Pirates of the Caribbean (film), 42
Piri Re'is map, 340
Pisces, 3233, 37, 49, 51, 56, 62, 65, 74, 81, 83-84, 91, 96, 103, 135-136, 177, 187, 189
Pistis Sophia, 232, 320
Pit, the, 9-10, 12, 56, 62, 74-75, 84, 88, 270. *See also* Abyss, Hades, Hell, Sheol, Tartaros
Pixels, 126
Planets, iii, 2-4, 7, 15-16, 24, 26, 39-42, 51, 53-56, 58, 73, 98, 101, 105, 150, 170, 192-193, 195-196, 277, 349, 357-358
Plato, Platonism, 136, 181, 191, 218-219, 294, 300, 304-307, 358, 361
Pleiades, 2-4
Plutarch (AD 45-AD 120), 48, 52, 188, 212, 218
Pneumatic initiate, 232
Polaris, 72
Pollux, 211, 269-270, 350
Polydeuces, 211
Polynesia, 12, 186, 275, 305
Pope, 253, 266, 278, 301, 348
Porphyrius (AD 347-AD 420), 255
Portolan maps, 340
Potentiality, 21, 23, 127, 157-158, 362-363, 368
Powder, 223
Praesepe, 66, 76-77
Praetextatus, Vectius Agorius (c. AD 315-AD 384), 263
Praetorian Guard, 247-248, 252, 254, 2579258, 280, 334, 343, 349
Pre-Socratic philosophers, 136
Precession, 30, 32-33, 46, 49, 62, 77, 81, 83, 91, 104-105, 186-188, 195, 201, 211-217, 227, 247-249, 251, 352, 383 (note 459)
Precessional constant, 105, 188
Precessional numbers, 81, 105, 188, 195

Stag, 35-36, 68
Standstill operation, 129, 155
Star Maps (Fix), 167
Stele of Qadesh. *See* Qadesh, stele of
Sterilization, 346-347, 364, 366
Stockholm syndrome, 358
Stonehenge, i, 107-114, 122-123, 176, 192, 256, 356
"Stonehenge-like Auditory Illusion," (Waller), 107-109, 114, 122
Strabo (64 BC-AD 24), 210
Styx, 102, 147, 329, 377 (note 259)
Subatomic particles, 21-22, 125, 152
Suetonius (AD 69-c. AD 122), 239
Sumer, 51, 84, 98-99, 206, 208, 210, 215, 275, 293
Summer solstice, June solstice, 29, 33-34, 70, 73-74, 84-85, 91, 94, 104, 109-110, 140-141, 287, 327
Sun, iii, 3-5, 7, 9, 14-16, 26-37, 39-40, 42, 44-46, 49, 51, 53-58, 60-65, 70-86, 88-90, 92-96, 98, 101, 103-105, 109-114, 135, 137, 146-147, 149-150, 159, 162, 178, 187-189, 192-196, 212-213, 217, 221, 245, 248-249, 252, 263, 269-270, 277, 280-281, 286-288, 290-291, 309, 327-330, 338, 349, 352, 357-358, 362, 366, 368, 374 (note 154)
Sun Temple Ring. See Ómahkiyáahkóhtóohp
Sunbird, 5
Sunday Sabbath, 585, 328, 338
Sunrise, 3, 40, 76, 79, 83, 110-112, 212, 352
Superposition, 21-23, 103, 114, 139, 157-159, 362-363
Superstition, 53, 100, 227, 268, 341
Susskind, Leonard, 124-127, 153
Sut. *See* Set
Swastika, 115-116
Sweden, 121
Symbolique, 18
Symplegades, 49-50
Syricius, 263
Syros, 211
T'Hooft, Gerard, 125
Tacitus (AD 56-after AD 117), 51
Tahn, 330

Talbot, Michael (1953-1992), 17, 105-106, 155-157, 172, 199-200, 223
Tallegewi, 332-333
Tallenbach, Gerd (1903-1999), 337
Tammuz, 84, 217
Tangier, 305
Tao Teh Ching, 367
Taricheae, 240
Tartaros, Tartarus, 74, 377 (note 259)
Tassili n'Ajjer, 194
Tat, Tat column, 286-291. *See also* Djed column
Tauroctony, 95, 248-250
Taurus, 3, 5-8, 56, 60, 62, 65, 67, 81, 91, 135, 183, 186-188, 212-214, 251, 327, 352
Taylor, Rev. Robert (1784-1844), 27, 39-40, 42-44, 47, 50-52, 54, 56-68, 70-73, 75-79, 84-86, 88-96, 98-100, 137, 139-141, 144-145, 149, 178, 185-186, 213, 221, 269-270, 287, 326-328, 371 (note 39)
Taylor, Thomas (1758-1835), 61, 139
"Teapot," 10-11. *See also* Sagittarius
Tehuty. *See* Thoth
Tel Aviv, 332
Telescopes, 52-54
Teletai, 202, 204
Tempest & Exodus (Ellis), 181, 189, 378 (note 290)
Temple of Jerusalem, 81, 91, 178-179, 182, 190, 229, 234, 237-238, 240-241, 243-248, 253-254, 263, 266-269, 275-276, 278, 280, 302, 311, 332, 337-338, 349
Ten Commandments, 180
Teotihuacan, 306
Terah 50, 52 179
Terra, 51
Tertullian (AD 160-AD 225), 298
Tet. *See* Djed
Tetrarchy, 261-262, 300
Texcoco, 342
Thai, Thailand 367
The Stars, A New Way to See Them (Rey) 8, 36
Thebes (Greece), 151
Thebes (Egypt), 229, 278
Thecoa, 235

About the Author

Fascinated by ancient Egypt at an early age – used up a lot of rolls of masking tape turning popsicle sticks into mummies. Parents inculcated a love of reading; Greek and Norse mythology a perennial favorite growing up. Early Montessori education was entirely allegorical and metaphorical – the Montessori method is a perfect example of what Gerald Massey described as the "thinging" of abstract concepts and knowledge. Loved looking at the stars as a child, guided by his father and the books of H. A. Rey. Influenced by outstanding literature and history teachers throughout primary and secondary schooling, ultimately leading to a degree in English literature from West Point, under the inspired guidance of Terry Freeman whose genius is to instill a "love of language" through the study of poetry, storytelling, Beowulf, and Shakespeare. Attended graduate school enroute to returning to West Point to teach in the Department of English; earned a masters degree in literature while studying Melville, Hawthorne, more Shakespeare, and translating Beowulf and other Old English literature.

The author has never been a member of any secret society, has never taken any oath of secrecy, and has arrived at the conclusions described herein through the study of publicly-available texts, primarily the book of the stars which is open to all men, women and children everywhere on the globe, every night and every morning.

He is directly descended from Reginald de Warren, William of Normandy, Charlemagne, Charles Martel, and other individuals mentioned in this book, through his mother's side of the family.

David Warner Mathisen asserts his natural-law right as a man to speak the truth in peace without being threatened with violence, incarceration, or assassination. He is not contemplating any violence against any person, including himself, nor does he condone violence in any way.

CPSIA information can be obtained at www.ICGtesting.com
Printed in the USA
LVOW07s2230080115

421933LV00001B/89/P